The International Business Environment

Third Edition

Leslie Hamilton and

Philip Webster

OXFORD
UNIVERSITY PRESS

OXFORD
UNIVERSITY PRESS

Great Clarendon Street, Oxford, OX2 6DP, United Kingdom

Oxford University Press is a department of the University of Oxford.

It furthers the University's objective of excellence in research, scholarship,
and education by publishing worldwide.

Published in the United States of America by Oxford University Press
198 Madison Avenue, New York, NY 10016, United States of America

British Library Cataloguing in Publication Data
Data available

Library of Congress Control Number: 2014954173

ISBN 978–0–19–870419–5

Printed in Great Britain by Bell & Bain Ltd., Glasgow

The International Business Environment

New to this edition

This third edition has been revised and updated throughout. The changes include more material on Africa and Latin America, updated and new case studies (including some extended end-of-chapter case studies), new mini case studies, and new learning tasks. The case studies are drawn from a wide range of geographical areas with a particular emphasis on emerging markets, especially Africa.

Pedagogical changes in this edition include questions added to 'counterpoint' boxes and mini case studies, and more assignment-style tasks added to review questions.

Author acknowledgements

We are indebted to all of the Oxford editorial team for their terrific support throughout, especially Angela Adams (Commissioning Editor) for encouraging us to develop the idea for the book, Helen Adams and Gina Policelli (Development Editors on the first and second editions), and Kirsten Shankland (Publishing Editor for this third edition) for her constant support and guidance.

Over the years spent teaching at Leeds Met we have been grateful for the comments and reflections of our domestic and foreign students who have taken the International Business Environment module and we hope that we have learned from these to produce a book which meets the needs of the intended wider audience of future students.

Oxford University Press acknowledgements

In listing those whom OUP would like to thank, we include the many reviewers who made a direct contribution to the way this book was put together. We express our gratitude to all who helped us. The authors and publisher are grateful to those who granted permission to reproduce copyright material. Every effort has been made to trace and contact copyright holders. If notified, the publisher will undertake to rectify any errors or omissions at the earliest opportunity.

Picture acknowledgements

The authors and publishers would like to extend thanks to the following for use of images in the book:

Part opening images

Part I: © chungking/ shutterstock.com; Part II: © jcarillet / istockphoto.com

Chapter opening images

Chapter 1: © zhu difeng/ shutterstock.com; Chapter 2: © OlgaNik / shutterstock.com; Chapter 3: © Mark III Photonics/ shutterstock.com; Chapter 4: © Konstantin Yolshin / shutterstock.com; Chapter 5: © tankbmb/ istockphoto.com; Chapter 6: © kawinnings / shutterstock.com; Chapter 7: © felixR / istockphoto.com; Chapter 8: © AntiMartina / istockphoto.com; Chapter 9: © Rob Wilson / shutterstock.com; Chapter 10: © argus / shutterstock.com; Chapter 11: © oonal / istock.com; Chapter 12: © DustyPixel / istockphoto.com

Brief contents

Detailed contents

PART ONE Global Context   1

PART TWO Global Issues   163

List of figures

List of tables

Guide to the book

This book is aimed at undergraduate students and Masters level students taking an introductory module on either the Business Environment or International Business Environment on business or related courses. It will provide a thorough underpinning for those modules which deal with International Business Management or Strategy.

The International Business Environment takes, as its starting point, a global perspective with a focus on understanding the global economy, the globalization process, and its impact on international business organizations. It examines the institutions and processes of the global economy and the economic, political, technological, and socio-cultural environment within which business organizations operate.

The International Business Environment is based on a module which the authors have successfully taught for a number of years. The authors have combined experience in academia of module development and delivery at undergraduate and postgraduate level and this has provided the foundation for this text. Les and Phil have vast experience of teaching International Business Environment and Business Strategy and the text benefits from this experience and the feedback from students, including many international students, on these modules.

Why use this book?

This book is aimed at undergraduate students studying the International Business Environment as part of a Business or International Business degree. It also offers an essential knowledge base for postgraduate students in Business, especially those specializing in the International Business Environment.

The text provides comprehensive coverage of the core topics that are central to the International Business Environment. Each topic is presented with a balance of theory, case studies, and exercises aimed to develop the reader's ability to understand and analyse the internal and external environmental factors affecting the business environment.

The case studies and examples used throughout the text identify the opportunities and threats to business organizations arising from changes in the global business environment. Detailed case studies, highlighting key concepts and issues from the chapter, are provided at the start and the end of each chapter.

Structure of the book

The book is divided into two parts. The first section, The Global Context, includes Chapters One to Five and sets the context for the international business environment, while in the second section, Global Issues, Chapters Six to Twelve deal with a range of global issues.

The first chapter of the book describes the process of the globalization of markets and production, and examines the key drivers and barriers to that process. It emphasizes the increasing complexity and interdependence of the world economy, concluding that the opportunities and threats arising from the global business environment can have consequences for all business organizations. Chapter Two examines in more detail some of the more important features of the world economy. It identifies the pattern of global wealth and poverty and the pattern of international trade. Chapters Three, Four, and Five include detailed analytical frameworks which provide the tools to enable students to undertake an analysis of external environmental issues and how these impact on business organizations. Chapter Three looks at the analysis of industries while Chapter Four places this analysis within an examination of the global macroenvironment using the familiar PESTLE framework. These frameworks are then used in Chapter Five to assess country attractiveness as markets or locations for production. Chapters Six to Twelve analyse in detail the issues in the socio-cultural, technological, political, legal, financial, and ecological environments, with Chapter Eleven providing an analysis of corporate social responsibility.

How to use this book

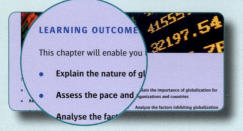

Learning outcomes

Identify what you can expect to learn from short bullet point lists at the beginning of every chapter. This feature can also be used to plan and organize your revision.

Case study

Connect key ideas to real-world examples from the outset. Reflect on the issues explored in the opening case study as you work through each chapter.

Counterpoint boxes

Develop your critical thinking skills and evaluate alternative viewpoints. Use the questions at the end of these boxes to focus your ideas for class discussion.

Mini case studies

Gain an understanding of the international business environment in practice and answer the accompanying questions to engage with the issues explored.

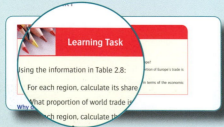

Learning tasks

Put your knowledge into practice with a range of learning activities designed to test and develop your understanding.

End-of-chapter case study

Apply what you have learnt by analysing a range of real-life international examples in more detail.

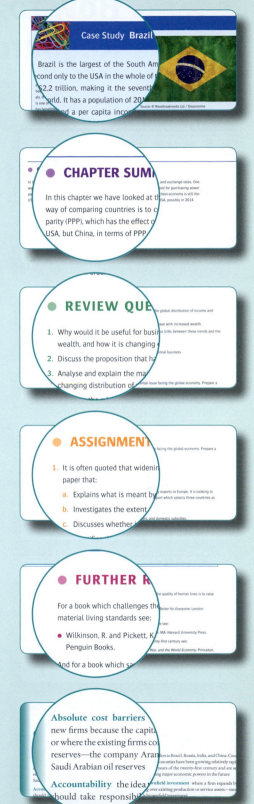

Chapter summary

Recap on key themes and review your understanding after every chapter.

Review questions

Test your knowledge and check your progress with these end-of-chapter questions. The review questions can also be used as the basis for seminar discussion and debate.

Assignment tasks

What would you do if you were a business manager? What solutions would you suggest as a researcher? Use these scenario-type questions to develop your analytical, reasoning, and problem-solving skills.

Further reading

Take your learning further with relevant supplementary reading, recommended by the authors.

Glossary

Check your understanding of key terms, highlighted in blue the first time they appear in the book. This is also a useful tool for revision.

How to use the Online Resource Centre

www.oxfordtextbooks.co.uk/orc/hamilton_webster3e/

For students

Multiple-choice questions

Test your understanding and receive instant feedback with our range of multiple-choice questions, organized by chapter.

Web exercises

Develop your research skills by answering questions linked to a range of relevant online articles and websites.

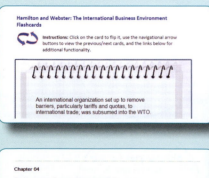

Glossary

Test your understanding of key terms from the book with this interactive flashcard glossary, ideal for revision. The complete glossary is also available to browse in PDF format.

Web links

Connect to relevant and reliable international business environment resources using these chapter-by-chapter web links.

The financial framework: additional links

Improve your understanding of the international financial environment by accessing links to additional material, supporting the financial and economic content from the book.

Hamilton & Webster: The International Business Environment 3e

The financial framework: additional links

Freakonomics article: 'The Economics of Happiness, Part 5: Will Raising the Incomes of All Raise the Happiness of All?' by Justin Wolfers
http://www.freakonomics.com/2008/04/23/the-economics-of-happiness-part-5-will-raising-the-incomes-of-all-raise-the-happiness-of-all/

Library of video links

View a range of video links connected to key topics and ideas introduced in the book.

Chapter 02

http://link.brightcove.com/services/player/bcpid439427290017bctid=658140244001
United Nations Development Programme: Interview with Amartya Sen.

http://www.chelseagreen.com/bookstore/item/limits_to_growth.paperback
/video_growth_vs_development
Chelsea Green Publishing: 'Limits to Growth' video by by Donella Meadows, Dennis

For registered lecturers

PowerPoint lecture slides

Adapt PowerPoint slides for use in your lecture presentations. The slides can be easily customized to match your own teaching, or can be used as hand-outs in class.

Learning Outcomes

This lecture on the global economy will enable you to:

- identify the global pattern of income
- analyse the pattern of international trade

Answers to review questions

Guide class debate with suggested solutions to the review questions from the book.

The review questions can be used as a basis for seminar discussion.

Review Questions

1. What is Globalization?

   This is a concept which should from the basis for a whole class discussion. A straightforward definition would be something like 'the process by which firms increasingly spread their activities across national boundaries and thereby increase the linkages between nations' or 'a process in which the physical, political, economic and cultural barriers between nations are reduced'. Students might be encouraged to think of some examples of how the term global is used, e.g. global industry, global competition, global strategy, global company and what is meant by each of these. Examples of 'global' companies might be used to explore to what extent they:

Answers to case study questions

Get the most from the end-of-chapter case studies with author guidance and suggested solutions.

The case study questions can be used as a basis for seminar discussion.

1. **Given that the alliance between Microsoft and Nokia is cross-border, what potential problems might be encountered?**

   - Students could be expected to use the material on cross-border mergers in Counterpoint Box 1.1 as a basis of their answer to this question. They could be expected to identify potential difficulties and/or costs around the following issues: differences in business cultures between the participating firms, including differences in language, differences in political and legal systems and consumer preferences (although in this alliance consumer preferences may not be an issue since both firms are big MNCs and have long experience of operating in different markets across the world).

Figures and tables

Download the figures and tables from the book, for use in assignments or exam material.

Exam and assignment questions

Use these additional questions in your group tutorial work, exams, and assignments.

About the authors

Leslie Hamilton is currently an associate member of staff at Leeds Beckett University (formerly Leeds Metropolitan University) and holds an MSc in Economics from the University of Hull. He has more than 30 years' experience of teaching at both undergraduate and postgraduate levels, mostly in the areas of the International Business Environment and the European Union. At Leeds Business School, Les was responsible for developing and leading a large module on the Global Business Context. He has taught in France, Germany, Hong Kong, Russia, and Spain. Les worked for two years in the Netherlands researching the economic and social implications of EU policies towards the regions, and examining issues around migration. His other publications cover a variety of topics including the EU, international business, and the business environment.

Philip Webster is an associate member of staff at Leeds Beckett University (formerly Leeds Metropolitan University). He was formerly Director for Undergraduate Studies at Leeds Business School and Principal Lecturer in Business Strategy and International Business. He graduated from the University of Leeds with an MA in Economic Development and worked in financial services and the computing industry before moving into education. Phil has over 30 years' experience of teaching International Business Environment, Business Strategy and Business Ethics, and Corporate Social Responsibility. He has taught mainly in the UK, but also in India, Sabah, and Hong Kong. Phil has also worked and lived in Malaysia.

Contributor

Dorron Otter is a Principal Lecturer in Economics at Leeds Beckett University. Dorron has extensive experience of developing new approaches to learning and teaching in introductory economics and business modules, and has led wider curriculum developments in these and other areas. While he has wider research interests, in the political economy of global development, and in his responsibilities as an academic manager, Dorron retains his passion and commitment to teaching issues relating to the business environment

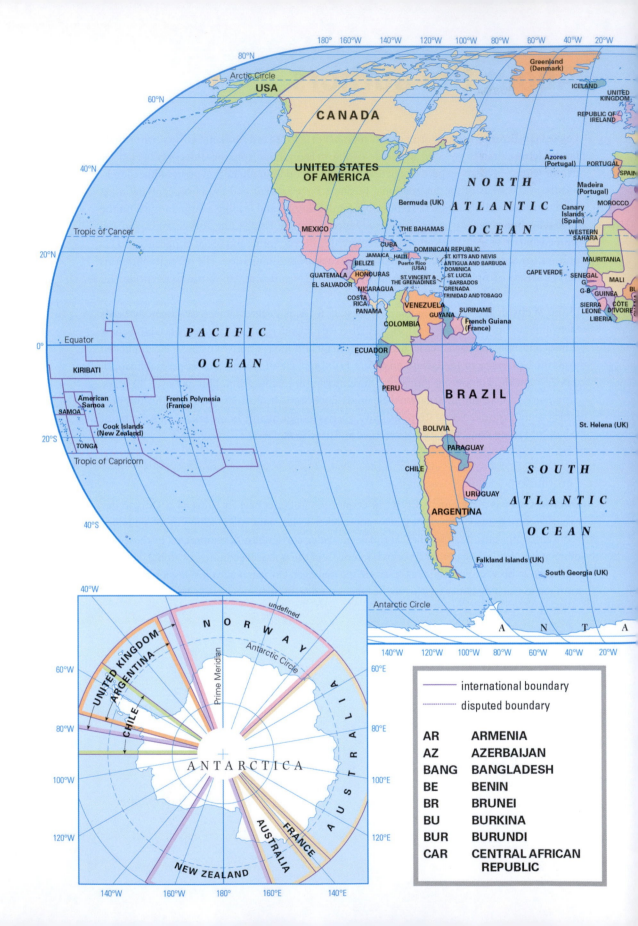

80°N

60°N

Arctic Circle

USA

CANADA

**UNITED STATES
OF AMERICA**

40°N

Tropic of Cancer

MEXICO

20°N

BELIZE
GUATEMALA
EL SALVADOR
COSTA
RICA
PANAMA

JAMAICA HAITI
HONDURAS
NICARAGUA

CUBA

Puerto Rico
(USA)

Bermuda (UK)

THE BAHAMAS

DOMINICAN REPUBLIC
ST. KITTS AND NEVIS
ANTIGUA AND BARBUDA
DOMINICA
ST. LUCIA
BARBADOS
GRENADA
TRINIDAD AND TOBAGO

ST. VINCENT &
THE GRENADINES

N O R T H

A T L A N T I C

O C E A N

Greenland
(Denmark)

ICELAND

UNITED
KINGDOM

REPUBLIC OF
IRELAND

Azores
(Portugal)

Madeira
(Portugal)

Canary
Islands
(Spain)

PORTUGAL

SPAIN

MOROCCO

WESTERN
SAHARA

MAURITANIA

CAPE VERDE

SENEGAL
G
G-B
GUINEA

MALI

BU

SIERRA
LEONE
LIBERIA

CÔTE
D'IVOIRE

P A C I F I C

O C E A N

Equator

0°

KIRIBATI

American
Samoa

SAMOA

Cook Islands
(New Zealand)

TONGA

French Polynesia
(France)

20°S

Tropic of Capricorn

VENEZUELA

COLOMBIA

GUYANA

SURINAME

French Guiana
(France)

ECUADOR

PERU

B R A Z I L

BOLIVIA

PARAGUAY

St. Helena (UK)

S O U T H

A T L A N T I C

CHILE

URUGUAY

O C E A N

ARGENTINA

40°S

Falkland Islands (UK)

South Georgia (UK)

Antarctic Circle

A N T A

180° 160°W 140°W 120°W 100°W 80°W 60°W 40°W 20°W

140°W 120°W 100°W 80°W 60°W 40°W 20°W

40°W

undefined

N O R W A Y

Antarctic Circle

60°W

UNITED KINGDOM
ARGENTINA

CHILE

Prime Meridian

80°W

60°E

A U S T R A L I A

60°E

80°E

A N T A R C T I C A

100°W

100°E

AUSTRALIA

FRANCE

120°W

120°E

NEW ZEALAND

140°W 160°W 180° 160°E 140°E

—— international boundary
- - - - disputed boundary

AR	ARMENIA
AZ	AZERBAIJAN
BANG	BANGLADESH
BE	BENIN
BR	BRUNEI
BU	BURKINA
BUR	BURUNDI
CAR	CENTRAL AFRICAN REPUBLIC

20°E 40°E 60°E 80°E 100°E 120°E 140°E 160°E 180°

80°N
Arctic Circle
60°N

RUSSIAN FEDERATION (RUSSIA)

NORWAY
SWEDEN FINLAND
DENMARK ESTONIA
LATVIA
LITHUANIA
GERMANY POLAND BELARUS
LUX UKRAINE KAZAKHSTAN MONGOLIA
CZ SK MOLDOVA UZBEKISTAN KYRGYZSTAN 40°N
AUST HUNG ROMANIA GEORGIA T NORTH
ITALY SLN CR BULGARIA TURKEY AR AZ TU T KOREA
ORRA MT KO GREECE SYRIA AFGHANISTAN CHINA SOUTH JAPAN
ALBANIA SE KOREA
MALTA CYPRUS L IRAQ IRAN
TUNISIA IS JORDAN PAKISTAN TAIWAN PACIFIC
KUWAIT NEPAL BHUTAN Tropic of Cancer
LIBYA EGYPT BAHRAIN Q BANG OCEAN
GERIA UAE INDIA MYANMAR LAOS Northern 20°N
SAUDI OMAN Marianas (USA)
NIGER CHAD ARABIA THAILAND Guam (USA) MARSHALL
SUDAN YEMEN VIETNAM ISLANDS
ERITREA REPUBLIC CAMBODIA PHILIPPINES
NIGERIA DJIBOUTI SRI LANKA PALAU FEDERATED STATES
CAR SOUTH ETHIOPIA MALDIVES OF MICRONESIA Equator 0°
GO CAMEROON SUDAN BR KIRIBATI
ATORIAL U KENYA MALAYSIA NAURU
GUINEA SOMALIA SINGAPORE I N D O N E S I A TUVALU
GABON R SEYCHELLES PAPUA NEW
Cabinda BUR GUINEA SOLOMON
(Angola) DEMOCRATIC TANZANIA EAST ISLANDS
REPUBLIC TIMOR
OF CONGO COMOROS I N D I A N VANUATU TUVALU
ANGOLA MALAWI O C E A N FIJI 20°S
ZAMBIA MOZAMBIQUE New
ZIM MADAGASCAR MAURITIUS Caledonia
NAMIBIA Réunion (France) (France) Tropic of Capricorn
BOTSWANA AUSTRALIA
SWAZILAND
REPUBLIC OF LESOTHO
SOUTH AFRICA NEW 40°S
ZEALAND

S O U T H E R N   O C E A N

R C T I C A

20°E 40°E 60°E 80°E 100°E 120°E 140°E

G	THE GAMBIA
G-B	GUINEA-BISSAU
IS	ISRAEL
L	LEBANON
Q	QATAR
R	RWANDA
T	TAJIKISTAN
TU	TURKMENISTAN
U	UGANDA
UAE	UNITED ARAB EMIRATES
ZIM	ZIMBABWE

SWEDEN ESTONIA RUSSIAN
FEDERATION
(RUSSIA)
DENMARK LATVIA
LITHUANIA
Kaliningrad BELARUS
NETHERLANDS (Russia)
GERMANY POLAND
BELGIUM UKRAINE
LUXEMBOURG CZECH REPUBLIC SLOVAKIA
FRANCE LIECHTENSTEIN MOLDOVA
AUSTRIA HUNGARY
SWITZERLAND SLOVENIA ROMANIA
ITALY CROATIA
BOSNIA-
HERZEGOVINA
MONACO SAN MARINO SERBIA
MONTENEGRO KOSOVO BULGARIA
FYRO
MACEDONIA TURKEY
ALBANIA 40°N
GREECE

20°E

PART ONE

Global Context

CHAPTER ONE

Globalization

LEARNING OUTCOMES

This chapter will enable you to:

- Explain the nature of globalization

- Assess the pace and extent of globalization

- Analyse the factors driving and facilitating globalization

- Explain the importance of globalization for organizations and countries

- Analyse the factors inhibiting globalization

Case Study Globalization—China and Latin America

Over several decades the Chinese economy has grown at around 10 per cent per year. Such dynamic growth has been a major factor in globalization through its impact on international trade and investment, and it is fundamentally changing the map of the world economy. To feed the rapid expansion of its industry, China massively increased its demand for raw materials particularly from developing economies in Latin America.

Since the turn of the century, interconnections between Latin America, including the Caribbean, and China have grown rapidly. China is becoming an increasingly important trading partner, investor, and source of finance in Latin America.

Between 2000 and 2012, bilateral trade in goods between China and Latin America increased from around $12 billion to $250 billion, a factor of 21. Latin American exports to China grew by a factor of 25 while imports multiplied by 18. Despite this exponential growth of its exports, Latin America has run a persistent and growing trade deficit with China (see Figure 1.1). In 2013 total trade reached $262 billion.

By 2012 China's share, by value, of Latin American trade had reached 9 per cent of exports and 14 per cent of imports. Latin America's share of Chinese trade was smaller (4.7 per cent and 6.4 per cent, respectively).

China is the main market for the exports of goods for Brazil, Chile, and Peru; the second largest destination for Colombia, Uruguay, and Venezuela; third largest for Argentina and fourth for

Source: © chungking / shutterstock.com

Mexico. Raw materials like oil, iron ore, copper, soya beans, scrap metal, wood, and sugar constitute the vast majority of exports to China (70 per cent in 2011). Manufactures incorporating some level of technology represent a very small proportion of these exports (7 per cent). As regards imports, China is one of the top four suppliers to the area. Over 90 per cent of imports from China are manufactures with some level of technology.

China's foreign direct investment (FDI) in Latin America and the Caribbean was very small up to 2010 ($7 billion in total). That year marked a major turning point with an inflow of about $14 billion, most of which was spent buying oil industry assets by

Figure 1.1 Latin American and Caribbean merchandise trade with China (2000–2012 $m)

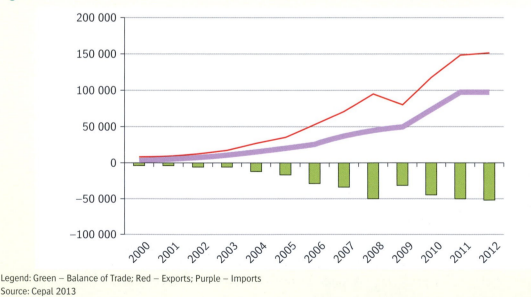

Legend: Green – Balance of Trade; Red – Exports; Purple – Imports
Source: Cepal 2013

→ Chinese state-owned entities, Sinopec in Brazil, and CNOOC (China National Offshore Oil Corporation) in Argentina. In subsequent years, China annually invested some $9 billion to $10 billion; 90 per cent of the investments went into the raw materials sector. China has not simply been involved in the extraction of resources such as fossil fuels but also in the expansion of large-scale agriculture, the processing of natural resources into intermediate goods, and big infrastructure projects involving the construction, for example, of railways and ports.

In 2014, China proposed the establishment of a $20 billion infrastructure fund for Latin America and the Caribbean. Also on offer was a $10 billion credit line and a further fund of $5 billion for investment. Baidu, China's answer to Google, set up a Portuguese language version in Brazil. China and Brazil, along with Russia and South Africa, other BRICS members, agreed to set up a development bank to fund infrastructure projects. This was seen as an alternative to the Western-dominated World Bank.

Analysts suggest that the burgeoning economic links with China create challenges for Latin America. While the effect has been to boost economic growth and reduce the income gap between it and richer industrialized countries, the resulting expansion of industries producing natural resource has not raised technological levels nor reduced the productivity gap between Latin America and leading countries, which, in fact, has increased (CEPAL 2013). Nacht (2013) says that some Latin American countries have taken advantage of the growing links with China to become more independent of the United States (US) and Europe, and have used some of the income to develop social welfare policies helping governments to create consensus in society. He warns of the danger of overdependence on a single customer and on natural resources whose prices, subject to the vagaries of global demand and supply, can fluctuate wildly. Concerns are also raised about competition from cheap Chinese manufactured imports undermining Latin America's industrialization process.

China and Latin America have not only become closer economically, but also politically and culturally. Thirty-two Confucius Institutes have been set up across Latin America, and China has observer status at the Organization of American States and is a member of the Inter-American Development Bank. The increasing influence of China causes much concern to the US, which historically has seen Latin America as part of its sphere of influence.

Sources: CEPAL 2013; ECLAC 2012; Yahoo News 17 July 2014; www.dw.de 14 October 2013; Nacht 2013

Introduction

How is it that a teenager in the UK can press a key on his computer and immediately bring chaos to Houston, the biggest US seaport? Why is it that a collapse in the US housing market causes banks to be nationalized in the UK? Why should a demand for democracy in the Middle East be bad news for Egypt's tourist industry but good news for Shell? Why should an earthquake in Japan cause an increase in the price of computer chips and a fall in stock markets worldwide; or the expansion of the Chinese economy cause unemployment among Dell employees in the USA? How can a court decision in Holland ordering the Russian government to pay $50 billion compensation to shareholders in a defunct Russian oil company result in a fall in BP's share price?

These are all examples of globalization—a major theme of the book. They show that events in one corner of the globe can have a major impact on others, sometimes good, sometimes bad. Business operates in a world where globalization is going on at an accelerating rate. As globalization progresses, it confronts business with significant new **threats** and **opportunities** in the external environment to which it has to respond. So globalization is important for business, but what is it and why is it so important?

The Process of Globalization

Globalization involves the creation of linkages or interconnections between nations. It is usually understood as a process in which barriers (physical, political, economic, cultural) separating different regions of the world are reduced or removed, thereby stimulating exchanges in goods, services, money, and people. Removal of these barriers is called **liberalization**.

As these exchanges grow, nations, and the businesses involved, become increasingly integrated and interdependent. Globalization promotes mutual reliance between countries. Globalization can have many advantages for business such as new markets, a wider choice of suppliers for goods and services, lower prices, cheaper locations for investment, and less costly labour. It can also carry dangers because dependence on foreign suppliers and markets leaves businesses vulnerable to events in foreign economies and markets outside their control.

Mini Case Study Russia, Ukraine, and the west, a new cold war?

In 2014, civil unrest led to the overthrow of the Russian-supported Ukrainian government. Russia subsequently assisted Ukrainian separatists to seize the Crimea, which it then annexed. The Russian president, Vladimir Putin, went on to support separatist elements in east and south-west Ukraine. These actions raised tensions between Russia and the West to a level unseen since the Cold War. Fears were created of a Russian invasion in some former communist bloc countries in Eastern Europe like Latvia and Lithuania.

In response, both the US and the European Union (EU) imposed increasingly tough economic sanctions. In July, the EU agreed to target Russia's finance, energy, and defence sectors by restricting trade, and access to financial markets and to sensitive technologies, for example in the energy sector. Russia retaliated by banning or restricting imports of certain food and agricultural products. Although Russia is dependent on Europe as its main market for oil and gas exports, the EU, in turn, imports around 40 per cent of its gas needs from Russia's state-controlled Gazprom.

It was estimated that the economic effect of the sanctions would hurt the Russian economy by €23 billion in 2014 (1.5 per cent of its gross domestic product (GDP)) and €75 billion in 2015 (4.8 per cent of its GDP). *The Economist* calculated that the sanctions could cost Russian firms up to one trillion US dollars in terms of their stock market value. For instance, the share price of Gazprom, the largest energy exporter to the EU, could have been hit by the sanctions and by the EU's attempts to reduce its energy reliance on Russia.

Russian state-owned financial institutions raised $16.4 billion (£9.7 billion) in EU capital markets between 2004 and 2012. In 2013 nearly half of all the bonds issued by those banks—about €7.5 billion (£5.9 billion)—were issued in the EU.

Russian arms sales to Eastern Europe were $3.2 billion, but bought just $300 million in exchange.

But the EU will also be hurt by the capital markets restrictions and trade bans for defence, high technology, and goods that can be used both for military and defence purposes. The EU Commission expected the EU to lose €40 billion (0.3 per cent of GDP) in 2014 and €50 billion in 2015—the equivalent of 0.4 per cent of EU GDP.

Western multinationals likely to be affected by the sanctions included BP, which had a 20 per cent stake in Russian state energy giant, Rosneft; Exxon Mobil, drilling with Rosneft for oil in Siberia; Shell, working with state-controlled Gazprom in the Far East; Boeing, importing a large proportion of metals like titanium form Russia; Unilever, which saw the Russian market as crucial to expanding its earnings; McDonalds, potentially facing an anti-American backlash in Russia which is among its top seven global markets; and the Austrian Raiffeisen Bank and France's Société Générale, two of the biggest foreign banks in Russia.

UK retailers were worried that the tensions between Russia and the EU would harm their business. Marks and Spencer had 41 stores in Russia, Kingfisher, the DIY chain, had 20 outlets, while Karen Miller, the women's fashion retailer, had 28 shops.

Sources: *EU Observer* 28 May and 28 July 2014; European Commission 2014; Communication from the Commission to the European Parliament and the Council, (COM) Commission - Statement/14/244 29 July 2014; *The Economist* 26 July 2014; *The Guardian* 28 July 2014; *Financial Times* 9 August 2014.

Questions
1. Analyse the implications of tensions between the EU and Russia for bank profits and growth.

Globalization also poses a threat insofar as it removes protection from domestic producers by opening up their markets to foreign competitors. Manufacturing in footwear, textile and clothing, and toys in the USA and the EU has shrunk as a result of competition from low-cost countries such as China, Vietnam, Pakistan, and Bangladesh.

Nations may also find that globalization causes them to specialize in producing those goods and services in which they are relatively more efficient. While this could generate benefits from **economies of scale** in production, it could also create dependence on a smaller range of products, and leave their economies more vulnerable to external events.

Globalization is not Global (yet)

Globalization is something of a misnomer because most foreign trade and investment takes place within and between four economic blocs:

- Western Europe, dominated by EU member states
- **North Atlantic Free Trade Area (NAFTA)** comprising the USA, Canada, and Mexico
- Japan
- China.

A significant proportion of world trade takes place either within Western Europe and NAFTA or between the blocs. However, much of this trade is internal: NAFTA is not heavily dependent on trade either with the EU or with Japan. Around 60 per cent of EU trade takes place between the member states (Eurostat 2012).

This situation is reflected in the strategies pursued by big Western and Japanese multinational companies. These organizations focus their strategies on the bloc where they produce. This concentration of trade in their own bloc is largely due to the size of their markets. Globally, rich countries make up less than a fifth of the world population but account for three-quarters of the consumption of goods and services (see www.globalissues.org).

For a long time NAFTA, the EU, and Japan dominated world trade, but their predominance came under threat from China whose share of world trade in manufacturing has grown very rapidly. China has joined Germany and the US among the leading traders. In 2012, it matched the US share of 21 per cent of world merchandise trade, with Germany trailing at 14 per cent. The 27 countries of the EU held about 30 per cent (WTO 2014).

The Indicators of Globalization

There are three main economic and financial indicators of globalization. These are:

- international trade in goods and services
- the transfer of **money** capital from one country to another
- the movement of people across national borders.

Of the three, international trade and foreign investment are the most important. Each of the three indicators will be examined in turn.

International Trade

International trade means that countries become more interconnected through the exchange of goods and services; that is, through imports and exports. Between 1950 and 2006, world trade grew

Figure 1.2 Growth in world exports by volume of goods and GDP %

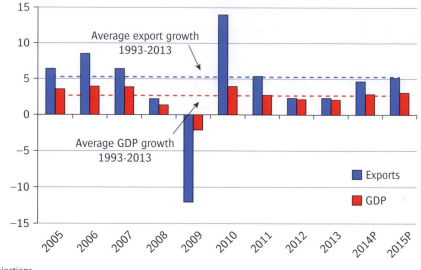

P = projections
Source: WTO 14 April 2014

27-fold in volume terms, three times faster than world output growth (WTO 2007). We can conclude from this that importing and exporting were becoming an ever more crucial component of global and national economic activity. Merchandise trade grew very quickly, particularly in manufactures, which increased tenfold between 1950 and 1975. As can be seen from Figure 1.2, export growth continued to exceed that of world output, i.e. GDP, the total value of the world's output of goods and services. Both went into hard reverse in 2009 due to the global recession with trade in intermediate goods, such as semi-finished products, and capital goods, like machinery, much more badly affected than consumption goods. World trade suffered its sharpest decline in 70 years but recovered strongly in 2010. The WTO forecast a return to the long-term growth trends by 2015 (Figure 1.2).

Trade in services grew exceptionally fast in the period between 2000 and 2008, at an average rate of 14 per cent per annum. But they, like merchandise trade, suffered a setback with the global crisis. Subsequently, growth resumed and was particularly rapid for developing countries (Figure 1.3).

In 2012, four countries, China, the US, Germany, and Japan, were the largest traders of goods with a share of more than 60 per cent. The US, the UK, and Germany are the major exporters of commercial services. China lags far behind in service exports (WTO 2014).

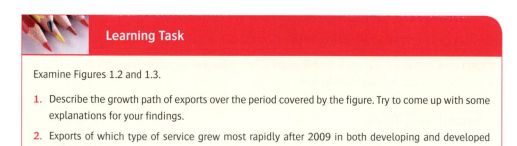

Learning Task

Examine Figures 1.2 and 1.3.

1. Describe the growth path of exports over the period covered by the figure. Try to come up with some explanations for your findings.

2. Exports of which type of service grew most rapidly after 2009 in both developing and developed economies? Give some reasons, paying particular attention to developing countries.

Figure 1.3 Exports of selected services categories, 2007–12 (2007 = 100)

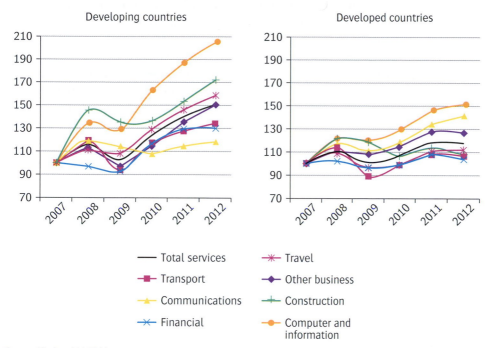

Source: Mashayekhi 2014

Some economies are particularly dependent on international trade. According to the **World Trade Organization** (WTO Trade Profiles), exports and imports together equate to 95 per cent of Germany's GDP, compared with around 54 per cent for China, 63 per cent for the UK, but only around 30 per cent for the USA. Furthermore, the UK depends on customers in only two countries, the US and Germany, for a quarter of its exports of goods (ONS 2014). Events in those economies are outside the control of UK business, but could have a major impact on it. For example, a rapid and simultaneous expansion of both economies would be very good news for sales of British manufactures but a **recession**, as occurred in 2008/09, could mean a significant fall in turnover and profits.

Multinational companies (MNCs) are major traders and account for a large proportion of international trade, with significant proportions accounted for by trade between subsidiaries within the same company—this is called intra-firm trade. So, for example, Ford makes gearboxes in its factory in Bordeaux and exports them to its assembly plants in other European countries. Almost one-half of world trade is intra-firm according to Altomonte et al. (2012). For the US, intra-firm trade flows are estimated at around one-half of imports, and one-third of exports. Intra-firm trade takes place in both goods and services, like bank and IT call centres which have been moved offshore (Maurer and Degain 2010; Lanz and Miroudot 2010).

Financial Flows

Foreign Indirect Investment

The second main driver is the transfer of money capital across borders.

This can take two forms. The first, **foreign indirect investment** (FII, or portfolio investment), occurs where money is used to purchase financial assets in another country. These assets can comprise foreign stocks, bonds issued by governments or companies, or even currency. Thus, UK financial institutions such as HSBC and Barclays often purchase bonds or company shares quoted on foreign stock exchanges such as New York or Tokyo. Purchasers buy them for the financial return they generate. This activity has been increasing very rapidly—in the 1990s such trading was expanding at more than 20 per cent per annum, helping to bring about an increased integration of **financial markets**. Growth faltered after the East Asian financial crisis of the late 1990s, but picked up again in the new century. The interlinkages created by FII were demonstrated in 2006 when it was estimated that foreign financial institutions held more than 10 per cent of the US$8 **trillion** in outstanding US residential mortgages in the form of mortgage-related securities. This left them vulnerable to the downturn in the US housing market which started in 2007, and led to a worldwide **credit crunch** (International Monetary Fund 2006) (see Chapter 10, Financial Crises). The International Monetary Fund (2014) estimated that the stock of cross-border portfolio investment amounted to around US$40 trillion. Developed countries like the USA and Eurozone members are by far the most popular sources and locations for this investment.

Activity on the foreign exchange market is enormous. The average daily turnover worldwide in 2001 was US$1.4 trillion with most business taking place in the main financial centres: New York, London, and Tokyo. By 2013, turnover had almost trebled to US$5.3 trillion. Only a very small proportion of currency trading is associated with the financing of trade in goods and services—most goes on the buying and selling of financial assets (Bank for International Settlements 2013).

Another example of cross-border flows of money is **migrant** remittances. Migrants often send money to their home countries, and the total amount has grown over time. They reached almost US$530 billion in 2012, big recipients being India and China with $69 billion and $60 billion, respectively, while Mexico received $23 billion. The USA was the biggest source, sending some US$123 billion in 2012 (World Bank, www.worldbank.org May 2013). Remittances are a vital source of foreign currency for some poor countries—Tajikistan, Liberia, and the Kyrgyz Republic are countries whose remittances from abroad equate to more than 25 per cent of GDP (World Bank).

Mini Case The global environment and tata motors

Tata Motors, a division of the Tata Group, the giant Indian multinational conglomerate, operates in over 175 markets, employs some 67,000 people, and produces around 700,000 vehicles per year in countries as far afield as India, South Korea, South Africa, Thailand, Bangladesh, Singapore, UK, Spain, Morocco, and Brazil. Research and development (R&D) facilities are located in India, South Korea, the UK, Italy, and Spain. Its products include heavy trucks, vans, and passenger cars such as Jaguar, Land Rover, and the ultra cheap Nano.

Tata reported in 2010 that the devastating global crisis of 2007–09 had hit car makers very hard especially in Continental Europe and in North America. By 2013–14, the world economy was strengthening, with the US economy speeding up but the Eurozone economies remaining weak. The economies of promising markets like China and India were expanding but at lower growth rates than in previous years. The more than 20 million vehicles sold in China in 2013 made it the world's largest automobile market.

→

➜ **Figure 1.4** Tata motors sales volume

Figure 1.5 Tata motors profits*

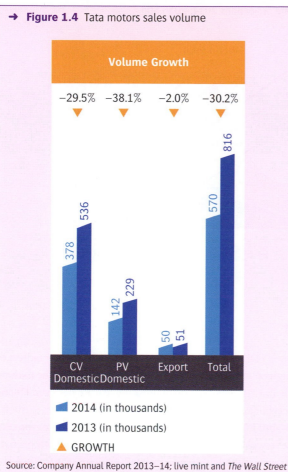

Volume Growth

−29.5% −38.1% −2.0% −30.2%
▼   ▼   ▼   ▼

CV Domestic: 378 / 536
PV Domestic: 142 / 229
Export: 50 / 51
Total: 570 / 816

CV Domestic | PV Domestic | Export | Total

▮ 2014 (in thousands)
▮ 2013 (in thousands)
▲ GROWTH

Source: Company Annual Report 2013–14; live mint and *The Wall Street Journal* 19 August 2013

Profits (EBITDA, PBT, PAT)

2010: 4,178 / 2,830 / 2,240
2011: 4,806 / 2,197 / 1,812
2012: 4,412 / 1,341 / 1,242
2013: 2,144 / 175 / 302
2014: (482) / (1,026) / 355

2010 | 2011 | 2012 | 2013 | 2014

▮ EBITDA (₹ crores)
▮ PBT (₹ crores)
▮ PAT (₹ crores)

*One crore = $163,532 in 2014. EBITDA: earnings before the deduction of interest, tax, depreciation, and amortization   PBT: Profit before tax
PAT: Profit after tax
Source: Company Annual Report 2013–14; live mint and *The Wall Street Journal* 19 August 2013

Tata's global sales of passenger and commercial vehicles in 2013–14 topped 570,000, a fall of over 30 per cent compared with the previous year (Figure 1.4). This was, in part, due to tough domestic market conditions in India where the company lost market share in both commercial and passenger vehicles. The company attributed declining performance to customers postponing the purchase of cars and vehicle finance companies tightening their lending conditions (Figure 1.5). But Tata was also facing fierce competition from South Korea's Hyundai, Maruti Suzuki and Honda, both of Japan, and India's Mahindra and Mahindra. Nonetheless, it was a good year for luxury car makers so Tata's poor performance was mitigated by the success of its Jaguar Land Rover operation, which posted record sales.

Tata responded by putting in a new management team. It identified the company's weaknesses as poor quality products,

a need to update the model line, and a customer perception that Tata's cars were only good for use as taxis. The new team set out to improve its products and restructure its dealer network.

Questions

1. What were the main causes of Tata's poor performance?
2. How did Tata's poor performance impact on its sales and profits?

Figure 1.6 Inflows of FDI 1995–2013 and projections 2014, 2015 $bn

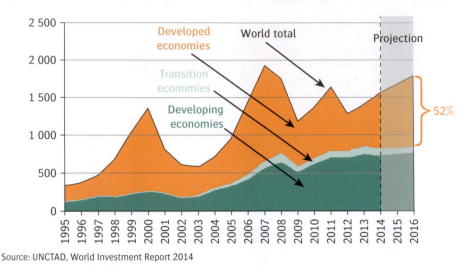

Source: UNCTAD, World Investment Report 2014

Foreign Direct Investment

The second form of capital movement is FDI. FDI occurs when a firm establishes, acquires, or increases production facilities in a foreign country. MNCs are responsible for FDI and the massive increase that has occurred in FDI in the last 50 years. The distinguishing feature between FII and FDI is that MNCs not only own the assets but also wish to exercise managerial control over them.

FDI grew spectacularly in the 1990s, but fluctuated widely in the opening decade of the century. It declined steeply after 2000 due to weak growth of the world economy. Following a five-year upward trend from 2003, FDI inflows declined by 16 per cent in 2008. This was followed by a further decline of 37 per cent in 2009 to US$1.1 trillion. Outflows from rich countries fell much more steeply than those from developing economies. After recovering in 2010, FDI inflows slumped once again. However, 2013 saw inflows rising by 9 per cent to $1.45 trillion (Figure 1.6; UNCTAD 2010 and 2014).

Countries can receive inflows of investment, but they can also be sources of investment. Until recently, the major recipients of FDI were the **developed countries**, mainly because of their large and affluent markets. In 2006, they received around 60 per cent of FDI inflows while accounting for the vast majority, more than four-fifths, of the outflows. By 2013, rich countries were receiving around 40 per cent of inflows, but continued to dominate outflows. Poorer countries received more than half of FDI inflows with much of the investment going to Asia and Latin America. (UNCTAD 2014; Figure 1.7).

The USA heads the league of FDI recipients, followed a long way behind by China (adding Hong Kong's figures to those of China reverses these rankings) and Russia. Brazil ranked fifth and Mexico tenth. The USA is also, by far, the biggest source of FDI followed by Japan, China, and Russia (Figures 1.7 and 1.8).

Up to 2010, FDI largely involved MNCs in rich countries investing in production facilities in other rich countries, the **developing countries** and Eastern Europe, having smaller and less lucrative markets, playing only a minor part. Where FDI did take place in poor countries it was

Figure 1.7 FDI Inflows—the top 20 host economies 2012 and 2013 (US$ billion)

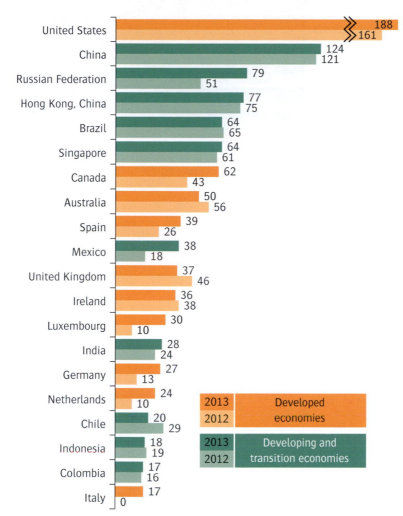

Source: UNCTAD, World Investment Report 2014

often to exploit natural resources such as oil or other minerals, to take advantage of cheap labour, or, sometimes, to penetrate a market. China was favoured by foreign multinationals because labour was cheap and there was great market potential. Firms like Volkswagen, Toyota, Caterpillar, and Tesco invested there to take advantage of cheap resources or to exploit the market. Now markets in countries like India, China, Brazil, South Africa, and Nigeria are large and fast-growing and a major attraction for MNCs.

According to UNCTAD figures (2010, 2014) there has been a fall in the number of MNCs and in the numbers they employ, but a rise in their foreign sales and assets. In 2013, there were some 55,000 multinational companies employing 71million workers with sales of $35 trillion and assets of £97 trillion. While the vast majority are based in rich countries, there are an increasing number of MNCs to be found in developing economies such as Tata of India, China's Lenovo, Vale of Brazil, and Russia's Gazprom. Most MNCs are privately owned, but

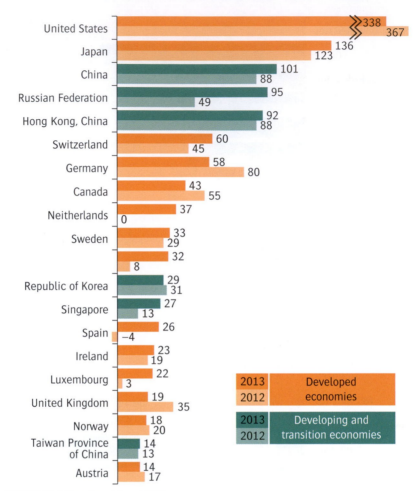

Figure 1.8 FDI Outflows—the top 20 home economies 2012 and 2013 (US$ billion)

Source: UNCTAD, World Investment Report 2014

there some 550 state-owned MNCs from both rich and poor countries with $2 trillion of foreign assets (UNCTAD 2014).

Big MNCs are the most important foreign direct investors. Table 1.1 shows the 20 biggest global companies ranked by the value of their foreign assets. The list is dominated by companies based in the **advanced economies**. Three are US companies, 10 are Western European (two German, two French, three British, two Italian, and one Swiss), and one is based in Japan. Many of the largest companies are extremely international in their operations. Oil companies like ExxonMobil, BP, Shell, and Total, and others such as Siemens and Vodafone, all generate more than 50 per cent of turnover from foreign sales.

However, the reality is that only a few of the 500 MNCs that dominate international business have a genuinely global presence. US MNCs concentrate on North America, European companies on Western Europe, and Japanese MNCs on Asia. However, FDI statistics show that the growth of developing economies such as China, India, and Brazil has caused many MNCs to invest there.

Table 1.1 The world's top 20 non-financial MNCs, ranked by foreign assets, 2012 (millions of dollars and number of employees)

Corporation	Home economy	Industry	Assets Foreign	Sales Foreign	Employment Foreign	TNI[a] (Per cent)
General Electric Co	United States	Electrical and electronic equipment	338 157	75 640	171 000	52.5
Royal Dutch Shell plc	United Kingdom	Petroleum expl./ ref./distr.*	307 938	282 930	73 000	76.6
BP plc	United Kingdom	Petroleum expl./ ref./distr.	270 247	300 216	69 853	83.8
Toyota Motor Corporation	Japan	Motor vehicles	233 193	170 486	126 536	54.7
Total SA	France	Petroleum expl./ ref./distr.	214 507	180 440	62 123	78.5
Exxon Mobil Corporation	United States	Petroleum expl./ ref./distr.	214 349	301 840	46 361	65.4
Vodafone Group Plc	United Kingdom	Telecommunications	199 003	62 065	78 599	90.4
GDF Suez	France	Utilities (electricity, gas and water)	175 057	78 555	110 308	59.2
Chevron Corporation	United States	Petroleum expl./ ref./distr.	158 865	132 743	31 508	59.5
Volkswagen Group	Germany	Motor vehicles	158 046	199 129	296 000	58.2
Eni SpA	Italy	Petroleum expl./ ref./distr.	133 445	85 867	51 034	63.3
Nestlé SA	Switzerland	Food, beverages, and tobacco	132 686	96 849	328 816	97.1
Enel SpA	Italy	Electricity, gas, and water	132 231	65 966	37 588	56.6
E.ON AG	Germany	Utilities (electricity, gas, and water)	128 310	117 973	40 535	65.0
Anheuser-Busch InBev NV	Belgium	Food, beverages, and tobacco	115 913	36 013	109 566	92.8
ArcelorMittal	Luxembourg	Metal and metal products	112 239	83 996	185 319	91.1
Siemens AG	Germany	Electrical and electronic equipment	111 570	87 236	250 000	77.9
Honda Motor Co Ltd	Japan	Motor vehicles	110 142	95 792	118 923	73.4
Mitsubishi Corporation	Japan	Wholesale trade	109 657	49 052	18 915	40.6
EDF SA	France	Utilities (electricity, gas, and water)	103 015	38 840	30 412	30.8

Source: UNCTAD 2014

*Petroleum expl./ref./distr. – petroleum exploration, refining and distribution

a TNI – Transnationality Index: the average of foreign assets/total assets; foreign sales/total sales/; foreign employment/ total employment

Learning Task

Referring to Figures 1.7 and 1.8, advance reasons why:

1. The US and Japan are the biggest foreign direct investors.
2. The US and China are the largest receivers of FDI.

Greenfield and Brownfield Investment

MNC investment overseas can be broken down into greenfield and brownfield investment. Greenfield investment involves the establishment of completely new production facilities, such as Ford setting up its new car factory near St Petersburg in Russia. Brownfield investment entails the purchase of already existing production facilities—the acquisition of Asda, the British supermarket chain, by Wal-Mart, is an example of brownfield investment. MNCs have undertaken massive brownfield investment. In 2000 they were involved in around 11,000 cross-border mergers and acquisitions (M&As) to a value of more than US$1.1 trillion, two to three times greater than the figures for 1995. However, after 2000 there was a significant drop in merger activity to around US$380 billion by 2004. Merger activity then started to pick up so that by 2007 the total had again reached US$1 trillion. The recovery was curtailed by the global crisis so much so that even by 2013 the total value at $349 billion was about one-third of the 2007 figure.

The main purchasers were rich country MNCs from the US, Canada, and Japan, but companies from China and Russia also played a prominent role. Over two-thirds of cross-border M&As by value still take place in rich countries, but the share of developing economies is on the increase reaching almost one-third in 2013. The service sector is the dominant player in cross-border mergers with finance firms like banks, hedge funds, and commodity firms playing a significant role. The food, beverages, and tobacco industries were also important players in M&As (UNCTAD 2007, 2011, 2014).

Counterpoint Box 1.1 Cross-border mergers and acquisitions

There have been huge waves of cross-border M&As at least up to the global crisis in 2008–09. It appeared that such mergers had become a fundamental tool of business strategy.

Cross-border mergers are argued to generate benefits. The firms to be acquired have an established market position and have experience of the local political, legal, and cultural environment. Efficiency benefits arise when takeovers increase economies of scale in production, finance, and marketing, or economies of scope leading to a reduction in unit costs. Strategic gains are generated if M&As, by reducing the number of competitors, permit the company to raise prices and profits. Horizontal mergers (i.e. between firms producing the same good or service) are the most likely type to yield these benefits. Another benefit stems from the spreading of risk over several markets. Furthermore, it is argued that firms with lots of intangible assets, such as technological know-how or marketing expertise, can best exploit these abroad through M&As that allow them to control the use of these assets rather than ceding, and perhaps losing control, to foreign firms through licensing or franchising. Mergers are →

→ a quicker method of expansion compared with internal growth.

However, cross-border mergers also pose significant challenges that threaten the ability to realize these gains. For example, the acquirer may face difficulties and extra costs in dealing with language barriers and cultural differences, customer preferences, business practices, and in the political and legal environment, which could act as major impediments to integrating the new business. The problems encountered in cross-border M&As can be exacerbated where: the firm moves into an activity of which it has little knowledge or experience, for example where it diversifies into another industry, such as Sony's takeover of Columbia Pictures in the US; the firm takes over another at a different stage of the supply chain in the industry in which it is currently operating by buying a supplier or a customer (a vertical merger), an example of this is Reliance of India which appears to have successfully integrated backwards from textile production to the supply of polyester fibres, into the refining of oil, and then into oil and gas exploration and production.

Research offers conflicting evidence on the results generated by cross-border mergers. For example, a survey of business in North America, Europe, and Asia by the consultancy firm, Accenture, found most firms had not achieved the expected cost and revenue gains from cross-border M&As. However, this has apparently not deterred business, which still sees cross-border M&As as an essential part of its competitive strategy.

Sources: Accenture (2006) *Globalization and the Rise of Cross-Border Mergers and Acquisitions*; Finkelstein 2009; Couerdacia et al. 2009; www.ril.com; Aybar and Ficici 2009; Conn et al. 2005; Chakrabarti et al. 2009; Steigner and Sutton 2011.

Questions

1. Assess whether cross-border mergers have been as popular with firms since the onset of the global financial crisis. Advance reasons for your response.

Migration

The globalization of markets has not been paralleled by the liberalization of labour flows. While globalization has led to the dismantling of barriers to trade in goods, services, and capital, barriers to cross-border labour movements are not falling as fast. Nevertheless, migration between developing and developed countries has risen. Historically, flows of migrants were greatest to North America and Europe—while Asia, Latin America, and Africa were major sources. The United Nations (UN) reports that, recently, migrant flows between developing countries are as common as those from poor to rich regions.

According to the UN, the number of migrants (people currently residing for more than a year in a country other than where they were born) is 232 million—which is around 3 per cent of the world's population (http://esa.un.org). This means that the migrant population more than doubled in 25 years. Europe has most migrants with 72 million (around 10 per cent of the population), Asia has 71 million (about 2 per cent), and North America 53 million (15 per cent) (http://esa.un.org/migration). This increase in numbers has occurred despite the fact that, during the last 30 years of the twentieth century, migration had become steadily more difficult—particularly for people in developing countries wanting to enter Europe. Migrants constitute a significant proportion of the population in some countries. In Australia, Canada, New Zealand, Luxembourg, and Switzerland the percentage exceeds 20 per cent. The USA, along with certain European countries such as the UK, France, Germany, the Netherlands, and Sweden, has a percentage, between 10 and 15 per cent, of immigrants. None of these compare with the Middle Eastern state of Qatar where more than four-fifths of the population are migrants. Care needs to be taken regarding the accuracy of migration statistics because countries differ in their definition of 'migrant' and clandestine migrants are unlikely to be picked up by official statistics. The official immigrant population in the USA for 2013 is 46 million, but Camarota and Jensenius (2009) suggest that official figures could underestimate the actual number by almost 25 per cent.

People move for a variety of economic, social, and political reasons. They may move voluntarily to find work, to earn higher wages, to study, or to reunite with their families. Widening inequalities in income and job opportunities increase the pressures to move. Movement may also be stimulated by employers in developed countries actively recruiting labour from abroad. At the start of the new century, the attitudes of certain governments towards migration changed as shortages of skilled workers emerged. For example, the USA, UK, and Germany started to look much more favourably on the entry of workers with high levels of education and skills in areas such as IT. The 2007 global crisis caused a hardening of attitudes to migration in rich countries.

Migration may also be involuntary where people, often in large numbers, are forced to migrate by political instability and violations of human rights—as we have seen, for example, in civil unrest in 2010/11 in North Africa and the conflicts in Syria and Iraq. Natural disasters, such as hurricanes, earthquakes, and floods can also force people to move. Global warming is expected to cause extensive flooding in coastal areas of South East Asia which will cause large waves of migration.

Large short-term movements of people also occur as a result of executives going on foreign business trips, students involved in study abroad, and tourism. UNWTO (2014) recorded over 1 billion international tourists in 2013. France, the most popular tourist destination, receives 83 million tourists annually, the USA around 70 million, Spain 61 million, and China 56 million. Some small countries, for example, in the Caribbean, St Lucia, Antigua and Barbuda, and the Bahamas, are heavily dependent on tourism for their income.

Learning Task Wal-Mart and the Movement of Labour

It was reported that more than 300 illegal workers had been arrested at 61 Wal-Mart stores in the USA as part of an investigation into contract cleaning crews at the world's largest retailer. The investigation involved allegations that a contractor had recruited illegal immigrants, mainly from Eastern Europe. The company ended up paying millions of dollars in fines in 2005. But the story did not end there. In 2010, a group of migrant workers took Wal-Mart to court for, among other things, failing to give them overtime pay and coercing them into forced labour. They claimed that Wal-Mart employed undocumented workers to evade taxes and government regulations and to avoid having to pay for health benefits.

1. What are the advantages to Wal-Mart of employing illegal migrants to clean its stores?

2. What risks might Wal-Mart face by taking on such workers?

3. Google the class action taken by the migrant workers to find the outcome of the 2010 case.

Source: *The Observer* 26 October 2003; *Financial Times* 24 October 2003; www.courthousenews.com

Globalization is All-Pervasive

Although globalization is often seen as an economic phenomenon involving trade and investment, it also has many other cultural and social dimensions. Held et al. (1999) argue that globalization is all-pervasive. They define globalization as:

> the widening, deepening and speeding up of worldwide interconnectedness in all aspects of contemporary social life, from the cultural to the criminal, the financial to the spiritual (1999:2).

As Held et al. observe, globalization is not confined to economic life but also influences many other areas of society. And they contend that each of these areas is becoming more deeply affected by the phenomenon. Cultural life involving the attitudes, behaviour, and values that are characteristic of a society, can be influenced by the process. Globalization can influence **culture** through the transfer of knowledge, ideas, and beliefs across national borders.

Mass media, such as television and film, illustrate how culture has been influenced by globalization. American programmes such as *The Simpsons* and *Breaking Bad* are watched worldwide. While the USA is by far the major exporter of TV programmes, countries with large internal markets, such as Brazil, Japan, and the UK, are also active exporters. Similarly, US films like *Iron Man* and *The Dark Knight Rises* are widely shown around the world. The collapse of communism in Eastern Europe and the arrival of cable and satellite systems opened up more markets to US media companies. However, commentators such as Tunstall (2008) see a challenge to the American TV and film industry from the growing capacity of China and India to become global media players, and the increasing competition from Latin America.

Diet is another area influenced by globalization. In France, the consumption of fast food such as hamburgers and soft drinks like Coca Cola has increased, and this is attributed by some commentators to the globalization of fast food chains like McDonald's, Subway, and Burger King. The movement of people can also have an impact on diet. In the second half of the twentieth century, many migrants came to the UK from India and Pakistan. With over 9,000 Indian restaurants in the UK, now almost all British towns and cities have an 'Indian' and it is claimed that the favourite meal, when eating out, is curry.

Another obvious route for transfer of culture across borders is through education. Universities in the USA, Western Europe, and Australia have enthusiastically embarked on campaigns to recruit students from abroad. Some have also gone in for FDI by setting up education facilities in other countries or have established partnerships with foreign colleges. The EU, through its Erasmus and Socrates programmes, has led to large numbers of students studying in other member states. In a further move to facilitate the movement of students and workers across borders, more than 40 European countries have initiated a programme of reform of their university systems. The idea is to standardize the structure of university studies with degrees taking from three to four years and the introduction of a common system of assessment, the European Credit and Transfer System.

Another conduit for such transfers is through the world of work. For example, the UK and the USA have been favoured locations for Japanese car companies; in other words, capital has been moved to these countries from Japan. The movement of capital across national borders brings with it different ways of working, such as Just-in-Time where suppliers deliver raw materials and components immediately before they are needed in the manufacturing process, or quality circles where small groups of employees meet together to identify how production could be improved. In turn, domestic firms have been influenced by new methods; for example, Nissan has persuaded suppliers to alter their production methods, and Toyota's rivals, such as General Motors and Ford, finding their market shares slipping because of their inability to compete with the Japanese, have responded to the threat by introducing some of their working methods. As a result, in the UK and USA, car industry working methods have become similar to those in Japan. Another example concerns McDonald's setting up in Moscow in partnership with the City Council. It had to devise a strategy for dealing with a Russian workforce that had a reputation for being surly and slovenly. McDonald's introduced expatriate managers and training programmes to show the Russian staff how things should be done. Moscow City Council officials could not believe that the employees in the fast food outlet were Russian because they were so friendly.

The globalization process can also be seen in sport, where football players like Lionel Messi and Cristiano Ronaldo cross borders to play abroad. In the 2014 World Cup, almost two-thirds of the Swiss team were of migrant descent. There has also been a rush of FDI into the English premier football league. Chelsea is owned by a Russian businessman, while Liverpool and Manchester United were acquired by US tycoons. Manchester United is promoted and known worldwide—it is marketed as an international brand and there is a lucrative trade in Manchester United team kit and other products outside the UK. Furthermore, many of the top teams in England are now managed by foreigners.

A further impact of globalization is on health. A new treatment for disease, discovered in one country, can be quickly transferred to others, helping to limit the spread of disease and improve the quality of health care. On the other hand, diseases may also spread more quickly as people move across borders; for example, the outbreak of the Ebola virus in 2014 that spread across several West African countries. Illness can also be spread through trade. In 2004 it was found that poultry farmers in Vietnam and Thailand had contracted the virus associated with avian flu. The infection spread to other countries through cross-border trade in poultry and the movement of migratory birds.

With regard to crime, globalization, by removing barriers to movement, can make it easier for criminals to operate in other countries. Criminals can move more easily across borders, as can pornography, prostitution, and illegal substances such as drugs. Large amounts of cocaine are produced in Colombia and gangs there ensure that the drug finds its way to users in the USA. The Russian mafia is involved in trafficking women for the vice trade in Amsterdam. Communications technology facilitates the electronic movement across borders of money generated by these illegal activities into countries where the criminals can portray it as being derived from a legitimate source. Or they may move the money to countries where the laws regulating such **money laundering** activities are deficient. The Internet makes it easier for criminals in one country to commit crime in another whether that is to sell pornography or to steal money from bank accounts (see Chapter 9, The Internet).

Religion, or the spiritual dimension as Held et al. call it, is another area that is globalized. Major religions, for example the Catholic, Anglican, Muslim, and Jewish faiths, all operate multinationally and have been spreading their values over large parts of the world for the last 2,000 years. In the UK, the established churches, such as the Church of England, are in decline in contrast to evangelical churches, which have their roots in the USA and, ironically, have their origin in English Puritanism. Evangelical churches are also expanding rapidly in parts of Africa and Latin America.

The Drivers of Globalization

In 1983 Theodore Levitt claimed:

> Gone are accustomed differences in national or regional preferences. Gone are the days when a company could sell last year's model—or lesser versions of advanced products—in the less developed world. Gone are the days when prices, margins and profits were generally higher than at home.

Although he was overstating the case, he was making the point that technology, through communication, transport, and travel, was driving the world towards convergence. In the business world the process of competition would drive firms to seek out these markets and force down prices by standardizing what was sold and how it was made in an effort to cut costs and to maintain profit. International competition is not a new business phenomenon, nor is FDI or international trade, but, as we have seen in the first section, the process of globalization appears to be accelerating. The organization of trade is also different, with much of it taking place between and within large multinational organizations across borders that are increasingly irrelevant. It is supported by international organizations like the WTO and agreements which did not exist a century ago.

The process has also embraced an increasing number of countries, as free market ideology was accepted as the dominant economic philosophy. The countries of South East Asia, Latin America, India, Central and Eastern Europe, and even China have one by one bowed to the power of market forces. However, the global financial crisis of 2007 did raise questions about giving markets free rein and led to calls for more government intervention (see Chapter 10 for discussion of this).

The big MNCs have not been passive participants in the liberalization process. They are usually to be found at the forefront, pushing governments to open up their economies by removing barriers to trade and investment. Indeed, Rugman and Hodgetts (2002) argue that their managers are the real drivers of globalization. MNCs encourage governments through pressure groups such as The European Round Table (ERT), set up by MNCs from 17 countries. It brings together leaders of around 50 of the biggest MNCs with a combined turnover exceeding US$1.3 trillion, supporting nearly 7 million jobs in Europe. It was instrumental in promoting the idea of a single market for the EU and is very keen to integrate the former communist countries and the developing nations into a globalized system (see the ERT website at www.ert.be). Similarly, the National Association of Manufacturers in the USA has pressed for markets to be opened up from Cape Horn, the southernmost tip in South America, to Alaska.

Competition is one of the dominant drivers in the process of globalization of the world economy. If your competitors are globalizing and capturing new growth opportunities, scale efficiencies, and gaining invaluable knowledge of global operations, then you may cease to exist or be forced into small domestic market niches unless you follow suit.

There are other drivers, although some might be more correctly labelled as 'facilitators'. In the next sections, we look at the forces driving the globalization of business, the facilitating factors, and those forces that act as barriers, helping to keep business 'local'.

Political/Regulatory

Governments have taken steps to remove barriers to trade and the movement of finance through international organizations such as the General Agreement on Tariffs and Trade (GATT) and its successor organization, the World Trade Organization (WTO), and they have also set up free trade areas, customs unions, or common markets.

- Free trade area—member states agree to remove tariffs and quotas on goods from other members of the area. Members have the freedom to set the level of tariff imposed on imports of goods from non-members of the area.

- Customs union—this is a free trade area, but with the addition that members agree to levy a common tariff on imports of goods from non-members.

- Common market—this is a customs union, but with the addition that member states agree to allow free movement of goods, services, capital, and labour.

There have been major reductions in the barriers to movement, particularly for goods and capital brought about by liberalization. These have been brought about multilaterally through negotiations in international institutions such as GATT and its successor organization, the WTO, or bilaterally between individual governments. Governments help bring about increased economic and political interlinkage by signing treaties setting up regional trade areas (RTAs), such as NAFTA with the involvement of the USA, Canada, and Mexico, where barriers to movement, such as tariffs and quotas, are abolished among the members. Other examples are: The Association of Southeast Asian Nations (ASEAN) incorporating ten countries in South East Asia, and Mercosur comprising four countries in South America. The number of RTAs rose dramatically from about 30 in 1990 to 379 in 2014 (www.wto.org), the vast majority being free trade areas and a much smaller number, customs unions. While such bodies do promote integration among the members, they often limit integration with non-members by maintaining barriers against imports from them.

Sometimes, governments push integration further by agreeing to the establishment of customs unions that comprise a free trade area plus a common import tariff against non-members. Or, they may set up a common market like the EU where there is complete freedom of movement for goods, services, capital, and people. One result of this removal of barriers to the movement of people in the EU is that someone in Southern Spain could drive to Lapland without necessarily having to stop at a single border. Some members of the EU have taken the integration process even further by removing currency as a barrier through agreement on the introduction of a common currency, the euro. Economic integration often then leads on to political integration. So, EU member states are subject not only to EU laws but also to common policies in areas such as agriculture, the regions, and social policy.

Changes in political regimes have also helped reduce barriers; for example, the collapse of communism in the late 1980s and early 1990s led to Eastern European countries becoming more interconnected economically, politically, and militarily particularly with Western Europe and the USA. Many of the former communist countries joined the North Atlantic Treaty Organization (NATO) and the EU. China opened up its economy to foreign investors and joined the WTO.

Governments, particularly in poorer countries in Asia, Africa, and Latin America, anxious to promote economic development, facilitate the movement of capital into their countries by setting up **export processing zones** (EPZs) where MNCs can invest, produce, and trade under favourable conditions. China has 15 zones employing 40 million people. Kenya has 45 zones, while Honduras has 24. MNCs are usually given financial incentives to invest and often they are allowed to import goods and produce output free of tax. Waters (2013) estimated that there were EPZs in over 119 countries employing around 68 million people, or about 3 per cent of the global workforce. There are also many tax-free free trade zones, or freeports, which are supposed to act as entrepots and be used for storage purposes.

Technological

Improvements in communications, and reductions in transport costs, have facilitated the movement of goods, services, capital, and people. Modern communications technology makes it easier for businesses to control far-flung empires. It further allows people to connect and interact over long distances, and, with transport becoming easier and cheaper, goods and people are able to travel long distances quickly and at a relatively low cost.

The Internet and cheaper telephony not only make it easier for MNCs to control their foreign operations, but also for migrants to maintain links with their countries of origin. Furthermore, it has been a major force in integrating the world's financial markets. A trader in a bank in New York can use the computer to monitor movements in share prices, **interest rates**, and currency rates in all the major financial markets, and can respond by buying and selling almost simultaneously. Vast amounts of money can be transferred across borders at the press of a button.

In 1930, it cost more than a week's average wage in the UK for a three-minute telephone call from London to New York. Now it costs a fraction of the average hourly wage. Demand for telecommunications has increased very rapidly. The number of mobile phone subscribers worldwide more than doubled between 2005 and 2010. Access to a mobile network is available to 90 per cent of the world population (World Bank 2014).

The growth in demand for telecommunications services has been driven by the development of the cellular technology associated with mobile phones. Another factor, the Internet, has revolutionized telecommunications. It has become a very cheap and reliable method of communicating text, data, and images and it is also being increasingly used for voice communication. The number of people in the world with Internet access grew more than tenfold from less than 100 million in the mid-1990s to around 3 billion in 2014. Access to the net is highest in the developed world with a penetration level of 78 per cent compared to 36 per cent in the Asia-Pacific region and 11 per cent in Africa (ITU, 'ICT Facts and Figures: The World in 2014').

India is a good example of a country that has benefitted from the impact of advances in communications technology. It has a ready supply of relatively cheap, educated labour and has become an increasingly popular location for call centre jobs. This has come about as a result of the advances in communication technology, which have significantly reduced the costs and improved the quality and reliability of telephony. Consequently, there has been a movement of IT and other business processes jobs from the UK and the USA to South East Asia, with India a particularly favoured location.

Technology can also have the effect of reducing movements of people. Improvements in the costs and quality of video links may mean that business executives do not need to attend meetings abroad. They can be virtual travellers, interacting electronically through teleconferencing with fellow managers in other countries.

Economic

In many modern industries, the scale of investment needed for R&D and production facilities can mean that the size of a single domestic market is insufficient to support that industry. The production of electronic components requires high levels of investment in both R&D and the manufacturing process, and this drives firms to go global. This is especially so when **product life cycles** are shortening, increasing the pressure to recover investment quickly. Competitive pressures on costs also push firms to reduce product lines and to expand globally to seek every possible saving from economies of scale in R&D, manufacturing, and marketing.

The desire to cut costs can be seen in the aluminium industry. Aluminium is a relatively expensive metal to produce as it takes a lot of electricity to turn ore into metal. This is why aluminium firms locate their smelters in locations with access to cheap energy. Other industries will seek out cheap sources of labour. In the footwear industry, which uses relatively simple technology and is therefore **labour intensive**, labour costs represent about 40 per cent of total costs. Hourly wages in some countries are very low; for example, in manufacturing, those in Mexico are just one-sixth and in Brazil just less than one-third of those in the USA (www.bls.gov figures for 2012). As a result, manufacturing has been relocating to countries with low labour costs.

Firms may globalize because they have outgrown their domestic market. Furthermore, the pace of growth in mature, developed economies for many industries is relatively modest. To maintain a rate of growth required by **capital markets** will mean for most of the world's leading companies that they must seek opportunities beyond their domestic borders. IKEA, based in Sweden and the world's largest furniture retailer, is an example of this. The Swedish market is relatively small, so, in order to grow, IKEA had to go abroad. In the new century it rapidly expanded to 345 stores in 42 countries in North America, Europe, Asia, and Australasia (IKEA, *2013 Facts and Figures*).

The rapid improvements in technology, and the consequent reduction in communication and transport costs, have enabled people to experience other societies' lifestyles first hand or through the medium of TV and film or the Internet. This has led to a convergence in tastes which MNCs have been quick to exploit by creating global brands such as Coca Cola, Levi, Sony, Nike, and McDonald's. This has been called the 'Californiazation' or 'McDonaldization' of society (Ohmae 1985; Ritzer 2004, respectively).

Global companies mean global customers. Global customers require basic supplies of input materials, global financial and accounting services, and global hotel chains to house travelling executives. Dealing with one supplier of a standard product or service has many advantages for the global buyer: lower purchase costs, a standard product of consistent quality, lower administration costs, and more opportunities for cooperation with suppliers. For example,

Counterpoint Box 1.2 Globalization: the free market

Supporters of globalization claim that free movement of goods, services, and capital increases economic growth and prosperity and leads to a more efficient allocation of resources with benefits to all countries involved. It results in more competition, lower prices, more employment, higher output, and higher standards of living. Countries, therefore should open up their economies to free movement by removing barriers such as tariffs, quotas, laws and regulations, subsidies, and the purchase by public bodies of goods and services on nationalist grounds. It is also argued that a liberalized world economy would eradicate global poverty.

Critics see an element of hypocrisy when rich countries use the arguments above to persuade poor countries to open up their economies to imports and inward investment. Historically, almost all rich countries, including the USA and UK, protected domestic industries from foreign competition with subsidies, tariffs, quotas, regulation, and through state-owned enterprises. Many, such as Japan, Finland, and South Korea, tightly controlled foreign investment while France, Austria, Finland, Singapore, and Taiwan developed key industries through state-owned enterprises. But, despite this, they grew rich. Critics also point to the period after 1980 when developing countries liberalized their economies and their economic growth rates fell compared with the 1960s and 1970s when they protected their domestic industries from foreign competition. Opponents claim that globalization increases inequality between countries and also results in economic instability, citing the 2007–09 financial crisis which spread rapidly from the USA around the world.

Sources: Sachs 2005; Bhagwati 2004; Wolf 2005 and 2010; Stiglitz 2002; Chang 2008 and 2010; Chua 2003

Questions

The World Bank reported in 2013 that globalization had benefitted the global middle class and the top 1 per cent of world earners. Earnings had almost stagnated for the bottom 5 per cent (World Bank (2013) 'The Winners and Losers of Globalization: Finding a Path to Shared Prosperity', 25 October. Available at: www.worldbank.org).

1. Discuss the Bank's findings in relation to the arguments in the Counterpoint Box.

Japanese banks became more global following the globalization of Japanese car manufacturers (an important customer).

Barriers to Globalization

Despite the fast pace of globalization, it remains the case that goods, services, capital, and people move more easily within nations than across borders. Trade between regions within nations is generally much higher than trade across borders, even when adjusted for income and distance levels. This occurs even when trading restrictions appear to be low; for example, between Canada and the USA.

Government Regulation

Governments pursue policies that can hinder the flow of goods and services and the movement of capital and people across borders. Surprisingly, the global economic crisis did not lead governments to resort to protectionism, the head of the WTO describing it as 'the dog that hasn't barked' (*The Guardian*, 27 January 2011). However, there remain a number of barriers to globalization.

Tariffs and Subsidies

There remain numerous tariffs on imports of goods. Rich countries impose particularly high tariffs on goods coming from poor countries. The EU and Japan levy high tariffs on imports of agricultural products that are important to developing economies while tariffs imposed on manufactured goods from other rich countries are lower. Such differences in tariffs help to explain why trade tends to take place within and between rich countries. Poor countries also impose tariffs. India and Brazil apply maximum average tariffs of over 30 per cent on imports of non-agricultural products (http://stat.wto.org figures for 2012).

Rich countries subsidize their farmers, with the EU, Japan, Norway, Switzerland, and South Korea contributing large proportions of their farmers' incomes (www.oecdilibrary.org, figures for 2012). Subsidies can also be used to promote globalization. In EPZs, they are often used to attract foreign investors.

Foreign Aid

Rich countries usually give financial assistance to poor countries. Frequently, such aid, for example from the USA and Japan, is used to promote the interests of domestic firms by requiring the recipients to buy goods and services produced by firms in the donor country irrespective of whether they give best value for money.

Controls on Capital

Controls on capital can take the form of either controls on inflows or on outflows of foreign direct and indirect investment.

Big steps have been made in liberalizing the movements of capital. However, some countries have been more amenable to this than others. Thus, India and South Korea have been reluctant to remove restrictions on capital inflows, and Japan has one of the most closed financial systems of all the advanced countries. In 2009, Brazil introduced controls on inflows of portfolio investment because they were driving up the value of the currency and affecting the country's international competitiveness (see Chapter 2, end of chapter Case Study). Countries are often reluctant to accept inflows of FDI where it involves sectors they regard as strategically important, such as the basic utilities of gas, electricity, and water. The USA and the EU are not prepared to cede control of their airline companies to foreign organizations. US law prevents foreign firms from buying more than 24.9 per cent of an American airline (the corresponding figure for the EU is 49 per cent).

Public Procurement

Government departments, nationalized industries, public utilities in telecommunications, gas, and water often spend large amounts of public money purchasing goods and services. **Public procurement** worldwide accounts for between 10 per cent and 25 per cent of GDP. In the EU it equates to 16 per cent of GDP (http://ec.europa.eu 7March 2013). Governments are very important customers for firms, particularly those producing goods and services for the defence, health, and education sectors. When issuing **contracts**, governments will often favour domestic producers over their foreign rivals, even when domestic firms are more expensive.

Border and Immigration Controls

Border controls affect trade in goods. They can require the filling in of export/import forms and also customs officers stopping vehicles and checking goods at the frontier. This can take time, add to traders' transport costs, and make goods less competitive in the foreign market.

Many barriers remain to the movement of people. These include stringent visa requirements, quotas requiring employers to search for a national employee before employing a foreign one, and refusal by the authorities to accredit foreign educational and vocational qualifications.

Technical Standards

Technical standards and regulations can be formidable barriers. There are thousands upon thousands of different technical specifications relating to goods and services which can effectively protect domestic markets from foreign competition and consequently restrict trade. The EU has tried to deal with this through its Single Market Programme. It uses the principle of mutual recognition whereby countries accept products from other member states so long as they do not constitute a danger to the consumer.

Companies in the service sector can be hampered by the myriad of technical standards and requirements. Financial institutions such as banks may find it difficult to use the Internet to sell their services in foreign markets because countries may lay down different solvency requirements, or different levels of liquidity for financial institutions operating in their territory.

In addition, new barriers can appear: where several companies are competing to develop a new product, the first to do so may establish its technical specifications as a standard for the new product which then acts as a barrier to trade for competitors.

Protection of Intellectual Property Rights

Different national policies towards what are called intellectual property rights (IPRs) could constitute barriers as well. IPRs relate to new products and production processes, brand names, and logos as well as books and films. Their owners argue that they should have the legal right to prevent others from commercially exploiting them. However, the extent of protection and enforcement of these rights varies widely around the world. Some countries, such as China and Malaysia, do not offer the firms creating the ideas and knowledge much protection against counterfeiting. Firms contend that the lack of protection of IPRs stunts their trade and FDI in those countries.

Cultural and Geographical Distance

Culture

Cultural distance can constitute an important barrier. Differences in language, religious beliefs, race, national and regional tastes, social norms and values, and business practices, which regulate what is regarded as acceptable behaviour and attitudes, can constitute major impediments to globalization. Culture can be an important influence on consumer behaviour, work culture, and business practices. Thus, McDonald's cannot sell Big Macs in India because to

Hindus the cow is sacred, nor can it assume that staff in Eastern Europe will have the same attitudes to work as its workers in the USA. Another example concerned Tyrrells, the UK crisp company: the founder described how it encountered difficulties when trying to sell parsnip crisps in France, not realizing that the French saw parsnips as pig feed (*Financial Times* 21 March 2011).

Some goods and services are more sensitive than others to cultural differences. Ghemawat (2001) researched the impact of culture and found that products such as meat, cereals, tobacco, and office machines had to be adapted to local cultures, whereas firms producing cameras, road vehicles, cork and wood, and electricity did not need to adapt their products—or were under less compulsion to do so.

Corruption

Another area where cultural distance can cause problems for firms is corruption. In some countries, in Africa and the Middle East for example, it is the norm for firms to reward individuals who help them to get business. However, in other countries such behaviour would be seen as corrupt and would be deemed illegal. The prospect of prosecution in their home countries might deter firms from trading with, and investing in, countries where such behaviour is the norm.

Cultural differences can be a significant barrier to globalization and ignoring them can be very costly (Ghemawat 2001).

Learning Task

Some goods and services are more sensitive than others to cultural differences. Ghemawat did some research on the impact of culture and found the following:

More Sensitive Products	Less Sensitive Products
Meat	Cameras
Cereals	Road vehicles
Tobacco	Cork and wood
Office machines	Electricity

1. Discuss and advance explanations for Ghemawat's findings.

Geography

Geographical distance can also be a barrier. It has been shown that the more distance there is between countries, the less will be the trade between them (Ghemawat 2001). Geographical distance can make trade difficult, particularly for firms producing goods that are low in value but high in bulk, such as cement or beer. The cost of transporting cement or beer over long distances would be prohibitive. Fragile or highly perishable products like glass and fruit may suffer similar problems. Firms respond to the barrier posed by geographical distance in various ways. Brewers have responded either by taking over a foreign brewer or by granting a licence to firms in foreign markets to brew their beer. Thus, barriers to one aspect of globalization, trade, result in globalization in another form, investment or licensing. Historically, geographical

Mini Case Study Removing barriers—TTIP and TISA

In 2014, in the absence of progress on the WTO Doha Round of trade negotiations (see Chapter 2, International Trade) the EU and the US embarked on the negotiation of the Transatlantic Trade and Investment Partnership (TTIP). The aim was to remove trade barriers, making it easier to export and import goods and services between the two blocs. The barriers in question were tariffs and non-tariff barriers such as different technical regulations, standards, and approval procedures. Supporters of the deal referred to cars—even though approved as safe in the EU—having to go through another safety approval process in the US despite both blocs having similar safety standards. The negotiators also hoped to remove barriers in services, public procurement, and the movement of capital.

The European Commission claimed that a comprehensive and ambitious agreement would open up the massive US market to EU business which could reduce company costs by millions of euros and create thousands of jobs. Exports to the US would rise by 28 per cent and EU GDP would be given an annual boost of 0.5 per cent, or €119 billion. Average household disposable income would benefit to the tune of €545 each year. US GDP would rise by €95 billion a year, with US families gaining €655. It was also claimed that economies other than the EU and US would benefit from the increased trade between the two blocs.

In 2013, frustration at the stalemate in the Doha Round led 23 WTO members, including the EU and the US, accounting for 70 per cent of world trade in commercial services, to start talks on reducing barriers to trade in services through the Trade in Services Agreement (TISA). Based on the principles of the WTO General Agreement on Trade in Services (GATS), TISA aimed to liberalize services trade by opening up markets and agreeing rules in areas such as licensing, financial services, telecoms, e-commerce, maritime transport, and workers moving abroad temporarily to provide services.

Services have become an increasingly important sector in the world economy, especially in the EU and the US. The EU, the world's largest exporter of services, saw TISA as a way of boosting service exports and generating economic growth and jobs.

TTIP and TISA have faced mounting opposition. Organizations on both sides of the Atlantic—including trade unions and pressure groups such as Friends of the Earth and the World Development Movement—fear that the deals would open up publicly provided services, like health and education, to privatization through the obligation to compete with foreign private sector companies. They go on to claim that the TTIP will threaten democratic rights by establishing a court where big business can sue governments whose democratic decisions jeopardize their profits. They also see standards being driven down in food, the environment, and workers' rights and a threat to democracy. Sauvé (2014) raises concerns about the TISA negotiations taking place outside the ambit of the WTO, and the possibility of countries not involved in the talks being marginalized.

Sources: ec.europa.eu/trade 15 March and 25 July 2014; François 2013; *The Guardian* 4 November 2013; Sauvé 2014; www.wdm.org.uk/trade 17 July 2014

Questions

1. Find out how far the negotiations on TTIP and TISA have progressed in reducing barriers and opening up markets.

distance is likely to have declined in importance as transport has become cheaper and techniques for carrying fragile or perishable products more effective.

The Benefits and Costs of Globalization for Business

Globalization can comprise major changes in the external environment of business. On the one hand, it creates opportunities for business, particularly for the big MNCs who are in the best position to take advantage. On the other hand, it can pose threats for business as well. We examine the benefits and costs in turn.

The Benefits for Business

Removal of barriers to trade or investment can:

- open up markets to businesses that were previously excluded, giving them the possibility of higher revenues and growth. The activities of car producers and tobacco firms in South East Asia illustrate this. As their traditional markets in North America and Western Europe have matured, General Motors, Ford, Volkswagen, Toyota, and others have all looked to the fast-expanding markets of South East Asia as a source of growth. China, with its rapidly growing car market, has been a particularly favoured location for car industry investment. Similarly, the fall of communism gave banks from the USA and Western Europe the opportunity to move into the former communist bloc countries and in many countries, such as the Czech Republic, Bulgaria, and Croatia, they have ended up controlling a majority of banking assets;

- give business access to cheaper supplies of final products, components, raw materials, or to other **factors of production**, such as labour, which lowers their costs and makes them more competitive. It is hardly surprising that firms such as HSBC, Tesco, ebookers, and BT have been relocating activities to India where graduates can be employed for a fraction of the corresponding salaries in the USA or the UK. The relatively low cost of IT professionals has also resulted in the biggest computer firms establishing operations in India. Similarly, China is not seen by Western MNCs simply in terms of its market potential but also as a very cheap source of supply. Many MNCs relocated manufacturing production to China where there was an abundant supply of cheap labour;

- allow firms to obtain previously denied natural resources. For many years Saudi Arabia was unwilling to give foreign firms access to its energy deposits. The Saudi authorities had a change of heart allowing Shell to explore for gas.

The Costs for Business

Globalization can also have costs for business.

- The environment is likely to become more complex and risky. Business is confronted by new sets of factors in the form of different political regimes, laws and regulations, tax systems, competition policies, and cultures. In extreme cases, they may find that the host government seizes their investment or takes discriminatory action against them. For example, Bolivia nationalized natural gas production and took four electricity generating companies, including power stations owned by France's GDF Suez and UK's Rurelec, into public ownership (PRS Group 2010).

- Inefficient firms may find that it removes the barriers protecting them from foreign competitors. National airlines such as Lufthansa, or telecommunications companies like France Telecom found it difficult to face up to the more intense competition engendered by the liberalization of civil aviation and telecommunications in the EU. Often, the endangered businesses will pressurize governments to leave the protective barriers in place or to reintroduce the barriers previously removed. Removal of the barriers may allow the entry of new competitors from abroad or it may permit existing customers to switch their custom to foreign suppliers who are cheaper or who can offer better product quality. Weaker domestic firms may find that their access to factors of production is threatened.

• Globalization can raise the dependence of plants and firms on foreign markets and suppliers. As a result of NAFTA, more than 3,000 plants (called **maquiladoras**) were set up along the Mexico/USA border employing some 1,300,000 workers, producing goods for the North American market. They accounted for half of Mexico's exports. When the US economy went into recession in 2008, the maquiladoras began shedding workers. By 2009, nearly 30 per cent of jobs had disappeared and exports had fallen by more than one-third (Muñoz Martinez 2010). In the Mexican border towns, they say that when the US economy catches cold, Mexico gets pneumonia (Rosen 2003).

• Globalization can cause the environment to become more volatile. Firms generally prefer to operate in an environment where the financial and macroeconomic systems are stable and predictable. However, there is evidence from global financial crises, for example in the late 1990s and in 2007–08, that the economies of developing economies, whose financial systems have integrated most with the rest of the world, are more subject to greater instability than other developing countries (Prasad et al. 2003; Green et al. 2010). Increasing integration of financial markets allows enormous sums of money to be moved effortlessly across borders, leaving financial markets more vulnerable to

Mini Case Study Globalization and football

This case shows the impact of globalization on the supply of scarce resources, here talented footballers to Brazilian and African football leagues.

Arguably one of the largest sources of football talent in the world, Brazil, itself has hardly any stars left. Fans and officials blame globalization. Brazil is a developing economy and is poor relative to its European counterparts, so the best Brazilian players seek greener grass in Europe. Similarly, talented African players grasp any chance to play in the top European leagues in Spain, England, and Italy. In the 2014 World Cup, only five of 150 squad players for Ivory Coast, Ghana, Algeria, Nigeria, and Mali played in their domestic leagues, while the Brazilians had four.

The process is not new. Brazilian football icons went abroad long before Pele was lured to the New York Cosmos in the 1970s. However, the exodus has reached new proportions in the twenty-first century. The attraction for foreign clubs is that recruiting or buying players from Brazil or Africa costs less than local footballers of equivalent talent. Top European clubs have scouting networks and academies across Africa.

Training with top European clubs may improve performances of the national football team—Ghana is seventeenth in the FIFA rankings—although Brazil's poor performance in the 2014 World Cup belies that. Brazilian football fans have long lamented the loss of their football stars as their best players leave for big contracts abroad. As the head of a Brazilian fan club put it, 'Brazil has the best football in the world but we are losing all our top players, we feel betrayed'. The mass exodus of African football players has crippled some domestic leagues, according to the Duke University website.

The tide may be changing. Increasing wealth generated by Brazil's rapidly growing economy could lead to players staying at home, and may even lead to players returning from abroad.

Sources: *The Economist* 20 January 2005; *Financial Times* 15 September 2003; www.bbc.co.uk 25 November 2010; http://soccerlens.com; http://sites.duke.edu Soccer Politics Pages; bbc.co.uk 3 June 2014

Questions
1. Explain how European football clubs go about competing for footballers in developing economies.
2. Looking at FIFA's world football rankings of Brazil and England, discuss the possible impacts of the recruitment of foreign footballers on the national team performance.

instability and the world financial system more prone to violent fluctuations in **exchange rates** and interest rates. Such fluctuations can pose a major risk to business costs, revenues, and profits.

● CHAPTER SUMMARY

In this chapter we have explained the nature of globalization as a process through which barriers between nations are reduced. Nations thereby become increasingly interdependent, although we point out that most of this interdependence is between members of the NAFTA, Western Europe, the EU, Japan, and China, with the rest of the world playing a minor role. Their dominance is under some challenge from India, Brazil, and Russia. Increased interdependence is indicated by increases in exchanges across borders of goods and services, financial capital, and people.

We also make the point that globalization is not just about economic exchanges, but also has a cultural and social dimension. The media, our diet, education, work practices, sport, health, crime, and religion all demonstrate the impact of globalization.

The main drivers of globalization are identified as competition, reduction in regulatory barriers, improvements in technology, saturated domestic markets, the desire to cut costs, and the growth of global customers. There still remain important barriers to the process, including regulation, technology, and cultural and geographic distance.

Globalization presents both opportunities and threats to business. On the one hand, it presents access to new and bigger markets and to different and cheaper sources of raw materials, components, and labour. On the other hand, the environment is more complex and less stable.

It is this environment and the implications for business that this book will explore. In Chapter 2 we will look at the global economy and explain in more depth some of the topics discussed in this chapter.

● REVIEW QUESTIONS

1. What is globalization?

2. Where is globalization mainly taking place? Why should that be the case?

3. Identify the main:

    a. indicators of globalization;

    b. drivers of globalization;

    c. facilitators of globalization;

    d. barriers to globalization.

● ASSIGNMENT TASKS

1. You are a reporter for a quality business newspaper. The editor asks you to write an article:

    a) explaining what TTIP or TISA is trying to achieve;

b) discussing the main benefits and challenges for business of the TTIP or TISA;

c) outlining the arguments of the opponents to TTIP or TISA.

See: the Europa website for information on TTIP and TISA; the report by François at: http://trade.ec.europa.eu/; articles by George Monbiot and Slavoj Žižek in *The Guardian* (/www.theguardian.com/), and Monbiot's website www.monbiot.com; the report by BEUC at: http://beuc.org/

2. You are employed in the purchasing department of a big German-based electricity company that uses a lot of gas in its power generation. Its main markets are Germany and neighbouring countries in Eastern Europe. Fearing that Russia might cut off supplies of gas to the EU, the head buyer asks you to write a report which:

a) shows the dependence of the EU as a whole on imports of Russian gas;

b) identifies which member states are most/least dependent on gas from Russia—see Figure 1.9;

c) discusses the implications of Russia cutting off gas supplies for your employer;

d) indicates some short-term and longer-term policy responses that your firm could make to a Russian embargo on gas imports.

See: http://ec.europa.eu/energy/

Figure 1.9 Dependency on natural gas supplies from Russia 2013

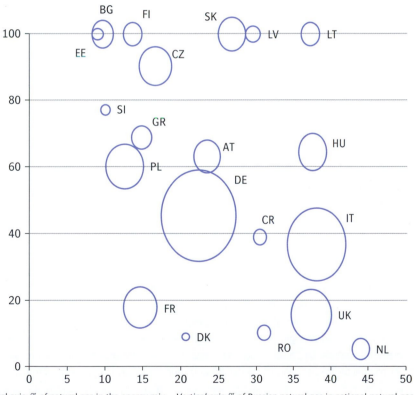

Horizontal axis: % of natural gas in the energy mix − *Vertical axis:* % of Russian natural gas in national natural gas consumption − *Size of the circles:* volume of imported Russian natural gas.

Source: European Commission 2014

Case Study Globalization, international hotel chains, and Africa

Africa is a growing tourist and business destination and is 'the next big thing', according to Starwood, the large US multinational hotel chain (*Financial Times* 11 January 2014). Hotel chains see Africa as a key growth market with an undersupply of hotel rooms caused by an increase in international tourists, the boom in the exploitation of the continent's natural resources, and a growing middle class.

In 2012, 53 million international tourists arrived generating revenues of $34 billion. The number of tourists was expected to reach 56 million the following year and to double by 2030, according to the UN World Tourism Organisation (2014).

The sub-Saharan economies of Botswana, Kenya, Mauritius, and Tanzania rely heavily on international tourism, offering splendid beach resorts and safaris. But not all countries enjoyed the same success. Before 2010, North African countries like Egypt and Tunisia were important tourist destinations, but the trade was badly affected by the civil unrest associated with the Arab Spring. In Egypt, industry takings more than halved from almost £8 billion in 2010 to £3.6 billion in 2013. Tourist numbers dropped from 14.7 million to 9.5 million over that period. Room occupancy rates in Cairo fell as low as 15 per cent during the troubles, and hotels around popular Red Sea resorts were also affected. Some hotel developments had to be postponed. On the other hand, the North African countries of Morocco and Algeria were relatively unscathed by the unrest.

Another attraction for hotel chains is the demand from business executives travelling around the continent. This demand is driven by the high growth rates of sub-Saharan economies based to a large extent on the increase in production and trade of their natural resource and agricultural sectors. The IMF (2014) has estimated that these economies will continue to show vigorous growth, while UNCTAD reported fast growth in African trade outstripping that of other developing regions in Latin America and Asia.

Africa, and especially sub-Saharan Africa, is becoming the new battleground for multinational hotel chains like US-based Hilton, Marriott, and Carlson Rezidor, Golden Tulip from Holland, and France's Accor. Some of the expansion has been through acquisition. For example, Marriott took over Protea, the biggest chain in Africa with 116 hotels in seven countries. But, given the lack of suitable takeover targets, most of the expansion will have to be organic; that is, setting up new hotels.

In 2013, 29 hotel chains operated about 90,000 rooms, the majority located across five countries in North Africa and the

Source: © kosmozoo / istockphoto.com

remainder in 49 sub-Saharan countries. The chains plan to speed up their expansion programmes, proposing to build an extra 40,000 rooms in 207 hotels in cities where there is a shortage of hotel accommodation. Hilton, which has around 11,000 rooms, intends to raise that number by almost 50 per cent in 17 new hotels. Carlson Rezidor, operating under the Radisson Blu brand, wants to increase its number of hotels from 49 to 61. Expansion will be concentrated in sub-Saharan Africa and in capital cities or major commercial centres. Nigeria is the most sought after location by the hotel chains, but countries like Kenya, Ghana, and Gabon are also popular.

South Africa will not see the same rate of expansion of hotel accommodation. Although South Africa is the continent's main financial centre and biggest tourist destination, it does not figure large in the hotel chains' expansion plans. Apparently, this is due to a high proportion of its tourists coming from low-income African countries like Zimbabwe, Lesotho, and Mozambique. Another possible factor is South Africa's high rate of crime and lack of security, which may act as deterrent to international tourists.

However, expansion is not straightforward in a continent with 54 countries and with many different languages and legal systems. There are also major infrastructure issues for tourist organizations. Air, road, rail, port, communication, water, sanitation, and power infrastructures are poor. Air travel tends to be expensive, few airfields are paved, and railway systems are not interconnected. According to the ➡

➜ World Bank, Africa's main infrastructure problem is the electricity sector, due to inadequate generation capacity, unreliable service, and high cost. As an example, South Africa has the most developed transport infrastructure in the region, but around half the road network is unpaved, in rural areas can be difficult to use in bad weather, and there are frequent power shortages.

Sources: IMF 2014a; *Financial Times* 11 January 2014; UNWTO 2014; UNCTAD 2013 www.wto.org/english/res_e/reser_e/wtr_e.htm; W Hospitality Group 2013; World Bank (nd); African Development Bank 2013; *The Guardian* 11 February 2014; *Travel and Tour World*, 2 September 2013; Business Monitor International Q4 2013.

Questions

1. What are the links between the case and globalization?

2. What is the connection between economic growth, trade, and the demand for hotel rooms from:
   a. international tourists?
   b. business executives?

3. Why are international hotel chains particularly interested in investing in sub-Saharan Africa?

4. Give reasons why outbreaks of civil unrest could affect supply of, and demand for, hotel rooms.

5. Why are infrastructure issues important for tourist organizations like hotel chains?

6. Discuss Kenya's infrastructure problems. What is it doing to deal with them and what are the implications for tourism?

7. Discuss the language, legal, and infrastructure obstacles international hotel chains are likely to encounter in Africa.

8. Go to the Transparency International Corruption Perceptions website and find out where sub-Saharan countries are placed in the rankings. What issues might this raise for hotel chains wishing to operate in these countries?

● FURTHER READING

For a discussion of the debates and controversies around globalization see:

● Held, D. and McGrew, A. (2007) *Globalization/Anti-Globalization: Beyond the Great Divide*, 2nd edn. Cambridge: Polity.

● Steger, M.B. (2013) *Globalization: A Very Short Introduction*. 3rd edn. Oxford: Oxford University Press.

For an examination of the various theories around globalization and how the world economy has been transformed by MNCs, states, and interest groups see:

● Dicken, P. (forthcoming 2015) *Global Shift: Mapping the Changing Contours of the World Economy*. 7th edn. London: Guildford Publications.

● REFERENCES

African Development Bank (2013), *The Africa Infrastructure Development Index*. Available at: http://www.afdb.org/en/documents/document/economic-brief-the-africa-infrastructure-development-index-may-2013-32369/.

Altomonte, C.Di Mauro, F., Ottaviano, G.I.P., Rungi, A., and Vicard, V. (2012) *Global Value Chains During the Great Collapse: A Bullwhip Effect?* European Central Bank Working Papers, 1412, January.

Aybar, B. and Ficici, A. (2009) 'Cross-border Acquisitions and Firm Value: An Analysis of Emerging-market Multinationals'. *Journal of International Business Studies* 40(8).

Bank for International Settlements (2013) 'Triennial Central Bank Survey of Foreign Exchange Turnover in April 2013'. Available at: www.bis.org/publ/rpfx13fx.pdf.

Bhagwati, J.N. (2004) *In Defence of Globalization*. Oxford: Oxford University Press.

Business Monitor International (Q4 2013) *South Africa Tourism Report*. Available at: http://www.businessmonitor.com/.

Camarota, S.A. and Jensenius, K. (2009) 'A Shifting Tide: Recent Trends in the Illegal Immigrant Population'. *Center for Immigration Studies* July.

CEPAL (2013), *Promoción del Comercio y la Inversión con China*. Available at: http://www.cepal.org/cgi-bin/getProd.asp?xml=/publicaciones/xml/2/51652/P51652.xml&xsl=/publicaciones/ficha.xsl&base=/publicaciones/top_publicaciones.xsl.

Chakrabarti, R., Gupta-Mukherjee, S., and Jayaraman, N. (2009) 'Mars−Venus Marriages: Culture and Cross border M&A'. *Journal of International Business Studies* 40.

Chang, H.-J. (2008) *The Myth of Free Trade and the Secret History of Capitalism*. New York: Bloomsbury Press.

Chang, H.-J. (2010) *23 Things They Don't Tell You About Capitalism*. London: Allen Lane.

Chua, A. (2003) *World on Fire: How Exporting Free Market Democracy Breeds Ethnic Hatred and Global Instability*. New York: Doubleday.

Conn, R., Cosh, A., Guest, A., and Hughes, A. (2005) 'The Impact on UK Acquirers of Domestic, Cross-border, Public, and Private Acquisitions'. *Journal of Business Finance & Accounting* 32.

Couerdacia, N., De Santis, R.A., and Aviat, A. (2009) 'Cross Border Mergers and Acquisitions: Financial and Institutional Forces'. Working Paper Series No. 1018/March. European Central Bank.

ECLAC (2012), *China and Latin America and the Caribbean*. Available at: http://www.cepal.org/publicaciones/xml/6/46566/China_Latin_America_Caribbean_trade_relationship_2012.pdf.

European Commission (2014) 'Communication from the Commission to The European Parliament and The Council: European Energy Security Strategy'. SWD (2014) 330 final.

Eurostat (2012) 'External Trade, Statistics in Focus 3/2012'. Available at: http://epp.eurostat.ec.europa.eu/portal/page/portal/eurostat/home.

Finkelstein, S. (2009) *Cross Border Mergers and Acquisitions*. Available at: www.tuck.dartmouth.edu.

François, J. (2013) 'Reducing Transatlantic Barriers to Trade and Investment: An Economic Assessment'. *Centre for Economic Policy Research*, March.

Ghemawat, P. (2001) 'Distance Still Matters: The Hard Reality of Global Expansion'. *Harvard Business Review* September: 137−47.

Green, D., King, R., and Miller-Dawkins, M. (2010) 'The Global Economic Crisis and Developing Countries: Impact and Response'. *Oxfam Research Report* January.

Held, D., McGrew, G., Goldbatt, D., and Perraton, J. (1999) *Global Transformations*. Stanford: Stanford University Press.

International Monetary Fund (2006) 'World Economic Outlook', September. Available at: http://www.imf.org/external/pubs/ft/weo/2006/02/.

International Monetary Fund (2014) 'Coordinated Portfolio Investment Survey', September. Available at: http://cpis.imf.org/.

International Monetary Fund (2014a) *World Economic Update* July 2014.

Lanz, R. and Miroudot, S. (2010)' Issues and Challenges for Measuring Intra-firm Trade'. OECD, 6 October. Available at: www.oecd.org/trade/its/46289076.ppt.

Levitt, T. (1983) 'The Globalization of Markets'. *Harvard Business Review* May-June: 91−102.

Mashayekhi, M. (2014) 'Trade, Services and Development: The Regulatory and Institutional Dimension'. UNCTAD Background Note 15−17 April.

Maurer, A. and Degain, C. (2010) 'Globalization and Trade Flows: What You See is Not What You Get!'. WTO, 22 June. Available at: http://www.wto.org/english/res_e/reser_e/ersd201012_e.pdf .

Muñoz Martinez, H. (2010) 'The Double Burden on Maquila Workers: Violence and Crisis in Northern Mexico'. Available at: www.global-labour-university.org .

Nacht, P.A. (2013) 'El Dragón en América Latina: las relaciones económico-comerciales y los riesgos para la región'. *Iconos, Revista de Ciencias Sociales*, 45(septiembre). Available at: http://www.redalyc.org/articulo.oa?id=50925659010 .

Ohmae, K. (1985) *Triad Power: The Coming Shape of Global Competition*. New York: Free Press.

ONS (2014) 'UK Trade April 2014'. Available at: http://www.ons.gov.uk/ons/rel/uktrade/uk-trade/april-2014/stb-uk-trade-april-2014.html .

PRS Group (2010) 'Bolivia: Country Report', 1 May. Available at: https://www.prsgroup.com/ .

Prasad, E., Rogoff, K., Wei S.-J., and Kose, M.A. (2003) 'Effects of Financial Globalization on Developing Countries: Some Empirical Evidence'. IMF Occasional Paper No. 220, 3 September.

Ritzer, G. (2004) *The McDonaldization of Society*. London: Pine Forge Press.

Rosen, D.H. (2003) 'How China Is Eating Mexico's Lunch'. *The International Economy* Spring, 78.

Rugman, A. and Hodgetts, R.M. (2002) *International Business*. London: Prentice Hall.

Sachs, J. (2005) *The End of Poverty*. New York: Penguin Press.

Sauvé, P. (2014) 'Towards a Plurilateral Trade in Services Agreement (TISA): Challenges and prospects. *Journal of International Commerce, Economics and Policy* 5(1).

Steigner, T. and Sutton, N.K. (2011) 'How Does National Culture Impact Internalization Benefits in Cross-Border Mergers and Acquisitions? '. *The Financial Review* 46.

Stiglitz, J. (2002) *Globalization and its Discontents*. London: Penguin.

Tunstall, J. (2008) *The Media were American: US Media in Decline*. Oxford: Oxford University Press.

UNCTAD (2010) 'International Trade After the Economic Crisis: Challenges and New Opportunities'. Available at: unctad.org/en/docs/ditctab20102_en.pdf .

UNCTAD (2007) 'World Investment Report'. Available at: www.wto.org/english/res_e/reser_e/wtr_e.htm.

UNCTAD (2011) 'Global Investment Trends Monitor', 17 January.

UNCTAD (2013) 'Economic Development in Africa', Report 2013.

UNCTAD (2014) 'World Investment Report'. Available at: http://unctad.org/en/pages/PublicationWebflyer.aspx?publicationid=937 .

UNWTO (2014) *Tourism Highlights: 2014 Edition*. Available at: http://mkt.unwto.org/publication/unwto-tourism-highlights-2014-edition .

W Hospitality Group (2013), *Hotel Chain Development Pipelines in Africa, 2013*. Available at: http://w-hospitalitygroup.com/?p=1943 .

Waters, J.J. (2013) 'Achieving World Trade Organization Compliance for Export Processing Zones While Maintaining Economic Competitiveness for Developing Countries'. *Duke Law Journal* 63.

Wolf, M. (2005) *Why Globalization Works*. Yale: Yale University Press.

Wolf, M. (2010) *Fixing Global Finance*. Baltimore: Johns Hopkins University Press.

World Bank (2014) 'Mobile Cellular Subscriptions (per 100 people)'. Available at: http://data.worldbank.org .

World Bank (nd) 'Fact Sheet: Infrastructure in Sub-Saharan Africa'. Available at: http://web.worldbank.org/WBSITE/EXTERNAL/COUNTRIES/AFRICAEXT/0,,contentMDK:21951811~pagePK:146736~piPK:146830~theSitePK:258644,00.html.

World Tourism Organisation (2014) *UNWTO Tourism Highlights*. Available at: http://mkt.unwto.org/publication/unwto-tourism-highlights-2014-edition.

WTO (2007) 'World Trade Report 2007'. Available at: www.wto.org/english/res_e/reser_e/wtr_e.htm .

WTO (2014) 'Trade Profiles 2014'. Available at: http://stat.wto.org/CountryProfile/WSDBCountryPFReporter.aspx?Language

CHAPTER TWO

The Global Economy

LEARNING OUTCOMES

This chapter will enable you to:

- **Identify the global pattern of wealth**

- **Analyse the pattern of international trade**

- **Explain why countries trade with each other**

- **Identify the controls on trade**

- **Assess the significance of exchange rates for the business environment**

Case Study China and the world economy

Globalization is a process whereby nations become increasingly interdependent largely through the exchange of goods and services, financial capital, and people. This case illustrates China's entry into the world economy. It shows how China transformed itself from a centralized, closed economy into a very open one and in the process became a leading world player; and also how growth has raised the living standards of some sectors of the economy but not all, and that rapid growth can also have its costs.

China joined the World Trade Organization (WTO) on 11 December 2001, submitting itself to a universal set of rules and giving up some of the independence it had for so long defended. The process of moving the centrally planned economy of China to a more market oriented economy actually started in 1978 with the phasing out of collectivized agriculture. Other liberalization measures in relation to state-owned enterprises, prices, domestic labour mobility, external trade, and foreign direct investment (FDI) followed and it is now the world's second largest economy with an estimated gross domestic product (GDP) of over US$14 trillion PPP (purchasing power parity—a measure which takes into account the relative cost of living). The USA is still the biggest at over US$17 trillion, but China is expected to become the biggest economy by 2019. Recent International Comparison Programme data from the World Bank suggest that this might happen earlier, even by the end of 2014.

The Chinese economy grew rapidly after 1978 averaging around 10 per cent per year, although with some wide fluctuations with growth as low as 4 per cent and as high as 14 per cent per annum. This resulted in a sixfold increase in GDP from 1984 to 2004. Growth has been much more stable since 2000 with 2007 being the fifth year in a row with growth above 10 per cent per annum. Growth has since slipped to below 10 per cent and seems to have stabilized at about 7.5 per cent in 2013–14, still more than double the world average. This has been very much an export led growth with exports growing at over 30 per cent per year for five years up to 2007 and 15 per cent from 2005 to 2012. It is also a very open economy with trade (imports plus exports) as a percentage of GDP measuring 53.6 per cent between 2010 and 2012, up from 44 per cent in 2001. Visit the supporting **Online Resource Centre** for a link to these statistics.

Source: © Wavebreakmedia Ltd / Dreamstime

China is now a major world player and changes there have a significant knock-on effect on the rest of the world economy. In 2004 China accounted for a third of the growth in world demand for oil and was a major reason for the dramatic rise in oil prices in that year. China is the world's second largest oil consumer, using one in every 10 barrels produced. China is also the top consumer of steel, copper, and aluminium accounting for around 40 per cent of global consumption for each.

The sectors of the economy to benefit have been industry and services, with agriculture now in decline. The main cities to benefit alongside Beijing have been those along the coastal region, and the well-to-do residents of those cities can now afford to buy imported luxury goods, such as Mercedes, and can choose from a greater variety of goods available in retail stores.

But it is not good news for all. The reduced tariffs on agricultural products have threatened the livelihoods of hundreds of millions of farmers. More than 100,000 people have lost jobs in state-owned banks as they adjust to a more competitive climate. China may well be the world's second largest economy, but, with a population of 1.3 billion, the average income is still only US$7,332 (2014) although this has risen significantly from US$285 in 1985 and US$1,290 in 2005. In 2012, according to the World Bank, 98.99 million people still lived below the national poverty line of RMB 2,300 per year (about $1 per day at current prices).

According to the World Health Organization, China has some of the world's most polluted cities although the worst are in India and Pakistan. Beijing is four times as polluted as New York, Paris, and London, and Shanghai almost three ➡

→ times. Coal is the major energy source and there are plans to build more than 500 coal-fired power stations to add to the 2,000 that already exist. Most of these are un-modernized and spew out clouds of carbon dioxide and sulphur dioxide. China's mines have the world's worst casualty rate. According to the China Labour Bulletin in 2002, there were over 4,000 accidents and nearly 7,000 deaths, but this figure has been decreasing each year since. In 2013, there were 589 accidents and 1,049 deaths.

Sources: IMF; World Bank; WTO; Coates and Luu 2012; China Labour Bulletin, April 2014; World Health Organisation

Introduction

What is going to happen to the world economy next year? Which economies will grow the fastest? Which are the richest? Which are the poorest? Where are the new markets of the world? What sort of goods and services do they require? Who trades with whom? What trade restrictions are in place? What is happening to exchange rates?

These are just a few of the many questions international businesses will be asking as globalization spurs the search for new markets and new locations to site increasingly global activities. This chapter seeks to answer some of these questions. It looks at the incidence of global wealth and poverty and how this is likely to change in the future. It examines the pattern of international trade, why countries trade, regulation of trade, and exchange rates.

Measuring the Size of the Global Economy

The most common method of measuring the size of an economy is by calculating GDP. This is the market value of total output of goods and services produced within a nation, by both residents and non-residents, over a period of time, usually a year.

In comparing the relative size of different economies, one obvious problem is that the calculation of GDP is in a country's national currency. A common currency is required and this is normally the US$, using foreign exchange rates to convert. This is not without its problems as foreign exchange rates reflect only internationally traded goods and services and are subject to short-term speculation and government intervention. For example, in the 1940s £1 sterling bought US$4. This rate was fixed as part of an international regime which considered that it was best for business if there was certainty about future exchange rates. In 1949, the UK government, for domestic reasons, decided to devalue sterling to US$2.80. It remained at this rate until 1967 when it was further devalued to US$2.41. In 1971, the USA moved to a floating exchange rate and other currencies followed suit. In the 1970s, sterling was floated and has varied from US$2.50 in the early 1970s to almost parity (US$1=£1) in 1984, back to about US$2 in 2007 and around US$1.70 in 2014. So measuring and comparing the wealth of the UK with the USA using foreign exchange rates would have indicated sudden changes in wealth, which is clearly not the case as the wealth of a mature economy such as the UK tends to change slowly, and fairly smoothly, over time.

This way of measuring GDP may indicate a country's international purchasing power but does not adequately reflect living standards. Most things, especially the basics of food, transport, and housing tend to be much cheaper in low-income countries than in high-income countries. A Western European travelling in much of Asia or Africa will find hotels, food, and drinks on average a lot cheaper than at home. The opposite, of course, is also true; people from those countries will find that their money does not go very far in Western Europe. A better indicator of living standards can be achieved by calculating GDP using what is known as the purchasing power parity (PPP) method. This calculates GDP on the basis of purchasing power within the respective domestic market, i.e. what you can buy with a unit of a country's currency. The International Comparison Program, housed in the World Bank, collects information from 199 countries to establish PPP estimates. When these rates are used, the relative size of developed economies is very much reduced and that of lower income countries much increased, as indicated in Table 2.1 (see http://icp.worldbank.org). This table compares GDP and GDP per capita, both at current prices and PPP, of some of the richest and the poorest countries of the world. The data is derived from the International Monetary Fund's World Economic Outlook database.

Learning Task

The World Bank, using a slightly different measure (Gross National Income which is GDP plus net income flows from abroad), classifies countries for 2014 into four different per capita income groups: low income, US$1,035 or less in 2012; lower middle income, US$1,036–US$4,085; upper middle income, US$4,086–US$12,615; and high income, US$12,196 or more (http://data.worldbank.org/about/country-classifications).

From the information in Table 2.1 complete the following tasks:

1. Explain why, if countries were ranked according to their nominal GDP or their PPP GDP, the rankings vary depending on which measure of income is used.

2. Use your answer to Q1 to explain why the USA is more than 7.5 times richer than China according to GDP per capita but just over 3.5 times richer using the PPP figures.

3. Group the countries according to the World Bank classification of different income groups. Comment on their regional spread.

GDP as an Indicator of the Standard of Living

GDP tells us the absolute size of an economy and will indicate that, in nominal terms, according to Table 2.1, India is slightly larger than Australia. If, however, we look at their respective GDPs using PPP, we can see that India's GDP is more than five times that of Australia. What does this tell us about the standard of living? Not a lot really, because India has a very big population, over 53 times more people than Australia. When we take this into account to calculate on average how much of that GDP accrues to each person then, using PPP we can see that Australia has a per capita income of US$44,345, over 10 times that of India's US$4,306. Does this mean that Australian citizens are 10 times as well off as Indian citizens? They might be, and some might be many more times better off than some Indian citizens, but not all, because many Indian citizens are also very wealthy. These figures are averages and say nothing about the distribution of wealth. According to some (see Piketty 2014), wealth in capitalist economies is becoming increasingly unequal and will continue to do so. Piketty's argument is that the return on wealth is higher than the rate of

Table 2.1 Gross domestic product, 2014 (IMF estimates)

	GDP current prices (US$ million)	GDP PPP (US$ million)	Population (,000)	GDP per capita current prices (US$)	GDP per capita US$ (PPP)
Australia	1,435,830	1,041,482	23,485	61,137	44,345
Benin	9,237	17,935	10,592	872	1,693
Bolivia	33,616	63,165	11,246	2,989	5,616
Botswana	15,112	35,989	2,104	7,183	17,106
Brazil	2,215,953	2,505,185	200,004	11,079	12,525
Bulgaria	55,330	108,257	7,202	7,682	15,031
China	10,027,558	14,625,212	1,365,520	7,332	10,694
Colombia	387,692	559,659	47,711	8,125	11,730
Egypt	286,112	574,717	85,833	3,333	6,695
France	2,885,692	2,336,609	63,951	45,123	36,537
Germany	3,875,755	3,338,019	80,925	47,892	41,248
Ghana	38,994	94,108	26,216	1,485	3,589
Haiti	8,980	14,328	10,461	858	1,369
India	1,995,776	5,425,430	1,258,695	1,584	4,306
Indonesia	859,339	1,382,994	251,490	3,416	5,498
Italy	2,171,482	1,846,941	59,960	36,215	30,803
Japan	4,846,327	4,834,998	127,061	38,141	38,052
Malaysia	343,009	561,481	30,124	11,386	18,639
Oman	82,254	99,717	3,288	25,014	30,325
Pakistan	241,411	601,943	186,289	1,295	3,231
Poland	544,746	855,570	38,537	14,135	22,201
Russia	2,092,205	2,629,691	142,857	14,645	18,407
Rwanda	8,058	17,865	10,685	741	1,644
South Africa	354,150	619,840	53,699	6,595	11,542
Spain	1,415,304	1,424,856	46,507	30,431	30,637
Sweden	580,195	414,056	9,714	59,726	42,624
Turkey	767,066	1,219,193	77,324	9,920	15,767
UK	2,827,514	2,497,254	64,511	43,829	38,710
USA	17,528,382	17,528,382	318,814	54,979	54,979
Venezuela	342,067	412,099	30,457	11,231	13,530
Vietnam	187,837	385,747	90,630	2,072	4,256

Source: International Monetary Fund, World Economic Outlook Database, April 2014

economic growth so that those with wealth will see income and wealth grow more quickly than those without (visit the **Online Resource Centre** for a video of Piketty discussing his work at Parliament in the UK).

GDP also only measures activity that takes place in the formal, officially recorded, economy. If an electrician does jobs for cash and does not declare the income to the tax authorities, then there is additional output in the economy but it is not recorded. This is an example of activity in the so-called 'shadow economy'. This would include all activities (legal and illegal) which produce an output but do not get recorded in official statistics. Most studies, including that of the Institute for Economic Affairs in the UK, use a narrower definition than this to include 'all market-based legal production of goods and services that are deliberately concealed from public authorities'. They found that the shadow economy was about 10 per cent of GDP in the UK, about 14 per cent in Nordic countries, and 20–30 per cent in many Southern European countries (Schneider and Williams 2013). Schneider et al. (2010), using the same narrower definition, in a survey of the shadow economies of 162 countries from 1999 to 2007 found that the unweighted average size of the shadow economy was 31 per cent in 2007 (down from 34 per cent in 1999).

The countries with the largest average size of shadow economy over the period were Zimbabwe (61.8 per cent), Georgia (65.8 per cent), and Bolivia (66.1 per cent). The lowest were Switzerland (8.5 per cent), USA (8.6 per cent), and Luxembourg (9.7 per cent). By region, sub-Saharan Africa has the highest estimate with a mean of 40.8 per cent, followed by Latin America and the Caribbean (38.7 per cent). The lowest is the OECD (Organization for Economic Co-operation and Development—33 of the most developed economies) at 16.8 per cent. Within the last group, Greece had an average of 27.5 per cent and Italy 27.0 per cent.

Learning Task

Explain why countries in sub-Saharan Africa have the highest average shadow economies.

Another problem is that GDP figures do not take into account environmental degradation and the depletion of natural resources. When oil is taken from the ground, it is irreplaceable. The value of that oil is added to GDP, but the depletion of reserves is not accounted for even though it will affect the welfare of future generations. When the oil is turned into petrol that again adds to GDP, but the damage done to the atmosphere when we use it in our cars is not deducted (see Chapter 12 for more discussion on the environment). GDP simply measures the additions to output without taking into account the negative effects of pollution, congestion, and resource depletion.

Economic Growth

Regardless of the comments in Counterpoint Box 2.1, growth in national output (economic growth) is a key objective for all national governments as they believe it is fundamental to raising standards of living. It is measured by the annual percentage change in a nation's gross domestic product at constant prices, as GDP can grow through the effects of inflation. Quite modest rates of growth can have a significant effect on living standards if they are maintained. A growth rate of 2 per cent would double real incomes every 36 years. We saw in the opening case study that China's GDP had increased sixfold in just 20 years from 1984.

According to the International Monetary Fund (IMF), world GDP between 2006 and 2014 grew on average by 3.5 per cent per year, but, as shown in Table 2.2, growth rates for individual countries

Counterpoint Box 2.1 GDP and the quality of life

GDP per person is often used as an indicator of human progress, welfare, and happiness, but GDP tells us only about income. It does not tell us if GDP is spent on health and education projects or on armaments or on space projects. To emphasize that development is about people, The United Nations Development Programme (UNDP) has developed a set of measures which capture some other elements of development, the **Human Development Index** (HDI). This is an aggregate measure of three features of development, life expectancy, education, and standard of living (PPP per capita income). Its purpose is to emphasize those other elements of development not captured by GDP. The top two countries in the 2013 HDI rankings were Norway and Australia. The latter would rank only seventeenth in a table ranked in order of GDP per capita, but does very well on the other measures of welfare. On the other hand, Qatar and Kuwait, with high per capita incomes, are thirty-first and forty-sixth, respectively, in HDI terms (see http://hdr.undp.org/en/ for more information and the full tables, or visit the **Online Resource Centre** for a video of an interview with Amartya Sen).

Does more money make people happier? In the 1970s Richard Easterlin (1974) drew attention to the fact that, within a society, rich people seemed to be happier than poor people, but that rich societies seemed no happier than poor societies, and getting richer did not necessarily make people happier. It became known as the Easterlin paradox. Others have claimed the evidence is not so clear, although Proto and Rustichini (2013) found that in rich countries life satisfaction peaked at an income somewhere between $26,000 and $30,000 per year (2005 USD in PPP) (visit the **Online Resource Centre** for a video link on this topic). The New Economics Foundation has established the Happy Planet Index, which measures which countries deliver long, happy, sustainable lives using data on life expectancy, experienced well-being, and ecological footprint (see http://www.happyplanetindex.org for a video on this).

Nicholas Sarkozy (President of France), at the time unhappy with current measures of economic performance (i.e. GDP), set up a commission in 2008, chaired by Joseph Stiglitz, to see if the present measures properly reflected societal well being as well as economic, environmental, and social sustainability. A link to this report can be found on the supporting **Online Resource Centre**.

Questions

1. Access the references mentioned above and advance reasons why more money might not make people happier.

can vary quite markedly, from country to country and year to year. Growth in the most advanced and mature economies of the developed world tends to be much lower than in the developing economies of the world. Table 2.2 shows that world growth rates since 2006 have varied from -0.38 per cent to 5.3 per cent, but for the G7 (the most advanced economies of the world) the corresponding figures are -3.7 per cent and 2.8 per cent, and for developing economies 3.1 per cent and 8.7 per cent. In late 2008 and 2009, after the financial crisis (see Chapter 10), the world economy went into recession. World output shrank in a recession which lasted longer and was deeper (the fall in output from its peak to its trough was about 4 per cent) than any other post-war recession.

This affected some economies more than others. The developed economies suffered worst with Japan, Germany, and the UK contracting by over 5 per cent. At the same time, China continued to grow at a slightly slower rate than hitherto, 9.2 per cent, India by 8.5 per cent, and Nigeria by 7 per cent. In 2010 the world economy began to recover and world growth rates have been above 3 per cent in each year since. The European debt crisis still threatened so that recovery and growth rates in the EU have been lower than for other advanced economies. Rates of growth in developing economies and sub-Saharan Africa have generally been lower than pre-crisis rates, but still well above advanced economy rates of growth. The World Bank expected global GDP to expand by 3.4 per cent and 3.5 per cent in 2015 and 2016, respectively. Again,

Table 2.2 Economic growth (annual percentage change in GDP)

	2006	2007	2008	2009	2010	2011	2012	2013	2014(e)
World	5.2	5.3	2.7	−0.38	5.2	3.9	3.2	3.0	3.6
G7	2.6	2.2	−0.3	−3.7	2.8	1.6	1.7	1.4	2.2
EU	3.6	3.4	0.6	−4.4	2.0	1.7	−0.3	0.2	1.6
Developing Economies	8.2	8.7	5.9	3.1	7.5	6.2	5.1	4.7	4.9
Sub-Saharan Africa	6.3	7.1	5.7	2.6	5.6	5.5	4.9	4.9	5.4
Australia	2.7	4.5	2.7	1.5	2.2	2.6	3.6	2.4	2.6
Brazil	4.0	6.1	5.2	−0.3	7.5	2.7	1.0	2.4	1.8
China	12.7	14.1	9.6	9.2	10.4	9.3	7.7	7.7(e)	7.5
Colombia	6.7	6.9	3.5	1.7	4.0	6.6	4.2	4.3(e)	4.5
Germany	3.9	3.4	0.8	−5.1	3.9	3.4	0.9	0.5	1.7
India	9.2	9.8	3.9	8.5	10.3	6.6	4.7	4.4	5.4
Indonesia	5.5	6.3	6.0	4.6	6.2	6.5	6.3	5.8	5.4
Japan	1.7	2.2	−1.0	−5.3	4.7	−0.5	1.4	1.5	1.4
Kenya	6.3	7.0	1.5	2.7	5.8	4.4	4.6	5.6	6.3
Mexico	5.0	3.1	1.4	−4.7	5.1	4.0	3.9	1.1	3.0
Nigeria	6.2	7.0	6.0	7.0	8.0	7.4	6.6	6.3(e)	7.1
Russia	8.2	8.5	5.2	−7.8	4.5	4.3	3.4	1.3	1.3
South Africa	5.6	5.5	3.6	−1.5	3.1	3.6	2.5	1.9(e)	2.3
Tanzania	6.7	7.1	7.4	6.0	7.0	6.4	6.9	7.0(e)	7.2
Thailand	5.1	5.0	2.5	−2.3	7.8	0.1	6.5	2.9	2.5
Turkey	6.9	4.7	0.7	−4.8	9.2	8.8	2.2	4.3(e)	2.3
UK	2.8	3.4	−0.8	−5.2	1.7	1.1	0.3	1.8	2.9
USA	2.7	1.8	−0.3	−2.8	2.5	1.9	2.8	1.8	2.9
Vietnam	7.0	7.1	5.7	5.4	6.4	6.2	5.2	5.4	5.6

(e) estimate

Source: International Monetary Fund, World Economic Outlook Database, April 2014

Counterpoint Box 2.2 Is economic growth a good thing?

Not everybody agrees that the pursuit of economic growth is necessarily a good thing. Edward Mishan, in his book, *The Costs of Economic Growth* (1967), pointed out that economic growth brought with it social costs such as pollution, traffic congestion, and 'the frantic pace of life'. In a later book (Meadows 1972), *The Limits to Growth*, the authors explored the relationship between growth and resources and concluded that, if growth continued at its present pace, then the limits to growth would be reached sometime in the twenty-first century.

Visit the link on our **Online Resource Centre** for an interview in January 2010 with Dennis Meadows, one of the authors (see Chapter 12 for a fuller discussion of these issues).

Nor is everybody agreed that growth is necessarily the solution for poverty as the benefits of growth can be highly unbalanced. For a recent discussion of this, and the problems of climate change and resource depletion, see Simms et al. (2010). You can find the link on the supporting **Online Resource Centre**.

Questions
1. Explain why economic growth is not necessarily the solution to poverty. How else could poverty be addressed?

developing countries were expected to grow faster (on average over 5 per cent) than high-income countries (around 2.5 per cent). Visit the **Online Resource Centre** for a link to the Global Economic Prospects Report on the World Bank's website.

The Changing World Economy

Looking further ahead, the OECD (2012) estimates that the world economy will grow at an annual rate of around 3 per cent over the next 50 years. Non-OECD countries will continue to grow faster than OECD countries, at over 7 per cent per year up to 2020, declining to around 5 per cent and then to about 2.5 per cent in the 2050s. OECD countries will grow at around 2 per cent. This will result in a fourfold increase in world output, but, because non-OECD countries will grow more quickly than OECD countries, their share of world output will grow. This will see major changes in the relative size of economies. The combined GDP of China and India will outstrip the G7 (Canada, France, Germany, Italy, Japan, the UK, and the USA) GDP by 2025 and by 2060 will be 1.5 times larger. By 2060, their combined GDP will be larger than the current 34 developed economies in the OECD. The output of the current developing world will be bigger (57.7 per cent) than the current developed world (42.3 per cent). China alone will account for 28 per cent of GDP, India 18 per cent, while the share of the USA will fall to16 per cent and the euro area to 9 per cent (see Figure 2.1). Per capita GDP will increase fourfold in developing economies and only double in advanced economies, so there will be some convergence of per capita GDP but there will still be a substantial gap between advanced and developing economies.

For China and India this would be more like their positions in the nineteenth century when they were the world's two biggest economies. In the nineteenth century, together they accounted for around 30 per cent of world GDP (Maddison 2003). Their populations were large then, as now, so per capita incomes were lower than Western Europe. In fact, China remained the largest economy until 1890 when the lead was lost to Western Europe and the USA following the

Figure 2.1 Percentage of World GDP

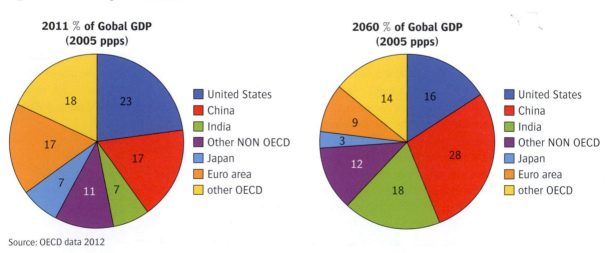

Source: OECD data 2012

industrial revolution that originated in the mid-eighteenth century in Britain. This transformed Western society from an agricultural economy with small-scale cottage industries to an industrialized economy with mass production carried out in factories in towns. There was mass migration from the countryside to the cities as a result of this.

The driver for all of this was the application of steam power, not just in factories but also for transport, allowing the movement of relatively low value goods across large distances over both land and water. The benefits of this transformation were confined to the industrialized nations of the time largely because they held the advantage in technological progress, but also because many of the countries of Africa, Asia, and Latin America were the colonies of the Western powers supplying primary products to the industrialized nations. In the case of Africa, they also supplied young men and women as unpaid, slave labour.

In the nineteenth century, the UK was the dominant power producing 30 per cent of total world industrial output, but this position was changing as the USA and other Western European powers developed. By 1913, the USA was producing 36 per cent of world industrial output and the UK only 14 per cent (Dicken 2004). This pattern continued until World War II when the world divided into three different spheres.

The first sphere was the Western world led by the USA and organized along capitalist lines. It set up world institutions such as the World Bank, the IMF, and the General Agreement on Tariffs and Trade (GATT) (later WTO) in order to aid recovery of the war-torn Western European economies and to establish a 'world system' to combat the power of the Soviet bloc. The 1950s also saw the emergence of Japan as a new competitor for the developed Western world so that the bi-polar world of trade in manufactures became a tri-polar world.

The second sphere to emerge after World War II was the Eastern communist bloc led by Russia. Russia had become a communist state after the 1917 revolution, but it was after World War II that communism took hold in other countries. Some Eastern and Central European countries were invaded by Russia and others, Cuba and China, experienced revolutions. The Soviet Union was a centrally planned economy and this system was imposed on the satellite states of Eastern and Central Europe so that trade and investment between the two spheres was minimal. China became the People's Republic of China in 1949 and for the next 30 years had little to do with the world economy, following a policy of self-reliance. The Soviet bloc ushered in some political and economic reforms in the 1980s in a move towards becoming a democratic market economy and this was a prelude to popular revolutions which swept across Eastern Europe following the withdrawal of Soviet Union support for the communist regimes. In 1991, the Baltic states declared themselves independent and by the end of that year the whole Soviet sphere unravelled with the Soviet Union itself ceasing to exist. China had started its move towards becoming a market economy in 1979, but, unlike the Soviet bloc, communism still prevails there.

The world is now less divided along political lines, but there is still an enormous gap between those who have and those who have not. In East Asia, a number of newly industrialized economies have emerged (initially South Korea, Taiwan, Singapore, and Hong Kong and later, Malaysia, Thailand, and Indonesia) to become global players, but, for much of the rest of the world, poverty remains a major problem and narrowing this gap will be a major challenge.

For business, business analysts, and fund managers these changes are of great interest as they seek new markets and investment opportunities. The growth and potential of Brazil, Russia, India, and China has been well documented, so much so that they are now well known by the acronym 'BRIC', a label given to them in 2001 by Jim O'Neill, former chief economist of Goldman Sachs (2003). Various other groupings have been identified as the next great wave of **emerging markets**. Goldman Sachs (2007) identified what they called the N11 (next eleven) economies with strong market growth potential. These countries were Bangladesh, Mexico, South Korea, Vietnam, Pakistan, Egypt, Philippines, Nigeria, Indonesia, Turkey, and Iran. Next came the Economic intelligence Unit's CIVETS, Colombia, Indonesia, Vietnam, Egypt, Turkey, and South Africa, and now we have MINTs, Mexico, Indonesia, Nigeria, and Turkey. What all these countries have in common is a large, youthful population in contrast to the ageing populations of the more advanced economies. Some, Mexico, Indonesia, and Turkey, are close to large markets, USA, China, and the EU. Some have abundant natural resources, but none have the potential to be the next BRICs. What critics say of these new acronyms is that they are no more than marketing ploys by fund managers to attract new investment funds. Although they form convenient groupings, they are all very diverse economies and tend to be much less stable than more advanced economies, often with weak governance and high levels of corruption (see Chapter 11). While they all, no doubt, have potential for business, further research needs to be undertaken before committing resources, as we shall see in Chapter 5.

In 2010, the BRICs became the BRICS with the inclusion of South Africa conveniently maintaining the acronym. This was not because of South Africa's prospects, as had been the case with the original members, but was a reflection of the rise of a new political grouping representing the emerging market countries of the world. The original members had begun meeting annually in 2006, but one problem was that Africa was not represented, hence the invitation to South Africa to join the original BRICs (see Mini Case Study: Africa to join the BRICS?).

Similar to the OECD study, Goldman Sachs (2011) estimated that by 2050 China and India will be the first and third largest economies, with Brazil and Russia taking fifth and sixth places. China's economy will be some 30 per cent bigger than the US economy and India's about 12 per cent smaller. Brazil, Russia, Indonesia, and Mexico will all be bigger than any of the European economies, with Turkey not far behind. These economies will provide opportunities for outsourcing manufacturing activities, opening new offices, mergers, acquisitions, and alliances; but of major significance will be the emergence of a global middle class. In 2050 Russia, Mexico, Brazil, Turkey, China, Indonesia, and India will still have per capita incomes less than the USA, Japan, and Western Europe, but they will be very much greater than today (see Figures 2.2 and 2.3).

Estimating the growth of the middle class is fraught with problems of definition, but what business is interested in mainly is 'spending power'. For this, per capita GDP is a good proxy measure of 'middle class'. The World Bank, as we saw above, separates the 'middle class' into 'lower middle' and 'upper middle' with a cut-off point at about $4,000 dollars per year or about $11 per day. The lower cut-off point of about $2.80 dollars per day is useful in terms of a measurement which takes people out of extreme poverty, but not very useful to businesses wanting to sell cars, washing machines, health care, and financial services. Kharas and Gertz (2010), using a measure of $10–100 per day, estimated that by 2015 the number of Asian middle class consumers will equal the number in Europe and North America, and that by 2021 there could be more than 2 billion Asians in middle class households. By 2030 they project that two-thirds of the global middle class will be in the Asia Pacific region (see Table 2.3).

This will mean that by 2030 there will be 5 billion members of the global middle class with only 21 per cent of them resident in North America and Europe. These new consumers in developing countries will have spending patterns similar to current residents of high-income

Figure 2.2 GDP level, 2010 ($US billion)

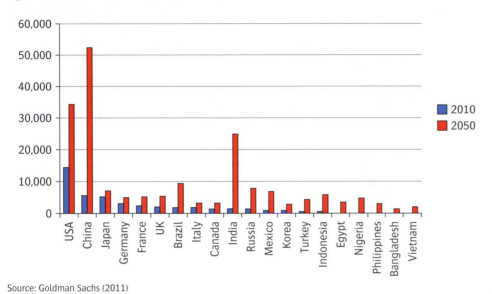

Source: Goldman Sachs (2011)

countries, providing enormous opportunities to international business in the form of new markets. According to Ernst and Young (2013) countries hit a 'sweet spot' of interest to businesses when per capita incomes move beyond, on average, about $6,000 per annum, although different industries have different 'sweet spots' and therefore need more specific information. They give as an example the automobile market in China, which, in 2001, was tiny but once per capita incomes hit $6,000 in 2008 it grew very quickly. General Motors in 2004 sold one

Figure 2.3 GDP per capita level, 2010 ($US)

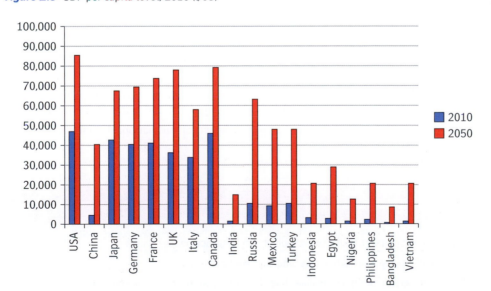

Source: Goldman Sachs (2011)

Table 2.3 The middle class: size and distribution

	2009		2020		2030	
	millions	%	millions	%	millions	%
North America	338	18	333	10	322	7
Europe	664	36	703	22	680	14
Central and South America	181	10	251	8	313	6
Asia Pacific	525	28	1,740	54	3,228	66
sub-Saharan Africa	32	2	57	2	107	2
Middle East and N. Africa	105	6	165	5	234	5
World	1,845	100	3,249	100	4,884	100

Source: Kharas and Gertz (2010)

Table 2.4 When will the emerging markets countries hit their sweet spots? (projected)

Country	Year
Egypt	2011
Indonesia	2015
India	2017
Philippines	2019
Vietnam	2019
Pakistan	2024
Nigeria	2025
Bangladesh	2029

Source: Economist Intelligence Unit quoted in Ernst and Young (2013)

car in China for every 10 sold in the USA. By 2009, this had reached parity. The estimated 'sweet spots' for various countries are shown in Table 2.4.

In the next section we go on to look at two other aspects of international business: trade flows and exchange rates.

Learning Task

1. Explain what is meant by the 'sweet spot' of per capita income.
2. Why might different industries have different sweet spots?
3. Why is the growth of a global middle class of such interest to international business?

Mini Case Study Africa to join the BRICS?

The World Bank uses as its extreme poverty line an income of about US$1.25 (at 2005 prices) per person per day. Using this measure, poverty has fallen in all regions since 1990 except in sub-Saharan Africa where, in 2010, nearly 400 million people still lived on less than US$1 per day, up from about 300 million in 1990, although as a proportion of the population this has fallen from 56.5 per cent to 48.5 per cent. Sub-Saharan Africa stands out as the poorest area and by 2030 it is predicted that most of the world's poor will be in Africa. The situation did not change much in the early nineties largely because of low and sometimes negative rates of economic growth, but since 1995 growth has been around 6 per cent (see Table 2.2). Some, such as Nigeria and Tanzania with growth rates of 10 per cent and 7 per cent, respectively, have done much better. This has lead Jim O'Neill of Goldman Sachs to speculate that Africa, thought of as a whole, could have the same bright future as the BRIC countries. He picks out South Africa, Nigeria, and Egypt as critical to this success.

Michael Keating (Executive Director of the Africa Progress Panel) writing in the *Financial Times* points out:

> The continent's advantages include abundant natural resources, whether commodities, land or energy, whose strategic and financial value is generally increasing. It also has a vast, inexpensive pool of labour; a growing middle class that brings growing demand for consumer goods (and better governance); and an increasing recognition that business can play a much greater role in reducing the costs of goods and services to all of Africa's billion people, including the hundreds of millions living on or below the poverty line (Keating 2010).

But as Leke et al. (2010) point out in a survey of African economies, Africa has over 50 individual economies which are extremely diverse. It identifies four different development paths. The diversified economies are the most advanced and have large manufacturing and services sectors (as a percentage of GDP). The four largest are Egypt, Morocco, South Africa, and Tunisia of which only South Africa is in sub-Saharan Africa. The oil exporters such as Angola, Equatorial Guinea, Chad, Libya, and Nigeria are the richest but least diversified and need to invest in infrastructure and education. The transition economies, e.g. Ghana, Kenya, and Tanzania, have begun the process of diversifying, but their income per head remains below the first two groups. The poorest countries such as the Democratic Republic of the Congo, Ethiopia, Mali, and Sierra Leone remain in the pre-transition stage.

According to the World Bank, economic growth, while averaging around 4.5 per cent from 1995–2013, was four times higher in the fast-growing regions than in the slow-growing regions. Among the best performers were the five oil exporters and eight non-oil but resource-abundant countries of Botswana, Ghana, Liberia, Mozambique, Namibia, Sierra Leone, Tanzania, and Zambia, but some non-resource countries did equally well, such as Rwanda, Uganda, Malawi, and Burkino Faso. The Bank points out that within Africa there are many internal and external uncertainties. Natural disasters occur more frequently and there is a continued threat of conflict. Exports tend to be concentrated on a few natural resources making them vulnerable to movements in price. There has, though, been diversification in trading partners with the BRIC countries, now accounting for 36 per cent of exports.

The BRIC countries have also become major sources of new investment, not just in resources but also in infrastructure projects. They also supply loans, aid, and arms and this is to the liking of many African countries as the BRIC countries are much less prescriptive about economic policy, unlike Western-backed institutions such as the World Bank and the IMF who often insist on free market economic reforms. They also have a policy of non-interference in the domestic policies of their partners, probably because of a shared history of colonial exploitation (Carmody 2013). In 2014, the BRICS nations agreed to establish the BRICS Development Bank to fund infrastructure and development projects and to rival the Western-dominated institutions of the World Bank and IMF.

Sources: *Financial Times International Business Insight*, 22 October 2010; FT.com 26 August 2010; *McKinsey Quarterly* June 2010; Carmody 2013; World Bank, *Africa's Pulse*, Vols. 8 and 9, 2013–2014.

Questions

1. Explain the different growth paths identified by McKinsey.
2. Which is the most sustainable and why?
3. Why might African economies prefer aid and investment from the BRIC economies rather than the World Bank and the IMF?

International Trade

One of the key drivers of globalization is international trade, the exchange of goods and services between nations. In this section we will look in more detail at the pattern of global trade and put forward several theories to answer the question, why do countries trade? We will also look at the regulation of trade through the WTO.

The Pattern of Trade

International trade grew very quickly in the second half of the twentieth century and more quickly than global output, which had been rising at 3 per cent per annum. It has grown especially quickly in the last 30 years at about 7.3 per cent per annum. In 1950, world exports were approximately US$0.5 trillion, rising to US$2.03 trillion dollars in 1980, and about US$22 trillion in 2012. Of this US$22 trillion, most (US$17.9 trillion) was in merchandise trade, and the rest (US$4.4 trillion) was in services. Generally, service trade has grown more quickly than merchandise trade (see Table 2.5). Exports as a percentage of world output were about 13 per cent in 1970, 25 per cent in 2005, and are predicted to be 34 per cent in 2030 (World Bank 2007). The main contributors to this growth are the reduction of trade barriers, the continuing reduction in transport and communications costs, and, not least, the growth in vertical specialization in production and the establishment of MNC global supply chains.

Merchandise trade comprises three categories: manufactured goods, mining, and agricultural products. The share of primary commodities in total world exports of merchandise trade has fallen dramatically. In 1960, primary commodities (excluding fuels) accounted for 38 per cent of world exports, but by 2012 had fallen to only 9 per cent. Over the same period, the share of manufactured goods has increased from 51 per cent to 64 per cent. Developing countries have increased their share of world trade in manufactured goods from less than 25 per cent in 1960 to about 39 per cent in 2012, with South East Asian countries being the main contributors to this growth. Other developing regions' exports did not see the same growth. African states' exports have averaged only 2 per cent growth since 1980, while world exports have grown at 6 per cent per annum. Developed economies still account for the majority of traffic—see Tables 2.6, 2.7, and 2.8. The WTO (2013) estimates that developing countries will see their share of world exports rise from 41 per cent in 2010 to 57 per cent in 2030, with developed economies dropping from 59 per cent to 43 per cent. China's share of world exports will increase from 9 per cent to 15 per cent over the same time period.

Table 2.5 World exports of merchandise and commercial services 2005–12 (billion dollars and percentage)

	Value 2012	Annual percentage change			
		2005–12	2010	2011	2012
Merchandise	17,930	3.5	14	5.5	2.5
Commercial Services	4,350	8	10	12	2

Source: WTO

Table 2.6 Leading exporters and importers in world merchandise trade 2012 (billion dollars and percentage)

Exports				Imports			
Rank		Value	Share	Rank		Value	Share
1	China	2,049	11.1	1	USA	2,336	12.6
2	USA	1,546	8.4	2	China	1,818	9.8
3	Germany	1,407	7.6	3	Germany	1167	6.3
4	Japan	799	4.3	4	Japan	886	4.8
5	Netherlands	656	3.6	5	UK	690	3.7
6	France	569	3.1	6	France	674	3.6
7	Korea, Republic of	548	3.0	7	Netherlands	591	3.2
8	Russian Federation	529	2.9	8	Hong Kong, China	553	3.0
					Retained imports	490	0.8
9	Italy	501	2.7	9	Korea, Republic of	520	2.8
10	Hong Kong, China	493	2.7	10	India	490	2.6
	Domestic exports	22	0.1				
	Re-exports	471	2.6				

Hong Kong imports includes re-exports
Source: WTO

Table 2.7 Leading exporters and importers in world service trade 2012 (billion dollars and percentage)

Exports				Imports			
Rank		Value	Share	Rank		Value	Share
1	USA	621	14.3	1	USA	411	9.9
2	UK	280	6.4	2	Germany	293	7.1
3	Germany	257	5.9	3	China	280	6.7
4	France	211	4.8	4	Japan	175	4.2
5	China	190	4.4	5	UK	174	4.2
6	Japan	142	3.3	6	France	172	4.1
7	India	141	3.2	7	India	127	3.1
8	Spain	136	3.1	8	Netherlands	119	2.9
9	Netherlands	131	3.0	9	Singapore	118	2.8
10	Hong Kong, China	123	2.8	10	Ireland	112	2.7

Source: WTO

Table 2.8 Intra- and inter-regional merchandise trade 2012 (billion dollars)

Origin	Destination							
	North America	S & C America	Europe	CIS	Africa	Middle East	Asia	World
North America	1151	217	380	18	38	75	488	2,371
S and Central America	187	202	128	8	21	17	172	750
Europe	492	124	4,383	245	211	208	643	6,385
CIS	37	7	430	149	14	20	127	805
Africa	74	30	240	2	81	17	160	630
Middle East	118	11	148	7	39	116	732	1,349
Asia	975	196	855	121	177	260	3,012	5,640
World	3.035	787	6,564	550	580	714	5,333	17,930

(Asia includes Japan, Australia, New Zealand, China, and other Asia)
Source: WTO

Learning Task

Using the information in Table 2.8:

1. For each region, calculate its share of world merchandise trade.

2. What proportion of world trade is accounted for by North America and Europe?

3. For each region, calculate the share of intra-regional trade, e.g. what proportion of Europe's trade is within Europe?

4. What conclusions can you draw from these and any other calculations in terms of the economic self-reliance of different regions?

Why do Countries Trade?

The earliest theory (seventeenth and eighteenth century) in relation to international trade was that of **mercantilism**, which held that countries should maximize exports and try to limit imports as much as possible. Mercantilists viewed the accumulation of precious metals (gold and silver being the medium for settling international debts) as the only way to increase the wealth of the nation. Generating a **trade surplus** (when the value of exports exceeds the value of imports) was the aim of governments, as this would result in an inflow of gold and silver. The governments of mercantilist nations, such as Britain, the Netherlands, France, Spain, and Portugal, restricted or banned imports with tariffs and quotas and subsidized domestic industries to encourage exports. At the same time, they developed large colonies which provided cheap raw materials to a growing manufacturing base. They, in turn, exported finished goods to the colonies at much higher prices.

Mercantilists viewed exports as a good thing, as they stimulated industry and increased the number of jobs at home, and imports as bad, as this was a loss of demand and jobs. Although the mercantilist era ended in the eighteenth century, **neo-mercantilism** or, as it is also known, **economic nationalism** continues. The USA and Germany, in the late nineteenth century, were able to erode Britain's dominance through protectionist policies. More recently, post-war Japan has subsidized its domestic industries and protected them from foreign imports. It also had very tight controls on foreign exchange and foreign investment within Japan. These policies resulted in large trade surpluses. The current problems besetting the world economy are threatening a new wave of mercantilist policies as countries look to exports of goods to deliver economic growth. Whereas mercantilists viewed trade as a zero sum game (i.e. one country could only gain if another lost), Adam Smith (1776) set out to prove that all could gain by engaging in free trade. Smith demonstrated that if countries specialized in producing the goods in which they were most efficient (i.e. in which they had an absolute advantage), then world output would be increased and the surpluses could be traded.

David Ricardo (1817) extended this theory to show that even when a country had an absolute advantage in the production of all goods, total output could still be increased if countries specialized in the production of a good in which they had a **comparative advantage**. A country has a comparative advantage over another country if it can produce at a lower **opportunity cost**. In other words, it has to forgo fewer resources than the other in order to produce it.

These theories help to explain the pattern of trade, but do not tell us why one country should be more efficient than another and therefore what that country should specialize in. The factor proportions theory (or factor endowment theory), developed by Eli Heckscher (1919) and Bertil Ohlin (1924), explains that countries will produce and export products that utilize resources which they have in abundance, and import products which utilize resources that are relatively scarce. So Australia, with lots of land and a small population, exports mainly minerals (about 40 per cent of total exports), beef, cereals, and dairy products. Its main imports are petrol, road vehicles, telecoms equipment, and industrial machinery (in total about 35 per cent of total imports). China and India export goods and services which take advantage of cheap labour, whereas in Western Europe (where labour is expensive) there tends to be a concentration on relatively high value capital intensive industries, such as the chemical industry.

Trade patterns seem to correspond quite well with this theory, but there are weaknesses which Wassily Leontieff (1953) discovered in a study of US exports, some of which he found to be highly labour intensive, and imports, which were capital intensive. This became known as the Leontieff paradox. A weakness of the Heckscher–Ohlin theory is that it treats all factors as homogeneous, when in fact they are not. Labour, for example, varies enormously in skill levels depending on the training and development undertaken. When this was taken into account, and skill intensity was measured, then the results were more as predicted. The theory is further complicated when technology is considered. It had been assumed that technology is universally available, but there are in fact major lags in the diffusion of technology. However, one of the features of globalization is that this diffusion is becoming more rapid, especially the reduction in cost of collecting, analysing, and communicating information.

For much of the less developed world, the pattern of trade predicted by these theories holds true, but this pattern has tended to favour the richer nations at the expense of the poor. This is especially the case for sub-Saharan Africa. These countries produce and export primary products (other than oil for most) for which they have a comparative advantage, and they import manufactured goods for which they are at a comparative disadvantage. The problem is that the theories predict that total output is increased, but say nothing about how that increase will be shared between countries. History shows that the demand for primary products does not rise as quickly as the total rise in demand for all goods and services, so there tends to be long-run deterioration in the terms at which primary products exchange for manufactured goods. In other words, the price of manufactured goods tends to rise more quickly than the price of primary products. This, together with a very narrow range of products, probably goes a long way to explaining the low levels of income in those countries. Uganda, for example, relies heavily on agriculture which forms almost 23 per cent of GDP, but 80 per cent of the population rely on it for their livelihood. It also forms 90 per cent of export earnings, with coffee being the major export crop (over 17 per cent of earnings in 2013)—consequently, the economy is very susceptible to variations in the price of coffee. The main imports are oil and manufactured goods (http://www.africaneconomicoutlook.org).

Another model to explain the pattern of trade in manufactured goods was developed by Raymond Vernon (1966), the International Product Life Cycle model. The different locations for production, and subsequent exports and imports, were explained according to stages in the International Product Life Cycle. According to this theory, products move through three phases: new product growth, maturing product, and standardized product.

The new product stage requires high levels of investment in research and design and a market with high purchasing power. Initial production volumes tend to be low with consumers paying a premium price for the new product. The market conditions for this scenario are found in the developed economies and this is where production is first located. During this stage, firms monitor demand and make modifications to the product. Towards the end of this stage, production increases and some exporting begins.

In the maturing product stage, overseas markets become more aware of the product and exports increase. As they begin to account for an increasing proportion of sales, then production facilities are set up in major markets either in subsidiaries or through licensing local manufacturers.

In the standardized stage, new competitors selling similar products appear, the technology is widely available, and, in order to maintain sales, prices are reduced. Companies seek low-cost production centres, often in developing economies. Products that were once exports now become imports.

Vernon was using this theory to explain the evolution of US firms and the associated pattern of US exports and imports, and, at the time, it fitted quite well. Since then, the pattern of international investment has become much more complex as we saw with the case of Tata Motors (see Chapter 1). Competition is much more international, product life cycles much shorter, and **innovation** may come from anywhere in the company's global production and marketing network. In an electronic age, some firms are said to be '**born global**' (see Chapter 5), in that they start international activities right from the outset and move into distant, and sometimes multiple, markets right away.

What none of this explained was, as noted earlier, that most trade takes place not between nations which are very different, but between similar, developed nations and that it is trade in similar goods—so-called intra-industry trade. **New trade theory** in the 1980s explained that there were gains to be made from **specialization** and economies of scale and that those who were first to enter the market could erect entry barriers to other firms and become the dominant firm. As output increases, the unit costs of production fall and new entrants are forced to produce at similar levels. Without a large domestic market to justify producing on that scale, cost then becomes a major barrier to entry (see Chapter 3 for a discussion of entry barriers). The end result can be a global market supporting very few competitors and thus new trade theory becomes a major factor in explaining the growth of globalization.

A feature of intra-industry trade is **product differentiation**. Much international trade theory regards products as homogeneous but modern manufacturing firms produce a range of similar products appealing to different consumer preferences. For example, a few car producers based in a few developed economies each manufacture a range of models and most of the trade in those products takes place between those countries.

According to the country similarity theory (Linder 1961), this trade is determined not so much by cost difference but by similarity in the markets. As identified in Chapter 1, there are many barriers to globalization: such as geography, cultural difference, and corruption. It follows that firms will tend to do business with countries which are geographically close, culturally similar, have similar economic and political interests, have similar demand patterns, and are at similar levels of development (see Chapter 5).

The Competitive Advantage of Nations

In the 1980s, Michael Porter (1990) undertook a study to find what made the major advanced nations competitive. He studied 10 of the most successful exporting nations and found that constant innovation and upgrading, in their broadest sense, were the key to **competitive advantage**. Constant, and often incremental, improvement is the key as almost any advantage could be replicated by others. According to Porter, this advantage comes from four related attributes which he called 'the diamond of national advantage'. They were factor conditions, demand conditions, related and supporting industries, and firm strategy, structure, and rivalry.

Factor conditions: traditional theory said that nations would export those goods which made most use of the factors in which they were relatively well endowed. Porter distinguished between basic and inherited factors (such as raw materials and a pool of labour) and the created factors (a skilled workforce and scientific base) essential in modern, knowledge-based industries. Where countries can create these advantages, then they will be successful. He gave Denmark, a world leader in the export of insulin, as an example where two specialist hospitals existed for the study and treatment of diabetes.

Demand conditions: what is important is the nature of demand rather than the size of the market. Sophisticated and demanding buyers keep sellers informed of buyers' wants and give them early warning signs of shifts in market demand. It helps companies, also, if consumer tastes and national values are being exported to other countries, as the USA has done so successfully.

Related and supporting industries: the third determinant is the existence of internationally competitive firms within the local supply chain. They provide cost effective inputs and information on what is happening in the industry. Clusters of mutually reinforcing organizations tend to grow within the same geographical area. Porter used the example of the Italian shoe industry, which benefits from the close proximity of world class leather-tanning and fashion-design industries.

Firm strategy, structure, and rivalry: the final determinant of national competitiveness refers to the ways in which companies are created, organized, and managed as well as the nature of domestic rivalry. Intense local competition leads firms to be innovative in seeking ways to outdo their domestic competitors. This, in turn, makes them more internationally competitive. The way in which firms are organized, managed, and the goals they set themselves as well as the structure of capital markets are all key to this rivalry.

Porter emphasizes the systemic nature of this diamond in that the points are dependent on each other. A nation may have sophisticated buyers, but if the other conditions are not present then this is likely to lead to imports rather than domestic production. Low cost supplies may be available, but if a firm easily dominates the market then this is not likely to lead to greater competitiveness. Domestic rivalry is probably the most important point of the diamond because of the improvement effect it has on all the others, but clustering is also important because it magnifies the effect of the other elements.

Porter also included two other variables as being important for the success of a nation: chance and government. Chance events are those outside the control of firms, and even governments, which can change very quickly the conditions in the 'diamond'. They include such things as wars, inventions, political decisions by foreign governments, shifts in the world financial markets or exchange rates, discontinuities in input costs such as oil price shocks, major technological breakthroughs, and surges in world or regional demand.

Governments can influence the four broad attributes either positively or negatively through various policies such as subsidies, incentives, capital market controls, education policy, environmental controls, tax laws, and competition laws. The complete model is shown in Figure 2.4.

Figure 2.4 Determinants of national competitive advantage

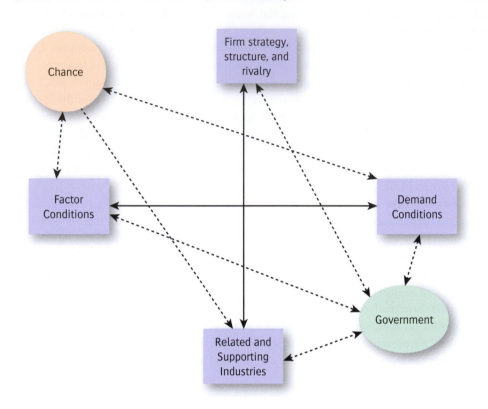

Source: Porter, M. (1990) The Competitive Advantage of Nations; Palgrave Macmillan

Trade Intervention

All of the theories and models make the assumption that trade takes place freely between nations, but, as noted in Chapter 1, this is far from the case. Every nation imposes trade restrictions of some description. Generally, their purpose is to limit imports by imposing tariff or non-tariff barriers, or to encourage exports by subsidizing exporting firms.

A tariff is a tax or duty placed on an imported good by a domestic government. Tariffs are usually levied as a percentage of the declared value of the good, similar to a sales tax. Unlike a sales tax, tariff rates are often different for every good and tariffs do not apply to domestically produced goods.

Non-tariff barriers can take a number of forms: quotas, licences, **rules of origin**, product requirements (standards, packaging, labelling and markings, product specifications), customs procedures and documentation requirements, local content rules, and exchange rate manipulation.

Subsidies can take many forms and can be difficult to identify and calculate. Financial assistance of any sort, including cash payments, low interest loans, tax breaks, **export credits** and **export guarantees**, export promotion agencies, free trade and export processing zones, all distort trade in favour of domestic producers. According to the OECD (2010) support to agricultural producers amounted to US$258 billion, or €201 billion, in 2012. This averaged about 19 per cent, but was as low as 1 per cent in some countries, for example New Zealand, and as high as 63 per cent in others, such as Norway.

Why Intervene?

National defence—it is argued that certain industries need defending from imports because they are vital in times of war. Weapons, transport, utilities, and food would probably fall into this category, but where would the line be drawn? Similar arguments have been put forward to ban exports of technically advanced, especially military, products. The USA banned exports of satellites to China because this would have given the Chinese access to US military technology. It resulted in a fall in the American share of world satellite sales.

When US firms sell high-tech products and military equipment to allies, the US government tries to prevent the selling-on of such technology to countries such as China and Venezuela. In July 2007, Saab withdrew from an international trade deal with Venezuela because of an arms ban imposed by the US on Venezuela. Bofors, a subsidiary of Saab, had supplied Venezuela with weapons for 20 years, but the ban meant they could not sell any weapons with US-made parts.

To protect fledgling domestic industries from foreign competition—it is argued that industries in their infancy may need protection until they can compete internationally. This gives them time to grow to a size where they can gain economies of scale, learn from doing business, and develop the supporting infrastructure discussed above. Some of the Asian economies, Japan, South Korea, and Taiwan, have successfully protected infant industries until they have grown to compete internationally and the barriers have been removed. On the other hand, some Japanese industries, such as banking, construction, and retailing, have remained protected and inefficient.

To protect domestic industries from foreign competition and thereby save jobs—governments often come under pressure to support industries in decline because the human cost involved in the event of sudden closure can be very high. Protection may be justified to delay the closure and allow time for adjustment.

To protect against over dependence on a narrow base of products—the law of comparative advantage tells us that countries should specialize in the production of goods in which they have a comparative advantage. For some countries, this will result in a range of primary products for which demand is income inelastic. This could condemn these countries to persistent poverty, so protection to expand the industrial base may be the only way to escape from poverty.

Political motives—the USA, for example, has an embargo on trade with Cuba because it disagrees with Cuba's politics.

To protect domestic producers from dumping by foreign companies or governments—dumping occurs when a foreign company charges a price in the domestic market which is 'too low'. In most instances, 'too low' is generally understood to be a price which is lower in a foreign market than the price in the domestic market. In other instances, 'too low' means a price which is below cost, so the producer is losing money. Vietnam took its first case to the WTO (having joined the WTO in 2006) accusing the USA of unfair duties on frozen shrimp imported from Vietnam. The USA has charged duties ranging from 2.5 per cent to 25.76 per cent because it fears dumping by the Vietnamese. The case was completed in April 2011 finding that the USA had acted inconsistently with the provisions of the Anti-Dumping Agreement and the GATT (key WTO accords). Firms in the USA have accused China of dumping by keeping the value of the Renminbi low (see this chapter, Exchange Rates).

Retaliation—to respond to another country's imposition of tariffs or some other restriction or against 'dumping'.

To prevent the import of undesirable products—drugs, live or endangered animals, and certain foodstuffs may be deemed undesirable.

To resist cultural imperialism and/or maintain a particular lifestyle—that is, the imposition of one country's culture, politics, systems of governance, and/or language on another. Quite often, the West, and in particular the USA, is accused of cultural imperialism. As we noted in Chapter 1, American movies and television programmes are watched worldwide and most of these promote American values and beliefs.

Learning Task

1. Which of the above reasons for trade intervention do you think is justified and which is not?
2. For each, identify the costs and the benefits of the policy for domestic consumers and producers and foreign producers and workers.

Control of Trade

On 26 June 2014, Yemen became the one hundred and sixtieth member of the WTO. The WTO was the successor organization to the GATT established in 1947 with just 23 members. In the depression of the 1930s, many countries had suffered from falling exports and had tried to solve their problems by restricting imports. Of course, others retaliated and the net effect was a reduction, by a third, of world trade in manufactured goods. These beggar-my-neighbour trade policies were in part responsible for WWII, so there was a determination to devise a system in which there was much more economic cooperation. A much more ambitious scheme, the International Trade Organization, was proposed—covering not only trading relations but also financial arrangements, but this was blocked by the USA. This left the GATT as the only mechanism for regulating trade until the establishment of the WTO. The aim of the GATT was the reduction of tariffs and liberalizing trade giving countries access to each other's markets.

GATT's, and now the WTO's, principles are:

- **Non-discrimination**: a country should not discriminate between trading parties. Under the 'most favoured nation' rule, a member has to grant to all members the most favourable conditions it allows trade in a particular product. Once goods have entered a country then the 'national treatment rule applies' in that they should be treated exactly the same as domestic goods.

- **Reciprocity**: if a member benefits from access and tariff reductions made by another member then it must reciprocate by making similar access and tariff reductions to that member.

- **Transparency**: members' trade regulations have to be published so all restrictions can be identified.

- **Predictability and stability**: members cannot raise existing tariffs without negotiation, so everyone can be confident there will be no sudden changes.

- **Freeing of trade**: general reduction of all barriers.

- **Special assistance and trade concessions for developing countries**.

Mini Case Study Yemen's entry to the WTO

On 26 June 2014, after 14 years of talks, Yemen became the one hundred and sixtieth member of the WTO. Yemen is located in the Middle East bordering the Arabian Sea with a strategic location linking the Suez Canal, Red Sea, and the Gulf of Aden. It is the poorest country in the Middle East and one of 48 countries that the UN classifies as 'least developed'. It defines this as 'low-income countries suffering from structural impediments to sustainable development'. Yemen's population is 27.5 million and growing quickly as it has one of the highest birth rates in the world and a young population (under 15) of 46 per cent. Its GDP is $US43 billion at current prices ($US65.9 billion PPP) and per capita GDP $US1,572 ($US2,399 PPP). It relies heavily on oil (25 per cent of GDP, 70 per cent of government revenues), but this is a declining resource. Yemen has a history of political violence including civil wars, violent protests, and as a base for terrorists. Following the Arab Spring in North Africa, growing protests in Yemen brought an end to the 33-year rule of President Ali Abdullah Saleh. The country has now embarked on a political transition into a federal state. According to the World Bank, poverty has risen from 42 per cent in 2009 to 54.5 per cent in 2012. It is one of the most food insecure countries in the world with 45 per cent of the population food insecure. It is also has scarce water resources.

Yemen wants to use its membership to overcome years of strife and to use its strategic location to transform itself into a maritime hub. It will also open up new investment opportunities. Not everybody is agreed that membership is a positive move. Yemen imports 85 per cent of its food commodities from abroad and does not produce many goods for export.

Sources: www.WTO.org; Gulfnews.com, 28 May 2014: *Yemen Times*, 5 December 2013: IMF World Economic Outlook Database, April 2014 estimates; www.un.org; www.worldbank.org

Questions

1. Explain why it took so long for Yemen to join the WTO.
2. Identify the benefits of Yemen's acquisition.
3. What effect will membership have on domestic producers?

Under the GATT, these principles were applied only to merchandise trade and then some sectors, such as agriculture and textiles, were ignored. These have now begun to be addressed under the WTO. Another weakness with the GATT was the lack of any effective process for settling disagreements and a deterrent against offenders. The WTO now has a dispute resolution process and is able to take sanctions against offenders, as it did against the USA in 2002. Under pressure from domestic steel producers, the American administration imposed tariffs on steel imports. WTO members reported this and the WTO allowed other members to impose retaliatory tariffs. The US tariffs were removed in 2004.

Trade negotiations have taken place in a series of 'rounds'. There have been nine of these rounds if we include the current and incomplete Doha round. These are summarized in Table 2.9.

The GATT was a fairly loose arrangement, but the WTO is a permanent organization dealing with a much wider range of issues. About three-quarters of its members are less developed countries. Its top-level decision-making body is the Ministerial Conference, which meets at least every two years, but below this are other committees, which meet on a regular basis. It has permanent offices in Geneva.

The GATT/WTO has been successful in reducing tariffs on industrial products from an average of about 40 per cent in 1947 to something like 4 per cent today, but whether it increases trade is the subject of debate. Trade has increased, as we have seen, faster than world GDP—but is this because of the measures taken by the GATT/WTO? Not according to Rose (2004), who found that trade had increased for members and non-members alike. On the other hand, Subramanian and Wei (2005) found that GATT/WTO had served to increase trade substantially (possibly by

Table 2.9 GATT/WTO rounds

Period	Round	Countries	Subjects
1947	Geneva	23	Tariffs
1949	Annecy	13	Tariffs
1950–51	Torquay	38	Tariffs
1955–56	Geneva	26	Tariffs
1960–61	Dillon	26	Tariffs
1964–67	Kennedy	62	Tariffs, anti-dumping measures
1973–79	Tokyo	102	Tariffs, non-tariff measures, and framework agreements
1986–94	Uruguay	123	Tariffs, agriculture, textiles, and clothing brought into GATT Agreement on services (GATS) Intellectual property (TRIPS) Trade related Investment (TRIMS) Creation of WTO and dispute settlement
2001–	Doha	141	'Bali package' accepted in December 2013 but possibly blocked by India in August 2014

Source: WTO

US$8 trillion in 2000 alone), but that the increase had been uneven. Industrial countries witnessed a larger increase in trade than did developing countries, bilateral trade was greater when both partners undertook liberalization, and those sectors that did not liberalize did not see an increase in trade.

The WTO is not without its critics, as we have witnessed with the demonstrations by anti-globalization protestors at the Ministerial Council meetings from Seattle in 1999 to Hong Kong in 2005. The major criticism is that it is a club favouring the developed countries, at the expense of the less developed countries. Decision-making is by consensus, often following many rounds of meetings most often attended by those countries with the resources to have representatives present at these meetings. Many of the less developed countries are excluded from this process. Other arguments against are: that market access in industry is still a problem for less developed countries; anti-dumping measures have increased; there are still enormous agricultural subsidies in the developed world; and labour standards and the environment are ignored.

Some of these problems have meant that the current round of negotiations has been difficult, with the talks suspended on more than one occasion. The previous round of talks in Seattle had ended in failure and a major disagreement between developed and developing countries—the latter accused the WTO of being for free trade whatever the cost, a charge which the WTO contests (see http://www.wto.org). Whatever their protestations, the package for discussion at the Doha round has been called the Doha Development Agenda. The concern is to ensure that developing economies benefit from the growth of trade by improving market access to developed economies for developing countries. The most significant differences are between developed countries, led by the EU, the USA, and Japan, and the major developing countries, led and represented mainly by China, Brazil, India, South Korea, and South Africa. There is also considerable contention against and between the EU and the USA over their maintenance of agricultural subsidies. Thirteen years after the talks started, agreement was reached in a deal in Bali in December 2013, but, just before

Mini Case Study The WTO dispute settlement

In July 2014, the WTO ruled against the USA for imposing punitive tariffs on the import of steel from China and India. China and India had disputed the way that the USA had imposed 'countervailing duties' against alleged illegal subsidies by public bodies.

For years, the USA insisted that the Chinese state-owned enterprises benefitted from public subsidies that lowered costs of production and that this was unfair competition. Others saw this as US protection of its own steel producers. The case has taken nearly two years to reach a decision and can still go to appeal.

The USA also lost on a separate, but related, case against Indian steel, although the case was not so clear cut. The US had claimed that steel firms in India, such as Tata, Jindal, and Essar, had benefitted from being supplied by the state-owned iron ore mining firm, NMDC.

This case underlines the differences in the way in which economies are structured. In the West, it is assumed there is a clear separation between corporations and the state, but in China (especially) and many emerging countries the separation is not so clear. And the assumption in the West is often that if the separation is not clear then there must be some sort of state subsidy.

Since China's accession to the WTO in 2001, the USA has brought 15 WTO cases against China (as of December 2013),

more than twice as many as any other WTO member has brought against China. The American view is that 'if China is going to deal successfully with its economic challenges at home, it must reduce the role of the state in planning the economy, reform state-owned enterprises, eliminate preferences for domestic national champions and remove market access barriers currently confronting foreign goods and services' (United States Trade Representative December 2013).

The issue for the WTO is whether Chinese state-owned enterprises are what the WTO classes as 'public bodies'; that is, organizations that can carry out government operations. In this case, it found that this was not the case and that a government simply owning an entity is not enough to establish that it is a 'public body'.

Sources: ft.com, 15 July 2014: Reuters, 14 July 2014: United States Trade Representative (2013)

Questions

1. What is the role of the WTO?
2. Why is it important for members to adhere to the rules of the WTO?
3. It is often argued that the WTO is a tool of powerful Western business interests. Is this the case?

the treaty was due to be signed, India, who had since elected a new government, blocked the deal. This is a crucial stage in the life of the WTO. Up to 60 countries are ready to implement the 'Bali package' outside the WTO. Many countries, such the US, the EU, and Japan, frustrated with the lack of any progress, are organizing their own regional trade initiatives covering more complex, non-tariff barriers to trade. If talks at the WTO make no further progress, then the WTO could be increasingly side-lined as an effective world organization (*FT* 2 August 2014).

Exchange Rates

An exchange rate is the price of one currency as expressed in another or, to put it another way, the rate at which one currency is exchanged for another. The way in which the value of a currency is determined is dependent upon the exchange rate regime in place. In a floating exchange rate system, the market value of a currency is determined by the demand for and the supply of a currency. Most of this supply and demand comes from speculators (see Chapter 10) with trade and investment flows having a minor role. Nevertheless, countries with trade surpluses, and those who attract inflows of capital, will see demand for their currency rise and therefore an appreciation in the value of the currency. The reverse is also true. According to the IMF (2013) there are 30 countries with a freely floating exchange rate. In this system, the rate could be very volatile and this could create problems for firms that are heavily involved in international trade and investment. They could face wild fluctuations in import prices and in the value of export earnings and foreign assets.

Countries may adopt a **fixed exchange rate** policy where they peg the value of their currency against another. Fixed rates give a degree of stability to business whether it is importer, exporter, or investor wishing to move capital in or out of the country.

There are also a number of systems which try to capture the benefits of both systems by allowing currencies to float within a preset band and/or where governments actively manage the exchange rate. It may be that the authorities decide that they are prepared to see the value of the currency fluctuate within prescribed bands against another currency. When the currency looks as if it is going to break through the bands, the authorities intervene to buy the domestic currency when it is sinking too low or to sell it when it is threatening to rise too high in value. This gives business less certainty than the fixed rate regime, but more certainty than a floating regime.

According to the IMF (2013), 13 countries, including El Salvador and Panama, use the US dollar as their domestic currency and 45 others peg their currency against it, while 27 countries peg theirs against the euro. Movements in exchange rates can be an important influence on the business environment—good news for some, bad for others. A rise in the exchange rate can make imports cheaper, which is good news for those firms buying a lot of goods and services from abroad. On the other hand, it is likely to be bad news for exporters as it could make them less competitive in foreign markets. Requena-Silvente and Walker (2007) found that car exporters to the UK reduced their mark up to keep prices stable and maintain market share when their currencies rose against sterling.

Similarly, for businesses producing abroad, a rise in the exchange rate could reduce the value of their foreign sales and assets when translated back into their domestic currency.

Adverse long-lasting realignments of exchange rates can have a major impact on business strategy. They may cause firms to: relocate production; change the source of supply; look for new product markets or strong currency markets; make products having a more global appeal to facilitate the switch from weak to strong currency markets; look for ways of increasing productivity.

A way of affecting both imports and exports is by exchange rate manipulation by governments. When two firms in different countries do business, the prices they quote will be determined by a combination of their domestic price converted to the other's currency using foreign exchange rates. If £1 exchanges for US$2, then a UK exporter with a domestic price of £100 will quote US$200 to an American buyer. Any change in the exchange rate will affect the foreign exchange price. If the £ strengthens to £1 = US$2.5, then the US price will be US$250. In a competitive market, a price rise might not be possible, which would then mean that if the UK firm could only charge US$200 then it would only receive £80 of revenue. One way of maintaining the competitiveness of a country's exports would be to keep the value of its currency low in relation to others (see Mini Case Study: China's exchange rate). Being a member of a currency union (i.e. sharing a common currency), such as the EU, not only eliminates transaction costs when exchanging currency but also reduces the risks associated with changes in exchange rates. It is also claimed that this reduction in uncertainty can promote investment (see text of a speech by Mark Carney, Governor of the Bank of England, on the economics of currency unions available on the **Online Resource Centre**).

Mini Case Study China's exchange rate

The Chinese government manages the value of the Chinese currency, the Renminbi. Many in the USA believe that the Renminbi is undervalued and that this is the cause of the large trade imbalance with China. The US authorities, worried about this burgeoning trade deficit, and believing that an appreciation in the Renminbi would solve this, boost the US economy, and reduce unemployment, put pressure on a reluctant China to intervene to raise the value of the Renminbi. In the annual US–China talks in July 2014, the US Treasury Secretary, Jack Lew, said that 'he would push China to speed up economic reforms and do more to let the Yuan (Renminbi) rise against the dollar'. From Figure 2.5, it can be seen that China has allowed the spot rate—the current exchange rate that the Renminbi could be bought at 'now'—to rise against the dollar. In June 2005, US$1 bought about 8.29 Renminbi. In 2014, US$1 only bought around 6.2 Renminbi (see

Figure 2.5). US goods exports to China have increased to a record $122 billion in 2013, but so have imports of goods to $440 billion. The US has a small trade surplus in services of $17 billion, but the overall trade deficit has grown. The US believes that China needs to do more.

1. Use the data in Figure 2.5 to calculate:
    a. how much the Renminbi went up against the US dollar between 2005 and 2014;
    b. how much the dollar depreciated against the Renminbi.
2. Explain why the USA would wish to see a rise in the value of the Renminbi against the dollar.
3. Explain the Chinese reluctance to let the Renminbi appreciate in value.
4. The dollar has depreciated against the Renminbi, but the trade surplus has grown. Explain how this could happen.

Figure 2.5 How many Chinese Renminbi for US$1

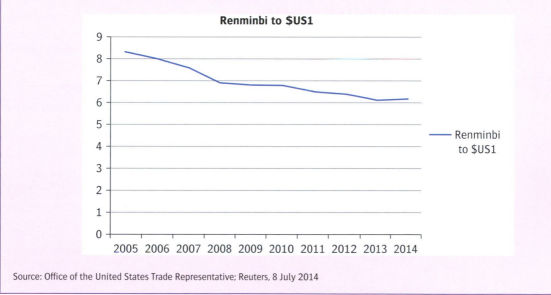

Source: Office of the United States Trade Representative; Reuters, 8 July 2014

● CHAPTER SUMMARY

In this chapter we have looked at the global pattern of wealth, international trade, and exchange rates. One way of comparing countries is to compare their respective GDP. This can be adjusted for purchasing power parity (PPP), which has the effect of narrowing the gap between rich and poor. The richest economy is still the USA, but China, in terms of PPP, is catching up quickly and will soon overtake the USA, possibly in 2014.

GDP indicates the different sizes of economies, but does not say much about the standard of living—population has to be taken into account to give income per capita. Even then, GDP per capita says nothing about the quality of life. In determining the degree of development, the UNDP also looks at other indicators such as income inequality, life expectancy, literacy rates, and school enrolments. On any of these measures, the world is still a very divided place when comparing the rich with the poor. Economic growth is seen as the key to raising standards of living. The world is changing and, by 2060, China will be the biggest economy, followed by India, with the USA in third place. Many current emerging nations will be as big as current advanced economies, but per capita incomes in those countries will still be lower. There will be an enormous global middle class by 2030 with two-thirds in the Asia Pacific region.

International trade has increased, with exports in 1970 just 13 per cent of world output whereas they are predicted to be 34 per cent by 2030. Developing countries are increasing their share of trade in manufactures, but this is still dominated by the developed nations. Countries trade with each other and world output increases, but history shows that the rich nations tend to benefit at the expense of the poor. There have been a number of theories put forward to explain the pattern of trade. Many countries impose restrictions, but the WTO works to liberalize trade. It has faced criticism because it is seen as a club that helps to maintain the established patterns of trade, which favour the rich.

An exchange rate is the price of one currency expressed in another. Fluctuations in exchange rates can have a major impact on business. Some countries have been accused of manipulating the exchange of their currencies in order to make their goods more competitive in overseas markets.

● REVIEW QUESTIONS

1. Why would it be useful for business to build up knowledge of the global distribution of income and wealth, and how it is changing over time?

2. Discuss the proposition that happiness does not necessarily increase with increased wealth.

3. Analyse and explain the major trends in international trade. Discuss links between these trends and the changing distribution of world income.

4. What are the advantages to countries of foreign trade?

5. Discuss why the level of exchange rates is important for international business.

● ASSIGNMENT TASKS

1. It is often quoted that widening inequality is a fundamental issue facing the global economy. Prepare a paper that:

   a) Explains what is meant by 'inequality'.

   b) Investigates the extent of this inequality.

   c) Discusses whether inequality is a problem or a benefit.

   d) Identifies the risks to international business of inequality.

2. You are working for a pharmaceutical business that currently only exports to Europe. It is looking to expand its export destinations and you are asked to prepare a report which selects three countries as suitable destinations. You should concentrate on:

   a) Economic growth prospects and associated risks.

   b) Any trade restrictions such as tariffs, non- tariff barriers, and domestic subsidies.

Case Study Brazil

Brazil is the largest of the South American economies and second only to the USA in the whole of the Americas. Its GDP is $US2.2 trillion, making it the seventh wealthiest economy in the world. It has a population of 201 million people (2013 estimate) and a per capita income of US$11,079 (2014), more than double that of 1990, with the result that more than 50 per cent of Brazil's population is now middle class. Brazil has a very young population and the growing workforce is likely to make a major contribution to future growth. Brazil's economy has been based largely on primary products, especially raw materials. It has some of the largest iron ore deposits in the world and is one of the largest producers of tin, quartz, and manganese. It has benefitted from increasing commodity prices brought about by Chinese growth. Brazil has discovered major offshore reserves of oil and gas, which could make it one of the top oil-exporting nations in the future. It has been diversifying and its industrial base has grown considerably. Its main exports are iron ore, crude petroleum, soybeans, raw sugar, and poultry meat to the EU27 (20.2 per cent), China (17.0 per cent), USA (11.1 per cent), and Argentina (7.4 per cent). Its main imports are machinery, electrical and transport equipment, chemical products, oil, and automotive parts from the EU27 (21.4 per cent), China (15.3 per cent), USA (14.6 per cent), and Argentina (7.4 per cent). Brazil is regarded by many as the one BRIC likely to be most challenged by the predictions for growth into the twenty-first century. Its growth record in the past has averaged around 2 per cent and has been erratic, swinging between -4 per cent and 5.8 per cent between 1990 and 2003. However, from 2004 to 2010 its performance was much improved save for 2009, the year of global recession. For these years, it has averaged nearer 5 per cent and in 2010 was 7.5 per cent. It was expected to be about 4 per cent per annum up to 2014, but turned out to vary between 1.0 per cent and 2.7 per cent.

One problem hindering the economy is the struggle to maintain a competitive exchange rate. In 1999, Brazil allowed its currency to 'float' on the foreign currency markets, but it is a 'dirty float' in which the authorities step into the market to 'manage' the exchange rate at about 2 Reals (the Brazilian currency) to $US1. Since 2008, the Real has varied from about 1.6 to over 2.4 Reals to $US1. It slipped to over 2.4 Reals to $US1 in July 2014, with the Brazilian government intervening to put a floor under the depreciation of the Real.

Source: © Wavebreakmedia Ltd / Dreamstime

As domestic demand in Brazil outstrips supply, inflation has also become a worry as the rate has risen to 6.52 per cent in July 2014, which is at the upper end of its target rate of 4.5 per cent plus or minus 2 per cent. The depreciating Real does not help as this has the effect of increasing import prices. To combat this, interest rates are very high. The central bank has a rate of 11 per cent, higher than any other major economy.

2014 was an election year in Brazil, with their first female President, Dilma Rousseff, standing for re-election in October 2014. It was also a year of the football World Cup and protests at the millions being spent on sports stadiums while education, housing, healthcare, and other social services go without. It is also a protest against corruption, poor infrastructure, and continuing inequality in a country that is now one of the richest in the world. Brazil still has one of the highest inequality levels in the world despite income inequality falling by 12 per cent between 1997 and 2011. Arnold and Jalles (2014) estimate it would take at least 20 years at the current rate of improvement for inequality to reach the levels of the USA, itself one of the most unequal of OECD countries. According to the World Bank, 11 per cent of the population still live on less than $US2 per day (2009).

Sources: http://www.worldbank.org/en/country/brazil/overview; IMF Economic Outlook Database April 2014; Arnold and Jalles (2014); http://country.eiu.com/brazil; http://www.economonitor.com/blog/2013/12/brazil-exchange-rate-policy/. ➔

● FURTHER READING

For a book which challenges the idea that the best way of improving the quality of human lives is to raise material living standards see:

- Wilkinson, R. and Pickett, K. (2009) *The Spirit Level: Why Equality is Better for Everyone*. London: Penguin Books.

And for a book which says that, under capitalism, inequality is inevitable see:

- Piketty, T. (2014) *Capitalism in the Twenty-First Century*. Cambridge, MA: Harvard University Press.

For a historical account of the evolution of world trade up to the twenty-first century see:

- Findlay, R. and O'Rourke, K.H. (2007) *Power and Plenty: Trade, War, and the World Economy*. Princeton, NJ: Princeton University Press.

- VanGrasstek, C. (2013) *The History and Future of the World Trade Organisation*. Geneva: WTO.

For an in-depth analysis of the Chinese economy, its relationship with global trade, and emerging economies and global trade see:

- Eichengreen, B., Chui, Y., and Wyplosz, C. (eds) (2008) *China, Asia, and the New World Economy*. Oxford: Oxford University Press.

- Hanson, G.H. (2012) *The Rise of Middle Kingdoms: Emerging Economies in Global Trade*. NBER Working Paper No. 17961. March 2012. JEL No. F10.

For an application and extension of the Porter diamond to national competitiveness see:

- Stone, H.B. and Ranchhod, A. (2006) 'Competitive Advantage of a Nation in the Global Arena: A Quantitative Advancement to Porter's Diamond Applied to the UK, USA and BRIC Nations'. *Strategic Change* 5(6).

- Özlem, Ö. (2002) The Case of Turkey: National Advantage'. *Journal of Business Research* 55(6).

Rugman et al. have been one of the main critics of the Porter diamond. See:

- Rugman, A., Verbeke, A., and Van Den Broeck, J. (eds) (1995) *Research in Global Strategic Management: Volume V Beyond the Diamond*. Greenwich, CT: JAI Press.

● REFERENCES

Arnold, J. and Jalles, J., (2014) *'Dividing the Pie in Brazil: Income Distribution, Social Policies and the New Middle Class'*. OECD Economics Department Working Papers no.1105, OECD Publishing.

Carmody, P. (2013) *The Rise of the BRICS in Africa, The Geopolitics of South-South Relations*. Zed Books.

Coates, B. and Luu, N. (2012) China's emergence in global commodity markets, *Economic Roundup*. Treasury Australian Government, May 2012. Available at: http://www.treasury.gov.au/~/media/Treasury/Publications%20and%20Media/Publications/2012/Economic%20Roundup%20Issue%201/Downloads/Economic%20Roundup%20Issue%201%202012.ashx.

Dicken, P. (2004) *Global Shift: Reshaping the Global Economic Map in the 21st Century*. London: SAGE Publications.

Easterlin. R. (1974) *'Does Economic Growth Improve the Human Lot? Some Empirical Evidence'*. In Paul A. David and Melvin W. Reder (eds) Nations and Households in Economic Growth: Essays in Honor of Moses Abramovitz. New York: Academic Press, Inc.

Ernst and Young (2013) *'Hitting the Sweet Spot. The Growth of the Middle Class in Emerging Markets'*. Available at: http://www.ey.com/Publication/vwLUAssets/Hitting_the_sweet_spot/$File/Hitting_the_sweet_spot.pdf.

Financial Times International Business Insight (2010) *'Part Three: Middle East and Africa'*, 22 October 2010.

FT., S com (2010) *'How Africa can Become the Next BRIC'*, Jim O'Neill, 26 August 2010.

Goldman Sachs (2003) 'Dreaming with BRICS: The Path to 2050'. Global Economics Paper No. 99. Available at: http://www.goldmansachs.com/korea/ideas/brics/99-dreaming.pdf.

Goldman Sachs (2007) The N-11: More than an Acronym'. Global Economics Paper No. 153. Available at: http://www.chicagobooth.edu/~/media/E60BDCEB6C5245E59B7ADA7C6B1B6F2B.pdf.

Goldman Sachs (2011) 'The BRICs 10 Years On: Halfway Through the Great Transformation'. Global Economics Paper No. 208. Available at: http://blogs.univ-poitiers.fr/o-bouba-olga/files/2012/11/Goldman-Sachs-Global-Economics-Paper-208.pdf.

Heckscher, E.F.(1919 [1991]) *'The Effect of Foreign Trade on the Distribution of Income. Economisk Tidsckrift'*. In Heckscher E.F. and Ohlin, B., Heckscher-Ohlin Trade Theory. Cambridge, MA: The MIT Press (translated, edited, and introduced by Harry Flam and M. June Flanders).

International Monetary Fund (2013) 'De Facto Classification of Exchange Rate Regimes and Monetary Policy Frameworks'. Available at: https://www.imf.org/external/np/mfd/er/2008/eng/0408.htm.

International Monetary Fund (2014) World Economic Outlook Database, April 2014. Available at: http://www.imf.org/external/pubs/ft/weo/2014/01/weodata/index.aspx.

Keating, M. (2010) 'Ways to Improve Africa's Business Culture'. *Financial Times* 21 October 2010.

Kharas, H. and Gertz, G. (2010) *The New Global Middle Class: A Cross-Over from West to East*. Wolfensohn Center for Development at Brookings. Available at: http://www.brookings.edu/~/media/research/files/papers/2010/3/china%20middle%20class%20kharas/03_china_middle_class_kharas.pdf.

Leke, A., Lund, S., Roxburgh, C., and Aend van Wamelen, A. (2010) 'What's Driving Africa's Growth' *McKinsey Quarterly* June 2010. Available at: http://www.mckinsey.com/insights/economic_studies/whats_driving_africas_growth.

Leontieff, W. (1953) 'Domestic Production and Foreign Trade: The American Capital Position Re-examined'. *Proceedings of the American Philosophical Society* 97 (November).

Linder, S.B. (1961) *An Essay on Trade and Transformation*. New York: Wiley.

Maddison, A. (2003) *The World Economy: Historical Statistics*. Paris: Development Centre Studies, OECD.

Meadows, D.H., Randers, J., and Behrens, William W. III, (1972) *The Limits to Growth*. New York: Universe Books.

Mishan, E. (1967) *The Costs of Economic Growth*. London: Staples Press.

OECD (2012) *'Looking to 2060: Long-term Global Growth Prospects, A Going for Growth Report'*, November 2012. Available at: http://www.oecd.org/eco/outlook/2060%20policy%20paper%20FINAL.pdf.

OECD (2010) *'Agricultural Policies in OECD Countries at a Glance'*. Available at: www.oecd.org/tad/agricultural-policies/45539870.pdf.

Ohlin, B. (1924 [1991]) *'The Theory of Trade'*. In Heckscher E.F. and Ohlin, B., Heckscher-Ohlin Trade Theory. Cambridge, MA: The MIT Press (translated, edited, and introduced by Harry Flam and M. June Flanders).

Piketty, T. (2014) *Capitalism in the Twenty-First Century*. Cambridge, MA: Harvard University Press.

Porter, M. (1990) *The Competitive Advantage of Nations*. London: Macmillan Press.

Proto, E. and Rustichini, A. (2013) 'A Reassessment of the Relationship between GDP and Life Satisfaction'. *PLOS ONE* 8(11): e79358. doi:10.1371/journal. pone.0079358

Ricardo, D. (1817) *On the Principles of Political Economy and Taxation*. London: John Murray.

Requena-Silvente, F. and Walker, J. (2007) 'The Impact of Exchange Rate Fluctuations on Profit Margins: The UK Car Market, 1971-2002'. *Journal of Applied Economics* X(1) May.

Rose, A. (2004) 'Do WTO Members have More Liberal Trade Policy?'. *Journal of International Economics* 63(2).

Schneider, F. and Williams C.C. (2013) *The Shadow Economy*. London: Institute of Economic Affairs.

Schneider, F., Buehn, A., and Montenegro, C.E. (2010) 'Shadow Economies All Over the World, New Estimates for 162 Countries from 1999 to 2007'. World Bank Working Paper WPS5356.Available at:IT http:// www-wds.worldbank.org/servlet/WDSContentServer/ WDSP/IB/2010/10/14/000158349_2010101416070 4/Rendered/PDF/WPPS5356.pdf.

Simms, A., Johnson, V., and Chowla, K. (2010) *Growth Isn't Possible*. London: New Economics Foundation.

Smith, A. (1776) *An Inquiry into the Nature and Causes of the Wealth of Nations*. Oxford: Clarendon Press.

Subramanian, A. and Wei, S.-J. (2005) *'The WTO Promotes Trade, Strongly But Unevenly'*. CEPR Discussion Papers 5122. Available at: http://www.cepr.org/content/ discussion-papers.

United States Trade Representative (Office of the) (2013), 'Report to Congress on China's WTO Compliance'. Available at: http://www.ustr.gov/about-us/ press-office/press-releases/2013/December/ US-Report-to-Congress-on-China-WTO-Compliance, accessed October 2014.

Vernon, R. (1966) 'International Investments and International Trade in the Product Life Cycle'. *Quarterly Journal of Economics* 80(2): 190–207.

World Bank (2006) *Global Economic Prospects: Managing the Next Wave of Globalization 2007*. Washington, DC: World Bank Publications.

World Bank (2014), *Africa's Pulse, An Analysis of Issues Shaping Africa's Future*, Volume 9, April, 2014. Available at: http://www.worldbank.org/content/dam/ Worldbank/document/Africa/Report/Africas-Pulse-brochure_Vol9.pdf.

World Trade Organization (2013) *World Trade Report 2013. Factors Shaping the Future of World Trade*. WTO. Available at: http://www.wto.org/english/res_e/ publications_e/wtr13_e.htm.

CHAPTER THREE

Analysing Global Industries

LEARNING OUTCOMES

This chapter will enable you to:

- Distinguish between the concept of market and industry

- Identify various market structures and their implications for competition and performance

- Measure market concentration, analyse it, and explain the link with market power

- Explain and use the Porter Five Forces model for industry analysis

Case Study Big pharma

The pharmaceutical industry researches, develops, manufactures, and markets drugs for use as medications. The industry includes biotech firms that harness genetic science to make products dealing with diseases. Such products started to come on stream in the 1980s and became an increasing threat to traditional pharma companies. Among top earning drugs are those used in the treatment of cancers, cholesterol, respiratory disorders, high blood pressure, diabetes, and mental health.

In 2012, global pharmaceutical sales were £511 billion. While there are thousands of firms in the industry, more than half of the global market is taken by the 15 largest (see Table 3.1). These are multinational corporations based in developed economies and heavily dependent on sales of patented and branded drugs. As the table shows, the global market for most of these companies shrank in 2012.

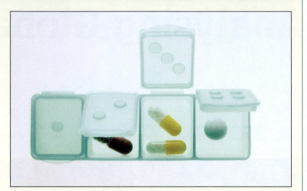

Source: © Corbis

The industry faces important challenges. Fricker (2013) notes that the pace of drug discoveries has been modest despite rapid advances in medical science and significant increases in R&D

Table 3.1 Global pharmaceutical industry—growth and market share

	Corporation	Nationality	2012 Growth (%)	2012 Global market share (%)
1	Novartis	Switzerland	−3	5.97
2	Pfizer	USA	−18	5.51
3	Merck & Co	USA	−1	4.72
4	Sanofi	France	−5	4.44
5	Roche	Switzerland	0	4.08
6	GlaxoSmithKline	UK	−4	3.84
7	AstraZeneca	UK	−15	3.76
8	Johnson & Johnson	USA	1	3.27
9	Abbott	USA	2	3.15
10	Teva	Israel	0	2.91
11	Lilly	USA	−9	2.58
12	Amgen	USA	2	2.02
13	Boeringer Ingel	Germany	5	2.01
14	Bayer	Germany	−1	1.90
15	Takeda	Japan	−13	1.89

→

Source: www.abpi.org

→ expenditure. The industry has found it increasingly difficult to find blockbuster drugs—these are drugs that generate annual sales of at least $1 billion. No surprise, then, that firms like Merck, AstraZeneca, Pfizer, and Johnson and Johnson are concerned about the expiry of patents that give them market exclusivity on existing drugs.

When patents expire, pharma firms often face competition from cheaper generic versions that eat into market shares and profit margins. Generic suppliers anticipate the expiry of patents and produce drugs that are copies of the branded and patented products. They are the fastest growing sector of the industry.

The industry also reports concerns about infringement of patents by, for example, generics suppliers marketing their products before the patent expiry date or by foreign governments overriding the patent. In such cases, firms usually try vigorously to protect their patents through litigation.

Revenues are also threatened in richer countries where governments, trying to control health spending, pressurize the industry for lower drug prices. Health care reforms in the US are another source of pressure on revenues. Merck also sees a risk of increased regulation by governments that could raise costs.

Big pharma has responded to the challenges through domestic and cross-border acquisitions, both of traditional rivals and of biotech firms. Pfizer is an active acquirer, having taken-over five pharma firms since 1999. In 2014, it bid unsuccessfully for UK-based AstraZeneca, and AbbVie, a US company spun off from Abbott, bid for Shire. Both aimed to boost their drugs portfolio and lower their tax liability by transferring their tax base from the US to the UK. In the same year, Abbott made acquisitions in Chile and Russia.

Further responses include the development of collaboration with other firms and universities, focusing on growth in emerging markets like China, and increasing operational efficiencies. Marketing is also undergoing major changes, with reductions in sales forces but significant increases in the use of digital tools like webinars, webcasts, and emails.

Sources: Fricker (2013); *The Guardian* 18 July 2014; www.bbc.co.uk 6 May 2014; www.pmlive.com 18 April 2013; Kirchhoff and Schiereck 2014; Cha and Lorriman 2014; Merck SEC 10-K filing 2014; *Financial Times* 3 May 2014

Introduction

In this chapter we develop the knowledge and skills necessary to carry out analyses of industries. We start off by examining the concepts of the market and the industry. In line with other authors, we see the terms 'market' and 'industry' as being interchangeable. Various market structures are then explored along with their implications for the nature and intensity of competition and company performance. We go on to look at **market concentration**, how it is measured, and the implications of different levels of concentration for the distribution of market power among firms in the industry. The Five Forces of Porter's model provide a set of tools that allow a systematic and comprehensive analysis of industries. Each force is explained and applied to various industries along with a sixth force, **complementary products**.

The term 'global' is used liberally in this chapter. We use it on occasions where multiple countries are involved. This usage varies from other authors, who interpret the word as meaning worldwide; that is, covering most countries in the world.

The Market and the Industry

Analysing markets and industries involves building up a detailed knowledge of the competing firms in the industry, the goods and services they are selling, and the geographical markets where they compete.

Defining the market involves several steps:

- deciding which goods or services to include;
- identifying the firms competing in the market;
- indicating the geographical area where those firms are competing.

First, it is important to identify products or services that customers see as very similar. Economists use a concept called the **cross elasticity of demand** which measures the response of customers when one firm changes its price. If the price of a product increases, and customers switch in large numbers to other, cheaper products, then economists conclude that the products can be classified to the same market. In other words, there is a high cross elasticity of demand because customers see the products as being very good alternatives. One would expect to see this effect were an oil company like BP to raise the price of petrol on the forecourt to a level higher than its competitors, Esso and Shell. This allows us to identify competitors because the firms making products with a high cross elasticity of demand are then defined as being part of the same industry. However, if very few customers transfer their business to the cheaper goods then the products are not seen by consumers as good alternatives and the firms cannot be classified to the same industry.

The concept of cross elasticity, while neat in a theoretical sense, can be difficult to use in practice. Usually, the information required to calculate cross elasticity is not available. In the absence of data on cross elasticity, some observers look for evidence showing businesses reacting regularly to decisions made by other firms. Signs of such interdependence among firms indicate that they see themselves as competitors. For example, if one firm lowers a price or increases spending on advertising and others regularly follow suit, then those firms who end up pursuing similar policies could be seen as members of the same industry. Another approach is to identify firms whose actions as regards, for example, pricing, advertising, and sales promotion are constrained by others. To take the example of low-cost airlines, it would be understandable were firms such as Ryanair and easyJet constrained in their pricing policies by the possible reaction of the other.

Classifying firms to a particular industry may not be as straightforward as it first appears. Car firms are often seen as operating in the same industry, but it would hardly be sensible to view the Rolls Royce as a direct competitor to a Mini or a Fiat Punto. It would make more sense, for our purposes, to consider car manufacturers as producing for a series of markets, from the most basic models to the luxury end of the market.

Diversified firms also complicate the picture. Companies selling a range of goods may end up being classified into several industries. Take domestic appliance manufacturers such as Whirlpool, Electrolux, or LG, the South Korean multinational. They make various appliances including washing machines, dishwashers, and electric cookers—these products can hardly be seen as close substitutes, so the companies could be seen as competing in various markets, for washing machines, dishwashers, and electric cookers. Of course, the fact that diversified firms such as these can offer customers like retailers the ability to source a range of products from a single company may put such firms at a competitive advantage against rivals offering a more limited range.

Companies operating at several stages of production of a product can also complicate the issue of how to classify them. Examples of such **vertically integrated firms** can be found in the oil industry where companies like Shell, Exxon, and BP drill for oil, refine it, and sell it on the forecourt. They could be classified to three industries: drilling, refining, and retailing. The media sector also provides an illustration with groups like 21st Century Fox producing films and distributing them through their television and satellite broadcasting companies.

Another aspect of the market that needs to be clarified is its geographical boundaries. Firms located in different places could be producing similar products, but not actually competing against each other in the same geographical market place. Geographical distance may mean that the cost of transporting goods from one area to the other is not economic so, in reality, the firms in one area are not competing with firms in the other. There are a variety of factors which keep markets separate, such as geographical distance or poor transport infrastructure. For example, in poor countries in Africa and South East Asia, the lack of road and rail networks may keep markets fragmented, whereas in the developed economies of Northern Europe improving transport links have integrated previously distinct markets. Firms may also set out deliberately to keep markets separate. Car producers do this in Western Europe. Traditionally, they have charged significantly higher prices in the UK than in countries like Belgium and the Netherlands. They hope that British customers will not realize that prices are cheaper across the Channel and therefore will not hop across to get their cars from Belgian or Dutch dealers. UK customers who recognize that they can get a lower price on the Continent, and try to buy there, have found that distributors may claim that they are out of supplies or that they do not have access to right-hand drive cars. The EU Commission found Volkswagen guilty of discriminating in price between customers in Southern Germany and those in Northern Italy. German consumers were richer than the Northern Italians so they could afford to pay more. VW, so long as it could keep the two markets separate, increased profits by charging more in Germany than in Italy. Economists identify the geographical boundaries of the market by assessing the extent to which a price increase in one area:

- attracts competition from firms elsewhere. For example, had the high prices charged by VW in Southern Germany attracted many car dealers from Northern Italy lured by the prospect of higher profits, then the two regions could be classified as one market;

- drives customers away to cheaper areas. VW's high prices in Germany could have led many German car buyers to go to Italy to get a better deal. The two areas could be seen as part of the same geographical market had many German consumers taken that route. Such behaviour can be seen in Southern England where consumers get the ferry across to France to buy cheaper alcohol and tobacco. Similarly, French buyers of alcohol and tobacco products flock to the small Spanish towns on the border where the prices of these products are much lower than in France.

Market Structures

There is a variety of market structures ranging from pure **monopoly** to the perfectly competitive (see Table 3.2). In a pure monopoly, one firm dominates the market usually protected from competition by high **barriers to entry** (barriers to entry are explained in more detail in this chapter, Force 2 Competition from New Entrants section). Such firms control the market and can set prices to extract maximum profit from their customers. Consumers have to pay the price because they have no alternative suppliers to turn to. In a globalizing world economy, one rarely encounters pure monopoly outside the pages of basic economics textbooks, although some

Table 3.2 Types of market structure

Type of market structure	Number of firms	Barriers to entry	Nature of product
Perfect competition	Very many	None	Homogeneous
Monopoly	One	High	Unique
Monopolistic competition	Many	None	Heterogeneous
Oligopoly	Few	Often high	Homogeneous/differentiated

markets, at times, may come close. For example, Wrigley, owned by Mars, accounts for around one-third of the global market but 84 per cent of the UK chewing gum market, while Microsoft accounts for more than 90 per cent of the world market for desktop operating software—this drops to 20 per cent when the market definition expands to include operating systems on tablets and smartphones (*Confectionery News* 20 May 2013; companiesandmarkets.com; netshare.com; *Forbes* 13 December 2012).

Market structure can be influenced by the costs incurred by business. Very high **fixed costs** can result in the creation of what is termed a **natural monopoly**. To survive, firms need to produce on a very large scale relative to the size of the market to generate sufficient revenues to cover their fixed costs. Examples of natural monopolies include gas, water, electricity, and telephone networks. It is very expensive to build transmission networks of pipelines for water and gas and electricity and telephone lines. The result is a single producer having an overwhelming cost advantage over potential competitors. Such rivals are deterred from entering the market by the high capital investment involved and the dominant market position of the monopolist.

In perfectly competitive markets, large numbers of firms are completely free to enter and to leave the market, no individual firm can control the market, price is set by the forces of supply and demand, and buyers and sellers have complete knowledge of market conditions. Profit levels are just enough to keep firms in business. Any profits above that level are quickly eroded away by competition from entrants attracted to the market by the prospect of high profits. **Perfect competition**, where there are many firms supplying identical products with no entry barriers, is difficult to find in the real world. In reality, markets are usually imperfect—they can be costly to enter and dominated by a small number of firms who set prices, differentiate their products, earn abnormally high profits, and comprise buyers and sellers who have gaps in their knowledge of market conditions.

Another market structure is **monopolistic competition** with large numbers of firms, no barriers to entry, and only a small degree of product differentiation. The corner shop or convenience store segment of the retail market could be seen as monopolistically competitive with a large number of outlets, ease of entry, and each differentiated by their location.

In reality, most manufacturing and many service sector industries operate in oligopolistic markets where there are few firms, often protected by high entry barriers and able to exercise some control over the market. In oligopolistic markets, firms often try to differentiate their products from those of their competitors in the branding, advertising, packaging, and design of their goods and services. Firms that are successful in convincing consumers that their products are different, such as Apple with its Mac computer, the iPod and the iPad, can charge higher prices and not lose custom. Oligopolists, when formulating their policies, have to take into account that their actions could affect their rivals' sales, market share, and profits and are therefore likely to provoke a reaction. For example, a price reduction by one of the players might spark off a price war where competitors try to undercut each other. The end-result could be cut-throat competition with some firms going out of business.

In order to avoid such competition, oligopolists sometimes set up cartels. These, usually operating in secret, aim to control competition through the firms in the market agreeing to set common prices or to divide the market geographically among cartel members. In the EU, 17 steel producers were found guilty of running a cartel for 18 years in which they fixed prices and shared markets (EU Commission press release IP/10/863). Work by Connor (2002) suggests that global cartels are widespread. He talks of 'a global pandemic' of international cartels and a 'resurgence of global price fixing' (2002: 1). His database records nearly 900 international cartels and he adds 90 to 100 new entries each year. He argues that, with cartels, crime pays (*The Chronicle of Higher Education* 16 September 2013).

Market structure can influence the behaviour of firms in the industry and the nature and intensity of competition. In perfect competition, firms cannot set their own pricing policy because price is determined by the market and there would be no point in trying to differentiate one's goods or services in a perfectly competitive market because consumers see the products as identical.

By contrast, a monopolist is free to pursue an independent pricing policy. In addition, monopolists, facing no competition, do not need to try to differentiate their products. On price, oligopolists can usually exercise some influence although they must take into account the possible reactions of their competitors. Furthermore, in oligopoly, especially when selling to the final consumer, firms make strenuous efforts to differentiate the product through, for example, their marketing and sales promotion activities. For instance, Procter and Gamble, a leading producer of toiletries and other personal care products, was the leading global advertiser in 2013 with an annual spend of nearly US$10 billion equal to 12 per cent of sales. By contrast, Coca Cola spent just over $3 billion, or 6 per cent of sales revenues (SEC 10-K filings 2013).

Market structure can also influence company performance. The intensity of competition can affect profitability. In very competitive markets, profits are likely to be lower than they would be were those markets to turn into an oligopoly or a monopoly.

Learning Task

The European Commission was asked to decide whether a proposed merger between a firm producing instant coffee and one making ground coffee had any implications for competition. To come to a decision, the Commission had to determine whether the firms were competing in the same market. There was no statistical information available to estimate the cross elasticity of demand between instant and ground coffee.

Do you think consumers see these products as good alternatives?

One way to determine this is to compare the prices for both products. A major price difference could indicate that they are not good alternatives. Check prices at your local supermarket. You could also survey your fellow students to find out whether they see the two products as significantly different. An important indication that they are in different markets would be the willingness of the students to pay more for one than the other.

Market Power

The distribution of power among firms in an industry is assessed by the level of market concentration which can be measured by looking at the market share of firms in the industry. Market concentration gives an indication of the competitive pressures in a market. High concentration levels usually indicate that competition will be of low intensity. Big firms in highly concentrated markets will be able to determine prices, the quantity and quality of output they are prepared to supply, and to force policies on reluctant customers.

In search engines, high levels of concentration indicate low intensity competition. Google dwarfs its rivals, holding around 72 per cent of the global search market while China's Baidu trailed far behind with 15 per cent (Netmarketshare.com accessed 15 March 2014). More than three-quarters of all web searchers click on the first three links in Google and only a small minority look past the first page of results. Consequently, Google has the power to make or break firms promoting their products on the web. Online travel firms like Expedia claim that Google ensures that its own travel services appear above Expedia in the rankings. Firms, generally having little bargaining power over Google, sometimes complain to the regulatory authorities. In the EU, where Google enjoys a 90 per cent market share, the Commission forced Google to give its rivals more prominence in specialized search results, like those for shopping, travel, and local business reviews (European Commission – Memo 14/87, 05/02/14).

Pure monopoly demonstrates the highest level of concentration with one firm holding 100 per cent of the market. At the other extreme, in perfect competition, power is distributed equally among firms and, as a result, the level of market concentration is low. In oligopoly, a few firms dominate the market and the level of market concentration is usually high. The world smartphone market is a good illustration of this. As can be seen in Table 3.3, the three largest firms, Samsung, Apple and Huawei, account for more than 40 per cent of the market.

Measuring Market Concentration

There are various ways of measuring market concentration. The most straightforward method is the **concentration ratio** (CR). This is usually calculated by taking the share of the largest firms in industry sales or output by value or by volume. CR2, CR3, CR10, and so on, indicate the concentration ratio for the two, three, and 10 largest firms in the industry. In 2014, the CR3 for the

Table 3.3 Global market share smartphones Q2 2014 (%)

Samsung	25.2
Apple	11.9
Huawei	6.9
Lenovo	5.4
Others	44.1

Source: IDC

global smartphone industry was 44 per cent. This had changed dramatically compared with 2010 when the top three firms were Nokia, RIM, the makers of Blackberry, and Apple, and the CR3 was 66 per cent (www.quirksmode.org). The change in concentration was mainly due to the great success of Samsung, the marked decline of Nokia and RIM, and aggressive competition from China's Huawei and Lenovo.

A second method of calculating market concentration is provided by the Herfindahl-Hirschmann Index (HHI). The HHI is calculated by summing the squares of the individual market shares of all the firms in the market. The HHI gives proportionately greater weight to the market shares of the larger firms. It gives a more accurate picture than the concentration ratio because it includes all firms in the calculation. Sometimes, there is a lack of information about the market shares of very small firms, but this will not be important when such firms do not affect the HHI significantly. For example, a market containing five firms with market shares of 40 per cent, 20 per cent, 15 per cent, 15 per cent, and 10 per cent, respectively, has an HHI of 2,550 $(40^2 + 20^2 + 15^2 + 15^2 + 10^2 = 2,550)$. The HHI ranges from close to zero in a perfectly competitive market to 10,000 in the case of a pure monopoly.

The EU Commission sees an HHI of more than 1,000 in a market as indicating a level of concentration that could have adverse effects on competition. The Commission is especially concerned where firms are also protected by high entry barriers and where their market position faces little threat from innovation. It feels the same way when the share of the largest firm in the market, that is the CR1, exceeds 40 per cent. Consequently, the Commission looks for evidence of firms abusing their market power and examines closely proposed mergers between firms in these markets that would raise concentration to an even higher level (see Verouden 2004; Pleatsikas and Teece 2001).

Concentration figures can also be affected by the geographical focus of the information. In 2014, Lenovo, the Chinese multinational, held about 5 per cent of the world market for smartphones (see Table 3.3). However, switching the focus to its domestic market changes the picture as it holds nearly 12 per cent of the Chinese market (www.bloomberg.com 29 January 2014).

Learning Task

1. Use the information on market shares in Table 3.3 to work out an HHI for the global smartphone market. Assume that the remaining firms in the market only hold tiny shares and that their inclusion would not significantly distort the result.

2. On the basis of your answer, discuss whether the EU Commission would be concerned, on competition grounds, were Samsung to propose a takeover of Huawei.

What this shows is that a market can appear to be quite highly concentrated at one geographical level but fragmented at another. While AB InBev holds around a fifth of the world market for beer, the figure is nearer 70 per cent in Brazil (businessinsider.com 14 February 2014; bloomberg.com 26 February 2014).

Counterpoint Box 3.1 Market power—good or bad?

Firms like to have market power because it reduces competitive risk and gives them more control over price and output decisions.

The traditional case against market power is that it concentrates control in the hands of one, or a few, firms. Low levels of competition and high barriers to entry allow firms to raise prices above the competitive level in order to reap abnormally high profits. High prices cause customers to buy less of the product, less is produced, and society as a whole is worse off. Furthermore, in facing light competitive pressures, monopolists may become lazy by not innovating or pressing down on costs of production, resulting in resources not being used to maximum efficiency. In short, prices are higher, output less, and average cost of production greater under monopoly.

On the other hand, the Austrian School argue that dominant firms gain their position through competing better in the market place whether that be through price, new or better products, more effective advertising or distribution channels, or lower costs due to economies of scale. And higher prices, rather than indicating abuse of market power, simply reflect the value that consumers place on the goods and services provided.

Etro (2008) contends that where a firm is dominant, but barriers to entry are low, the leading firm will produce more and at a higher quality, set lower prices, and spend more on R&D.

Schumpeter (1976) and Galbraith (1967) assert that firms need to be large, have a significant market share, and be protected by barriers to entry to induce them to invest in the risky R&D that society needs to advance technologically (also see Threats and Challenges in Chapter 7).

Sources: Stigler (nd) 'Monopoly', *The Concise Encyclopedia of Economics*, available at: http://www.econlib.org/library/Enc/Monopoly.html; Leibenstein 1978; Armentano (nd [1978]) A Critique of Neoclassical and Austrian Monopoly Theory, available at: https://mises.org/etexts/armentanomonopoly.pdf; Schumpeter 1976; Galbraith 1967; Etro 2008

Questions

1. Microsoft has a virtual monopoly of desktop operating systems. Research the company and assess whether it is a lazy monopolist.

Analysing Industries—A Framework

Porter provides a useful framework for analysing the competitive environment of an industry (Porter 1979; 2008). His Five Forces model can be used to identify and evaluate the main threats to the firms in an industry (see Figure 3.1).

The Porter model is often used in combination with other complementary tools such as the PESTLE model (see Chapter 4) that focuses on the wider environment, or the resource-based view (RBV). While Porter focuses on the firm's external environment, the RBV tool concentrates on evaluating how the firm's internal resources and capabilities, such as patents and trademarks, or the success of the company in establishing a successful reputation for itself and its brands, can be used to achieve and sustain competitive advantage (see Fahy 2001).

Three of the forces are concerned with competition. The first, and most important, is industry rivalry, which involves competition from rivals already established in the industry. Next, there is competition from new entrants to the industry. Third, the industry may have to confront competition from products that carry out the same function for customers but provide the service in a radically different way. For example, trains and planes both transport customers from points A to B but in a different way, and consumers can get access to music by buying

Figure 3.1 Porter's 'Five Forces' model

Source: Porter 2008

CDs or downloading it from the Internet—it is a substitution in use. Porter calls these products, substitutes. The inclusion of this particular force helps get around problems of a precise identification of the industry. For example, in the market for luxury cars we might include firms producing Rolls Royces, Bentleys, and Mercedes because we see them as having a high cross elasticity of demand. Such a definition would exclude competition from sailing yachts or motorized vessels but these could be analysed using the substitution force in the Porter model.

The other forces are concerned with the industry customers and suppliers. We go through each of the forces in turn.

Force 1 Industry Rivalry

Industry rivalry can vary in form and intensity from one industry to another and in particular industries over time. At one point in the 1980s, telecommunications companies like BT, France Telecom, and Deutsche Telecom in Germany were seen as national flagship companies, with very powerful market positions and protected by the law preventing other firms entering the industry. There was little competition to speak of. This changed in the subsequent 20 years as barriers to entry fell and they faced up to fiercer competition generated by new entrants, like Vodafone, to the industry.

Competition usually occurs in one or more of the following areas: price, advertising, and sales promotion, distribution, improvements in existing goods and services, or the introduction of completely new products. New and improved products are particularly important in industries such as electronics—as illustrated in the oligopolistic battle between Sony with its PlayStation,

Nintendo's Wii, and Microsoft's Xbox in the console market. In 2013–14, Microsoft sold 5 million of the Xbox One compared with sales of 7 million for Sony's PlayStation4. Microsoft lost out because it tried to make the Xbox an entertainment system when console consumers wanted video games (www.forbes.com 9 June 2014).

Rivalry can also take the form of a struggle for resources. Firms in the oil industry also have to compete for reserves. In 1970 international oil companies controlled 85 per cent of the world's oil reserves, whereas, nowadays, state-owned oil companies control 70 per cent of reserves (*Financial Times Magazine*, 15 December 2007; www.forbes.com 16 July 2012). The difficulties that big oil firms like BP and Shell confront in their relationships with oil-rich countries like Russia and Venezuela force them to seek out reserves elsewhere. The Economist Intelligence Unit (10 July 2014) reports that companies in fast growing countries in sub-Saharan Africa desperately compete with each other for the best graduates.

Firms, especially international firms, increasingly strive for competitive advantage through mergers and alliances. There were over 1,000 cross-border M&As in the first quarter of 2014 with a total value of US$263 billion (mergermarketgroup.com 24 June 2014). While the global recession blunted the business appetite for acquisitions, cross-border merger activity started to recover very rapidly in 2010.

Horizontal mergers, that is between firms at the same stage of production of a product, boost market share and reduce competition. An example of this was the Air France merger with the Dutch carrier, KLM, which made it, in revenue terms, the largest airline in the world. Subsequently, it set up an alliance with Delta Air Lines of the USA to make it one of the most powerful forces in North Atlantic aviation, posing a tough competitive challenge for other transatlantic carriers such as BA. BA, in turn, responded by setting up a joint venture with American Airlines and merging with Iberia (www.bbc.co.uk; *Financial Times*, 18 October 2007; www.britishairways.com). Horizontal mergers facilitate the movement into new geographical markets.

Vertical mergers, where companies move closer to their supplies of raw materials or to their final customers, guarantee supplies of materials or distribution. In the late 1990s, with the Internet offering new methods of distributing news, music, and film, media companies in newspaper publishing, TV, radio, and film moved to integrate different levels of production and distribution in order to place their products in the largest possible number of different platforms. The motto appeared to be 'Create Once, Place Everywhere!' This enabled companies to produce films or music, register them in DVDs or CDs and distribute them not only through retail outlets but also through the cable, satellite, or mobile telephony networks they owned. Such vertically integrated companies were in a position to exploit their products at every single level of the value chain. Thus, Time Warner, the US media giant, merged with Internet service provider, AOL, and Vivendi got together with Universal. In 2014, Comcast, the large US cable TV company, bid for Time Warner. While vertical integration may allow firms to make efficiencies in the supply chain, it may also allow them to squeeze rivals where those rivals have to come to them for supplies or for distribution (see Pleatsikas and Teece 2000).

Competition intensity can range from being cut-throat to weak and depends on the following:

- The number of competing firms—the larger the number of competitors, the more likely is rivalry to be fierce. Conversely, the lower the number of rivals, the weaker the competition is likely to be.

- The relative size of firms—where rivals are of similar size or have equal market shares, then competition can be expected to be strong. This situation can be found in oligopolies such as cars where a small number of leading firms, including General Motors, Ford, Volkswagen, and Toyota, compete hard for sales. By contrast, in markets where one dominant firm competes with a number of smaller rivals, competition is likely to be less intense.

- Market growth rate—when the market is growing slowly, firms, wishing to grow faster than the market, will try to take market share away from their rivals by competing more fiercely. This is the case in the traditional markets of North America and Western Europe for the beer and car industries. If a beer firm wants to grow in those markets it has to up its competitive performance or take over a rival.

- The extent of product differentiation—when firms have been successful in persuading customers that their products are different from those of their rivals, then competition is likely to be less intense. In the beer market, Anheuser-Busch InBev has five well-established international brands, Budweiser, Stella Artois, Beck's, Skol, and Leffe, and more than 200 local brands, while Heineken manages a large portfolio of beer brands, such as Heineken, Amstel, Cruzcampo, and Tiger. Some firms, like Hoover, Sellotape, and Google, are so successful that their brand becomes the generic name for the product.

- The importance of fixed costs—fixed costs are those which do not change with output and include, for example, depreciation, rent, and interest payments. Industries operating with large, expensive pieces of capital equipment often have high fixed costs and relatively low running, or variable, costs. Examples include oil refining, nuclear power generation, and mass car production. In such industries, firms will be under pressure to sell their output in order to generate some contribution to their fixed costs. This pressure will be particularly intense when there is spare capacity in the industry; in other words, where firms are not using the resources to produce to their full potential, a situation faced by the big car producers in the traditional markets of North America and Western Europe.

- Where production capacity needs to be added in large chunks, then expansion by firms can add significantly to the industry's ability to supply and could result in supply outstripping demand, leading to more competition. This is a particular problem for the car industry given that new factories could add significantly to supply in an industry suffering from over-capacity. To be competitive, new factories have to be able to produce several hundred thousand units a year in order to take advantage of economies of scale.

If most or all of the above conditions are met, then competition in an industry will be fierce. Conversely, if none of these conditions prevail, then firms in the industry are unlikely to be competing fiercely against each other.

Often oligopolists faced with the unpalatable prospect of competition will make efforts to avoid it. There are various devices they can use to achieve this, such as forming a cartel, which, in many countries, is illegal. The members of the cartel agree to follow certain competition-avoiding policies.

One price-fixing cartel involved several large multinational producers of vitamins, including Roche of Switzerland, BASF of Germany, and Daiichi of Japan (European Commission

IPO/01/1625; also see Chapter 9, Case Study International Banks and the Law, for banking cartels). The USA and the EU found that major airlines, including British Airways, Air France, Lufthansa, and Japan Airlines, were operating a cartel to fix the prices for carrying cargo (*Financial Times*, 22 December 2007).

Often, cartels are established by firms producing undifferentiated products where buyers will take their custom to the cheapest supplier. When supply threatens to outstrip demand in such industries, firms fear the outbreak of fierce competition and sometimes set up a cartel to prevent this happening. Alternatively, competitors can avoid competition by resorting to **price leadership**. While cartels bring firms together in an explicit agreement, price leadership can result from implicit understandings within the industry. Under price leadership, one firm raises prices and the others follow suit. Price leadership takes two forms. The first is dominant price leadership where the biggest firm in the industry changes price and others, either willingly or through fear of the consequences, follow suit. Barometric is the second type of price leadership. This occurs when firms in the industry are of similar size and the identity of the price leader changes from one period to another.

Mini Case Study Food retailing—Brazil

Brazil, with a population of over 200 million, is the fifth largest country in the world. Its fast growing population, rising incomes, and a growing middle class has attracted the two largest global supermarket chains, Wal-Mart of the US and France's Carrefour—both with 500 or more stores. Brazil is important to Carrefour, being its second largest market. Total revenues of the food retail industry were around $146 billion in 2013, representing a compound growth rate close to 7 per cent per year between 2009 and 2013, around double the growth of food retailing in the US and the UK.

Sales of food through supermarkets and hypermarkets accounted for 52 per cent of the market in 2013. The five biggest food retailers are all foreign. Carrefour is the market leader followed by Grupo Pão de Açúcar, owned by France's Casino Group, then comes Wal-Mart. Fourth and fifth in the ranking is the Chilean chain, Cencosud, and Spain's Dia. The next five places in the league are taken by Brazilian supermarket chains.

The market is fragmented, with the top 10 supermarkets holding only 18 per cent of the market between them. The big chains benefit from economies of scale and their ability to price aggressively, unlike their smaller rivals.

Competition is intense. Customers can switch their custom from one chain to another at negligible cost. They tend to see the products and services offered by the chains as being similar despite efforts by supermarkets to differentiate themselves from their rivals through products and prices. To be competitive, supermarkets have to compete on price. Another issue for chains like Carrefour, who have gone in for hypermarket developments, is the increasing popularity of convenience and discount stores.

There are also well-established regional supermarkets that are expanding within their regions to deter the entry of the large supermarket chains.

In addition, supermarkets compete against a large number of independent and speciality retailers. A further threat comes from the fast expanding warehouse clubs which, operating in cheaper locations outside cities, offer lower income groups the possibility of buying in bulk at low prices. There are also a large number of informal sellers operating through street markets and small businesses.

Sources: www.chainstoreage.com 3 October 2013; igd.com 3 July 2014; Carrefour Annual Report 2013; thebrazilbusiness.com 3 May 2012; MarketLine Industry Profile 2014; Gain Report 2013;justfood.com 30 August 2013

Questions
1. What is the attraction of Brazil to foreign supermarket chains?
2. Why is rivalry intense in the food retail market in Brazil?

Counterpoint Box 3.2 International joint ventures—cooperation not competition

During the past decade, international joint ventures (IJVs) have become increasingly popular, particularly for MNCs trying to enter emerging economies, driven as these MNCs are by sluggish growth in developed economies, increased market competition, and rapid technological change. IJVs involve firms agreeing to combine resources in R&D, or production, or marketing, or distribution. In some emerging economies, foreign firms may be obliged to take on a local partner as a condition of entry. Studies on the performance of individual IJVs have shown mixed results.

The plus points of IJVs for business include: reducing political and business risks to facilitate faster, cheaper, and more reliable entry for IJVs into new geographical or product markets and access to technology; greater ability to obtain economies of scale and/or scope in areas like R&D, production, marketing, and distribution; more rapid development of new products; mitigation of competition; and faster growth. Gaining partners who have knowledge of local markets can help foreign firms navigate unfamiliar business practices and policies, increase a firm's credibility in the eyes of local consumers, and make connections with government.

The minuses include: difficulties of managing due to the IJV being owned by parent companies that could have very different cultures, managerial styles, or conflicting goals, with the added complexities associated with a different political and legal environment; loss of control over strategic and operational decisions; difficulties in monitoring, maintaining, and enforcing intellectual property rights, particularly in emerging economies where little protection may be given to them (see Chapter 7, Protecting Technology, and Chapter 9, International Law and IPRs).

Sources: Teece (1986); Beamish and Lupton (2009); Zhang et al. (2007); Burgers and Padgett (2009)

Questions
1. Why did foreign companies entering China initially favour joint ventures with Chinese firms?
2. What lessons have been learned about such an approach in China?

Force 2 Competition from New Entrants

The entry of new firms is another threat to established firms in the industry. New entrants will be attracted into industries by the prospects of high profits and growth. It may be that established firms are not making high profits, but that the entrants can see the potential for profit—this was the case with low-cost entry to the airline industry. Entry increases the number of firms and, if it takes the form of greenfield investment, adds to industry capacity. As a result, competition could become more intense. On the other hand, low growth industries with poor profits are unlikely to be threatened by a rush of new firms. Established firms are likely to leave such industries, looking for more profitable pastures elsewhere.

The probability of new entrants to the industry is dependent on the height of barriers to entry. Industries protected by very high barriers face little threat of new entry. The following are examples of barriers to entry.

- **Absolute cost barriers**—these are advantages which established firms have over newcomers. In the world of five star hotels, where location is of utmost importance, it would be difficult for a new entrant to find a sufficient number of prime sites to set up an extensive chain of hotels because many of these sites would be already occupied by established hotel chains. Similarly, firms trying to enter the telecommunications, electricity generation, or rail industries could have problems because existing operators control the physical networks.

- Legal barriers—laws and regulations can constitute insurmountable barriers. Before the telecommunications and airline industries were liberalized, the legal and regulatory framework protected existing firms from new entry. In many countries, firms wishing to enter banking usually have to pass a series of legal tests to get permission to set up in business.

- Product differentiation—this can be a major barrier when firms manage to convince customers that their products are significantly different from those of their competitors. Some firms, especially in consumer goods industries like cars, food, soft drinks, and computer software, spend large amounts of money on advertising, sales promotion, and packaging to differentiate their products. Apple spent just over $1 billion in 2012–13, but this was dwarfed by Volkswagen's $3 billion advertising spend (Apple SEC-10K filing 2013; *New York Times* 6 April 2014).

- Spending on advertising is increasing very fast in countries like China. McKinsey (2013) forecast that spending would more than double to $73 billion between 2011 and 2016, TV being the main medium but with the Internet catching up fast.

Promotional expenditure in the pharmaceutical industry is one of its main areas of cost. Some pharma companies spend more on promotion than they do on R&D. Massive promotional expenditures can build up brand loyalty and recognition to such an extent that the brands become very valuable. As can be seen in Table 3.4, it is estimated that the Apple, Google, Coca Cola, IBM, and Microsoft brands are each worth more than US$50 billion. Product differentiation can be a significant deterrent to new firms entering an industry.

- Economies of scale—these occur when an increase in the scale of the organization, say from a small factory to a large factory, leads to a fall in unit costs. In some industries, such as cars, firms need to operate on a large scale in order to compete with their rivals. If not, then they will suffer a major competitive disadvantage and some may find it hard to survive. This appears to be happening in China. Car sales in China, the world's largest car market, exceeded 20 million in 2013 (businessinsider.com 9 January 2014). However, sales are divided up between some 170 companies, few of whom are anywhere near achieving

Table 3.4 Rank and value of international brands 2013

Rank	Brand	Value (US$m)
1	Apple (US)	98,316
2	Google (US)	93,291
3	Coca Cola (US)	79,213
4	IBM (US)	78,808
5	Microsoft (US)	59,546
6	GE (US)	46,947
7	McDonald's (US)	41,992
8	Samsung (S. Korea)	39,610
9	Intel (US)	37,257
10	Toyota (Japan)	35,346

Source: Interbrand

Mini Case Study De-cluttering brands

Kumar (2003), in his study of four MNCs, found a 'surprising truth' that 80–90 per cent of profits came from fewer than 20 per cent of their brands, while other brands were losing money or just covering their costs.

Many multinationals, especially in the consumer goods sector, globalized by acquiring local brands. As a result, they found themselves with large portfolios of brands. There was an assumption that giving the consumer more choice would encourage them to spend more.

At the turn of the century, three-quarters of Unilever's brands, across 150 countries, were contributing less than one tenth of company sales. Diageo, the large producer of spirits, wine, and beer, sold 35 brands in 170 countries, but eight of them, including Smirnoff vodka and Baileys liqueur, generated more than half of sales and 70 per cent of profits. Nestlé, selling more than 8,000 brands in 190 countries, found that most of its profits came from around 200 brands. Procter & Gamble's 10 biggest and fastest growing brands, like Pampers nappies and Crest toothpaste, accounted for half of sales and more than half of profits.

No surprise, then, that companies such as Unilever and Procter & Gamble set about rationalizing their brands. Unilever aimed to remove the least profitable brands by reducing the number from 1,600 to the most profitable 400 by 2010. In 2014, Procter & Gamble declared an end to brand proliferation by announcing that it would cull up to 100 brands, like Oral B toothbrushes and Wash & Go shampoo, accounting for a tenth of sales revenue. The company wanted to concentrate on 70–80 big brands, 23 of them with annual sales of between $1 billion and $10 billion. According the chief executive, 20 per cent of the brands accounted for 80 per cent of sales.

De-cluttering of brands and cutting down choice for shoppers fits with the thesis of social scientists, such as Barry Schwartz, who argue that too much choice can overwhelm consumers, cause stress, and lead them to buy less. He illustrates this by recounting an attempt to buy a pair of jeans. The sales assistant asked if he wanted slim fit, easy fit, relaxed fit, baggy, or extra baggy . . . stone-washed, acid-washed, or distressed . . . button fly or zipper fly . . . faded or regular?

Questions

1. How could de-cluttering of brands enhance competitive advantage?
2. Discuss whether there might be pitfalls in getting rid of brands. See Professor Holt's comments at: brandchannel. com 7 March 2005.

Sources: Kumar 2003; brandchannel.com 7 March 2005; *Financial Times* 2 August 2014; Schwartz 2004

the economies of scale needed to guarantee long-term survival (*The Wall Street Journal* 9 April 2014).

Other factors deterring entry to an industry are **excess capacity**, declining demand, the ability of established firms to freeze out new entrants by controlling supply of materials, and distribution through vertical integration or long-term contracts with suppliers and customers. The actual or anticipated reaction of established firms can also be an obstacle to entry, especially where those companies are large and powerful. The EU found that French banks used discriminatory prices to block the entry of Internet banks and supermarket chains who wished to issue credit cards (*Financial Times*, 18 October 2007). Ellison and Ellison (2011) found some evidence that pharmaceutical firms deterred entry of generic rivals through their pricing and advertising policies.

Firms need to be ready to respond to new entrants. In the first decade of the new century, domestic banks in Singapore embarked on a frenzy of mergers when the authorities carried out further liberalization which was expected to lead to the entry of foreign competitors (*Asia Pacific Bulletin* 17 August 2001). The Chinese car industry cut prices when China's membership of the WTO meant that the measures previously protecting them from foreign competition would have to be removed (*Asia Pacific Bulletin* 25 January 2002). India's big retailers, like Reliance Industries, fearful that the Indian government would open up the market completely to foreign firms, expanded very rapidly in order to steal a march on rivals such as Wal-Mart and Tesco (*Time* 15 May 2009).

Force 3 Substitutes

An industry may face competition from substitutes. In the Porter model, substitutes are goods or services produced by firms in an apparently different industry and delivering a similar service to the consumer but in a different way. In the airline industry, firms sell flights to transport customers from point A to B, say London to Paris. All firms selling flights, such as BA, Air France, Lufthansa, and easyJet, would be seen as part of the same industry competing in the same market. But trains, ferries, coaches, and private cars could also be used by travellers to get to Paris. If the consumer sees the trains run by Eurostar as being an acceptable alternative to the services provided by airlines, then it would seem sensible to include them in any analysis of an industry's competitive environment.

The threat from substitutes will be influenced by the cost and ease with which customers can switch to the substitute product. For example, as oil prices rise, customers with central heating might consider switching to a cheaper form of energy. However, the costs, time, and inconvenience of changing the equipment could deter switching. In addition, switching may be deterred by firms using what is called confusion pricing. This occurs where the deals offered to customers are so complicated that it is virtually impossible to compare the value of one firm's offer against another. Examples can be seen in the competitive struggle in the telecommunications sector between mobile and fixed-line telephones. Customers are offered a bewildering variety of tariffs, services, and handsets with different technical capabilities making it difficult to judge which is the best deal for them (see Leek and Chansawatkit 2006).

One problem faced by the industry analyst is that, often, the information is not available to assess whether customers do see different goods or services as being good substitutes; in other words, whether there is a high cross elasticity of demand.

Force 4 Customers

Firms sell their output to customers who could be other businesses or the final consumer. For companies like Intel, business customers will be the main purchasers of its computer chips. On the other hand, supermarkets sell to the final consumer. Some firms, such as Microsoft, sell both to other businesses and to the final consumer. The power relationships that firms have with their customers depend on a combination of factors:

- The number and size of firms: when an industry comprises a small number of large firms facing a large number of small customers, then the industry will be in a powerful position. Losing a customer, in this situation, would not be very costly in terms of sales. This is the position of supermarket chains in Western Europe. They are large, few in number, but have millions of customers. It is also the case for accountancy services in the Asia Pacific region, which includes Australia, China, Japan, India, Singapore, South Korea, and Taiwan. Four major players dominate the market: PricewaterhouseCoopers, KPMG, Deloitte Touche Tohmatsu, and Ernst & Young (MarketLine Industry Profile, 'Accountancy in Asia-Pacific', August 2013). On the other hand, where many firms in an industry have a small number of large customers, then the power switches to the buyer because loss of a single client could cause much damage to revenues and profits. Firms producing defence equipment, such as BAE in the UK or Mitsubishi and Kawasaki in Japan, are in this position. Usually their domestic governments are, by far, the biggest purchasers of arms and other defence equipment such as tanks, submarines, and aircraft carriers. A situation of only a single customer is called a monopsony.

- The proportion of customer costs constituted by the product: when a product constitutes a large proportion of a business customer's total costs, the more sensitive they will be to price because price increases will have a big impact on their costs and, if they are unable to pass this on, their profits. These buyers, when faced by a variety of sellers, can shop around and play suppliers off against each other in order to get the most favourable prices. Where customers are dealing with only a few suppliers, then their bargaining power is reduced. This is the case in Europe for intensive energy users like steel makers whose energy bills are a large proportion of their total costs. The EU energy sector is highly concentrated, indicating low bargaining power for buyers such as those in the steel industry.

- The extent of product differentiation: the less differentiated the product, the easier it is for customers to switch to a cheaper supplier. Farmers supplying supermarket chains with meat, fruit, and vegetables will be in a much less powerful bargaining position than firms selling branded washing powders.

- The ability of customers to integrate vertically: sellers will be at a disadvantage where customers are big enough to produce their own supplies, either by taking over their suppliers or by setting up new production facilities. Wal-Mart and other supermarket chains built giant warehouses to take over the distribution of supplies direct from the manufacturer thereby cutting out the wholesalers that previously carried out this task. Apple is also vertically integrated because it not only designs and markets Macs, iPhones, and iPads, but also distributes them through its retail outlets. In contrast, buyers will have less power when they are unable to integrate vertically.

Force 5 Suppliers

'Suppliers' refers to businesses selling inputs, such as fuel, raw materials, and components to the firms in an industry. The position of suppliers can be analysed in a similar way to those of buyers, but in reverse. The only difference, as Grant (2005a) points out, is that it is now the firms in the industry that are the customers and the sellers of inputs that are the suppliers. To illustrate, if the supplier industry is dominated by a few large firms, compared to the buying industry, then the ability of suppliers to get away with price increases, reductions in quality, and a worsening of the terms and conditions of sale will be high. Firms producing computers have little bargaining power faced as they are by the world's dominant producer of microprocessors, Intel. Conversely, where the supply side is more fragmented than the buying side, then the advantage will lie in the hands of the customer. This was the case in the European dairy industry where suppliers of milk, cheese, and yoghurt were faced by a smaller number of big, powerful customers like Tesco, Aldi, and Leclerc. The dairy industry responded to this inequality by consolidating. For example, in the UK, Arla took over Express Dairies while Campina, a Dutch firm, took over Germany's Sator (see www. FoodandDrinkEurope.com; www.FoodNavigator.com). To see Porter discussing his Five Forces model and its application to the airline industry, visit the link on our **Online Resource Centre**.

Mini Case Study Market power in the global seed market

ETC (2008) reports that in the first half of the twentieth century seed production was under the control of farmers and public sector bodies. Nowadays, a large proportion of the world's seeds are produced by a few large agro-chemical multinationals (see Table 3.5). Table 3.5 shows that the CR9 for the seed market increased from around 13 per cent in 1985 to 62 per cent in 2012.

Table 3.5 World seed market—global market shares

1985	$M	Share of global seed maket	1996	$M	Share of global seed maket	2009	$M	Share of global seed maket	2012	$M	$M
Company	Net sales		Company	Net sales		Company	Net sales		Company	Net sales	
PIONEER	735	4.1%	PIONEER	1500	5.0%	MONSANTO	7297	17.4%	MONSANTO (USA)	9800	21.8%
SANDOZ	290	1.6%	NOVARTIS	900	3.0%	DUPONT PIONEER	4700	11.2%	DUPONT PIONEER (USA)	7000	15.5%
DEKALB	201	1.1%	LIMAGRAIN	650	2.2%	SYNGENTA	2564	6.1%	SYNGENTA (CH)	3200	7.1%
URJOHN ASGROW	200	1.1%	ADVANTA	460	1.5%	LIMAGRAIN	1155	2.8%	LIMAGRAIN (FRANCE)	1700	3.8%
LIMAGRAIN	180	1.0%	SEMINIS	375	1.3%	KWS	920	2.2%	WINFIELD (USA)	1300	3.5%
SHELL NICXERSON	175	1.0%	TAKII	320	1.1%	BAYER	645	1.5%	KWS (DENMARK)	1300	2.9%
TAKII	175	1.0%	SAKATA	300	1.0%	DOW	635	1.5%	DOW (USA)	1000	2.9%
CIBA GEIGY	152	0.8%	KWS	255	0.9%	SAKATA	485	1.2%	BAYER (GERMANY)	0.4	2.2%
VANDERHAVE	150	0.8%	DEKALB	250	0.8%	LAND O'LAKES	?	?	SAKATA (JAPAN)	0.4	1.0%
SHARE IN GLOBAL SEED MARKET (GSM)		12.5%			16.7%			43.8%			62%

Source: Mammana 2014

The level of concentration for particular seeds is even more highly concentrated (see Figure 3.2).

Changes in concentration have come about through the various growth strategies used by the large corporations. They have gone in for horizontal integration by the acquisition of rivals. Since the 1990s, France's Limagrain has taken-over 14 large seed companies. Bayer of Germany bought Nuhmens. The US MNC, Monsanto, acquired Seminis, De Ruiters, and Delta and Pine Land Company. The big operators have also established joint ventures and alliances with competitors in areas such as R&D and distribution; for example, Monsanto and Dow came together to develop genetically engineered maize seeds. Vertical integration is another part of the strategic toolbox. Mammana reports that companies have taken-over seed distributors. He adds that suppliers tie in farmers through the sale of genetically modified and highly productive seeds. The plants grown from these produce seeds giving a lower yield requiring farmers to buy new seed each year.

Figure 3.2 Global market share of seeds—maize, sugar beet, vegetables

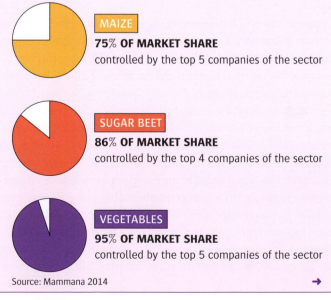

MAIZE
75% OF MARKET SHARE
controlled by the top 5 companies of the sector

SUGAR BEET
86% OF MARKET SHARE
controlled by the top 4 companies of the sector

VEGETABLES
95% OF MARKET SHARE
controlled by the top 5 companies of the sector

Source: Mammana 2014

➜ Sources: ETC 2008; Mammana 2014; Howard 2009; see video at: cookingupastory.com/seeds-of-life-consolidation-in-the-seed-industry-video

Questions

1. Assess the market power of the big seed companies.

A Sixth Force: Complementary Products

The Porter model pays particular attention to the relationships between competitors' products and also the threat from substitute products. It does not deal with the complementary relationship that can exist between products. Complementary products are those that are used together by customers, in other words they do not compete with each other but operate in tandem.

There are numerous examples of complementary products: mobile phones need service providers; DVDs need equipment to play them; computers need software; cars need petrol; and printers require ink cartridges. The suppliers of complementary products can play an important role in the competitive environment for firms in an industry, first, because the firms making the products depend on the efforts of the other, for example, in relation to product development. Second, there can be conflict over who gets most of the spoils.

Such a relationship is illustrated in the case of software vendors and the producers of PCs and PC components. Most PC manufacturers want new, exciting software to be developed that requires customers to upgrade to new PCs, but software providers generally prefer to target the larger market of customers with their existing computers. The schizophrenic nature of complementarity can be seen in the case of Intel, the maker of computer chips, and Microsoft. According to Casadeus-Masanell and Yoffie (2007: 584), they are 'joined at the hip' because more than four-fifths of the personal computers sold worldwide contain an Intel microprocessor running Microsoft's Windows operating system. The companies are dependent on each other because consumer demand and revenues depend on how well the different software and hardware components work together. This means that the R&D programmes for both players have got to complement each other. Casadeus-Masanell and Yoffie report that the two companies have been in conflict over pricing, the timing of investments, and who captures the greatest share of the value of the product. An Intel manager puts it thus:

> Intel is always trying to innovate on hardware platform and thus, always needs software. When software lags, it creates a bottleneck for Intel. Microsoft, on the other hand, wants to serve the installed base of computers in addition to demand for new computers. Therefore, a natural conflict exists between both companies. In addition, the question always remains—Who will get the bigger piece of the pie? The success of one is seen as ultimately taking money away from the other (Casadeus-Masanell and Yoffie 2007: 584).

Grant (2005b) shows how Nintendo managed to keep the upper hand in its relationships with the suppliers of games software for its video games console. Nintendo used various methods of establishing a dominant position over developers of games. It maintained control of its operating system, avoided becoming over-dependent on any single supplier by issuing licences to many developers, and established a firm hold over the manufacture and distribution of games cartridges.

Analysing an industry using the Six Forces: a checklist

- Are there many firms or only a few?
- Are firms a similar size?
- Is the market growing or declining?
- Is product differentiation important?
- How high are fixed costs as a percentage of total costs?
- Do additions to production capacity increase total industry capacity significantly?
- Are there any significant barriers to entry?
- Is there significant excess capacity in the industry?
- Do existing firms have the power to prevent entry?
- Is there any significant competition from substitutes?
- Is there a large number of small buyers/suppliers or a few large buyers/suppliers?
- Does the product constitute a large proportion of customer costs?
- Do input purchases constitute a large proportion of supplier revenues?
- Do customers/suppliers have the ability to take over firms in the industry?
- Are firms in the industry dependent on complementary products?

Counterpoint Box 3.3 Porter's 'Five Forces' model and its critics

Porter's Five Forces model has become part of the standard toolkit for managers and industrial analysts. However, it has been criticized on several grounds.

Critics claim that economic conditions have changed dramatically since the appearance of the model in the 1980s, when the business environment was much more certain, thereby making it easier for firms to plan ahead. They cite three developments that have made the environment much more dynamic and uncertain for business:

- digitalization and, in particular, the development of the Internet and e-business;
- globalization, resulting in firms finding themselves increasingly in a global market where customers can shop around and compare prices, and where rivals, buyers, and suppliers may decide to move production to cheaper locations;
- extensive deregulation, which led to a reduction in government influence over industries such as airlines and utilities in the energy, telecoms, and finance sectors and helped lead to major restructuring in these sectors.

A further line of criticism holds that a firm cannot be evaluated simply by reference to five forces in its external environment. These critics, supporting a resource-based view, argue that internal strengths and weaknesses of the firm also need to be taken into account.

Porter's supporters, while accepting the validity of some criticisms, argue that the idea that all firms operate in an environment characterized by rivals, buyers, suppliers, entry barriers, and substitutes remains valid. Some attempts have been made to extend the model. The inclusion of a sixth force, complementary products, has been proposed, while others have suggested adding government (national and regional) and pressure groups as another force.

The message for managers is that, while the model remains a useful tool enabling them to think about the current situation of their industry in a structured, easy-to-understand way, they need to be aware of its limitations when applying it.

Sources: Coyne and Sujit Balakrishnan 1996; Downes 1997; Brandenburger and Nalebuff 1996; Porter 2008

● CHAPTER SUMMARY

In this chapter we set out to explain the concepts and tools that are indispensable to the industry analyst and to show how they can be used to analyse industries. We started off with the concepts of the industry and the market. It was shown that any satisfactory definition of the market needs to specify a set of products and its geographical boundaries. The next issue to be addressed was the various market structures and their implications for business behaviour and industry performance. It was shown that the more highly concentrated is the market, the more power is concentrated in the hands of a few firms able to manipulate prices, the quantity and quality of the good or service, and the terms and conditions of sale. This was followed by an explanation of the Porter Five Forces model and how this could be used to analyse industries. As part of the analysis of Porter's force of rivalry, it was demonstrated how firms sometimes make strenuous efforts to avoid price competition through the establishment of cartels and systems of price leadership. We also revealed the importance of product differentiation as a major element of competitive strategy and as a barrier to entry in certain industries. A sixth force, complementary products, was added to the Porter model to make it an even more effective analytical tool.

● REVIEW QUESTIONS

1. Identify the main global companies producing oil, gas, and coal.

   a. Do these products compete against each other in the same market? For example, discuss whether customers in the transport industry and the power generation sector see them as good alternatives.

   b. Research online and assess whether the shale gas produced in the US competes in the global energy market.

2. Rexam, the UK MNC, is the world's largest producer of cans for the beverage market and is also a major manufacturer of plastic containers. Rexam has a particularly strong position in South America (see Figure 3.3). Giant global brewers like AB InBev and SAB Miller are major purchasers of beverage packaging in South America.

Figure 3.3 Company market shares global beverage can market

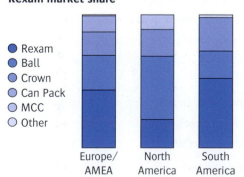

Source: Rexam (2014) 'Factsheet 2014', www.rexam.com/files/pdf/investor_factsheet.pdf

Figure 3.4 Market share by type of pack, South America

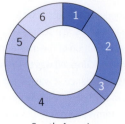

South America

1. Cans 2. Returnable glass 3. Non-returnable glass 4. PET 5. Bulk/draught 6. Other
Source: Rexam (2014) 'Factsheet 2014', www.rexam.com/files/pdf/investor_factsheet.pdf

   a. Looking at Figure 3.3, how powerful is Rexam in the South American market against its rivals?

   b. Figure 3.4 shows the market breakdown by type of container. Which type of pack is most popular?

   c. Assess how easy it would be for the brewers to switch from that type to other forms of packaging for their beers.

   d. In the light of your answer to b), analyse the buyer power of Rexam's biggest customers.

3. Online companies offering travel services, maps, weather forecasts, price comparison sites, and news complain that Google gives pride of place in its search results to its own services in these areas. With reference to the structure of the online search market, explain why companies such as Expedia and MapQuest are so incensed by this.

● ASSIGNMENT TASKS

1. Jeff Bezos, the founder of Amazon, has talked about 'eliminating all the gatekeepers' between authors and public; that is, the book publishers (Stone 2013: 315).

   a) How would you decide whether e-books and physical books were part of the same market?

   b) Discuss whether Amazon has a monopsony of the retail market for e-books.

   c) What are the implications of Amazon's power in the e-book market for publishers?

   d) Does Amazon have the same power in the retail market for physical books?

Visit the **Online Resource Centre** for articles on Amazon and the e-book market.

2. Construct a profile of the computer tablet industry. In the profile you must include discussion of:

   a) market growth;

   b) market structure, paying particular attention to market concentration;

   c) performance of the leading players;

   d) the nature and intensity of competition;

e) the identity of possible substitutes (see the Five Forces model);

f) barriers to entry.

For information, see the websites for: Business Insider; Tech Crunch; Apple Insider; Android Headlines.There are several sites giving up-to-date statistics on the tablet market: www.idc.com; www.gartner.com.

Case Study The smartphone industry

Between 2007 and 2014 the market for smartphone makers more than doubled because the number of people with mobile broadband expanded from over 3 billion to nearly 7billion (see Figure 3.5) The number of subscribers in the developing world almost quadruples those in developed economies.

Sales of smartphones exceeded 1 billion units for the first time in 2013, an annual increase of nearly 40 per cent. The main drivers of growth are low-cost phones in markets such as India, China, and Indonesia. It was estimated that more than 500 million smartphones would be sold in India and China alone in 2014. Many Indians will be buying smartphones for the first time. In developed economies and China, sales are usually purchased by consumers replacing their phones.

Two companies, Samsung and Apple, stand out as the biggest sellers. In 2013, Samsung was by far the market leader, holding more than one-quarter, followed by Apple, with around half that at about 12 per cent. Three firms, Huawei, LG, and Lenovo, together hold less than a fifth of the market (see Table 3.6).

Source: © imageCORE / shutterstock.com

There is a war of platforms among the major sellers between Apple's iOS, the open source Android developed and promoted by Google, Windows Phone, and Blackberry. It looks as if the war is being won by Android. Fearful that Apple would end up

Figure 3.5 Active mobile broadband subscribers (m) *Estimate

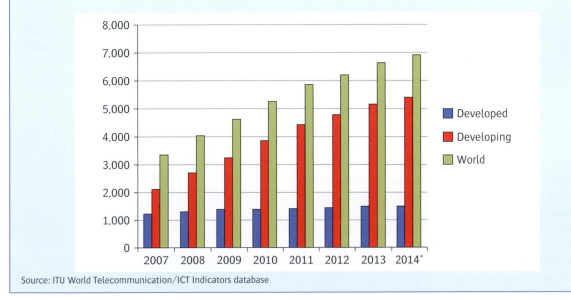

Source: ITU World Telecommunication/ICT Indicators database

→ **Table 3.6** Top five smartphone sellers, shipments in millions, and market share (second quarter 2013 and 2014)

Vendor	2Q14 Shipment volume	2Q14 Market share	2Q13 Shipment volume	2Q13 Market share	2Q14/2Q13 Growth
1. Samsung	74.3	25.2%	77.3	32.3%	−3.9%
2. Apple	35.1	11.9%	31.2	13.0%	12.4%
3. Huawei	20.3	6.9%	10.4	4.3%	95.1%
4.lenovo	15.8	5.4%	11.4	4.7%	38.7%
5. LG	14.5	4.9%	12.1	5.0%	19.8%
Others	135.3	45.8%	97.5	40.6%	38.7%
Total	295.3	100%	240.0	100%	23.1%

Source: IDC Worldwide Mobile Phone Tracker

dominating the mobile world and locking out access to its online services, Google gives Android away for free. Shipment figures in the second quarter of 2014 showed that around 85 per cent of smartphones were equipped with the Android system, an increase from 80 per cent a year before. iOS held 12 per cent of the market, with Microsoft and Blackberry trailing with 3 per cent and less than 1 per cent, respectively.

Samsung and Apple sell upmarket products. Samsung spends lots of money on R&D, which helps generate innovative products attractive to customers. It has gained market share by trimming profit margins. It also has a good geographical spread in terms of markets. A potential weakness is its almost complete dependence on Google's Android system.

Apple spends a smaller proportion of revenues than Samsung on R&D, but still manages to produce products seen as superior by their high value customer base. Apple does not compete on price, but on product design and a quality and content that is shared across all its devices. Vertical integration is seen as a formidable competitive strength for Apple through its offer of hardware, software, content, services, and retail outlets. Huawei, the fast growing Chinese producer, and Lenovo sell at the bottom end of the market. Losers in the smartphone market include Microsoft, which, following its unsuccessful partnership with Nokia, took over that company's handset business in 2014. Blackberry, which used to have very competitive products and was especially attractive to business customers, was unable to keep pace with a rapidly evolving market due to delays in introducing new products. As a result, its market share fell, big losses were incurred, and its very survival was threatened. HTC,

of Taiwan, is another that appears to have fallen by the wayside. It could not compete with Apple and Samsung and, after 2013, was retrenching through shedding assets and employees.

In 2012, Google moved into the smartphone market by concluding its takeover of Motorola with a primary aim of acquiring patents that would allow it to protect phone manufacturers using Android from litigation. By 2014, it had sold the handset business to Lenovo.

Intellectual property is important in the mobile phone markets, and sellers have shown themselves to be very litigious. Apple and Samsung have been fighting for years in courts around the world. In 2012, Samsung had to pay Apple $930 million, and a further $120 million in 2014 for violations of smartphone patents. Apple was also found to have infringed one of Samsung's patents. Some commentators see companies like Apple using litigation as a competitive tool; for example, to slow down the growth of competitive operating systems.

Source: © imageCORE / shutterstock.comSources: Rusko 2014; bgr.com 31 July 2014; blogs.strategyanalytics.com 30 July 2014; www.forbes.com 29 January 2014; *The Guardian* 3 May 2014; idc.com 27 January 2014; https://www.google.com/press/motorola; arstechnica.com 21 October 2013

Questions

1. Is the smartphone market an example of perfect competition, monopoly, monopolistic competition, or oligopoly? Explain the reasons for your answer.

2. In 2014, Amazon entered the market with its Fire Phone. What are the barriers for an entrant like Amazon trying to compete with Samsung and Apple?

3. What form does rivalry take:
    a) for customers in the smartphone handset market?
    b) in the market for operating systems?

4. a) Why is Apple's vertically integrated structure viewed as a 'formidable competitive strength'?
    b) How does the sharing of services across Apple's devices affect its competitive position?

5. Google is said to have 'an iron grip' on Android. Why might Samsung's dependence on Android be a weakness?

6. Discuss why litigation is so important in this market.

● FURTHER READING

For further discussion of market definition and market power see:

● Weinstein, A. (2006) 'A Strategic Framework for Defining and Segmenting Markets'. *Journal of Strategic Marketing* 14(June).

● Fennell, G. and Allenby, G.M. (2004) 'An Integrated Approach'. *Marketing Research* 16 (4).Pleatsikas, C. and Teece, D. (2001) 'The Analysis of Market Definition and Market Power in the Context of Rapid Innovation'. *International Journal of Industrial Organization* 19 (5).

● Verouden, V. (2004) 'The Role of Market Shares and Market Concentration Indices in the European Commission's Guidelines on the Assessment of Horizontal Mergers under the EC Merger Regulation'. FTC and US DOJ Merger Enforcement Workshop, Washington, DC, 17-19 February.

For discussion and application of Porter's Five Forces model see:

● Dobbs, M.E. (2014) 'Guidelines for applying Porter's Five Forces Framework: A Set of Industry Analysis Templates'. *Competitiveness Review* 24 (1).

● Siaw, I. (2004) 'An Analysis of the Impact of the Internet on Competition in the Banking Industry, using Porter's Five Forces Model'. *International Journal of Management* 21 (4).

● REFERENCES

Beamish, P.W. and Lupton, N.C. (2009) 'Managing Joint Ventures'. *Academy of Management Perspectives* May.

Brandenburger, A.M. and Nalebuff, B.J. (1996) *Co-Opetition*. London: Profile Books.

Burgers, W. and Padgett, D. (2009) 'Understanding Environmental Risk for IJVs in China'. *Management International Review* May.

Casadeus-Masanell, R. and Yoffie, D.B. (2007) 'Wintel: Cooperation and Conflict'. *Added Management Science* 53(4).

Cha, M. and Lorriman, T. (2014) 'Why Pharma Megamergers Work'. McKinsey & Co., February. Available at: http://www.mckinsey.com/insights/health_systems_and_services/why_pharma_megamergers_work.

Connor, J.M. (2002) *The Food and Agricultural Global Cartels of the 1990s: Overview and Update.* Purdue University Staff Paper #02-4, August. Available at: http://ageconsearch.umn.edu/bitstream/28631/1/sp02-04.pdf.

Coyne, K.P. and Sujit Balakrishnan (1996) 'Bringing Discipline to Strategy'. *The McKinsey Quarterly* 4.

Downes, L. (1997) 'Beyond Porter'. *Context Magazine* Fall.

Ellison, G. and Ellison, S.F. (2011) 'Strategic Entry Deterrence and the Behavior of Pharmaceutical Incumbents Prior to Patent Expiration'. *American Economic Journal, Microeconomics 3 February*.

ETC (2008) 'Who Owns Nature? Corporate Power and the Final Frontier in the Commodification of Life'. Available at: www.etcgroup.org/content/who-owns-nature.

Etro, F. (2008) 'Stackelberg Competition with Endogenous Entry'. *The Economic Journal* (118:532): 1670-1697.

Fahy, J. (2001) *The Role of Resources in Global Competition*. London: Routledge.

Fricker, L.D. (2013) 'Drug Discovery over the Past Thirty Years: Why Aren't There More New Drugs?'. The Einstein Journal of Biology and Medicine 29: 61-65. Available at: www.einstein.yu.edu/uploadedFiles/Pulications/EJBM/EJBM%2029.1%20Fricker.pdf.

Gain Report (2013) 'Brazil'. USDA, Gain Report Number BR 13011, 12/4/2013.

Galbraith, J.K. (1967) *The New Industrial State*. Woodstock: Princeton University Press.

Grant, R. (2005a) *Contemporary Strategy Analysis*, 5th edn. Oxford: Blackwell.

Grant, R. (2005b) *Cases in Contemporary Strategy Analysis*. Oxford: Blackwell.

Howard, P.H. (2009) 'Visualizing Consolidation in the Global Seed Industry: 1996–2008'. *Sustainability* 1(4).

Kirchhoff, M. and Schiereck, D. (2011) 'Determinants of M&A Success in the Pharmaceutical and Biotechnological Industry'. *The IUP Journal of Business Strategy* VIII (1).

Kumar, N. (2003) 'Kill a Brand, Keep a Customer'. *Harvard Business Review* 81(12).

Leek, S. and Chansawatkit, S. (2006) 'Consumer Confusion in the Thai Mobile Phone Market'. *Journal of Consumer Behaviour* 5(6).

Leibenstein, H. (1978) *General X-Efficiency Theory and Economic Development*. Oxford: Oxford University Press.

Mammana, I. (2014) 'Concentration of Market power in the EU Seed Market'. The Greens/EFA in the European Parliament. Available at: https://www.arche-noah.at/files/seeds-study_uk_28-01v3.pdf.

MarketLine Industry Profile (2014) 'Food Retail in Brazil', June. Available at: http://www.marketline.com/overview/industry-information/.

McKinsey (2013) 'Taking the Pulse of China's Ad Spending'. *McKinsey Quarterly* June. Available at: http://www.mckinsey.com/insights/media_entertainment/taking_the_pulse_of_chinas_ad_spending.

Pleatsikas, C. and Teece, D. (2000) 'The Competitive Assessment of Vertical Long-Term Contracts'. Presented at the Trade Practices Workshop, Business Law Section, Law Council of Australia, Queensland, 12 August.

Pleatsikas, C. and Teece, D. (2001) 'The Analysis of Market Definition and Market Power in the Context of Rapid Innovation'. *International Journal of Industrial Organization* 19(5).

Porter, M.E. (1979) 'How Competitive Forces Shape Strategy'. *Harvard Business Review* March-April.

Porter, M.E. (2008) 'The Five Competitive Forces that Shape Strategy'. *Harvard Business Review* 86(1).

Rusko, R. (2014) 'Mapping the Perspectives of Co-Opetition and Technology-based Strategic Networks: A Case of Smartphones. *Industrial Marketing Management* 43.

Schumpeter, J. (1976) *Capitalism, Socialism and Democracy*. London: Routledge.

Schwartz. B. (2004) *The Paradox of Choice: Why More is Less*. New York: HarperCollins.

Stigler, G.J. (nd) 'Monopoly'. *The Concise Encyclopedia of Economics*. Available at: www.econlib.org/library/Enc/Monopoly.html.

Stone, B. (2013) *The Everything Store*. London: Bantam Press.

Teece, D.J. (1986) 'Profiting from Technological Innovation: Implications for Integration, Collaboration, Licensing, and Public Policy'. *Research Policy* 15(6).

Verouden, V. (2004) 'The Role of Market Shares and Market Concentration Indices in the European Commission's Guidelines on the Assessment of Horizontal Mergers under the EC Merger Regulation'. FTC and US DOJ Merger Enforcement Workshop, Washington, DC, 17-19 February.

Zhang, Y., Li, H., Hitt, M.A., and Cui, G. (2007) 'R&D Intensity and International Joint Venture Performance in an Emerging Market: Moderating Effects of Market Focus and Ownership Structure'. *Journal of International Business Studies* 38: 944–60.

CHAPTER FOUR

The Global Business Environment

LEARNING OUTCOMES

This chapter will enable you to:

- **Explain the nature of the global business environment**

- **Understand and apply the PESTLE analytical framework**

- **Identify organizational stakeholders and construct a stakeholder map**

- **Analyse the impact on business of changes in the external environment**

Case Study **Telecommunications and India**

This case demonstrates the difficulties multinational companies face in dealing with diverse political, legal, and regulatory environments.

In 2007, Vodafone, the UK-based MNC, paid nearly US$11 billion for a 67 per cent stake in Hutchison Essar, India's third largest mobile operator. Vodafone was delighted to get such a powerful foothold in the world's second largest, and fastest growing, telecoms market where prices, and profit margins of 35 per cent, were high. However, within three years prices had fallen by more than 50 per cent and revenues had collapsed. Vodafone was forced to write down the value of its investment in India by US$3.3 billion, or by more than one-quarter. The company found itself in this position due to the intensity of competition in India. Vodafone was not alone in its suffering. All 15 telecoms operators in India, including the market leader, Bharti Airtel, were feeling the pain.

Government regulation was also an issue for telecoms operators. The Indian authorities were accused of implementing a series of policy switches that led to an influx of new entrants and a scarcity of spectrum—the precious airwaves on which mobile calls are transmitted. Bernstein Research, a US investment research company, commented that India was not a good choice for telecoms firms looking to exploit emerging markets: 'The country . . . is a competitive mess, and its regulation grows more capricious and nonsensical by the day' (*Financial Times* 25 May 2010).

Inhospitable market conditions made foreign investors wary of pumping money into Indian telecoms. This wariness was compounded after the eruption of a major corruption scandal in 2010. In 2011, the telecommunications minister was arrested on allegations that he had been bribed to allocate 122 mobile phone frequency licences at discount rates to a select group of firms. Several of these firms had no experience in the telecoms sector. Auditors estimated that the alleged mis-selling of the licences cost the Indian government nearly US$40 billion in lost revenue. As a result of the scandal, foreign multinationals started to distance themselves from their local partners whose licences were cancelled by the Indian Supreme Court. The subsequent regulatory uncertainty created chaos, but, by 2013, the situation was starting to settle down as disputes were gradually resolved by the Indian legal system. In terms of doing business in India, there is a suspicion of widespread corruption especially when dealing with government. India ranks 94 out of 177 countries in the 2013 Transparency International Corruption Perceptions Index.

Source: © Flickr / Klaus W. Saue

It was not meant to be this way. India is the world's second largest telecommunications market with, in 2013, almost 900 million mobile subscribers, and it is the fastest growing market adding more than 16 million subscribers every month. It has been predicted that India's mobile subscriber base will grow from 795 million in 2013 to 1,145 million in 2020. Unlike China, India welcomes foreign ownership of mobile companies, moving the cap for ownership from 74 per cent to 100 per cent in 2013. The Indian authorities see telecoms as one of the country's primary drivers of development. There is not only huge investment in the national infrastructure, but millions of rupees have also been invested in satellite earth stations, fibre optic submarine cables, and microwave systems to satisfy the demand for international bandwidth and high-quality connectivity. The National Telecom Policy (2012) has targeted 100 per cent tele-density and 600 million broadband connections by 2020, and, in the process, the generation of an additional 4.1 million jobs. Millions of farmers and urban poor, from Calcutta rickshaw pullers to Himalayan yak herders, now carry mobile phones. Mobiles enable them to do more business and gives them better access to services, such as health care. Every 10 percentage points increase in mobile penetration produces 0.81 per cent economic growth, according to a 2009 World Bank study.

Sources: India Telecom News 13 April 2011; *Financial Times* 25 May 2010; bbc.co.uk 15 November 2010 and 4 April 2011; Transparency International Corruption Perceptions Index 2013 Results; www.dot. gov.in; www.ibef.org/industry/telecommunications.aspx; www.budde. com.au/Research/India-Telecommunications-Infrastructure-and-Forecasts.html

Introduction

In this chapter we are going to examine the global macroenvironment and the tools which firms use to analyse it. By macroenvironment, we mean the wider external (or general) environment rather than the microenvironment (sometimes referred to as the task environment or industry analysis), the subject of Chapter 3. In this chapter, we will refer to the macroenvironment as the 'external environment'. The external environment is changing radically and becoming much less predictable due to:

- the accelerating rate of globalization;
- the information technology revolution;
- the increasing economic and political weight of countries such as China, India, and Russia;
- international institutions like the WTO and the EU becoming increasingly important influences on the global environment; as have non-governmental organizations(NGOs) with their vocal opposition to free trade and investment, and their success in getting environmental issues, such as climate change, onto the political agenda of national governments and international agencies.

Firms face great difficulty in monitoring, analysing, and responding to an external environment subject to literally thousands of different forces, both domestic and international. The increasing pace of globalization in recent decades has made the task of monitoring the external environment much more complex and turbulent. Firms can find themselves operating in countries with very disparate histories, political and legal institutions and processes, economic, financial, and socio-cultural environments, and physical and technological infrastructures. Firms have to be prepared to cope with various languages, different trading rules and currencies, and volatile exchange rates. Given this complexity, organizations may find it difficult to identify forces that could have a critical impact, as opposed to those that can be safely ignored. This ability to evaluate the external forces is vital because the environment creates opportunities for firms to achieve crucial objectives, such as profits and growth. However, it can also pose dangers to firms that could result, ultimately, in them failing. At the global level, the external environment can force organizations to alter policies on prices, modify products, and adapt promotional policies. It may oblige them to restructure the organization, to change strategies regarding moves into new product or geographical markets, and it can make them vulnerable to take-over. These can be seen as indirect costs for business when operating abroad.

The External Environment

The external environment of the firm comprises all the external influences that affect its decisions and performance. Such influences can vary from firm to firm and industry to industry and can change, sometimes very rapidly, over time. According to many observers, the environment for international business is changing faster than ever in two particular aspects, complexity and turbulence. Complexity relates to the increasing diversity of customers, rivals, and suppliers, and of socio-cultural, political, legal, and technological elements confronting international business. Complexity is increased by the forces in the external environment continuously interacting with, and impacting on, each other. An increasingly complex external environment makes it more difficult for firms to make sense of, and to evaluate, information on changes in the environment, and to anticipate their impact on the business. This, in turn, makes it more of a problem formulating an appropriate response. The problems created by complexity are aggravated by the growing turbulence of the environment. A turbulent environment is one where there is rapid, unexpected change, in contrast to a stable environment where change is slow and predictable. Turbulence has increased with the rapid widening and deepening of the political, economic, socio-cultural, and technological interconnections brought about by globalization and facilitated by advances in telecommunications.

What was a fairly static environment may become turbulent and subject to violent change. In the 1990s, the relatively tranquil environment faced by EU airlines like BA, Air France, and Lufthansa was disturbed by the decision made by the EU to liberalize entry into the industry. New, aggressive rivals in the form of the low-cost airlines like Ryanair, easyJet, and Air Berlin entered the industry competing away the established firms' market shares on short- and medium-haul flights. Business operating on a purely domestic basis is likely to confront a safer environment than its international counterparts. Some firms, like small local retail establishments, face a relatively simple and certain environment whereas multinationals, like Nestlé, operating in almost 100 countries, have to deal with one that is much more dynamic, complex, and, in some cases, dangerous and uncertain.

Growing complexity and turbulence in the environment makes it more difficult for firms to predict demand. It leads to competition becoming more disorderly, shortens the time available to make decisions, increases the risk of product obsolescence, and forces business to speed up the innovation process. Mason (2007) suggests that most managers have not been trained to cope with an environment of complexity, uncertainty, and turbulence and goes on to claim that such an environment is not conducive to traditional authoritarian, top-down, command and control styles of management.

However, it would be unwise to see firms as simply being the subject of the macroenvironment. Business, especially big businesses like Microsoft, General Electric, ExxonMobil, and Deutsche Bank, can exercise influence over their macroenvironment.

The US presidential election in 2000 shows how firms attempt to do this. Large oil companies in the USA, along with other energy interests, gave around US$50 million to the Republican Party in the run up to the presidential election. George W. Bush was elected, with Dick Cheney as Vice President. Both Bush and Cheney had previously been involved in the oil industry. Cheney had been the CEO of Halliburton, the world's largest oil field services company (www.bbc.co.uk 1 May 2001). On his election, the President abandoned the Kyoto Protocol on global warming and moved to allow oil drilling in the Arctic National Wildlife Refuge in Alaska.

Just before the EU was about to slap a €300 million fine on Microsoft for abusing its dominant position in computer operating systems, US diplomats lobbied the EU to take a softer line (*EU Observer* 27 September 2006).

Mini Case Study Indonesia complexity and turbulence

Indonesia is an ex Dutch colony situated in South East Asia between the Indian Ocean and the South Pacific, straddling the equator. It includes over 17,000 islands, although only 6,000 are inhabited. It has a tropical climate that is hot and humid. It lies on shifting tectonic plates and so suffers from frequent earthquakes and volcanic eruptions. In 2004, there was a massive undersea earthquake in the Indian Ocean which caused a tsunami killing 220,000 people in Indonesia.

The country has a population of 251 million people and the world's largest Muslim population. Its capital is Jakarta and its currency is the Indonesian Rupiah. The dominant language is Indonesian Bahasa, although Dutch and English are spoken together with over 300 local languages, the most common of which is Javanese.

Indonesia has a per capita GDP of $US3,416 in current terms, or US$5,498 in PPP terms (2014). Driven by domestic demand, the economy has been growing at a rate of around 6 per cent since 2006. It is regarded as a lower middle-income country, but the gap between the poor and the rich is widening. More than 32 million Indonesians live below the poverty line, set at about $22 per month, and 70 per cent of the poor live in rural communities. Inflation and unemployment are both relatively high.

Indonesia has a history of political and economic instability. Independence from the Dutch was gained in 1949. In 1965 there was a failed coup following which President Suharto took control and ruled for the next 33 years. His was an authoritarian rule with the army involved at all levels of society. Economic progress was made with some industrialization, but it was also a very corrupt regime. In 1997, the Indonesian Rupiah plummeted as part of the Asian economic crisis. Protests followed and Suharto was toppled. Since then, the country has become a democracy with the third presidential election in 16 years held in July 2014. It is now much more stable and one of the fastest growing economies. This has attracted strong FDI, although there are infrastructure problems and corruption is still endemic. There are a number of secessionist movements still active, notably in Aceh and Papua. East Timor became an independent nation in 2002. Islamist militancy is also a problem with a number of bombings, the worst of which was the 2002 Bali bombing in which 202 people died.

Sources: globaledge.msu.edu; bbc.co.uk; www.worldbank.org/en/country; IMF World Economic Outlook Database April 2014

Questions

1. Identify and list all the external issues you think a business should consider if thinking of setting up in Indonesia.

Opportunities and Threats

Globalization, associated with the increased cross-border movement of goods, services, capital, and people, is creating a more closely interdependent world characterized by growing networks, and has been a major influence in shaping the external environment of business. The widening and deepening of globalization means that local environments are not solely shaped by domestic events. Equally, increased interdependence causes local, regional, or national events, such as the 2007 credit crunch which originated in the USA, swine flu with its origins in Latin America, and bird flu originating in South East Asia, to become global problems. Increasing interconnectedness means that threats and opportunities are magnified, especially for organizations operating internationally.

Opportunities

Globalization generates opportunities for business to enter new markets, take advantage of differences in the costs and quality of labour and other resources, gain economies of scale, and get access to raw materials. Over the last decade, China and India have opened up their economies to foreign trade and investment. Foreign companies, including Tesco, Heineken, Disney, General Motors, and Toyota, have taken advantage of the opportunity to invest in China and India.

Many firms have responded to the new environment by globalizing production and reorganizing their supply chains to take advantage of low-cost labour, cheap international transport, and less regulated operating environments. Wal-Mart, the largest retailer in the world, has located its global procurement headquarters in China, and purchases many of its supplies of toys, clothes, and electronic goods there. Other large retail multinationals, like Carrefour and Auchan of France, Metro in Germany, Makro of the Netherlands, UK-based B&Q, IKEA of Sweden, and the US firm Home Depot, also source extensively from China (Coe et al. 2007). Boeing is another example, with the three million parts in a 777 being provided by more than 900 suppliers from 17 countries around the world (*The Guardian* 18 January 2008). In order to reduce development time and costs for the 787 Dreamliner, Boeing changed the way it outsourced. Instead of using hundreds of firms supplying direct to Boeing for final assembly, a number of tier suppliers were set up. An implication of this trend is that the fates of these companies, and their customers, become intertwined with their foreign suppliers and subject to the external environments in which they operate (see this chapter, Case Study Boeing's Dreamliner).

Threats

Globalization is also accompanied by threats that can have devastating effects on business, causing long-term damage or even leading to the collapse of the business. In the past, threats for international firms tended to be seen as country-specific, arising from:

- financial risks—for example, currency crises, inflation;
- political risks associated with events such as expropriation of assets by foreign governments or unwelcome regulations; and
- natural disasters such as earthquakes and tsunamis.

For example, the 1999 earthquake in Taiwan cut the supply of computer chips to HP, Dell, and Compaq, and the Chinese earthquake in 2008 forced Toyota to halt production there. In 2011 the Japanese earthquake and tsunami restricted the flow of many components to industry around the world, and later that year Thailand, a hub for electronic and car parts, suffered from severe floods. In 2014, riots in Vietnam targeted crucial manufacturing centres owned by Chinese and other foreign companies, disrupting global supply chains. This was in a country viewed as stable and an attractive alternative to China. But now there is an additional set of threats—these include terrorism, hacker attacks on computer networks, and global diseases such as Aids, bird flu, and the Ebola virus.

Terrorists are more likely to attack business than other targets, particularly US business. Two-thirds of terrorist attacks are against US businesses in the Middle East, South America, and Asia (*Financial Times* 25 April 2006; Enderwick 2006). Czinkota et al. (2010) identifies the main threats to business from terrorism as: interruptions in international supply chains, resulting in shortages or delays in critical inputs; government policies to deal with terrorism that alter the business environment and the ease with which global commerce takes place, for example at ports and airports; and declines in inflows of FDI caused by high rates of global terrorism as observed in Greece, Spain, Israel, Latin America, Middle East, and Pakistan.

As firms become more international they become more vulnerable to threats. For example, with the move towards global sourcing, supply chains can become stretched as they straddle multiple borders and involve more parties (see Braithwaite (2003) for a discussion of global sourcing and its risks). This leaves the supply chain more liable to disruption.

The growth in world trade in goods has resulted, according to the World Bank (www.data.worldbank.org), in the growth of container trips from around 200 million units per year in 2000 to over 600 million in 2012. The 9/11 terrorist attacks led the USA, along with other governments, to tighten up on security at ports. This resulted in a more rigorous inspection of cargoes, which led to increased delivery times. As a result, costs rose for firms who, often facing fiercer competition as a result of globalization, were trying to reduce delivery times and minimize stockholding through the introduction of just-in-time. It also raised costs for shipping firms as it increased the time taken to turn round their vessels.

Another effect of 9/11 was to make it more difficult, and sometimes even impossible, to get insurance cover. Enderwick (2006) reports that Delta Airlines' insurance premium against terrorism in 2002 rose from US$2 million to US$152 million after the attack. In a survey (by Marsh) it was found that more than 60 per cent of businesses bought insurance cover against terrorism. (You can view The Marsh Report, Terrorism Risk Insurance 2013 through the link on our **Online Resource Centre**.) In 2002 the American government introduced the Terrorism Risk Insurance Act to support the insurance industry providing cover for loss from terrorist acts as losses from terrorism are difficult to predict and quantify and therefore probably uninsurable. This was supposed to be a temporary measure, but was extended in 2007 and again in 2014 even though no claims have been paid.

Increased international sourcing of supplies means that firms need to pay particular attention to the maintenance of quality standards. In 2007, the giant US toy firms Mattell and Hasbro had to recall millions of toys made for them in China because of hazards, such as the use of lead and small magnets that could be swallowed by children (*Financial Times* 30 August and 10 September 2007).

Threats for some firms and industries can be opportunities for others. In 2005, the US states of Florida and Louisiana, along with the Gulf of Mexico, were devastated by several hurricanes—the city of New Orleans had to be evacuated. Oil firms, operating in the Gulf, suffered extreme losses as a result of extensive damage to oil rigs and onshore pipelines and refineries. The supply of oil was adversely affected and prices rose, hitting big consumers of oil such as shipping and airline companies. On the other hand, some firms benefited. With power lines down, and many houses destroyed, producers of portable power generators experienced a surge in demand, as did producers of mobile homes. In 2006, Shell, which had only suffered limited hurricane damage, announced its largest profits ever. The Japanese Tsunami in 2011 caused widespread damage and estimates are that reconstruction will cost £181 billion over a decade, good news for construction companies. Most nuclear plants have remained closed and some companies are planning safer and cleaner methods of power generation, such as solar plants.

Financial risks have become increasingly important because, over the last 40 years, there have been increasing levels of volatility in financial markets. Unexpected movements in exchange rates, interest rates, and commodity and equity prices are major sources of risk for most MNCs. Surveys show that many large MNCs see the management of foreign exchange risks to be as important as the management of other risks.

Mini Case Study Global threats—cybercrime

Increasing global interconnectedness has been accompanied by the development of new threats that can have a devastating impact on business. Advances in communications technology have made it easier to commit crimes using computers and the Internet. This fast-growing threat is called cyber-crime. It is attractive because it can be done at a distance, with anonymity, and is relatively low risk. It includes identity theft where personal information is stolen, for example, from customers. Users are lured to fake websites where they are asked to enter personal information such as usernames and passwords, phone numbers, addresses, credit card numbers, and bank account numbers. The information can be used to drain bank accounts or to buy goods and services using fraudulently obtained credit card details. It also includes hacking into computers to get access to confidential business information and /or personal information, the creation and distribution of viruses and worms on business computers, and a distributed denial of service, as in the case when a program repeatedly tried to access a website from various computers around the world to stop the intended users gaining access. Companies may find themselves being blackmailed by cyber-criminals threatening to use the information they have stolen to attack their systems. It used to be carried out by individuals, but, increasingly, criminal gangs are committing cyber-crimes. For example, in 2014 cyber criminals hacked into a well-protected ticketing system called StubHub. They stole personal information and used the credit cards fraudulently to buy tickets that were then sold on. In another attack, the GameOver Zeus Crew used phishing emails masquerading as official bodies to access individuals' and business machines. They then stole money from bank accounts, blackmailed the victims, and used their computers to attack other targets. It netted the gang half a billion pounds, with one firm losing £100,000 in under three minutes.

Illegally downloaded films and music cost film and music companies billions of pounds in lost revenues every year, although this figure is much disputed. Some estimates say the cost of piracy in the US alone is $12.5 billion to the music industry and $20.5 billion to the film industry.

Although cybercrime tends to be under-reported (for obvious reasons) and estimating the cost fraught with difficulties, such

as incomplete data, McAfee (2014) estimate the cost to the global economy from cybercrime is more than $400 billion although it could be as high as $575 billion. They say that most countries and most companies underestimate both the risk they face and how quickly the risk can grow.

As Web technology develops, and companies increasingly open their networks to involve communities of customers and suppliers as well as employees, so the opportunity for abuse of the systems increases.

Pandalabs and Symantec both agree that, in 2013, the focus switched to cyber-espionage conducted by governments around the world, most of which was overshadowed by the release of information by the National Security Agency contractor, Edward Snowden (see Chapter 8, opening Case Study). Pandalabs reported that, in 2013, cybercriminals created 30 million new malware strains, bringing the total of all malware in existence to 145 million. Trojans dominated (71 per cent) followed by worms and viruses. Countries with the most infected computers were China (54 per cent), Turkey (42 per cent), and Ecuador (40 per cent). Increasingly, social media sites (where users tend to be less security conscious) were attacked. Twitter, Facebook, Apple, and Google all admitted to being targeted.

In 2010 a worm called Stuxnet was discovered. This worm targeted industrial systems, such as power stations, water plants, and industrial units, with the purpose of destroying them. It seems to have been aimed at disrupting Iran's nuclear programme, although it was not the only country attacked and experts seem to be agreed that only a state could have engineered something as complex as this worm—no state has as yet confessed. Since then, other variants (Flame, DUQU) have been discovered, probably developed by nation states for use in espionage, such as stealing information about industrial control systems, and they are now out in the open and hackers can use elements of these programs for their own devices. In 2014, Symantec reported that, since 2011, the Dragonfly group had been spying on defence and aviation companies in the USA, but in 2103 switched their interest to focus on US and European energy firms and, more recently, industrial control systems. These activities involve spying, but they do have sabotage capabilities.   ➜

→ Sources: *The Guardian* 6 May 2014, 23 July 2014; McAfee (Intel Security) (2014) 'Net Losses: Estimating the Global Cost of Cybercrime'. Center for Strategic and International Studies, June www.mcafee.com/uk/resources/reports/rp-economic-impact-cybercrime2.pdf; Kushner, D. (2013) 'The Real Story of Stuxnet. How Kaspersky Lab tracked down the malware that stymied Iran's nuclear-fuel enrichment program'. IEEE Spectrum, posted 26 Feb 2013 http://archive.today/RpY2X; Symantec Security Response (2014) 'Dragonfly: Cyber-espionage Attacks Against Energy Suppliers', Version 1.21: 7 July 2014 www.symantec.com/content/en/us/ enterprise/media/security_response/whitepapers/Dragonfly_Threat_Against_Western_Energy_Suppliers.pdf; www.channel4.com/news/cybercrime-a-bigger-threat-than-nuclear-attack

Questions

1. Access the various reports and websites listed above and identify the consequences of industrial espionage for firms in the energy sector.
2. What steps can these firms take to mitigate these consequences?

There are various overlapping risks associated with exchange rate movements that need to be managed. Contractual risk occurs when firms enter into contracts where the revenues or outgoings take place in a foreign currency. A Eurozone firm may agree to buy a good from a US supplier and pay in dollars, or may accept dollars in payment from US customers. If the dollar falls against the euro, then purchasers in the Eurozone benefit because they need to exchange fewer euros to buy the goods. On the other hand, French champagne producers, selling to the USA, will lose out because the dollars they receive will buy fewer euros.

The next risk arises when firms earn money abroad and have to translate that into their domestic currency for the purposes of the reports and accounts. Movements in the exchange rate could have a major impact on the profit and loss account and on the balance sheet value of assets held abroad. Acer, the large Taiwanese IT firm, reported a loss of US$45 million on foreign currency exchange and other financial instruments in the first nine months of 2010. (An article on this topic can be located on the supporting **Online Resource Centre**.) In 2014, China's major state airline suffered big exchange losses because of the weakness of the Renminbi. When buying aircraft they take on finance denominated in US dollars so when their currency declines their debts become costlier to finance in the local currency.

Fluctuations in exchange rates make it difficult to evaluate company performance. Some companies get round this by stripping out the effects of movements in rates by translating the current year's turnover and operating profit using the previous year's exchange rate, or stating the sales and profits in the appropriate foreign currencies or, like Unilever, stating how much sales or profits were reduced or increased as a result of exchange rate changes.

Scanning the Environment

Big international firms spend time and resources regularly scanning their environment in order to identify forces that will have a major influence on them. In particular, they will be looking out for changes in the environment that could have an impact on their operations in terms of helping or hindering them to achieve their objectives. These objectives, for industrial and commercial firms, usually include profits and growth, and they may also set themselves targets with regard to market share or becoming the leading brand. Thus, firms will be particularly sensitive to aspects of the external environment that will affect their ability to achieve their objectives.

This scanning of the external environment is part of what is known as 'strategy', that is the process by which firms arrive at decisions about the direction the firm should take. Essential parts of that process are understanding the goals of the organization and analysing the resources and capabilities of the firm and the external environment. Indeed, strategy is the link between these elements.

Thinking about strategic management has gone through several phases. In the fifties and sixties, when the external environment was much more stable, the emphasis was on planning, with detailed operational plans being set typically for five years ahead. Instability in the macroenvironment in the seventies made forecasting difficult and so the emphasis changed from planning to position the firm in the market to maximize the potential for profit using techniques such as Porter's Five Forces (see Chapter 3). This became known as the **industry based view** (IBV), emphasizing that a firm's performance was determined by the macro- and microenvironment. In the nineties, the emphasis shifted again from external analysis to internal analysis of resources and capabilities in order to identify what was different about the firm and to look at ways of exploiting those differences—the **resource based view** (RBV). In the first decade of this century, change, as noted in the Introduction to this chapter, is much less predictable and so there is now increasing emphasis on flexibility and creating short term, rather than sustained, competitive advantage often in alliances with other organizations (see Grant and Jordan (2012): Chapter 1). It could be argued, then, that knowledge of the external environment, and identification of the main drivers of change for the organization, are more important than ever. Indeed, strategy must start from an understanding of the major trends in society, where your markets are going to be, who your suppliers will be and where, what new technology is on the horizon, and how it will affect products and processes and the way you organize your business (see Figure 4.1).

There has also been a questioning of the role of business in society in the wake of corporate scandals such as Enron, and the impact of business on the natural environment that strategists must consider. This questions whether business exists simply to make profits for owners (or increased shareholder value) or if there should be some wider purpose in serving society. At the heart of this debate is the notion of **stakeholders**. According to Freeman (1984), a stakeholder is any individual, group, or organization that is affected by or can affect the activities of a business (visit the **Online Resource Centre** for a video of Freeman explaining

Figure 4.1 Strategy

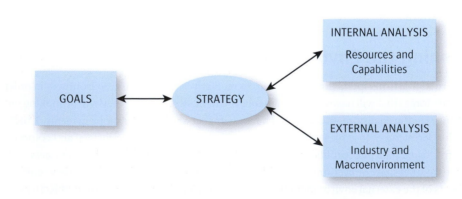

Counterpoint Box 4.1 What's wrong with stakeholder management?

Proponents of stakeholder management argue that, when making decisions, managers should consider the interests of all stakeholders, including shareholders, rather than just shareholders. In other words, all stakeholders should be treated like shareholders. Boatright (2006) argues that the interests of each group are actually better served by other means. For example, employees' interests would be better protected by contractual arrangements and the law rather than by management decisions. As he puts it, 'corporate governance, which is designed to solve specific problems of economic

organization, is simply the wrong tool, like using a screwdriver to hammer a nail'.

Source: Boatright J (2006) 'What's Wrong—and What's Right—with Stakeholder Management'. *Journal of Private Enterprise* XXI(2)

Questions
Look up Boatright's article, and any other appropriate resources, and answer the following:
1. What's right with stakeholder management?

stakeholder theory). Therefore, they have an interest in the decisions of the business, and equally, it is argued, the determination of strategy should take into account the actions and wishes of stakeholders. This would be true whatever the motivations of the firm, but for those who argue that firms should have an obligation to society other than their economic role in maximizing shareholder value then the recognition of who and what is affected is fundamental to the realization of that obligation (see Chapter 11 for a much fuller discussion of the debates around corporate social responsibility and Chapter 12 for an analysis of the relationship between business and ecology). Stakeholder analysis, or mapping, aims to identify a firm's stakeholders likely to be affected by the activities and outcomes of a firm's decisions and to assess how those stakeholders are likely to be affected.

Post et al. (2002), embracing the concept of the stakeholder, put forward a new strategic approach to managing what they called the 'Extended Enterprise' (see Figure 4.2). They stressed the role of recognizing stakeholder relationships in managing wealth creation in today's complex 'extended enterprise'. This approach recognized the futility of the controversy between those who preached the RBV rather than the IBV approach to strategy and that both of those approaches ignored the socio-political environment. This approach, it is claimed, integrates all three aspects. It recognizes that a network of relationships exists that is not just a matter of contracts, but also needs to be managed through building relationships and that these relationships exist not just between the organization and its stakeholders but also between stakeholders. For this, they put forward a new definition of stakeholders as:

individuals and constituencies that contribute, either voluntarily or involuntarily, to its wealth-creating capacity and activities, and who are therefore its potential beneficiaries and/or risk bearers (2002).

Stakeholders for each firm will differ, but Post et al. put forward typical groups within each of the three dimensions as demonstrated in Figure 4.2.

This idea of the extended enterprise, along with the industry structure (see Chapter 3), provides a useful framework for assessing the impact of changes in the external macroenvironment on the structure of the industry and ultimately on the stakeholders of the organization. This

Figure 4.2 The stakeholder view of the corporation

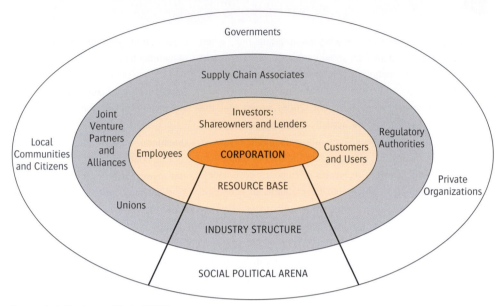

Source: Post, Preston, and Sachs (2002)

approach could also be used for assessing the impact of particular courses of action or future scenarios. The steps are:

1. Identify the macroenvironmental issues.
2. Assess the urgency and likely occurrence of the issues.
3. Analyse the impact on the structure of the industry.
4. Identify the relevant stakeholders.
5. Identify the most important by assessing their impact on the organization.
6. Assess the impact of the issue on each of the stakeholders.

One method of classifying the importance of stakeholders is to map them on to a 2 × 2 matrix according to their power and their interest. Those with the highest level of power and interest are the key stakeholders and need most attention. Others will need to be kept satisfied or informed (see Figure 4.3).

Learning Task

Shell and BP work in the very sensitive area of non-renewable resources and therefore have to be aware of the negative impacts their operations might cause. Choose one of these companies and:

1. Identify their stakeholders, classifying them into the various categories of the extended enterprise.
2. Construct a stakeholder map such as that in Figure 4.3.

Figure 4.3 Stakeholder mapping

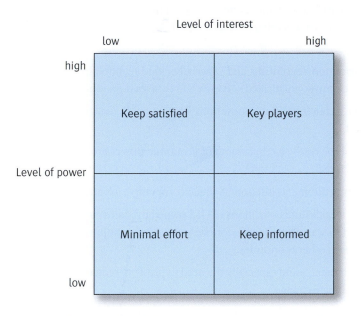

Source: Adapted from A. Mendelow, 'Proceedings of the Second International Conference on Information Systems, Cambridge, MA, 1991' cited in Johnson, G., Scholes, K., and Whittington, R. (2009) *Fundamentals of Strategy*. Pearson Education Ltd

Of course, the situation regarding stakeholders is not a static one, and stakeholder positions change according to the situation. Firms involved in stakeholder engagement keep up a constant dialogue with their stakeholders. Royal Dutch Shell, for example, has incorporated responsibilities to its stakeholders into its Business Principles. Visit the **Online Resource Centre** for a link to Principle 7, Communication and Engagement, on this topic.

Following embarrassing experiences in the 1990s over the proposed disposal of the Brent Spar Oil storage terminal by sinking it in the sea, and its relationships with the Nigerian government and local communities in Nigeria, Shell now make it a requirement that any new project has a stakeholder engagement plan. Since 2007 Shell has been discussing the decommissioning of the Brent Oil and Gas Field, and has held a series of meetings with over 140 invited stakeholders and also published a series of e-newsletters.

Shell, and other organizations, make full use of social media to keep in touch with their stakeholders by developing surveys, websites, chat rooms, emails, e-newsletters, bulletin boards, blogs, and podcasts.

This **impact analysis**, when done early enough, allows firms the time to consider a range of responses to exploit the opportunities and defuse the threats. This helps organizations recognize and adapt policies and strategies to their changing regional, national, and global environments. Because of increasing volatility and turbulence in the external environment, firms have got to expect/prepare for the unexpected. Kotler and Caslione (2009) claim that turbulence, with its consequent chaos, risk, and uncertainty, is now the 'new normality' for industries, markets, and companies. Globalization, together with communications technology, mean the world is now, as we noted in Chapter 1, more interdependent than ever so that change in one country can soon lead to change in many others. According to Kotler and Caslione, the factors that can cause chaos are:

- The **information revolution** and especially cloud technology which allows instant and flexible access to sophisticated software and data storage, especially useful for new firms.

- Disruptive technologies and innovations which quickly render 'old' technologies/products redundant.

- The 'rise of the rest'—a rebalancing of economic power around the world; for example, China and India.

- Hyper-competition—a situation in which competitive advantage is short lived.

- Sovereign wealth funds—trillions of US$ owned by states such as China, Singapore, Abu Dhabi, and Kuwait and available for overseas investment purposes, increasing the role of some states in other economies.

- The environment—and especially the need to preserve scarce resources and deal with the effects of climate change.

- Consumer and stakeholder empowerment gained through the information revolution.

They state that 'even more unsettling is the harsh recognition that whenever chaos arrives, you'll have little more than a fig leaf to hide behind—unless you can anticipate it and react fast enough to lead your company, your business unit, your region, or your department through it safely' (2009: 11).

Much of the above accords with McKinsey's assessment of the key trends in global forces. They identify five forces, which they label as follows:

- The 'great rebalancing', which, as we have noted, refers to the likelihood that most growth will come from emerging markets that will create a wave of new middle class consumers (as we saw in Chapter 2) and new innovations in product design, market infrastructure, and value chains.

- The productivity imperative—to continue to grow, developed economies will need to generate major gains in productivity.

- The global grid in which the global economy is ever more connected through vast complex networks. Information barriers break down as the walls between private and public information become blurred and economic volatility becomes more likely. The world, more than ever before, is becoming a single market place.

- Pricing the planet, rising from the tension between increasing demand for resources and **sustainability**. This will put pressure on using resources more efficiently, cleanly, and in dealing with new regulations.

- The market state in which the role of the state increases rather than withers in protecting individuals from the effect of globalization, intervening to stabilize economies (as in the recent financial crisis), and in bilateral agreements as multilateral agreements become more difficult as more economies demand their say at places such as the WTO and IMF.

(Visit the **Online Resource Centre** for a useful link related to this topic and see Chapter 1, Mini Case Study Removing barriers—TTIP and TISA.)

Given that forecasting and prediction become ever more unreliable in turbulent and chaotic times, one way of anticipating or being prepared for change is through what is known as scenario planning. Scenario planning is an approach to thinking about the future looking at stories relating different possible futures so that strategic responses can be considered and managers better prepared to deal with the issues. Shell has been developing scenarios since the 1970s, initially on a three-year cycle but now, indicative of the pace of change, annually. They have developed a tool called Global Scenario which is used to explore various scenarios relating to the legal environment, the role and importance of the market and the state, non-governmental organizations in society, forces bringing about global integration, and the factors leading to fragmentation and economic growth. It is also interested in the impact of the growing concerns about environmental issues, such as global warming, on the demand for fossil fuels such as coal, oil, and gas and consequently produces separate energy scenarios. For more information on these scenarios, and how Shell approaches scenario building, see the link on our **Online Resource Centre**.

From an American perspective, an organization busy developing scenarios is the National Intelligence Council of the USA which issued a report in 2012 looking at global trends to 2030. A link to this report can be found on the **Online Resource Centre**. From a European perspective, and concerned with the impact on the environment, the European Environment Agency has made its assessment of global megatrends, finding 11 which it conveniently organizes into five clusters: political, economic, social, technological, and environmental.

The Macroenvironment

Macroenvironmental forces comprise the wider influences on the business environment and, together with the microenvironment, complete the external environment (see Figure 4.4). For the purpose of analysis, the macroenvironment can be classified under the headings of political and legal, economic and financial, socio-cultural, technological, and ecological. Each of these can be examined as independent elements, but often changes in one area of the external environment can have an impact on others. For example, a government may take a policy decision to carry out a big expansion of public spending on infrastructure. This could influence the economic environment by increasing the total demand for goods and services in the economy and boost the rate of economic growth. If the economy is close to operating at full capacity then it could also lead to an increase in inflation and/or suck in more imports or divert exports to the domestic market. The balance of payments might suffer, which could result in a fall in the exchange rate. An instance of the interconnection between the various elements in the external environment occurred when the Chinese and Indian authorities made a decision to open up their economies to foreign trade and investment. These decisions changed the political environment and helped transform the economic environment as their rates of economic growth soared. This, in turn, had an impact on the microenvironment of business because rapid growth of income and demand for goods and services in China and India made them very attractive

Figure 4.4 The external environment

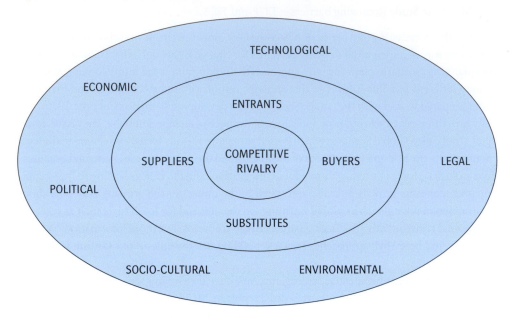

markets for foreign firms. On the other hand, the microenvironment can lead to changes in the macroenvironment—the credit crunch of 2007–08 lead to tighter government regulation of financial services. What is important for the individual firm, of course, is not just to identify the relevant **external factors** but also to analyse what the implications are of any change for their industry environment and their stakeholders.

Constant monitoring of all external issues might seem desirable, but it would not only be very time consuming but also very expensive. It would probably also result in a mass of information much of which might not be very useful. It is usually sufficient to identify the key drivers of change for an organization and monitor those. We are going to examine each element of the macroenvironment in turn, looking in particular at their potential impacts on business. For this, we use PESTLE as an analytical framework. PESTLE is an acronym for the political, economic/financial, social, technological, legal, and ecological factors which fashion the environment within which business operates. This external analysis is often used to identify opportunities (O) and threats (T) which can be combined with an internal analysis of a firm's strengths (S) and weaknesses (W), to produce a **SWOT** analysis, although internal analysis is not the subject of this book. The second part of this book deals with each section of the PESTLE in much more detail.

Political and Legal Environment

The political and legal environment is made up of the various political and legal systems under which business operates. We treat these together here because political institutions, such as governments and parliaments, pass laws and establish regulations which shape the legal environment

Counterpoint Box 4.2 What's wrong with PESTLE?

It is common to refer to this kind of analysis as a PESTLE (and there are many more acronyms, PEST, PESTEL, EPISTLE, LE PEST C are a few) analysis, but the great danger of this terminology is that the purpose of the analysis is forgotten; that is, to identify key external drivers and their implications for the industry environment and the organization's stakeholders. Too often, the exercise ends up with a long list of external issues with something in each section of the PESTLE, but with no appreciation or analysis of their implications. Moreover, it is often difficult to classify some as say, political, social, legal, or economic. A rise in taxes could be classified in any one of those four categories. The truth is that it does not matter. There does not need to be something in each section and it does not matter whether issues are political or economic, etc. As long as the main issues are identified and a careful analysis is undertaken of the impact, then that is all that is required. It is also sometimes difficult to classify issues as opportunities or threats as often an issue can be both. Again, it does not matter. Global warming may be a threat in that it is likely to increase energy bills, but it could also be an opportunity in the search for new products and new and more efficient production methods. The same could be said about the classification of internal issues as strengths or weaknesses but that is not the subject of this book.

Questions

1. Identify three external environmental issues and explain how they could be both an opportunity and a threat for business.

within which business operates. The courts, the police, and prisons ensure that the laws are enforced and lawbreakers are punished. Political regimes range from the liberal democratic systems of North America and Europe, to the Communist regimes of China and Vietnam, to military dictatorship in Burma (Chapter 8 deals with political regimes in more depth).

Some industries, like oil, need to pay particular attention to their political environment because they operate in a very politically sensitive sector, energy. Politicians and civil servants need to be kept 'on-side' because they are the people who decide whether oil companies are given the opportunity to search for, and exploit, oil reserves. Like other areas of the external environment, the political environment can turn nasty. Countries such as Russia, Venezuela, Bolivia, and Ecuador have been taking back control of their energy reserves from the oil majors. BP is a company with many reasons to nurture relationships with political institutions, and the people within them—it was nationalized in Iran, Iraq, and Nigeria, fined millions of dollars for illegally fixing propane prices in the USA, and for oil spills in Alaska. It has so far paid out over $30 billion dollars as a result of the 2010 oil spill in the Gulf of Mexico and is still facing action in the US courts which may cost billions more (*The Guardian* 4 July 2014).

Business also often looks to its domestic government to protect it from threats abroad (see next Learning Task). Governments in powerful countries such as the USA can exercise their influence over other countries to provide protection for home-based firms. This is particularly reassuring for MNCs given that the majority of the largest multinationals are based in the USA. However, commentators such as Haass (2008) see the USA losing position as the dominant world power. After the collapse of the Soviet Union, the USA was the dominant economic, political, and military power in the world. But in the twenty-first century, US dominance is being challenged economically and politically by countries such as China, whose share of the world economy is growing rapidly (for conflicting views of change in the global balance of power see Wallerstein (2007) and Wohlforth (2007)). Going along with this line of reasoning would suggest that the USA will not be able to offer the same degree of protection to its international companies.

Learning Task

Examine Table 4.1, which shows the average level of tariff protection afforded by the authorities in lesser developed countries (LDCs) and developed economies.

1. Compare and contrast the level of protection given by governments to their domestic producers in developing/emerging economies and developed/rich economies.

2. Discuss the protection given to farmers by developing countries.

   a) Advance reasons for this.

   b) Japan heavily protects its rice farmers. Why should that be the case?

3. A more detailed breakdown of tariff protection shows that Vietnam provides a very high level of protection to its processed food sector. What are the implications of that level of protection for domestic producers of processed food products in Vietnam, and for foreign food processors wishing to enter the Vietnamese market?

Table 4.1 Average tariffs on imports 2011

	Average tariffs on imports 2011		
	Total	**Agriculture**	**Non-Agriculture**
China	9.6	15.6	8.7
Colombia	8.8	14.9	7.8
Japan	4.6	16.6	2.6
New Zealand	2.0	1.4	2.2
Nigeria	11.7	15.5	11.2
USA	3.4	4.7	3.2
Vietnam	9.5	16.1	8.4

Source: WTO http://stat.wto.org/TariffProfile/WSDBTariffPFHome.aspx?Language=E

Firms also have to take account of the increasing importance in the political and legal environment of international institutions like the WTO, the EU, and the substantial number of regional trading blocs that have been established, and bodies such as the International Accounting Standards Board that has the task of setting international accounting standards. Countries get together in the WTO to agree the rules and regulations around international trade and investment. The WTO then acts to ensure respect for the rules. In 2008, a WTO panel ruled, in a case brought by the USA, the EU, and Canada, that China had broken the rules by using tax policy to restrict imports of car parts and, as we saw in Chapter 2, in 2014 the WTO found that the USA had unfairly placed high tariffs on Chinese exports of steel. Saner and Guilherme (2007) point out that the common approach used by the International Monetary Fund and the World Bank towards developing countries included:

- reducing budget deficits by raising taxes and cutting public expenditure;
- giving up control of interest rates;

- reducing barriers to trade and foreign direct investment;
- setting a stable and competitive exchange rate; and
- privatizing public enterprise.

All of these could have significant effects for domestic and foreign firms on the intensity of competition, market shares, prices, costs, and profits. There are signs, though, that the developing world, headed by China, is fighting back. The World Bank 'Doing Business Report' (see Chapter 5) ranks business according to the ease of doing business. China is ranked 96th out of 189 countries (2014) and reflects the fact that a more highly regulated economy scores lowly in the rankings. Critics argue that the rankings have a built-in bias towards deregulation, believing that the private sector is the main driver for growth. Opposition to the index comes from China, India, Brazil, and Argentina, among others, and is an indication of the possible shift in power mentioned above (*Financial Times* 6 May 2013; *The Guardian* 31 May 2013).

Economic and Financial Environment

The economic and financial environment comprises forces that affect large areas of the economy, like the rate of economic growth, interest rates, exchange rates, and inflation, and the policies of domestic and international institutions that influence these economic variables. The rate of economic growth is important for business because it indicates the speed at which the total level of demand for goods and services is changing. In fast-growing economies, income and purchasing power is increasing rapidly, leading to an expansion in demand. By contrast, slow growth means that markets are not expanding so quickly and are therefore not so attractive for business. Institutions like the IMF produce information on the world economy and its component parts. Its figures show that advanced economies have been growing relatively slowly whilst developing countries are expanding at a more rapid rate—Chinese growth, for example, topped 14 per cent in 2007 and was over 9 per cent in 2008 and 2009, when most developed economies' GDPs were shrinking (IMF 2014). The IMF also makes predictions of growth rates that could be of use for business trying to identify which markets will be fastest growing. They estimate that the world economy will grow at an average of over 3 per cent per annum to 2019 but, as we saw in Chapter 2, growth in emerging economies will be faster than growth in advanced economies. China is expected to grow at around 7 per cent per annum and India at 6.5 per cent compared to the USA's nearly 3 per cent (see Figure 4.5). Economic forecasting, however, is a tricky business and figures for future growth are regularly revised.

Learning Task

Using the IMF World Economic Outlook Database, look up the estimated future growth rates for the following countries: Colombia, Indonesia, Vietnam, Egypt, Turkey, and South Africa (the so-called CIVETS countries).

1. Analyse the market implications for foreign producers of telecoms, processed foods, roads, ports, and airports.

Figure 4.5 Estimated annual growth rate

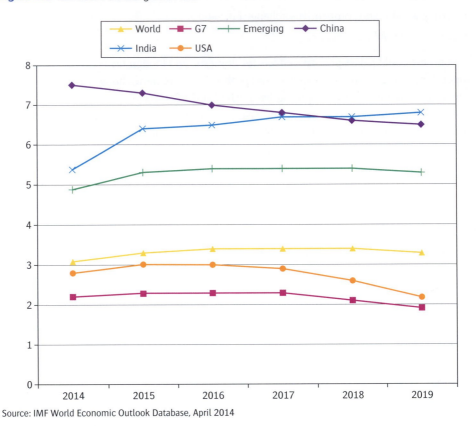

Source: IMF World Economic Outlook Database, April 2014

Despite the higher rates of economic growth in poorer countries, they still account for a relatively small proportion of world income and purchasing power, indicating that the biggest markets continue to be located in richer regions. IMF data (2014) show that the advanced economies generate 61 per cent of **global income** (down from 69 per cent in 2009), the USA alone leading the way with around 23 per cent of world GDP. Japan, Germany, the UK, and France together make up a further 19 per cent of income (see Table 4.2). China accounts for 13 per cent of the total (up from 9 per cent in 2009) but sub-Saharan Africa as a whole only 1.8 per cent; however, as we saw in Chapter 2, this will change considerably in the next 30 years.

Business can also be affected by volatility in the economic and financial environment. In the 20 years after the late 1980s, there were seven periods of turmoil in financial markets:

- the US stock market crash of 1987;
- the crisis in the European Monetary System in 1992 when sterling and the Italian lira were removed and several other currencies had to be devalued;
- Russia defaulting on debt repayments and the collapse of Long Term Capital Management in 1998;
- the financial crisis in East Asia of the late 1990s;
- the dotcom crash of 2000;

Table 4.2 Total gross domestic product 2014 ($US billions)

Ranking	Economy	US$ millions
1	USA	17,528,382
2	China	10,027,558
3	Japan	4,846,327
4	Germany	3,875,755
5	France	2,885,692
6	UK	2,827,514
7	Brazil	2,215,953
8	Italy	2,171,482
9	Russia	2.092,205
10	India	1,995,776
	Advanced	47,121,068
	Emerging	29,654,941
	sub-Saharan Africa	1,401,672
	World	76,776,008

Source: International Monetary Fund, World Economic Outlook Database April 2014

- the impact of the attacks on the Twin Towers in 2001;
- the 2007–08 credit crunch.

Such events cause a sudden and, because of globalization, geographically widespread increase in uncertainty in business and finance. Markets become volatile and make the assessment of risk more difficult. As a result, there is a flight from, what are deemed to be, risky to safer assets. Lenders steer away from providing credit to the private sector into lending to governments. It can become more difficult and costly for business and financial institutions to borrow money. Confidence takes a hit, which has a knock-on effect on economic growth because business and consumers become less willing to invest or buy goods and services. The inability to borrow, combined with contracting markets, could result in companies going out of business. These effects can be alleviated, to an extent, when institutions such as central banks, take action to boost confidence by, for instance, reducing interest rates and providing credit to banks, as happened in the USA and the UK during the 2007–08 credit crunch (see Chapter 10 for a more detailed analysis of these events).

Socio-cultural Environment

The socio-cultural environment is concerned with the social organization and structure of society. This includes many social and cultural characteristics which can vary significantly from one society to another. Social aspects include the distribution of income and wealth, the structures of employment and unemployment, living and working conditions, health, education, population characteristics including size and breakdown by age, gender, and ethnic group, social class, the degree of urbanization, and the provision of welfare for the population in the form of education, health care, unemployment benefits, pensions, and so on. The cultural components cover areas like language, religion, diet, values and norms, attitudes, beliefs and practices, social relationships, how people interact, and lifestyles (for more discussion of the socio-cultural framework see Chapter 6). Responding to cultural differences, whether that is producing packaging in various languages or changing ingredients in food products due to different diets, can incur costs for firms.

Mini Case Study Japan's demographic time bomb

Japan's population in 2012 was 127.5 million but this was 277,000 fewer than in 2004 when Japan's population peaked. It is now in decline with, since 2005, deaths exceeding births and by 2050 it is estimated that it will be just 97,076,000, over 32 million fewer people than in 2004. The birth rate measured as live births per 1,000 of the population was 28.1 in 1950, but has more or less declined continuously since then and in 2012 was only 8.2. The population is also ageing, as the Japanese are famous for their longevity. In 2012, the life expectancy for a female was 86.4 years and for a male 79.9 years compared to 81.1 and 76.3 for the USA. It means that there are many more elderly households (households with all occupants over 65). In

1975, 3.3 per cent of households were elderly, but by 2014 that figure had reached 25.6 per cent and children accounted for just 12.8 per cent of the population.

So, with a declining birth rate the proportion of the younger age population (0–14) is shrinking as is that of working age (15–64) and the only age group which is growing is the over 65s. Consequently, the total dependency ratio, measured as the sum of the young and the elderly divided by those of working age, will increase from 56 per cent in 2010 to an estimated 93 per cent in 2050. The old age dependency ratio will increase from 36 per cent in 2010 to 76 per cent in 2050, far higher than other developed economies (see Figure 4.6).

Figure 4.6 Old age dependency ratios

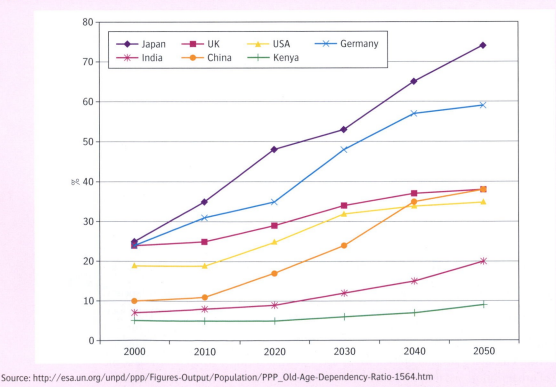

→ **Table 4.3** Japan's declining and ageing population

Year	Population ('000)	Age composition (%)			Average annual rate of increase
		0–14	15–64	65+	
2010	128,057	13.2	63.8	23.0	0.05
2020	124,100	11.7	59.2	29.1	−0.34
2030	116,618	10.3	58.1	31.6	−0.62
2040	107,276	10.0	53.9	36.1	−0.83
2050	97,076	9.7	51.5	38.8	−0.99

Source: Statistical Yearbook of Japan

Japan is not the only country facing this demographic problem. As the graph shows Germany has a similar profile and Italy, Greece, and Spain will all have dependency ratios of around 60 per cent by 2050 so they will be looking to Japan to see how they deal with the problem.

Sources: 'Statistical Handbook of Japan' available at www.stat.go.jp/english/data/handbook/index.htm; United Nations, 'World Populations Prospects: The 2012 Revision Population' database available at: http://esa.un.org/wpp/

Questions
1. Explain what is meant by an ageing population.
2. What are the implications for Japanese policy makers?
3. What are the implications for Japanese businesses?

Technological Environment

In simple terms, technology refers to the know-how or the pool of ideas or knowledge available to society. Business is particularly interested in advances in knowledge that it can exploit commercially. Technology offers business the prospect of:

- turning new ideas into new or improved products or production techniques;
- entering new markets;
- boosting revenues;
- cutting costs;
- increasing profits.

However, **technological advance** has been a fundamental force in changing and shaping the patterns of business as regards what it does and how it does it. The advent of microelectronics is a good illustration. In the production process it has cut down the amount of labour and capital required to produce a certain level of output, allowed firms to hold fewer components in stock, improved product quality by increasing the accuracy of production processes and facilitating quality testing, and reduced energy use by replacing machinery with moving parts with microchips (see Chapter 7 for more detailed discussion of the technological framework).

However, technology involves much uncertainty. Firms can pump lots of resources into research and development, be at the cutting edge of technology with new products that technically excel from those of their competitors, but that does not guarantee success. Big pharmaceutical companies have increased their spending on research and development significantly. In 2013, five of the top 10 R&D spenders were pharmaceutical companies, with the sector spending 18.1 per cent of all R&D spending (European Union 2013), but R&D productivity has plummeted. Deloitte (2013) found that the return on investment had declined from 10.5 per cent in 2010 to 4.8 per cent in 2013. The cost of launching a new medicine had increased 18 per cent over the four-year period to $1.3 billion with total development time increasing from 13.2 years to 14 years. PWC (2011) believe that the old strategy of discovering blockbuster medicines

Mini Case Study New technology

Skype is typical of a new technology company developing cheap global communications as part of what McKinsey refers to as the global grid. It was one of the pioneers of voice communication over the Internet and provides a service that allows consumers to make free voice calls between computers. It also allows voice and video calling, video conferencing, instant messaging, and SMS. In 2010, it launched a video calling app for the iPhone, iPad, and iPod Touch so their owners can make free Skype-to-Skype video calls wherever they are. Low-cost calls can also be made to landlines using a prepaid account or annual subscription.

Skype was founded in 2003 by Niklas Zennström and Janus Friis, Swedish and Danish entrepreneurs, respectively. The software was developed in Estonia and most of its engineers are still based in Estonia. In 2005, Skype was sold to eBay for US$2.6 billion, but, in 2009, 70 per cent was sold to a consortium of Silver Lake Partners, Canada Pension Plan Investment Board, Andreessen Horowitz, and Joltid (owned by the original Skype founders). In 2011, Skype was acquired by Microsoft for $8.5 billion.

Skype is now the world's largest carrier of transnational phone calls with over 500 million registered users worldwide and over 25 million users at peak times. According to TeleGeography (www.telegeography.com) Skype's international traffic volume continues to soar. In 2013, Skype added about 54 billion minutes of international traffic, 50 per cent more than the combined international volume of growth of every telephone company in the world.

McKinsey calls Skype 'a disruptive newcomer', but it also makes clear to businesses that 'even if they eschew such radical business models, they need to think strategically about how to use these new networks to advance their existing business models'.

Sources: http://about.skype.com/; 'The Global Grid', *McKinsey Quarterly*, available at: www.mckinseyquarterly.com/The_global_grid_2626;; www.telegeography.com

Questions

1. What opportunities does Skype present for small businesses?
2. Skype is a software product that uses existing hardware and the Internet to operate. Does this pose any potential problems for these businesses?

worked for many years, but the environment is changing, hence the reduction in return on investment. To survive, pharmaceutical companies will need to recognize these changes and adapt their strategies accordingly (see Chapter 3, opening Case Study).

McKinsey (2013) published a report identifying 12 technologies it describes as 'disruptive' because they have the power to 'transform life, business, and the global economy'. They include, inter alia, advanced robotics, next-generation genomics, and energy storage. These technology uncertainties make it much more difficult for business to carry out long-range planning.

The Ecological Environment

In recent decades there has been increasing concern, both nationally and globally, about the interaction between human beings, the economic systems they establish, and the earth's natural environment. Business forms a major part of economic systems that impact on the environment by using up resources and altering the ecological systems on which the world depends. The damage to the ozone layer, the impact of global warming, and the rise in sea levels due to greenhouse gases emitted by power generation, industrial, transport, and agricultural sectors, have been of growing concern.

Environmental challenges are a global phenomenon. Global warming is not confined within national borders, it affects the whole world. There is widespread recognition that economic growth is harming the environment irrevocably, and that we need to move towards a system that values the natural environment and protects it for future generations.

There is growing pressure on the political authorities to respond to these ecological threats. There are a number of possible policy responses, all of which have implications for business:

- tax the polluter;
- subsidize firms who manage to reduce activities that harm the environment, for example by switching to non-polluting sources of energy;
- use regulations to control the amount of pollution generated by business;
- promote the creation of environmentally friendly technologies.

For more discussion on the ecological environment see Chapter 12.

● CHAPTER SUMMARY

In this chapter we examined the global external business environment. The factors in this environment are highly interdependent but can usefully be analysed in the following categories: political, economic and financial, socio-cultural, technological, legal, and ecological, the various elements that make up the PESTLE model. This environment is increasingly complex, dynamic, uncertain, and can be hostile. Firms need to scan the environment in order to identify opportunities for new markets, for cost reductions, and for new sources of supply. They also need to look out for the many threats, not just from competitors but also from economic and financial volatility, political instability, new technology, and natural disasters. Organizations can assess the impact of external issues by analysing the effect of these issues on the structure of the industry and on the stakeholders of the organization.

● REVIEW QUESTIONS

1. Explain why operating in the international business environment is much more complex than in a firm's domestic business environment.

2. What implications does your answer to question 1 have for planning a firm's strategy?

3. Using the various reports mentioned in the chapter, summarize what you think are the most important issues affecting business in the next 20 years and their consequences for business.

● ASSIGNMENT TASKS

Select an organization of your choice operating internationally.

1. Identify the major external environmental issues.

2. Analyse the impact on the structure of the industry.

3. Assess the impact on the organization.

Case Study Boeing's Dreamliner

Boeing and Airbus produce every large commercial passenger airliner in the world and so in that market form a duopoly. They also produce smaller aircraft and these are important to their total revenue stream. In the smaller aircraft sector (single aisle with, on average, 155 seats), Embraer of Brazil and Bombardier of Canada are important competitors, but Japan, Russia, and China also produce smaller aircraft. Building on this experience, Russia and China are trying to enter the large aircraft sector and both have spent years developing suitable planes. China is set to enter the market with the state-owned Commercial Aircraft Corporation of China (Comac) as the Asian market is expected to grow rapidly in the next 20 years. Although the barriers to entry are very high in this sector, Chinese and Russian demand will guarantee some sales because of protected access to the market.

There are a number of key drivers of growth for passenger aircraft, of which the principal is economic growth. Increasing urbanization and the growth of the middle classes are also key drivers. Although there has been some turbulence in the market, particularly the global recession of 2008–09, orders have revived and revenues have grown. The world economy is expected to grow for the next 20 years at an average of 3.2 per cent per annum. This should, according to historic relationships, drive passenger growth by 5 per cent per annum. This is a doubling of passenger numbers every 15 years. This will continue to fuel demand for new and replacement planes. Boeing and Airbus differ in their predictions for demand in the next 20 years, but agree that it will be between 29,000 and 36,000 new planes. Growth in emerging markets and expansion of low-cost carriers mean that 70 per cent of the increased demand will be for single-aisle planes. The rest will be wide-bodied planes, around 9,000 or 450 per year.

Although there are only two major competitors in the large plane market, competition is said to be very keen. The industry's customers are the airline companies around the world and, with ticketing prices continuously falling in real terms (by 43 per cent between 1980 and 2012), they are looking to cut costs, especially in the fuel they burn. Fuel is the major cost of airline operations, about 34 per cent, and so producing more-efficient planes is a key selling point. Research into alternative fuel mixes using biofuel is also important. Other key issues are environmental regulations, market liberalization, infrastructure, and alternative transport.

Source: © Lakeview Images / shutterstock.com

Quality is obviously very important in airline construction as hundreds of lives are at risk every time one of these big planes takes off. The latest models from the two companies are the Airbus A380 and the Boeing 787 Dreamliner. The Airbus A380 costs $403.9 million and normally seats 525 passengers, whereas the Dreamliner costs £290 million and seats between 300 and 330 passengers. As of July 2014, Airbus had total orders for this plane of 318 with 138 having been delivered. Corresponding figures for the Dreamliner were 1,057 orders with 170 deliveries.

To conceive the idea and design, produce, and deliver a new aircraft can take years. The 787 was started in 2003 with a planned delivery date of 2008. The Dreamliner included many new innovations, such as a new electrical system and the use of composite materials that are much lighter and therefore improve fuel efficiency and aircraft speed. It also allows long haul flights without stopovers, and higher humidity in the cabin increases the comfort level for passengers. In order to reduce development cost from $10 billion to $6 billion, and speed up the development time from six to four years, Boeing increased outsourcing from 35–50 per cent for its earlier models to 70 per cent, and developed a new supply chain based on that used by car manufacturers. Traditionally, Boeing had assembled planes from thousands of parts supplied by firms all over the world. For the 787, more responsibility for development and assembly was given to what they called Tier 1 suppliers, of which there were about 50. These strategic Tier 1 suppliers, in turn, assembled parts from Tier 2 suppliers, and so on down the line. This meant that final assembly at Boeing's US sites was much quicker (three rather than 30 days) because, rather ➔

→ than assembling parts, they were assembling completed sections of the plane. This new strategy involved many risks that Boeing failed to foresee, resulting in a three-year delay in deliveries and billions of dollars in overspending.

There are now more than 140 Dreamliners flying across the world, but there have been problems. The first was with the skin of the fuselage and then, in 2013, battery fires grounded the whole fleet for three months. Boeing is using new lithium-ion batteries and their problems bring into question how well they have been tested. Other problems involved cracks in the windshield, fuel leaks, and engine failures. Some put these problems down to the new supply chain. Although all new aircraft experience some problems, the Dreamliner's reliability, at 98 per cent, is below expectations and at the reliability level of earlier models.

Sources: www.bbc.co.uk 10 February 2014; Boeing, Current Market Outlook 2013–2032; Airbus, 'Global Market Forecast, Future Journeys, 2013–2032'; Tang and Zimmerman 2009; *The Wall Street Journal* 13 July 2014

Questions
1. Explain what is meant by a duopoly.
2. What are the barriers to entry in this industry?
3. Draw up a stakeholder map for Boeing.
4. What risks was Boeing taking in developing its new supply chain?
5. Undertake an external environmental analysis for Boeing.
6. For each element in your analysis, identify the opportunities and threats for Boeing.

● FURTHER READING

For a very readable view of possible political, social, economic, and technological developments in the global economy, see:

- Moynagh, M. and Worsley, R. (2008) *Going Global: Key Questions for the 21st Century*. London: A&C Black Publishers.

The next two articles give alternative views on the changing world power of the USA:

- Wallerstein, I. (2007) 'Precipitate Decline'. *Harvard International Review* 29(1).

- Wohlforth, W. (2007) 'Unipolar Stability'. *Harvard International Review* 29(1).

For an introductory text to strategy, see:

- Johnson, G., Scholes, K., and Whittington, R. (2009) *Fundamentals of Strategy*. Harlow: Pearson Education Ltd.

● REFERENCES

Braithwaite, A. (2003) 'The Supply Chain Risks of Global Sourcing'. *Stanford Global Supply Chain* October.

Coe, N.M., Kelly, P.F., and Yeung, H.W.C. (2007) *Economic Geography*. Malden: Blackwell.

Czinkota, M.R., Knight, G., Liesch, P.W., and Steen, J. (2010) 'Terrorism and International Business: A Research Agenda'. *Journal of International Business Studies* 14(5).

Deloitte and Thomson Reuters (2013) 'Measuring the Return from Pharmaceutical Innovation 2013: Weathering the Storm?'. Deloitte UK Centre for Health Solutions.

Available at: www.deloitte.com/view/en_GB/uk/research-and-intelligence/deloitte-research-uk/deloitte-uk-centre-for-health-solutions/pharmaceutical-innovation-2013/index.htm.

Enderwick, P. (2006) 'Managing the Global Threats'. *University of Auckland Business Review* 8(2).

European Union (2013) 'The 2013 EU Industrial R&D Investment Scoreboard'. Brussels: EU.

Freeman, E. (1984) *Strategic Management: A Stakeholder Approach*. Boston: Pitman.

Grant, R. and Jordan, J. (2012) *Foundations of Strategy*. Chichester, UK: John Wiley & Sons.

Haass, R. (2008) 'A Political Education for Business: An Interview with the Head of the Council on Foreign Relations'. *McKinsey Quarterly* February.

International Monetary Fund (2014) World Economic Outlook Database April 2014. Available at: http://www.imf.org/external/pubs/ft/weo/2014/01/weodata/index.aspx.

Kotler, P. and Caslione, J. (2009) *Chaotics: The Business of Managing and Marketing in the Age of Turbulence*. New York: American Management Association.

Marsh (2013) 'Terrorism Risk Insurance Report'. Marsh Risk Management Research, May 2013.

Mason, R.B. (2007) 'The External Environment's Effects on Management and Strategy: A Complexity Theory Approach'. *Management Decision* 45(1).

McAfee (2014) 'Net Losses: Estimating the Global Cost of Cybercrime'. Economic Impact of Cybercrime II. Center for Strategic and International Studies, June.

McKinsey (2013) 'Disruptive Technologies: Advances that will Transform Life, Business, and the Global Economy'. McKinsey Global Institute. Available at: http://www.mckinsey.com/insights/business_technology/disruptive_technologies.

Post, J.E., Preston, L.E., and Sachs, S. (2002) 'Managing the Extended Enterprise: The New Stakeholder View'. *California Management Review* 45(1).

PWC (2011) 'Introducing the Pharma 2020 Series', Available at: www.pwc.com/pharma2020.

Saner, R. and Guilherme, R. (2007) 'The International Monetary Fund's Influence on Trade Policies of Low-Income Countries: A Valid Undertaking? '. *Journal of World Trade* 41(5).

Tang, S. and Zimmerman, J.D. (2009) 'Managing New Product Development and Supply Chain Risks: The Boeing 787 Case'. *Supply Chain Forum An International Journal* 10(2).

Wallerstein, I. (2007) 'Precipitate Decline'. *Harvard International Review* 29(1).

Wohlforth, W. (2007) 'Unipolar Stability'. *Harvard International Review* 29(1).

CHAPTER FIVE

Assessing Country Attractiveness

LEARNING OUTCOMES

This chapter will enable you to:

- **Explain the process of internationalization**

- **Identify reasons for FDI**

- **Select target markets and sites for exporting and FDI**

- **Assess global risks**

Case Study Tesco—the ups and downs of globalization

This case illustrates some of the issues faced by firms when entering foreign markets. It shows how Tesco entered foreign markets and, once in, some of the political/legal, cultural, financial, geographical, and competition issues it faced and their impact on success or failure.

Tesco, based in the UK, by turnover is the third largest supermarket chain in the world after Wal-Mart of the US and Carrefour of France. After the turn of the millennium, it embarked on an ambitious programme of expansion abroad. By 2013, it was operating in a number of markets outside its home base: the US, Czech Republic, Hungary, Ireland, Poland, Slovakia, China, South Korea, Turkey, Thailand, India, and Malaysia. In eight of these, it was the market leader. In most markets, Tesco worked with a local partner and, in most cases, it retained that partner's store identity. In 2013, 32 per cent of its sales and 29 per cent of profit came from outside the UK.

Tesco prospered in Eastern Europe, although sales in these markets fell as a result of the recession caused by the Eurozone debt crisis. Furthermore, in Hungary, retailers came under pressure from a sales tax, while the Czech Republic increased VAT from 10 per cent to 14 per cent. The company has strong market positions and saw much potential for growth in Thailand, Malaysia, and South Korea, although in the latter, Tesco's largest overseas market, profits in 2012–13 had been hit by legislation restricting large store shopping hours – the law allowed local authorities to close large supermarkets for two Sundays every month to help traditional markets.

Expansion in India became easier when the authorities eased regulations on foreign direct investment (FDI) in the highly protected retail sector. The new regulations allowed foreign retailers like Tesco to buy up to a 51 per cent stake in Indian retailers. Previously, it had been compulsory for foreign supermarkets to source 30 per cent of their products from small Indian firms. The new regulations gave them five years to reach that target and also allowed them to set up shop in cities with a population of less than one million. Tesco, seeing major growth opportunities in India, announced its intention to set up a chain of supermarkets in partnership with the Indian Tata Group.

However, Tesco found the going tough in several of its foreign markets. The company pulled out of Japan in 2011 and the US in 2013 because, according to the CEO, 'we had small market shares in markets with very strong competitors' (*The Guardian*

Source: © aimy27feb / shutterstock.com.

3October 2013). The US experience was particularly disastrous for Tesco. Rather than go into partnership with an existing US retailer in 2007, it set up a new venture, Fresh & Easy, in California, which was meant to break even in its second year of operation. Tesco did much preparation for its entry to the US. It spent three years and $1 billion researching the market. The research identified that its strengths in affordable fresh food products resonated with the US consumer and that there were gaps in the grocery market. Tesco, on the basis of the findings, added US recipes into their ready-made-meal range. But its stores, according to some analysts, were seen as urban food deserts that did not connect with the consumers it was targeting. In addition, the company ran up against cultural barriers with fresh ready-made-meals. These were a big seller in the UK market, but did not appeal to American customers who saw them as reminders of 1950's TV dinners and associated them with weight-loss packaged meals.

As it struggled to succeed, Tesco spent money remodelling stores. The company wanted to sell freshly prepared food at competitive prices, but found the US supply chain incapable of doing this. Consequently, Tesco pumped in more capital to build its own food preparation centre. The result was to inflate Tesco's cost base resulting in more stores having to be opened to generate the sales necessary to justify the extra expenditure. As this was going on, Fresh & Easy sales were hit by the recession in California. While Tesco was diverting more financial capital and managerial time to 200 Fresh & Easy stores in its faltering US operation, its rivals in its domestic market were getting stronger. The withdrawal cost the company close to ➜

→ £1 billion in profits and another £1billion in write-downs, and left it more vulnerable to competitors in the UK. Tesco joined a list of foreign retailers, with the major exception of Germany's Aldi, failing to make the grade in the US.

In the rapidly growing Turkish market, Tesco, like other foreign retailers, such as Praktiker of Germany, France's Carrefour, and Best Buy of the US, hit problems. The market was fragmented, with traditional corner shops accounting for around one-half of grocery sales, and competition was very strong. Foreign companies also struggled with the volatile Turkish lira, which could cause problems when buying goods in other currencies. However, analysts argue that the biggest issue, for foreign firms employing expatriate managers, is cultural differences, particularly in the food sector. Consumers, traditionally cooking their food from scratch, did not go for own-label, chilled, and pre-prepared food. Very high petrol prices also deterred consumers from driving to out-of-town shopping centres. According to one analyst, 'Grocery retail in Turkey is becoming more local . . . Given the fairly homogeneous food choices in Turkey from retailer to retailer, and a culture of scratch cooking, the expectation or need for own-label chilled

and prepared food innovation is less—this makes retail very "copiable" in Turkey, and arguably gives the global guys less advantage' (*Financial Times* 12 October 2013). In 2013, Tesco sold a major share of its operation to a local competitor.

The company also decided to cut its losses on its hugely ambitious expansion programme in China. Annual sales in this fast growing market had declined by 3 per cent and the company gave up control by putting its 134 loss-making Chinese stores into a joint venture with state-backed China Resources Enterprise, the country's biggest retailer. Tesco paid £354 million for a 20 per cent stake in the venture. China is a difficult market for foreign grocery chains because the vast distances between markets makes expansion costly and because of the fierce competition in fresh foods from local rivals.

Sources: Tesco Annual Report 2013; *The Guardian* 3 October and 10 August 2013; *Financial Times* 13 April, 10 August, and 12 October 2013; bbc.co.uk 14 September 2012, 31 December 2013; Open to Export 19 April 2013 http://opentoexport.com/article/why-did-tesco-fail-in-the-us/; www.telegraph.co.uk 29 September 2012.

Introduction

In Chapter 4 we looked at tools that could be used for making sense of the international business environment. In this chapter, we are going explain the internationalization process and why companies would want to invest overseas (FDI). We then go on to show how organizations can assess the attractiveness of countries as markets or production locations.

The Internationalization Process

International business includes firms undertaking imports and exports, producing abroad, or being involved in joint ventures, licensing, or franchising arrangements with a foreign partner. It ranges from firms producing goods and services in a single country and exporting them to another, to firms like Dell with complex global production and distribution networks across dozens of countries.

The traditional view of international business is that firms initially establish a stable domestic base before venturing overseas. Arenius (2005), quoting a Finnish company executive, provides a reason for this:

it seems easier for a fellow countryman to sell to a fellow countryman . . . It's easier for a Swedish company to do business with a Swedish person, who is located in the nice city of Stockholm and speaks their native language . . . There are cultural differences. You need to have an American to sell to an American company.

Carrefour, a French company, is the world's second largest retailer with 10,105 stores in 34 countries. The Carrefour name came into being in 1959, but it was not until 1969 that it took its first venture outside France, and that was in Belgium—a country, in terms of its business environment, very similar to France. Its next venture was to Spain and then in 1975 to South America. It was not until 1989, when it entered the Taiwanese market, that it ventured into a very different business environment. However, in 2013, nearly 73 per cent of turnover was still being made in France and other European countries (www.carrefour.com).

Traditionally, companies are seen as internationalizing incrementally in three stages, the Uppsala model (see Johanson and Vahlne 1977). From their domestic base, firms develop gradually by exporting to another country geographically and culturally similar. Initially, exporting takes place either directly through the company's own export department or indirectly via an external export agency. Then, as overseas business expands, and with it the experience and confidence of operating in overseas markets, the firm becomes more committed to foreign activities. This can take the form of exporting to more distant and less culturally similar countries and perhaps setting up an overseas sales company. Success, combined with the greater knowledge of foreign markets, according to the traditional model, leads ultimately to the setting up of production facilities across the world that can be done with partner firms through joint ventures or totally owned foreign subsidiaries (see Table 5.1). Whichever the mode of operations, expanding overseas is always challenging.

This traditional model of slow and incremental development of international business has been challenged in a number of ways. Benito et al. (2009) argue that the reality is much 'messier' and that, rather than a simple sequential process, firms may often operate different modes at the same time. Malhotra and Hinings (2010) argue that different types of organization follow different processes of internationalization. The Uppsala model was based on the study of Swedish manufacturing firms, but now many different organizations are internationalizing their operations. Many are consumer and professional service organizations such as hotels, restaurants, accountants, solicitors, retailers, and management consultants for whom the process is likely to be quite different. Professional service firms often follow clients into new markets, and for consumer services, such as retailing and hotels, the nature of the service demands a physical presence in the host market.

Many empirical studies of the internationalization process, especially in technology-based, knowledge-intensive sectors, contradict the predictions of the three-stage model and it is now

Table 5.1 The traditional model of internationalization

Entry mode	
Export from domestic base	Directly through export department or via overseas agent
Licensing/Franchising	An agreement to allow a partner to manufacture or sell abroad
Joint Venture	An alliance in which an equity investment is made with a partner
Wholly owned subsidiary	Either acquisition of existing firms (brownfield investment) or entirely new facilities (greenfield investment)

claimed that many firms are 'born global'. A born-global company is one in which foreign sales account for at least 25 per cent of the total within three years of its inception and looks to derive significant competitive advantage from operating multinationally (Andersson and Evangelista 2006). Such firms take an international perspective from the outset with the intention of trading internationally immediately or within a short period of time. 'These firms view the world as their marketplace from the outset and see the domestic market as a support for their international business' (Rennie 1993). They globalize their business rapidly, entering physically distant markets from an early stage in their life cycle (Prashantham 2005). Such companies are usually small, with limited resources but with a global vision (Gabrielson 2005). They tend to be high technology companies, focused on market niches. Companies in small, open economies, like Denmark, Sweden, and Switzerland, because of the limited size of their domestic market and the pressure of competition, are likely to come under more pressure to enter global markets than are firms based in bigger markets. Andersson and Evangelista (2006) use the example of Rubber, a Swedish company producing advanced cable entries and seals. From the start-up in 1990, the company saw the whole world as its market. It entered around 10 new markets each year, and by 2001 it was present in 80 nations.

The most important macro-trends encouraging the widespread emergence of born-globals are globalization and advanced **information and communications technologies (ICT)**. Globalization provides market opportunities and, along with the widespread diffusion of new communications technology and falling transport costs, lowers the costs of entering foreign markets. Born-global firms use technology to achieve competitive advantage and develop a range of alliances and collaborative partnerships with suppliers, distributors, and customers. This helps them overcome the traditional constraints to internationalization: being too small to gain economies of scale; lack of resources, both financial and knowledge; and an aversion to risk-taking. The financial burden and risk is shared with alliance partners and the partners provide knowledge about foreign markets (Freeman et al. 2006). Although still small in relation to the total, such firms are taking up an increasing share of world trade (Knight et al. 2004). Fan and Phan (2007) argue that they are not such a distinct breed and that these firms are subject to many of the same influences as in the traditional pattern of internationalization.

Learning Task

Research the history of an international business organization of your choice. Trace the steps in its growth and see if it fits the traditional path suggested in this chapter.

The Reasons for FDI

Businesses invest abroad for various reasons. The main motives can be summarized as:

- the need to get market access;
- the search for lower production costs; and
- a quest for natural resources and other assets.

Market Access

Business is interested in gaining entry to big markets or markets with the potential for growth and profit. According to the Trade Policy Unit (TPU) (2014) the UK is second only to the US in investing abroad, with the US being the largest recipient. Europe is the next largest, and in particular, France, the Netherlands, Luxembourg, and Ireland, although some of this is companies channelling funds through low tax regimes. The BRICS countries account for only 4 per cent of FDI stocks despite them being an attractive proposition. The TPU suggests this may be because of 'concerns about the existence and enforcement of property rights, inefficient bureaucracy, poor developed infrastructure or restrictions on the type, level and location of investment' (2014: 5). They point out, though, that in 2011, 16 per cent of net outward flows were to BRIC countries and that their share of the UK's stock of outward investment has grown every year since 2002.

These, and other emerging markets, are particularly attractive markets because of their relatively high rates of economic growth and purchasing power at a time when developed country markets are growing only slowly. As we saw in Chapter 2, emerging markets are estimated to grow at over 5 per cent per annum for the next five years whereas the estimate for developed economies is only just above 2 per cent. China and India are estimated to increase by around 7 per cent.

A problem confronted by business is that attractive markets are sometimes protected from imports by barriers such as tariffs the USA levies on imports of steel, quotas such as those imposed by the EU on Chinese clothing and footwear, and countries such as China and Indonesia trying to ensure that a certain proportion of the cars sold there is manufactured locally. One way of circumventing these barriers is for firms to set up production facilities in the market. Another reason for locating near the market is that, for bulky, low value goods, transport costs can be prohibitive and it becomes imperative that firms produce close to their customers. Or it may be that retail firms like Tesco and Wal-Mart, construction companies, or providers of medical or education services have to be in face-to-face contact with their customers. It may also be that important customers can precipitate a decision to invest abroad. When big car firms like Volkswagen and Fiat moved into Eastern Europe following the collapse of Communism, a large number of car component suppliers felt obliged to follow, given their customers' requirements for just-in-time deliveries (van Tulder and Ruigrok undated).

Other firms may feel the need to be close enough to respond quickly to alterations in market conditions, such as changes in taste, or to provide speedy after-sales service.

Lower Production Costs

Firms are often driven abroad by the need to find cheaper factors of production in order to cut costs. When jobs are transferred abroad, it is referred to as offshoring. This has gone on to such an extent that it was estimated that around 40 per cent of US imports are produced by US companies, many of them in China (*Financial Times* 10 July 2007). Although this trend has continued, and is much complained about by US workers, some reshoring is taking place. Falling labour rates in the US and increasing labour rates in Asia, plus the strengthening of the Chinese currency, have made it more cost effective to bring production back to the US (Forbes 27 February 2014).

With the increasing cost of labour in rich countries, industries, particularly labour intensive industries including textiles, clothing, and footwear and firms assembling electronic components, have looked abroad for cheaper locations. Financial institutions have also relocated data processing and call centre activities to countries such as India, as have computer manufacturers and Internet service providers. Initially, firms transferred low level, unskilled or semi-skilled work to countries where labour was cheap, labour market regulation loose, and there was a low level of unionization of the work force. However, with the passage of time, firms have started to transfer higher level activities, such as product design and development, as they discovered that developing countries also had pools of highly educated, technically qualified, and relatively cheap labour. In India, there is an abundance of well-trained programming, software-developer, and systems-engineering talent while China and Taiwan are developing world-class design expertise in specific technologies. Design is one of the most popular subjects at Chinese universities, and hundreds of design consulting firms have sprung up in cities such as Shanghai and Beijing.

The savings in labour costs from offshoring can be substantial. In 2012, a manufacturing worker in the UK cost US$31.23 per hour, in the USA US$35.67. A comparable worker in Mexico cost US$6.48 per hour, in Taiwan US$9.46 per hour, and in Brazil US$11.20 (www.bls.gov/fls/ichcc.pdf). Data for China and India is not directly comparable because of data gaps and methodological reasons, but BLS estimates that in 2009 hourly compensation costs in manufacturing in China were $1.74 and in India $1.24. Labour savings also apply to white-collar work. Project managers, software engineers, and accountants can all be much cheaper in developing countries.

The advantages of cheap labour in developing countries are likely to be offset to an extent by lower levels of **productivity**. Productivity measured in terms of output (GDP) per person employed is much lower in Mexico and Brazil than in the USA or UK. In 2012, in Mexico it was US$ 20,275, in Brazil US$23,114, in the UK US$49,428, and in the USA US$68,374 (GDP per person employed at constant 1990 PPP $). In China it was $15,250 and in India $9,200 (http://data.worldbank.org). The OECD (2014) says productivity growth is the key to narrowing the income gap between middle- and high-income countries, but productivity levels in middle-income countries are low, not rising quickly enough, and in some cases—Brazil, Mexico, and Turkey—the productivity gap in recent years has widened.

One effect of these fast expanding economies is that wages and salaries have been increasing in countries like China, as demand for educated and technically skilled workers starts to outstrip the supply of suitable candidates. Although the productivity of Chinese workers is rising, in many industries it is not keeping pace with wages. Consequently, some MNCs may look elsewhere, like the Philippines, Thailand, and Vietnam, where wages and other costs are much lower than in China (www.business-in-asia.com/investment_comparison.html). Foxconn, for example, is moving all of its assembly operations for Apple products to Indonesia (www.china-briefing.com). According to *The Economist* (October 2012) the China 'plus one' strategy (a strategy where Western firms had the bulk of their Asian operations in China but were also active in one other Asian country to hold down costs or reduce over dependence) has widened to a 'China plus' strategy because the options have widened to include Indonesia, Myanmar, Vietnam, Cambodia, the Philippines, and India.

It has also been argued that MNCs, to avoid environmental regulations at home, have intentionally relocated polluting activities to developing countries, including China, where the authorities turn a blind eye to environmental damage (Zheng and Chen 2006). Christmann and Taylor (2001) contend that pollution-intensive MNCs have not taken advantage of lax environmental regulation in China. They found that MNCs were more likely than were local firms to comply with local regulations and to adopt internationally recognized environmental standards.

Learning Task

Find an organization that has offshored some of its activities. Explain the reason for the offshoring activity.

Natural Resources

Businesses in the primary sector are the principal seekers of deposits of natural resources such as oil, gas, and other minerals. But, deposits of natural resources are not spread evenly across the globe, so resource-seeking firms, such as mining groups like Rio Tinto and BHP Billiton, and oil companies like Shell and Exxon, must locate near deposits of natural resources.

With increasing demand for raw materials from the fast growing economies of China and India pulling up prices, combined with a lack of new deposits, mining companies are also looking to expand their deposits of mineral ores and their capacity to refine them. The main driver of the demand for metals is the growth of urbanization as this creates a demand for infrastructure projects, and increased wealth also increases demand for consumer durables such as fridges and cars. Rio Tinto expects that, by 2025, emerging markets will account for over two-thirds of total copper demand with, for example, the Chinese power grid doubling its use of copper over the next 12 years (http://m2m.riotinto.com/issue/3/article/copper-solving-societys-challenges).

The UN (2012) predicts that, by 2050, urban dwellers will likely account for 85.9 per cent of the population in the more developed regions and for 64 per cent in the less developed regions. Overall, the world urban population is expected to almost double from 3.6 billion in 2011 to 6.3 billion in 2050, which would mean that two out of every three people in the world would be living in towns and cities (see Figure 5.1).

To increase production capacity, in 2007 Rio Tinto (one of the world's largest mining companies; mines for coal, copper, iron, bauxite, gold, titanium, lead, zinc, cobalt, nickel, and uranium) put in a successful bid for the Canadian aluminium company, Alcan. This acquisition made it a global leader in aluminium production which, with copper and iron ore, gave it a major role in the key metals associated with growth and urbanization in emerging markets, and especially China. In 2011, it also gained a majority shareholding in an Australian coal mining company, Riversdale. Rio Tinto, in turn, was the subject of an unsuccessful bid by BHP Billiton in 2010.

Competition from Developing Country MNCs

Western and Japanese MNCs not only compete with each other for access to natural resources, but also face increasing competition from companies based in poorer countries. In 2005, the Brazilian mining company, Vale S.A., bought Inco of Canada to become the second biggest mining group in

Figure 5.1 World urban and rural population

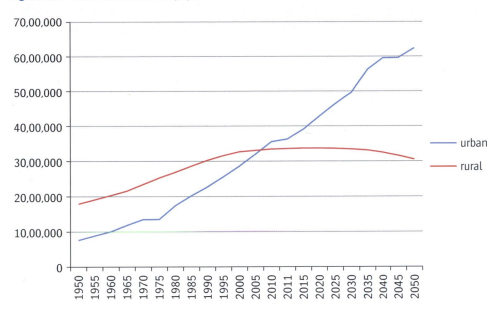

Source: UN (2012) The World Urbanization Prospects: The 2011 revision

the world. The following year, Mittal Steel, whose founder Lakshmi Mittal is of Indian origin, bought Luxembourg rival, Arcelor, for US$34 billion—thereby creating the world's biggest steel maker. Rusal, the Russian minerals company, became the largest aluminium company in the world when it took over another Russian company, SUAL, and the aluminium assets of the Swiss firm, Glencore. In the same year, Tata, one of India's biggest conglomerate firms, took over Corus, the European steel firm (Yahoo Finance; *Financial Times* 22 November 2006 and 6 July 2007).

There is also fierce competition from China for resources. With just over 1.3 billion people, China is the world's most populous country and the second largest consumer of global oil supplies after the USA.

China's oil reserves are limited, and its oil consumption, growing at 7 per cent per annum, is almost double that of its output. By 2020, it is forecast that China will need to import 60 per cent of its energy requirements. By 2030, it is expected to have more cars than the USA, and to be one of the world's largest importers of oil. The Chinese authorities, well aware of their increasing dependence on imported oil, especially from the Middle East, have made aggressive efforts to secure oil and gas supplies all over the globe, in Africa, Latin America, and Central Asia. In 2012, the China National Offshore Oil Co. (CNOOC) paid $15 billion for the Canadian oil company, Nexen, and in 2013 China's top three oil companies spent more than $32 billion on oil and gas acquisitions, mainly in South America, Africa, and the Middle East (*Wall Street Journal* 20 January 2014).

Other assets

Another reason for FDI is to gain other assets, such as technological and managerial knowhow. Firms can set up in other countries to monitor competitor activities more closely, as Kodak did in Japan to learn from their Japanese competitors. They can also enter into joint ventures to learn from others or acquire the assets of another firm, and in so doing acquire access to technology, brand names, local distribution systems, and expertise. A good example of this kind of FDI activity was the acquisition of IBM's personal computer business by Lenovo of China in 2004. Lenovo was able to acquire a foothold in the American market and easier access to Europe (market seeking activities), but also acquired a famous brand (the 'Think' brand), technological and management expertise, and a distribution network. Similarly, China has the world's largest shale-gas reserves, but not the technology to exploit them. The acquisition of Nexen, mentioned above, may have been one way of tapping into Western technology.

Mini Case Study China and Brazil—FDI and trade

China has become a major force in FDI. In 2009, with outflows of US$48 billion, it was the sixth largest foreign direct investor and by 2013 had become the third largest with outflows of $US101 billion, after the USA and Japan. This has been driven by a search for natural resources and by the opportunities to acquire foreign companies created by global restructuring (UNCTAD 2014).

Brazil, with vast mineral resources and a well-developed agricultural sector, has been a major recipient of Chinese FDI. In 2010, China became the biggest foreign direct investor in Brazil—accounting for about US$17 billion of Brazil's total FDI inflows in 2010 of US$49 billion, up from less than US$30 million in 2009. The biggest transaction was Chinese oil major Sinopec's US$7.1 billion purchase of a 40 per cent stake in Repsol Brazil. The Chinese have also invested in infrastructural projects such as the building of an enormous port complex in the state of Rio de Janeiro. This will allow China to transport iron ore for its fast expanding steel industry. The complex will include a steel mill, shipyards, an automobile plant, and factories manufacturing oil and gas equipment. Chinese companies have also invested heavily in Brazil's electric power supply business with the purchase of stakes in the country's power grid. Others are looking to buy land in Brazil for the production of soya beans.

From 2011 to 2013, Chinese investment in Brazil fell or projects were put on hold because of the sluggish Brazilian economy, uncertainty about policy on mining laws and foreign ownership of land, and some political and popular backlash against the Chinese. In 2014, with the visit of President Xi Jinping, new commitments were made in both trade and investment. China promised to buy 60 passenger jets from Embraer, invest $7.5 billion in Vale, and promised new investment in infrastructure and a raft of other deals.

China is now also Brazil's main trade partner, accounting for 19 per cent of exports and 16 per cent of imports. It is an example of the growing so-called South–South trade, although it has a flavour of the traditional North–South trade in that Brazil exports commodities to China and imports manufactured products. This causes tensions because not all see this as a benefit. While welcoming investment, there are those who fear de-industrialization and over dependence on a single partner (also see opening Case Study in Chapter 1).

Sources: UNCTAD *World Investment Report 2014* http://unctad. org/en/pages/PublicationWebflyer.aspx?publicationid=937; Reuters 1 November 2013 and 17 July 2014

Questions
1. How will Brazil benefit from Chinese investment?
2. What impact will the relationship have on Brazilian manufacturers?
3. What other tensions might the relationship generate?

Screening and Evaluating Foreign Markets

In Chapter 4, we talked about environmental analysis being part of the strategic process. The decision to 'go abroad' is another aspect of strategy that involves a matching of internal resources with external opportunities aimed at achieving the organization's goals. Although the basic principles of strategy apply, the decision-making in international strategy is much more complex because of the 'barriers created by distance' (Ghemawat 2001: 138). Ghemawat identified four dimensions of distance—geographic, cultural, administrative, and economic—all of which, in different ways, add complexity to decision-making. Managers have to decide not just which countries to target, but how they are going to target those countries, and they need some idea of the global systems and structures appropriate for their organization. How companies organize will depend very much on the type of product/service they produce. For products, such as commercial aircraft, which are transportable, subject to substantial economies of scale, and do not have to accommodate local tastes, then final production is likely to take place in a small number of sites and output exported. Boeing Commercial Airlines, for example, has just three main assembly sites in Renton and Everett in Washington and the most recent, built for the Dreamliner, in North Carolina. As we saw in Chapter 4, Boeing imports many of its components from manufacturers across the world for final assembly in the USA. It then exports completed planes. For service industries where production and consumption are inseparable, then direct investment has to take place in the host economy. This will also be the case where products need to be adapted to local tastes and where there are few economies of scale, such as in packaged foods. Products such as telecommunications equipment, cars, computers, mobile phones, and pharmaceuticals, where some local adaptation is probably necessary, and for which there will be some economies of scale (but which can be produced anywhere and shipped around the world), then both direct investment and trade are important. Increasingly, firms try to locate each part of the production chain where resource availability and cost is the lowest, and this global mode of operations is becoming dominant. It is the most complex form of organization, requiring decisions on the most appropriate locations for all aspects of the organization's operations. Whatever method they choose, they are faced with the complex task of **screening** and evaluating foreign markets/countries and this is the subject of this section.

What makes an attractive market or production location? To begin with, there has to be an expectation of profit, but this must be weighed against the risk of operating in the country. However, there is usually a trade-off to be made between risk and return. High attractiveness and high returns are usually associated with high risk, and low attractiveness and low returns with low risk. Countries differ in terms of their attractiveness as a result of variations in the economic environment, growth rates, political stability, **disposable income** levels, available resources, government incentives, and level of competition, and they also differ in the associated risk according to economic and political stability.

In this section we are going to build on the general macroenvironmental analysis already established in Chapter 4, together with the industry analysis of Chapter 3, to provide a framework to assess 'attractiveness'. We concentrate here on attractiveness as a market or a production site (or for many managers in an increasingly globalized world, both) rather than for sourcing or partners. Much of the literature about evaluating countries is from the marketing world and focuses on international market selection (e.g. Cavusgil 1985) rather than production location, but many direct investment decisions are heavily influenced by target market potential (Papadopoulos and Martin 2011) and the sequential process they advocate can also be applied to decisions to locate, albeit with some different considerations. Target market selection will, inter alia, be concerned primarily with indicators such as the size and growth of the market, whereas location decisions will be more concerned with the ease of doing business. Deciding between more then 200 possible country locations is a daunting task, and so the process which is usually recommended is that a general screening is undertaken, which narrows down the choice to a group or cluster of countries, possibly a region, against some given criteria for which the data is readily available from public sources (Cavusgil et al. 2004). These selected countries may well be ranked before a more detailed analysis takes place in which those countries are compared with each other. For market selection, information on a range of variables which indicate market size and potential growth will be needed, as well as information about potential competition and the general macroenvironment and how that might affect demand. For site location, information about the competition, resources, infrastructure, and any government incentives will need to be collected. Some information collected will be relevant to both decisions; for example, the ease of doing business and the general attitude of government to business. Infrastructure will also be a common concern, as both will require transport, communications, and power to operate. Once the field has been narrowed down to one or two possibilities, then the final stage is to select the market or site. At this stage, site visits and field research will probably be needed to collect more detailed and specific information and to talk to possible partners and/or suppliers and distributors. This can be an expensive process, so thorough initial screening is important. Alongside all of this, managers will also need to undertake a risk analysis to weigh against the possible returns before a decision can be made.

Collecting Data

In order to undertake an assessment of country attractiveness for markets and production sites companies have to undertake research and analysis that can be both time consuming and expensive. Like all research, there has to be a balance between the cost of research and the benefits from the research, as it is impossible to gather all the information and this may anyway result in information overload. There is a lot of information that can be obtained from the Internet and for companies there are many private sector organizations providing country and industry reports at a price.

IMD World Competitiveness Yearbook

The IMD ranks 60 of the most competitive countries according to economic performance, government efficiency, business efficiency, and infrastructure. (A link to the IMD World Competitiveness Yearbook is located in the **Online Resource Centre**.) Each of these four factors is then broken down into a number of sub-factors (over 300 in all) and scores given to each of these sub-factors. From this, an overall total is calculated. These totals are then formed into indices with the most competitive given a score of 100 and the rest ranked below this with their relative score. Of course, that is only 60 out of over 200 countries, although these countries do account for the bulk of investment and trade. In 2014, the USA topped their list with a score of 100. Switzerland was second and Singapore third. Bottom of their 60 countries was Venezuela with a score of 34.2 (http://www.imd.org/uupload/IMD.WebSite/wcc/WCYResults/1/scoreboard_2014.pdf).

The Economist Intelligence Unit (EIU)

The EIU ranks 82 countries according to the attractiveness of their business environment (www.eiu.com/public). Their model covers 10 different factors, political environment, the macroeconomic environment, market opportunities, policy towards free enterprise and competition, policy towards foreign investment, foreign trade and exchange controls, taxes, financing, the labour market, and infrastructure. These categories are then broken down into between five and 10 indicators and assessed for the last five years and the next five years. As with the IMD index, overall scores are calculated and then countries are ranked. They also produce country reports from over 200 countries.

For students trying to collect information, these costly sources are not an option, but, fortunately, there are now many sources of information available free of charge over the Internet. The first to mention is the interactive map that is part of the **Online Resource Centre** attached to this textbook. Here you will readily find information on the economy, people, geography, and government of over 50 countries across all the continents of the world.

GlobalEDGE

GlobalEDGE is created and maintained by the International Business Centre Michigan State University. (See the **Online Resource Centre** for a link to this resource.) This is a very extensive resource bank and links to many other sites of interest. In its Global Insights database there are entries for over 200 countries with information on the history, government, and culture of each country as well as a range of statistics on the economy. You can find, for example, that Nigeria has a population of 170 million people with a GDP per capita (PPP) of $5,863 (2013 current $US). GDP is growing at a rate of 7.4 per cent. It is an oil-based economy, accounting for 20 per cent of GDP, 95 per cent of foreign earnings, and 80 per cent of budgetary revenues coming from oil. Its main trading partners are the USA and UK. It is ranked 144 out of 175 countries in Transparency International's Corruptions Perceptions Index (see Chapter 11) and 147 out of 189 in the World Bank's Ease of Doing Business Index. It has a high risk political and economic situation and an often difficult business environment.

GlobalEDGE also ranks the market potential of 87 markets, albeit with a US focus. It uses eight factors in its assessment, market size, market growth rate, market intensity, market consumption capacity, commercial infrastructure, economic freedom, market receptivity, and country risk, scoring countries out of 100. In 2014, China was ranked first with a score of 100 followed by Hong Kong (56) and Japan(54). There is also an industry database with an overview of each industry, trade statistics, main corporations, and links to other resources.

The World Economic Forum (WEF)

The World Economic Forum (WEF) Global Competitiveness Report ranks 148 economies, based on publicly available information and its own survey, according to national competitiveness as well as a detailed profile for each of the economies. (See the accompanying **Online Resource Centre** for a link to this report.) It takes into account the microeconomic and macroeconomic foundations of national competitiveness based on the ideas outlined in Porter's diamond and the stages of development (see Chapter 2, The Competitive Advantage of Nations). The WEF identifies '12 pillars of competitiveness' as:

- Institutions—the legal framework, government attitudes to markets and freedom, excessive bureaucracy, overregulation, and corruption.

- Infrastructure—quality roads, railroads, ports, airports, electricity supply, and telecommunications.
- Macroeconomy—economic stability.
- Health and Primary Education—a healthy workforce with a basic education.
- Higher education and training—higher grade skills necessary for the economy to move up the value chain.
- Goods market efficiency—sophisticated customers and competitive domestic and foreign markets.
- Labour market efficiency—flexible labour markets with appropriate reward systems.
- Financial market sophistication—with savings channelled to productive investment.
- Technological readiness—access to ICT.
- Market size—domestic and foreign markets allow economies of scale.
- Business sophistication—quality of business networks and individual firms' operations and strategy.
- Innovation—high levels of R&D expenditure, collaboration between universities and industry, protection of intellectual property.

According to the WEF, these 12 pillars are the key to national competitiveness, but they are only separated in order to be measured (see Figure 5.2). They are interdependent and reinforce each other. For example, the twelfth pillar of innovation is impossible without an advanced higher education system, or without the protection of intellectual property rights.

The WEF identifies three stages of development linked to the pillars and includes the factor-driven stage, efficiency-driven stage, and the innovation-driven stage. The WEF allocates countries to each stage according to two criteria. The first is the level of GDP per capita (see Table 5.2) and the second is the share of exports of primary goods in total exports with the assumption that countries with a ratio of 70 per cent or more are factor driven. Those falling in between are said to be 'in transition'. The full list of countries and which stage they are in can be found in the report.

In 2007–08, the USA topped the overall ranking of the 131 countries included at that time, but this spot was taken by Switzerland in 2009 and 2010 with the USA relegated to fourth spot behind Sweden and Singapore. For 2013, Switzerland remained in top spot followed by Singapore, Finland, Germany, and the USA (see Table 5.3).

Doing Business

The World Bank has a very useful website called 'Doing Business' (www.doingbusiness.org). Again, this gives basic information for 189 economies, but its major focus is about starting a business in a particular economy and provides answers to such questions as dealing with construction permits, registering property, getting credit, paying taxes, enforcing contracts, and closing a business—as they apply to domestic small and medium-size enterprises. More detailed information about national and international statistics and trends in the world economy can be found at another World Bank site, www.worldbank.org, with information

Figure 5.2 The 12 pillars of competitiveness

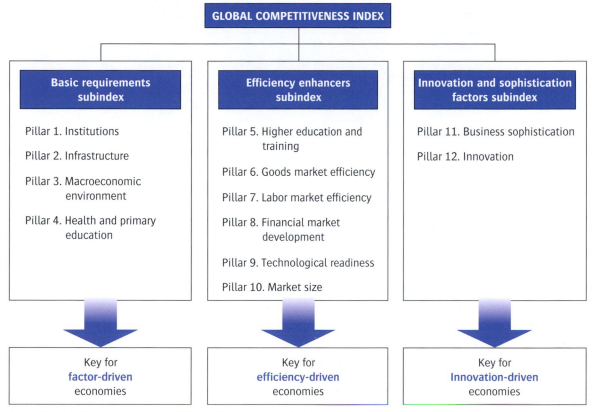

Source: The Global Competitiveness Report 2013–2014, World Economic Forum

Table 5.2 Income thresholds for establishing stages of development

Stage of development	GDP per capita (in US$)
Stage 1: Factor driven	<2,000
Transition from stage 1 to stage 2	*2,000–2,999*
Stage 2: Efficiency driven	3,000–8,999
Transition from stage 2 to stage 3	*9,000–17,000*
Stage 3: Innovation driven	>17,000

Source: The Global Competitiveness Report 2013–14, World Economic Forum

on over 200 countries. The World Bank is particularly interested in the development of countries and so it provides a lot of indicators of development such as figures on health, education, literacy, the environment, and infrastructure many of which can be good indicators of market potential. For example, the number of Internet users per 100 people in 2013 was 6.0 for Cambodia, 59.9 for Argentina, but 83.0 for Australia (http://data.worldbank.org/indicator/).

Table 5.3 Global Competitiveness Index rankings 2013–14

Country	Rank	Score/7	Country	Rank	Score/7
Switzerland	1	5.67	Italy	49	4.41
Singapore	2	5.61	Kazakhstan	50	4.41
Finland	3	5.54	India	60	4.28
Germany	4	5. 51	Vietnam	70	4.18
United States	5	5.48	Seychelles	80	4.10
UK	10	5.37	Namibia	90	3.93
Saudi Arabia	20	5.10	Algeria	100	3.79
Puerto Rico	30	4.67	Bangladesh	110	3.71
Spain	35	4.57	Nigeria	120	3.57
Panama	40	4.50	Benin	130	3.45
Mauritius	45	4.45	Chad	148	2.85

Source: The Global Competitiveness Report 2013–14, World Economic Forum

Counterpoint Box 5.1 How useful are competitiveness indices?

Competitiveness is at the top of business and political agendas all over the world. On the basis of the indices, several countries and regions have established policies and institutions devoted to improving competitiveness. Despite its popularity in business and management literature and public policy, the concept of national economic competitiveness remains unclear and the object of criticism.

Critics of the field of competitiveness research argue that there are limitations to the indices. They often fail to include a national economy's unique characteristics, such as geography, culture, and demographics. In addition, the choice of variables and their weight is based on a particular concept of competitiveness and, therefore, a country's competitive rank will be different depending on which index is used. Sabadie and Johansen (2010) specifically contend that indices like that of the WEF pay too little attention to the importance of human capital in national competitiveness indices. They argue that indices risk diverting country attention towards areas with a lesser potential impact on competitiveness, with critical consequences particularly in developing and transi-

tion countries because the indexes can have a major impact on policy-making in these countries. This could lead to an inappropriate allocation of resources, an even less competitive economy, and possibly to protectionism.

Krugman (1994) questions the very concept of competitiveness rankings, challenging the basic assumption that countries compete with each other like companies and that a country's prosperity is based on its success in international markets. A firm can go out of business if it is uncompetitive, but an economy does not. This is because all economies produce the bulk of their goods and services for domestic consumption and however uncompetitive an economy may be, most of its business continues, regardless. Furthermore, when two firms compete, one wins and the other loses, but when two economies compete, through trade, both can gain thanks to the law of comparative advantage. Finally, while an uncompetitive firm may be unable to lower its costs, an uncompetitive economy will do so through a deflation of the economy, or a depreciation of the exchange rate, or a combination of both.   ➔

→ Sources: Sabadie, J.A. and Johansen, J. (2010) 'How Do National Economic Competitiveness Indices View Human Capital?' *European Journal of Education* 45(2): 236; Krugman, P. (1994) 'Competitiveness: A Dangerous Obsession'. *Foreign Affairs* March/April.

Questions

1. The WEF ranks the BRIC countries, China, Brazil, India, and Russia, twenty-ninth, fifty-sixth, sixtieth, and sixty-fourth, respectively, in its global competitiveness rankings. Using these countries as examples discuss the usefulness of competitive indices.

Mini Case Study Investing in Italy

Italy is the world's eighth largest economy with a GDP of US$2,171 billion (see Table 2.1) and a per capita income of US$36,215. It has a history of weak political structures and, recently, a declining economic base. It struggles to attract inward investment. In a survey by EY (2014) to establish the most attractive countries to establish operations in Western Europe, Italy came last and did not even appear in the top 15 countries in Europe by FDI projects. Total FDI project numbers in Italy have declined by 19 per cent per year on average since 2010.

Why? The WEF lists tax rates, access to financing, inefficient government bureaucracy, restrictive labour practices, tax regulations, political instability, and corruption (in that order) as the most problematic obstacles to doing business in Italy. In the WEF rankings, Italy comes forty-ninth and scores poorly in institutions, macroeconomic stability, labour market efficiency, and financial market sophistication.

Many tourists will see the Italian towns that retain their traditional shops as quaint, unlike many other European towns and cities which look very much alike with global retail chains and their familiar facades. But the reason for the absence of these chains is not that they do not want to be there, it is because it is made so difficult to invest there. There is a mass of regulations, selective application, and long drawn-out processes for settling disputes. Italy is ranked eighty-sixth in the Heritage Foundation's Index of economic freedom.

All this means that many organizations feel Italy is not an attractive country in which to invest, with the consequence being economic growth below the European average. According to the IMF, the Italian economy contracted in 2012 and 2013 and will grow by only 0.6 per cent in 2014.

Sources: World Economic Forum; *Financial Times*; EY (2014) 'European Attractiveness Survey 2014, Back in the Game' http://www.ey.com/GL/en/Issues/Business-environment/Ernst---Young-attractiveness-surveys; Economist Intelligence Unit; Heritage Foundation

Questions

1. Access the WEF, GlobalEDGE and World Bank sites and build up a picture of 'doing business' in Italy.
2. The new government in Italy (February 2014) has made FDI a priority with its policy 'Destination Italy' (See ft.com 13 January 2014 'Italy Faces Challenge in Trying to Lure Foreign Investors'). Research the measures Italy has put in place and assess how successful they have been.

Other useful sources

The International Monetary Fund has a freely accessible database (www.imf.org/external/data.htm) providing data on economic and financial indicators such as GDP, GDP per capita, economic growth, inflation, government finance, balance of payments, and population.

Other useful sources of data from world organizations:

OECD (www.oecd.org/index.htm)

UNCTAD (http://unctad.org/en/Pages/Home.aspx)

World Trade Organization (www.wto.org/)

The UK Data Service (formerly the Economic and Social Data Service (ESDS)) is hosted by Manchester and Essex Universities and provides a useful link to many international datasets (http://ukdataservice.ac.uk/about-us.aspx).

UK Trade and Investment also has a useful website (www.ukti.gov.uk/export.html) aimed at supporting UK business to expand internationally through exporting. It offers detailed guides on how to do business in many countries across the world. The USA has a similar site at www.export.gov/index.asp.

The Central Intelligence Agency's World Factbook has information on every country recognized by the USA (https://www.cia.gov/library/publications/the-world-factbook/index.html). It covers each country's geography, people, system of government, climate, natural resources, infrastructure, and economic conditions and is a most useful source of information to extract data for country screening. Moreover, it is regularly updated.

International Data Problems

When collecting international data, it is important to consider some of the problems associated with the data. Using the IMF World Economic Outlook Database as an example, most of the information comes from national datasets and the IMF advises countries on the compilation of the statistics in such areas as analytical frameworks, concepts, definitions, classifications, and valuations. Nevertheless, compilation of national statistics is highly complex and not all governments have the same resources to allocate to the process, so governments with limited funds and/or skills at their disposal may not place too high a priority on collecting information. Often, information is not available or is out of date and sometimes it can be 'managed' for political purposes.

There are also definitional problems. Poverty, literacy, and unemployment, for example, can have very different meanings depending on the context or country. Unemployment in sub-Saharan Africa is not reported in many of the 45 countries included in the IMF database. In any case, many 'unemployed' workers may not be captured by the official employment statistics as they form part of the informal economy or, even if captured, there tends to be considerable underemployment in low productivity jobs more concerned with survival.

Even where there is common understanding of the terms, capturing the data only takes place in the official recorded economy. Some economies have large, informal economies and some have shadow economies where the production of goods and services is deliberately concealed from the authorities. As we saw in Chapter 2, this can amount to over 60 per cent for some economies.

Difficulties also arise in comparison when converting to a common currency, usually the dollar. Again, as we saw in Chapter 2, variations in exchange rates can lead to changes in GDP reported in US dollars when no change has actually taken place. Even when GDPs are converted to PPP terms, comparison is difficult to make and care needs to be taken, especially when trying to estimate market size.

(See Center for Global Development Report (2014) for a discussion of the need for accurate data and the weaknesses of data collection in sub-Saharan Africa.)

The Process of Assessing Country Attractiveness

This section will be divided into the assessment activities shown in Figure 5.3.

Figure 5.3 Country Assessment

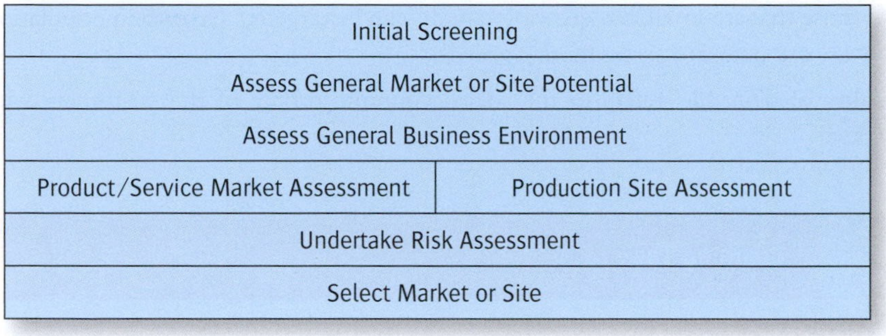

Initial Screening
Assess General Market or Site Potential
Assess General Business Environment
Product/Service Market Assessment	Production Site Assessment
Undertake Risk Assessment
Select Market or Site

Initial Screening

The first stage in any screening process is to eliminate those countries which have little chance of being markets or production sites by assessing if there is a basic demand for the company's products or if the basic resources required are present and the business environment is acceptable. This is a fairly obvious first step that can eliminate many countries from the search. For example, a country's climate can be a significant influence on the pattern of demand. There is no demand for heating in Malaysia, a tropical country with an average year round temperature above 30 degrees Celsius, but a substantial demand for air conditioning. This makes screening fairly straightforward for specialized goods of this nature, but less so for other, more widely consumed products such as confectionery, computers, and games.

Many businesses, as previously noted, target countries which are close not only geographically but also in language, culture, and business environment, and this can be a simple way of arriving at a handful of countries on which to do more detailed analysis. Of course, this could ignore many potentially good targets, and is no guarantee of success. The USA would be considered to have more in common with the UK than does Thailand, but, as we noted in the opening case study, Tesco entered Thailand with far fewer problems than it did the USA.

Assessing General Market or Site Potential

Market Potential

At this stage, the objective is to develop a number of indicators which help firms assess the general potential of a market so that further countries can be eliminated. This assessment often uses broad economic, social, or infrastructural indicators as proxy measures. This is not intended to assess the size of markets for particular products, but to be an overall assessment of the market potential of a country. In particular, companies will want an indication of:

- Market size—the relative size of the overall economy. Population size can be a useful indicator of the number of potential customers, while GDP per head and disposable income per head indicates whether there is a sufficient level of purchasing power—the overall buying power of those within the economy is referred to as market intensity. The distribution of income tells us about whether purchasing power is evenly spread.

- Market growth—size is important, but the rate at which the market is growing is also important; so, markets that are large, but shrinking, or growing very slowly, can be avoided and those that are small, but growing rapidly, can be targeted. Growth in population and GDP are often used to assess market growth.

- Quality of demand—refers to the socio-economic profile of the customers within a market.

Learning Task

Using Table 2.1 in Chapter 2, select a high income, a middle income, and a low income country. Using the statistics in that table, and any other secondary data you can obtain, compare the potential markets of the three countries.

A common method of assessing basic potential is to look at macroeconomic indicators such as GDP, GDP growth, and GDP per capita. If you are selling digital cameras, flat screen televisions, and DVD recorders, then Australia, with a per capita income in 2014 of US$61,137, is a better starting point than Haiti with a per capita income of only US$858 (IMF World Economic Outlook Database 2014). Other proxy indicators of wealth may also be used to assess market potential, such as the ownership of cars, energy usage, televisions, computers, telephones, and Internet usage, usually measured per head of population. These indicators are often associated with an expanding middle class (see Chapter 2) and this is often a good indicator of market potential. These types of figures are often used in combination with other indicators, such as demographic changes (population size, growth, and age structure), degree of urbanization, and income distribution. The type of indicator used will depend on the industry. Financial service firms require countries where the population has considerable disposable income.

Another way of targeting countries is to use trade statistics, such as the United Nations' *International Trade Statistics Yearbook*, to look at the goods and services a country is importing from abroad, or to identify to which countries your domestic competitors are exporting. Looking at the domestic output of an economy to see what local producers are selling is another indicator. Many businesses will also follow their customers into new markets.

Site Potential

Similarly, companies intending to produce abroad can do a quick scan of what they consider are essential resources to undertake production. Availability of raw materials is one such consideration, but access to labour and finance are other important considerations. As the reduction in costs is often a major reason for going abroad, then the cost of doing business is also an important factor. This refers not just to labour but also the cost of finance, the price of energy, communications, transport, and tax rates. Against the low cost of labour, the availability, skill level, and productivity must also be considered. A quick consideration of country risk can also eliminate many countries from the equation.

Assess the General Business Environment

Assessing the general business environment can further eliminate some countries and provide useful information to be incorporated into the next steps in the process. In this section, the PESTLE framework from Chapter 4 is a useful framework to use.

Political and Legal Environment

The main factors in any assessment of the political and legal forces are government regulation, government bureaucracy, and law and order.

Most governments impose ownership restrictions which hinder FDI, according to the World Bank (World Bank 2010). In their report, 'Investing Across Borders', the World Bank claim that of the 87 countries surveyed 'almost 90% of countries limit foreign companies' ability to participate in some sectors of their economies' (2010:8). It was the removal of such restrictions in the retailing sector by the Thai government in the late 1990s that allowed Tesco to enter the country through a joint venture. Governments may also impose trade barriers, so a scan for any barriers can soon eliminate a country. In a globalizing world with countries eager for FDI, a ban is much less likely than a range of incentives trying to attract FDI.

Typical of the type of incentives are:

- financial incentives—investment grants or credit guarantees;
- fiscal incentives—reduced corporation tax;
- regulatory incentives—easing of health and safety or environmental regulations;
- subsidized services—water, electricity, communications;
- market privileges—preferential government contracts; and
- foreign exchange privileges—special exchange rates.

Other features of the regulatory and legal regime to consider are the tax regime, employment laws, health and safety laws, environmental policy, and competition policy.

Government bureaucracy, in relation to business, refers to the difficulties faced by business in day-to-day operations because of the number of regulations that they have to comply with, and the rigidity with which they are enforced, commonly referred to as 'red tape'. For example, how long does it take to obtain licences to operate and how many forms have to be completed and submitted to government, how often, and in how much detail?

The Heritage Foundation in the USA, a libertarian think-tank, assesses countries according to various measures of freedom—business freedom, freedom to trade, freedom from tax, regulation and corruption, the strength of property rights, and labour, financial, and investment freedom. It then ranks countries according to their scores out of 100. Those scoring between 80 and 100 are classified as free, from 70–79.9 mostly free, 60–69.9 moderately free, 50–59.9 mostly unfree, and less than 50 repressed. Hong Kong, with a score of 90.1, was ranked first in 2014. The USA, with a score almost 15 points below Hong Kong, was ranked twelfth, and North Korea, with a score of 1, was ranked one hundred and seventy-eighth (see Table 5.4 for the scores of a selection of countries). This is used in several of the country rankings, including the GlobalEDGE rankings.

Learning Task

From Table 5.4, select one country in the top 10 and one ranked above 100. Using any secondary data you can obtain, explain the differences in the rankings.

Secondary data is available in World Development Indicators on the World Bank website. The IMF produces country reports and the OECD carries out country surveys, reviews, and guides that are available on their websites. More information is also on the Heritage site under each of the country profiles.

Table 5.4 Economic Freedom Index 2014 (%)

Country	Rank	Score	Country	Rank	Score
Hong Kong	1	90.1	Italy	86	60.9
Singapore	2	89.4	Uganda	91	59.9
Australia	3	82.0	Tanzania	106	57.8
Switzerland	4	81.6	Cambodia	108	57.4
New Zealand	5	81.2	Kenya	111	57.1
Canada	6	80.2	Brazil	114	56.9
Chile	7	78.7	Greece	119	56.7
Mauritius	8	76.5	India	120	55.7
Ireland	9	76.2	China	137	52.5
Denmark	10	76.1	Liberia	138	52.4
USA	12	75.5	Russia	140	51.9
United Kingdom	14	74.9	Vietnam	147	50.8
Germany	18	73.4	Angola	160	47.7
Qatar	30	71.2	Argentina	166	44.6
Malaysia	37	69.6	Korea, North	179	1.0

Source: www.heritage.org

Economic and Financial Environment

The major financial considerations will be rates of inflation, interest rates, exchange rates, credit availability, financial stability, and returns on investment. High and variable rates of inflation might increase earnings in money terms at least, but make forecasting and planning difficult, adding to the risk of operations. Similarly, exchange rate volatility adds to the uncertainty surrounding the value of any repatriated earnings and how much capital is needed for investment. On the other hand, some firms in the financial sector depend on volatility to make a living. Large industrial and commercial firms quite often have Treasury departments not only trying to protect earnings, but also trying to make money out of movements in exchange and interest rates.

Equally important are the policies that governments use to try and control their economies and how successful they are, as poor economic management can lead to volatility in the above.

Socio-cultural Environment

In assessing countries for markets and industrial locations, socio-cultural factors also have to be taken into account. The cultural elements of language, religion, diet, values and norms, attitudes, beliefs, customs, and social relationships can all be important in terms of employment, and in the acceptability of the product and any adaptations which need to be considered, including labelling and instructions on use of the product. Social factors, such as the distribution of income, modes of employment, living, and working conditions, population characteristics, such as ethnicity, the degree of urbanization, the availability and skill level of labour, the motivational basis of work, levels of pay, working hours, and the level of trade unionization, are all important.

The growth of a 'middle class' in many emerging markets is boosting world demand for mass consumer goods and is making these countries the target for global multinational companies. China is at the forefront of this, although estimates of the growth of its middle class vary. What all seem to agree is that during the next 20 years a huge middle class with enormous spending power will emerge. Wal-Mart, Carrefour, Tesco, IKEA, and Kingfisher's B&Q are all already well established in China.

Technological Environment

Another key feature of country attractiveness is the development of the infrastructure. An efficient transport and communications network is necessary for markets to function properly, and, if the intention is to export, a well-developed port infrastructure is also necessary. Key elements to assess in the infrastructure are:

- Science and technology infrastructure.
- Extent and quality of road network.
- Extent and quality of public transport network.
- Telephony network.
- Internet capacity.
- Water supply.
- Air transport.
- Quality of ports.
- Electricity production and certainty of supply.

Countries with well-developed infrastructures are attractive to business because they facilitate market growth and offer cheaper and better transport and communication networks. Developing countries with poorer infrastructures in Africa, Asia, or Latin America are less appealing.

Ecological Environment

The natural environment is the source of essential raw materials, which are part of any basic screening, but the natural environment is also the source of major but difficult-to-predict risks. Natural catastrophes such as earthquakes, flooding, and hurricanes are all unpredictable, although certain areas are more prone to these occurrences than others.

Mini Case Study Doing business in South Africa

South Africa (SA) is located at the southern tip of Africa. There is scrubland in the interior, desert in the northwest and tropics in the southeast. It also has something like 1,700 miles of coastline. It has a population of nearly 54 million made up of predominantly black African (79 per cent) plus a much smaller white (9.6 per cent) and coloured (8.9 per cent) population. Unusually, SA has three capitals. Bloemfontein is the capital of the judiciary, Cape Town is the legislative capital, and Pretoria is the administrative capital. The largest city is Johannesburg. Its currency is the Rand. The most common spoken language in official and commercial life is English, but it only ranks joint fifth as a home language. The state recognizes 11 official languages.

Until 1994, SA had a system of apartheid in which racial discrimination was institutionalized by a white minority ruling over the black majority. Under this system, non-white South Africans were forced to live in separate areas from whites and use separate public facilities. It was not until 1991 that much of the legislation began to be repealed and now a democratic culture has emerged.

SA has one of the continent's largest economies with a GDP of $US354 billion ($US620 billion PPP) and a per capita GDP of US$6,595 (US$11,542 in PPP terms). The economy went into recession in 2009, but since then has been growing at about 3 per cent per annum. Although the economy has been growing at a reasonable pace (although low by African standards), there remains much poverty, especially in the black population and in the townships. The poverty rate has declined from 50.8 per cent

of the population in 2000 to 34.5 per cent in 2010. Public health facilities are poor, as is education and infrastructure services. Job prospects are also poor. SA has one of the highest inequality rates in the world.

Mining has been the major driving force in the development of the South African economy, especially gold and diamonds, and SA remains an international leader in the mining industry. While those two elements are now not so important, SA (although still the fifth largest producer of gold) is the world's leader in the production of platinum, manganese, vanadium, and chrome and an important producer of many other minerals. Its main exports are minerals to China, USA, India, and the UK.

SA was ranked 41 in the World Bank's ease of doing business rankings compared with an average ranking for sub-Saharan Africa of 142. Getting electricity seems particularly time consuming, taking up to 226 days from application to completion. Registering property and trading across borders are other categories in the lower half of rankings.

For market potential, GlobalEDGE ranks South Africa 70 out of the 87 countries it ranks.

Sources: IMF World Economic Outlook Database, April 2014; GlobalEDGE Country reports; World Bank 2013; www.southafrica.info. ?

Questions

1. Assess the market potential and general business environment for South Africa.

Product/Service Market Assessment

Having reduced the number of countries for consideration in the first stage, the next stage is to undertake a more detailed assessment of the potential within each of the selected markets. Initial screening is undertaken using broad indicators, but at this stage much more specific industry indicators are called for in attempting to measure the total market demand in a particular industry and gaining as much information as possible about the market in each of the countries selected after stage 1. Data is more likely to be available for developed economies than for emerging economies, but, again, this information is likely to cost money. A Euromonitor report on alcoholic drinks in the Czech Republic, for example, would cost, in July 2014, £1,250 (www.euromonitor.com/alcoholic-drinks). It is worth searching your library to see if it has subscriptions to such organizations as Mintel, Datamonitor, and Key Note.

The information that will be needed includes:

- size and growth rate of the market;
- major competitors, products, and market shares;
- prices, marketing, and promotions of competitors;
- distribution networks;
- local standards and regulations, including trade mark rules and product liability;
- value of imports and exports of the product;
- tariffs and other trade regulations; and
- local cultural factors that may require product adaptation.

Information on the size of the market may not be readily available and often it is necessary to look at other indicators. For example, a UK company producing protective coverings for transporting high value but bulky audio equipment wanted to investigate export markets in Europe. There was no information available on the products they produced, but a lot on the music industry they supplied and so comparing this market with the UK market gave them an indication of the potential demand in Europe.

Competitive Forces

As well as information on the size of the market, an analysis of the competitive environment will be required using a model such as Porter's Five (Six) Forces. This was explained in Chapter 3 and a checklist was provided to help in the process.

Production Site Assessment

If FDI is taking place, then a more detailed analysis of doing business in each market is required. This will include information on setting up the business, the quality and cost of the resources available, the infrastructure, regulations, taxation, financial reporting, and legal system. In addition, it is important to find information on a whole host of practical issues, as detailed in the following checklist:

- Foreign ownership of enterprises. What are the regulations restricting the ownership of enterprises and what type of businesses are permitted? What regulations exist concerning governance, procedures, and liability?
- Financial system—how developed is the banking system? What currency is used? Are there any foreign exchange controls? Is there a stock exchange?
- Investment—are there any investment guarantees? Are there any incentives? What business registration procedures exist?
- Labour regulations—what regulations are there covering expatriate employees? Are there social, health, and unemployment insurance payments to be made for local and expatriate employees? Is there a minimum wage?
- Disputes—how are disputes settled? Are there any regulations protecting intellectual property rights? Is there any competition law?

- Taxation—what taxes exist and what are the rates?
- Reporting—what are the statutory requirements for financial reporting?
- Expatriate employees—are entry visas and work permits required? What housing, education, and medical facilities are there for expatriate employees?

Counterpoint Box 5.2 Investing in Africa

According to Ha-Joon Chang (2010), the perceived image of Africa is that it is 'destined for underdevelopment'. It has a poor climate, lousy geography, small markets, violent conflicts, corruption, and poor-quality institutions. It is ethnically divided, making people difficult to manage, and has a bad culture in which people do not work hard, do not save, and they cannot cooperate with each other.

These are sweeping generalizations for a group of over 50 countries, but, nevertheless, are probably most people's image of the prospects for Africa. However, real GDP growth in Africa averaged 4.9 per cent per annum from 2000 to 2008, dipped in 2008–09 along with the rest of the world, but has rebounded and has averaged above 4 per cent since, compared to the world average of 3 per cent. The average hides some varied performance. Sub-Saharan growth excluding South Africa was above 6 per cent with East and West Africa recording the highest rates of growth. The growth was driven by exports, rising public expenditure on infrastructure, increasing FDI, good harvests, and increasing agricultural productivity. Average GDP growth for sub-Saharan Africa is expected to be nearly 6 per cent from 2015 to 2019. For some countries, such as Ethiopia, Ghana, Liberia, Mozambique, Nigeria, Rwanda, Tanzania, Uganda, and Zambia, growth will be significantly higher than this.

McKinsey is optimistic about prospects for Africa. It highlighted 'government action to end armed conflicts, improved macroeconomic conditions, and microeconomic reforms' (2010) as key reasons behind the growth. Although recognizing individual economies may struggle, the analysis suggested that:

> Africa has strong long-term growth prospects, propelled both by external trends in the global economy and internal changes in the continent's societies and economies.

Sources: Chang, Ha-Joon (2010) *23 Things They Don't Tell You About Capitalism.* Allen Lane; IMF World Economic Outlook Database April 2014 www.imf.org/external/pubs/ft/weo/2014/01/weodata/index.aspx; 'What's Driving Africa's Growth', *McKinsey Quarterly* June 2010; UNCTAD, African Economic Outlook www.mckinsey.com/insights/econoic_studies/whats_driving_africas_growth

Questions

1. Rwanda and Uganda are predicted to have growth of over 7 per cent to 2019 whereas growth in Chad, Equatorial Guinea, Guinea-Bissau, Namibia, and Zimbabwe is forecast to be much lower. Select one country from each group and account for the different expectations.

Risk

All of the above must be weighed against the risks of doing business.

Wars, hurricanes, terror attacks, uprisings, crime, earthquakes, and stock market crashes can bring companies to the brink, and sometimes tip them over the edge. The Gulf oil spill in 2010 has cost BP upwards of US$40 billion, and rising, and severely damaged its future operations in the USA. Earlier, Hurricanes Katrina and Rita left the global insurance industry with a bill for US$80 billion. The price of insurance and re-insurance cover for areas of the world exposed to US hurricanes has also rocketed. A construction company agreed a contract in Nepal without seriously considering the implications of the uprising by Maoist rebels. Within weeks, a couple of its workers had died at the hands of rebels, and the roads on which the project relied had been blown up. The company was forced to pull out. More recently, uprisings across North Africa and tensions in the Middle East have pushed up further the price of oil and, following the earthquake in Japan, stock markets suffered their biggest two-day fall for 40 years. Worldwide floods have caused major disruption and cost billions of $US and it is estimated that climate change combined with rapid population change, economic growth, and land subsidence could lead to a more than 9-fold increase in the global risk of floods in large port cities between now and 2050. Average global flood losses estimated at about $US6 billion per year in 2005 could rise to $US52 billion per year by 2050 (www.oecd.org/newsroom/future-flood-losses-in-major-coastal-cities.htm).

In today's more interconnected world, uncertainties can emerge almost anywhere as a result of product innovation, political change, changes in the law, or market deregulation. As business becomes more globalized, moving into new markets and transferring production to lower cost locations, it opens itself up to more risks, especially in countries with political instability, and more vulnerability to natural catastrophes. International business needs to weigh up the risk factors when making strategic decisions on FDI.

Country Risk

Country risk refers to the possibility of the business climate changing in such a way as to negatively affect the way in which business operates. Sources of risk include:

- change in political leadership;
- radical change in philosophy of political leadership;
- civil unrest between ethnic groups, races, and religions;
- corrupt political leadership;
- weak political leadership;
- reliability of the infrastructure;
- supply chain disruption;
- economic risks such as the volatility of the economy and foreign exchange problems;
- organized crime;
- poor relationships with other countries;
- wars;
- terrorism; and
- piracy.

One source of risk is a change in political leadership. Elections take place every four or five years in all of the advanced industrialized economies of the world, and with this can come relatively minor changes in attitude to business. This might result in changes in trade agreements or general changes in policies and regulations towards business. This is risk which is fairly predictable and should not therefore be a problem. It is risk that is unpredictable that is the bigger problem. Although past patterns can be analysed to assess the risk, this also has its dangers. Kenya was generally considered as one of Africa's more politically stable countries with a thriving tourist industry bringing in about US$1 billion per year. Controversial elections in December 2007 triggered a wave of violent unrest resulting in more than 1,000 deaths and 250,000 forced from their homes. The World Bank was predicting growth in real GDP of 6.5 per cent for Kenya in 2008 (Global Economic Outlook—October 2007), but the violence hit the economy by reducing the number of tourists to a trickle. Horticulture was Kenya's other big earner, but this also depended on the tourist industry as did the many local handicraft sellers. According to the IMF, estimated growth in 2008 was just 1.5 per cent increasing to 2.4 per cent in 2009. The economy is now (2014) growing at around 5 per cent and projected to grow in the medium term at about 6 per cent. According to the World Bank (www.worldbank.org/en/country/kenya/overview#1), the economy remains vulnerable to internal and external risk. In September 2013, terrorists attacked a shopping mall killing 67 people and injuring 175. These security threats continue to have a negative impact on tourism.

It is the other sources of political instability that form the biggest risk. The possible consequences are:

- property seizure by:
  - confiscation—assets seized by government without compensation;
  - expropriation—assets seized with compensation;
- nationalization—takeover by government of an entire industry;
- property destruction;
- freezing of funds;
- kidnapping of employees;
- market disruption;
- labour unrest;
- supply shortages; and
- racketeering.

Risk Assessments

Again, many commercial organizations provide assessment of risk, but at a price.

The EIU assesses countries for a variety of risks and sells the results to business, although summary information on each of 180 countries is available on their website. Countries are assessed for risk based on 10 issues:

- security;
- political stability;
- government effectiveness;
- legal and regulatory;
- macroeconomic;
- foreign trade and payments;
- financial;
- tax policy;
- labour market; and
- infrastructure.

The least risky countries tend to be the most advanced economies, while poorer countries dominate the ranks of the most risky. Countries with good records on economic policy-making, such as Singapore, Hong Kong, and Chile, tend to do well. Those with poor payment records, institutional failings, and civil violence are the worst rated.

The World Bank has a worldwide governance indicator project that reports governance indicators for 215 economies between 1996 and 2012 for the following:

- voice and **accountability**;
- political stability and absence of violence;
- government effectiveness;
- regulatory quality;
- the rule of law; and
- control of corruption.

See http://info.worldbank.org/governance/wgi/index.aspx#home.

The WEF also produces a global risks report available at (www.weforum.org/issues/global-risks). The 2014 report takes a 10-year view and organizes risks into the PESTE framework (no legal). It identifies 31 global risks. The 10 global risks of highest concern for 2014 are shown in Table 5.5.

Over the next 10 years, it sees income disparity as the risk most likely to cause significant problems globally, such as social unrest, followed by extreme weather events, unemployment and underemployment, climate change, and cyberattacks. The most potentially impactful risks

Table 5.5 The 10 global risks of highest concern

No.	Global risk
1	Fiscal crises in key economies
2	Structurally high unemployment/underemployment
3	Water crises
4	Severe income disparity
5	Failure of climate change mitigation and adaptation
6	Greater incidence of extreme weather events
7	Global governance failure
8	Food crises
9	Failure of a major financial mechanism/institution
10	Profound political and social instability

Source: World Economic Forum, Global Risks 2014, Ninth Edition

Learning Task

Using the sources mentioned prior to Table 5.5, compare the risks of doing business in China and Australia.

it sees as fiscal crises, climate change, water crises, unemployment and underemployment, and critical information infrastructure breakdown.

Select market and/or site

Having reduced the number of countries to a few, and undertaken detailed analysis of the market and business environment in those few countries, a decision has to be made about which country or countries to enter. This decision will require an estimate to be made of the market share the company is likely to gain.

One useful mechanism for comparing countries is to compile a grid using factors judged important to the decision, giving each of them a weight, according to the importance to the company, and then scoring each country. The factors will be different for a company just considering exporting from one considering FDI, and will be different for each company. This idea can be used at any stage of the process, with earlier grids using fewer and broader measures of potential. The grid at this stage is likely to be in at least two sections and probably three. One would be for market potential, one for the ease of doing business, and one for potential risk. At its simplest, the grid could be just three rows with a score taken from published ranking tables for each of the above three categories, but this is unlikely to capture all the factors a company might want to take into account. A grid might look like that at Table 5.6, scoring each factor out of five and taking into account the weighting. In the first two categories, higher numbers are preferable, indicating higher potential and greater ease of doing business. In the third category, a low score is preferred.

From this grid, country B and country D would seem to be ruled out given that their total score for the first two sections is 19 and 20, respectively, with a risk score of 8 and therefore a net score of 11 and 12. Country A has a net score of 21 (14 + 12 - 5) and country C scores 24 (16 + 14 - 6) and would seem to be the preferred choice, although the risk is slightly higher. At this stage, it is likely that managers would want to undertake field trips to each of the countries in order get a 'feel' for those countries, check the assessments, and meet potential customers, suppliers, and workforce. Only then, will the final decision be made and contracts negotiated.

Table 5.6 Country attractiveness grid

Factor	Weight	Country A	Country B	Country C	Country D
Market potential					
Size of market	0.3	4	3	3	2
Growth rate	0.2	2	3	4	2
Market share	0.3	3	1	3	2
Investment required	0.4	3	1	4	2
Tax rates	0.1	2	2	2	2
TOTAL		14	10	16	10
Ease of doing business					
Starting a business	0.3	3	3	4	3
Getting credit	0.1	3	2	3	3

Paying taxes	0.1	3	2	3	2
Employing labour	0.3	3	2	4	2
TOTAL		12	9	14	10
Risks					
Political risk	0.4	1	3	2	3
Supply chain disruption	0.2	2	3	2	3
Foreign exchange risks	0.2	2	2	2	2
TOTAL		5	8	6	8

Learning Task

Carry out a screening of Venezuela for firms involved in:

- the production of newspapers and magazines; or

- oil production.

Comment on the conditions to be faced by US businesses considering setting up operations in Venezuela.

● CHAPTER SUMMARY

In this chapter we examined a process for assessing the attractiveness of countries. We saw that firms tend to follow a gradual process of internationalization, starting by exporting and gradually progressing to the establishment of overseas subsidiaries, although we noted that some firms appear to be 'born global'. Reasons for FDI include market access, lower production costs, and access to resources. China is leading the way in scouring the world for raw materials.

Firms intending to export or invest abroad can systematically screen countries to assess their attractiveness as new markets and/or production locations. This should include an initial assessment of the need for exports or investment before an analysis of the general business environment and the ease of doing business. Many commercial organizations specialize in country and market analysis, but at a price. Once the initial need is established, then a more detailed analysis of industry potential and operations is required before a final decision can be made.

● REVIEW QUESTIONS

1. The internationalization process is normally a gradual transition from exporting to FDI, but some firms may be 'born global'. Explain what this means and why firms should want or need to be 'born global'.

2. Why is it that some firms locate their investments close to their markets while others appear to have the luxury of a much greater choice of location? Illustrate your answer with examples.

3. Discuss the problems of collecting international data.

4. Explain what is meant by political risk. Use examples to illustrate your answer.

● ASSIGNMENT TASKS

1. The UK is renowned for its creative industries. As part of the drive to promote exports from small- and medium-sized businesses, the government announced the Music Export Growth Scheme. Under this scheme, 15 British music acts that have had their first success in the UK will receive funding for touring overseas. Management companies will have to put together a marketing plan to be judged by a selection board. As part of this plan, they will have to identify target markets. Research suitable target markets to present to the management company as part of their marketing plan. You will need to justify your choices.

2. Your company is looking for investment opportunities abroad and wishes to evaluate various country locations. Select three countries, one from South America (not Venezuela), one from Africa, and one from Asia, and compare the attractiveness of these countries for foreign direct investment.

Case Study The emerging Turkish economy

Turkey is strategically located between the two continents of Asia and Europe with control over the entrance to the Black Sea. It shares borders with, among others, Syria, Iraq, and Iran on the Asian side, and Greece and Bulgaria on the European side.

It is a predominantly Muslim (Sunni) country with a population of 77.3 million people. Over 42 per cent are below the age of 24. Most are Turkish, but there is a sizeable, about 18 per cent, Kurdish population in the southeast of the country. There has been a long-running dispute between the Kurds and the Turkish state that, over the years, has cost many lives. A cease-fire was agreed as recently as 2013.

Modern Turkey was founded in 1923 under the leadership of Mustafa Kemal, who later became President Ataturk (leader of the Turks). He died in 1938 and since then Turkey has become a democracy, but the army has always been a powerful presence and has used its powers to oust governments, in 1960, 1971, and 1980. In 2002, the Justice and Development Party (AKP), under the leadership of Tayyip Erdogan, came to power. It was the first time that a single party had won sufficient votes to form a government. He has been prime minister ever since, winning two more general elections. In 2014, he was elected as president of Turkey.

Source: © bedo / istockphoto.com.

Under Erdogan's rule, millions have been lifted out of poverty, which some say accounts for the popularity of somebody who has become increasingly autocratic. Turkey, the 'T' in CIVETS, has undergone an economic transformation since 2002 with average per capita incomes almost trebling from $US3,500 in 2002 to $US9,920 ($US15,767 PPP) in 2014. In this time, the economy has averaged growth of 6 per cent per annum; although growth dipped in the global recession, it bounced back in 2010–11 to around 9 per cent. It has a GDP of ➜

→ $US767 billion, making it the seventeenth largest economy in the world. The World Bank classes Turkey as middle income with a large and growing middle class. Turkey has climbed the rankings in the WEF competitiveness index from fifty-ninth in 2006 to forty-fourth place in 2014. It could climb further if it was able to address weaknesses in the labour market such as restrictive labour regulations, an inadequately trained workforce as well as a low attraction to foreign talent, and a very low ratio of women to men in the labour force, where it ranks one hundred and thirty-fourth.

Turkey has undergone a privatization programme that has reduced state involvement in the economy considerably and created a new wave of export-oriented entrepreneurs, known as the 'Anatolian tigers'. Agriculture is an important element of the Turkish economy and still employs 25 per cent of the workforce, although it accounts for only 9 per cent of output. Corresponding figures for industry are 26 per cent and 27 per cent, and for services, 48 per cent and 64 per cent. It is a world leader in the production of dried figs, hazelnuts, sultanas/raisins, and apricots. Tobacco, cotton, grain, and olives are other important crops. The top industries are textiles, food processing, automobiles, electronics, mining, and steel and these have now overtaken textiles in Turkey's export mix. Encouraged by Turkey's growth, FDI into the country has boomed from just over $US1 billion in 2002 to, at its peak in 2007, $US22 billion. By this date there were over 32,000 foreign firms operating in the Turkish economy.

Turkey has been a part of the EU customs union since 1995 and a candidate to join the EU since 1999, but its membership has been hotly contested. One of the major obstacles is the disputed territory of Northern Cyprus that the EU sees as occupied territory (by Turkey) of one of its member states. Another factor is the threat to democracy many see from an increasingly authoritarian prime minister whose suppression of the freedom of speech has drawn criticism from allies in the US and Europe.

In 2013, protests were put down violently by the authorities. The government has also faced corruption charges, has censored the Internet, jailed many journalists, and banned Twitter and YouTube. The economy is now not nearly as healthy as it was. Economic growth slowed to 2.2 per cent in 2012 and predictions by the IMF for the next few years are around 3 per cent. Inflation is above 7 per cent and unemployment above 10 per cent. The current account deficit is financed by bonds and loans and growth is fuelled mainly by domestic demand based on credit growth. It is open to question how sustainable is Turkey's economic progress.

Sources: WEF; GlobalEDGE; FT Special Report, Turkey, 7 May 2014; IMF Economic Outlook database, April 2014

Questions

Using the above case, and any other resources mentioned in the chapter, answer the following:

1. Over 42 per cent of Turkey's population is under 24. Why is this an important factor in the future growth of Turkey's economy?
2. What is meant by a 'customs union'? How would full membership of the EU differ?
3. Explain the attraction of the Turkish economy as an investment location.
4. Investigate how easy it would be for a Western company to establish a new business in Turkey.
5. What risks would be faced in setting up business in Turkey?
6. Undertake a country assessment of Turkey for firms in one of the following sectors:
   a. Management training;
   b. ICT;
   c. Renewable energy;
   d. Defence technology.

● FURTHER READING

For a book about born-globals, see:

● Cavusgil, S.T. and Knight, G. (2009) 'Born Global Firms. A New International Enterprise'. *Business Expert Press* 2009.

For further discussion and ideas about assessing country and market attractiveness see:

● Cavusgil, S.T., Knight, G., and Reisenberger, J.R. (2010) *International Business: The New Realities,* 2nd edn. Harlow: Pearson.

- Daniels, J.D., Radebaugh, L.H., and Sullivan, D.P. (2014) *International Business*, 15th edn. Harlow: Pearson.

For the issues around doing business in China:

- Xiaowen Tian (2007) *Managing International Business in China*. Cambridge: Cambridge University Press.

- Buckley, P.J., Clegg, L.J., Cross, A.R., Liu, X., Voss, H., and Zheng, P. (2007) 'The Determinants of Chinese Outward Foreign Direct Investment'. *Journal of International Business Studies* 38 (4): 499.

- Morck, R., Yeung, B., and Zhao, M. (2008) 'Perspectives on China's Outward Foreign Direct Investment'. *Journal of International Business Studies* 39 (3): 337.

● REFERENCES

Andersson, S. and Evangelista, F. (2006) 'The Entrepreneur in the Born Global Firm in Australia and Sweden'. *Journal of Small Business and Enterprise Development* 13(4): 642.

Arenius, P. (2005) 'The Psychic Distance Postulate Revised: From Market Selection to Speed of Market Penetration'. *Journal of International Entrepreneurship* 3(2).

Benito, G.R.G., Peterson, B., and Welch, L.S. (2009) 'Towards More Realistic Conceptualisations of Foreign Operation Modes'. *Journal of International Business Studies* 40: 1455.

Cavusgil, S.T. (1985) 'Guidelines for Export Market Research'. *Business Horizons* 28(6): 27.

Cavusgil, S.T., Kiyak, T., and Yeniyurt, S. (2004) 'Complementary Approaches to Preliminary Foreign Market Opportunity Assessment: Country Clustering and Country Ranking'. *Industrial Marketing Management* 33: 607.

Center for Global Development and The African Population and Health Research Center (2014) 'Delivering on the Data Revolution in Sub-Saharan Africa', Final Report of the Data for African Development Working Group. Center for Global Development, Washington, DC.

Christmann, P. and Taylor, G. (2001) 'Globalization and the Environment: Determinants of Firm Self-Regulation in China'. *Journal of International Business Studies* 32(3).

Fan, T. and Phan, P. (2007) 'International New Ventures: Revisiting the Influences behind the "Born-Global" Firm'. *Journal of International Business Studies* 38: 1113.

Freeman, S., Edwards, R., and Schroder, B. (2006) 'How Smaller Born-Global Firms Use Networks and Alliances to Overcome Constraints to Rapid Internationalization'. *Journal of International Marketing* 14(3): 33.

Gabrielson, G. (2005) 'Branding Strategies of Born Globals'. *Journal of International Entrepreneurship* 3(3): 199.

Ghemawat, P. (2001) 'Distance Still Matters: The Hard Reality of Global Expansion'. *Harvard Business Review* September: 137–147.

IMF (2014) World Economic Outlook Database April 2014. Available at: www.imf.org/external/pubs/ft/weo/2014/01/weodata/index.aspx.

Johanson, J. and Vahlne, J.E. (1977) 'The Internationalization Process of the Firm—A Model of Knowledge Development and Increasing Foreign Commitments'. *Journal of International Business Studies* 8 (Spring/Summer): 23.

Knight, G., Madsen, T.K., and Servais, P. (2004) 'An Inquiry into Born-Global Firms in Europe and the USA'. *International Marketing Review* 21(6): 645.

Malhotra, N. and Hinings, C.R. (2010) 'An Organizational Model for Understanding Internalization Processes'. *Journal of International Business Studies* 41: 330.

OECD (2014) *Perspectives on Global Development 2014, Boosting Productivity to Meet the Middle-Income-Challenge*. Paris: OECD.

Papadopoulos, N. and Martin, O.M. (2011) 'International Market Selection and Segmentation: Perspectives and Challenges'. *International Marketing Review* Special Issue 28(2).

Prashantham, S. (2005) 'Toward a Knowledge-Based Conceptualization of Internationalization'. *Journal of International Entrepreneurship* 3: 37–52.

Rennie, M.W. (1993) 'Born Global'. *McKinsey Quarterly* 4.

Trade Policy Unit (2014) 'Outward Investment: Selected Economic Issues'. Trade and Investment Analytical Papers: Topic 15 of 18: 1–27. Department for Business Innovation and Skills.

UN (2012) *World Urbanization Prospects: The 2011 Revision*. UN Department of Economics and Social Affairs, Population Division.

van Tulder, R. and Ruigrok, W. (undated) 'International Production Networks in the Auto Industry: Central and Eastern Europe as the Low End of the West European Car Complexes'. Available at: http://repositories.cdlib.org.

World Bank (2010) *Investing Across Borders, Indicators of Foreign Direct Investment Regulation in 87 Economies*. Available at: http://iab.worldbank.org/.

World Bank (2013) *Doing Business 2014: Understanding Regulations for Small and Medium-Size Enterprises*. Washington, DC: World Bank Group.

Zheng, Y. and Chen, M. (2006) 'China Moves to Enhance Corporate Social Responsibility in Multinational Companies'. *Briefing Series, Issue 11, August*. University of Nottingham: China Policy Institute.

PART TWO

Global Issues

CHAPTER SIX

The Socio-cultural Framework

LEARNING OUTCOMES

This chapter will enable you to:

- Explain the importance of the social and cultural environment for business

- Apply concepts of cultural theory to international business

- Analyse major social and cultural elements such as demography, youth unemployment,

- religion, and language and their implications for business

- Compare and contrast the liberal, conservative, and social democratic social models

Case Study   Obesity—a global issue

This case shows the rapid increase in obesity around the globe and its implications for health. It illustrates the opportunities and challenges this social issue poses for business.

The Overseas Development Institute (Keats and Wiggins 2014) reports that, globally, over one-third of adults are obese, i.e. those having a body mass index of more than 25. The percentage of adults who are obese had grown from 23 per cent to 34 per cent between 1980 and 2008. The increase is particularly marked in developing countries, where the number of obese has risen to 904 million, from 250 million in 1980, and especially in countries like Mexico and Egypt with rising incomes. In richer countries, 557 million are overweight. Child obesity is also a concern in high-income countries and is increasingly being seen in middle-income economies (see Figure 6.1).

The regions of North Africa, the Middle East, and Latin America saw large increases in overweight and obesity rates in adults to a level on a par with Europe, at around 58 per cent. While North America still has the highest percentage of overweight adults at 70 per cent, regions such as Australasia and southern Latin America are now not far behind with 63 per cent.

The ODI identifies changing diets with a shift from eating cereals and grains to the consumption of more fats, sugar, oils, and animal produce as causes of obesity. The consumption of fat, salt, and sugar is a significant factor in cardiovascular disease, diabetes, and some cancers and reduces life expectancy.

Source: © Amanda Grandfield / istockphoto.com

One of the report authors, Steve Wiggins, said there were likely to be multiple reasons for the increases: 'People with higher incomes have the ability to choose the kind of foods they want. Changes in lifestyle, the increasing availability of processed foods, advertising, media influences . . . have all led to dietary changes' (www.bbc.co.uk). Other contributory factors include urbanization, which has led people to switch from a traditional healthy diet, and people being less physically active, and globalization which has led to a gradual homogenization of diets. Some commentators argue that falling incomes and rising unemployment caused by the global economic crisis has led to an increase in consumption of cheap junk food.

Figure 6.1 Percentage of overweight and obese adults with BMI greater than 25, by region

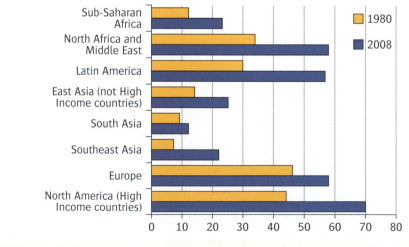

Source: Overseas Development Institute

→   Stewart and Wild (2014) predicted that the number of new cancer cases could soar 70 per cent to nearly 25 million a year, half being preventable because of their link to lifestyle.

The explosion in obesity generates opportunities, but also poses challenges for organizations in various sectors. Hospitals and medical insurance companies have to adjust to dealing with more cases of diabetes, strokes, and heart attacks. In private health care systems, the cost is being borne by the individual and private sector firms. Reportedly, $190 billion a year is spent in the US treating conditions related to obesity. In publicly funded health care systems, the financial burden is borne by the tax-payer. For pharmaceutical firms, the obesity epidemic opens up opportunities to sell more drugs, to treat the conditions caused by obesity, and more slimming products.

In developed countries, soft drinks manufacturers like Coke and Pepsi and fast-food outlets such as McDonald's and Subway are accused of being major contributors to the rise in obesity. In the US, soft drinks makers and the fast-food industry spend bil-lions of dollars every year advertising their products. Critics in the health professions say that much of the advertising is aimed at children and have called for increased taxes on carbonated drinks along with greater controls on TV advertising promoting food and drinks high in saturated fat, sugar, and salt. Demands have also been made to reduce numbers of fast-food outlets near schools and leisure centres.

Long used to such attacks, and with a history of effective government lobbying, these moves have been vigorously opposed by the food and drink industries. The British Soft Drinks Association (BSDA) argues that consumption of soft drinks con-taining added sugar had fallen by 9 per cent, while the inci-dence of obesity increased by 15 per cent in the 10 years up to 2012. It added that 61 per cent of soft drinks sold in the UK contained no added sugar. Critics claimed that this was mis-leading, pointing to the fact that the figure of 61 per cent included bottled water. However, the industries continue to resist the charges against their products arguing that sugars consumed as part of a varied and balanced diet are not a cause of obesity. Firms like Coke, Pepsi, McDonald's, Nestlé, and Mars have all stressed the need for people to be more physically active. The sponsorship by Cadbury, McDonald's, and Coke of the 2012 London Olympics is seen by critics as an attempt to shift the blame away from their unhealthy products. Apparently acknowledging some of the criticism, firms have taken steps to reduce salt and saturated fat in their products and to substitute artificial sweeteners for sugar.

Sources: Keats and Wiggins 2014; WHO 2014; www.bbc.co.uk 3 January 2014; *Marketing* 18 and 19 February 2013; Harvard School of Public Health, Nutrition Source accessed 7 January 2014; BSDA website www.britishsoftdrinks.com/ 1 November 2013; Rudd Radar 2013; www.theguardian.com 7 August 2013; PLOS 2012; Food and Drink Federation, News Article 9 January 2014; American Beverage Association, News Release 5 August 2013; Stewart and Wild 2014; McClure et. al. 2013

Introduction

Why do cross-border mergers fail? How is it that mergers such as that between two advertising giants, France's Publicis and Omnicom from the US, collapse before being finalized? Why do pro-ducers of alcoholic drinks, such as Diageo and InBev, flourish in some countries but find it difficult to develop markets in others? Why does KFC have to serve Peking Duck burgers for lunch in Shanghai? Often it comes down to national differences in social characteristics, cultural attitudes, and values.

This chapter examines the social and cultural environment. This encompasses a vast range of social and cultural characteristics, which can vary significantly both within societies and between one society and another. Social aspects include the distribution of income and wealth, the structures of employment and unemployment, living and working conditions, health, edu-cation, population characteristics including size and breakdown by age, gender, ethnic group, the degree of urbanization, and the provision of welfare for the population in the form of educa-tion, health care, unemployment benefits, pensions, and so on. The cultural components cover areas like language, religion, diet, values and norms, attitudes, beliefs and practices, social rela-tionships, and how people interact. There are links between certain aspects of culture and social conditions; for example, between diet and certain types of disease, values and norms and the role of women in society, religious beliefs, and attitudes to contraception and their effect on birth rates. To be successful, business has to be aware of socio-cultural differences that could be important regarding levels and patterns of demand, the quality and quantity of labour, and the policies and strategies to be adopted.

There are far too many elements to be addressed comprehensively in a single chapter. Therefore, the chapter focuses on a limited number of social and cultural aspects. We start off by considering culture and then go on to consider some important elements in the social environment.

Culture

Culture can be seen as a system of shared beliefs, values, customs, and behaviours prevalent in a society that are transmitted from generation to generation through a multitude of channels, the family, religion, books, newspapers, television, and the Web (see Bates and Plog 1990). Hofstede (1994: 5), the management scientist, described these elements of culture as the software of the mind, 'the collective programming of the mind which distinguishes the members of one category of people from another' and which influences how people think and behave. The values in the culture are enforced by a set of norms, which lay down rules of behaviour. These rules are usually supplemented by a set of sanctions to ensure that the norms are respected. Culture comprises a whole variety of different aspects, including religion, language, non-verbal communication, diet, dress, and institutions, ensuring that the values and beliefs are transmitted from one generation to another. Culture is dynamic; in other words, it changes over time not least due to the process of globalization with the increasing cross-border movement of goods, services, capital, and the migration of people.

Different cultures can have significantly different attitudes and beliefs on a whole range of issues. As we will see later, when discussing the various social models, there is a significant divide between the USA and Continental Europe on attitudes to social issues such as poverty. In the USA poverty tends to be seen as the fault of the poor, whereas in Europe the poor tend more to be seen as victims of the system. Cultural attitudes can also vary toward issues such as corruption, women at work, sexuality, violence, suicide, and time.

Cultural attitudes can have important implications for business. Some of the most influential research on culture and the workplace was carried out by Hofstede (1991, 2001). He surveyed over 100,000 workers in IBM subsidiaries in 40 countries, looking for cultural explanations of differences in employee attitudes and behaviour. He concluded that the norms and values embedded in national culture were a very powerful influence on the workplace, and that different approaches would be necessary when managing people from different cultural backgrounds. Hofstede (1994) concludes that the workplace can only change people's values to a limited extent (see Mini Case Study Hofstede and consumers, below). The message for multinational companies was that they would be unwise to assume that an organizational culture that was successful in one cultural context, for example that of the USA, would be equally successful in a completely different cultural context in, say, China (see Counterpoint Box 6.1 for a different view).

Hofstede's work (2007) also contains another message for multinationals. He contends that countries, especially big countries like China, India, Indonesia, and Brazil, do not have a single national culture but rather a variety of cultures that can vary significantly from region to region. A similar point could be made for smaller countries, in Western Europe for instance, where different cultures may be based on ethnic group rather than region.

Counterpoint Box 6.1 Homogenization of management?

Multinationals face a dilemma when they operate abroad whether to standardize their managerial style or adopt local practices.

Work by academics such as Kerr et al. (1960) suggest that this issue should become less important for MNCs as best managerial theory and practice are universally valid and applicable irrespective of the cultural, political, or legal context. According to this school of thought, best practice inevitably spreads across borders leading to a convergence of managerial approach. The idea that shareholder value should be maximized, resources allocated rationally, human resources systematically selected and developed, and their performance objectively appraised and rewarded are seen as universally acceptable managerial concepts. They see managerial convergence being driven by the forces of globalization and the international diffusion of technology. And because all humans share common needs, so motivation theories also have universal validity, independent of any cultural context, examples being Maslow's hierarchy of needs model, Herzberg's two-factor theory, McClelland's achievement motivation theory, and Porter and Lawler's expectancy theory.

An alternative body of thought, propounded by Hofstede (2003) and many others, holds that managerial practices are heavily influenced by their particular cultural and institutional contexts and cannot simply be transferred willy-nilly from one culture to another. They cite significant differences in managerial style between rich and poor countries but also between nations such as Japan and the USA, which they attribute to important cultural, political, and legal factors. Such authors also point to fundamental differences within the West, particularly between the managerial model operational in the US and that in Europe. Work by Maurice indicates major disparities in approach even between European countries. This school emphasizes the continuing national differences in management practices and is sceptical about the possibility of international transfer of best practice. Their message to MNCs is that there is little room for the international convergence of management processes.

Researchers like Shimoni (2006) steer a middle course, arguing that a hybrid form of management is developing across borders.

Sources: Hickson and Pugh 2001; Hofstede 1980, 2003; Kerr et al. 1960; Child 2002; Shimoni with Bergmann 2006

Questions

1. A US multinational fast-food retailer wishes to establish outlets in Nigeria, but finds that its human resource and marketing policies are not transferable. How would you suggest the company prepares for the new venture?

Research has revealed fundamental cultural differences between East and West that have important implications for Western executives trying to do business in the East. Psychologists have shown that Eastern and Western cultures can vary significantly in terms of perception, logic, and how they see the world around them. Apparently, Westerners focus more on detail while Easterners tend to look at things in the round. For example, when American students were asked to look at a picture of a tiger in a forest, they focused on the tiger while Chinese students concentrated more on the background, that is, the context within which the tiger was located.

Researchers attribute this to different social environments. In East Asia, social environments are more complex, collective, and constrained. As a result, Easterners need to pay attention to the social context if they are to operate effectively. On the other hand, Western societies prize individual freedom and there is not the same need to pay heed to the social environment. With their focus on the individual, Westerners tend to view events as the result of specific agents, while those raised in the East set the events in a broader context.

Cultural differences influence the way firms in the East and West do business. For example, when an applicant for a job appears uneasy, Westerners are likely to see that as an undesirable characteristic of the interviewee, which makes them unsuitable for stressful jobs. In the East, they will tend to view the uneasiness in the context of a stressful situation, the interview, and thus be less likely to attribute it to the character of the applicant. Similarly, North Americans, when posing a question, expect a trustworthy person to respond immediately, with any delay inspiring mistrust. In contrast, the Japanese view more favourably those individuals who take time to ponder before giving a reply.

Attitudes toward contracts also vary. Once a contract is signed, Westerners regard them as agreements set in stone while Easterners, such as the Japanese, take a more flexible view. They are quite happy to renegotiate if circumstances change. They look at the situation of their customers or suppliers in the round and may renegotiate in order to maintain a long-term relationship.

In the East, there is a desire for consensus and harmony. Westerners sometimes perceive Japanese managers as incompetent or indecisive because, in pursuit of consensus, they continually consult their team and are usually reluctant to challenge the decisions made by others (Nisbett 2005). One of the authors came across an example of this in an interview with the Scottish executive put in charge of Mazda, the Japanese car company, by the parent company, Ford. Coming from a Western culture, he was used to debate, discussion, and disagreement when arriving at decisions. In Mazda, he found the reluctance to disagree among his senior managers extremely frustrating.

Hofstede and National Cultures

National cultures can vary significantly from one country to another and the differences can be reflected by employees in the workplace and by consumers in the market. Such variations in the psychology of work and organizations and in the marketplace have major implications for management. Managerial systems and approaches that work well in one country may be inappropriate for another.

Geert Hofstede, when working with IBM, noted that, while the company promoted an organizational culture in the form of common values, assumptions, and beliefs, there remained differences in attitudes and behaviour among IBM's international subsidiaries. He concluded that organizational culture is less influential than the attitudes and values prevalent in the national culture. In his research, he identified five dimensions of culture:

- **Individualism**: reflects the degree to which people in a country act as individuals rather than as members of a group. Individualistic cultures value the rights of the individual over those of the group. By contrast, cultures low in individualism and high in collectivism emphasize the interests of the group rather than the individual. The USA, the Netherlands, France, and Germany are highly individualistic while countries in Asia, Africa, and Latin America score low on this dimension.

- **Uncertainty avoidance**: refers to the extent to which people prefer structured to unstructured situations. Societies tolerant of ambiguity, the unknown, and the unfamiliar score highly on this dimension. They operate with fewer rules and do not attempt to control all events or outcomes. Cultures with an aversion to uncertainty try to cling to rules and seek ways to control their environment. Latin America, Africa, France, Germany, and Japan have low tolerance levels of uncertainty in contrast to China and the UK. The USA lies somewhere in the middle.

- **Masculinity**: reflects the degree to which masculine values such as competition, assertiveness, a clear role distinction between men and women, money, income, job promotions, and status dominate over feminine values like cooperation, quality of life, and human relationships. In masculine countries, men are favoured for positions of power in organizations. The USA, Japan, and certain South American countries, like Venezuela, score highly on masculinity while Nordic countries and Africa score low.

- **Power distance**: shows the degree of inequality accepted as normal in a society. High power-distance cultures accept, and are marked by, significant levels of inequality and hierarchy, such as differences in social class. Low power-distance societies value equality and egalitarianism. In Latin America, Africa, Thailand, and Arab countries, hierarchies are very important and power is distributed very unequally. Less powerful members of organizations, those on the lower rungs of the hierarchy, expect and accept the unequal distribution of power. In the USA and Nordic countries, there is low acceptance of power differences and a greater desire for equality.

- **Long term/short term**: long-term cultures make decisions based on long-term thinking, value perseverance, and thrifty behaviour, such as saving for the future. Short-term losses may be taken to ensure long-term gain. Brazil, India, and China have a long-term orientation. At the other extreme, the USA, Britain, Spain, Nigeria, and Pakistan focus on the short term, while most European countries lie somewhere in the middle.

Subsequently, Hofstede expanded the long-term/short-term dimension and renamed it, Pragmatic versus Normative. Pragmatic cultures have long-term characteristics. People do not feel the need to explain everything, and operate on the basis that this is impossible given the complex lives that they lead. Truth is not an absolute but depends on things like context and situation. They can accept contradictions. Indonesia is an example of a pragmatic society. Normative societies have short-term characteristics. Their peoples wish to be able to explain everything and have a desire for the absolute truth. They desire social stability and respect social conventions and traditions. Nigerian society is heavily normative.

Implications for Business

Cultural characteristics have important implications for international business. According to Hofstede, centralized corporate control is more feasible in societies with large power distances, while decentralization fits better in small power distance cultures. Collectivism is more likely to favour group rewards and family enterprises, while job-hopping and individual remuneration systems are more acceptable in individualistic cultures. Masculine cultures prize competition and survival of the fittest, while feminine cultures favour solidarity and sympathy for the weak. Uncertainty-avoiding cultures are comfortable with strict adherence to rules and principles, while their counterparts are happy to shape policies according to particular circumstances and are more tolerant of deviant behaviour (Hofstede 1994). Studies in many countries show that culture has implications for human resource management, the management of change, entry strategies into foreign markets, the targeting of consumers, and selling to industrial customers (see An and Kim 2007; Eby et al. 2000; Ramamoorthy and Carroll 1998; Fisher and Ranasinghe 2001; Hewett et al. 2006).

Counterpoint Box 6.2 Hofstede and his critics

Hofstede's research is widely recognized as a major contribution to the understanding of cross-cultural relationships. He has described his work as paradigm shifting. However, his work has also been criticized on five major grounds:

1) Surveys are not a suitable way to measure cultural differences. It is not a good way of measuring phenomena that are subjective and culturally sensitive. Hofstede's response is that methods additional to surveys were also used.

2) Nations are not the best units for studying culture. Hofstede retorts that national identities are the only way of identifying and measuring cultural disparities.

3) Studying the subsidiaries of a single multinational, IBM, is not a valid method of uncovering the secrets of entire national cultures.

4) Cultures are dynamic and change over time so the data are old and obsolete. Hofstede claims that over 200 other studies have supported his country rankings.

5) Five dimensions are not enough to represent the complexity of culture. Hofstede accepts the criticism that five dimensions are too few and that more should be added.

Critics point out that cultures are not limited to the confines of national frontiers, but can straddle national boundaries.

Hofstede's assumption that the population of a country is culturally homogeneous has also drawn criticism on the basis that most countries comprise a variety of different ethnic groups. In his 2007 article, Hofstede goes along with this argument. Some researchers claim that the study data are too old to be of relevance to modern times, particularly given the subsequent changes brought about by the impact of rapid globalization and the collapse of communism. Hofstede has refuted this by claiming that cultural change occurs only very slowly and that cross-cultural differences are inherently stable and based on the evolution of societies over centuries.

Sources: Bond 2002; Hofstede and Bond 1998; Hofstede 2001, 2007; McSweeney 2002, 2002a; Redpath 1997; Jones 2007

Questions

1. Choose a country with which you are familiar and consider whether there are cultural differences:
   a. across regions;
   b. between different ethnic groups;
   c. between different age groups.

Business meetings in North America or Europe have formal agendas setting the order in which items are discussed, and each item is resolved prior to proceeding to the next. The Japanese, rather than deal with agenda items in a rigid sequence, may prefer a more flexible approach that enables them to get a better overview. To Westerners, meetings in Japan may appear unstructured, chaotic, and even threatening. However, Japanese managers are well used to such ambiguity.

Differences in approach can also be seen in negotiations. Westerners expect to focus on contentious issues and try to achieve the most beneficial outcomes for themselves. In contrast, the Japanese prefer to discuss areas of agreement, with the expectation that harmony will lead to the resolution of details. Such differences can lead to bad feeling in negotiations. Lee (2004) quotes a senior South Korean official involved in trade negotiations with Australia. Even though Australia was running a large trade surplus in agricultural products with South Korea, which was of serious concern to the Koreans, 'Australia, nevertheless, continuously puts pressure on Korea to buy more off them . . . they are self-centred, one-sided, only concerned with self-interest, not in considering another's situation or position' (2004: 76).

The upshot is that business has to take cultural differences into account when considering entry to foreign markets through exports, joint ventures, or through takeover or greenfield investment. Similarities between the domestic and foreign cultural norms and values may

Mini Case Study Hofstede and consumers

Hofstede's findings on culture have implications for the choice of effective marketing strategies. In countries scoring high on individualism, taking personal responsibility is important. Personal preferences are a main driver for consumers in their purchasing decisions. People in individualistic cultures, much more than those in collectivist countries, tend to see Internet messages as manipulative. Countries with high power-distance stress respect hierarchy, authority, and paternalism and each person has a specific social status. Particular goods and services are not simply bought for their functional use, but are also a visible reflection of social status. Cultures scoring high on uncertainty avoidance favour a system of rules, structure, and formality and people tend to be risk averse, like to rely on expert advice, and are reluctant to try new or different products. For countries scoring high on masculinity, where the dominant values are success, money, and material wealth, people strive to have more than others and demonstrate their success through the ownership and frequent purchase of particular goods and services. On the other hand, feminine cultures value modesty, shun conspicuous consumption, and try to avoid provoking envy. People are less assertive than in masculine cultures and are more likely to be sceptical of advertising.

Sources: Watson et al. 1999; Kyoungmi and Shavitt 2006; Güliz and Belk 1996; Hofstede and Bond 1984; de Mooij and Hofstede 2010; Möller and Eisend 2010

Questions

Refer to the country comparisons on Hofstede's website to help you answer these questions.

1. Discuss whether it would be a good idea to use the Web to market a good or service in:
    a. the USA;
    b. Brazil.
2. Compare and contrast how you might go about marketing a new product in Indonesia and Argentina.

make entry for a firm easier, whereas large differences may cause major difficulties due to misunderstandings and conflict where social groups do not want to give up valued elements of their culture (van Oudenhoven and van der See 2002).

Religion

A core element of the culture in many societies is religion. In such societies, religion is a major influence on the attitudes and beliefs that regulate behaviour. Christianity has the ten commandments, Islam has five pillars, and Buddhism has eight precepts. Each religion has a system of rewards for those who are good and punishment for those who are evil. Although there are hundreds of religions in the world, five of them, accounting for around 75 per cent of the world population, predominate. Christianity with 2.1 billion followers has the greatest number of adherents, followed by Islam with 1.5 billion, Hinduism at 900 million, Buddhism with 376 million, followed a long way behind by Judaism with 14 million. Christianity and Islam together account for more than half of the world's population and operate in more regions of the world than all the other religions. Even in China, where religion declined after the Communist revolution, it is estimated that around 400 million Chinese practise some religion, with 100 million of them Buddhists, 20 million Muslims, and up to 90 million Christians (www.adherents.com; www.bbc.co.uk).

Some religions lay down rules about which foods can and cannot be eaten, and how they should be prepared. For instance, Muslims are not supposed to consume pork, alcohol, foods

Learning Task

In 2012, one year after the onset of the Arab Spring, Pew carried out a survey of attitudes in six predominantly Muslim countries toward gender equality. The results are shown in Table 6.1.

Table 6.1   Gender equality in Muslim countries

	Women should have equal rights as men %	Men have more right to jobs when scarce %	Men make better political leaders %	Family should have say over women's husbands* %
Lebanon	93	50	32	51
Turkey	84	67	52	35
Pakistan	76	81	62	87
Tunisia	74	86	75	14
Egypt	58	79	42	–
Jordan	63	66	50	73

*Percentages include those who say the family should decide who a woman will marry and those who say the woman and her family should both decide.

Source: Pew Research Centre 2012

Questions

1. Looking at column 1 in the table, what is the attitude generally across the six countries to gender equality?

2. To what extent are the attitudes represented in columns 2, 3, and 4 consistent with those in column 1?

3. These countries often have high levels of unemployment. In which of them might a large Western multinational retailer, with a strong ethical commitment to equal employment opportunities, encounter most/least difficulty?

that contain animal fats, tinned vegetables that include animal fat, frozen vegetables with sauce, particular margarines, and bread or bread products containing dried yeast. Animals have to be slaughtered in a particular way. In Judaism, meat from cattle, sheep, goats, and deer can be eaten, but not from pigs, and there are rules forbidding the mixing and consumption of dairy products with meats. As in Islam, animals must be slaughtered in a certain way. Only fish with scales and fins can be eaten. Hindus do not eat meat, but dairy products including milk, butter, and yoghurt are considered to enhance spiritual purity, and most Buddhists are vegetarian. There can be differences in dietary rules among faiths of the same religion. Some Christian faiths, such as Protestantism, do not have dietary rules, while others, such as the Mormons, avoid alcohol and caffeinated drinks like coffee, and most Seventh Day Adventists do not eat meat or dairy products. The various rules and rituals around eating help religions reinforce their identity and distinguish them from other religions. These rules have implications for food manufacturers and retailers wishing to operate in countries with large numbers of practising Muslims, Jews, Hindus, and Buddhists (Better Health Channel).

Learning Task

The map in Figure 6.2 shows the geographical location of major world religions (note that space limitations make it impossible for the map to represent the large number of Muslims in areas like Western Europe and North America).

Figure 6.2 Major religions of the world

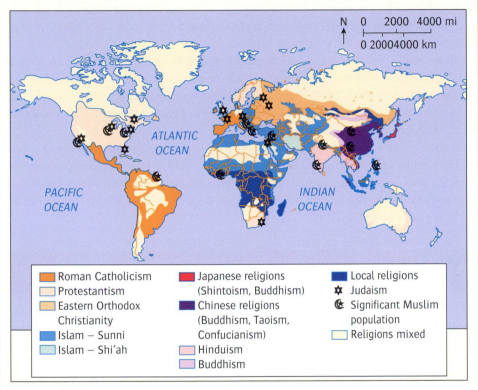

Source: www.justmaps.org

Questions

1. Comment on the geographical spread of Christianity, Islam, and Judaism.

2. Discuss the implications for firms such as McDonald's or Burger King of expanding in the Middle East.

3. Where are the major markets for firms producing goods specifically aimed at Jewish consumers?

Language

Another important distinguishing feature for many cultures is language.

There is no agreed total on the number of languages spoken in the world today. Estimates vary, but Ethnologue suggests a figure around 7,000 (www.ethnologue.org). Estimating the number of speakers is complicated because it can vary widely from one decade to another, due to factors such as population growth and armed conflicts. The Asian population is forecast to grow by more than 20 per cent to over 5 billion in 2050, while the number of European inhabitants is expected to fall by some 33 million (UN www.unpopulation.org). As a result, the number of speakers of Asian languages like Chinese, Hindi, and Bengali will increase dramatically while those speaking German, French, and Italian will fall. War, civil unrest, abuses of human rights, political instability, and people moving across borders to find work can also cause the figures to change significantly. Climate change could also play an increasing part in causing people to move across borders. The UN estimated the number of refugees at more than 15 million people in 2012, with the vast majority coming from Asia and Africa. Pakistan was the largest host, with Afghanistan the biggest source (UNHCR 2013; Global Trends 2013). It is obvious from the figures given that major changes are occurring in the number and location of speakers of particular languages.

While estimates vary of the most commonly spoken languages, most research identifies Mandarin/Chinese, with over 1 billion speakers, as first in the rankings. Other languages in the top five are Arabic, Hindi, English, and Spanish. The top languages are spoken across many countries. Chinese is spoken in 31 countries, English in 112, and Spanish in 44 mainly Latin American countries (www.ethnologue.com).

Business will be interested in the speakers of a particular language especially when they congregate together in large enough numbers to constitute a market worth exploiting or present an attractive pool of labour. In the past, language speakers, even where there were lots of them, were not attractive to firms when they were widely dispersed geographically, because of high marketing and distribution costs.

Learning Task   The Chinese diaspora

There are more Chinese living outside China than the population of France. Estimates, which some regard as far too low, suggest that there are at least 40 million Chinese living outside China, spread around the globe with over 1 million in South Africa, between 6 and 8 million in each of Indonesia, Malaysia, and Thailand, 1 million in Russia, 1.3 million in Peru, 3.5 million in the US, 700,000 in Australia, and 300,000 in the UK. Some of these communities are long established. It is claimed that members of the Chinese diaspora have a very strong sense of shared identity as well as a powerful attachment to China, the latter reflected in the remittances they send back to China and their major contribution to foreign direct investment there. Some recent Chinese emigration is associated with the quest by China for raw materials in Africa and Latin America (see Chapter 1, opening Case Study)

Sources: *The Guardian* 11 June 2008; *The Economist* 17 November 2011; Skeldon 1996

Questions

1. What opportunities does the presence of a diaspora of 40 million people of Chinese origin abroad offer to Chinese business in terms of:

   a. markets
   b. investment
   c. labour

 See **Online Resource Centre** for more information.

Countries Speaking the Same Language

Even where a single language is the mother tongue in several countries, business may still encounter certain difficulties. English is the mother tongue in the UK, the USA, Australia, and the major part of Canada, but that does not mean that communication is always straightforward. Words used in one country may not be understood in another. The British talk about multi-storey car parks while the Americans refer to a parking garage and the Canadians to a parkade. Similarly, Americans go to a convenience store, the British to a corner shop, and the Canadians go to a depanneur. Australians, like Americans, drive on freeways while the British drive on motorways. And some words have completely different meanings. American cars run on gas, but British vehicles run on petrol. In the UK, mufflers are scarves that are put round the neck for warmth, but in the USA it is part of the car exhaust system that deadens noise. Similar concerns are likely to arise with Spanish, which is also spoken in many Latin American countries.

Issues also arise in countries where English is an official language, for example in India, Pakistan, and South Africa, or where it is widely spoken as a second language. Firms would be foolish to assume that they can conduct business effectively in English because levels of proficiency in the language can vary dramatically. Some may have the ability to read the language, but have difficulties speaking or listening to it. Even where people have a good level of proficiency, it does not figure that they can understand it to the required level, especially where the topic of discussion is technical or legal, for instance around product specifications or patents and copyright.

Facing such difficulties, business will often turn to translators and interpreters. However, according to Crystal (2003), translation always involves some loss of information because it is impossible to get an exact equivalence. The slogan 'Come alive with Pepsi' appeared in a Chinese newspaper as 'Pepsi brings your ancestors back from the grave' (2003: 347). Even big multinational companies can slip up with language. One of the most well-known gaffes was when General Motors sold the Nova model in Spain. Nova, in Spanish, means 'it does not go'. Toyota offered the MR2 in France which, when pronounced, means excrement (*The Times* 9 November 2002).

For a long time, British and American firms have come in for much criticism for their linguistic insularity, their assumption that English is the global language of business, and that foreigners will be happy and able to communicate in English. Therefore, for them, building up competence in foreign languages is not a priority. The situation may have improved to a degree, but one US senator said that his country was 'linguistically malnourished' (www.eric.digests.org). International surveys of language skills across Europe tell a consistent tale: the UK is bottom of the league in terms of competence in other languages.

While English is the most widely spoken foreign language throughout Europe, and can be seen as the global language of business, it does seem as if competence in foreign languages is essential for international commerce. Evidence suggests that if companies want to buy anything from anywhere in the world, they can manage with only English; if they want to sell something abroad, they need to learn the language of their customers.

Time

Different cultures vary in their attitudes to time. In some cultures, the clock directs behaviour, in others behaviour is determined by the natural course of events in which people find themselves. In cultures where people follow the clock, they are careful to turn up on time for meetings and are likely to be irritated and frustrated if others do not. In other cultures, people behave according to event time, which means that they organize their time around various events, participate in one event until it reaches its natural end, and then begin the next event.

It has been found that the clock directs behaviour in North America, Western Europe, East Asia, Australia, and New Zealand. Event time is often found in South America, South Asia, Mediterranean countries, and in developing economies with big agricultural sectors—in which people operate according to the seasons rather than the clock, and clock time is not yet fully part of people's work habits. North Americans will schedule a meeting for 9 a.m., turn up on time and apologize if they are a few minutes late. In countries like Saudi Arabia, people may turn up 20 minutes late and feel no need to apologize. It may be that, in cultures where status is important, this is demonstrated by the high status participants turning up late. In event time countries, a higher proportion of time at work is likely to be devoted to social activities such as chatting and having cups of tea or coffee. People from clock time cultures will often get frustrated by this behaviour, seeing it as time wasting or an inefficient use of resources. However, these activities could be useful for a business because they may help to build up supportive groups so that when someone comes under pressure, colleagues will be happy to help out on a voluntary basis. Also, it may be that important business relationships are made during what appears to be aimless social activity (Brislin and Eugene 2003).

The Social Environment

In this section we move on to examine various elements of the social environment. We start off by examining social divisions and then go on to compare three social models that show how the state looks after the welfare of its citizens. Subsequently, we consider demography, the process of urbanization, and then health and education.

Social Models

In different countries, the state takes on varying degrees of responsibility for the welfare of its citizens. Today, in most developed economies the state spends more on welfare than all other programmes. This spending takes the forms of benefits to the elderly, the disabled, the sick, the unemployed, and the young. It also usually involves spending on health care and education. Welfare policies may vary from country to country in terms of their aims, the amount of money spent on them, the priority given to different programmes, and the identity of the beneficiaries. In some countries, the state intervenes only to provide a limited level of support to those who are regarded as deserving of help. This tends to be the dominant system in Anglo-Saxon countries. In others, such as in Scandinavia, benefits are universal, relatively generous, and open to the entire population. In poor countries, the provision of welfare is often left to the family. Influences on the various approaches are the levels of economic wealth, different attitudes toward poverty, and the proper role of the state.

In the West, there are three social models in operation: the liberal, the corporatist, and the social democratic. Trying to classify different welfare states neatly into separate pigeon-holes is not straightforward because they are continually adjusting to factors like globalization, to demographic change such as the ageing population, or to the feminization of the labour force. And, sometimes, a country will contain elements of several models. For example, the UK has aspects of both the liberal and the social democratic models. On one hand, as in the USA, unemployment benefits are not tied to incomes and require those out of work actively to seek employment or training, or perform community service. On the other hand, the provision of universally provided social services in the UK, such as the National Health Service, and in-work benefits for those who take low-paid jobs, a policy underpinned by a minimum wage, are more akin to the social democratic model prevalent in countries such as Denmark and the Netherlands.

The Liberal Social Model

The liberal social model, found in the USA, Canada, Australia, and also, to an extent, the UK, is based on a clear distinction between the deserving and undeserving poor, with limits on the level of benefit payments. In liberal welfare states like the USA and the UK there is a sharp cut-off in unemployment benefits to discourage dependency and to force people back to work.

There is a commitment to keep taxes low and to encourage people to stay in work. While everyone is treated equally, there is a low level of welfare provision as expressed in the level of social expenditure (see Figure 6.3). There is a belief that people can better themselves through their own efforts, and that they may be poor because they do not try hard enough. In the USA, and to a lesser extent in the UK, there is scepticism about the state's effectiveness in tackling poverty. The welfare system, by giving benefits to single parents, is also believed to discourage marriage and to encourage single motherhood (see Lang (2007) on the US system).

Even in countries operating the liberal model, there can be major differences in the level and nature of welfare provision. For example, in the UK and Canada publicly funded health care is provided free to all at the point of delivery. All citizens qualify for health coverage, regardless of medical history, personal income, or standard of living. By contrast, the US system is a combination of private insurance paid for by workers through their employer, publicly provided insurance for the elderly (Medicare), the military, veterans, the poor, and disabled (Medicaid). The implementation of Medicaid varies greatly state by state. In the run up to the 2010 health care reforms, around 43 million people in the USA did not have private health insurance, which made it the only developed country not providing health care for all of its citizens. Large government budget deficits, brought about by the global financial crisis, have led to countries such as the UK to cut back on welfare benefits. See the **Online Resource Centre** for more details.

Now we look at the corporatist and social democratic models operating in many European countries. They share certain distinctive characteristics. There is a commitment to social justice. Neither system abandons those who fail. They aspire to high levels of employment, universal access to health care and education, adequate social insurance for sickness, disability, unemployment, and old age, and have a well-developed system of workers' rights. These systems seem better at tackling poverty than the liberal model operating in the UK and the USA (Hemerijck 2002).

The Corporatist Model

The corporatist social model is typical of continental European countries such as Germany, France, Austria, and Italy. Japan and other EU countries, for example in Southern Europe, also display elements of the corporatist model, but spending is not as generous as in France or

Figure 6.3 Social expenditure, percentage of GDP 1960–2012

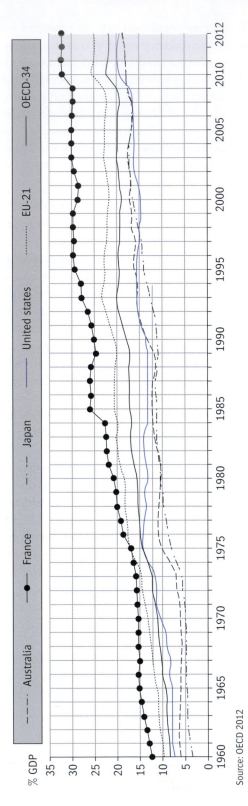

Source: OECD 2012

Germany (see Figure 6.3). In the past, the Church played an influential role in the model with its commitment to the preservation of the traditional family. Thus, wives who were not working were excluded while family benefits were paid to those having children. The model emphasizes the importance of work, and benefits are based on individual contributions. Benefits are generous relative to those provided in countries operating under the liberal model. In contrast to the liberal model, poverty is viewed as either inevitable or as a result of social injustice. This is why, in Germany and the Netherlands, political parties of both the right and the left support an extensive welfare state. While around one in five households in Britain are poor, the rate for Germany is one in eight.

In corporatist systems, there is a belief in the value of partnership and dialogue between the government and the various interest groups in society (sometimes called the social partners) such as trade unions and employers' associations. This is seen as a way of avoiding and reconciling conflicts over economic and social policy. It emphasizes solidarity between the various social groups and gives an important role to voluntary organizations such as churches and charities. In Germany, for example, church bodies are important providers of welfare services to groups such as migrants and young people.

The Social Democratic Model

The social democratic model, found in Scandinavian countries, has several defining characteristics. Sweden, where total state spending makes up 60 per cent of the economy, spends almost twice as much on social welfare as the USA. Britain falls between the low-spending USA and the high-spending continental European countries.

There are much lower levels of child poverty in Scandinavia compared to the UK and the USA. According to UNICEF (2012), around 7 per cent of Swedish children live in poverty while almost one in five are in that position in the USA.

Support is provided through generous welfare benefits for all those who are poor, old, young, disabled, and unemployed, and there is universal access to education and health care. There is a heavy commitment to helping families and to mothers wishing to work. This is financed by high levels of taxation. Also, unlike the liberal model, governments usually commit themselves to generating and maintaining high levels of employment and low levels of unemployment. There is an emphasis on taxation and spending policies that redistribute income from the rich to the poor and an active approach is taken to finding jobs for the citizens. As in the corporatist model, dialogue between the social partners is valued (UNICEF 2005).

Latin America

Social expenditure has been rising gradually in Latin America (see Figure 6.4). Social security systems in Latin America tend to be funded by payroll taxes, so the amount of funding available is determined by the number of people officially in work; this in a region with the lowest rates of salaried work and the lowest minimum wages in the world. Government-supported health care programmes depend on social security funding and a patchwork of health insurance packages put together by various, and sometimes unregulated, private providers. As a result, citizens requiring health care often have to pay, which, given the high levels of poverty, they can rarely afford. Recent reforms aim to extend health insurance protecting low- to middle-income households from financial disaster (Knaul et al. 2011). Governments have also been

Counterpoint Box 6.3 **The clash of social models**

Critics have launched bitter attacks on the social democratic and corporatist social models of Western Europe and blame them for the inferior economic performance of Europe compared with the USA; for example, as regards economic growth.

They attribute high and persistent unemployment in France and Germany, declining productivity growth, growing fiscal strains, and the mediocre and inflexible services provided by the state to high tax and spend policies and over-zealous interference with market forces, for example, the setting of a minimum wage. The essence of the argument is that high taxes and benefits discourage people from seeking employment and working hard and discourage businesses from taking risks. The result is mediocrity—people who do well are penalized by high taxes while nobody is allowed to fail. The answer is to move toward a liberal regime where market forces are allowed much freer rein. Critics accept that the free market can result in undesirable outcomes, but argue that it leads to a more creative, flexible, and productive economy. In their view, people should take responsibility for their lives and not be protected by the state from the consequences of their own decisions. Thus, if individuals decide not to buy health insurance then they, not the state, must bear the consequences when they become ill.

Defenders of the social democratic model challenge claims of superior US performance. They argue that growth of GDP per head has grown at roughly the same rate in the USA and the majority of European countries, and that a European country like Sweden is richer than the USA as measured by per capita income, even though its economy is more highly regulated and has a larger welfare state. They also claim that French and German productivity levels are higher than in the USA and that inequality, poverty, and crime rates are much lower. They point to the 15 per cent of the US population not covered by private health insurance despite President Obama's Affordable Care Act (*The New York Times* 17 September 2013).

Sources: Green 1999; Navarro and Schmitt 2005; Pierson et al. 2014

improving rudimentary employment services to connect workers to jobs, training, and social services. They are of particular importance in Latin America where the public listing of jobs is not widespread, so large numbers of disadvantaged workers are left to seek work inefficiently through informal contacts (Mazza 2013).

Asia

Asian countries spend much less as a proportion of their **national income** on social programmes (see Figure 6.5).

Some authors have noted that several East Asian societies do not fit in with any of the models outlined above. In Japan and the four 'tiger' economies of Hong Kong, Singapore, South Korea, and Taiwan, priority has been given to economic growth, and welfare policies have been subordinated to that. They do engage in social policy, but only after attending to their main objective of growth, and social policies are often geared to the achievement of economic objectives. While welfare arrangements do vary in each of these countries, there are some common elements. In these societies, there is hostility toward the concept of the welfare state, public expenditure on social welfare is low, social rights and benefits tend to be limited, and the family is expected to play a central role in social support.

The Japanese Constitution accords its citizens a minimum standard of healthy civilized life. They have a right to basic health care, and pensions are almost universal. However, benefits are limited and the family is expected to play a role (Holliday 2000). Compared with other OECD

Figure 6.4 Social expenditure in 21 Latin America and Caribbean countries 1992 –2011 %*

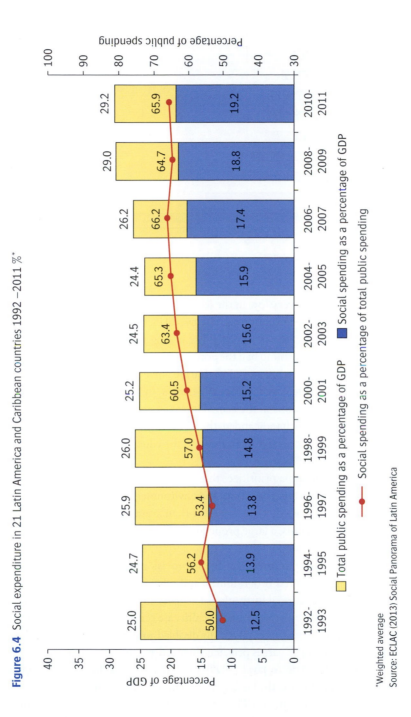

*Weighted average

Source: ECLAC (2013) Social Panorama of Latin America

Percentage of public spending

Percentage of GDP

☐ Total public spending as a percentage of GDP ■ Social spending as a percentage of GDP

Social spending as a percentage of total public spending

	1992-1993	1994-1995	1996-1997	1998-1999	2000-2001	2002-2003	2004-2005	2006-2007	2008-2009	2010-2011
Total public spending	25.0	24.7	25.9	26.0	25.2	24.5	24.4	26.2	29.0	29.2
Social spending % of total public spending	50.0	56.2	53.4	57.0	60.5	63.4	65.3	66.2	64.7	65.9
Social spending % of GDP	12.5	13.9	13.8	14.8	15.2	15.6	15.9	17.4	18.8	19.2

Figure 6.5 Asia social protection expenditure as percentage of GDP, 2009

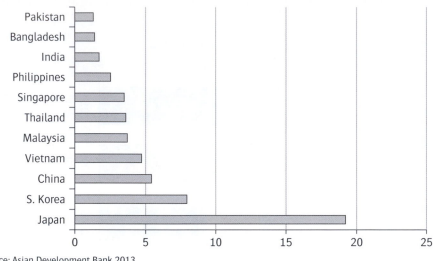

Source: Asian Development Bank 2013

members, Japan ranks very low in the level of social assistance it provides (see Figure 6.3) but high relative to other Asian countries. The level of income inequality and relative poverty among the working-age population in Japan has been rising and is higher than the OECD average (Jones 2007a). In Hong Kong, around half the population live in rented housing provided by the authorities, and rights to health care and education are universal but limited. The state does not provide pensions, unemployment benefit, or child benefit. In Taiwan, the bulk of welfare spending predominantly goes to groups in the armed forces, state bureaucrats, and teachers, while the less fortunate, the poor, the handicapped, the old, and the young receive almost nothing (Holliday 2000). A lot of resources have been put into the education system in pursuit of the country's economic objectives (Chow 2001).

Welfare policy in China prioritizes three aspects: high growth at the expense of other public goods such as health care, education, and environmental protection; the favouring of those in occupations and sectors that are better off than average, for example, civil servants and high ranking military veterans; a large proportion of expenditures on pensions compared to health care and unemployment (Frazier 2006).

In India, social programmes include the provision of education, housing schemes, income and employment-oriented programmes, and schemes for providing jobs in government and places in higher educational institutions for lower castes. Social security takes the form of primary health care through government health care centres, nutrition schemes, and old age pensions for the destitute, widows, physically disabled, and informal sector workers. In India, more than four-fifths of health care is privately financed, putting it out of reach of the poor (Ma 2008; OECD 2009). According to Jayal (1999), the Indian state adheres, philosophically, to welfare based on need. In practice, the basis is one of charity, benevolence, and paternalism.

According to the International Labour Organisation (2012), only one-third of countries provide comprehensive social protection, covering some 20 per cent of the world's population of working age. Nearly one-third of the world's population has no access to health care.

Learning Task

Examine Table 6.2, which shows some health indicators in the USA, Sweden, China, Brazil, and Nigeria.

1. The USA and Sweden have much higher average incomes than the other countries in the table. Compare and contrast its indicators of health with those of the other countries.

2. Use your knowledge of the different social models to come up with explanations for your findings.

3. What other explanations might be advanced?

Table 6.2 Health indicators for the USA, Sweden, China, Brazil, and Nigeria 2011

	Life expectancy at birth (years)[1]	Life expectancy at age 60	Infant mortality rate[2]
USA	79	23	4
Sweden	82	24	1
China	76	20	20
Brazil	74	21	21
Nigeria	53	16	16

[1] Life expectancy influenced by both positive and negative biological and social factors. Negative biological factors tend to show up quite early after birth so that death rates tend to be higher during the first year of life. Social factors are the main determinants of life expectancy. Positive elements include shelter, health care, educational provision, working conditions. Malnutrition, poverty, armed conflict, stress, and depression are examples of negative social aspects (Chattopadhyay and Sinha 2010)

[2] infant mortality = per 1,000 live births

Source: WHO (2013)

Demography

Demography is the study of population. It looks, among other things, at the size of the population, its rate of growth, the breakdown by age, gender, and ethnic group, and the geographical distribution of the population.

World population was 7.2 billion in 2013, around 1.2 billion more than in 2000. More than 80 per cent of the world's population live in poorer regions, and just less than one-fifth in the more developed regions. By contrast, in 1950 almost one-third of the world population lived in rich countries. Poorer countries have increased their share of world population because they have been growing almost three times as fast as the more developed regions (see Table 6.3).

The number of people and their geographical location are of interest to business. Large populations may indicate that markets are there to be exploited. However, to be attractive to business, incomes in such populous areas need to be high enough for consumers to be able to afford to buy goods and services.

The most highly populated countries tend to be found in the less developed regions of the world. China and India are the most populous, each with over 1 billion people. Together, they account for more than one-fifth of the world population. The USA and Japan are the only rich countries to make the top 10 in terms of population (see Table 6.4).

Table 6.3 World population 1950, 1975, 2013

Area	Population (million)		
	1950	1975	2013
World	2,535	4,076	7,162
More developed regions	814	1,048	1,233
Less developed regions	1,722	3,028	5,909
Least developed countries	200	358	898
Other less developed countries	1,521	2,670	5,010
Africa	224	416	1,110
Asia	1,411	2,394	4,298
Europe	548	676	742
Latin America and the Caribbean	168	325	617
Northern America	172	243	355
Oceania	13	21	38

Source: UN 2013

Table 6.4 The 10 most populous countries (millions)

1. China	1,356	6. Pakistan	196
2. India	1,236	7. Nigeria	177
3. United States	319	8. Bangladesh	166
4. Indonesia	254	9. Russia	142
5. Brazil	203	10. Japan	127

Source: US Census Bureau website, accessed 14 April 2014

Changes in Population Size

Population size is affected by the death rate, the birth rate, and net migration.

With increasing prosperity and advances in sanitation, diet, and medical knowledge, death rates have been declining, not only in the richer countries of the developed world, but also in Asia, Latin America, and the Caribbean. However, in some former Communist countries, like Russia and the Ukraine, rates have been increasing, largely as a result of deteriorating social and economic conditions, and in some African countries because of the spread of HIV/AIDS.

Birth rates at a world level have fallen to 2.53 children per woman—half the level they were in the 1950s. Women in the least developed countries have more than three times the number of children as their counterparts in the rich world (UN Population Division June 2013). Birth rates tend to fall as countries become richer. In poor countries, where incomes are low and there is minimal or no welfare provision, people have large families to support them in their old age. Increasing incomes in these countries reduces the need for large families. The OECD suggests that the changing role of women also has a big influence on the number of children they have.

As the level of education of women increases, along with their greater participation in the workforce, so the birth rate declines. The attitudes of women, especially in the developed world, are moving away from their traditional role as bearers and nurturers of children. Even in supposedly Catholic countries such as Poland, Italy, and Spain, where the Church condemns contraception, there have been significant declines in the birth rate (d'Addio and d'Ercole 2005).

As regards international migration, it has been increasing since the 1970s, with the vast majority going to richer countries, particularly the USA, and many fewer to developing regions. As Martin (2008) points out, this movement has led to a significant growth in the labour force of the developed economies. In Europe, Northern America, and Oceania, net migration increased population growth from 1950, while natural increase became less important—in Europe, natural increase became negative after 1990 and the UN sees net migration offsetting population decline until 2020 (UN 2013a).

The Ageing Population

Increased life expectancy and falling birth rates mean that the average age of the population in many countries will rise, and this has become a major demographic concern. In some countries, this will lead to stagnation and even decline in the population. Europe is the first region in the world to experience demographic ageing. By 2050 it is expected that the population share in the EU of those aged 65 and over will increase from over one-quarter in 2013 to just under one-half (Eurostat http://epp.eurostat.ec.europa.eu/portal/page/portal/eurostat/home/). Populations of other regions in Europe, Africa, the Middle East, and Asia, excepting Japan, will start to age later because their populations are much younger.

The OECD reckons that the ageing population could lead to shortages of labour, wage inflation, increased pressures on taxation and public expenditures, and a fall in the rate of economic growth. Unless something is done to alleviate the problem, taxes will have to rise to meet the

Mini Case Study Hispanic spending power in the USA

One of the major demographic changes in the USA has been the increase in the Hispanic* population. In 2012, there were around 53 million Hispanics in the USA, some 16 per cent of the total population. According to the US Census Bureau, the number of Hispanics is projected to more than double to 129 million, nearly one in three of the population by 2060. Hispanics are particularly concentrated in California, Texas, and Florida. Around 38 million US residents speak Spanish at home and in California one in seven of the population speak only Spanish.

For business, this means that the Hispanic market is one of the fastest growing in the USA. The spending power of these consumers, estimated at US$1 trillion, is growing much faster than that of non-Hispanic groups. It is estimated that Hispanics will be the main driver of consumer sales in the US, particularly in the area of cars and beverages. No surprise, then, that companies like McDonald's, Budweiser, and AT&T spend large amounts attracting Hispanic consumers.

Source: US Census Bureau, National Population; Ortman and Shin (2011); Forbes 18 July 2012, 9 March 2013

Questions

1. What are the possible implications of the increasingly important Hispanic market for television channels?
2. How might companies need to change their product and promotion strategies to appeal to Hispanic consumers?

*the US authorities define Hispanics as persons of Mexican, Puerto Rican, Cuban, Central or South American, or other Spanish Culture (US Census Bureau)

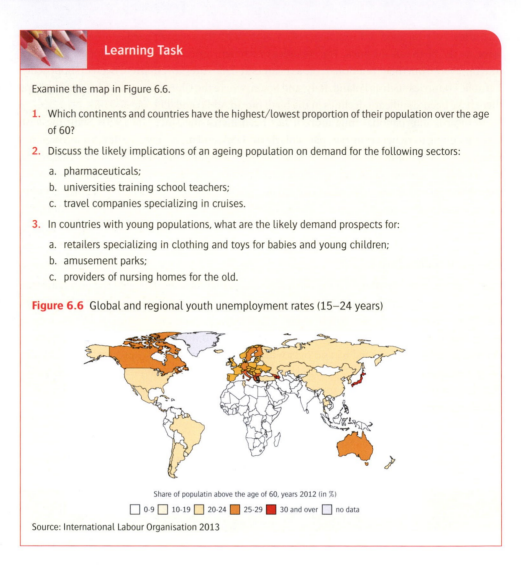

Learning Task

Examine the map in Figure 6.6.

1. Which continents and countries have the highest/lowest proportion of their population over the age of 60?

2. Discuss the likely implications of an ageing population on demand for the following sectors:

   a. pharmaceuticals;
   b. universities training school teachers;
   c. travel companies specializing in cruises.

3. In countries with young populations, what are the likely demand prospects for:

   a. retailers specializing in clothing and toys for babies and young children;
   b. amusement parks;
   c. providers of nursing homes for the old.

Figure 6.6 Global and regional youth unemployment rates (15–24 years)

Share of populatin above the age of 60, years 2012 (in %)

☐ 0-9   ☐ 10-19   ☐ 20-24   ☐ 25-29   ☐ 30 and over   ☐ no data

Source: International Labour Organisation 2013

increasing cost of pensions and health care, or public expenditure and benefits will have to be cut. Global growth could fall to less than 2 per cent per year, which is almost one-third less than for the period from 1970 to 2000. Possible responses could involve encouraging older people to work longer, getting more women to enter the labour force, and attracting more young immigrants. This could be accompanied by a rise in the age of retirement, as has occurred in the public services in the UK. However, employers would need to change their negative attitudes to the employment of older workers. There would need to be more opportunities for flexible working and retraining for older people to help them develop new skills.

Youth Employment and Unemployment—The Lost Generation

In 2013, it was estimated that over 75 million young people were unemployed across the globe, an increase of 3.5 million compared with the pre-financial crisis year of 2007 (International Labour Organisation 2014). Youth unemployment was particularly prevalent in rich economies, where the unemployment rate was 18 per cent, the Middle East with 29 per cent, and North Africa with 24 per cent. The International Labour Organisation (2013) predicted that high unemployment would persist for years in these regions (see Figure 6.7). By contrast, in East and South Asia fewer than 1 in 10 young people were unemployed. Even young people who find work face a proliferation of precarious jobs that are low paid, part time, and temporary in advanced economies; and poor quality, informal, subsistence jobs in developing countries. Young people who are unemployed for a long time suffer long-term debilitating effects, called scarring (see Mini Case Study Youth unemployment—a social time bomb).

Figure 6.7 Global and regional youth unemployment rates (15–24 years)

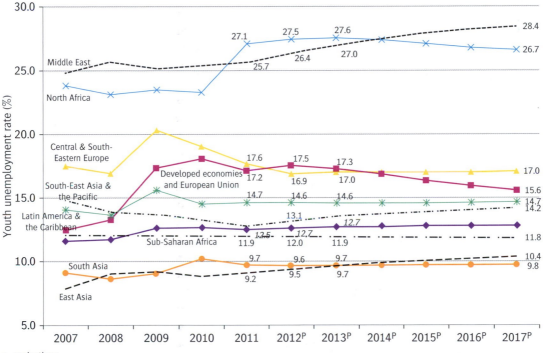

p= projections
Source: International Labour Organisation 2013

Mini Case Study Youth unemployment—a social time bomb

Unemployment for young people is a global epidemic that has many negative effects. Those who experience unemployment early in their life are more likely to be unemployed again in later years. Moreover, they are likely to earn less over their working life than those finding jobs more easily. The difference in earnings can amount to as much as 20 per cent, and

this deficit can last for as long as 20 years. It has also been found that unemployment can have long-term effects on mental and physical health and levels of job satisfaction. Blanchflower (2009) says that unemployment tends to be associated with malnutrition, illness, mental stress, depression, increases in the suicide rate, poor physical health in ➔

➔ later life, and reductions in life expectancy. Marmot, a professor of public health, described persistent high youth unemployment as 'a public health time bomb waiting to explode' (cited in *The Lancet* 9 November 2013).

Young, long-term unemployed may find it difficult to get work because some employers see them as not productive. Morsy (2012) argues that unemployment can lead to social exclusion, poverty, violence, crime, and social unrest. The young unemployed may also be tempted to take illegal jobs in the black economy. Hoffman and Jamal (2012) point out that the youth unemployment rate in some parts of the Middle East and North Africa is as high as 80 per cent, and they see this as a contributory factor to the civil unrest associated with the Arab Spring.

Standing (2014) attributes the increase in precarious jobs in both young and older people to the spread of neo-liberal policies pursued across the world and the adoption of policies of austerity. He sounds a warning that the jobs situation makes the young ready to listen to dangerous extremist political views. Reports by the National Institute of Economic and Social Research show that, in the UK, underemployment, that is workers wanting to work more hours than employers will give, is particularly concentrated among the young and that pay for young people after 2008 had fallen by more than 14 per cent

back to 1998 levels (Bell and Blanchflower 2013; *The Guardian* 1 May 2014).

Countries suffering high youth unemployment are likely to experience increased rates of emigration, particularly of young educated people, which some characterize as a brain drain.

Sources: Hoffman and Jamal (2012); Standing (2014); Blanchflower (2009); Morsy (2012); Bell and Blanchflower (2013)

Questions

In 2014, almost a quarter of young people in the EU were unemployed. The figure was 35 per cent in Portugal and 55 per cent in Spain (European Commission, Eurostat).

1. Unemployment, particularly of young people, is very high in Spain and Portugal. Find out whether there is any evidence of a brain drain from Spain and Portugal.

See *The Guardian* 30 January 2014; *Financial Times* 8 June 2011; www.bbc.co.uk 31 October 2013, 30 April 2014.

2. Discuss whether large outflows of highly educated young people would be good for economies such as Spain and Portugal.

3. Consider whether the black economy might make the prospect of civil unrest less likely.

● CHAPTER SUMMARY

We can see from our analysis that the international social and cultural environment offers major opportunities, but also poses many threats and challenges to business.

One conclusion to be drawn is that business ignores cultural differences at its peril. Hofstede has pointed out that, for companies, culture more often leads to conflict than synergy and that cultural differences can be a nuisance at best and are frequently a disaster. Firms need, as a matter of course, to take into account the varying national attitudes to such factors as hierarchy and power distance when considering entry to foreign markets through exports, joint ventures, takeover, or when setting up completely new production facilities. To be successful abroad, firms need to be aware of the impact of culture on the conduct of business meetings, how negotiations are carried out, and on attitudes to contracts. Different national cultures may require business to respond to the local culture by changing their approach to the management of personnel, to the products they produce, and to the methods used to market their products. Failure to do so can lead to higher costs, lower levels of productivity, and poor sales and profits.

Our examination of the social environment demonstrated how social models vary from one country to another, from the less generous liberal approach in the USA to the more generous Swedish social democratic model. The debate continues to rage between the supporters of these models as to which model provides the best environment for business and which promotes economic performance and social cohesion. We have seen how changes in the social environment can be of importance for business. Demographic changes, for example, population growth in Asia and Africa, an ageing population in Europe, youth unemployment and underemployment, and different national levels of health and education, all have implications for the quantity and quality of the labour supply as well as for the economic growth rate and the pattern of demand for goods and services.

● REVIEW QUESTIONS

1. Table 6.5 shows social spending as a percentage of GDP from 1990 to 2013.

   a. What is the trend in social spending over the period from 1990 to 2013? To answer this, look first at the OECD average. Do any countries buck the trend?

Table 6.5 Public social expenditure (as a percentage of GDP)

	1990	2000	2005	2010	2013
Australia	13.2	17.3	16.5	17.9	19.5
Canada	18.1	16.5	16.9	18.7	18.2
Chile	9.9	12.8	10.1	10.8	–
Czech Republic	15.3	19.1	18.7	20.8	21.8
Denmark	25.1	26.4	27.7	30.6	30.8
Finland	24.1	24.2	26.2	29.6	30.5
France	25.1	28.6	30.1	32.4	33.0
Germany	21.7	26.6	27.3	27.1	26.2
Greece	16.6	19.3	21.1	23.3	22
Hungary	–	20.0	22.5	22.9	21.6
Ireland	17.3	13.4	16.0	23.7	21.6
Italy	19.9	23.1	24.9	27.7	28.4
Japan	11.1	16.3	18.6	22.3	–
Korea	2.8	4.8	6.5	9.2	9.3
Mexico	3.3	5.3	6.9	8.1	7.4
Poland	14.9	20.5	21.0	21.8	20.9
Portugal	12.5	18.9	23.0	25.4	26.4
Spain	19.9	20.2	21.1	23.6	23.8
Sweden	30.2	28.4	29.1	28.3	28.6
Turkey	5.7	–	9.9	12.8a	–
United Kingdom	16.7	18.6	20.5	23.8	23.8
United States	13.6	14.5	16.0	19.8	20.0
OECD average	17.6	18.9	19.7	22.1	21.9

– not available
Source: OECD.StatExtracts http://stats.oecd.org/

b. Group the countries into continents, North America, South America, Europe, Asia, and Australia, and compare spending in each. Comment on your findings.

c. How would you explain Sweden's high levels of expenditures compared to those of the US?

d. Some commentators argue that globalization is leading to a 'race to the bottom' with regard to welfare spending. Explain what they mean and assess whether the figures lend support to that argument.

2. What major challenges does an ageing population pose for business?

3. Which countries are particularly affected by high youth unemployment? Analyse the economic and social impact of persistently high youth unemployment.

4. Möller and Eisend carried out a survey of nearly 8,000 consumers in 34 countries on the effectiveness of online advertising, typically containing graphics, text, and a link to the advertiser's website. They analysed the results using Hofstede's cultural dimensions. The research showed that consumers from individualist societies are not appreciative of banner advertising and are less likely to click on banner advertisements than those from collectivist societies.

a. draw on your knowledge of the individualist and collectivist dimensions to explain the results of the research.

b. in which of the following countries would consumers be most receptive to online banner advertising?

- Indonesia;
- Australia;
- South Africa;
- Brazil.

c. what methods could companies use to market their goods and services in individualist cultures?

● ASSIGNMENT TASKS

1. In 2013, reports from the New York Film Academy and Centre for the Study of Women in Television and Film in San Diego found a large degree of gender inequality in the Hollywood film industry. You are employed by a government agency responsible for funding the arts, including film. One of the main elements of your mission statement is a commitment to equal treatment irrespective of gender, race, or sexuality. Your manager, under pressure from the government minister responsible for the arts, gives you a remit to read the reports (visit the **Online Resource Centre**) and:

a) identify which areas of the film industry are affected by gender inequality;

b) propose steps the agency could take in its funding policies to promote positive discrimination in the film industry.

2. You are employed in the communications department of a multinational producer of alcoholic drinks. Your boss has come across an article in the *Financial Times* referring to Hofstede's work on national cultures. He asks you to write a report explaining how Hofstede's research could help the firm manage its foreign operations more effectively.

Case Study Sweden and China—worlds apart

Hofstede holds that national cultures have a strong influence on how organizations operate. In his research he found major differences between Sweden and China (see Table 6.6).

Table 6.6 Hofstede's research showing major differences between Sweden and China

	Power distance	Individualism	Masculinity
Sweden	31	71	5
China	80	20	66

Source: Hofstede http://geert-hofstede.com/china.html

Source: © esfera / shutterstock.com

Power distance: Chinese society expects and accepts as normal a high degree of inequality. In such high power distance countries, power in organizations is centralized and hierarchical where workers, with little power, know their place and are ready and willing to obey their managers, whom they look to for leadership and as sources of authority. Managers are free to abuse their power. By contrast, Sweden scores low on this concept. Organizational structures are flat, power is decentralized, with hierarchies being accepted only when appropriate. Managers see employees as members of a team, value their experience, and accept their participation in business decisions.

Individualism: China scores low on this dimension, being a highly collectivist culture with employees acting in the interest of the group rather than themselves. The group takes care of its members in return for loyalty. Cooperation occurs within the group, but employees can be cool or even hostile to other groups. The group gets preferential treatment when it comes to the hiring of staff and promotion. Employees are committed to other group members rather than the company and prioritize personal relationships over the job task or the organization. Sweden is an individualist society. In such societies, employees are expected to look after themselves and their direct families. Both managers and employees view their relationship as a mutually advantageous contract, while recruitment and promotion decisions are made on merit.

Masculinity: Hofstede's research found that China is a masculine society where people focus on winning through competition and achievement. China, being success oriented and driven, scores highly on this concept. According to Hofstede, many

Chinese sacrifice family and leisure to achieve their goals at work. Managers in such cultures assume the right to make decisions and this is what employees expect. Sweden has the lowest score of any country on masculinity. It is regarded as a feminine society where it is important to maintain a balance between life and work. Managers are supportive of employees, try to involve employees in decision making, and operate with a consensus. Conflict is resolved through negotiation and compromise. Equality, solidarity, and quality of working life are highly valued.

He and Liu (2010) carried out research on a Swedish multinational manufacturer of office equipment and its Chinese subsidiary operating in Shanghai. The Chinese company had been operating for 70 years and had a good reputation. The authors set out to apply elements of Hofstede's model to compare and contrast national cultures and their effects on management style, staff behaviour, and communication systems.

In one instance, the Swedish company supplied the specifications of a new design and asked its Chinese subsidiary to make a production ready model. This was done, but with a 1mm error. The Chinese company asked the Swedish product manager what it should do. His reaction: 'Do they need to ask such a question? . . . Why are they waiting for orders instead of taking initiatives?' They also found that, on being asked by Swedish HQ to meet unattainable product standards, the Chinese had agreed.

At home, the Swedish company preferred to make decisions and deal with issues through employees and departments working together in groups. When this was tried in Shanghai, people just sat around waiting for the management to make decisions. The Swedes also tried to draw on the long experi- ➡

→ ence of employees in the Chinese subsidiary to help make better decisions, but got little response.

Swedish managers, unlike their Shanghai counterparts, were proud of what they did, with the job becoming part of their identity. The authors found that the parent company had embarked on a policy of recruiting employees in Shanghai with higher standards in English and of taking increasing numbers of Chinese employees to Sweden to enhance their skills and to experience the Swedish approach to management.

Sources: http://geert-hofstede.com; He and Liu (2010)

Questions

1. He and Liu found that the Swedish company had not carried out any research on Chinese culture before moving in to China. Use Hofstede's research on the two countries to identify issues the Swedish company was likely to encounter in China.

2. Use Hofstede's concepts to analyse the problems encountered by the Swedish company in China.

3. Why is the company recruiting employees in Shanghai who can speak English and giving them experience in Sweden? To what extent is the company likely to be successful? (to help with this task, reread Counterpoint Box 6.1).

4. Assume that the Swedish company decides to move in to Hong Kong. To what extent could it simply apply its knowledge and experience of Chinese culture gained in Shanghai to an operation Hong Kong?

5. Hofstede claims that Chinese society is collectivist, i.e. where people's self-image is defined in terms of 'we', the group, rather than 'I', the individual. On the other hand, he says that many Chinese sacrifice family, for example by leaving them to go to cities to achieve their goals. How would you explain this apparent contradiction?

● FURTHER READING

For discussion of the impact of national cultures on company performance see:

● Hammerich, K. and Lewis, R.D. (2013) *Fish Can't See Water: How National Culture Can Make Or Break Your Corporate Strategy*. Chichester: John Wiley & Sons.

For results of a survey of business culture in 13 countries in Europe, Asia, and the Americas see:

● Ardichvili, A., Jondle, D., and Kowske, B. (2010) 'Dimensions of Ethical Business Cultures: Comparing Data from 13 Countries of Europe, Asia, and the Americas'. Human Resource Development International 13(3).

The World Health Organisation publishes statistics and a review of health issues every year:

● World Health Organisation *World Health Report*, annual.

For two different views on the challenges of the increasing population see:

● Dorling, D. (2013) *Population 10 Billion*. London: Constable & Robinson.

● Emmott, S. (2013) *10 Billion*. London: Penguin Books.

● REFERENCES

d'Addio, A.C. and d'Ercole, M.M. (2005) 'Trends and Determinants of Fertility Rates in OECD Countries: The Role of Policies'. OECD Social, Employment and Migration Working Papers 27, November.

An, D. and Kim, S. (2007) 'Relating Hofstede's Masculinity Dimension to Gender Role Portrayals in Advertising: A Cross-Cultural Comparison of Web Advertisements'. *International Marketing Review* 24(2).

Asian Development Bank (2013) 'The Social Protection Index: Assessing Results for Asia and the Pacific'.

Bates, D. and Plog, F. (1990) *Cultural Anthropology*. Maidenhead: McGraw-Hill.

Bell, D. and Blanchflower, D. (2013) 'Underemployment in the UK Revisited'. *National Institute Economic Review* 224 (May).

Blanchflower, D. (2009) 'What Should be Done about Rising Unemployment in the UK?'. Lecture presented at The University of Stirling, 25 February 2009. Available at: www.bankofengland.co.uk

Bond, M.H. (2002) 'Reclaiming the Individual From Hofstede's Ecological Analysis—A 20-Year Odyssey: Comment on Oyserman et al.'. *Psychological Bulletin* 128(1).

Brislin, R.W. and Eugene, K. (2003) 'Cultural Diversity in People's Understanding and Uses of Time'. *Applied Psychology: An International Review* 52(3).

Child, J. (2002) 'Theorizing About Organization Cross-Nationally: Part 1—An Introduction'. In: M. Warner and P. Joynt, *Managing Across Cultures. Issues and Perspectives*, 2nd edn, 26–39. London: Thomson Learning.

Chattopadhyay, A. and Sinha, K.C. (2010) 'Spatial and Gender Scenario of Literate Life Expectancy at Birth in India'. *Asia Pacific Journal of Public Health* 22: 477.

Chow, P.C.Y. (2001) 'Social Expenditures in Taiwan (China)'. World Bank Institute. Available at: http://siteresources.worldbank.org/WBI/Resources/wbi37167.pdf.

Crystal, D. (2003) *The Cambridge Encyclopedia of Language*. Cambridge: Cambridge University Press.

de Mooij, M. and Hofstede, G. (2010) 'The Hofstede Model: Applications to Global Branding and Advertising Strategy and Research'. *International Journal of Advertising* 29(1).

Eby, L.T., Adams, D.M., Russell, J.E.A., and Gaby, S.H. (2000) 'Perceptions of Organizational Readiness for Change Factors Related to Employees' Reactions to the Implementation of Team-Based Selling'. *Human Relations* 53(1).

ECLAC (2013) *Social Panorama of Latin America*. United Nations Economic Commission for Latin America and the Caribbean. Available at: www.cepal.org/cgi-bin/getprod.asp?xml=/publicaciones/xml/8/51768/P51768.xml&xsl=/publicaciones/ficha-i.xsl&base=/publicaciones/top_publicaciones-i.xsl.

Fisher, T.F. and Ranasinghe, M. (2001) 'Culture and Foreign Companies' Choice of Entry Mode: The Case of the Singapore Building and Construction Industry'. *Construction Management and Economics* 19(4).

Frazier, M.W. (2006) 'Welfare State Building: China in Comparative Perspective'. Paper presented at the Annual Meeting of the American Political Science Association, 31 August-3 September.

Green, D.G. (1999) *Benefit Dependency: How Welfare Undermines Independence*. London: Civitas.

Güliz, G. and Belk, R.W. (1996) 'Cross-Cultural Differences in Materialism'. *Journal of Economic Psychology* 17(1).

He, R. and Liu, J. (2010) *Barriers of Cross Cultural Communication in Multinational Firms: A Case Study of Swedish Company and its Subsidiary in China*. Halmstad, Sweden: Halmstad School of Business and Engineering.

Hemerijck, A. (2002) 'The Self-Transformation of the European Social Model'. Available at www.fas.umontreal.ca.

Hewett, K., Money, R.B., and Sharma, S. (2006) 'National Culture and Industrial Buyer-Seller Relationships in the United States and Latin America'. *Journal of the Academy of Marketing Science* 34(3).

Hickson, D.J. and Pugh, D.S. (2001) *Management Worldwide: Distinctive Styles Amid Globalization*. London: Penguin Books.

Hoffman, M. and Jamal, A. (2012) 'The Youth and the Arab Spring: Cohort Differences and Similarities'. *Middle East Law and Governance* 4.

Hofstede, G. (1980) *Culture's Consequences: International Differences in Work-Related Values*. Beverly Hills, CA: SAGE Publications.

Hofstede, G. (1991) *Cultures and Organizations: Software of the Mind*. New York: McGraw-Hill.

Hofstede, G. (1994) 'Business Cultures: Every Organization has its Symbols, Rituals and Heroes'. *UNESCO Courier* 47(4).

Hofstede, G. (2001) *Culture's Consequences: Comparing Values, Behaviors, Institutions and Organizations Across Nations*. Thousand Oaks, CA: SAGE Publications.

Hofstede, G. (2003) *Culture's Consequences. Comparing Values, Behaviors, Institutions*. London: SAGE Publications.

Hofstede, G. (2007) 'A European in Asia'. *Asian Journal of Social Psychology* 10.

Hofstede, G. and Bond, M.H. (1984) 'Hofstede's Culture Dimensions: An Independent Validation Using Rokeach's Value Survey'. *Journal of Cross-Cultural Psychology* 15.

Hofstede, G. and Bond, M.H. (1998) 'The Confucius Connection: From Cultural Roots to Economic Growth'. *Organizational Dynamics* 16(4).

Holliday, I. (2000) 'Productivist Welfare Capitalism: Social Policy in East Asia'. *Political Studies* 48 (September).

International Labour Organisation (2012) 'World Social Security Report 2010/11: Providing Coverage in Times of Crisis and Beyond', 10 April. Available at: www.socialsecurityextension.org/gimi/gess/ShowTheme.action;jsessionid=c1a4949c085773247e158b43e05b1c70dee818aed4825fb9533dabaf97fac860.e3aTbhuLbNmSe34MchaRah8Tchr0?th.themeId=1985.

International Labour Organisation (2013) 'Employment and Social Protection in the New Demographic Context'. Available at: www.ilo.org/ilc/ILCSessions/102/on-the-agenda/employment-social-protection/lang--en/index.htm.

International Labour Organisation (2014) 'Global Employment Trends 2014: Risk of a Jobless Recovery?'. Available at: www.ilo.org/wcmsp5/groups/public/---dgreports/---dcomm/---publ/documents/publication/wcms_233953.pdf.

Jayal, N.G. (1999) *Democracy and the State: Welfare, Secularism and Development in Contemporary India.* New Delhi: Oxford University Press.

Jones, M.L. (2007) 'Hofstede – Culturally Questionable', Oxford Business & Economics Conference Oxford, UK, 24-26 June.

Jones, R.S. (2007a) 'Income Inequality, Poverty and Social Spending in Japan'. OECD Economics Department Working Paper No 556, June.

Keats, S. and Wiggins, S. (2014) *Future Diets. Implications for Agriculture and Food Prices.* Overseas Development Institute. Available at: www.odi.org/sites/odi.org.uk/files/odi-assets/publications-opinion-files/8776.pdf.

Kerr, C., Dunlop, J.T., Harbison, F.H., and Myers, C.A. (1960) *Industrialism and Industrial Man.* Cambridge, MA: Harvard University Press.

Knaul, F.M., Wong, R., and Arreola-Ornelas, H. (eds) (2011) *Financing Health in Latin America, Volume I: Household Spending and Impoverishment.* Cambridge, MA: Harvard University Press.

Kyoungmi L. and Shavitt S. (2006) 'The Use of Cues Depends on Goals: Store Reputation Affects Product Judgments when Social Identity Goals Are Salient'. *Journal of Consumer Psychology* 16(3).

Lang, K. (2007) *Poverty and Discrimination.* Princeton and Oxford: Princeton University Press.

Lee, H.-S. (2004) 'Outstanding Issues in Bilateral Economic Relations between Australia and South Korea'. *Australian Journal of International Affairs* 58 (March).

Ma, S. (2008) 'Sustainability of India's Welfare System in the Context of Globalization'. MPSA Paper presented at the Midwest Political Science Association 66th Annual National Conference, 3-6 April.

Martin, J.P. (2008) 'Migration and the Global Economy: Some Stylised Facts'. OECD. Available at: www.oecd.org/migration/mig/40196342.pdf.

Mazza, J. (2013) 'Connecting Workers to Jobs: Latin American Innovations in Labor Intermediation Services'. *Latin American Policy* 4(2): 269–84.

McClure, A., Tanski, S.E., Gilbert-Diamond, D., Adachi-Mejia A.M. Li, Z., Li, Z., Sargent, J.D. (2013) 'Receptivity to Television Fast-Food Restaurant Marketing and Obesity Among US Youth'. *American Journal of Preventive Medicine* 45(5).

McSweeney, B. (2002) 'Hofstede's Model of National Cultural Differences and their Consequences: A Triumph of Faith—A Failure of Analysis'. *Human Relations* 55.

McSweeney, B. (2002a), 'The Essentials of Scholarship: A Reply to Geert Hofstede'. *Human Relations* 55: 11.

Möller, J. and Eisend, M. (2010) 'A Global Investigation into the Cultural and Individual Antecedents of Banner Advertising Effectiveness'. *Journal of International Marketing* 18(2).

Morsy, H. (2012) 'Scarred Generation'. *Finance & Development* 49(1).

Navarro, V. and Schmitt, J. (2005) 'Economic Efficiency versus Social Equality? The US Liberal Model versus the European Social Model'. *International Journal of Health Services* 35(4).

Nisbett, R.E. (2005) *The Geography of Thought: How Asians and Westerners Think Differently—and Why.* London: Nicholas Brealey.

OECD (2009) *Society at a Glance – India.* OECD/Korea Policy Centre—Asia/Pacific Edition.

OECD (2012) 'Social Expenditure During the Crisis'.

Ortman, J.M. and Shin, H.B. (2011) 'Language Projections: 2010 to 2020'. Paper presented at the Annual Meetings of the American Sociological Association, 20–23 August 2011.

Pew Research Center (2012) 'Most Muslims Want Democracy, Personal Freedoms, and Islam in Political Life: Few Believe US Backs Democracy'. Global Attitudes Project, 10 July. Available at: www.pewglobal.

org/2012/07/10/most-muslims-want-democracy-personal-freedoms-and-islam-in-political-life/.

Pierson, C., Castles, F., and Naumann, I.K. (eds) (2014) *The Welfare State Reader*, 3rd edn. Cambridge: Polity Press.

PLOS (2012) 'Is Obesity Simply About a Lack of "Balance"? Why Big Food Wants You to Be Fit', 5 July. Available at: http://blogs.plos.org/speakingofmedicine/2012/07/05/is-obesity-simply-about-a-lack-of-balance-why-big-food-wants-you-to-be-fit/.

Ramamoorthy, N. and Carroll, S.J. (1998) 'Individualism/Collectivism Orientations and Reactions Toward Alternative Human Resource Management Practices'. *Human Relations* 51(5).

Redpath, L. (1997) 'A Comparison of Native Culture, Non-Native Culture and New Management Ideology'. *Revue Canadienne des Sciences de l'Administration* 14(3).

Rudd Radar (2013) 'Fast Food Facts 201: Fast Food Companies Still Target Kids with Marketing for Unhealthy Products', 5 November. Available at: www.yaleruddcenter.org/fast-food-facts-2013-fast-food-companies-still-target-kids-with-marketing-for-unhealthy-products.

Skeldon, R. (1996) 'Migration from China'. *Journal of International Affairs* 49(2).

Shimoni, B. with Bergmann, H. (2006) 'Managing in a Changing World: From Multiculturalism to Hybridization—The Production of Hybrid Management Cultures in Israel, Thailand, and Mexico'. *Academy of Management Perspectives* August.

Standing, G. (2014) *The Precariat*, 2nd edn. London: Bloomsbury.

Stewart, B.W. and Wild, C.P. (eds) (2014) *World Cancer Report 2014*. World Health Organisation.

UN (2013) 'World Population 2012'. Available at: http://www.un.org/en/development/desa/population/publications/pdf/trends/WPP2012_Wallchart.pdf.

UN (2013a) 'International Migration Report 2013'. Available at: http://www.un.org/en/development/desa/population/publications/migration/migration-report-2013.shtml.

UNICEF (2005) 'Child Poverty in Rich Countries'. Innocenti Report Card 6.

UNICEF (2012) 'Measuring Child Poverty in Rich Countries: New Tables of Child Poverty in the World's Richest Countries'. Innocenti Report Card 10.

UN Population Division (2013) *World Population 2012*.

van Oudenhoven, J.P. and van der Zee, K.I. (2002) 'Predicting Multicultural Effectiveness of International Students: The Multicultural Personality Questionnaire'. *International Journal of Intercultural Relations* 26(6).

Watson, J.J., Rayner, R.S., Lysonski, S., Durvasula, S. (1999) 'Vanity and Advertising: A Study of the Impact of Appearance-Related, Sex, and Achievement Appeals'. *Advances in Consumer Research* 26.

WHO (2013) 'World Health Statistics 2013'. Available at: http://www.who.int/gho/publications/world_health_statistics/2013/en/.

CHAPTER SEVEN

The Technological Framework

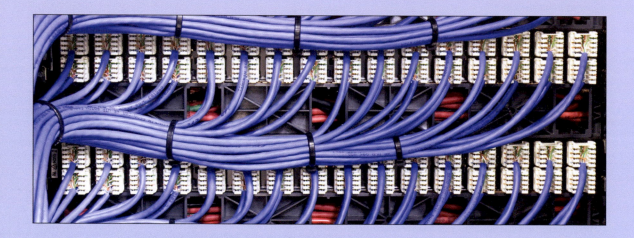

LEARNING OUTCOMES

This chapter will enable you to:

- **Explain the meaning of technology and associated concepts**

- **Identify and explain the sources of technology and how firms go about innovating**

- **Explain why the intensity of technological activity varies by firm size, sector, and country base**

- **Analyse the importance of the technological environment, both domestic and foreign, for business decisions and performance**

- **Explain how the external environment allows business to protect its technology in an international context**

Case Study **Twitter**

Twitter was incorporated in Delaware in April 2007. Through the Internet it provides an online social networking and microblogging service. Users can send messages limited to 140 characters. Videos and photographs can also be shared on Twitter.

By 2013 it had around 3,000 employees. It floated on the New York Stock Exchange in November 2013 and, despite rising losses, the share price soared. By the end of the first day of trading, it was valued at $30 billion (*The Independent* 7 November 2013). Because Twitter was the home to hundreds of millions of users, stock exchange analysts were apparently salivating over the prospect of it making money by selling adverts and using its data to help advertisers target Twitter users wherever they were on the Web.

The number of Twitter users has grown very rapidly. It doubled to 138 million users in 2011–12 and by the end of 2013 had reached 241 million see (see Figure 7.1). Revenue increased from $28 million in 2010 to $665 million in 2013, while losses grew almost tenfold over the same period to $645 million (see Figure 7.2). Revenue is not generated directly from users or organizations using Twitter as a platform, such as the BBC, CNN, and *The Times of India*. The increasing number of users and level of activity create, through so-called network effects, more content attracting more users and more organizations wishing to use it as

Source: © MicroWorks / istockphoto.com.

a platform, such as advertising agencies like Publicis, whose clients include Microsoft, Coca Cola, and Proctor and Gamble, and firms such as GM and Budweiser, who pay to promote their brands.

Mobile technology has been vital to the success of Twitter. In the last quarter of 2013, 76 per cent of active users were accessing Twitter from a mobile device and over 75 per cent of advertising revenue was generated from mobile devices.

In Internet technology sectors, intellectual property (IP) and its protection is vital against infringement by rivals. To that end, Twitter holds around 1,000 patents and is filing for more in the

Figure 7.1 Monthly active Twitter users worldwide

Source: Twitter SEC-10K filing

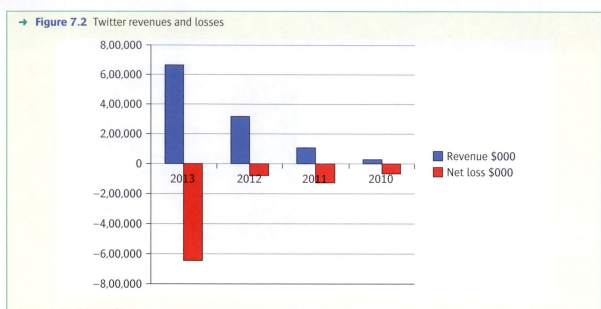

→ **Figure 7.2** Twitter revenues and losses

Source: Twitter SEC-10K filing

US and abroad relating to message distribution, graphical user interfaces, and security.

It is also very concerned about patent vultures/trolls/innovation hijackers. These are organizations who buy up patents from holders who have no interest in bringing the product to market or who may be going out of business. They look for firms who have invested heavily in the technology, accuse them of infringing their patents, and threaten them with a lawsuit to obtain licensing royalties. In 2014, Twitter was involved in a number of these cases and expected more to arise in future.

Twitter has also protected its IP by obliging employees, consultants, and its founders to sign an Innovators Patent Agreement.

The company recognizes its dependence on other technology firms and the consequent risks. Its services are made available across various operating systems and websites over which it has no control. Therefore, it needs to ensure the interoperability of its services with desktops, laptops, tablets, and mobiles, and browsers such as Mac OS, Windows, Android, Chrome, and Firefox from powerful players such as Microsoft, Google, Apple, Samsung, and Vodafone.

Sources: Twitter SEC 10K filings; Bloomberg Businessweek 1March 2011; *Financial Times* 15 October 2013; *The Independent* 7 November 2013; www.bbc.co.uk 23 April 2013.

Introduction

New technology is most visible in personal computers, laptops, tablets, smartphones, portable digital audio players like the iPod, digital cameras, and high definition flat panel TVs produced by the information and communications industry. It can also be seen in the products of other high-tech industries such as pharmaceuticals and **biotechnology**. Technology has become internationalized through trade, investment, migration, and digitization. Thus, consumer goods like smartphones, iPads, and BMWs can be seen on the streets of Mumbai as well as those of Berlin and Tokyo. Multinational companies, such as Microsoft, General Motors, and Sony, transfer production technologies from their domestic base to foreign operations and many, like Samsung and Alcatel-Lucent, take opportunities offered by the international environment to develop global research strategies, carrying out research and development both at home and abroad.

Technology is a double-edged sword for business, offering many opportunities but also challenges. On the one hand, it opens up a variety of opportunities for business in terms of new products, processes, and markets. On the other, it leaves firms more open to a range of competitive threats, such as takeover, increased competition, and even to the theft of their technologies. The rapid internationalization of technology means that firms need to monitor both their domestic and their foreign technological environments. For many industries, technology is of the utmost importance and can determine whether firms prosper or fall by the wayside.

What is Technology?

In simple terms, technology refers to the know-how or pool of ideas or knowledge available to society. Some is codifiable, meaning it can be written down and transferred easily to others, but there is also tacit knowledge which is carried about in the heads of a firm's employees and therefore not easy to transfer.

Technological advance comprises new knowledge or additions to the pool of knowledge and can lead to changes in how businesses behave; for example, changes in how goods and services are produced, how production processes are managed, the characteristics of the good or service, and how products are distributed and marketed. Technical change can refer to ground-breaking advances in knowledge or simply to minor modifications of products and processes.

There are a number of terms associated with technology and it is useful to have an understanding of these. **Research and Development** (R&D) refers to the discovery of new knowledge (research) about products, processes, and services, and the application of that knowledge to create new and improved products, processes, and services that fill market needs (development).

Basic research is the pursuit of knowledge for the sake of it. In other words, it is carried out to push back the frontiers of knowledge with no thought of its commercial application. Such research is commonly funded by governments and is most often undertaken in universities or research institutes. It can be very expensive, take an inordinate length of time to yield results, and may produce no results at all.

An example of basic research was that carried out by Crick and Watson at Cambridge University. In 1953, they announced the most important biological discovery of the twentieth century, the structure of deoxyribonucleic acid, DNA, the chemical of life. Crick and Watson's discovery of DNA spawned the biotechnology industry producing new treatments for genetic diseases such as cancer, multiple sclerosis, and cystic fibrosis. It led to numerous scientific discoveries that have changed our lives, from the food we eat to the seeds that farmers use in their fields, and to the DNA testing used by the police to help identify criminals.

While there are businesses, for example in the electronics and pharmaceuticals industries, helping to fund basic research in the hope that some commercially exploitable ideas will be generated, firms, as a rule, do not usually get involved. Companies are normally more interested in **applied research**; that is, activities intended to lead to new or improved products and processes with clear and more immediate commercial uses. Even in applied research, there is no guarantee that results will be exploitable commercially. Scientists at General Electric (GE)—one of the biggest companies in the world, with interests ranging from jet engines to nuclear power stations to financial services—estimate that around 20 per cent of the company research projects are scrapped each year.

Innovation is the commercial exploitation of new knowledge; in other words, developing new ideas into products and production processes and selling them on to customers. It is often measured by R&D spending or by the number of patents—a patent gives its owner the exclusive right to exploit the idea and gives the legal right to stop others from using it. But innovation can also arise through investment in new machinery and equipment, market development, skills, brands, new ways of working, new business processes, and linkages with other organizations. It can involve the implementation of major advances in technical knowledge such as the digitization of electronic equipment, or small incremental changes such as a minor improvement in a production process. When firms come up with new ideas for products, processes, brands, and so on, these become part of their IP.

The spread of innovation from one firm and industry to another, nationally and internationally, is known as **technological diffusion**. Diffusion has been growing at a rapid pace as is shown by the growth of high-technology exports, foreign licensing agreements, and the foreign ownership of patents. After 1990, high-technology exports worldwide grew very rapidly, with Chinese manufacturing industries performing particularly well. By 2013, China accounted for more than one-third of such exports, with the contribution of Hong Kong taking the share to around 50 per cent, far outstripping the USA's 10 per cent, Japan's 7 per cent, and Germany at 4 per cent (*Financial Times* 18 March 2014).

The intensity of cross-border technological diffusion has been increasing, but appears to have tailed off since 2005 as measured by the foreign ownership of new inventions (OECD StatExtracts http://stats.oecd.org/). Nonetheless, in the USA, foreigners accounted for more than half the

Mini Case Study The global crisis and R&D

Dachs and Zahradnik (2014) reported that the global crisis, after three decades of increasing spending on foreign R&D, led MNCs, the driving force for diffusion, to cut back. The increasing share of foreign firms in total R&D expenditure in almost all countries was brought to a halt by the global crisis starting in 2007. They report that foreign firms' R&D was more affected by the crisis than the research spending of domestic firms, and that the downward trend continued until 2010, but then started to recover (see Figure 7.3). US MNCs, the largest overseas investors in R&D, saw a drop in expenditure abroad from about

Figure 7.3 R&D expenditures of foreign firms as a percentage of total business R&D expenditure in OECD member countries, 1999–2011, unweighted median and mean

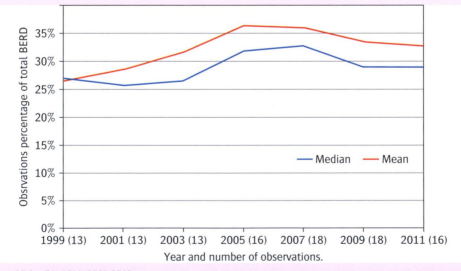

Source: Dachs and Zahradkin 2014; OECD 2012

→ $42 billion to $39 billion between 2008 and 2009, but bounced back to $46 billion in 2010. The main losers from the fall in US R&D were EU countries, but not Asia. Belgium, Sweden, the Czech Republic, and Spain were particularly affected by the fall in inward R&D. By contrast, France, Poland, and the UK bucked the trend. The World Intellectual Property Organisation (WIPO) (2013) reported that, with the global crisis, patent filings worldwide fell by about 4 per cent in 2009.

Reasons for the cutbacks in foreign R&D were probably due to MNCs being more dependent on exports than domestic firms. During the crisis, exports and FDI contracted more rapidly than domestic markets. This is likely to have caused MNCs to be pessimistic about future market growth and led to a reduction in R&D expenditure. The OECD (2012) says that innovative and high-tech businesses suffered particularly badly with the drop in demand for higher quality innovative products, which is characteristic of recessions. It also suggested that the crisis in the banking system could have affected the ability of innovative business to raise external finance. Since MNCs also tend to operate their main R&D activities at home, they may be more reluctant to retrench there.

Questions

1. Why did US MNCs cut back their R&D hardest in EU countries but not Asia?

patents granted in 2013 compared with 46 per cent before 2000 (US Patent and Trademark Office 2014). However, foreign ownership as a proportion of all US patents remains low, as it does for Japan, South Korea, and China, but is high in Belgium, Ireland, and Hungary. Less than 5 per cent of patents in Japan and South Korea are foreign-owned. Foreign owners, predominantly MNCs based in the USA, the EU, or Japan, have a tendency to own patents in countries with close historical and cultural links as well as geographical proximity to their home country.

The degree of internationalization varies across different technologies. R&D in pharmaceuticals, motor vehicles, chemicals, and the manufacturing of information and communication technologies are more internationalized than other sectors. Furthermore, some countries are dependent on foreign companies for their R&D capabilities. Foreign MNCs account for a significant proportion of R&D spending in Ireland, Sweden, Spain, Canada, and the UK as compared with the USA and Japan. The R&D activities of US MNCs are much more internationalized than Japanese companies. Dachs and Zahradnik (2014) identify MNC motives for foreign R&D as a desire to adapt products to foreign markets and to take advantage of high quality R&D resources based in, for example, research institutes or universities.

Globalization in general, and multinational companies in particular, are important vehicles for the international diffusion of new knowledge through their trading, investment, and competitive strategies. Their influence is illustrated by the international spread of lean manufacturing in the car industry. This sets out to eliminate waste and to decrease the time between receipt of a customer order and delivery. It was pioneered by car makers in Japan and subsequently adopted by Western companies, such as GM, Ford, and VW, as a result of the fierce competition they faced from their more efficient Japanese rivals.

Learning Task

The British government is proud of the foreign contribution to UK R&D (See Figure 7.4)

1. Using Figure 7.4, compare and contrast the evolution of UK R&D financed from abroad with the USA and South Korea.

2. Discuss the pros and cons for the UK economy of its dependence on foreign R&D finance.

Figure 7.4 Percentage of business R&D financed from abroad 2000–2012

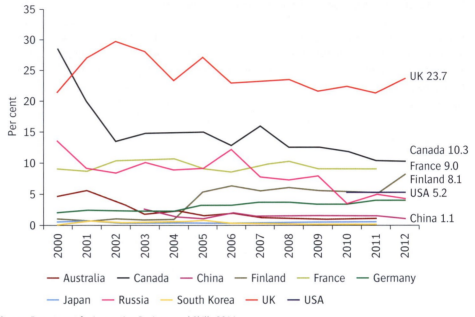

Source: Department for Innovation Business and Skills 2014

Waves of Innovation

History has seen waves of major innovations:

- The Industrial Revolution, starting in Britain in the second half of the eighteenth century, involved machines such as water-driven spinning jennies and looms.

- The next wave saw steam power being used to drive the machines used in the production of manufactured goods in the second half of the nineteenth century, particularly in Britain.

- The third wave occurred at the end of the nineteenth century with enormous expansion in chemical industries, with the introduction of products such as synthetic dyestuffs and high explosives. An important advance in communications occurred with the invention of the telephone.

- In the first half of the twentieth century we moved into the age of oil and the application of electricity to industrial processes.

The second half of the twentieth century and the first decade of the twenty-first saw rapid developments in electronics, communications, computers, aerospace, pharmaceuticals, biotechnology, petrochemicals, and synthetic materials. There have been major advances in body imaging technology embodied in scanners using ultrasound, gamma rays, or X-rays. These permit scientists to obtain detailed pictures of areas inside the body, the pictures being created by a computer linked to the imaging machine. Surgeons can identify potential tumours, the damage following a stroke, and signs of incipient dementia. Firms, such as Coca Cola and BMW, have used this new technology to examine areas of the brain that are used when confronted with new designs or brands or when choosing between competing products on supermarket shelves.

Some commentators, like Wonglimpiyarat (2005), suggest that another wave could be sparked by nanotechnology, the science of the ultra-small. Nanotechnology is the ability to manipulate and manufacture things using individual particles of materials when the dimensions of the particles are 100 nanometres or less. The width of a human hair is about 100,000 nanometres (http://science.howstuffworks.com/462-how-nanotechnology-works-video.htm). This is already having a big impact on firms producing computer chips, integrated circuit boards, flat displays in products like computers, televisions, and mobile phones, and in textiles and biotechnology.

Information and Communications Technology

Information and communications technology (ICT) has become increasingly important in the business world. ICT is a term that encompasses all forms of technology used to create, store, exchange, and use information in its various forms whether that be business data, voice conversations, still images, motion pictures, or multimedia presentations. It involves the use of machines such as computers, telephone exchanges, robots, satellites, automatic cash dispensers, and cable TV along with the software installed in them. ICT is all-pervasive affecting the home, the office, and the factory and it has major implications for business both large and small from the small shop with its computerized accounts to supermarket chains such as Wal-Mart and Tesco who use electronic links with their suppliers to ensure that their shelves are always stocked with sufficient quantities of the appropriate goods.

The pace of change in ICT has been extraordinary due to a variety of factors. The needs of the military have been a major impetus for developing computers to solve problems related to encryption, decoding, and missile trajectory. The development of microelectronic technologies owes much to the space race between the USA and the USSR. US rockets were smaller than Soviet rockets, so they could not carry as much computer equipment. Miniaturization provided the solution and led to the computer chip.

With the power and speed of computer chips doubling every 18 months, and their cost falling by 50 per cent, many new products have emerged, like laptop computers, tablets, mobile phones, global positioning systems, and satellite TV. An important development has been the Internet, which is an enormous international computer network initially developed in the US defence sector. It links a vast number of pages of information on the worldwide Web, which is expanding at an exponential rate. It has led to the emergence of auction companies like eBay, search engines such as Google, and social networking sites like Facebook and Twitter. In 2002, it was estimated that about 10 per cent of the world population was using the Internet. By 2012, at over two billion people, this had risen to around 34 per cent. The highest number of users was in Asia, with well over 1 billion, followed by Europe with 519 million, North America with 274 million, Latin America with 255 million, and Africa with 167 million (www.internetworldstats.com).

Digitization is breaking down boundaries between different media. Smartphones are increasingly used to take photographs and record videos, and television programmes can be viewed on PCs, laptops, and tablets.

Web 2.0

There have been a number of important technological developments on the worldwide Web known as Web 2.0 (see O'Reilly 2005; also see video on this topic by visiting the link on the **Online Resource Centre** for this book). These rely on user collaboration and include peer-to-peer networking, blogs, podcasts, wikis, video sharing, and social platforms like Facebook, WhatsApp, YouTube, Flickr, and Twitter. Web 2.0 is creating global systems that make it much easier for business-to-business and business-to-customer interaction. One place to see the application of these advances in action is in the mobile phone market, where manufacturers and service providers are creating 'apps' which users can download to their smartphones. They allow users to play games, locate nearby restaurants or friends, listen to music, find the best deals online, and access countless sources of specific information. Apple claims more than 75 billion apps downloads between 2008 and 2014. By 2014, Facebook had more than 1.3 billion users, of whom almost 1 billion accessed the site with a mobile (www.statista.com). That year around 4.5 billion people in the world were using mobile phones, and smartphone user numbers were expected to exceed 1.75 billion (www.statisticbrain.com; www.emarketer.com).

Mini Case Study   Data is the new oil

Internet usage has grown explosively and has led to the faster and cheaper accumulation of masses of data, now commonly known as 'big data' (see Table 7.1). Some firms recognized the potential benefits of such a treasure trove, but the volume of data was so vast that it outstripped the ability of existing software programs to analyse it. This led to the development of new processing technologies, such as Hadoop used by Yahoo and Facebook. Microsoft, IBM, Amazon, and Oracle all now offer database management services.

The new database technologies analyse the data, looking for statistical relationships; that is, correlations between different data which can be quantitative, text, images, and moving images. Big data analysts are not interested in finding out why the relationships exist.

UK finance firms, like Lloyds Bank, found that customers who are careful with cash are less likely to have car accidents, and it therefore offers them a lower insurance premium. Amazon uses its huge database to predict what its customers will buy, whether that be books, shoes, music, tablets, or smartphones. Reportedly, FedEx can identify which customers are likely to defect to a competitor.

McKinsey (2013a) estimated that the use of big data could generate $3 trillion to $5 trillion of benefits in seven sectors of the US economy through raising productivity, improving products and services, introducing new products, and increasing cost and price transparency.

Table 7.1 The growth of global Internet traffic

Year	Number of gigabytes	
1992	100	per day
2002	100	per second
2007	2,000	per second
2012	12,000	per second
2014	23,272	per second

Source: *The Guardian* 24 August 2103; www.internetlivestats.com

Sources: Mayer-Schönberger and Cukier 2013; *InformationWeek* 30 January 2014; *Financial Times* 28 March, 12 July 2014; McKinsey 2013a; Hayashi 2013

Questions

1. Some commentators are concerned about the hyping of big data. Explain why. To answer this, look up the *Financial Times* article 28 March 2014 by Tim Harford and the article by Hayashi.

McKinsey (2013) reported that 82 per cent of surveyed companies were using social media, with two-thirds using mobile networks. Companies can use Web 2.0 to communicate with employees and also invite customers to rate products and recommend improvements. Social media gives companies powerful new insights into how to position products, create new ones, and decide on pricing strategies. More than 40 per cent of firms surveyed were using video conferencing, social networking, collaborative document editing, video sharing, and blogs. Tools like wikis and podcasts were less popular. McKinsey found that after years of rapid growth, use of social technology had plateaued.

The Cloud

Cloud computing offers business the possibility of using software from the Internet. This means that firms do not need to have software, such as Windows, installed on their own computers. Company data can also be stored in the cloud. Cloud services are provided by companies like Google, Amazon, Microsoft, HP, and Tata. Cloud computing reduces the amount of money firms need to spend on IT personnel and infrastructure, such as air-conditioned rooms to store servers, and upgrades on software and hardware. This makes it easier for small- and medium-sized firms to compete because they only need to pay for the IT services they need, when they need them, and they can access the same IT services as their larger competitors. It is argued by commentators, such as Kotler and Caslione (2009), that cloud computing could make it easier for developing countries to compete with richer economies.

A potential drawback is that firms could become dependent on the cloud company to hold their confidential data and for the provision of IT services. Problems could arise were the service provider to have a breakdown (as happened with Google and Amazon—*The Observer* 1 March 2009), leak confidential information, or go out of business.

Theorists, like Schumpeter (1976), have attempted to explain why technological innovation occurs in cycles. He built on the work of the Russian economist, Kondratieff, who had noted a tendency for economies to go through cycles of expansion and then contraction, each cycle or wave lasting around 50 years. Schumpeter argued that the growth phase of the cycle arose from a bunching of innovations that brought about a technological revolution and led to the creation of completely new markets and industries through the invention of new products, production processes, or the discovery of new sources of raw materials or energy.

For the waves to occur, there have to be people willing to take the risks of exploiting the new ideas commercially. Schumpeter saw the entrepreneur as playing this vital role. Nowadays, we look to firms to carry out that function.

Who Innovates?

The EU R&D Scoreboard 2013 found that R&D spending for the world's top 2,000 companies had risen by 6.2 per cent to about €540 billion. Research intensity, that is R&D as a percentage of sales, varies from sector to sector, industry to industry, by size of firm, and by geographical location. The Scoreboard found that in the US, the EU, and Japan, the most research intensive sectors

Mini Case Study China and the internet

Between 2000 and 2014, the number of Internet users in China increased 30-fold to 642 million, and there are 500 million mobile users. The Chinese have embraced Internet shopping with a passion. In 2013, 271 million Chinese were shopping online and increasingly using smartphones to do this (see Figure 7.5).

A Boston Consulting Group study (2014) found that a majority of online shoppers use the Internet as the main source of information on products, brands, and prices with a significant proportion depending on both online and offline sources. But they shy away from getting that information from actual company websites, preferring to obtain that information elsewhere on the Web; for example, from e-commerce sites like Alibaba with huge stocks and low prices, blogs, and social networking sites. Most consumers spend up to 80 per cent of their time on a few sites like Youku, a local video-streaming website, Sina.com, a news portal, QQ, an instant messaging service, Taobao, an e-commerce site, and Baidu. Internet users in China also like to follow celebrities on Weibo, a microblogging service with more than half a billion users. However, consumers are sceptical of heavily commercialized blogs and those purporting to represent a celebrity promoting shoddy products. Product recommendations from grass roots bloggers are seen as more genuine and can help product sales.

Consumer purchasing behaviour varies from one product category to another. Clothing tends to be bought on impulse. With small appliances and packaged foods, consumers are likely to research online, but make most purchases offline. Skin care products are compared online and offline, but purchased online only if a lower price is on offer and the product is not counterfeit.

Daily peak times for online purchases are 10am, 2pm, and 9pm. The Boston survey points to Uniqlo, the Japanese clothing retailer, as an example of good practice to foreign MNCs in China. It promotes its products in a coordinated way both online and offline through activities like interactive games.

Sources: www.internetlivestats.com; Boston Consulting Group, The Chinese Digital Consumer in a Multichannel World, www.bcg. perspectives 17 April 2014; Forbes 28 April 2014

Questions

1. What advice would you give to a foreign MNC wishing to sell online in China?

Figure 7.5 China—Number of users of digital platforms

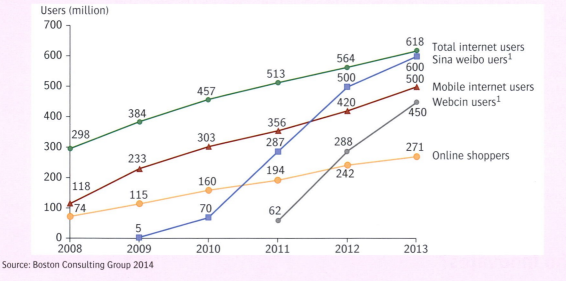

Source: Boston Consulting Group 2014

were pharmaceuticals and biotechnology, technology hardware and equipment, and automobiles, involving big companies like Merck, Sony, and Volkswagen. Sectors with a low research intensity include oil and gas, tobacco, and mining. In terms of firm size, the larger the firm, the more likely it is to do research, even in low-tech industries.

Counterpoint Box 7.1 This time technology will kill jobs?

Recently, high levels of prolonged unemployment in rich countries have reignited the debate about technological unemployment.

For years, economists have reassured society that technology creates rather than destroys jobs. The argument holds that technology replacing workers increases productivity. Increased efficiency in the production of a range of goods can reduce their prices causing a rise in real income and an increase in demand for other goods and services. This demand creates new jobs for workers displaced by technology. Industrialization in the nineteenth and twentieth centuries in the UK is used as proof that technology, rather than reducing total employment, created large numbers of new jobs for an increasing population. For much of the twentieth century, those arguing that technology generated more jobs and prosperity looked to have won the debate.

Brynjolfsson and McAfee (2011) go along with this view, at least up towards the end of the twentieth century, pointing out that over the previous 200 years the number of US jobs increased despite the huge automation of the workplace. But they go on to argue that the rapid technological advances in the digital era have changed the situation. Technology involving, for example, data visualization and high-speed communications is associated with an increased demand for skilled labour. Technologies like robotics, numerically controlled machines, and computerized stock control replace jobs involving routine tasks, causing a reduction in demand for unskilled and semi-skilled workers. Frey and Osborne (2013) argue that it is not simply routine manual work in jeopardy. They estimate that 47 per cent of US jobs are at high risk of being automated. White collar occupations, including accountancy, legal work, technical writing, and real estate jobs, are amongst the areas most under threat.

Brynjolfsson and McAfee (2013) go on to claim that the benefits of technology are not evenly spread, noting that, in the digital era, wage inequality between the most and least educated workers has been accelerating. This is supported by Autor and Dorn (2013) who found workers moving from middle-income manufacturing jobs to low-income service occupations.

Sources: Brynjolfsson and McAfee 2013; Frey and Osborne 2013; Autor and Dorn 2013

Questions

1. Supermarkets have increasingly been automating checkouts in their stores. Who benefits and who loses? To help answer this, search online for: *The Grocer* 8 June 2012, *The Telegraph* 29 January 2014, and http://web.mit.edu/2.744

Big manufacturing firms spend a much larger proportion of their turnover on innovation activities than small firms. Table 7.2 shows the top 10 innovators as measured by US patent applications. The sector filing most patents was electrical engineering, including the IT and telecoms industries.

However, using measures of innovation other than R&D and patents shows that small and medium-sized firms can also be important innovators. Historically, manufacturing firms have carried out most R&D. However, research activity in the service sector is on the increase, particularly in telecommunications, information technology, networking, and consultancy.

However, industries are not all equally affected by the competition arising from technological change and the opportunities and threats that it poses. Firms operating in industries where technology evolves and diffuses rapidly need to stay very aware of their technological environment. Such high-technology industries include aerospace, computers and office equipment, radio, TV, and communications equipment, and pharmaceuticals. A firm in these industries failing to respond effectively to its technological environment runs the risk of falling sales, market share, and profits, and even takeover or bankruptcy. This is particularly so in markets where, due to customer preference, only the latest product sells. There are some industries that are less sensitive to technological change. These are classified as medium technology industries and include motor vehicles, electrical (other than communications equipment), and non-electrical machines, chemicals excluding drugs, cars, rubber and plastics products, and shipbuilding and repairing.

Table 7.2 Top 10 innovators by US patent filings, 2013

Number of patents filed in the US 2013		
IBM	US	6,788
Samsung	South Korea	4,652
Canon	Japan	3,820
Sony	Japan	3,073
Microsoft	US	2,659
Panasonic	Japan	2,582
Toshiba	Japan	2,365
Qualcomm	US	2,103
LG	South Korea	1,945
Google	US	1,851

Source: US Patents and Trademark Office 2014 http://www.uspto.gov/

Finally, there are the low-tech industries that are relatively unaffected by competition in the area of technology, such as paper products, textiles, non-fashion clothes and leather goods, food, beverages and tobacco, wood products, and furniture.

The high- and medium- high-tech sectors together usually account for most R&D and contribute a disproportionately large share of sales of new and improved products.

Learning Task

Globally, it is the largest companies, in the richest countries, in a limited number of sectors that account for the vast majority of the money spent on R&D. Examine Table 7.3 and answer the questions below to test the validity of this claim.

1. Are the 10 companies amongst the biggest multinationals in the world? To answer this, go to the latest World Investment Report at www.unctad.org.

2. Which countries dominate the list? Give some reasons for this.

3. In which sectors do these firms operate? Why should R&D spending be high in these sectors?

Geographical Location of R&D

R&D expenditure is geographically concentrated. In 2014 the US, China, Japan, and Europe accounted for about 78 per cent of the $1.6 trillion global total. The share of the US and Europe has been in decline while that of Asia, especially China and South Korea, has been on the rise (see Figure 7.6).

Sources of Technological Advance

Technological advances can come from a variety of sources both inside and outside the organization. New ideas for commercial exploitation may be generated in the wider environment by scientists and technologists working in universities or research centres, or from individual

Table 7.3 Top 10 global companies by R&D expenditure, 2012

Rank 2012	Company	Sector	Country	R&D €m (rounded)	Growth in R&D over last three years (%) (rounded)	R&D % of sales
1	Volkswagen	Automobiles	Germany	9,515	18	4.9
2	Samsung	Electronics	S. Korea	8,344	14	5.9
3	Microsoft	Software and computer services	USA	7,891	6	13.4
4	Intel	Technology hardware and equipment	USA	7,691	20	19.0
5	Toyota	Automobiles	Japan	7,071	4	3.7
6	Roche	Pharmaceuticals and biotechnology	Switzerland	7,001	−4	18.6
7	Novartis	Pharmaceuticals and biotechnology	Switzerland	6,923	6	16.1
8	Merck	Pharmaceuticals and biotechnology	USA	5,996	9	16.7
9	Johnson & Johnson	Pharmaceuticals and biotechnology	USA	5,810	2	11.4
10	Pfizer	Pharmaceuticals and biotechnology	USA	5,741	−2	12.8

Source: EU R&D Scoreboard 2013 http://iri.jrc.ec.europa.eu/scoreboard13.html

Figure 7.6 Share of total global R&D spending 2012–2014[*]

Share of total global R&D spending			
	2012	2013	2014
Americas (21)	34.5%	34.0%	33.9%
U.S.	32.0%	31.4%	31.1%
Asia (20)	37.0%	38.3%	39.1%
China	15.3%	16.5%	17.5%
Japan	10.5%	10.5%	10.2%
India	2.7%	2.7%	2.7%
Europe (34)	23.1%	22.4%	21.7%
Germany	6.1%	5.9%	5.7%
Rest of world (36)	5.4%	5.3%	5.3%

Numbers in brackets = number of countries

[*]2014 = forecast

Source: Batelle *2014 Global R&D Funding Forecast* December 2013

http://www.battelle.org/docs/tpp/2014_global_rd_funding_forecast.pdf?sfvrsn=4

inventors. Scientists at Manchester University discovered how to extract graphene from graphite. It is one molecule thick, 200 times stronger and six times lighter than steel, and is a better electricity conductor than copper. It can be used to make folding mobile phones and batteries that charge up in minutes, and is added to paints, plastics, and lubricants. Technologists at the University of Oxford invented a direct-drive engine allowing car manufacturers to reduce weight and improve the range of electric and hybrid vehicles by removing heavy gearbox components from the transmission (www.isis-innovation.com). Sometimes businesses establish research links with universities to give them first call on new ideas generated by the university. Huawei, the giant Chinese telecoms company, financially supports six UK universities for research in areas such as advanced multimedia, optical technology, and 5G technologies.

Big firms in industries such as pharmaceuticals and electronics have their own R&D facilities that generate ideas for new goods and services. GE spends billions of dollars annually on R&D in the US, India, China, and Germany (www.ge.com/research). As part of its research effort, it runs a Global Research Centre employing thousands of researchers in the USA, India, China, Germany, and Brazil. The centre pioneered very successful breakthroughs in lasers, optical lenses, and digital X-rays, which allowed doctors a more accurate view of organs and bones and did away with the need for film and light boxes (www.ge.globalresearch.com).

Business can also look to the more immediate environment as a way of facilitating the innovation process. For example, firms may cooperate with domestic or foreign rivals when the costs of innovation are high or to improve their ability to innovate. Collaboration can help lower the costs and risks of innovation as well as facilitating the commercialization of new scientific and technical knowledge and can therefore be an attractive strategy for small- and medium-sized firms. The Italian furniture and textile industries, comprising mainly small firms, have formed networks of producers allowing them to cooperate on technology and ensuring that they maintain their competitive edge in the market place. Examples of cross-border collaboration can be seen in the car industry where even financially powerful big car producers feel obliged to cooperate to develop costly new models and components; for example, GM's joint venture with DaimlerChrysler to develop new transmission systems and Peugeot's joint venture with BMW to develop parts for electric cars. Technology, particularly the Internet, facilitates the process of collaboration—it is easy, speedy, and cheap for R&D units based in different countries to exchange information in the form of text, graphics, design drawings, video images, and so on.

Firms often try to involve suppliers, distributors, and customers (the supply chain in other words) in the innovation process to develop and share innovative ideas or to share in the development of new products or processes. In the aerospace sector, Supply Chain Relationships in Aerospace (SCRIA) is an example of such networking.

Some companies, particularly Japanese firms such as Nissan and Toyota, look to stakeholders such as their employees to come up with ideas for improving products and processes. Every year, Toyota, the world's largest car company, receives literally thousands of suggestions from assembly line workers about how it could do things even better. Workers are encouraged to find ways of shaving as little as one-tenth of a second off routine tasks. Most suggestions involve tiny modifications to existing practices, for example performing a particular task while standing up rather than sitting down. If the modifications work, they are adopted throughout Toyota's factories.

Finally, the acquisition of new machinery and equipment can be an important source of product or process innovation for small- and medium-sized enterprises. The new equipment may require the business to change the way it produces the product or to produce new or improved products.

Learning Task

Advance reasons why firms involved in expensive, risky, or complex research projects, such as those in the pharmaceutical industry, would seek cooperation in R&D with other organizations.

Visit the **Online Resource Centre** for a useful link to Hagedorn's paper to help with this task.

What Motivates Business to Innovate?

Technical advance is driven by a complex combination of factors in the firm's external environment: the intensity of competition, relationships with customers and suppliers, and government policies.

The Intensity of Competition

Since the mid-1980s, the pace of globalization in the world economy has accelerated. The reduction in the barriers to the movement of goods, services, and capital across borders has meant that markets have become increasingly integrated, innovation has diffused much more quickly, and technological competition has grown more intense. Increasing competition from emerging economies such as China and India has also contributed to the process. Competition means that when one firm innovates, competitors may be forced to react, often in creative ways. This could involve major ground-breaking advances or, more likely, improvements and innovations around the first innovator's design; for example, 'me-too' drugs in the pharmaceutical industry. Technological competition may drive firms to launch new products and at a faster rate, add features, enter, or even create new markets. In this way, technological competition begets more innovation and more competition. The increase in technological competition makes life more risky for business because one of the persistent characteristics of innovation is that most attempts to innovate fail in the marketplace. When the rate of innovation accelerates, it has the effect of shortening the length of the product life cycle. The period of time from conception to the death of the product is reduced and this increases pressure on business to innovate to stay ahead of the competition.

Customers and Suppliers

Some industries may find that the pressure to innovate comes from customers or suppliers. Car components producers, hoping for contracts with big manufacturers like Nissan, get business on condition that they change their mode of operation to meet Nissan's cost and quality requirements. Nissan advises suppliers on how to go about changing their production processes in order to increase efficiency. In the North East of England, where Nissan manufactures cars, it has set up a high-tech learning centre which suppliers use to develop their skills and to improve their productivity. For example, through the centre, suppliers can find out about Kaizen, a Japanese management technique embracing the concept of continuous improvement.

On the other hand, suppliers can be the instigators of innovation. Taking health care as an example, we can see that advances in body imaging has led to new and much more sophisticated scanning techniques being used in hospitals which has implications for the treatments offered, and also for the training of staff.

Government Policy

Increasingly governments have become aware of the importance of technical progress to the performance of their economies. To this end, they can pursue policies which remove or mitigate the effects of some of the barriers or give a positive impetus to innovation. Some innovations never get started or suffer serious delays because of their cost, or the inability to secure finance for what financial institutions view as too risky projects. This is a particular problem for small firms who may also suffer because they are often unaware of the information that is being generated, for example in universities and research institutes, that could be commercially exploited. Lack of qualified scientific and technical personnel can be another barrier to the development and exploitation of new ideas, as can the high cost of protecting intellectual property rights (IPRs), or where the degree of protection awarded to intellectual property is low. However, the regulatory framework can also be a positive influence. For example, stringent environmental and consumer regulation, as found in several EU countries, can force firms to raise their game regarding innovation. Labour laws making it difficult to fire employees may cause firms, when they innovate, to search for less labour-intensive production methods.

In 2000, the EU embarked on its **Lisbon Strategy**, a 10-year plan to improve competitiveness, with innovation and the knowledge economy as two of its central planks. Member states agreed to pursue policies that would help reduce some of the important barriers to innovation with the aim of making the EU the most competitive economy in the world. To that end, the EU agreed to aim for an increase in R&D spending to 3 per cent of GDP per year, with two-thirds of that coming from private sector firms, and to coordinate R&D programmes across the members of the union. The Strategy also saw education and training as crucial in providing a workforce capable of creating knowledge-intensive industries and services. However, a review in 2010 found that its main targets had not been reached. In particular, it had failed to reach the 3 per cent target for R&D as a percentage of GDP or to close the productivity gap with its main competitors (EU Commission 2010). The EU then initiated the Europe 2020 Strategy once again prioritizing an increase in R&D to boost competitiveness and economic growth (http://ec.europa.eu/europe2020/index_en.htm).

Businesses operating in developed economies are likely to be at an advantage because of the well-developed school, higher education, and training systems which mean that a high proportion of the population is literate and numerate. Conversely, firms operating in poor countries will be at a disadvantage, although countries like China and India, focusing on closing the innovation gap with richer economies, are producing increasing numbers of highly skilled and technically qualified graduates.

Governments, following the prescriptions of Michael Porter (1998) for improved competitiveness, promote the emergence of industrial clusters of associated firms including suppliers, customers, competitors, and other related institutions to which rivals in other locations do not have access. Clusters allow firms to boost their competitiveness by taking advantage of the intimate knowledge of, and interaction with, other businesses located in the cluster. These are visible in countries like Italy where a textile cluster comprises not merely fabric and garment manufacture, but also supporting industries like textile machinery and design, all located within a compact 200–300 square kilometres. In Andhra Pradesh, in India, the state has, through public–private partnerships, encouraged the creation of clusters in the IT, biotechnology, pharmaceutical, and textile sectors. Similar attempts to develop clusters have occurred in Latin America and in the Basque country in Spain.

Governments can pursue tax, subsidy, and **equity support regimes** that make finance more easily available, and cut the costs and risks associated with innovation. Almost all rich countries provide tax incentives and subsidies for innovation, although the focus is usually on promoting research, which tends to favour big business and to discriminate against SMEs.

Why Technology is Important for Business

Technology opens up all sorts of domestic and foreign opportunities for businesses who are ready to take advantage of them. On the other hand, it can also pose many threats to firms who are unaware of, and unprepared for, technical change. It can, as we will see from the example of the Internet, erode boundaries between markets and industries.

Technology can be a principal factor determining the size and growth of firms, the structure of industry on a global scale, its location and ownership, and the organization of production. According to Held et al. (1999), technology has played a part in the global restructuring of production. It has helped MNCs slice up the value chain by facilitating the location of segments of the production process to lower cost countries or to subcontract production activities to cheaper suppliers in Asia or Latin America.

Competitive advantage regarding productivity, costs, and products can all be heavily influenced by new ideas and knowledge. Those ideas and knowledge can result in new inventions, designs, trade marks, literary, and artistic works. These are the firm's IP. In reality, not many companies invent wholly new products; most of them adapt and extend ideas that others have already tried. Apple's iPod was not the first MP3 player, but the company added enough to make its version innovative (see Case Study Apple and technology, at the end of this chapter). Similarly, drugs companies often build on each other's breakthroughs to produce 'me-too' drugs.

Opportunities

New goods and services—firms can create new and improved goods and services, revive tired products and consequently penetrate new markets, and, as a result, can end up with powerful market shares and controlling valuable processes, products, designs, and brand names. Danish firm, Lego, is a good example of a firm using technology to revive a flagging product, the toy building brick. The brick is now sold with electronic technology allowing customers to build a range of moving robots.

Global organization—technology makes it increasingly easy to extend globally and to integrate economic activity in many widely separated locations. Technology has thus facilitated the rapid growth of the multinational corporation with subsidiaries in many countries, but with business strategies, production, and distribution still being determined and controlled by head office in a single nation. So, MNCs like Unilever are able to employ more than 160,000 people and sell its products in 170 countries (www.unilever.co.uk).

Learning Task

This task requires you to examine links between R&D expenditure and company performance.

Improved performance arising from technology can enhance a company's share performance. The R&D Scoreboard suggests that share prices (and sales growth) in companies with the highest R&D intensity perform better than the average. The list below, taken from the 2013 EU Scoreboard, shows R&D expenditure in large UK-based firms as a percentage of sales revenue.

• Vodafone (telecoms)	0.7
• AstraZeneca (pharmaceuticals and biotech)	15.9
• Delphi (automobiles)	7.7
• MISYS (software)	26.1
• Royal Dutch Shell (energy)	0.3

1. Choose a high spending and a low spending company from the table. Construct a graph of changes in their share prices over the last five years.

2. Comment on the relative share performance of the two companies. Identify a range of technological and other factors that could have influenced their share price.

Small firms—technology can make it easier for small firms to compete with large. The Internet, for example, enables all firms to communicate with customers both at national and at international level and to sell goods and services at relatively low cost. Small companies can design their own websites for as little as a few thousand pounds. Firms, producing for niche markets, can use the Web to reach customers who are of little interest to conventional distributors such as Wal-Mart. eBay provides opportunities for small firms to compete with the big boys. In the USA, the biggest music retailer is Wal-Mart. Given the need to make a return on its shelf space, it is only interested in carrying the biggest hits and cannot afford to carry a CD or DVD that sells only a handful of copies a year. The Web offers firms the opportunity to tap into customers interested in the 'non-hits'; and, in some areas, non-hits can often be a bigger market than the best sellers.

Freezing out competitors—exclusive control of technology can give firms the ability to freeze out their rivals by excluding them from using the same knowledge or techniques. That is why, in industries such as pharmaceuticals, IT hardware, and software, firms readily apply for patents which, if granted, will give them control of a technology. Microsoft, in 2013, filed for around 3,000 patents when in 1990 it received a mere five (see Table 7.2). Companies may deliberately set out to hoard patents purely to frustrate rivals by preventing them from getting access to new technology. This can be a very powerful competitive tool in certain sectors such as IT software and hardware where there has got to be technical compatibility, sometimes called interoperability, between programs and equipment. In the telecommunications industry, compatibility is vital for a firm to be able to connect to the network.

Apple was particularly effective in freezing out competition when it set up iTunes. The company made it technically impossible for songs bought on iTunes to be played on competitors' equipment. Shortly after Apple launched its service in Europe, it announced that it had sold 800,000 songs in the first week of operation. Both iTunes and the iPod won a market share of about 80 per cent in the USA and the UK, as well as a substantial market share in many European countries. The iPod's strong market position gave Apple the bargaining power to strike a deal with the four biggest record companies to sell songs through iTunes for around 54 pence each. The agreement was widely seen as a defeat for record companies.

Another tactic used by firms to exclude rivals is to get their technical standards accepted as the norm. Microsoft has done this very successfully by managing to get Windows accepted as the standard computer operating system, and then bundling in additional software such as Internet Explorer, which makes it very difficult for rival browsers to get a foothold in the market. And success breeds success. People buy Microsoft Office because they know they can take their knowledge anywhere, and because they want to be able to share their work with other users. Microsoft's dominance in operating systems has been subject to intense scrutiny by regulatory bodies, particularly in the EU and the USA.

Licensing—can be used to control the diffusion of a firm's technology and also to generate significant additional income streams. Qualcomm, the US wireless technology firm, earned about US$2 billion in licensing revenues in 2013 (SEC 10K filing). Microsoft went in for extensive licensing of its patented technology when growth in its core products started to slow down. This move by Microsoft also allowed the company to counter charges of abusing its monopoly by claiming that it was making its technology available to competitors.

Related products—a firm with a powerful technological position in one product may be able to oblige purchasers of that product to buy related products, thus generating additional income. For example, a manufacturer of photocopying machines could require the customer to take its own brand of ink or toner, or a computer maker could ensure that its own peripheral equipment was used with its machines. Microsoft consumers can only use Microsoft games in their Microsoft Xbox, but these games cannot be used in a Sony PlayStation (such behaviour could be seen as anti-competitive and attract the interest of the regulatory authorities—see Chapter 9, Competition Law).

Increased productivity—there is empirical evidence indicating that those countries and companies more rapidly adopting information and communication technologies tend to show higher levels of growth in productivity. For example, US companies have invested more in ICT than their European counterparts and, consequently, have experienced particularly strong productivity growth in sectors that make intensive use of ICT.

Reducing costs—telecommunication operators such as BT or France Telecom have also been major beneficiaries of technology. Automation of the exchanges permitted reductions in the workforce, while the miniaturization of computer equipment created savings in the amount of floor space required. The replacement of mechanical by electronic parts in the equipment economized on maintenance because electronic parts are more reliable than mechanical components and also because electronic machinery is now constructed in modules—any problems can be diagnosed electronically, the faulty module identified, removed, and replaced by another. As regards new products, technology enabled telecoms firms to offer a plethora of new services to their customers, such as ring back, answering services, and the ability to use wireless-free telephones and computers.

One can also see this in the driverless metros in cities such as Hong Kong, and in airport trains like those in Stansted airport in the UK. Another advantage is that technology could help firms deal with labour shortages. John Smedley, a medium-sized British manufacturer of luxury knitwear, had a costly labour-intensive production process and faced a shortage of skilled textile workers. The company could have cut costs and dealt with its labour shortage by getting its sweaters made in South East Asia. It was reluctant to do this because it would mean sacrificing the Made in England label, the hallmark of John Smedley knitwear and the reason why the company could demand high margins on its products. The company solution was to invest in new, technologically advanced knitting machinery that did away with the labour needed for panel stitchers. It enabled more of its workers to focus on the design and hand finishing of its products and, additionally, allowed the company to manufacture patterned designs, which permitted it to tap into new markets. The previous technology only allowed it to produce single colour items.

Job design—technology can facilitate the redesign of jobs and change the pattern of skills required by business. ICT in the newspaper industry has led to a disappearance of the traditional skills of the printer and a reduction in wage costs. Printing was a job traditionally done by a highly unionized workforce with skills being built up over a period of five or more years. These days, news information is keyed in by the journalist via the computer, while photographs and advertisements are input by less highly unionized and lower paid workers with computer skills that can be learned much more quickly. In this way, technology can reduce the skill levels required, which means that employers do not have to pay the same levels of wages and salaries.

Monitoring and control—ICT also enhances the ability of business to monitor and control what is going on in the workplace. In call centres, employers can monitor the number of calls workers take, how long it takes to deal with customers, what is said in the conversation with clients, and the outcomes; for example, how successfully staff exploit sales opportunities and the length of time staff are logged off on breaks. They can use the data to evaluate the performance of individual employees, or teams, and also for the call centre as a whole. Additional information can be gathered on the average length of time a caller has to wait before he or she is put through and the number of callers who ring off before they are put through. Similarly, such technology can make it easier for firms to monitor employees who are working from home or workers whose job entails them moving from one location to another, such as salesmen or lorry drivers.

Internal communications—ICT can be used to improve internal communications. E-mail, wikis, and blogs (a blog is an online diary or journal) can be used cheaply and easily to reach thousands of employees simultaneously. Investment banks like Dresdner Kleinwort and law firms such as Allen & Overy introduced blogging to facilitate communication and to allow online collaboration. Some firms, such as Motorola and Apple, use their technology as a tool to improve competitiveness. Workers are encouraged to use computers to exchange information. As a result, the workforce becomes more knowledgeable and more willing to accept and adapt to new ideas and change. Businesses who are successful with this approach are called learning organizations.

Threats and Challenges

While technology offers many opportunities for business to meet the objectives of generating sales and profits, it can also pose many threats and challenges.

Business organizations have to prepare for, and learn to cope with, new technology and to take advantage of the opportunities offered by technology to devise new consumer goods and new methods of production and distribution, to create new markets, and to take advantage of new forms of industrial organization. Innovation involves change in products or processes and it can be risky, especially for firms who are not good at managing change effectively, because new products may not catch on in the market place and new production processes may not deliver the expected benefits. While Castellion and Markham (2013) refute the contention that most product innovations fail, they still report failure rates of 35 per cent in capital goods and 45 per cent in consumer goods and services (see Table 7.4).

If firms are not properly prepared, then new technology can cause them to go out of business. Schumpeter (1976) called this the process of **creative destruction**. He argued that innovation over a period of time, by bringing in new products, new sources of supply, and new types of organization, could create a form of competition that strikes not simply at profits and market shares, but also at their very existence. Schumpeter's notion of creative destruction is neatly encapsulated by the chief executive of Procter & Gamble, who said, 'People ask me what I lose sleep over. If somebody announced an alternative to solution chemistry (i.e. washing powder) for laundry, all of a sudden I've got an US$11 billion business that's at risk' (*Financial Times* 22 December 2005). HMV, the UK music retailer, underestimated the threat from online competition both in terms of physical CDs and in music downloading. Sales fell sharply, its share price was undermined, and in 2013 it went into administration.

A classic case of creative destruction was Kodak, which was severely punished for reacting too late to important advances in photographic technology. In the 1990s, it was a very

Table 7.4 New product failure rate by industry

Industry	Percent failure
Chemicals	44%
Other materials	39%
Industrial services	43%
Consumer goods	45%
Consumer services	45%
Capital goods	35%
Healthcare	36%
Software & services	39%
Technology	42%
Average	41%
Highest	45%
Lowest	35%

Source: Castellion and Markham 2013

profitable world leader in the production of traditional cameras, film, and photographic paper. In the first decade of the new century, disruptive digital technology began to wreak havoc on Kodak's business. As sales of digital cameras zoomed, Kodak's sales plummeted. It took until 2003 for Kodak to recognize the problem and embark on a digital strategy. In the process, it closed several factories, cutting tens of thousands of jobs.

Even firms sitting on comfortable monopoly positions can find such positions threatened by new technology. The telecommunications industry is a case in point where national monopolists such as BT, Deutsche Telekom, and France Telecom, who owned networks of telephone lines, found themselves under severe attack from mobile phone companies and from firms using satellite systems.

As in telecommunications, such competition may not arise from within the existing boundaries of an industry. Companies like Amazon, using the Web as a new business model, have made a significant impact on traditional book retailers like Waterstones and Barnes and Noble. Not only does Amazon provide a greater choice of books in its 33 million print and digital titles, it also uses digital technology that permits customers to read excerpts from millions of pages of its titles. In the travel business, one of the most successful areas for e-commerce, the Internet has pitted travel agents and established airlines against online providers in an intense battle to win customers. Online agents such as Expedia and Travelocity have shaken up the travel booking business, while low cost airlines like Ryanair and easyJet have used the Internet to cut the costs of their reservation systems. This has made them even more price competitive, and has forced their established rivals, such as BA, Air France, and Lufthansa, to extend their online reservation service. As a consequence, more and more flights and trips are being booked over the Internet rather than through call centres or high-street travel agents.

The increasing use of ICT has made business more vulnerable to cybercrime, which has been growing exponentially. Electronic crime takes various forms such as fraud, commercial espionage, blackmail, money laundering, and the rigging of gambling on online sites. It can be used to swamp a company's website with external communications. The website either fails completely or slows down to such an extent that service is denied to legitimate customers (see Chapter 4, Mini Case Study Global threats—cybercrime; Chapter 9, The Internet).

R&D—A Guarantee of Success?

Conventional wisdom assumes that company spending on R&D is a good thing, with the implied assumption that it will lead to innovative success. According to this view, the more a company spends on research the better the result is. But Burton Malkiel, an economics professor at Princeton and a company director in the biotechnology industry, described the risks rather colourfully, calling biotechnology a 'crapshoot' and going on to say that, 'Even biotech companies themselves don't know which one is going to make it' (*Financial Times* 3 July 2007).

However, R&D is an input and its impact, like any other input, such as labour and machinery, depends on how efficiently it is deployed. The productivity of R&D expenditure in terms of new products and processes is determined by the quality of the inputs, and those who are managing it. Consequently, there is no automatic correlation between high R&D spending and company performance.

A survey of the world's top 1,000 R&D companies by Jaruzelski and Dehoff (2010) failed to find any significant relationship between R&D spending and business success as measured by growth in sales, profit, the value of the firm on the stock market, or total shareholder return. The top 10 per cent of R&D spenders enjoyed no consistent performance advantage over companies that spent less on R&D. However, the survey did find that companies spending relatively little on R&D significantly underperformed compared with their competitors. Jaruzelski similarly reported in 2013 that business performance of the top R&D spenders did not match that of companies like Apple, with its AppleMac, iPod, iTunes, and iBook, who spent less but were classed as more innovative. Pantagakis et al. (2012) found that the market value of EU computer companies was maximized when they spent 41 per cent of their revenues on R&D. The market value of firms decreased when R&D exceeded that figure.

By contrast, Ehie and Olibe (2010), in a study of nearly 70,000 US firms, found that R&D expenditures had a persistently positive effect on market value for both manufacturing and service firms, with a more pronounced effect on manufacturing.

Protecting Technology

Bill Gates reflects the importance of technology when he claims that, 'it has become imperative for chief executives to have not just a general understanding of the intellectual property issues facing their business and their industry, but to have quite a refined expertise relating to those issues' (*Financial Times* 12 November 2004). The globalization of markets means that firms have to look for protection not just at home but also abroad.

Technology can be so important to company performance that business often spends much time and effort in ensuring that its IP is protected and in pursuing those who infringe it. The external environment offers organizations the possibility of protecting their codifiable technology.

Methods of Protection

In richer countries, the owners of IPRs are normally accorded the protection of the law. Legally, the IP system covers five areas, aims to provide legal protection against counterfeiters and copiers, and is vital in many fields, such as music, film, biotechnology, and nanotechnology, and in consumer goods where branding is important in gaining and retaining competitive advantage.

Patents—a patent can be taken out on inventions. When firms come up with a commercially exploitable idea for a new product, such as the iPod, they will often apply for a patent. Patents can be granted on new inventions for a period of up to 20 years in the UK, Germany, Japan, and the USA.

Designs—designs comprise the characteristics of the product, such as the shape, pattern, and colour, and the law allows companies to prevent others using their designs.

Trade marks—brand names like Perrier or Persil, or logos such as the Nike swish can also be protected. Trade marks comprise any signs capable of being represented graphically, particularly words, designs, letters, numerals, the shape of goods, or of their packaging, provided that such signs are capable of distinguishing the goods or services of one firm from those of other businesses.

Copyright—book publishers, film, television, and music companies can take out a copyright on original literary, dramatic, musical, artistic works, sound recordings, films, and television broadcasts that they have produced and, more controversially, firms can also copyright information on genetic data. So, music by Shakira or Coldplay, and television programmes such as *Game of Thrones* or *Breaking Bad* can be protected, as can cartoon characters such as Disney's Buzz Lightyear and Mickey Mouse.

Industrial espionage—this involves the theft of a firm's secret information, which is normally protected by the law. A striking example of attempted espionage concerned Coca Cola, which treats its product formulae as closely guarded secrets. An employee at its headquarters tried to steal a sample of a secret new product with the intention of selling it to Coke's bitter rival, Pepsi. Pepsi, refusing to take advantage of this, reported the approach to Coke, who called in the police. The employee was charged with unlawfully stealing and selling trade secrets.

WIPO (2013) reports a steady growth in patenting activity particularly in the areas of computer technology, digital communications, nanotechnology, electrical machinery, and energy, especially relating to green technology.

Counterpoint Box 7.2 Patents—a help or hindrance to innovation?

At issue here is the role which patents play in innovation. Those who argue for strong patent protection claim that such protection of IP is essential to promote innovation and investment in new technologies. The monopoly conferred by a patent allows innovators to cover the costs of R&D and obtain an economic return on their investment, which, in turn, provides incentives for more innovation and its commercialization. The result is new and better products and new and more efficient production processes, which help boost productivity, economic growth, and consumer welfare.

On the other hand, it is claimed that, by conferring a monopoly on the holder, patents lead to higher prices, stifle competition, and, consequently, innovation. Stiglitz, in evidence to the Federal Trade Commission hearings on innovation, argued that overly broad patents will deter other firms from pursuing follow-on innovations. They make new entry more difficult and stifle competition. In the same hearings, Heckman stated that most innovations are not new, but build on work done by others, citing the famous quote from Newton that we stand on the shoulders of our predecessors. He felt that firms wanting to improve on the original ideas contained in

the patent rightly saw it as ridiculous to be forced to start from scratch. Opponents of the patent system often raise the argument that inventions would be developed even without a patent system, because there is still a significant competitive advantage from being first-to-market with a new product. Finally, critics also see the system as loaded against developing countries since they, primarily users rather than generators of innovation, have to pay the price. The TRIPS (Trade-Related Agreement on Intellectual Property Rights) agreed at the WTO exacerbates the problem by strengthening patent protection. The World Bank calculated that the increase in technology licensing payments alone would cost poor countries US$45 billion a year.

Sources: Dumont and Holmes 2002; Federal Trade Commission 1996; Chang 2008; Bessen and Meurer 2008

Questions

1. What are the arguments for and against the patenting of software? To help you with your answer research patents online.

Problems in Protecting Technology

Even though rich countries usually provide a degree of legal protection for technology, firms, particularly small and medium-sized enterprises, may still encounter problems in protecting their IPRs.

Cost—the cost of filing a patent can be high and can vary considerably from one country to another. It is, for example, more expensive to obtain patent protection across Europe than in the USA. The EU Commission calculated that obtaining a patent across the EU cost €36,000. However, the unitary patent system, agreed in 2012, reduces the cost to around €5,000, compared with €2,000 in the US and €500 in China

Multiple applications—these must be made in different countries to get legal protection. Patent applications usually have to be translated into the language of the country where the patent is to be registered. Getting highly technical application documents translated into various languages, such as Chinese, Portuguese, Hungarian, and so on, could be a very costly exercise. The EU unitary patent system affords supranational protection for inventions in 25 member states and contributes to translation costs (www.epo.org).

In 2013, the Global Patent Prosecution Highway pilot scheme was announced, giving multinational protection for patents across 30 countries including North America, several European countries, Australia, Japan, and South Korea (WIPO 1 June 2014).

Differing protection periods—in Japan designs are protected for 15 years, but in Germany the period is 20 years. In the USA, owners of copyright are given 95 years, while the period in the EU is 70 years. The situation is further complicated by the situation in some countries, including Australia and Germany, where firms can be granted minor patents that allow them to apply for protection for a shorter time than a full patent.

Application time—the entire procedure from application to grant will generally take more than 12, and in many cases, over 18 months and that time period may be further extended where the law provides for other parties to oppose the granting of the patent.

Enforcement problems—firms may have to pursue infringements through various national courts, which could also be time-consuming and expensive. Once again, the cost can vary country by country. In the US, enforcing a patent through the courts can cost millions of dollars, whereas it is much cheaper in Europe and in countries like China and India. In some countries, the level of legal protection is either low, or non-existent, or the authorities do not enforce the law. China is a particular source of concern in this regard, being seen as the counterfeiting capital of the world and berated regularly by the US authorities for its lax enforcement of IPRs.

While the issues outlined above can pose challenges for big firms, it can make it virtually impossible for poorer small and medium-sized firms to protect their technology. The consequence of all these issues is that the system excludes small businesses because they cannot afford to defend their IP in court.

● CHAPTER SUMMARY

In this chapter we have shown how technology refers to ideas and knowledge that business can exploit commercially. The sources of new ideas on which companies can call are many and varied, ranging from universities and research institutes to competitors, customers and suppliers, and employees.

Globalization and technology make foreign sources of new ideas more accessible and have made it easier for business to tap in to foreign sources through, for example, cross-border R&D partnerships.

Innovations tend to be concentrated in big firms operating in the high-tech manufacturing sector. The rate of innovation varies from firm to firm, sector by sector, and country to country. Firms are motivated to innovate by increasingly fierce competition from rivals, both domestic and foreign, other elements in the supply chain, developments in the ICT sector, and the policies pursued by governments.

Technology offers opportunities to business organizations to increase their profits and growth through the introduction of new and improved goods and services and through changes to their production processes. Technology also helps firms to restructure their global patterns of production through investment in low cost locations or by sub-contracting to cheaper suppliers. However, as we have seen with Kodak, technology can also pose threats and challenges for firms, particularly if they allow themselves to fall behind their competitors. Technological advance, because it involves change in products or production processes, is a risky business, particularly for firms that do not manage change well.

Finally, the external environment offers business the means to protect its IP, although the degree and cost of protection can vary significantly from one country to another. In countries like China and some other South East Asian countries, where the level of protection is low, there are significant problems with the theft of IPRs, the counterfeiting of goods, and the piracy of films, music, and books. Attempts to provide protection internationally have been slow to progress and are relatively underdeveloped. Industries and firms differ to the extent to which they protect their IP, with companies in the IT and electronic sectors having a high propensity to protect their technology compared with firms in the car industry.

● REVIEW QUESTIONS

1. Review your understanding of the following terms:
    a. technological advance;
    b. applied research;
    c. innovation;
    d. technological diffusion;
    e. intellectual property.

2. Discuss how multinational companies could contribute to the international diffusion of technology. Illustrate your answer with examples.

3. Explain why innovation is important for big firms in the consumer electronics/pharmaceutical industry.

● ASSIGNMENT TASKS

1. It is claimed that big data can generate lots of benefits for business.
    a) What is big data?
    b) Explain how mobile telecoms companies like China Telecom are in a strong position to benefit from big data. Illustrate your answer with examples.
    c) Explain how Wal-Mart, the world's biggest retailer, takes advantage of big data.

d) Discuss the issues around privacy faced by mobile firms or Wal-Mart and how they might deal with them.

2. Analyse Nokia's performance in mobile handsets after 2008. Assess whether Nokia is an illustration of Schumpeter's concept of creative destruction.

Case Study Apple and technology

Apple, the giant US multinational, designs, manufactures, and markets mobile communication and media devices, personal computers, and portable digital music players, and sells related software and services. In 2013, it was the world's most valuable brand (Forbes 11 June 2013). In mid-2014, it had a market value of $564 billion (YCHARTS 1 July 2014) and employed over 80,000 workers.

Apple is seen by many as a brilliant technological pioneer. An IT journalist put it thus:

> While all the other technology firms were churning out products with all the wow factor of a tumble dryer, Apple set out to change the world with innovative computers and gadgets, again and again and again . . . Apple products have revolutionized the way we work and play and listen to music (techradar.computing 10 March 2013).

He illustrated his claim by indicating 10 ways in which Apple had changed the world, giving examples such as the iMac first introduced in 1998, iPhone (2007), iPod + iTunes (2003), iPad (2010), and the Apps Store (2008). In 2007 the iPhone and iPod Touch featured the company's new mobile

Source: apple.com.

operating system, iOS, including a multi-touch screen and virtual keyboard. Mazzucato (2013) refers to the 'visionary products' conceived and marketed by Steve Jobs, the founder of Apple, and says that its products have altered the competitive landscape.

Table 7.5 shows Apple's performance since the turn of the century.

Table 7.5 Apple performance 1999–2013

	1999	2001	2003	2005	2007	2009	2012	2013
Global sales ($m)	6,134	5,363	6,207	13,931	24,006	36,537	156,508	170,910
Net income ($m)	601	−25	69	1,335	3,495	5,704	41,733	37,037
R&D/sales (%)	5.12	8.02	7.59	3.83	3.26	3.65	2.00	3.00
iPod unit sales (m)	n/a	n/a	0.939	51,630	22,487	54,132	35,165	26,379
iPhone unit sales (m)	n/a	n/a	n/a	n/a	1,389	20,731	125,046	150,257
iPad unit sales (m)	n/a	n/a	n/a	n/a	n/a	n/a	58,310	71,033
Mac unit sales (m)	3,448	3,087	3,012	4,534	7,051	10,396	18,158	16,341

Sources: Apple SEC 10-K filings

→

With the exception of one year, 2001, Apple has seen dramatic rates of growth in global sales and net income over the period.

However, it has not been all plain sailing for Apple. Figures for the last quarter of 2013 show that Apple was losing market share in Europe, USA, Latin America, China, and Japan to Android, its main competitor in smartphone operating systems that was developed by Google. In Europe, Android held 69 per cent of the market against Apple's 19 per cent. Nonetheless, it retained strong positions in Japan with nearly 70 per cent of the market and 44 per cent in the USA.

Apple sees itself as operating in highly competitive global markets characterized by aggressive price cutting and downward pressure on gross margins, frequent introduction of new products, short product life cycles, changing industry standards, continual improvement in product price/performance characteristics, rapid adoption of technological and product advancements by competitors, and price sensitivity on the part of consumers.

To be competitive, Apple needs to develop and market innovative new hardware, software, and service technologies. As a result, it claims to give great importance to investment in R&D and to the need to protect its IP with numerous patents, copyrights, and trade marks, and also through litigation against rivals both in the US and internationally. In 2013, Apple held 6,462 patents in the US.

There is an apparent paradox here because Apple does not spend as much as some of its main competitors on R&D. While Apple spent around 2 per cent of sales revenue in 2012, the figure for Google was 13.1 per cent and for China's Huawei almost one-quarter (see Table 7.6). Nevertheless, Apple is still seen by some as the world's most innovative company (www.strategyand.pwc.com/global/home/what-we-think/multimedia/video/mm-video_display/global-Innovation-1000-2013).

Mazzucato (2013) argues that Apple would not have been a global success without the investment and intervention of governments. In support of her claim, she points to the equity investment put in by a US federal agency in the early stages of Apple's development. Second, she highlights Apple's access to technology resulting from government research programmes in publicly funded institutions—the iPod, with its tiny but enormous capacity hard drives, owes its existence to the invention by two European research scientists of giant magnetoresistance (GMR). She claims that this allowed Apple to take on Sony and to recover from a long period of stagnant growth. Multi-touch

Table 7.6 R&D expenditure as percentage of sales revenue, 2012

Huawei (China)	23
Ericsson (Sweden)	14.6
Microsoft (US)	13.4
Nokia (Finland)*	13.8
Google (US)	13.1
HTC (Taiwan)	5.4
Samsung (South Korea)	4.3
HP (US)	2.8
Apple (US)	2.2
Dell (US)	1.9

Source: European Commission (2013) 'The 2013 EU Industrial R&D Scoreboard'
*Microsoft acquired Nokia's handset division in 2014

screens were developed at the publicly funded University of Delaware. Mazzucato also identifies military projects and state purchases of goods and services as being important factors in Apple's success. Lastly, she says that the US government played a critical role in protecting the IP of US tech companies against foreign violations and in ensuring their access to foreign consumer markets. Mazzucato concludes that Apple's success is mainly because of its ability to:

> ride the wave of massive State investments in the 'revolutionary' technologies that underpinned the iPhone, and iPad: the Internet, GPS, touch-screen displays and communication technologies (2013: 88).

Sources: Mazzucato 2013; EU Commission 2013; www.kantarworldpanel.com 27 January 2014; Apple SEC 10-K filings; www.uspto.gov.

Questions
1.
   a) Chart Apple's performance in terms of growth rates in sales and net income between 1999 and 2013.
   b) Now call up Apple's subsequent SEC 10-K filings. Compare Apple's subsequent growth with previous growth rates.
2. Discuss the unit sales performance of the:
   a. Mac;
   b. iPod;

c. iPhone;
d. iPad.

3. Compare Apple's spending on R&D with its competitors. In the light of your comparison, give some explanations for Apple's success.

4. Assess Apple's iOS smartphone system performance against Android.

5. Why is Apple's IP so important to the company?

6. Apple, like many of its competitors, uses litigation like a tool of competition. Research the litigation between Apple and Motorola, owned by Google. What was the issue at stake and the outcome? See: Apple Inc. v. Motorola, Inc. at the Justia US Law website; and the case at: http://docs.justia.com/cases/federal/appellate-courts/cafc/12-1548/12-1548-2014-04-25.pdf.

7. Discuss the importance of the State to companies like Apple.

● FURTHER READING

Anderson shows how the Web helps create new markets and small firms to survive and prosper.

● Anderson, C. (2009) *The Long Tail: How Endless Choice is Creating Unlimited Demand.* London: Random House.

Edgerton analyses the importance of technology to twentieth-century society at the global level.

● Edgerton, D. (2007) *The Shock of the Old: Technology in Global History Since 1900.* London: Profile Books.

Tidd and Bessant advise business how to manage the innovation process.

● Tidd, J. and Bessant, J. (2011) *Managing Innovation; Integrating Technological, Market and Organizational Change,* 4th edn. Chichester: John Wiley and Sons.

Siegel and Davenport look at how big data can help business predict human behaviour.

● Siegel, E. and Davenport, T. (2013) *Predictive Analytics: The Power to Predict who will Click, Lie, Buy, or Die.* Hoboken: John Wiley and Sons.

● REFERENCES

Autor, D. and Dorn, D. (2013) 'The Growth of Low Skill Service Jobs and the Polarization of the US Labor Market'. *American Economic Review* 103(5).

Bessen, J. and Meurer, M.J. (2009) *Patent Failure: How Judges, Bureaucrats, and Lawyers Put Innovators at Risk.* Princeton: Princeton University Press.

Brynjolfsson, E. and McAfee, A. (2011). *Race Against the Machine: How the Digital Revolution is Accelerating Innovation, Driving Productivity, and Irreversibly Transforming Employment and the Economy.* Lexington: Digital Frontier Press.

Castellion, G. and Markham, S.K. (2013) 'Perspective: New Product Failure Rates: Influence of *Argumentum ad Populum* and Self-Interest'. *Journal of Product Innovation Management* 30(5).

Chang, H.-J. (2008) *The Myth of Free Trade and the Secret History of Capitalism.* London: Bloomsbury Press.

Dachs, B. and Zahradnik, G. (2014) 'R&D Internationalisation during the Global Crisis'. *Vox 6* July 2014. Available at: www.voxeu.org/article/rd-internationalisation-during-global-crisis.

Department for Business, Innovation & Skills (2014) *Innovation Report 2014: Innovation, Research and Growth,* March.

Dumont, B. and Holmes, P. (2002) 'The Scope of Intellectual Property Rights and their Interface with Competition Law: Divergent Paths to the Same Goal?'. *Economics of Innovation and New Technology* 11(2).

Ehie, I. and Olibe, K. (2010) 'The Effect of R&D Investment on Firm Value: An Examination of US Manufacturing and Service Industries'. *International Journal of Production Economics*, 128(1).

EU Commission (2010) 'Lisbon Strategy Evaluation Document SEC (2010) 114 final'.

EU Commission (2013) 'The 2013 EU Industrial R&D Scoreboard'.

Federal Trade Commission (1996) 'Selected Themes from the FTC'S Hearings on Global and Innovation-Based Competition'. The 1996 Antitrust Conference: Antitrust Issues in Today's Economy, 7 March.

Frey, C.B. and Osborne, M.A. (2013) 'The Future of Employment: How Susceptible are Jobs to Computerisation?'. Available at: www.oxfordmartin. ox.ac.uk.

Hayashi, A.M. (2013) 'Thriving in a Big Data World'. *MITSloan Management Review* Winter 2014. Available at: http://sloanreview.mit.edu/article/thriving-in-a-big-data-world/.

Held, D., McGrew, A., Goldblatt, D., Perraton, J. (1999) *Global Transformations: Politics, Economics and Culture*. Stanford: Stanford University Press.

Jaruzelski, B. and Dehoff, D. (2010) 'The Global Innovation 1000: How the Top Innovators Keep Winning'. *Strategy + Business* 61 (Winter).

Jaruzelski, B. (2013) 'The Global Innovation 1000: Navigating the Digital Future'. *Strategy + Business* 73 (Winter).

Kotler, P. and Caslione, J.A. (2009) *Chaotics: The Business of Managing and Marketing in the Age of Turbulence*. New York: Amacom.

Mayer-Schönberger, V. and Cukier, K. (2013) *Big Data: A Revolution that will Transform how we Live*. London: John Murray.

Mazzucato, M. (2013) *The Entrepreneurial State*. London: Anthem Press.

McKinsey Global Research Institute (2013) 'Organizing for Change Through Social Technologies: McKinsey Global Survey Results', November. Available at: http://www. mckinsey.com/insights/high_tech_telecoms_internet/ organizing_for_change_through_social_technologies_ mckinsey_global_survey_results.

McKinsey Global Research Institute (2013a) 'Open Data: Unlocking Innovation and Performance with Liquid Information, October. Available at: http://www. mckinsey.com/insights/business_technology/open_ data_unlocking_innovation_and_performance_with_ liquid_information.

OECD (2012) 'Science, Technology and Industry Outlook 2012: Recent Trends in the Internationalisation of R&D in the Enterprise Sector'. Special Session on Globalization, 13 March.

O'Reilly, T. (2005) 'What is Web 2.0: Design Patterns and Business Models for the Next Generation of Software', 30 September. Available at: http://oreilly.com/web2/ archive/what-is-web-20.html.

Pantagakis, E., Terzakis, D., and Arvanitis, S. (2012) 'R&D Investments and Firm Performance: An Empirical Investigation of the High Technology Sector (Software and Hardware) in the EU'. Working Paper, University of Crete, 21 November.

Porter, M.E. (1998) *The Competitive Advantage of Nations*. Basingstoke: Palgrave MacMillan.

Schumpeter, J.A. (1976) *Capitalism, Socialism & Democracy*. London: Routledge.

US Patent and Trademark Office (2014) 'Technology Assessment and Forecast Report'. http://www.uspto.gov/.

WIPO (2013) 'World Intellectual Property Indicators, 2013 Edition'. Available at: http://www.wipo.int/ipstats/en/ wipi/.

Wonglimpiyarat, J. (2005) 'The Nano-Revolution of Schumpeter's Kondratieff Cycle'. *Technovation* 25(11).

CHAPTER EIGHT

The Political Environment

LEARNING OUTCOMES

This chapter will enable you to:

- **Identify and explain the functions performed by the institutions of the state**

- **Analyse the characteristics of different political systems and understand their importance for business**

- **Evaluate the arguments regarding the demise of the nation state**

- **Assess the importance of the state for business**

- **Analyse how business can influence the state**

Case Study Intelligence agencies and industrial espionage

In 2013, Edward Snowden, a former employee contracted to work for the US government's National Security Agency (NSA) disclosed 1.7 million top-secret NSA documents revealing that global surveillance was being carried out by the NSA with intelligence agencies in four other countries: the UK with the involvement of GCHQ, Australia, Canada, and New Zealand.

It was alleged that the NSA was ordering technology firms to hand over customer telephone and Internet records and directly accessing the servers of big US technology companies: Google, Apple, Microsoft, Facebook, AOL, PalTalk, and Yahoo. The NSA encouraged technology companies to allow it secret access to their commercially available, supposedly secure products. It emerged that several major telecoms companies had given GCHQ unlimited access to their network of undersea cables.

It also appeared that the NSA and GCHQ were cracking the encryption technology that underpins the safety and security of the Internet, protecting e-mails, banking, commercial transactions, and company records. The result was that telephones, smartphones, email, texts, social media, laptops, PCs, and tablets could all be accessed by the security services. The top-secret documents revealed that surveillance targets included the EU's competition commissioner in charge of important antitrust cases including one involving Google. The commissioner has access to highly confidential commercial information: he is charged with breaking up cartels, approving mergers, and imposing fines on those who break the bloc's antitrust rules. In other prominent cases involving US companies, the commissioner blocked the NYSE's planned takeover of Deutsche Börse and UPS's bid for TNT.

It also emerged that the e-mails and phone calls of the large state-controlled Brazilian energy multinational, Petrobras, had also been hacked by the NSA, much to the fury of the Brazilian president. Snowden claimed that the NSA also carried out industrial espionage citing the giant German multinational, Siemens, as a particular target. According to Snowden, money was set aside to spy on other countries' adherence to trade agreements. It also transpired that political leaders were being bugged. Angela Merkel, Germany's Chancellor, discovered that her mobile was being monitored by the NSA.

Source: © ER_Creative / istockphoto.com

Implications for Business

The revelations had serious implications for the business community. One fear of non-US companies was that the NSA was passing on their business secrets to US competitors. An expert panel, appointed by the White House, warned that forcing US firms such as Google, Microsoft, ISPs, and telecoms companies to hand over business records or compelling them to allow the NSA to access their servers, allowing it to intercept communications, could have a serious impact on these companies. It threatened their ability to guarantee the privacy of their international customers, which could cause them to lose their share of the world's communications market.

The panel pointed out that the cloud computing market was expanding rapidly and was expected to more than double in size to $207 billion annually between 2012 and 2017. US companies dominating the cloud, like Google, Microsoft, and Amazon, would find it difficult to retain existing customers and recruit new ones to maintain market share.

In contrast, Neelie Kroes, the EU commissioner for digital affairs, saw the furore as an opportunity for EU companies to take business in the cloud computing market from US firms.

The world's leading technology companies have united to demand sweeping changes to US surveillance laws, urging an international ban on bulk collection of data to help preserve public trust in the Internet. AOL, Twitter, Yahoo, Microsoft, Facebook, Google, Apple, and LinkedIn called for reforms, saying that: 'The balance in many countries has tipped too far in favour of the state and away from the rights of the individual'. They blamed spy agencies for the resulting threat to their business →

→ interests. The eight technology companies also hinted at new fears, particularly that national responses to the Snowden revelations would not only damage their commercial interests, but also lead to a balkanization of the Web as governments try to prevent Internet companies from escaping overseas.

The companies argued that, '[t]he ability of data to flow or be accessed across borders is essential to a robust, 21st century, global economy'. 'Governments should permit the transfer of data and should not inhibit access by companies or individuals to lawfully available information that is stored outside of the country. Governments should not require service providers to locate infrastructure within a country's borders or operate locally"' (*The Guardian* 9 December 2013).

Microsoft, Yahoo, Facebook, and LinkedIn filed legal motions seeking permission to publish details about the government orders. The US responded by allowing the companies to disclose details about orders compelling them to give the government e-mails and other Internet data about their users.

Vodafone, the world's second largest mobile phone company with operations in 25 countries, also expressed deep concern: 'We want all of our customers worldwide to feel they are at liberty to communicate with each other as they see fit. We want our networks to be big and busy with people who are confident they can communicate with each other freely; anything that inhibits that is very bad for any commercial operator' (*The Guardian* 16 January 2014). '...this is anathema because our whole business is founded on protecting privacy as a fundamental imperative' (*The Guardian* 17 January 2014).

Sources: Greenwald 2014; *Financial Times* 15 June 2013; *The Guardian* 9 December 2013, 16,17, 27 January 2014; *The Guardian* and *Financial Times* 21 December 2013; Report and Recommendations of the President's Review; *The Guardian* 'The Snowden Files' 5 June 2013; Group on Intelligence and Communications Technologies 2013; Bloomberg 9 September 2013, 27 January 2014.

Introduction

> Few relationships are as critical to the business enterprise itself as the relationship to government. The manager has responsibility for this relationship as part of his responsibility to the enterprise itself (Drucker 1999: 283).

This quote from Drucker, seen by some as the inventor of modern management, indicates the importance of the political environment to business. It is no surprise, in the light of Drucker's comment, that firms spend so much time and money trying to influence governments and politicians like Barack Obama, David Cameron, Angela Merkel, Li Keqiang of China, Vladimir Putin, and India's Narendra Modi. They are major decision-makers in a powerful entity called the state. Knowledge of where decision-making power lies in the state is very important for business, whether that be a firm wishing to influence the process of formulating laws or regulations, or to get permission to drill for oil, or a contract for building roads and airports.

The political environment has major implications for both the macro- and microenvironments of business. State institutions establish and enforce the legal and regulatory framework within which business operates. They can have a significant influence on a whole range of business decisions. As we have seen in the opening case study, they can stop firms doing what they want to do or force them to do things they do not want to do, for example, by forcing technology firms to hand over customers' communication records.

The political environment is significant for business because the decisions emanating from it can generate important opportunities for firms and also pose significant threats, not only domestically but also abroad. The ability of the state to wage wars, pursue diplomacy, agree treaties and alliances, establish policies as regards migration, taxation, interest rates, the exchange rate, the balance of payments, inflation, education, health, the environment, maintaining law

and order, and guaranteeing the right to buy and sell private property all have important implications for business.

As globalization proceeds, business increasingly finds itself affected by political events outside its home base. It is important that firms build up an understanding of the diverse nature
of different political systems and how they operate. This knowledge will make it easier for
business to grasp better the opportunities the systems provide as well as coping with the challenges they pose.

In this chapter, we examine the different types of political system, the size of the state, and
how it has grown. We also consider the impact the political environment can have on business
and, in the final section, we look at how firms go about influencing their political environment.

What is the Political Environment?

An important entity in the political environment is the nation state where political parties fight
elections, form governments, and make laws and enforce them. National governments are
indeed an important part of the political environment, but they are only one element of a much
broader concept called the state. As you will see later, the state comprises institutions such as the
civil service and the judiciary as well as governments. Governments come and go, but the other
elements of the state tend to be more permanent. Basically, the political environment is made up
of those institutions which make political decisions and implement them. The political environment not only comprises institutions operating at the national level, but also, as we will see,
bodies at local, regional, and supranational (above the nation state) levels.

The Institutions of the State

The core of the state can be seen as a set of institutions having the legal power, ultimately backed
up by coercion (the power to make people do or stop doing things), to make decisions in matters
of government over a specific geographical area and over the population living there. The state
comprises the following institutions:

- The **legislative branch**, which includes those institutions that make the laws, e.g. Parliament in the UK, Congress in the USA and Brazil, the Diet in Japan. An important role in
  such bodies is played by the leading politician—the President in the USA, France, and
  Russia, the Prime Minister in the UK, Japan, Italy, and Spain, and the Chancellor in
  Germany—along with cabinet members, ministers, and senior civil servants because
  they determine and direct government policy.

Parliaments pass policies, laws, and regulations, which are then implemented by the executive
branch. The EU Parliament is an example of a legislative body but at the supranational level (see
Mini Case Study EU institutions and decision-making).

- The **executive branch** puts the laws into effect and ensures the desired outcomes.
  It gives policy advice to government ministers. This branch includes administrative bodies, such as the civil service in the UK and the European Commission in the

EU—uniquely, the Commission has the power to initiate policy. Regulatory agencies, which operate, to an extent, separately from central government, also form part of the executive branch. Examples include the Federal Communications Commission in the USA, the Office of the Communications Regulator (OFCOM) in the UK, and NERSA the energy regulator in South Africa. In Britain, they are known as Quasi Autonomous Non-Governmental Organizations, often referred to as Quangos. In developed countries, the executive branch is usually large, running to thousands of people. Heads of government, such as the US President or the British Prime Minister, are commonly the chief executive of this branch.

• The judicial branch interprets and applies the laws—this branch comprises the judiciary, the police, and the armed forces, which give the state its capacity to enforce the laws that it makes. Businesses operating in the geographical area are required to accept that the state has the authority to make decisions and to maintain order. If they are not prepared to accept this authority then the state can try to compel them to do so through the judicial system of police, courts, and prisons. At the EU level, the Court of First Instance and the European Court of Justice (ECJ) interpret and apply the laws of the Union (for more discussion of EU law see Chapter 9, European Union).

Mini Case Study EU institutions and decision-making

This case study identifies and explains the decision-making power of institutions in the EU. Various institutions participate in EU decision-making. The most important are:

• the **European Commission**: this is the civil service of the EU with powers that are wide and varied. It is the only institution having the power to initiate laws and is responsible for enforcing them. It negotiates international treaties on behalf of the EU as well as the entry of new members. It is headed by a president and a number of commissioners, each with responsibility for a particular area such as the internal market, trade, and transport. While the Commission proposes new legislation, it is up to the Council of the European Union and the Parliament whether those proposals become law. The Commission seeks to uphold the interest of the EU as a whole.

• the **Council of the European Union**: this represents individual member states and comprises ministers from national governments. It meets on a regular basis and is arguably the most important decision-making institution. It plays a vital role in the development of EU law. It has to approve all laws and budget proposals, but cannot make new laws on its own. It must get the agreement of the Parliament. The Council has the power to sign international agreements with non-EU countries.

Each country's voting power in the Council is based on its population size, with the smaller, less populous countries, like Malta and Cyprus, being given more votes than their population would warrant. In some areas, such as common foreign and security policy, taxation, asylum, and immigration policy, Council decisions have to be unanimous. In other words, each member state has the power to veto any new proposals in these areas. On most issues, however, the Council takes decisions by qualified majority voting (QMV). QMV requires around three-quarters of the votes to be cast in favour of a proposal. In addition, a member state may ask for confirmation that the votes in favour represent at least 62 per cent of the total population of the Union. If this is found not to be the case, the decision will not be adopted.

• the **European Parliament** (EP): this is made up of representatives elected by the citizens of each member state. Each member state has a number of seats allocated on the basis of the size of its population. The EP does not have the same powers as national parliaments. For example, it cannot propose new laws nor has it the power to legislate on matters of taxation, agricultural policy, or industrial policy. Instead, it can only discuss and vote on laws proposed by the Commission. In order for a new EU law to pass, it has to have the support of both the Parliament and the Council of the European Union. The EP also has the power to accept or reject Commissioners and to sack the entire Commission through a vote of censure.

There are two other important institutions. The first is the European Council. This brings together the heads of government and the Commission President four times a year. They map out the overall direction of the Union, for example regarding enlargement, and deal with issues that have not been resolved because of their contentious nature, such as the size of the budget and how it is to be spent. It decides who will be President of the Commission. Like the Commission, the Council also has a President. Under the Lisbon Treaty, a politician will be chosen to be President of the European Council for 2.5 years.

The second institution is the ECJ. The Court upholds EU law and, in EU matters, is the highest court in all of the member states. It arbitrates between member states, institutions, and individuals in cases relating to EU law. There is no right of appeal against ECJ judgments.

Sources: Europa, European institutions, and other bodies; available at: http://europa.eu; www.civitas.org.uk

Questions

1. In 2014, the ECJ ruled that, under EU data protection law, individuals have the 'right to be forgotten' by search engines like Google.
   a) Explain what is meant by the 'right to be forgotten'.
   b) Discuss the implications of the Court's ruling for search engines like Google and Bing.

Learning Task

This task lets you review your understanding of the different branches of the state. Allocate the following people to the appropriate branch of the state.

	Legislative	Executive	Judicial
Premier of China			
The Cabinet Secretary (UK)			
President of the EU Commission			
The Chief of Police			
Chief Executive of Google			
Supreme Court judge in the USA			
Governor of the Punjab			
Commander of the armed forces			
The Queen of the United Kingdom			

Different Political Systems

We start off by considering the political environment at the level of the nation state. If we take membership of the United Nations (UN) as an indicator of the number of independent countries in the world, then there are 193. These nations operate under a variety of political systems, but in each of them a national government exercises the right to make laws and to ensure that they are enforced in society. In some countries, power is concentrated in the hands of one or a few people while, in others, power is spread over a large number of different groups.

No two countries have identical political regimes. We examine four different types of political system, liberal democracy, authoritarian and absolutist, communist, and theocratic. You will see that, in the real world, these regimes sometimes do not exist in their pure form. Subsequently, we go on to look at the differences between unitary states and federal states.

Liberal Democracy

There are two main characteristics of liberal democracies. The first is the right of citizens to elect governments to represent their interests. The second is the right to individual freedom. More specifically, such societies comprise:

- Governmental institutions based on majority rule, with members drawn from a variety of political parties winning their positions through free elections. This occurs, for example, in the countries of Western Europe, North America, Latin American countries such as Argentina and Brazil, and Asian countries like India and Japan where voters have the choice of candidates from several political parties. The party that wins the majority of votes or seats usually becomes the party of government.

- State institutions, which are constrained in their powers by other institutions. In the USA, this is reflected in the separation of powers among different bodies. Power and responsibility is divided between the President, the Congress, the executive, and the judges. Each acts as a check and a balance on the others in the exercise of power. So, the President may wish the USA to implement measures to deal with climate change—for example, in 2014, President Barack Obama wanted to implement an action plan to cut emissions from new power plants, but he had to get the approval of Congress to do so.

- Governments that are accountable to the electorate. This means that citizens can vote governments out of office if they do not like what they are doing. In the UK, India, South Africa, and Japan, the electorate have the opportunity to do this in national elections that are held every four or five years.

- The right to personal freedom and to express views freely. In liberal democracies, television, radio, and the press are not under the sole control of the state, so a range of views can be expressed. There is also the right to assembly, which means that people can gather peacefully and demonstrate to make their views known. These rights are guaranteed by an independent judiciary.

- A permanent, skilled, and impartial public service, for example, the civil service, responsible to the government and through it to the electorate.

Mini Case Study **Mexico**

Mexico is the second largest economy in Latin America. It is an emerging economy with a population of 121 million and income per head of around $10,000. It is a federal republic comprising 31 states. For 70 years, up to 2000, it was governed by a single party, the PRI. According to the historian, Enrique Krauze, it was an oligarchy, not a democracy. For him, Mexico now has the characteristics of a liberal democracy to a 'great degree' (*The World Post* 23 January 2013).

Three main political parties, PRI, PRD, and PAN, compete every six years for power, with the latter breaking the PRI monopoly of power in 2000. There is universal suffrage, the president is constrained in his powers by the constitution, congress is independent, and trade unions are no longer subservient to the president.

On the down side, the press is not free, ranking 153 out of 179 countries in the Press Freedom Index 2013, which notes that censorship during the 2012 elections, when the PRI regained power, was high. Journalists are subject to violence, particularly from drug cartels, and political parties are linked with these cartels. A US academic overheard representatives of the three main parties discussing the differing ways they used money from the cartels, one claiming that it was for voter education (TakePart 7 April 2014). At the state level, Frontera NorteSur reported that organized crime had overtaken state power in Michoacán (20 January 2014). Billions of dollars of drug money flow over the border from the US funding the activities of the drugs cartels.

The Economist talks about 'the murky relationship between politics and justice in Mexico' (5 April 2014). The World Economic Forum (2014) scores Mexico eighty-eighth out of 144 countries as regards judicial independence. It also cites corruption and inefficient government bureaucracy as two of the main problems of doing business. Corruption is endemic and pervasive, according to the Heritage Foundation, influencing the judicial system and bolstering the power of party bosses, monopolistic businesses and criminals—of 177 countries, Mexico ranks 106 in the corruption league table (www.heritage.org; Transparency International 2014). Mexico also rates poorly on favouritism in government decisions and reliability of police services, but scores better on protection of property and intellectual assets (World Economic Forum 2014).

Sources: CIA World Factbook 2014 www.cia.gov/library/publications/the-world-factbook/docs/didyouknow.html; Reporters without Borders 2013 http://en.rsf.org/press-freedom-index-2013,1054.html; TakePart www.takepart.com/article/2014/04/07/mexico; World Economic Forum 2014 http://www.weforum.org/events/world-economic-forum-annual-meeting-2014; Transparency International 2014, Corruption Perceptions Index 2013 http://cpi.transparency.org/cpi2013/

Questions

1. Why can Mexico be seen as a flawed liberal democracy?

- Most liberal democracies operate a mixed economy. That is true whether one looks at the countries of North America and Europe, and nations such as Argentina, India, South Africa, and Japan. In these nations, the majority of economic activity is carried out in the private sector with business and the consumer having the freedom to buy and sell goods and services. However, the state can also play an important economic role through taxation and public expenditure and ownership of, or significant shareholdings in, certain industries. It can also limit the freedom of business to trade and to make profit through the laws and regulations that it passes.

Of the 193 nations in the UN, it seems that less than half are full liberal democracies. Liberal democracy is more likely to be found in rich, politically stable countries such as those in North America and in Northern and Western Europe and in Japan. This is obviously of interest to business because stability and prosperity make liberal democratic economies and their markets very attractive for business. It is therefore no surprise to find that the vast bulk of trade and foreign investment takes place among liberal democracies. Liberal democracy is found less often in countries with a low level of income per head of population. Such countries frequently experience political instability and this can be a deterrent to business getting involved in their economies. While there are countries that are clearly liberal democracies, there are others, like Egypt, that are moving, sometimes rather unsteadily, towards it.

Authoritarian and Absolutist Systems

A relatively small number of countries operate under authoritarian or absolutist regimes. These are forms of government in which one person or a group of people exercise power unrestrained by laws or opposition. These countries are usually characterized by:

- restrictions on the activities of political parties. It may be that only one political party is allowed to operate, which gives total support to the ruler. Such is the case in China and Cuba;
- the state headed by one or several people who have unbridled power to make decisions;
- an absence of checks and balances on the power of the ruler. In Saudi Arabia, the royal family holds power with little constraint from parliament or the judiciary;
- a system where support for the ruler is based on patronage. Patronage, or Clientelism, as it is sometimes called, occurs where favours are doled out in return for political support. Such favours can take a variety of forms such as money, jobs in government offices, or public contracts. Alternatively, the system could be based on inheritance where power and privilege is passed on from one member of the ruling family to another—once again, Saudi Arabia is a good example of this. Saudi law declares the country to be a monarchy ruled by the sons and grandsons of King Abd Al Aziz Al Saud, so when King Fahd died in 2005, his crown passed to his half-brother, Abdullah.

Of course, patronage is not confined to authoritarian and absolutist regimes. It also occurs in some liberal democracies. In the USA, the slang expression 'pork barrel politics' is often used to describe members of Congress lobbying to get publicly funded projects that bring money and jobs to their own districts. In Italy, there has been a history of Christian Democrat governments distributing state jobs, tax relief, and preferential pension treatment to blocs of reliable supporters.

Countries operating under authoritarian or absolutist regimes only constitute a small proportion of the world's population and income. Thus, as far as business is concerned, their markets are not that important. However, firms may be interested in producing goods and services in these countries because resources like labour are often cheap. And for some primary sector industries, a number of these countries are vital because they are rich in natural resources. For example, several countries in the Middle East are sitting on vast reserves of oil. Saudi Arabia is the world's single largest oil producer and has, by far, the biggest oil reserves. This makes it attractive to the big multinational oil companies such as Exxon, Shell, and BP. Oil companies need to be aware of the identity of those exercising power in these nations. Such knowledge is invaluable for these companies because it indicates where they need to apply influence when, for example, they are trying to obtain permission to drill for oil (for more on the oil industry and its political environment see Chapter 4, Political and Legal Environment).

Communist Regimes

Communist regimes tend to have the following characteristics:

- The production of most goods and services is owned and controlled by the state. In China, even though companies such as VW and General Motors have been allowed to invest there, the state continues to exercise a very significant degree of economic control over what is produced, how much is produced, where it is produced, and who will produce it. The system is dominated by one political party. Vietnam is another example of a one-party state where the Communist Party has tight control of the political system.

- In addition to controlling the economy, the Party controls the legislative, executive, and judicial branches of the state as well as trade unions and the media. In North Korea, for example, the Communist Party controls television and the press. (Chapter 7 discusses some of the difficulties confronted by firms like Google in dealings with the Chinese political and legal system.)

Unlike liberal democracies, communist regimes do not value so highly the right to personal freedoms. They put more emphasis on meeting the needs of society as a whole. Examples include China, Vietnam, and Cuba.

Counterpoint Box 8.1 Liberal democracy—global convergence?

There is a debate as to whether liberal democracy will become the world's predominant political system. Commentators such as Fukuyama (1993) argue that when a country gets past a certain level of economic development the citizens will increasingly demand democratic participation and democratic political institutions. Others disagree, seeing increasing rivalry between liberal democracy and authoritarian states like China and Russia.

Wright (2006) found that public demands for democracy in China fell as the economy prospered. Deng and Kennedy (2010) also refute the idea that China's capitalist transition is generating pressure for democratization from business. However, Reinicki (2013) sees the continuance of the Chinese model not as a sign of strength but more as a reflection of the weakness of its major competitor, liberal democracy, wracked as it is by crises of increasing inequality, poverty, and the environment. These, along with the global financial crisis, have undermined civil society's faith in the ability of liberal democracies to deliver sustainable social and economic benefits. He also sees Western liberal democracies adopting elements of the Chinese model in their massive intervention to bail out the banks and their imposition of non-elected officials to head up heavily indebted Italy and Greece.

Deudney and Ikenberry (2009) claim that internal pressures in autocratic countries like China will cause them to move towards liberal democracy. These include the growth of a middle class with a growing interest in political accountability; high levels of inequality, illustrated by the many landless peasants, marginalized migrants, and underpaid workers, leading to the rise of political parties to represent their cause; and undemocratic systems being prone to pursue bad policies will consequently face challenges to their political legitimacy. They accept that China and Russia are not liberal democracies, but assert that they are now much more liberal and democratic than ever before.

Sources: Fukuyama 1993; Wright 2006; Reinicki 2013; Deudney and Ikenberry 2009

Questions

1. In the discussion of liberal democracy, we highlighted six characteristics of the system. Using as many of those characteristics as possible, assess the extent, if any, to which China, Russia, Vietnam or Cuba are moving towards becoming liberal democracies.

The political system operating in China does not apply in Hong Kong. When Britain handed the colony over to China in 1997, the Chinese authorities agreed to an arrangement under which the territory was granted more freedoms and democracy than the mainland. That is why China is described as being 'one-nation, two-systems'. While the mainland is communist, Hong Kong is seen by some as a glittering showpiece of capitalism.

Theocratic Regimes

In theocratic regimes:

- religion or faith plays a dominant role in the government;
- the rulers in government are normally the same people who lead the dominant religion;
- policies pursued by government are either identical with, or strongly influenced by, the principles of the majority religion, and, typically, the government claims to rule on behalf of God or a higher power, as specified by the local religion.

There are no more than a handful of theocratic states. Iran is one example of a theocratic regime where the political process is heavily influenced by Islam. The policies of the Islamic political parties are founded on the Koran, and the ayatollahs and mullahs, the religious leaders, are very influential in the formulation of policies. They, along with Islamic lawyers, sit on a council that has the power of veto over laws proposed by parliament. A priority in Iran is to resist what is seen as the corruption inherent in Western materialism, which makes it difficult for big Western MNCs to operate there given that they are seen as the agents of the materialist culture.

The Vatican City is another example of theocracy. It is an independent sovereign state with the Pope as its elected head. Its policies are based on the teachings of the Bible. Power is concentrated in the hands of the Pope, who holds supreme legislative, executive, and judicial power. The Vatican describes itself as an 'absolute monarchy' meaning that the Pope cannot be sued or prosecuted. It has 'non-member state' status at the UN. It has no permanent population, no jurisdiction over crimes committed in its territory, and depends on Italy for essential services (Robertson 2010).

Unitary and Federal Systems

Political regimes may also be classified according to the distribution of power at different levels. The regime may be unitary where most decision-making power is held by the institutions of central government and where the regions and localities have little or no autonomy. In unitary states, the institutions of central government normally are responsible for important policy decisions, for the majority of public expenditure, and for the raising of taxes, with the regions having fewer powers in this regard. The great majority of countries in the world have a unitary system. France, Italy, Japan, and China are examples of unitary states.

On the other hand, the system may be federal where power is shared between the centre and the component regions. In such systems, regions may have significant decision-making powers in relation to areas such as spending and taxation. Friction between the centre and the regions in federations is not unusual, the tension between Catalonia, the Basque country, and the Spanish central government being a particular example. More than 2 billion people live in federal states and they comprise half the world's land area. Examples of federations are the USA, Germany, Brazil, and India. In unitary systems, those who award contracts for goods and services and decide rates and levels of tax are located at the centre of the regime. Thus, firms wishing to be given government contracts or to influence taxation decisions have to be in a position to affect the decision-making process at the centre. In federal systems businesses may find themselves dealing with decision-makers at both the centre and in the various regions of the federation.

Learning Task

In federal systems, national governments often run into conflict with the regions.

1. Come up with reasons for the conflict between central government and the regions.

2. What is the Affordable Care Act? Discuss the resistance from US states to President Obama's Health Act. See 'Google Privacy Ruling is Just the Thin End of a Censorship Wedge', by John Naughton, *The Observer* 17 May 2014.

The Size of the State

In this section we examine the size of the state relative to the economy. This is most commonly done by looking at the amount of money the state is spending and what it takes in tax as a proportion of the total income generated in the country, i.e. gross domestic product. As we will see, the size and importance of the state varies from one country to another.

Public Expenditure

The three decades after the end of the Second World War in 1945 saw the biggest increase, historically, in public spending. This mainly reflected the fact of governments taking on responsibility for maintaining high levels of employment and adequate living standards. One result of this was a major expansion of the welfare state. Spending also increased significantly on defence arising from the Cold War between the West and the Communist bloc of countries. By 1980, in developed economies the state's average slice of the economy had leapt to 43 per cent (in the US the percentage topped 30 per cent; in many small European countries it breached 50 per cent). Up to the mid-1980s, it continued to grow, but then levelled off. Towards the end of the first decade of the twenty-first century, the financial crisis caused OECD countries to increase spending to around 40 per cent of GDP. In the EU, it was just over half of GDP and more than 40 per cent in the US and Japan (see Table 8.1). In developing economies, government spending has also risen during the past few decades, and now represents about 30 per cent of GDP in emerging market economies and 25 per cent in low-income countries (IMF 2014).

Table 8.1 General government expenditures as a percentage of GDP

	2000	2005	2010	2012
Australia	35.7	34.1	36.4	32.3
Austria	51.9	50.0	52.8	51.7
Belgium	49.1	51.9	52.6	55.0
Canada	39.7	37.6	42.3	40.6
Chile	..	..	..	..
Czech Republic	41.6	43.0	43.7	44.5
Denmark	53.7	52.8	57.7	59.4
Estonia	36.1	33.6	40.5	39.5
Finland	48.3	50.3	55.8	56.7
France	51.7	53.6	56.6	56.6
Germany	45.1	46.9	47.9	44.7
Greece	..	44.6	51.4	53.6
Hungary	47.8	50.1	50.0	48.7
Iceland	41.9	42.2	51.6	47.4
Ireland	31.1	33.9	65.5	42.6
Israel	..	..	42.3	41.7
Italy	45.9	47.9	50.4	50.6
Japan	38.8	36.4	40.7	42.0
Korea	22.4	26.6	30.1	..
Luxembourg	37.6	41.5	43.5	44.3
Mexico	..	19.0	23.1	24.7
Netherlands	44.2	44.8	51.3	50.4
New Zealand	..	..	..	..
Norway	42.3	41.8	45.2	43.3
Poland	41.1	43.4	45.4	42.2
Portugal	41.6	46.6	51.5	47.4
Slovak Republic	52.1	38.0	40.0	37.8
Slovenia	46.5	45.1	49.4	48.1
Spain	39.2	38.4	46.3	47.8
Sweden	55.1	53.9	52.3	52.0
Switzerland	35.6	35.2	33.9	34.1
Turkey	..	..	40.2	..
United Kingdom	36.4	43.4	49.9	47.9
United States	33.7	36.4	42.6	40.0
Euro area	46.2	47.3	51.0	49.9
EU 28	44.7	46.7	50.6	49.3

Source: OECD Factbook 2014

Where does the Money Go?

The largest amounts of public spending go on subsidies and transfers, for example, pensions, social security, and unemployment benefits. This is followed by spending on defence, law and order, education, and health, often referred to as public or government consumption.

How the Money is Raised—Taxation and Borrowing

A clear trend since the mid-1970s was a steady increase in the proportion of total income taken by taxes. The tax-to-GDP ratio across most of the developed economies rose despite many countries cutting tax rates on personal and company income. Some countries have tried to offset the effects of cuts in tax rates by drawing more sectors and people into the tax net and reducing the degree of **tax evasion** and **tax avoidance** (www.oecd.org). Tax revenues fell in most countries as a result of the financial crisis, but started to recover after 2009 (see Table 8.2).

The tax take tends to be higher in Western European countries. In Austria, Norway, Denmark, Sweden, Finland, and France it is greater than 40 per cent of GDP. Chile and Mexico have the lowest tax ratio at around 20 per cent, somewhat below countries like South Korea, the USA, and Japan (see Table 8.2).

More than 90 per cent of the tax revenues raised in the developed economies come from three main sources: direct taxes on the income of individuals and business, indirect taxes on goods and services such as VAT and excise duties on the likes of tobacco and alcohol, and another form of direct tax, social security contributions.

Businesses pay tax on their net income, i.e. their profits. There has been a widespread tendency for tax rates on profits to drop in the advanced economies. Devereux and Sørenson (2005) describe the reduction in the tax rate on profits as remarkable. In 1982, they reported that 15 countries had tax rates in excess of 40 per cent. In Germany, Sweden, Finland, and Austria the rate was around 60 per cent. By 2010, rates had fallen significantly across many countries (see Figure 8.1). This trend may be due to the spread of globalization and the wish by countries to attract and retain foreign direct investment. A further reason is that host countries want to encourage those businesses to retain their earnings in the host country. The USA had the highest rate of 40 per cent, with Japan in second place with 36 per cent, the lowest being tax havens such as the Cayman Islands with a tax rate of zero.

When spending is greater than the taxes raised, governments usually borrow to cover the deficit. The USA has been running large budget deficits for a number of years. In 2010, in the aftermath of the financial crisis, the deficit in OECD countries was at a record level: in the US it was US$1.5 trillion, or over 10 per cent of GDP, while the figure for the UK was around £60 billion (OECD 2014; www.usgovernmentspending.com; www.ons.gov.uk). On the other hand, India and China were running significant budget surpluses, showing that tax receipts were higher than public expenditure.

The Global Crisis and Government Finances

The global financial crisis and economic downturn caused a dramatic increase in developed country government deficits as tax revenues fell and massive expenditure on bailing out the

Table 8.2 Tax revenue as a percentage of GDP

	2000	2007	2010	2012 provisional
Australia	30.4	29.7	25.6	n/a
Austria	43.0	41.8	42.2	43.2
Belgium	44.7	43.6	43.5	45.3
Canada	34.9	32.3	30.6	30.7
Chile	18.8	22.8	19.5	20.8
Czech Republic	34.0	35.9	33.9	35.5
Denmark	49.4	48.9	47.4	48.0
Estonia	31.0	31.4	34.0	32.5
Finland	47.2	43.0	42.5	44.1
France	44.4	43.7	42.9	45.3
Germany	37.5	36.1	36.2	37.6
Greece	34.3	32.5	31.6	33.8
Hungary	39.3	40.3	38.0	38.9
Iceland	37.2	40.6	35.2	37.2
Ireland	30.9	31.1	27.4	28.3
Israel	37.0	36.4	32.4	31.6
Italy	42.0	43.2	43.0	44.4
Japan	26.6	28.5	27.6	n/a
Korea	22.6	26.5	25.1	26.8
Luxembourg	39.1	35.6	37.3	37.8
Mexico	16.9	17.7	18.9	19.6
Netherlands	39.6	38.7	38.9	n/a
New Zealand	32.9	34.5	31.1	32.9
Norway	42.6	42.9	42.6	42.2
Poland	32.8	34.8	31.7	n/a
Portugal	30.9	32.5	31.2	32.5
Slovak Republic	34.1	29.5	28.3	28.5
Slovenia	37.3	37.7	38.1	37.4
Spain[1]	34.3	37.3	32.5	32.9
Sweden	51.4	47.4	45.4	44.3
Switzerland	29.3	27.7	28.1	28.2
Turkey	24.2	24.1	26.2	27.7
United Kingdom	36.4	35.7	34.9	35.2
United States	28.4	26.9	23.8	24.3
Unweighted average:				
OECD Total	**35.2**	**35.0**	**33.8**	**34.6**

Source: OECD www.oecd.org/ctp/tax-policy/revenue-statistics-ratio-change-latest-years.htm
Revenue Statistics tax-to-GDP ratio changes between 2007 and provisional 2012 data

Figure 8.1 Average corporate tax rates %

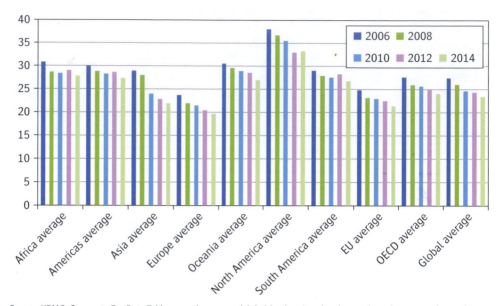

Source: KPMG, Corporate Tax Rate Tables www.kpmg.com/global/en/services/tax/tax-tools-and-resources/pages/corporate-tax-rates-table.aspx

banks and on unemployment benefits rose. Most developed countries tried to stimulate their economies through tax and spending policies. Finland, Korea, and the United States cut taxes significantly, while Australia, Denmark, Japan, Korea, and Turkey planned for large increases in spending. China gave a massive fiscal stimulus to its economy to the tune of 2.5 per cent of GDP by increasing investment in infrastructure and social welfare. Then, the Eurozone, UK, Hungary, and Iceland, trying to cut large budget deficits, pursued austerity programmes by raising taxes and cutting spending.

The Demise of the Nation State?

Commentators including Ohmae (2005) and, to an extent, Held and McGrew (2007), argue that the state has become increasingly powerless in the face of globalization. They contend that the increasing and all-pervasive interconnectedness of national economies is fatal to the effective power of individual states. National governments can no longer manage their domestic economies because they are subject to the forces that shape the international economy, for example through business decisions made by powerful MNCs. So, if an individual government set profit tax on business at a much higher level than other countries, then firms would relocate or ensure that their profits were earned in countries with a lower profits tax. Tax revenues would fall and the government would be obliged to revert to a lower level of profit tax.

Similarly, if a government wanted to have a relatively low rate of interest, then this would be undermined by investors moving their money out of the country to take advantage of higher rates elsewhere. This would reduce the supply of money available for borrowers and put upward pressure on interest rates.

A government wanting to prohibit dangerous or undesirable working practices might find the affected industries moving abroad or shutting down, because the new regulation would put domestic firms at a disadvantage in competition with foreign producers.

Some commentators supported their arguments with the case of Germany, where welfare benefits were high relative to other countries. Generous benefits meant that, for each worker, employers had to pay a high level of social security tax on top of wages. This pushed up labour costs and made the German economy less competitive internationally. As a result, Germany, it was claimed, suffered slow growth and high levels of unemployment. It was thus no surprise to the commentators that Germany cut back on the welfare benefit system. They saw the reforms as an indication that countries cannot buck global market forces and that the market will enforce a convergence of taxation and public expenditure among countries; in other words, there will be a race to the bottom.

Tanzi (1998) contends that the growing influence of supranational organizations like the WTO and the EU reduces the sovereignty of the nation state. Both these institutions set rules on trade and investment that reduce the power of national governments to influence them through measures such as tariffs, quotas, subsidies, and local content requirements. Ohma (2005) also foresaw globalization leading to cultural homogenization and a loss of national identity.

Learning Task

Examine Tables 8.1 and 8.2 and answer the following questions:

1. Identify and explain changes in the size of the state in terms of spending and taxation after 2005.

2. Advance reasons for the high tax rate in Scandinavian countries and the low tax rates in the USA and Japan.

Functions of the State and their Importance for Business

Earlier on, we looked at the different branches of the state. However, the boundaries of the state are not always clear-cut and, as we now discover, they can extend much further than the narrow description given above. Modern governments perform many functions besides the traditional ones of maintaining law and order and protecting the country from external attack.

A crucial role for the state is the preservation of the economic and financial system. A striking example of this occurred during the global credit crunch in 2008–09 when the US and European banking systems were in turmoil. Financial institutions, unable to borrow money, went bust or, like Northern Rock in the UK, were taken into public ownership (see Chapter 10, Mini Case Study Northern Rock—a credit crunch casualty). In the USA, several major financial institutions failed

Counterpoint Box 8.2 The nation state—dead or alive?

Critics of Ohmae's view, such as Hirst and Thompson (2005) and Scholte (2005), argue that the demise of the nation state is much exaggerated. Hirst and Thompson point out that the actual net flows between major economies are considerably less than a century ago. They contend that the main test of globalization is whether world economic trends confirm the existence of a single global economy. In this respect, they suggest, the evidence falls far short of any such claim.

Others argue that globalization has not weakened the most powerful states such as the USA, Japan, and those in Western Europe who are the parent states and political voices of most of the major multinational corporations. These countries, powerful in their own right and even more so when they coordinate their policies, exercise influence through their continued domination of decision-making in the international financial institutions and forums such as the IMF, World Bank, and G20. Countries like China, Brazil, and India are also increasingly making their weight felt in the international arena. Scholte says that the most one can argue is that globalization has severely constrained the bargaining positions of smaller and weaker states, mainly in the underdeveloped world (2005). This is hardly a new situation since small and poorer states have always had to consider the potential responses of more powerful states to the policies they adopt.

Neither does it appear that globalization has destroyed national identity. Harttgen and Opfinger (2012), using a survey of 69 countries, found a majority of respondents being very proud of their country while 73 per cent said that they were willing to fight for their country.

Rodrik concludes, 'the nation state refuses to wither away. It has proved remarkably resilient, and remains the main determinant of the global distribution of income, the primary locus of market-supporting institutions, and the chief repository of personal attachments and affiliations' (2012: 4).

Sources: Hirst and Thompson 2005; Scholte 2005; Held and McGrew 2007; Paczynska 2009; Harttgen and Opfinger 2012; Rodrik 2012

Questions

1. National identity reflects one's sense of belonging to a state or nation. To what extent is this manifest in international events like the Olympic games or the football World Cup in your country?

including Bear Stearns, Indy Mac, and Washington Mutual, and Lehman Brothers went bankrupt. Stock markets gyrated wildly and the dollar plunged against other currencies. Governments could not allow the global financial system to crash because the money and credit provided by banks is a vital lubricant for business in a modern economy. The IMF (2014) reports that the financial sector in 10 advanced economies was supported to the tune of around $2 trillion, with the US government alone disbursing more than $400 billion to stem the panic and stabilize the financial system (see US Dept of the Treasury 2013) (see Chapter 10, Financial Crises).

We are now going to look in more detail at other functions that can have a significant impact on the external environment of business. By carrying out these functions, state institutions can make decisions that constrain the ability of business to meet its objectives, such as making profits and increasing sales or market share. On the other hand, they can also provide opportunities which firms are able to exploit for commercial gain.

Law of Contract

The state has a major part to play in establishing the wider environment within which business operates. It passes laws and adopts regulations that set the legal framework or rules of the game for business, some of which are especially important. For example, in liberal democracies the state usually guarantees the right to own and to buy and sell capital assets and goods and services, the lifeblood of all commercial businesses.

One particularly important aspect is the law of contract, where the state lays down and enforces rules and obligations relating to transactions around the buying and selling of goods and services. The law of contract ensures that if a business sells goods or services, it will be able to use the law to pursue the customer for payment, were that to be necessary. Similarly, a firm contracting to buy a certain quantity and quality of goods wants to be sure that it is able to use the law to remedy any shortfalls or deficiencies on the part of the supplier. Business will be reluctant to operate in countries where it is not able to enforce the terms of its contract. A good example of such a country is the Congo in Africa, which the big oil multinational, Shell, classifies as a country where state institutions are ineffective. The absence of an effective judicial system makes it virtually impossible for firms to enforce the law of contract (for more on contract law, see Chapter 9).

Law and Order and External Attack

Another function of the state is to protect its geographical area from both external and internal threats. The intelligence services manage both categories of threat. The army, navy, and air force deal with external threats, for example military threats from other countries. The police, courts, and prisons help maintain law and order within the geographical frontiers of the state. States that can effectively protect themselves from external threat and maintain law and order internally are seen by business as providing a more stable and attractive operating environment.

Spending and Taxation

Economically, the state is the largest and most important single player in developed countries. This is reflected in the amount of money governments spend and take in tax in relation to the whole economy. Governments spend money on buying goods and services, paying the wages of state employees, and providing welfare benefits. Taxation takes the form of direct taxes, those on incomes, and indirect taxes, which are levied on expenditure.

The state can use its spending on goods and services and welfare benefits, and taxing, along with other policies, towards interest rates and the exchange rate to influence the level of total demand for the goods and services produced by business. When the economy is going into recession, the state can increase demand by raising its own spending on goods and services, or it can cut taxes or lower interest rates to encourage consumers and business to increase their spending. Alternatively, when the economy is booming, and there is a danger of inflation going out of control, the state can cut spending or raise taxes and interest rates to reduce consumer spending and relieve inflationary pressures.

Such decisions can have major implications for business. For example, a decision to raise interest rates increases the cost of borrowing for firms and is often greeted by them with dismay. The higher cost of borrowing may also cause consumers to cut back on spending on goods, such as consumer durables which they would normally buy on credit. On the other hand, organizations such as the retail banks may welcome such an increase in rates because it allows them to charge their customers more for loans. Rising interest rates often mean that banks can widen the gap between the interest they pay their customers on their current accounts and the income they can earn on their depositors' money.

Negotiator

The state acts as a negotiator with other states. Negotiations can be bilateral where two countries are involved, or multilateral where more than two participate. The WTO is a multilateral body where important negotiations take place on reductions in barriers to trade and to the movement of capital across borders. Such negotiations can be very good for business, particularly when they open up new markets. On the other hand, they can remove barriers that protect domestic firms from foreign competition (see Chapter 2, International Trade).

Regulator

Regulation can affect a very wide range of business activities. For instance, regulations could constrain the ability of the firm to take out patents, or set its own prices, for example in the telecommunications and water industries in the UK. It could also affect the level of competition and market entry. For instance, in both the EU and the USA the authorities liberalized entry into the civil aviation market, which led to new entry and a much fiercer degree of competition.

Regulations could increase a firm's costs by stipulating requirements relating to consumer health and safety, to employment contracts, and to the natural environment or by requiring companies to fill in certain forms and to meet certain administrative formalities, i.e. red tape (for more discussion of the impact of regulations on business see Chapter 9).

In its role as a regulator, the state can take the power to grant or refuse a firm a licence to operate or to guarantee it a monopoly. In the developed world, banks and other financial institutions usually need to get a licence to sell financial services. Tighter regulation, following the global financial crisis, means that compliance costs for banks will increase. Regulations can also determine whether or not firms can merge—the US Justice Department moved to block a merger between American Airlines and US Airways.

Firms may also find that regulations lay down the technical specifications to which their products must conform. There are examples of drugs regulators, concerned about safety, demanding more rigorous testing, prohibiting the launch of a new drug, or ordering pharmaceutical companies to withdraw products from the market place. The main forms of regulation are at the national level, but supranational regulation is becoming increasingly important through bodies such as the WTO and the EU.

Deregulator

Just as the state can regulate so can it deregulate, or liberalize. The USA and EU liberalized their civil aviation sectors. Now EU airlines have the freedom to set their own prices, to fly over the territory of member states, to operate flights within those countries, and to set up routes between them. As a result, numerous low cost airlines emerged, such as easyJet and Ryanair, that caused all sorts of competitive problems to the established national carriers like British Airways and Lufthansa.

At the global level, Western governments and the WTO, through measures like the General Agreement on Trade in Services (GATS), have encouraged developing countries to open up their markets in services such as telecommunications and banking.

Arbitrator

The state also acts as an arbitrator, or referee, between firms who are in dispute with each other. Thus, business may look to state institutions, such as the courts or other regulatory agencies, to resolve disputes with other firms or to take action against them. Such disputes could relate to a whole range of issues such as breach of contract, abuse of market power, and patent infringement.

Microsoft's competitors have complained on numerous occasions to the competition authorities in both the USA and the EU about Microsoft abusing its market power, making it very difficult for them to compete in the software market. Between 2004 and 2013, the software giant paid fines to the EU of over $3 billion (www.neowin.net 6 March 2013).

Customer for Goods and Services

The state can also play a vital role as a customer for business. Governments, especially those in developed economies, spend a significant proportion of GDP on the purchase of goods and services.

In the UK, the public sector spends some £230 billion on the purchase of goods and services from thousands of suppliers (www.gov.uk/government/policies/buying-and-managing-government-goods-and-services-more-efficiently-and-effectively#background). Some firms, such as MNCs like Serco and G4S, are heavily dependent in the UK on such contracts. For industries like pharmaceuticals and armaments, the single most important customer is the state, and the purchasing policies pursued by the state towards those industries is of paramount importance. This can be seen in those countries with ageing populations, where the state is trying to control public expenditure through pressure on pharmaceutical firms to lower prices and by turning to lower priced generic drugs. Governments are major customers for firms in the IT sector and for consultancies such as PwC and McKinsey.

The state can also be an important client for the financial sector. When governments run budget deficits, they borrow money from financial institutions in exchange for financial instruments such as bonds and Treasury Bills. This can make governments major customers for lending institutions—in 2013, US government interest payments were around $416 billion, while, in 2014, the UK was paying out almost £1 billion per week (www.treasurydirect.gov/govt/reports/ir/ir_expense.htm; www.ukpublicspending.co.uk).

The purchasing strategies pursued by the state can have important implications for suppliers. For example, there are claims in the UK that government procurement policies favour large companies at the expense of small and medium-sized enterprises. There is also much evidence that many states pursue nationalistic purchasing policies, favouring domestic producers over their foreign counterparts even when the foreign firms offer better value.

Supplier of Goods and Services

In many countries the state takes on the job of producing and selling goods and services. Sectors where the state often carries out these activities are energy, water, sanitation, transport, postal services, and telecommunications. The organizations responsible for producing in these sectors are frequently publicly owned and controlled.

In times of emergency, governments sometimes take businesses into public ownership because the economic and social impact of them going out of business would be very serious. The global financial meltdown and the subsequent economic crisis gave a good illustration of this. Banks were nationalized in the USA, the UK, the Benelux countries, Iceland, and Ireland (see discussion on the global financial crisis in Chapter 10, Anatomy of the Financial Crisis 2007 Onwards). In the summer of 2009, General Motors, the giant car maker, went bankrupt and was nationalized by the US government, which, in the process, spent nearly US$60 billion of taxpayers' money.

Other areas of production where the state is usually heavily involved is in the provision of welfare services, with health and education services being two prime examples. In developed economies, the state often exercises a high degree of control over the finances and policies pursued by schools, universities, and hospitals. The policies adopted by governments in those areas could be important for business since they could have implications for the quality of the labour force in terms of health and education levels.

As we have seen, the state supplies some goods and services essential for private sector production. For business to operate effectively, there has got to be a transport infrastructure in the form of road and rail networks, ports, and airports. Usually, the state is involved in providing these and also some of the services associated with them, such as rail or air travel. Similarly, state agencies can be suppliers of such vital elements as energy and telecommunications as well as basic research and development and economic statistics.

Financial services may also be provided by state agencies. In the UK, the Export Credit Guarantee Department (ECGD) insures exporters against the risk of not getting paid by their overseas buyer for reasons such as insolvency, war, or lack of foreign exchange.

The policies pursued by these state-owned suppliers as regards pricing and investment can have a significant impact on the performance of their customers in the private sector. For example, big energy consuming firms in the steel and chemicals industries in France will be very sensitive to the prices charged by the state monopoly suppliers, Electricité de France (EDF) or Gaz de France (GDF), because energy counts for a large proportion of their costs.

Competitor

State organizations may be important competitors for private sector firms in, for example, energy, transport, and telecommunications, and in areas such as health and education. Often, private sector firms complain that they face unfair competition from their state rivals. This can take several forms. State firms may be subsidized, allowing them to charge artificially low prices. Most of France's electricity is produced by nuclear power, which receives great dollops of subsidy from the French government. State firms may be able to raise finance at much lower rates of interest than private sector rivals simply because they are state agencies and regarded as less risky by the financial markets. Foreign private sector energy companies wishing to

Counterpoint Box 8.3 India and liberalization

In 1991, India, suffering a crisis in the balance of payments and unable to borrow, was forced to go the IMF for a bail-out of several billion dollars. In return, India agreed to embark on structural reforms of the economy. Up until then, the Indian economy was to a great degree closed. The currency, the rupee, was not convertible into other currencies, high tariffs and import licensing limited the access of foreign goods to the Indian market, and there were tight controls on inward foreign investment. Entrepreneurship was stifled by a labyrinthine state bureaucracy, and inefficient state-owned enterprises accounted for a significant share of the economy.

The government embarked on a programme of what turned out to be a gradual liberalization. It drastically reduced the number of licenses to start a firm, cut tariffs, devalued the rupee, leaving the exchange rate to be determined by the market, and opened up the economy to foreign direct investment. Capital markets were liberalized and taxes reduced.

Supporters of the programme point to the subsequent increase in economic growth and exports, rises in per capita income, increases in adult literacy, and reductions in poverty. Bhagwati and Panagariya (2013) argue that growth directly benefits the poor by generating income and employment. Despite the progress, liberalizers say that India could do with another dose of reform.

Critics point out that the average annual growth rate of 5.8 per cent in the eight years after liberalization was not that much higher than the 5.6 per cent achieved in the 1980s. They also claim that growth in the industrial sector actually fell in the 1990s. While accepting that economic growth was impressive in the noughties, they argue that growth has not benefited all sections of society and that widespread poverty persists among large swathes of the population. Inequality has risen, with Kwashik Basu, chief economist at the World Bank, saying that, '[t]he bulk of India's aggregate growth is occurring through a disproportionate rise in incomes at the upper end of the incomes ladder' (cited in Mishra 2013). Critics are also concerned that inequality has not only widened between social classes, but also between regions, and rural and urban areas and these seem intractable due to the lack of adequate education and public health.

Sources: Drèze and Sen 2013; Bhagwati and Panagariya 2013; Kalirajan and Singh 2010; Panda and Ganesh-Kumar 2009; Mishra 2013; *The Economist* 21 July 2011; www.bbc.co.uk 12 February 1998

Questions

1. How could the Indian government ensure that the benefits of economic growth are more widely distributed?

enter the French market could face formidable competition from their state-owned rivals, EDF, one of the world's largest electricity companies, and GDF. EDF has entered markets in both Western and Eastern Europe, but foreign energy firms trying to penetrate the French market have run up against barriers to entry put up by the French state despite EU efforts to liberalize the energy market.

Subsidizer

The state often subsidizes business in the form of grants, tax reliefs, and cheap loans to maintain or generate employment or to maintain the production of goods and services regarded as important to the national economy. For example, 62 per cent of R&D in the aerospace sector, where R&D outcomes are uncertain and may take a long time to pay off, is provided by the US government (ECSIP 2013). In 2012, EU state aid to the railways was around €40 billion. Following the onset of the global financial crisis in 2007, EU member states supported the financial sector with €592 billion and also gave hefty loan guarantees to keep the sector afloat (European Commission (2013) 'State Aid Scoreboard 2013').

Subsidies are not confined to rich countries, but are also often given by poorer countries to domestic producers. In 2014, India announced a €54 a ton subsidy for sugar exports (www.blooomberg.com 12 February 2014).

In summary, we can see that the exercise of the functions outlined above can have an impact on industry structure, ownership, and control; for example, through the control of mergers and acquisitions or through policies to remove barriers to entry in industries such as airlines and telecommunications. It can also have a significant influence on the decisions organizations make in areas like pricing, product, and investment. Such influences may then have important implications for the performance of a company in areas such as profit performance, market share, and growth rate.

How Organizations Influence the State

As trade, overseas investment, and foreign competition have grown in importance, so firms, particularly those with international operations, have perceived the increasing importance of their relationships with state institutions. While decades of international negotiations may have made trade and the movement of capital freer, companies in many sectors confront increasing competition in their domestic markets and still face barriers in foreign markets. To protect themselves against foreign competition, to get the barriers removed, or to keep them in place for that matter, companies often appeal to forces in their political environment that could help. As the chief executive of BP said, 'We've always got to be in a position to turn to the government in power' (*Financial Times* 2 August 2002).

Because the state can have such an important impact, firms often make big efforts to influence the decisions it makes and are often prepared to devote very large amounts of resources to ensure a successful outcome to their attempts to do so. Big firms like Apple, Ford, and Microsoft have a global political strategy, overseen by senior executives with a substantial budget usually reporting directly to the chief executive. Where very important public policy issues arise, the chief executive often intervenes to represent and advocate the company's interests to the state.

Big firms are in the best position to exercise an influence on the state. One reason for this is the possible reluctance of the state to cause hostility in businesses whose decisions on pricing, production, investment, employment, imports, and exports can have a major influence on the ability of the state to achieve its goals of economic prosperity, high levels of investment and employment, low inflation, and a healthy balance of payments. Some industries, by their nature, are also well positioned to influence the state. For example, governments may be averse to taking decisions that will provoke a critical reaction in the press or on television. This gives the people who run the media the power to influence politicians, especially in the run-up to national elections.

The authorities may be reluctant to incur the wrath of firms operating in high technology, high growth industries for fear of losing their contribution to jobs and to economic growth. Such sensitivities may cause governments to consult business before embarking on new policies.

The pharmaceutical industry is a good example of an industry that is often treated with care by state institutions such as the UK Medicines and Healthcare Products Regulatory Authority (MHRA). Pharmaceutical firms are major suppliers to the National Health Service (NHS). The NHS depends on the industry as providers of existing and new medicines that are important in the provision and quality of health care. The UK government is very keen to promote innovation by encouraging firms to invest in research and development. The pharmaceutical industry is a major source of R&D and innovation within the UK. Its investment in R&D is 28 per cent of the total carried out by UK business. The industry is a major exporter, running an annual trade surplus of £5 billion. Finally, pharmaceutical firms directly employ some 68,000 people in the UK (www.abpi.org.uk).

Methods of Influencing the State

According to the executive chairman of Google: 'The average American doesn't realize how much of the laws are written by lobbyists' (www.brainyquote.com). Business employs a variety of methods to influence decision-makers in the institutions of the state to protect and promote their interests. We will now examine some of these methods.

Lobbying

Businesses try to exert influence over the state by lobbying individually or collectively with other firms. To do this, they set up offices or employ professional lobbyists in the cities where state institutions make their decisions. A good example is Washington in the USA, where the institutions of the federal government are located. The pharmaceutical industry has more than twice as many lobbyists in Washington as the number of elected representatives in Congress. It wields considerable power over its regulator, the Food and Drugs Administration, and donates millions of dollars each year to members of Congress sitting on important safety committees. In 2013, the industry spent more than US$140 million to influence lawmakers and federal agencies (www.opensecrets.org).

Where businesses succeed in getting regulatory agencies to serve their interests rather than that of the wider society they are said to have captured the regulator. According to some commentators, the pharmaceutical industry has been one of the more effective in this regard with the regulatory agencies appearing to identify their interests very closely with the industries they are supposed to regulate.

Brussels, as the location for many EU institutions, is another major lobbying focus for business. Hundreds of trade associations have offices there, ranging from the International Federation of Industrial Energy Consumers, to the Liaison Committee of European Bicycle Manufacturers, to the International Confederation of European Beet Growers, to the Union of European Railway Industries.

Companies such as Google, Siemens, Microsoft, Intel, Procter & Gamble, General Electric, and General Motors have offices in Brussels to lobby the Commission, the European Parliament, and the Council of Ministers—the three important decision-making institutions in the EU capital. Their desire to influence the political and regulatory process in Brussels has swelled the ranks of the professional lobbyists in the city. Corporate Europe Observatory estimates that around 30,000 lobbyists compete for the attention of the EU institutions, the vast majority of them representing business (www.corporateeurope.org; see Klüver 2013)

When deciding how to lobby, businesses have to take a number of factors into account. They must choose whether to act alone or in alliance with others in the industry, the state institutions to be influenced, the nature and amount of pressure to be exerted on the agencies, and the degree of publicity that is advisable.

Big firms are usually powerful enough to lobby on their own account. Boeing, the giant producer of commercial and military aircraft, spends much time and resources lobbying the US government to increase defence spending, to win military contracts, and to protect it from its main European competitor, Airbus (www.opensecrets.org).

Small and medium-sized firms, on the other hand, often find it more effective to lobby along with other firms in the same industry through, for example, trade associations operating either at national or supranational levels. At the national level in Britain, for example, the trade association for the consumer electronics industry is the British Radio and Electronic Equipment Manufacturers' Association (BREMA). BREMA is also associated with the European Association of Consumer Electronics Manufacturers (EACEM), which represents the industry in the EU.

In addition to lobbying on an industry basis, firms can also lobby through national bodies which represent business more generally, like the Confederation of British Industry (CBI) in Britain, the Bundesvereinigung der Deutschen Arbeitgebervebaende (BDA) in Germany, or the Business Council of Australia, when trying to influence the state at the country level. Or they may subscribe to supranational associations, such as the Union of Industrial and Employers Confederation of Europe (UNICE) or the European Round Table (ERT), at the European level.

State Consultation with Business

Frequently, business does not spend time and money lobbying in expectation of the state seeking its views on proposed policies, regulations, and laws. In the UK, government departments, as a matter of course, consult bodies representing the construction and vehicle industries on draft regulations. The obligation to consult business is written into the EC Treaty. It requires the Commission to consult firms when preparing proposals, particularly in the areas of social policy such as employment rights, working conditions, and equal opportunities, and in public health legislation relating to fields like biotechnology. The intention in the EU is for business to play a substantial role both in drafting and in implementing new measures (see the europa website for examples of business being consulted by the EU).

Promises or Threats

Occasionally, firms try to influence the state by using promises or threats. Big MNCs are able to offer countries the attractive prospect of large investment projects generating much income and many jobs. It is no surprise that governments fall over themselves in their attempts to attract such MNC investment, especially in times of high unemployment.

When energy companies offer to exploit large oil and gas reserves in poor countries like Equatorial Guinea or Nigeria they hold out the promise of vast income from gas and oil revenues, which gives them a deal of bargaining power in negotiations with government.

On the other hand, if business does not like the current or proposed policies of a particular country, it can threaten to cut down investment or relocate production, thereby reducing numbers of jobs. For example, the chairman of Ford Europe issued such a warning stating that his company would not hesitate to close down major assembly operations in countries wishing to give workers longer holidays or a shorter working week. Another possibility is for the firm to refuse to supply goods and services. Insurers in the USA threatened to withdraw from certain areas of health insurance if President Obama did not modify his reforms to the US health care system (www.consumerwatchdog.org).

Direct Access to Government Ministers and Civil Servants

Firms, especially large ones, are often able to get representation on government advisory committees where the concerns of business can be aired with the other committee members, civil servants, and government ministers. In the EU, business has representation on the European Economic and Social Committee, which is consulted by the various institutions of the union, the Commission, Council, and the Parliament. Over and above these formal structures, big business is also in a good position to get informal access to civil servants and ministers. A refusal would be highly unlikely were Google or Shell to ask for a meeting with a government minister or high-ranking civil servant.

Employment and Exchange of Personnel

Commentators often refer to the revolving door between industry and the state in terms of personnel. Some companies see major benefits in offering jobs to ex-members of the legislative or executive branches of the state such as former government ministers and high-ranking civil servants. The reason given is that such people bring invaluable knowledge of how the state operates and therefore could be very useful when companies are trying to win contracts or influence policy. Others suspect that the jobs may be pay-offs for past favours to the company or that the new employees will be able to exploit their links with the state to gain improper advantage for the firm.

Etzion and Davis (2008) did a study of the comings and goings of senior personnel between US government and business during the reign of Presidents Clinton and Bush. They found that employment in government could serve as a way of joining the corporate elite. All but one head of the US armed forces ended up serving on the boards of defence companies like Boeing and Northrop Grumman. Their research also showed a flow of people from business to high-level positions in government service. LaPira and Thomas (2012), in a survey of US lobbyists, found that more than half had held positions in the executive or legislative branches of government.

Learning Task

1. Why should defence companies, in particular, be among the largest hirers of ex-civil servants and former government officials?

2. Discuss the pros and cons for companies of employing civil servants and government officials previously involved in negotiations with them.

Mini Case Study Influencing the state in China

Just as in other countries, business tries to influence the state in China. This activity is even more important there because of the desire and ability of the Communist authorities to regulate and control economic activities.

While national laws are often written in broad terms, their implementation is left to regional and local Governments who therefore have a great degree of influence over economic activities in their areas. Business, both domestic and foreign, therefore needs to influence both central and provincial governments. Holtbrugge and Berg (2004) stated that the most important methods used by business in China were lobbying, bribery, codes of conduct, public relations, and sponsorship. Deng and Kennedy (2010), in a survey of large domestic and foreign firms, found that, for the vast majority of both Chinese and foreign-owned companies, lobbying is an integral part of the country's policy making process at local and national level, for company success or failure depends on thousands of regulations and laws. Guanxi—the use of social networks and personal relationships—was widely recognized as important by companies, especially in dealings with local authorities. They also discovered that firms recruited ex-government officials for their knowledge of how the political system worked.

Yongqiang (2007) compared and contrasted the successful attempts by Motorola with those of Microsoft to influence the authorities. Before the company entered China, the president of Motorola visited government officials to sound out their opinions on the firm's entry. It made a very good impression by donating mobile phones to officials in the Great Hall of the

People in Beijing in the presence of the Chinese Premier. When company executives visited, they always met up with high-ranking officials. Motorola even set up branches of the Communist Party and gave priority to Party members when hiring workers.

In contrast, Bill Gates did not visit China until a year after Microsoft's entry. The Chinese thought that he looked down on their domestic market and found him overbearing. Motorola also made a good impression by offering to train thousands of technicians and managers for state-owned enterprises, committing to the purchase of billions of dollars worth of parts and services from domestic suppliers, and to reaching targets on investment and output. Microsoft, in comparison, did not make any initial commitments only wishing to sell goods and services and to earn profits.

Government officials would not support Microsoft and it got a bad name with the public. Eventually, the firm did enter into joint ventures with Chinese companies and agreed to help promote the software industry and train professionals. Motorola sponsored schools and sports, helped China join the WTO, and publicized itself as a Chinese company. Unlike Microsoft, Motorola was happy to adapt its codes of conduct to Chinese social and business culture.

Sources: Holtbrugge and Berg 2004; Yongqiang 2007; Deng and Kennedy 2010

Questions

1. Explain why lobbying by business could be more important in China than in liberal democracies.

In some countries, the UK for example, there is a well-developed arrangement for the temporary exchange of managers and civil servants. Here, managers give up their jobs to work for a time in the civil service while senior civil servants move in the opposite direction. The benefits for business are that managers can learn how the civil service operates, shape policy advice to ministers, and make useful networks of contacts in the administrative branch, while civil servants who have transferred to private firms can be persuaded of the values and methods of the business community, which they then take back to the civil service.

Giving Money or Gifts

Companies donate money openly to political parties, particularly in the run-up to elections. Firms often justify this support by insisting that they are helping those parties who will create a better environment for the effective functioning of the market economy. Historically, in the USA the party traditionally favoured by business has been the Republicans, in the UK the Conservatives, and in Japan the dominant LDP. During the 2012 American presidential election, the finance and real estate sector donated US$68 million to political parties, with more than three-quarters going to the Republican party (www.opensecrets.org).

Firms may also give money illegally to political parties or state officials. In 2014, an Israeli prime minister was jailed for taking a bribe from real estate developers (www.bbc.co.uk 13 May 2014). Pei refers to the 'vast scale of corruption' of Chinese political officials (www.project-syndicate.org/commentary/minxin-pei-considers-the-main-economic–political–and-strategic-issues-facing-chinese-president-xi-jingping-this-year). BAE, Britain's biggest arms manufacturer, has regularly been accused of paying bribes. A BBC investigation revealed that the company had made £60 million of corrupt payments to Saudi officials, including providing prostitutes, Rolls-Royces, and Californian holidays while *The Guardian* reported that BAE had been identified as secretly paying more than £1 million through American banks to General Pinochet, the former Chilean dictator, in return for defence contracts. (Chapter 11 examines the issue of corruption in more depth.)

● CHAPTER SUMMARY

In this chapter we examined the characteristics of various political systems, the liberal democracies of Europe and North America, Communism in China, the authoritarian regime in Saudi Arabia, and the theocratic system in Iran. We saw how the political organization of countries into unitary or federal systems can have significant implications for business as regards the locus of important political decisions, for instance regarding taxing and spending. We identified and explained the different functions carried out by the state and showed how important they can be, for example, in preventing the collapse of the economic and financial system and in setting the legal and regulatory rules of the game for business. We also considered the arguments for and against the thesis that globalization had led to the demise of the nation state. Finally, we considered the variety of methods, from lobbying to the donation of money, that firms use to influence their political environment.

While relationships between business and the state can be difficult, there is a great degree of interdependence between the two. On the one hand, governments depend on business to deliver economic growth, low inflation, a healthy balance of payments, and to create jobs. On the other hand, business depends on the state to create and maintain an environment that provides opportunities to produce and sell goods and services and to make profits.

● REVIEW QUESTIONS

1. What is the state? Why is it important for the aerospace industry? Explain with examples.

2. Compare and contrast the characteristics of liberal democratic and communist states. Discuss which of these types of state would be more attractive for a Western MNC.

3. To what extent do you agree that globalization has undermined the power of the nation state? Give evidence to support your arguments.

4. The Economist Intelligence Unit (EIU) produces an Index of Democracy that charts the progress of democracy in the world. It reported in 2012 that global democracy was at a standstill (https://portoncv. gov.cv/dhub/porton.por_global.open_file?p_doc_id=1034).

   a) Which countries were the main cause of the standstill?

   b) Identify the principal reasons for the standstill.

   c) Has global democracy advanced since 2012? Give reasons for your answers.

   d) What, if any, are the implications of the standstill in democracy for press and broadcasting organizations?

● ASSIGNMENT TASKS

1. According to Edward Snowden, the NSA policy towards information collection is, 'Sniff it all, Know it all, Collect it all, Process it all, Exploit it all . . .' (Greenwald 2014). You are the PA to an executive in a German multinational which stores its data in the cloud with a big US technology firm. The same US firm also provides your company with telecoms services. Your boss asks you to write a report that:

   a) Gives a brief background to the Snowden disclosures.

   b) Analyses the implications of the disclosures for your company.

2. You work in the mergers and acquisitions section of a big multinational bank. One of your clients is a large mobile phone company considering moving into India. You are given the task of researching the political environment in India. Your specific remit is to:

   a) examine the experiences of foreign mobile phone companies with the political authorities in India in the decade up to 2014;

   b) outline the attitudes towards foreign business of the political party that took power in the 2014 national elections;

   c) in the light of your research, assess whether the political environment makes India a good location for your client.

Case Study The Arab spring—social and political upheaval

In the spring of 2011, a series of unprecedented popular uprisings took place in several Arab countries from North Africa to the Middle East. The first protests occurred in Tunisia and quickly spread to Libya, Egypt, Yemen, and Syria.

All of these societies were characterized by significant social and economic inequality, corruption, abuse of power by the political rulers, repression of political freedoms and civil rights, and conspicuous privileges accorded to government employees. The media was controlled by the state or the military, trade unions were restricted, and freedom of expression and of association was limited. Imprisonment without trial and torture were widespread. These countries had also been suffering from steady increases in food and transport costs.

Source: © jcarillet / istockphoto.com   →

→ Many of the protesters questioning the legitimacy of the regimes were the disaffected young, both men and women. Of the population in the Arab world, 60 per cent is under 30 years of age. Unemployment is rife, with youth unemployment as high as 80 per cent in some areas. Some commentators estimate that around half a million people join the unemployment queues each year. Research shows that the young are less religious than their parents. In the 1970s and 1980s, many Arab states launched massive educational reforms, which improved access to education and led to significant increases in participation in educational programmes. Women, in particular, benefited, for literacy rates for women are now higher than for men and they outnumber men in higher education.

Some analysts saw a substantial increase in the use of social media like Facebook and Twitter as helping to mobilize protests. They were used both by pro and anti regime supporters to organize demonstrations, disseminate information through their networks, and to encourage participation in the protests. Governments responded by monitoring and controlling information on the sites, and trying to block access to them. Other commentators suggest that social media were important where the demonstrators were more cosmopolitan, as in Egypt, but less significant in countries like Tunisia where the protests originated among the rural poor.

Anderson (2011) points out that the patterns of protest and the identities of those involved varied from one country to the other. Among the protesters there was no political consensus as to what should replace the old regimes. Some protesters in monarchies like Jordan and Morocco wanted immediate reform under the current rulers while others called for a more gradual transition. In republics, like Egypt and Tunisia, demonstrators wanted to overthrow the president and have free elections, but seemingly had little idea on what should follow.

While the long-term effects of the Arab Spring are unclear, it did result in the collapse of authoritarian regimes in Tunisia, Egypt, and Yemen that had been in power for decades. Dictators such as Egypt's Mubarak and Ben Ali in Tunisia were ousted, while Gaddafi in Libya was killed, and Assad's power in Syria was severely shaken.

The Muslim Brotherhood was victorious in Egyptian elections, but was then toppled by a military coup followed by a bloody crackdown on the Brotherhood. A subsequent election saw the military commander who had led the coup becoming president. Civil wars ensued in Libya and Syria. According to Dodge (2012), dictators had been deposed, but the ruling elites, the powerful secret services and the crony capitalists, remained.

Sources: Anderson 2011; Al Kaylani 2012; Dubai School of Government 2011; Soengas 2013; Mulderig 2013; Hoffman and Jamal 2012; Dodge (2012)

Questions

1. Which characteristics indicate that the Arab Spring countries were authoritarian?
2. Discuss the significance in the uprisings of a young, educated, but less religious population suffering high levels of unemployment.
3. Explore the potential role of social media in uprisings like the Arab Spring. Explain why social media might play a more important part in uprisings in countries where the population is cosmopolitan and educated.
4. What might be the implications of such uprisings for social media companies?

You need to carry out further research for the remaining questions.

5. To what extent, if any, do Egypt and Tunisia now resemble liberal democracies?
6. Find out whether Saudi Arabia was affected by the Arab Spring. Come up with some explanations for your findings.

● FURTHER READING

This textbook examines a variety of different political systems and concepts:

● Caramani, D. (2011) *Comparative Politics*, 2nd edn. Oxford: Oxford University Press.

For a text on global politics see:

● Edkins, J. and Zehfuss, M. (2014) *Global Politics: A New Introduction*, 2nd edn. Abingdon: Routledge.

For a useful overview of different political regimes see:

- 'The Keele Guide to Political Science on the Internet' www.keele.ac.uk/depts/por/psbase.htm. It is wide-ranging, covering the Americas, Europe, Asia, Africa, and Oceania.

● REFERENCES

Al Kaylani, H. (2012) 'Beyond the Arab Spring'. *OECD Observer* No 290-91, Q1-Q2.

Anderson, L. (2011) 'Demystifying the Arab Spring'. *Foreign Affairs* May/June.

Bhagwati, J. and Panagariya, A. (2013) *Why Growth Matters: How Economic Growth in India Reduced Poverty and the Lessons for Other Developing Countries*. New York: Public Affairs.

Deng, G. and Kennedy, S. (2010) 'Big Business and Industry Association Lobbying in China: The Paradox of Contrasting Styles'. *China Journal* 63 (January).

Deudney, D. and Ikenberry, G.J. (2009) 'The Myth of the Autocratic Revival: Why Liberal Democracy will Prevail'. *Foreign Affairs* 88(1).

Devereux, M.P. and Sørensen, P.B. (2005) 'The Corporate Income Tax: International Trends and Options for Fundamental Reform', October. Available at: www.sbs.ox.ac.uk.

Dodge, T. (2012) 'Conclusion: The Middle East After the Arab Spring'. Available at: www.lse.ac.uk/ideas/publications.

Drèze, J. and Sen, A. (2013) *An Uncertain Glory: India and Its Contradiction*. London: Penguin.

Drucker, P. (1999) *Management: Tasks, Responsibilities, Practices*. Oxford: Butterworth-Heinemann.

Dubai School of Government (2011) 'Civil Movements: The Impact of Facebook and Twitter'. *Arab Social Media Report* 1 (2).

ECSIP (2013) 'National State Aid in Support of Innovation and SMEs: Strengths and Weaknesses of the EU State Aid Control System', 29 April. Available at: http://ec.europa.eu/enterprise/policies/industrial-competitiveness/documents/files/state-aid-in-support-of-innovation_en.pdf.

Etzion, D. and Davis, G.F. (2008) 'Revolving Doors: A Network Analysis of Corporate Officers and US Government Officials'. *Journal of Management Inquiry* 17(3).

Fukuyama, F. (1993) *The End of History and the Last Man*. London: Penguin.

Greenwald, G. (2014) *No Place to Hide: Edward Snowden, and the US Surveillance State*. London: Hamish Hamilton.

Group on Intelligence and Communications Technologies (2013) 'Liberty and Security in a Changing World', 12 December.

Harttgen, K. and Opfinger, M. (2012) 'National Identity and Religious Diversity', Research Papers in Economics 7/12, University of Trier.

Held, D. and McGrew, A.G. (2007) *Globalisation Theories: Approaches and Controversies*. Cambridge: Polity Press.

Hirst, P. and Thompson, G. (2005) *Globalization in Question: The International Economy and the Possibilities of Governance*, 3rd edn. London: Polity Press.

Hoffman, M. and Jamal, A. (2012), 'The Youth and the Arab Spring: Cohort Differences and Similarities'. *Middle East Law and Governance* 4.

Holtbrugge, D. and Berg, N. (2004) 'How Multinational Corporations Deal with Their Socio-Political Stakeholders: An Empirical Study in Asia, Europe, and the US'. *Asian Business & Management* (3).

IMF (2014) 'Fiscal Monitor, Public Expenditure Reform: Making Difficult Choices', April. Available at: www.imf.org/external/pubs/ft/fm/2014/01/fmindex.htm.

Kalirajan, K. and Singh, K. (2010) 'Liberalization Strategies and Poverty Reduction in India'. *Asian-Pacific Economic Literature* 24(1).

Klüver, H. (2013) *Lobbying in the European Union; Interest Groups, Lobbying Coalitions, and Policy Change*. Oxford: Oxford University Press.

LaPira, T.M. and Thomas, H.F. (2012) 'Revolving Doors: Lobbyists' Government Experience, Expertise and Access in Political Context'. Paper to the American Political Science Association Conference, 12 September.

Mishra, P. (2013) 'The New York Review of Books', 21 November. Available at: www.nybooks.com/articles/archives/2013/nov/21/which-india-matters/.

Mulderig, M.C. (2013) 'An Uncertain Future: Youth Frustration and the Arab Spring'. The Pardee Papers/No16/April.

OECD 2014, *OECD Factbook 2014: Economic, Environmental and Social Statistics*. OECD Publishing.

Ohmae, K. (2005) *The Next Global Stage: The Challenges and Opportunities in Our Borderless World*. New Jersey: Wharton School Publishing.

Panda, M. and Ganesh-Kumar, A. (2009) 'Trade Liberalization, Poverty and Food Security in India'. IFPRI Discussion Paper 00930, November. Available at: www.ifpri.org/sites/default/files/publications/ifpridp00930.pdf.

Paczynska, A. (2009) 'Globalisation and Globality'. (IPS) Conference Papers—International Studies Association, 2009 Annual Meeting.

Reinicki, W.H. (2013) 'Purpose beyond Power'. Brookings, Fall 2013. Available at: www.brookings.edu/research/articles/2013/10/globalization-liberal-democracy-society-reinicke.

Robertson, G. (2010) *The Case of the Pope: Vatican Accountability for Human Rights Abuses*. London: Penguin.

Rodrik, D. (2012) 'Who Needs the Nation State?'. Harvard University, May. Available at: www.hks.harvard.edu/fs/drodrik/Research%20papers/Who%20Needs%20the%20Nation%20State.pdf.

Scholte, J.A. (2005) *Globalization: A Critical Introduction*. London: Palgrave MacMillan.

Soengas, X. (2013) 'The Role of the Internet and Social Networks in the Arab Uprisings: An Alternative to Official Press Censorship'. *Comunicar* 21 (41).

Tanzi, V. (1998) 'The Demise of the Nation State'. IMF Working Paper, WP/98/120, August.

US Dept of the Treasury (2013) Monthly 'Report to Congress: Troubled Asset Relief Program', 10 September. Available at: www.treasury.gov/initiatives/financial-stability/reports/Documents/Monthly%20Report%20to%20Congress%20August%202013.pdf.

Wright, T. (2006) 'Why Hasn't Economic Development Brought Democracy to China?'. Available at: www.eastwestcenter.org.

Yongqiang, G. (2007) 'Dealing with Non-Market Stakeholders in the International Market: Case Studies of US-Based Multinational Enterprises in China'. *Singapore Management Review* 29(2).

CHAPTER NINE

The Legal Environment

LEARNING OUTCOMES

This chapter will enable you to:

- Explain the importance of the legal environment for business

- Compare and contrast the different systems of law and their implications for international business

- Assess the importance of contract, tort, and criminal law for business behaviour

- Demonstrate the significance of international arbitration for firms involved in international trade and investment

- Recognize the lack of development of the law around the Internet and the difficulties this raises for firms involved in e-commerce

Case Study International banks and the law

Banks have come under increasing scrutiny since the 2007–08 financial crisis. International banks have been beset by a series of scandals, with regulators across the world from the US, the EU, Japan, and South Korea investigating their activities. The allegations faced by the banks include the rigging of interest rates and foreign exchange rates, money laundering for drug dealers, and circumventing legal restrictions on dealings with Iran, North Korea, and other states subject to US sanctions. This case study analyses the repercussions for banks for breaking the law.

Interest Rate and Foreign Exchange Rate Rigging

Banks were accused of manipulation of lending rates such as Libor, the London Interbank Offered Rate, and Euribor, its euro equivalent. These set the interest rates at which banks lend money to each other. Libor is used to price £800 trillion of financial products ranging from adjustable-rate mortgages, business loans, and credit cards.

Dealers joked or offered small favours by e-mail in the rigging of Libor. One trader promised another, 'Dude. I owe you big time!... I'm opening a bottle of Bollinger' (*The Guardian* 27 June 2012). Another said, 'I'll pay you...50,000 dollars, 100,000 dollars...whatever you want...I'm a man of my word' (*Time* 20 December 2012).

It was argued by regulators that the rigging by banks of key benchmarks such as Libor and Euribor, and the interest rate on European and Japanese financial products, could seriously undermine trust in the integrity of financial markets and could result in significant losses to consumers and investors, or distort the real economy through financial resources being allocated on the basis of rigged, artificially high or low interest rates on financial products.

The banks came under fierce attack, particularly from EU and US regulators. Such collusion between competitors is prohibited by Article 101 of the Treaty on the Functioning of the European Union (TFEU) and Article 53 of the European Economic Area Agreement. The European Commission fined eight international financial institutions a total of €1.7 billion for participating in illegal cartels in markets covering the European Economic Area (EEA). The banks involved were Deutsche Bank (Germany), Société Générale (France), RBS (UK), JP Morgan (US), Citigroup (US), and UK broker, RP Martin. Barclays (UK), previously fined £59.5 million by the UK Financial Services Authority for rigging Libor, would have been fined around €690 million and UBS

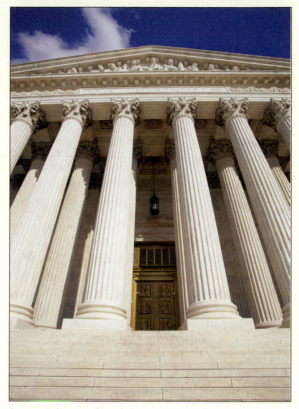

Source: © dynasoar / istockphoto.com

(Switzerland) €2.5 billion, but were given immunity for revealing the existence of the cartels to the EU authorities. The other companies' fines were reduced by 10 per cent for agreeing to settle. At the time of writing (summer 2014), criminal prosecutions of individual bankers involved in Libor rigging were ongoing in the UK. Following the scandal, the chairman and chief executive of Barclays resigned and three former Barclays' employees in the UK faced criminal charges of conspiracy to defraud.

In the US, Barclays was fined $360 million, while UBS paid $1.5 billion, and ICAP, a UK-based multinational financial broker, paid $77 million in total to US and UK regulators, with three of ICAP's ex employers being charged with conspiracy to commit fraud by the US Department of Justice. They faced up to 30 years in prison.

In 2014, a New York banking regulator launched an investigation into more than a dozen banks following allegations of them price rigging the $5.3 trillion a day spot foreign currency market. The banks included Deutsche Bank, Goldman Sachs (US), Lloyds (UK), RBS, and Standard Chartered (UK). It emerged that ➜

→ several employees had left Deutsche Bank following the launch of the probe. London is the most important centre for foreign exchange trading, accounting for 40 per cent of the global market, so it was no surprise when the UK's Financial Conduct Authority announced an investigation of 10 banks and said that the allegations of exchange rate fixing were 'every bit as bad' as that of the Libor scandal (www.bbc.co.uk). Barclays and RBS responded to the allegations by suspending a number of foreign exchange traders. Citigroup and JP Morgan were also being investigated.

Money Laundering and Sanctions Busting

HSBC could have faced criminal charges after a US senate subcommittee reported that the US section of the UK-based bank had:

- transported $7 billion in US bank notes from its Mexican bank to HSBC in the US, more than any other Mexican bank, but had not considered that to be suspicious despite Mexico's history of money laundering and drug trafficking;
- circumvented US safeguards designed to block transactions involving terrorists, drug barons, and rogue states, including allowing 25,000 transactions, involving $19.4 billion, over seven years without disclosing their links to Iran. The bank also provided US dollars and banking services to some banks in Saudi Arabia despite their links to terrorist financing;
- cleared $290 million in 'obviously suspicious' US travellers' cheques for a Japanese bank, benefiting Russians who claimed to be in the used car business.

However, the US, rather than prosecute HSBC, levied a record fine of £1.2 billion. The US authorities feared that pressing criminal charges would lead to HSBC losing its banking licence in the US, threatening the future of the institution and destabilizing the entire banking system.

Other banks also fell foul of US regulators for breaching sanctions. RBS was fined £60 million for dealings with Iran, Burma, Cuba, and other countries. Standard Chartered agreed to pay £220 million to regulators, while Lloyds paid over £200 million, and Barclays around £180 million.

Sources: EU Commission IP/12/846 25 July 2012, IP/13/1208 04 December 2013; US Permanent Subcommittee on Investigations 16 July 2012; *Time* 20 December 2012; *The Guardian* Wednesday 11 December 2013; FT 17 December 2013, 5 February 2014; *The Economist* 7 July 2012; www.theguardian.com 11 December 2012; www.bbc.co.uk 31 October and 1 November 2013, 4 and 17 February 2014; *The Wall Street Journal* 17 February 2014.

Introduction

In this chapter we examine the legal environment within which international business operates. We show the importance of the legal framework and how its rules and regulations can impinge on business, literally, from the cradle to the grave. The law can have a major influence on business behaviour; for instance, when forming a company or negotiating a contract. It can require firms to compensate those whom they injure and it can forbid business, under the threat of penalty, from undertaking certain types of behaviour such as mergers and acquisitions, colluding with competitors, and polluting the environment. We go on to consider the major systems of law prevailing across the globe and we conclude by outlining some important aspects and institutions in international law and their implications for the business community.

Changes in the legal environment can provide business opportunities, but can also generate risk. The firm may find itself the subject of a claim by, for instance, a rival, a customer, or a supplier, which could result in loss. This could take the form of a financial loss and could also result in damage to the company reputation. Companies may feel that they are protected by the law only to find that judges put a different interpretation on the law, or it may be that the law is not rigorously enforced. Finally, changes in the law could leave the company exposed to legal action for actions previously regarded as permissible.

Knowledge of different legal and regulatory systems operating at national and international levels is invaluable for business in a world where foreign trade, investment and outsourcing, and international e-commerce are growing rapidly.

The Importance of Law for Business

The legal environment forms a vital element of the external environment of business. Firms producing everything from laptop computers, mobile phones, air flights, toys, cosmetics, financial products, drugs, fertilizers, food, and drink are all subject to requirements laid down by the law. The legal environment sets the rules of the game within which business operates. It can influence a business from its inception, by laying down certain legal steps which must be undertaken to set the business up, to its death, with rules relating to the winding up of the company. When the firm is up and running, the law cannot only tell it what to do, but also what not to do. The law is a double-edged sword for business because it offers both threats and opportunities. On the one hand, it can leave firms open to legal action, but, on the other, it also gives them the possibility of pursuing others to protect and promote their interests. Business is also subject to regulations. These are not laws as such, but rules that take their authority from statutes and are usually issued by governmental agencies at all levels, national, regional, and local. In most developed countries, utilities companies in the energy sector and in telecoms and water are regulated. In the UK, for example, OFWAT regulates the water industry and OFGEM the energy sector, while, in the USA, the Federal Aviation Administration (FAA) deals with aviation and the Federal Trade Commission (FTC) is responsible for protecting the consumer and dealing with monopolies.

The legal environment, both domestic and international, can influence the whole process of production and sale regarding:

- **Production techniques**: how firms produce goods and services can be influenced by laws and regulations. The aerospace industry in the EU is regulated both globally, through the International Civil Aviation Organisation (ICAO), and in Europe, by the European Aviation Safety Agency (EASA). In the EU, passenger safety is of paramount importance, so aircraft and components must meet standards of airworthiness.

  Increasingly, car makers have been obliged to change their methods of production to meet emissions control regulations introduced by the US, the EU, Japan, China, and India.

  Africa, facing high rates of population growth, urbanization, and increasing industrialization, suffers from deteriorating urban air quality. Foreign car manufacturers and domestic industries using heavily polluting production techniques, such as steel mills and coal-fired power stations, in countries producing the largest amounts of greenhouse gases, Nigeria, Egypt, and South Africa, are likely to face increasingly stringent emissions controls.

- **Product characteristics**: the law can determine product characteristics from the materials used to the product specifications. Asbestos is used as an insulator in the construction and energy sectors. However, many advanced countries, like the USA, the UK, South Korea, and Singapore, along with some emerging economies, such as Saudi Arabia and Turkey, have banned asbestos since it was found to cause lung cancer and other respiratory diseases. Its use is allowed in countries like China, India, and most African countries.

- **Packaging and labels**: most major economies, like the USA, EU, Japan, and China, have rules relating to the packaging and labelling of products such as food and hazardous chemicals. Nonetheless, in 2011, Thailand became the first country to introduce mandatory stop light labelling on certain food products. Nutritional content values are depicted using traffic lights—red for high, amber for moderate, and green for low. In 2012, Chile proposed limits for fat, calories, sugar, and salt in food that, if exceeded, would require the product to wear a prominent stop sign on the label.

- **Content and placement of advertising and sales promotion**: tobacco and alcohol are two industries that are heavily regulated in this regard. Tobacco advertising is banned on radio and television in the USA and EU, with the EU ban extending to print media and the Internet. It is not allowed at all in Canada and New Zealand. South Africa bans advertising and promotion of tobacco and restricts smoking in public spaces.

  In order to counter the effects of the advertising bans on sales, tobacco firms, like British American Tobacco and Philip Morris, have had to find other ways of promoting their products. They have made more use of billboards and direct mailing, got their products placed in films, and sponsored music-oriented events particularly attractive to young people; for example, discos, 'raves', and concerts. Squeezed in rich world markets by advertising restrictions and bans on smoking in public places, tobacco firms have also looked to markets in poorer countries from China and India to Africa and Latin America. China, Brazil, and Argentina banned smoking in public places. Law makers are becoming increasingly concerned about the push by big tobacco firms into the electronic cigarette market and, worried about the effect on consumer health, are pushing for regulations to be introduced.

- **Treatment of workers**: many countries, including the USA, the UK, China, Japan, Brazil, Colombia, South Africa, and Russia, prescribe a minimum wage. The EU has a longstanding commitment to equal pay for equal work and lays down the maximum number of hours that can be worked. Both Japan and the EU have laws protecting the security of employment of older people.

- **Terms and conditions of trade with customers and suppliers**: these cover issues such as delivery dates, terms of payment, return policies for defective products, warranties, and so on. Most countries have statutes relating to the sale of goods and services. Usually, the law requires the terms of sale to be clear, consistent, and reasonable. Low cost airlines Ryanair and EasyJet were fined by the Italian authorities for not supplying adequate information, or giving misleading information, on the travel insurance policies sold via their websites. Information was lacking on policy excesses and the fact that taxes and airport charges were covered. Customers also faced obstacles when making claims (*The Guardian* 18 February 2014).

- **Tools of competition**: this relates to how firms compete with rivals and treat customers. Many developed economies have competition laws regulating business behaviour. In the USA and the EU, for example, the law is hostile to powerful firms exploiting their monopoly power by charging customers high prices or tying them in through the imposition of exclusive contracts which force them to buy all their requirements from the same supplier. EU and US law also disapproves of firms squeezing rivals through, for example, artificially low prices. Companies wishing to go in for takeovers can also be affected by the legal environment. Both the USA and the EU prohibit cartels where firms come to an agreement to avoid competition by agreeing a common price or by sharing the market out geographically. The OECD has been active in promoting competition policy in Latin American countries such as Brazil, Argentina, and Mexico. Emerging economies tend not to have competition laws, Russia, India, and China being three exceptions.

The law may also protect firms from competition from the **grey market**. The grey market refers to trade in goods through distribution channels that have not been authorized by the manufacturer. This often occurs when the price of the product varies from country to country. The good is bought in the country where it is cheap and sold at below market price in the country where price is high. It is sometimes called parallel importing. The practice is particularly prevalent in cigarettes, pharmaceuticals, cars, music and films, satellite television, and in electronic goods such as cameras and games consoles.

In the UK, some pub managers were buying satellite TV cheap decoder cards from Greece to view live Premier League matches. The Premier League decided to use the law to protect its lucrative television revenues, arguing that pubs were breaching strict copyright rules by showing live matches during which the Premier League's distinctive logo was depicted ('C-403/08 - Football Association Premier League and Others' http://curia. europa.eu/juris/). The European Court of Justice ruled that national legislation prohibiting the import and use of foreign decoding cards is contrary to the freedom to provide services conferred by EU law. The English High Court therefore allowed suppliers of foreign satellite systems to carry on business on condition that they prevented copyright elements associated with branding, such as the logo and Premier League anthem, from being shown in a public place. The result was that pubs could legally continue to buy cheap foreign viewing cards from other EU countries, but were stopped from showing matches because brands were protected by copyright law.

Most countries have laws against bribery and these laws can be applied against firms even when the crime has occurred abroad. Smith & Nephew, a UK-based medical device manufacturer with operations in the US, paid over $22 million to the authorities there for breaching the Foreign Corrupt Practices Act even though the offences, bribing doctors in Greece, had been committed outside the US.

• **Ownership of assets**: legal systems usually confer and protect rights of ownership and possession of company assets, both physical, like buildings and machinery, and intellectual assets. For example, the law will often protect intellectual property by giving the holder exclusive rights to exploit the asset for a certain period of time. Protection may also be accorded to holders of copyright covering creative and artistic works, including books, films, music, paintings, photographs, software, product designs, and on trade marks which are signs distinguishing the products or services of firms. Trade secrets may also be protected by the law. In 2012 the UK firm, Dyson, initiated English court proceedings against Korea's Samsung, accusing its rival of a 'cynical rip-off' of Dyson's intellectual property, its vacuum cleaner technology. Dyson subsequently dropped the case. Samsung then responded by filing a lawsuit in Korea against Dyson for around £6 million, arguing that Dyson's lawsuit had adversely affected Samsung's reputation (*The Guardian* 10 September 2013, 17 February 2014).

• **Financial reporting**: many countries lay down rules and regulations regarding the reporting of the financial state of the company and its performance. There are also moves afoot to establish international reporting standards. Around 120 countries require, are moving towards, or allow the use of the International Financial Reporting Standards (IFRS) which establish a framework for the preparation and presentation of financial statements so that financial information provided by companies is transparent and comparable. This harmonization of reporting standards has become more important for companies as they increasingly look overseas not only for market and investment opportunities but also to raise finance. Harmonized reporting allows firms to evaluate more easily potential distributors and candidates for joint ventures and takeovers. While the EU and many other countries around the world now subscribe to IFRS, the USA stands alone with its own generally accepted accounting principles (GAAP) (the International Accounting Standards Board is responsible for establishing the IFRS, see www.iasb.org).

Counterpoint Box 9.1   How big a role for law?

Neoliberals argue that the law should play a minimalist role in society. It should act as the guarantor of private property. Property in this sense refers to assets such as land, housing, company shares, works of art, intellectual property, and so on. The law should protect the rights to property—in other words, the right to own, sell, lend, give away, or bequeath assets—and should enforce contractual agreements. Friedman (2002:xviii), referring to the privatization programme in Russia, said:

> Privatization is meaningless if you don't have the rule of law. What does it mean to privatize if you do not have security of property, if you can't use your property as you want to?

Neoliberals argue that the rule of law is vital for the operation of the market by, for example, facilitating transactions between buyers and sellers. They also accept that the law should protect the citizen against violence, theft, and fraud. These views draw heavily on the ideas of Hayek, Von Mises, Schumpeter, and Friedman.

Critics of the neoliberal position argue that the law has got to do much more than guarantee private property. According to

this school of thought, markets can lead to undesirable outcomes that domestic and international law should try to prevent; for example, the behaviour of financial institutions that led to the global financial crisis, the creation of monopolies, or damage to the environment. Ownership of an asset should not give the right to do as one pleases. The law should stop owners of coal-fired power stations from polluting the air. Furthermore, the law needs to respond to major disparities in income and wealth and gender inequalities, and to ensure the human right to health and education.

Sources: Glinavos 2008; Friedman 2002; Stiglitz 2010; Patel 2009; Nozick 1977

Questions

1. To what extent should owners of assets such as:
   a. large circulation national newspapers;
   b. land producing the coca plant used in the making of cocaine;
   c. be free to do as they wish with their property?

Learning Task

The tobacco industry has been under attack for many years from health campaigners arguing for more stringent legal regulation of the industry.

1. Indicate the reasons why health campaigners want more regulation of the tobacco industry.

2. How have the regulations affected the industry?

3. Analyse the response of the tobacco industry to its legal environment.

   See World Health Organization website for more information.

Systems and Sources of Law

In an increasingly globalized world, firms buying, selling, and investing outside their domestic market confront a variety of laws and regulations in the countries where they operate. In this section, we discuss the major systems of law firms are likely to encounter. Contrary to a widespread misapprehension, laws are not simply the product of decisions made by governments and parliaments.

There are four major legal systems in the world, which are drawn, in large degree, from different sources. They comprise civil law, common law, **customary law**, and **religious law**. Civil law and **common law systems** are predominant in the world and, for that reason, are of most importance to business.

The particular systems operating in countries or regions are the result of the interaction of many historical forces, socio-cultural, political, economic, and technological. One particularly important influence in many countries is the historical legacy of empire. Thus, countries in Africa that were part of the French empire are likely to have a law based on the French system, while former British colonies tend to have systems based on English law. Furthermore, the boundaries between the different systems can break down as the systems evolve over time. Globalization contributes to this blurring of the boundaries because one country's legal system can end up incorporating elements from others. Thus, the system in Japan has been heavily influenced by the German legal code and has also been subject to English and American influences. Similarly, the Chinese system reflects, to a degree, Soviet and Continental legal principles.

Business can find that the various legal systems create very different legal environments within which to operate. Laws, regulations, procedures, and outcomes may vary enormously from one system to another.

Civil Law Systems

Most legal systems in the world have their basis in civil law (see Figure 9.1), the primary source of which is legislation. Civil law is a body of laws and legal concepts which have their basis in the legal codes of the Roman Empire. **Civil law systems** give precedence to written law, sometimes called codified law. Judges apply and interpret the law, which is drawn from legal codes and statutes—statutes are written laws passed by legislative bodies such as national or regional parliaments.

The legal systems in Continental Europe and in Central and South America are largely codified and set out in legislation. In the USA, Louisiana is the sole state having a legal structure based on civil law, with Quebec being in a similar position in Canada. Scottish law is heavily influenced by Roman law, but has not gone in for the extensive codification so prevalent on the continent. Other countries, for example in Scandinavia, while not so influenced by Roman law, have systems akin to civil law because of their heavy dependence on the laws written into statutes.

The procedure in civil law systems is inquisitorial where judges collect evidence and question witnesses to discover the truth. Rather than orally presenting their case, each side must provide written statements of it to the judge. A consequence of this emphasis on the written word is that lawyers act as advisors rather than as oral advocates of their client's case to the

Figure 9.1 Legal systems across the world

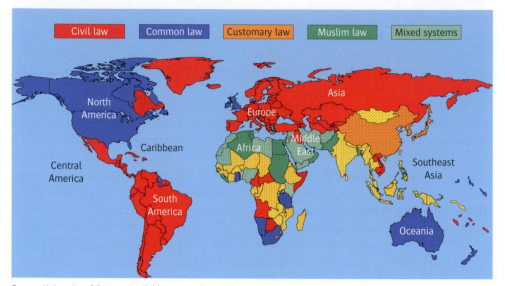

Source: University of Ottawa. Available at www.droitcivil.uottawa.ca

judge. Judges then decide, on the basis of the evidence, whether the case should go to trial, but trials are relatively rare. Should a trial occur, panels of judges or lay assessors review the written evidence gathered by the judge and come to a decision. Juries are used in some criminal trials. In civil systems, court decisions applying the law may influence subsequent decisions, but do not become binding.

One advantage to business of civil law systems is that, because the law is codified in written form, it is easier to find and to articulate clearly. On the other hand, the emphasis on written evidence means that there must be effective document storage and retrieval systems to handle all the paperwork generated by the system if the law is to be properly applied. While this may be the case in Continental Europe, many poorer countries, say in Africa or Latin America, do not have efficient bureaucratic systems, and, as a result, are not in a good position to apply the law effectively.

To avoid confusion, it is useful to note that the term civil law is also used to refer to law dealing with the rights and duties of one individual to another, for instance, in relation to the law of contract.

Common Law Systems

Common law is a legal system based on English law that accords greater importance to judgments in court cases than to written codes and statutes. Common law is also known as case law or judge-made law inasmuch as legal principles are determined by judgments in court cases (Mayson et al. 2013).

Courts, by interpreting and applying the law, determine its meaning and, through their judgments, fill in gaps in the legislative code. Court judgments can set precedents which are binding on themselves and on lower courts when judging similar cases—in other words, it becomes the

Mini Case Study Indonesia

Indonesia is one of the top 20 of the world's largest econo- mies. It is a developing economy with a population of 234 million spread over 17,500 islands. GDP per head is around $3,500 and the growth rate is between 5 per cent and 6 per cent per year. It is rich in natural resources such as copper, coal, oil, gas, and palm oil. The vast majority of the population is Muslim.

Being a former colony of the Netherlands, it has a civil legal system based on Roman and Dutch law. However, it is made more complex by the influence of customary law, traditionally used to resolve interpersonal village disputes in areas such as family and inheritance issues, and Islamic law, often used in disputes between Muslims.

In Indonesia, the rule of law is weak. Business executives do not see the judiciary as operating independently of govern- ment and it therefore remains vulnerable to political interfer- ence. The enforcement of property rights is weak and inconsistent. A company trying to enforce a contract has to go through 40 procedures, which, on average, takes 498 days and costs 139 per cent of the claim. Corruption is seen as the most important problem in doing business in the country. In 2013, the chief oil and gas regulator was arrested on corruption charges and, in 2014, a former chief justice was accused of making rulings that rigged election results and was charged with bribery and money laundering.

Table 9.1 The rule of law—Indonesia

Issue	Score (1 is low)	Country ranking
Judicial independence (1)	3.7/7	74/148
Efficiency in settling disputes (1)	4.1/7	49/148
Protection of property (1)	4.1/7	79/148
Protection of intellectual property (1)	3.9/7	55/148
Protecting investors (1)	6/10	41/148
Enforcing contracts (2)	n/a	147/189
Corruption (3)	32/100	114/177

Sources: (1) World Economic Forum 2014; (2) World Bank 2014a; (3) Transparency International 2014

Sources: World Bank 2014b; *The Jakarta Globe* 6 April 2014; Heritage Foundation 2014

The Indonesian legal system has been ranked by various international organizations and these can be seen in Table 9.1.

Questions
1. What might make Indonesia an attractive location for multinationals looking for foreign investment opportunities?
2. Use the Table to explain why investors might be deterred by the legal environment in Indonesia.

law for everyone to follow. Binding **precedents** are usually made by courts at the higher levels. Judges in lower level courts cannot usually issue binding precedents.

Precedent has a very important role in the common law. From the perspective of business, it has the advantage of ensuring certainty and consistent application of the law. Unlike civil law, precedent allows the law to develop and to respond to changes in society. At the same time, it may be very difficult to find or to state as it is spread across many cases. It may also give rise to laws based on court decisions in extreme, unusual, or unevenly argued cases—to put it another way, a case may be decided not on the relative merits of the evidence but because a lawyer has made an effective presentation of the case in court.

Common law systems are found in countries that have had close ties with Britain, such as the USA, Canada, India, and Australia. In some of these countries, the common law system may sit alongside codes and statutes, but it remains the fundamental basis of the legal system.

Where there is a clash between legislative statutes and common law, statutes take precedence. So, statutes generally have the power to change the established common law, but the common law cannot overrule or change statues (www.leeds.ac.uk/law).

Mini Case Study Argentina and Repsol

The Argentinian legal system is a combination of civil and common law. Heavily influenced by the Spanish legal system, the laws are contained in detailed codes. The judiciary is seen as weak, politicized, and prone to corruption, while court proceedings are slow and inefficient. To avoid using the domestic legal system, many foreign investors resort to international arbitration.

As regards the ease of doing business, the World Bank ranks Argentina 126 out of 189 economies in the world. However, Argentina's foreign investment regime appears to be one of the world's most liberal. The Foreign Investment Law lays down that foreign investors are to be treated like domestic investors so long as they invest in productive activities. Nonetheless, business executives do not see it that way, giving protection of property rights a low score of 2.5 out of 7 (Global Competitiveness Report 2013–14). As we see in the Repsol case below, some foreign investors would argue that their property rights have suffered at the hands of the Argentinian authorities.

Repsol, a Spanish multinational energy company, held a controlling stake in YPF, an energy firm operating in Argentina. In 2011, YPF found massive reserves of shale gas. In 2012, the Argentinian government announced that it would take control of YPF by seizing 51 per cent of its shares, wiping out Repsol's majority stake. It then passed a law in May 2012 legalizing the expropriation of the company. Argentina, with some of the world's largest reserves of shale oil and gas, accused YPF of not investing enough to increase output from its oil fields, which would have reduced the need for imports.

Repsol rejected the accusation and demanded compensation of $10.5 billion. It also said that it was exploring legal action against Argentina. The enforced nationalization of YPF provoked EU protests, and the Spanish government, in support of Repsol, threatened retaliation against Argentina. Spain, followed by other EU countries, raised tariffs on Argentinian exports of biodiesel.

Two years after the nationalization, negotiations between the Argentinian authorities, the Spanish and Mexican governments, and the company led to compensation of $5 billion being awarded to Repsol. The compensation was paid in the form of Argentinian government bonds.

Following the expropriation, Argentina set out to attract other foreign investors to exploit its gas reserves.

Sources: CIA World Factbook 2014; Heritage Foundation 2014; Transparency International 2014; Baker & McKenzie 2012; Repsol press release 25 February 2014 www.repsol.com; World Bank 2014a; www.bbc.co.uk; *El País* 1 November 2013 and 26 February 2014

Questions

1. Discuss the effects of Repsol's experience of the Argentinian legal system.
2. Read the related articles on the **Online Resource Centre**. In the light of the articles, discuss the implications for Repsol's compensation payments.
3. It was estimated by Repsol that $25 billion a year would be needed to exploit the Argentinian gas reserves. Some commentators thought that the nationalization of YPF would deter foreign energy companies. Others disagreed, arguing that energy firms were used to operating in such turbulent environments. Find out whether other investors have been attracted, and advance explanations for your findings.

Learning Task

Look at the map in Figure 9.1 showing the legal systems in the world.

1. Which is the dominant legal system in Latin America?
2. What are the main characteristics of that dominant system?
3. What legal issues might be encountered by a Brazilian firm wishing to do business in the US?

Common law, in contrast to civil law systems, is adversarial in nature. Thus, both sides are in competition to persuade judge and jury of the legitimacy of their case. In proceedings, lawyers act as the principal advocate of their client's case and witnesses are called to give oral testimony. Oral argument plays a more important role in common law. In court cases, the judge plays the role of impartial arbiter.

Customary Law Systems

There is no single agreed definition of customary law. It can be seen as a body of rules, values, and traditions based on knowledge gained from life experiences or on religious or philosophical principles. It establishes standards or procedures to be followed when dealing with social relationships such as marriage, adultery, and divorce, but can also play a part in the ownership and use of land and issues around fishing rights. Customary law, like common law, is often not written into statutes and can be fluid and evolutionary. While hardly any countries operate under a legal system which is wholly customary, there are a large number of countries where it plays an important role. This is true in a number of African countries, in some of which it operates in combination with either civil or common law systems depending on whether the area was colonized by France or Britain. It also plays a part in the legal systems of China and India as well as islands in the South Pacific.

Muslim Law Systems

Muslim law systems are codes of law mainly based on Sharia law, which is derived from the religious principles contained in the Koran and in the teachings and example of Mohammed. In some Muslim countries, the law is limited to regulating personal behaviour, while in others its impact is much more wide-ranging. Examples of the latter include countries such as Iran, Saudi Arabia, Sudan, Libya, and parts of Nigeria. This regulates all aspects of life, both public and private. The law forbids consumption of alcohol and pork as well as gambling, fraud, slander, the making of images, and usury (that is, lending money and charging the borrower interest), especially at an exorbitant or illegally high rate (*Britannica Concise Encyclopaedia* www.britannica.com).

Globally, the finance markets operated under Islamic law and untouched by the global financial crisis, have grown by more than 10 to15 per cent annually, from 2000–12. Islamic finance investments, while still less than 2 per cent of global financial assets, are now worth $1.6 trillion and are forecast to increase to $2.5 trillion by 2015 (National Bureau of Asian Research 7 November 2013).

Important Aspects of the Law for Business

There is a wide range of laws applicable to business, such as the law of contract, tort, criminal law, and international law. Contract law and the law of tort deal with disputes between business and the firms and individuals it deals with. Both give rise to actions by the concerned/aggrieved parties through the civil courts. Criminal liability, on the other hand, involves a business committing a crime against the state. Cases are initiated by state bodies, such as the Crown Prosecution Service in the UK or the Department of Justice in the USA, and are heard in the criminal courts.

Mini Case Study Nigeria

Businesses in Nigeria face a complex legal system. There are three distinct legal systems:

- laws based on English style common law, stemming from its past as British colony;
- Sharia, or Islamic, law operating in 12 of the northern states—in some states it applies only in issues of personal status, in the southern states Sharia law forms no part of the judicial system;
- and customary law, where various ethnic groups have their own distinctive customary laws.

In litigation between Nigerians and non-Nigerians, the general rule is that English law applies. Superior courts include the Sharia Courts of Appeal, Customary Courts of Appeal, the High Courts, the Court of Appeal, and the Supreme Court. The three latter courts apply common laws, rules, and procedures. Judges are appointed by the President on the advice of a Judicial Council. Some analysts argue that politicians have too much influence on the judiciary with their power to appoint and dismiss judges—in the Global Competitiveness Index 2013–14 it scores a poor 3.2 out of 7 for the independence of its judiciary.

Corruption is a big headache in Nigeria despite legal attempts by government to combat it. In 2013, in the Transparency International Corruption Perceptions Index it ranked 94 out of 177 countries. The Corrupt Practices and Other Related Offences Act (ICPC) was passed in 2000. However, administration and enforcement of the laws is ineffective. Since its inception, the ICPC has been unable to secure the conviction of high profile public officials for corruption in spite of several investigations and prosecutions. The Nigerian Chief Justice recognizes that there are corrupt elements in the judiciary.

In bribery scandals involving the US firm, Haliburton, and the German giant, Siemens, the prosecution of the Nigerian officials and companies involved was only commenced after the companies were convicted in the US and Europe. For example, after a German court found Siemens guilty of bribery in several countries including Nigeria, the company agreed to pay €30.5 million to the Nigerian government as part of a plea bargain deal that allowed the company to escape prosecution for bribing Nigerian officials in order to secure contracts.

Nigeria, at 147 out of 189 economies, fares badly in the World Bank ranking for doing business. It has a poorly developed road system and experiences regular breakdowns in power supply. Nonetheless, its significant reserves of gas and oil and other natural resources, large population, and economic growth rates averaging 8 per cent per year make it attractive to foreign investors, who have been reluctant to use Nigerian courts. As a result, arbitration proceedings, both domestic and international, have been on the increase.

Sources: CIA World Factbook 2014; Point Blank News 17 November 2012 www.pointblanknews.com; Aigbovo 2013; Transparency International 2014; Taddia 2013 www.lawgazette.co.uk/analysis/nigeria-risks-and-growth/70235.fullarticle; Abdulmumini 2011; World Bank 2013, 2014a

Questions

1. Why might a foreign investor, with a grievance against a Nigerian supplier, be reluctant to take the case through the Nigerian courts?
2. Advance reasons for foreign investors like Haliburton and Siemens bribing Nigerian government officials.
3. To what extent do you consider that weaknesses in the Nigerian legal system would deter foreign investors?

Contract Law

When firms do business, they are constantly entering into contracts. Essentially, contracts are struck when a firm buys or sells goods or services from a supplier or a customer, or takes on employees. The contract is a legally binding agreement between the parties concerned and may be formal, informal, written, or oral. The contract is likely to cover such elements as price, payment terms, contract duration, the consequences of breaching the contract, the process for resolving disputes between the parties, and what will happen if there are unforeseen events such as wars or revolutions (see Hagedoorn and Hesen (2007) for a discussion of contract issues in technology partnerships between firms). The contract obliges those involved to fulfil their side of the agreement. If they fail to do so, then they are in breach of contract and may be pursued by the aggrieved party through the courts.

Tort Law

Tort is an area of the law concerned with injuries to people or damage to their assets. The law obliges firms to ensure that their activities do not cause damage, intentional or accidental, to others and is in addition to any contractual arrangement that may exist. Business activities, therefore, that involve, for example, negligence leading to injury to a customer, selling defective goods, or counterfeiting another company's product is a tort (The Stationery Office *Business Law*).

A very famous tort case was the McDonald's coffee case in the USA. A customer called Liebeck won millions of dollars of damages against McDonald's when she claimed that the company's negligence had caused her to get burned with coffee that was far too hot. A more recent tort case was brought by Alcatel-Lucent, a French-based multinational communications company employing around 80,000 people and operating in 130 countries. Alcatel took Microsoft to court claiming an infringement of two of its MP3 technology patents that allowed for digital encoding and compression of music which could then be sent over the Internet. The US court found in favour of Alcatel and ordered the software giant to pay US$1.5 billion in damages (*Financial Times* 23 February 2007).

Mini Case Study Tort—big pharma on edge

In 2013, the Supreme Court in Alabama ruled that a man claiming to have been injured by the generic version of Reglan, the acid reflux drug produced by pharmaceutical giant, Pfizer, could sue Pfizer for its failure to warn his doctor about the drug's risks. The man claimed that the drug had caused him to develop a movement disorder of the muscles.

The Court came to its view even though the patient had taken a version of the product that Pfizer did not make. The Court decided that, 'it is not fundamentally unfair to hold the brand-name manufacturer liable for warnings on a product it did not produce' (Medical Marketing & Media 1 March 2013).

Pfizer held that the ruling applied only to Alabama and pointed to the decision of four federal appeals courts that innovator companies like Pfizer were not liable for injuries to consumers who took generic Reglan. It also argued that, since the patient had taken a generic version of the drug, it had no means of informing the patient of the drug's side effects. It asked the Court to rehear the case.

Big pharma companies were alarmed by the Alabama decision because they saw it as encouraging others to pursue further law suits there. Furthermore, it followed a ruling by the Supreme Court, the highest court in the US, that generic drugs makers could not be sued for failing to alert patients to such risks. The ruling was based on US regulations forbidding generic drug makers from updating labelling, even after becoming aware of a potential risk not mentioned in the labelling on the branded product.

Pfizer put it thus:

> If allowed to stand, the court's decision will radically alter the financial realities of drug innovation, forcing brand-name manufacturers to anticipate that, after their period of exclusivity has expired, they will, nonetheless, be responsible for an ever-growing generic market over which they have no control and from which they derive no profit.

Sources: Forbes 25 February 2013; *The New York Times* 11 January 2013; Medical Marketing & Media 1 March 2013

Questions

1. What is the tort in this case?
2. Who should be held responsible for causing the tort?
3. Why are big pharmaceutical companies concerned about the court decisions identified in the case?

Criminal Law

Criminal law applies across many business activities and has become increasingly important in areas such as financial reporting, the proper description and pricing of goods and services, the safety of goods and services, particularly food, and environmental impacts. In the USA, after several business scandals involving the likes of Enron and WorldCom—both of whom were involved in fraudulent accounting (WorldCom artificially inflated its profits by billions of dollars)—Congress introduced more criminal legislation. This tightened the rules in areas such as financial reporting, tax crimes, foreign currency violations, health and safety in the workplace, and crimes against the environment. The purpose of these legal requirements is usually the protection of life, or health, or the environment, the prevention of deceptive practices, or to ensure the quality of products, the preservation of competition, and the promotion of technological advance.

As we saw with the Smith and Nephew case, one country's criminal law can apply even when the offence occurs outside that country and also when the company involved is not based in the country. The Japanese multinational, Marubeni, under the US Foreign Corrupt Practices Act, agreed to pay the US Department of Justice around $55 million in criminal penalties for involvement in an alleged conspiracy to bribe Nigerian officials (Sivachenko 2013).

Learning Task

In 2013, Lush, a small company making handmade cosmetics, took the giant, Amazon, to court. Lush did not allow Amazon to sell its products. However, when customers typed the word 'Lush' into Amazon's search facility, they were directed to other products they might like to buy instead. Lush argued that Amazon was infringing its trademark. Lush said that it had cost it £500,000 to defend its intellectual property.

1. On what aspect of the law, contract, tort, or criminal, is the Lush case based?

2. What issues are small and medium-sized businesses likely to face when considering taking legal action against giants like Amazon?

3. Previously, Interflora, a network of companies delivering flowers, had pursued a similar case against Marks & Spencer (http://www.theguardian.com/business/2013/may/21/interflora-wins-trademark-case-against-marks-spencer ; www.ashurst.com/publication-item.aspx?id_Content=9164).

In the light of the result in that case, discuss the likelihood of Lush winning its case against Amazon.

International Law

Usually, when operating in foreign countries, business has to follow the law of the land. However, international law is playing an increasingly important role in the world of international business. As business has become more globalized, so has the law, developing in ways aimed at facilitating international trade and investment. Another development is that international contracts are increasingly being written in English (Jennings 2006).

Counterpoint Box 9.2 Business and the criminal law

There is a debate on whether corporations should be subject to the criminal law and the sanctions it can impose, such as imprisonment and fines.

Legal scholars, such as Khanna (1996), argue that firms do not have an independent identity, but are associations of individuals under contract to the business. They conclude that corporate criminal liability, from society's point of view, should only be pursued in the rarest of circumstances, and argues that it serves almost no purpose. They claim that firms cannot be imprisoned and only act through the conduct of their employees, so it is the individual who should be pursued through the civil courts. Companies being fined under the criminal law would reduce the money available for innocent stakeholders, such as employees and shareholders. Khanna rejects the claim that criminal sanctions invariably adversely affect a firm's reputation or confer a moral stigma with its customers. He contends that a firm, fined for emitting pollution that does not affect its customers, would not suffer any reputational damage. Subjecting firms to the criminal law simply leads, in this view, to a waste of public resources. He concludes that civil liability regimes are more efficient and effective in dealing with unlawful conduct by firms.

Opponents counter these arguments by claiming that firms are social entities and that their managers are usually protective of their reputation and know the difference between morally correct and incorrect behaviour. In fact, many companies make a point of advertising their policies on corporate social responsibility. Kelly (2012) argues that business, like individuals, should be held accountable for criminal behaviour. He claims that multinationals have been complicit in genocides over many years, citing the involvement of multinational companies in supplying mustard gas to Saddam Hussein's regime in Iraq to be used on the Kurds. There is no international tribunal or law to impose criminal responsibility on firms, and Kelly maintains that this needs to be rectified, given the increasing trend of globalization and the burgeoning power of multinationals.

Sources: Khanna 1996; Kelly 2012; Paraschiv 2013; Etzioni with Mitchell 2014

Questions

1. Discuss whether firms supplying military equipment to totalitarian regimes should be subject to criminal responsibility when the regime uses their equipment to commit crimes like genocide.

International law can reduce the uncertainty, costs, and the disputes associated with international commerce when there are doubts about which country's laws apply. In such situations, firms, unsure of their rights, could be less willing to go in for foreign trade and investment. There are a variety of organizations, conventions, codes, and treaties that play a role in international commerce. We now look at some of the most important.

Codes and Conventions

Some national laws have ended up being used by firms involved in international business. One example is the **Uniform Commercial Code** in the USA. It sets down standard rules governing the sale of goods, is in force in many US states, and has been adopted by other countries (www.ilpf.org).

Another element of international contract law is the United Nations **Convention on Contracts for the International Sale of Goods** (CISG) of 1980. It is very similar in content to the Uniform Commercial Code. It aims to make international trade as convenient and economical as trading across state borders in the USA. By 2014, 79 states, accounting for around two-thirds of world trade, had signed up to this convention. The CISG establishes a set of rules governing sales of goods between professional sellers and buyers who have their places of business in different countries. By adopting it, a country undertakes to treat the Convention's rules as part of its law. The Convention aims to reduce the uncertainty and the disagreements that arise when the sales law of one country differs from that of another (http://law.pace.edu).

Given that so many countries have signed up to it, the CISG might seem like a significant advance in the law relating to international trade. However, the reality is that many firms deliberately do not use the convention. In the EU, this is true of producers of oils, seeds, fats, and grain and of most large Dutch companies. This unwillingness to use the agreement appears due to some of the terms used in the convention being open to differing interpretations. Also, it may be that firms are ignorant of various elements of the CISG and are not prepared to invest time and money to find out. Another deterrent factor is that the convention only covers some aspects of the relationship between the buyer and seller so that, in other areas, national laws apply. Finally, countries such as the UK, Nigeria, India, Indonesia, Portugal, and South Africa are not party to the convention (Smits 2005; www.unilex.info; for discussion of the UK position, see Hoffmann 2010 and Moss 2005–06).

An organization trying to facilitate the legal processes around international commerce is the International Institute for the Unification of Private Law (Unidroit), which lays down principles for international commercial contracts. It is an independent, intergovernmental organization whose purpose is to help modernize, harmonize, and coordinate commercial law between its 63 member states. Only three African countries are members, Egypt, Nigeria, and South Africa. In 1964, a convention was signed relating to the Law on the International Sale of Goods. However, the agreement did not apply to the sale of all products. For example, it did not cover sales of financial products, such as stocks and shares, or sales of electricity. In 2002, a law relating to franchises was agreed (see www.unidroit.org).

International Arbitration

Sometimes, disputes arise between firms based in one country and firms or governments of other countries. For example, there can be disagreement between the firms as to which national law should apply. That such disputes arise is hardly surprising given the rapid growth of international trade and investment. In these situations, international arbitration has become increasingly popular for businesses. There are a number of international agencies who will arbitrate between the warring parties. For example, firms can use commercial arbitration under the New York Convention set up in 1958 under the aegis of the United Nations and called Uncitral (see United Nations Commission on International Trade Law at www.uncitral.org). Uncitral was used in a dispute between BP and its Russian partners in the TNK BP joint venture over BP's agreement to swap shares with Rosneft, the Russian energy giant (BP Group Results 1st Quarter 2011).

Another international body helping to resolve disputes between governments and foreign business around investment, is the International Centre for the Settlement of Investment Disputes (ICSID) which is based at the World Bank in Washington. It deals with cases such as that involving three Italian mining companies who filed a complaint against South Africa, saying that the Pretoria government's positive racial discrimination laws violated investment treaties with other countries. The companies complained that their granite mining operations had been expropriated because they were not conforming to South Africa's black economic empowerment policy and that this violated treaties that South Africa had signed with Italy and Luxembourg (*Financial Times* 9 March 2007; for other cases and information about ICSID, go to www.worldbank.org/icsid).

The World Trade Organization, where its rules have been broken, also arbitrates in disputes on matters of foreign trade, investment, and intellectual property rights. Firms cannot take a complaint direct to the WTO, for the disputes procedures can only be activated at the request of a member government. This is illustrated by the dispute brought to the WTO by Japan, the US, and the EU against China for restricting the export of rare earth minerals used in the production of computer hard drives and mobile phones. China, the world's largest producers of rare earth minerals, argued that controls were necessary to limit the environmental damage caused by mining, but also wanted to promote the expansion of its domestic processing of these minerals, which caused the WTO to rule in favour of the complainants (see dispute DS431 at www.wto.org).

When companies agree to insert an international arbitration clause into a contract, it means that disputes between them are dealt with by an independent arbitrator rather than a court. This has a number of advantages over litigation through national courts. The first advantage is neutrality because arbitrators have to meet strict independence tests and can be drawn from countries other than those of the firms concerned. The second is confidentiality. Proceedings, unlike court cases, are normally private so that there is no public washing of dirty linen. Third, the procedures are flexible, and lastly, awards made, for instance under the New York Convention, can be widely enforced in almost all trading countries, unlike national court decisions. The disadvantages are that it can be more costly than court litigation, there is normally no right of appeal, it does not work so well when there are more than two companies involved, and, finally, there is no possibility of a quick decision even when there is no justifiable defence.

Learning Task

The World Bank carries out research on the problems associated with doing business in different countries. It researches various legal issues, such as the enforcement of contracts. In its 2014 report, it found that enforcing a contract in the US took 370 days, 731 in Brazil, 406 in China, and 447 in Nigeria. It also found very large variations between countries in terms of the efficiency of the judicial system in resolving a commercial dispute. For example, the cost of enforcing the claim in the US was about 19 per cent of the total value of the contract, whereas in Nigeria the figure was 92 per cent. The Bank collects information on two indicators:

- time in calendar days to resolve a dispute and the cost in court fees; and

- lawyer fees, where the use of lawyers is mandatory or common, expressed as a percentage of the value of the claim.

Go to the latest Country Tables in Doing Business on the World Bank website and carry out the tasks below.

1. Compare and contrast the time taken and the cost of enforcing contracts in Argentina and South Africa.

2. How might the time and cost of enforcing contracts in Argentina and South Africa affect the decision of an MNC on where to invest?

3. Discuss how MNCs could deal with problems of enforcing contracts in countries where it takes a lot of time and costs a lot of money.

International Law and IPRs

Globalization has put an onus on firms to find ways of protecting intellectual property rights abroad. This has become particularly important in certain sectors such as film, music, and software where the growth of the Internet and digitization makes copying much easier. Such protection is relatively well-developed in the rich economies of North America and Europe, but much less so in poorer countries such as China and India—a further deterrent in pursuing cases in China is the corruption of the judiciary, and, in India, the time it takes for the wheels of justice to turn. It is therefore hardly surprising that companies prefer to pursue infringements of their IPRs in countries with well-developed systems of protection where cases are dealt with in a timely fashion and where the judiciary is not tainted by corruption. Thus, 3M, the US technology multinational, chose to file an IPR lawsuit with a federal court in Minnesota and the US International Trade Commission against other producers of laptops including Sony, Matsushita, Hitachi of Japan, and Lenovo of China. 3M complained that the laptop makers had infringed the technology it used in its lithium-ion batteries (www.techworld.com).

As pointed out in Chapter 7, Protecting Technology, the costs of taking out protection can vary significantly from one country to another, as can the time taken to get protection, the level of protection given, and the ease with which firms can pursue violators of their property rights.

So, intellectual property laws can vary from country to country—even in the EU, there is still no single system of granting patents. Usually, an application in one country for protection of a firm's IPRs only results in the granting of protection in that country. In the past, firms seeking protection in other countries had to make separate applications in each, which could be very costly in terms of money and time.

However, the situation is changing. Two systems now exist that reduce the need for separate national applications. The Patent Cooperation Treaty allows firms to file a single application indicating in which countries it is seeking protection. The European Patent Convention allows for an application to be filed at the European Patents Office in Munich. The Office can grant separate national patents for specified countries. There have also been some moves towards harmonization of laws as a result of international treaties, including the Agreement on Trade-Related Aspects of Intellectual Property Rights (TRIPS) agreed through the WTO. It aims to establish minimum levels of protection that each government has to give to the intellectual property of other WTO members. Member governments have to ensure that their intellectual property rights systems do not discriminate against foreigners, that they can be enforced in law, and that the penalties for infringement are tough enough to deter further violations. The procedures must not be unnecessarily complicated, costly, or time-consuming (www.wto.org).

European Union

The European Union (EU) comprises 28 members, all of whom are bound by EU laws. The primary source of EU law comes from treaties such as the Treaty of Rome as modified by the Single European Act, the Treaties of Maastricht, Amsterdam, Nice, and Lisbon. The secondary source of EU law consists of directives that are binding on the member states, but whose implementation is their responsibility, regulations that are binding and implemented consistently across the EU, and, finally, decisions which are made by European institutions like the Commission, the

Council of Ministers, and the European Parliament dealing with specific issues, countries, institutions, or individuals. European law develops through a combination of case law setting precedents and statutory law. In any clash with national law, EU law takes precedence. The European Court of Justice (ECJ) interprets EU law and ensures that is applied the same way across the Union. In the Lush versus Amazon case, it was asked by the UK High Court for an interpretation of the law regarding intellectual property rights.

Single Market Programme

An essential element of the EU project is the Single Market programme. The programme—by removing internal barriers such as frontier checks, different technical standards for goods and services, and obliging members to recognize academic or vocational qualifications gained in another member state—tries to ensure that goods, services, capital, and people can move freely across borders. The Single Market requires that laws of the various member states do not favour domestic firms over those of other members in areas such as trade, investment, the establishment of businesses on their territory, or the movement of workers.

The EU has seen that different national contract laws can constitute a barrier to the movement of goods and services so it has passed several directives, at least 12 according to Smits (2005), to deal with this. However, they do not replace national laws by laying down a general law of contract, but only apply to certain types of contract and to specific areas of contract law, such as that relating to the sale of tour packages and timeshares, on combating late payment in commercial transactions, or in the distance marketing of financial services.

For example, the Consumer Sales Directive does not attempt to harmonize different national laws nor does it require firms to offer the same product guarantee throughout the EU. However, it does require firms to provide specific information on product guarantees. The information has to be written in plain and intelligible language regarding the consumer's legal rights under the national legislation and has to make clear that these rights are unaffected by the product guarantee. The guarantee also needs to indicate the duration and territorial scope of the guarantee and how to make a claim (Schulte-Nölke 2007). The EU is trying to enable consumers to pursue EU-wide claims against firms providing faulty goods or services. As the Commissioner responsible for consumer affairs put it, 'I want a citizen in Birmingham to feel as comfortable shopping for a digital camera from a website in Berlin or Budapest as they would in their high street' (*Financial Times* 14 March 2007). The Commission wants to encourage consumers to buy more abroad.

Smits (2005) points out that EU directives in the field of contract law allow member states to create more stringent rules in the area covered by the directive. In particular, in the area of consumer protection some member states tend to enact rules that are tougher than the directives prescribe. This means that business still has to deal with differences in national legislation among the member states, which may make it less convenient and more costly to do business abroad.

The result is that there remain significant differences in contract law within the EU, with each country in the EU having its own contract law. These can be classified in three main groups. First, England, Ireland, and Cyprus have common law systems that emphasize judge-made law. The second type is the civil law system that holds sway in France, Belgium, Luxemburg, Spain, Portugal, Italy, Malta, Germany, Austria, Greece, and the Netherlands. The civil law is in place in nearly all of the former Communist countries of Eastern Europe that entered the EU in 2004 such as Poland, the Czech Republic, Slovakia, Hungary, Estonia, Lithuania, Latvia, Slovenia, and Croatia (see Smits (2005) who sees the new entrants as somewhat distinct from the other members operating civil law systems). Finally, the Scandinavian countries of Denmark, Sweden, and Finland form the third group, which has a number of common statutes relating to contract.

Competition Law

Business operating in the EU is also subject to the competition laws that are important in helping to maintain a barrier-free single market. These laws, which are policed by the Commission, cover four main areas.

First, cartels that prevent or distort competition in the EU are strictly forbidden by Article 101 (ex Article 81) of the Treaty. Cartels are often popular with firms because they allow them to avoid competition by agreeing to set the same price for their products or by sharing the market out between them (see Table 9.2). Firms are tempted to set up price-fixing cartels by the significant hike they can make in their prices. It has been calculated that international cartels overcharge their customers by an extra 30–33 per cent on average (*Financial Times* 9 May 2006). In 2014, the EU fined the four major producers of polyurethane foam, Vita, Carpenter, Recticel, and Eurofoam, €114 million for participating in a price-fixing cartel in 10 EU member states (IP/14/88 http://europa.eu/rapid/press-release_IP-14-88_en.htm).

Second, Article 102 (ex Article 82) prohibits firms with a strong market position from abusing their dominant position by, for instance, exploiting customers through high prices or squeezing their rivals through artificially low prices. The Commission imposed a fine of over €1 billion on Intel for abuse of its dominant position in the market for a certain type of computer chip, the x86 CPU, for which Intel held a 70 per cent share of the €22 billion world market. The fine was levied on two grounds: for giving illegal rebates to customers if they bought all their requirements of a

Table 9.2 The 10 highest cartel fines by company

Year	Undertaking	Case	Amount in €m
2008	Saint Gobain	Car glass	880
2012	Phillips	TV and computer monitor tubes	705
2012	LG Electronics	TV and computer monitor tubes	688
2013	Deutsche Bank	Euro interest rate derivatives	466
2001	F. Hoffman La-Roche	Vitamins	462
2013	Société Générale	Euro interest rate derivatives	446
2007	Siemens AG	Gas insulated switchgear	397
2008	Pilkington	Car glass	357
2009	E.ON	Gas	320
2009	GDF Suez	Gas	320

Source: http://ec.europa.eu

particular chip from Intel; and paying customers like Dell, Acer, HP, and Lenovo to stop or delay the launch of competitors' products—in this case the main rival to Intel was AMD (IP/09/745 http://europa.eu/rapid/press-release_IP-09-745_en.htm?locale=en).

The third area of the law covers mergers. Under the EC Merger Regulation, the Commission has the power to regulate big mergers. Firms have to notify the Commission of proposed mergers. The Commission can wave the merger through, as it did with the takeover of Scottish Power by the Spanish firm Iberdrola, or it can approve the merger subject to certain conditions. When Nestlé wanted to take over Perrier, it had to agree to sell off some of its brands before the Commission would give its approval. The EU, fearful that a merger would lead to reduced competition and increased prices, allowed Unilever to acquire the household and body care products divisions of Sara Lee on condition that it sell off a number of body care brands. Finally, permission can be refused where the acquisition would reduce competition in the market place. Thus, the merger between Tetra Laval, the dominant producer of packaging for carton drinks, and Sidel, a market leader in the production of machines used for making PET plastic bottles, was turned down (see http://ec.europa.eu and www.freshfields.com).

Finally, Article 107 (ex Article 87) of the Treaty frowns on assistance given by governments to firms that distort or threaten competition and impede the smooth functioning of the Single Market programme. It wants to avoid governments giving aid to domestic firms to the detriment of their foreign rivals. In 2013, the Commission ruled that that an Italian maritime firm, Saremar, should pay back €10.8 million it had received which had not been made available to its competitors (IP/14/59 http://europa.eu/rapid/press-release_IP-14-59_en.htm). To ensure no breach of Article 107, the Commission monitored closely the many government financial support schemes, amounting to a massive €4 trillion, that were put in place across the EU to help the banking sector face up to the damage wreaked by the global financial crisis (IP/10/623 http://europa.eu/rapid/press-release_IP-10-623_en.htm?locale=en).

The Internet

There has been a massive growth of e-commerce. However, no single code of law applies to the Internet alone. Hedley (2006) sees the laws that apply as 'a bewildering mix of the specific, the general and the metaphorical' (2006: 1). Some legal commentators see Internet law as incomprehensible.

Legislation, either national or international, makes very few specific references to the Internet, but many areas of law can be applied to it; for example, legislation on communications in the areas of trade, defamation, and pornography. Contract law is also problematic since the extent to which it applies to the Internet is a matter of debate. For example, traditionally, contracts require a signature to be legally valid, but there is, as yet, no agreed definition on what constitutes a legally valid electronic signature. The rise of the Internet has been accompanied by the increased use of standard electronic contracts. Some academics, like Friedman (2004), are concerned that these are slanted against the consumer because the Internet, much more than paper contracts, allows retailers to hide pro-seller clauses. However, a survey of 55 Internet retailers found that less than 10 per cent had sites where contracts were even enforceable and that relatively few included terms detrimental to the consumer (Mann and Siebeneicher 2008).

According to Schwabach (2006), the area of law most affected by the Internet is that related to intellectual property rights because these are ownership rights of information. There is much evidence that illegal downloading of software, music, and films costs the respective industries billions of pounds. A survey of the commercial software industry estimated that it was losing over $60 billion in one year alone (www.vilabs.com/resource-section/stat-watch/).

While it is widely accepted that certain activities on the Net breach criminal law, there can be great obstacles to enforcing it. For instance, the victim of someone hacking into their computer systems may be based in one country, say the USA, and the perpetrator thousands of miles away in another, say China. A 2013 survey of global cybercrime found that it was costing business an annual average of $7.2 million with each company experiencing between one and two successful attacks per week, a 20 per cent increase on the previous year. The most costly attacks involved malicious employees, denials of service, and web-based attacks (Ponemon Institute 2013).

Moreover, there is no obvious means for any one government to control the Net. Individual states find it difficult to control the activities of Internet users when the activity is taking place outside their territory, and Hedley (2006) questions their ability even when the activity occurs within their national frontiers. He goes on to argue that effective legal control can only be exercised at the international level. To that end, an International Convention on Cybercrime came into effect in 2004. By 2014, 42 countries had ratified the Convention—that is, approved in accordance with domestic law and thus rendered enforceable—while 11 have signed, but not yet ratified. The majority of signatories are European, but other countries, like the USA, Canada, Japan, and South Africa, have signed up (Council of Europe http://conventions.coe.int/Treaty/EN/Treaties/html/185.htm). The Convention requires countries to include a range of Internet-related activities in their domestic laws, for example relating to computer hacking, child pornography, computer-related fraud, and infringements of copyright (Council of Europe).

Up to now, Internet service providers (ISPs), like China Telecom, Telefonica, TalkTalk, Comcast, and MSN, have borne the main burden of regulation and control. They have been obliged by national police and intelligence services to spy on customers and to provide data, such as telephone conversations, e-mail records, and web pages viewed, to the authorities.

● Chapter Summary

As we have seen, the law constitutes a very important element of the environment within which firms must operate. Every aspect of a business operation can be affected by the law from its inception to its demise. The law can have a major influence on what firms produce, the production processes used, the prices they charge, where they sell, and how they go about advertising and promoting their goods and services. The strategies and policies that firms pursue to boost revenues, cut costs, and increase profits are shaped by the legal environments within which they operate. However, the law should not be seen solely as a constraint on business activities. It acts as a protection to firms and offers opportunities, as we saw with the easier access to markets created by the removal of barriers within the EU Single Market.

Companies wishing to get involved in international trade and investment find very different legal environments across the world. The principles on which the systems are based, and the procedures under which they operate, can vary widely depending on the prevailing legal system. Business can find that what is acceptable in common or civil law systems may not be permissible in countries where the system of Sharia law prevails. Even where countries have a similar legal tradition, firms may encounter very different experiences in each.

For example, Germany, Italy, and Colombia all have civil law systems, but the time taken to enforce a contract through the local courts varies enormously.

Some of the problems of dealing with different national legal frameworks are being eased by the development of international laws and arbitration procedures under the auspices of institutions such as the WTO, EU, and the World Bank.

The law relating to the Internet is seriously underdeveloped at both national and international level. There is no code of generally accepted internationally agreed laws to which business can have recourse, and the mixture of laws which do seem to apply are complex. As a result, firms involved in e-commerce face much risk and uncertainty when wishing to have recourse to the law or when they themselves are being pursued through the courts.

Business operating internationally, whether through trade or investment, has to be aware of the national and international systems of law. It needs to monitor how the law is changing and must be prepared to deal effectively with the constraints and opportunities generated by the legal environment.

● REVIEW QUESTIONS

1. Why is the legal environment important for international business?

2. Explain why knowledge of different legal systems would be useful for firms involved in international trade and investment.

3. Explain why firms involved in international trade might use international arbitration bodies to settle disputes.

● Assignment Tasks

1. In 2010, the European Commission launched an antitrust investigation into Google.

   a) Find out:

   - who were the main complainants in the case;

   - under which article of the EU Treaty was Google being investigated;

   - the reasons why the EU Commission initiated the case.

   b) Check Europa, the official EU website, to find out what has happened in the case.

   c) The complainants were unhappy with the Commission decision. Find out why and, on the basis of your research, write on behalf of the complainants to the Commission outlining your reasons for disagreeing with the outcome of the case.

2. Biwater Gauff, a jointly owned UK and German water company, was given a contract by the Tanzanian government to overhaul and operate the water and sewerage system of the capital, Dar es Salaam. The government became unhappy with Biwater's performance on the project and took it back into public hands. Arbitration in the dispute took place, under Uncitral rules, in London. The company subsequently filed a dispute with ICSID (Case No. ARB/05/22) against the Tanzanian government.

   a) What was the legal justification for the Tanzanian government taking back the project?

   b) What was the outcome of the London arbitration procedure (see www.theguardian.com Friday 11 January 2008)?

c) Biwater took its case to ICSID. On what legal grounds did the company base its case?

d) What was the outcome of the ICSID case (see Triantafilou, E.E. *International Disputes Quarterly*, winter 2009)?

e) Assume you are employed in the project management section of a multinational construction company. Your boss asks you to write a brief report of 300 words analysing whether the company should bid for infrastructure projects in Tanzania.

Case Study Apple, e-books, and price fixing

In 2011–12 both the US Department of Justice (DoJ) and the European Commission started antitrust proceedings against a cartel operated by Apple and five large multinational publishers, Simon & Schuster, Harper Collins, Hachette, Holtzbrinck/ MacMillan, and Pearson/Penguin. They were accused of conspiring to raise the prices of e-books. The US Sherman Act and Article 101 of the Treaty on the Functioning of the European Union prohibit firms from such collusion. The penalties for violating the Sherman Act can be severe. Although most enforcement actions are civil, the Sherman Act is also a criminal law. The Act imposes criminal penalties of up to $100 million for a corporation along with up to 10 years in prison. Under federal law, the maximum fine may be increased to twice the amount the conspirators gained from the illegal acts or twice the money lost by the victims of the crime, if either of those amounts is over $100 million. US Attorney General Eric Holder believed that the alleged collusion had led consumers to pay millions of dollars more for some of the most popular books. The EU Commission can impose a fine of up to 10 per cent of a firm's annual worldwide turnover.

Publishers were unhappy about the behaviour of a very powerful customer, Amazon, fearing that it was establishing a monopoly position in the e-book market. Amazon was offering big discounts on their e-books. They particularly disliked Amazon's decision to price newly released and best-selling e-books at $9.99, which was often below cost. The publishers were concerned that book buyers would come to expect this price point and that this would make it more difficult for them to raise prices in future. After Amazon started reaching out directly to authors, one publishing executive expressed his desire 'to screw Amazon'. Publishers were right to be worried, for Jeff Bezos, Amazon's founder, suggested that 'Amazon should approach...small publishers the way a cheetah would pursue a sickly gazelle' (Stone 2013: 243). An ex-employee of

Source: © Photodisc

Amazon said that its managers saw book publishers as 'antediluvian losers' with outdated inventory systems and 'warehouses full of crap' (Business Insider 10 February 2014).

The DoJ claimed that top publishing managers met regularly in expensive restaurants and also called and e-mailed each other in order to come up with a response to Amazon.

Apple launched the first iPad tablet in 2010 and wanted to offer e-books on its new iBookstore. Publishers realized that they would make losses on many books were Apple to charge prices similar to Amazon. According to the DoJ, Apple, recognizing the discontent of publishers with Amazon, agreed with them to raise the price of many best-selling e-books to $12.99 or $14.99. Apple went along with this on condition that the publishers together imposed the same deal on Amazon and other retailers. Steve Jobs, the chief executive of Apple, called this his 'aikido move'.

As a result of the investigation, three publishers, Simon & Schuster, Hachette, and Harper Collins, settled with the DoJ, agreeing to terminate their agreements with Apple and to let Amazon and other retailers resume discounting of e-books. They agreed to refrain from limiting any retailer's ability to ➔

→ set e-book prices for two years. That allowed Amazon to resume deep discounts on new e-books. Amazon called the settlement a victory for consumers and users of its Kindle e-reading device, and looked forward to discounting more Kindle books.

However, unlike in Europe, the companies in the US also faced a lawsuit by 49 states, which led to $75 million compensation to US customers who had bought e-books at the higher prices.

The DoJ continued to pursue Apple, Holtzbrinck/Macmillan, and Pearson/Penguin. In 2013, a US court found Apple guilty of conspiring with publishers to set e-book prices at the launch of the iBookstore and an injunction was issued in the US prohibiting Apple from repeating attempts to fix the prices of e-books. Apple was also required to allow retailers such as Amazon and Barnes & Noble to sell e-books directly through their iOS apps, a practice previously banned by Apple. It also established an external monitor to ensure that Apple complied with the judgment. Apple continued to protest its innocence, arguing that '[t]he iBookstore gave customers more choice and injected much needed innovation and competition into the market'. In

the EU, the publishers and Apple agreed to stop price fixing for the ensuing five years.

Sources: EU IP/12/1367 13/12/2012; U.S. v. Apple Inc. et al., US District Court, Southern District of New York, No. 12-02826; *The Wall Street Journal* April 11 2012; AppleInsider Friday 6 September 2013; The Register 8 August 2013; Federal Trade Commission, Antitrust Laws, State of Connecticut, Office of the Attorney General 22 May 2013 www.ct.gov/ag/lib/ag/about_us/annualreportfy2012-13.pdf.

Questions

1. Why do many countries prohibit cartels?
2. Use the case to compare and contrast the treatment of cartels in the US and EU.
3. Why did the publishers feel it necessary to act collectively to impose the deal on Amazon?
4. Explain the reasons for Apple getting involved in the cartel.
5. Discuss the constraints imposed by the US and EU decisions on participants in the cartel.
6. What opportunities did the decisions provide for e-book retailers?

● FURTHER READING

For sources of EU law see Europa, the official website of the EU, and the Cornell University site at http://library.lawschool.cornell.edu.

Carr covers the main legal aspects of overseas sales. It includes an examination of the developments in e-commerce.

- Carr, I. (2014) *International Trade Law*, 5th edn. Abingdon: Routledge-Cavendish.

- Salacuse provides an analytical tool to examine laws governing foreign investment and shows how countries influence such investment.

- Salacuse, J. (2013) *The Three Laws of International Investment*. Oxford: Oxford University Press.

Glenn gives a global view of the traditions of various legal systems, for example Islamic and Jewish. It examines national laws in the wider context of legal traditions.

- Glenn, H.P. (2014) *Legal Traditions of the World: Sustainable Diversity in Law*, 5th edn. Oxford: Oxford University Press.

The following reference is a standard text on international commercial law. It examines the legal framework and its application to commercial cases.

- Goode, R. (2010) *Transnational Commercial Law: Text, Cases and Materials*, 4th edn. Oxford: Oxford University Press.

Poole is a standard text on contract law.

● Poole, J. (2014) *Textbook on Contract Law*, 12th edn. Oxford: Oxford University Press

Van den Bossche and Zdouc give an overview of the laws and policies pursued by the WTO.

● Van den Bossche, P. and Zdouc, W. (2013) *The Law and Policy of the World Trade Organization*. Cambridge: Cambridge University Press.

Rogers covers major legal issues raised by the Internet for business.

● Rogers, K.M. (2011) *The Internet and the Law*. Basingstoke: Palgrave MacMillan.

● REFERENCES

Abdulmumini, A. (2011) 'Religious and Customary Laws in Nigeria'. *Emory International Law Review* 1 October.

Aigbovo, O. (2013) 'Nigerian Anti-corruption Statutes: An Impact Assessment'. *Journal of Money Laundering Control* 16(1).

Baker & McKenzie (2012) 'Doing Business in Argentina 2012'. Available at: www.bakermckenzie.com/files/Uploads/Documents/North%20America/DoingBusinessGuide/Dallas/br_dbi_argentina_13.PDF.

CIA (2014) The World Factbook. Available at: www.cia.gov/library/publications/the-world-factbook/docs/didyouknow.html.

Etzioni, A. with Mitchell, D. (2014) 'Corporate Crime'. Available at: www2.gwu.edu/~ccps/etzioni/documents/A366.pdf.

Friedman, M. (2002) 'Preface'. *Economic Freedom of the World: 2002 Annual Report*. Cato Institute. Available at: www.cato.org/pubs/efw/efw2002/efw02-intro.pdf.

Friedman, S.E. (2004) 'Text and Circumstance: Warranty Disclaimers in a World of Rolling Contracts'. *Arizona Law Review* 46: 677.

Glinavos, I. (2008) 'Neoliberal Law: Unintended Consequences of Market-Friendly Law Reforms'. *Third World Quarterly* 29(6).

Hagedoorn, J. and Hesen, G. (2007) 'Contract Law and the Governance of Inter-Firm Technology Partnerships: An Analysis of Different Modes of Partnering and Their Contractual Implications'. *Journal of Management Studies* 44: 3. Available at: http://core.kmi.open.ac.uk/download/pdf/6460436.pdf.

Hedley, S. (2006) *The Law of Electronic Commerce and the Internet in the UK and Ireland*. London: Cavendish Publishing.

Heritage Foundation (2014) *2014 Index of Economic Freedom*. Available at: www.heritage.org/index/.

Hofmann, N. (2010) 'Interpretation Rules and Good Faith as Obstacles to the UK's Ratification of the CISG and to the Harmonization of Contract Law in Europe'. *Pace International Law Review* (Winter).

Jennings, M.M. (2006) *Business: Its Legal, Ethical, and Global Environment*, 7th edn. Ohio: Thomson West.

Kelly, M.J. (2012) 'Prosecuting Corporations for Genocide Under International Law'. *Harvard Law & Policy Review* 6.

Khanna, V.S. (1996) 'Corporate Criminal Liability: What Purpose Does It Serve?'. *Harvard Law Review* 109(7).

Mann, R.J. and Siebeneicher, T. (2008) 'Just One Click: The Reality of Internet Retail Contracting'. *Columbia Law Review* 108(4).

Mayson, S., French, D., and Ryan, C. (2013) *Mayson, French and Ryan on Company Law*, 30th edn. Oxford: Oxford University Press.

Moss, S. (2005-06) 'Why the United Kingdom Has Not Ratified the CISG'. *Journal of Law and Commerce* 25. Available at: www.uncitral.org/pdf/english/CISG25/Moss.pdf.

Nozick, R. (1977) *Anarchy, State, and Utopia*. New York: Basic Books.

Paraschiv, D.-S. (2013) 'Corporate Criminal Liability in Comparative Law'. *Contemporary Readings in Law and Social Justice* 5(1).

Patel, R. (2009) *The Value of Nothing*. London: Portobello Books.

Ponemon Institute (2013) '2013 Cost of Cybercrime Study: Global Report', October. Available at: http://media.scmagazine.com/documents/54/2013_us_ccc_report_final_6-1_13455.pdf.

Schulte-Nölke, H. (ed) (2007) 'EC Consumer Law Compendium—Comparative Analysis'. December. Available at: http://ec.europa.eu/consumers/archive/cons_int/safe_shop/acquis/comp_analysis_en.pdf.

Schwabach, A. (2006) *Internet and the Law: Technology, Society and Compromise*s. Santa Barbara, CA: ABC-CLIO.

Sivachenko, I. (2013) 'Corporate Victims of "Victimless Crime": How the FCPA's Statutory Ambiguity, Coupled with Strict Liability, Hurts Businesses and Discourages Compliance'. *Boston College Law Review* 20.

Smits, J.M. (2005) 'Diversity of Contract Law and the European Internal Market'. Maastricht Faculty of Law Working Paper 2005/9. Available at: www.unimaas.nl.

Stiglitz, J. (2010) *Freefall: Free Markets and the Sinking of the Global Economy*. London: Penguin.

US Permanent Subcommittee on Investigations (2012) 'HSBC Exposed US Financial System to Money Laundering, Drug, Terrorist Financing Risks', 16 July 2012. Available at: www.hsgac.senate.gov/subcommittees/investigations/media/hsbc-exposed-us-finacial-system-to-money-laundering-drug-terrorist-financing-risks.

Stone, B. (2013) *The Everything Store: Jeff Bezos and the Age of Amazon*. London: Bantam Press.

Transparency International (2014) *Corruption Perceptions Index 2013*. Available at: http://cpi.transparency.org/cpi2013/.

World Economic Forum (2014) *Global Competitiveness Report 2013-2014*. Available at: www.weforum.org/reports/global-competitiveness-report-2013-2014.

World Bank (2013) 'Nigeria Economic Report', No. 1, May. Available at: https://openknowledge.worldbank.org/bitstream/handle/10986/16568/776840WP0Niger0Box0342041B00PUBLIC0.pdf?sequence=1.

World Bank (2014a) *Doing Business 2014: Understanding Regulations for Small and Medium-Size Enterprises*. Available at: www.doingbusiness.org/~/media/GIAWB/Doing%20Business/Documents/Annual-reports/English/DB14-Full-Report.pdf.

World Bank (2014b) 'Indonesia Economic Quarterly, March 2014: Investment in Flux'. Available at: www.worldbank.org/en/news/feature/2014/03/18/indonesia-economic-quarterly-march-2014.

CHAPTER TEN

The Financial Framework

LEARNING OUTCOMES

This chapter will enable you to

- Explain what money is and its importance for business

- Assess the significance of inflation and interest rates for the business environment

- Analyse the role and importance of international financial institutions and markets

- Explain the restructuring and the increasing integration of the international financial system

- Explain the characteristics and impact of the global financial crisis

- Assess the challenges faced by financial regulators

Case Study The VW bubble

This case examines financial manoeuvrings on the stock exchange leading to a massive increase in the share price of Volkswagen (VW), which had no connection with that company's performance in the car market.

In October 2008, Volkswagen, albeit briefly, became the most valuable company in the world despite the fact that prospects for the car industry looked bleak, facing as it did Western economies suffering from the worst financial crash in history and heading for a deep recession. How had this come about?

Financial traders, many of them working for hedge funds, looked at Volkswagen and the dismal economic situation in its main markets and could only see one way for its share price to go, down. Traders therefore decided to sell VW shares with the intention of making a profit by buying them back when the price fell—this practice is called shorting. They did this by paying a fee to borrow between 10 per cent and 15 per cent of VW shares from institutional investors, like pension funds, with a promise to return the shares in the near future.

Unfortunately for the traders, VW's rival, Porsche, had been quietly buying VW shares, including those borrowed by traders, with the aim of building up a 75 per cent stake in the company and taking it over. VW's home state of Lower Saxony owned another 20 per cent of the shares. Porsche had built up its stake partially through buying options on VW shares, giving it the right to buy VW shares at an agreed price. The result of Porsche's purchases was that the VW share price did not drop. When Porsche's strategy became known, traders that had bet on the VW share price falling realized that there were few shares left for them to buy to return to institutional investors. There was a desperate rush to buy, at any price, the 5 per cent or so of shares that were left causing the price to rise. They were joined in the rush by speculators trying to profit from the increase in the share price. The result was a bubble in VW shares, whose price rose 348 per cent over a two day period.

The rise in VW's value forced it into the top 30 companies on the DAX, the German stock exchange. This prompted another buying bout of VW shares, but this time by conservative institutional investors whose policy was to spread risk by having a stake in the largest blue-chip corporations. The result was that the VW share price soared from €200 to €1,000 in

Source: © shaunl / istock.com.

one week causing the value of the company to increase by €300 billion.

The BBC reported that hedge funds had made an £18 billion loss on VW shares. Subsequently, a number of hedge funds took Porsche to court in both the US and Germany. They claimed that Porsche had misled investors by denying in a press release and in phone calls any desire to take over VW. By March 2014, Porsche had scored victories against the hedge funds in two regional court cases in Germany. Other cases were still pending. The judge in the Stuttgart court ruled that the funds had not proved they actually invested because of the information in the press release. She continued that losses were at least partly caused by the hedge funds' decision to engage in 'highly speculative and naked short selling' (Bloomberg).

This case raises questions about the rationale for the valuation of companies by financial markets. It also has implications for business. Overvaluation could make it easier for companies to take over others by offering their overvalued shares, undervaluation could make the firm more vulnerable to take-over. Incorrect valuation is also likely to affect how company performance is measured, for example profit on shareholders' equity.

As a postscript, in 2012 VW took over Porsche.

Sources: Patel 2009; Bloomberg www.mobile.bloomberg.com 17 March 2014; www.bbc.co.uk 29 October 2008, 3 February 2014; *The Guardian* 5 July 2012.

Introduction

In this chapter we are going to look at the international financial environment, that part of the international economy concerned with money, interest rates, and financial assets such as deposits, company shares, bonds, derivatives, and foreign currencies. We examine the major private financial institutions and the markets where they operate and the extraordinarily fast rate at which these institutions and markets have grown, both at home and abroad. We also look at the operation of organizations such as the Bank for International Settlements, the International Monetary Fund, the World Bank, and the European Central Bank.

We go on to examine the characteristics of the 2007 global financial crisis that shook the international monetary system. Finally, we consider how the financial system is regulated and the effectiveness of regulation in maintaining stability in the international financial system.

Money

Money is an essential element of the international financial environment, playing, as it does, a number of vitally important roles for business:

- A medium of exchange—money allows businesses to receive payment from customers both at home and abroad and to pay their suppliers.

- A common measure of value—money enables firms to place a value on the goods and services that they buy and sell.

- Divisibility—money can be broken down into different units of value, cents and dollars or pence and pounds, facilitating the process of exchange.

- A store of wealth—money gives business the ability to store wealth. Businesses can build up reserves of money now which can then be used later to buy goods and services or to invest.

The Importance of Confidence

Underpinning the idea of money is an agreement to accept something that, in itself, may have no fundamental use to us.

Normally, we have confidence that it can be exchanged in the market for something that does have use, goods and services. Were that confidence to melt away, the whole financial and economic system would be under threat. In such a situation, neither individuals nor businesses would be prepared to accept money in exchange for goods and services and the system of monetary exchange would collapse with drastic consequences for the economy in general, and business in particular.

Money takes various forms, moving from the more to the less liquid. Liquidity refers to how quickly and cheaply an asset can be converted into cash. Thus, paper money or cash is the most liquid asset because it can be exchanged very easily for goods and services. Current bank accounts are another example of high liquidity insofar as the money in them is quickly and easily accessible and also because it can be easily transferred by cheque or electronic means.

Mini Case Study Bitcoin

The bitcoin is a digital currency in which transactions can be performed without the need for a central bank—the unit of account is the bitcoin. Transactions take place between individuals, but bitcoins are also accepted by some e-businesses, including some operating illegally, partly because transactions can be carried out anonymously and partly because the fees are lower than those charged by credit card companies, which can be anything from 2.5 per cent to 5 per cent. Transactions are recorded in a public digital ledger. In November 2013, it was reported that the number of firms accepting bitcoins had risen to 1,000 worldwide (www.coindesk.com).

Many individuals and companies buy and sell bitcoins, and such transactions occur in a variety of different currencies. The supply of bitcoins is determined by an algorithm; that is, a mathematical equation. New bitcoins are created every 10 minutes in batches of 25 (Quartz www.qz.com). The value of the bitcoin varies quite dramatically. According to Quartz, it topped $1,000 in the autumn of 2013. By 7 June 2014, the value had dropped to $655 (http://preev.com).

Some businesses quickly saw that security could be a major barrier to the growth of bitcoins so they set up what were claimed to be secure online wallet services where users could deposit their bitcoins. This reassured individual users that their bitcoins were safe with a trusted third party, at the same time allowing payments to be made easily and lowering the technical know-how required to get and store the currency. However, online wallet providers became the target of hackers. In October 2013, one company, Inputs.io, lost over $1 million worth of bitcoins and others suffered the same fate. In February 2014, MtGox, a leading bitcoin exchange, filed for bankruptcy claiming that its computer systems had been hacked and 750,000 bitcoins stolen.

Some national authorities are concerned about bitcoins, one reason being the threat it poses to their control of the money supply. *The Economist* (12 April 2014) reported that China was the 'promised land' for bitcoin with the country estimated to account for half of the world trade in the coin in 2013. The Chinese market collapsed when the central bank declared that bitcoins were not a currency and banned commercial banks from dealing with bitcoin cyber-exchange companies. The Japanese authorities were considering taxing the digital currency, but wanted to do so in cooperation with other governments. The Bank of England (McLeay et al. 2014) does not see the bitcoin as money because it is not accepted on the high street and its popularity derives from its ability to act as an asset like gold.

Sources: *The Guardian* 5 and 18 March 2014; McLeay et al. 2014; useBitcoins www.usebitcoins.info

Questions

1. Reread the section above on money. Assess whether bitcoins are money. In your answer, consider the extent to which bitcoins are:
    a. a good medium of exchange and store of wealth;
    b. divisible into smaller units

Less liquid are savings accounts and deposits that need notice before money can be withdrawn. Even less liquid are a variety of financial assets, such as stocks and bonds, which may not be turned into cash so easily.

Inflation and Interest Rates

Inflation

Inflation can be defined as an increase in the overall price level of goods and services in an economy over a particular period of time or as a reduction in the value of money. It is usually measured by collecting price information on a representative sample of goods and services and using the information to calculate a Price Index that shows the change in the general price level. Businesses operating in countries with relatively high rates of inflation can find their international competitiveness undermined as the rising costs of goods and services feed higher costs of production. This process may be exacerbated when workers respond to rising prices by demanding higher wages. On the other hand, this could open up selling opportunities for firms operating out of low inflation economies. They are likely to find it easier to compete with firms operating in countries suffering from high inflation.

The rate of inflation in rich countries started to pick up after 2004 with vigorous growth in the global economy. Rapid growth, particularly in countries like China, led to increases in demand for commodities such as oil and other raw materials, which pushed up their prices. Up to then, low import prices had helped to hold down rich country inflation rates. The Federal Reserve estimated that falling import prices had reduced US inflation by between 0.5 and 1 percentage point a year from the mid-1990s. Rising inflation was viewed with concern in most countries, with the major exception of Japan where economic growth had been stalled for many years. The rise in inflation above zero was seen as finally signalling the end of that country's 15 years of stagnation.

The onset of the global financial crisis in 2007 led to a slowdown in inflation globally to the point where, in 2009, price levels were deflating, i.e. dropping, in the USA, UK, Japan, and Switzerland, and commodity prices, with the exception of oil, dropped by around one-fifth over 2008. Figure 10.1 shows world inflation peaking in 2011 at around 5 per cent and then, with falls in commodity and food prices, declining to about 3 per cent (www.dataworldbank.org).

Inflation generally runs at a higher rate in emerging economies. In early 2014, inflation in Nigeria was running at nearly 8 per cent and in Brazil at just above 6 per cent. This compares with the UK and the US with rates of less than 2 per cent (www.tradingeconomics.com; if you wish to compare inflation rates, go to the Trading Economics or World Bank websites). High inflation rates are not unusual in countries like Nigeria and Brazil where economies are growing fast, wages are increasing, and the public may be more accepting of rising prices. Another reason could be that governments in poor countries, like Zimbabwe, finance their activities by simply printing more and more money, causing demand for goods and services to outstrip supply.

Figure 10.1 World inflation rate (%)

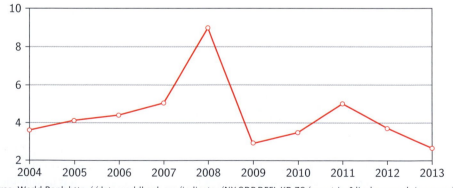

Source: World Bank http://data.worldbank.org/indicator/NY.GDP.DEFL.KD.ZG/countries?display=graph (accessed 10 October 2014)

Interest Rates

An interest rate is the price paid for the temporary use of someone else's money. Interest is a cost to borrowers but income to lenders. When interest rates rise in a country then this increases the cost of borrowing to business. Business could, given the removal of barriers to the movement of capital, shop around in other countries for cheaper rates. A hike in interest rates may also depress demand for goods and services as consumers find it more expensive to borrow to buy consumer durables such as cars, computers, plasma TVs, and so forth. On the other hand, rising interest rates could benefit financial institutions who lend money because they can charge more for their loans.

All the world's leading central banks, concerned about rising inflation after 2004, increased interest rates. However, the global financial crisis raised fears of a collapse of the international financial system and caused them to reverse the policy. Even by 2014, seven years after the crisis started, with developed economies still sluggish, central banks in the Eurozone, the USA, the UK, and Japan all had interest rates at 1 per cent or less, unlike Brazil and Russia with rates of 11 per cent and 7.5 per cent, respectively (www.global-rates.com).

Financial Institutions—Who Are They and What Do They Do?

The functioning of the international economy, and the production and the trading and investment activities of the organizations and individuals within it, are dependent on the effective operation of a variety of financial institutions, both public and private. We look first of all at several international financial institutions and their functions, and then we examine an array of other organizations in the financial sector.

International Financial Institutions

There are several international financial institutions whose main aim is to facilitate the effective operation of the international payments mechanism and to ensure stability in the international financial system.

Bank for International Settlements

The Bank for International Settlements (BIS) has 60 members, 59 of which are countries represented at the BIS by their central banks, the other being the European Central Bank. The BIS fosters international monetary and financial cooperation and stability. It serves as an international central bank for national central banks such as the Federal Reserve, the European Central Bank, and the Bank of China. It acts as a forum to promote discussion and policy analysis among central banks and in the international financial community.

The BIS deals with the central banks on a daily basis and, by buying and selling foreign currencies and gold, helps them manage their foreign currency and gold reserves. It also advises the central banks and other international institutions on how to prevent financial fraud. In 2013, the BIS held currency deposits representing around 2 per cent of world currency reserves. In times of financial crisis, the BIS offers short-term credits to central banks and may also coordinate emergency short-term lending to countries.

The Bank played a key role in establishing BASEL I, II, and III, which recommended levels of capital banks need to guard against the risk of collapse. The BIS hosts the Financial Stability Board (FSB), set up in 2009 in the aftermath of the global financial crisis. The FSB promotes international financial stability by monitoring the world financial system and advising on effective regulation.

International Monetary Fund

The International Monetary Fund (IMF), which has 188 members, was established to preserve international financial stability; in other words, to avoid financial crises that could threaten the international financial system. Up to the early 1970s that meant sustaining the system of fixed currency exchange rates set up by the Bretton Woods Agreement. Member countries contribute funds to a pool from which they can borrow on a temporary basis when running balance of payments deficits. Applicants for loans in the past have faced IMF demands for changes in government policy such as cutting public expenditures on social programmes, reducing subsidies on basic necessities, increasing taxes, eliminating import tariffs, and the privatization of publicly owned assets.

The move in the 1970s away from fixed exchange rates seemed to remove one of the main reasons for the IMF's existence. However, its services are still required; for example, in the mid-1990s when the stability of the international financial system came under threat due to a wave of financial crises in Mexico, South East Asia, Russia, Brazil, Turkey, and Argentina. In the cases of Brazil, Russia, and Argentina, the IMF intervened massively in the currency markets by pumping in millions of dollars to support their exchange rates.

It has some very ambitious aims: to promote global monetary cooperation, secure financial stability, facilitate international trade, promote high employment and sustainable economic growth, and reduce poverty. The IMF differs from the BIS insofar as it can provide temporary financial assistance to members to enable them to correct international payment imbalances. The idea is that such assistance discourages countries from trying to rectify their balance of payments deficits by resorting to policies such as competitive currency **devaluations** that could have disruptive effects on the international trading and financial systems, exchange controls, or trade protection.

During the latest global financial crisis, the IMF came to the rescue of countries with large amounts of financial assistance. For example, Greece was given a loan of US$30 billion, Hungary and Ukraine each got support of around US$16 billion, while Latvia secured an IMF stand-by arrangement worth more than US$2.3 billion (www.imf.org). These loans came with conditions forcing countries to implement austerity measures. The deal forced Latvia to: cut local government employees' wages by an immediate 15 per cent; agree a 30 per cent cut in nominal spending on wages from 2008 to 2009; reduce government spending by the equivalent of 4.5 per cent of GDP; and impose a pension freeze and a rise in value-added tax (www.brettonwoodsproject.org). In 2009, in the aftermath of the crisis, IMF members agreed to double the resources available to the IMF to US$1 trillion. While this represented a significant increase in resources, they remained minuscule compared with the cost to banks of the financial crisis. The Fund estimated that for the USA alone, banks had to write down loans and make provisions for losses to the sum of US$588 billion as a result of the financial crisis. The figure for Eurozone banks was US$442 billion (IMF 2010).

While the ability of the IMF to deal with global financial crises has been strengthened, it is difficult to envisage it making a significant difference were there to be another full-blown financial crisis of global dimensions such as that starting in autumn 2007.

World Bank

The World Bank, with 188 member countries, was set up to reduce global poverty and to improve standards of living. Currently, its specific aims are to reduce extreme poverty to no more than 3 per cent of the world population and to promote income growth for the bottom 40 per cent of each country's population.

It provides low cost loans and interest-free credit to developing countries for education, health, and for the development of infrastructure projects in water supply, transport, and communications. World Bank projects can be a source of lucrative contracts for businesses such as water, energy, and telecommunications utilities as well as construction companies.

It provides over US$30 billion of assistance to developing countries each year (www.bicusa.org). Like the IMF, the Bank may have the capacity to bring about change in individual countries, but its budget does not equip it to have a major impact on the billions of people who continue to live in poverty.

European Central Bank

The European Central Bank (ECB) is the central bank for countries that are members of the Eurozone (18 in 2014). Its main job is the control of inflation. It uses the tools of **monetary policy**, in other words the **money supply** and interest rates to achieve price stability. The ECB

Counterpoint Box 10.1 The IMF and World Bank

The World Bank, along with the IMF, has come in for criticism. The critics claim that neither institution works in the best interest of poor countries but on behalf of the rich economies. They provide assistance to debt-ridden or near-bankrupt developing countries that are powerless to resist their demands for the introduction of reforms that remove barriers to business in advanced economies wishing to export goods or services to those poor countries, import raw materials from them, or to invest there. In addition, poor countries are pressurized to cut public expenditure, remove state monopolies, and prioritize repayment of debt to foreign banks and investors. This hits the poor in those countries as jobs are cut, health and education budgets reduced, price supports removed, and food and natural resources exported abroad. In addition, the Bretton Woods Project (2014) found that the World Bank had, in the four years up 2013, given more aid to banks than to health and education, casting doubt on its ability to meet its poverty targets. This occurred despite the contribution of the banks to the global financial crisis.

Supporters argue that the removal of barriers to trade, public monopolies, and subsidies increases competition, leading to a more efficient allocation of resources and economic growth. Countries would be in an even worse state were they not forced to adopt responsible budgetary policies. The IMF has made efforts to protect the vulnerable during the latest crisis by inclusion of a commitment to strengthen the provision of social safety nets. On aid to the financial sector, defenders claim that the money can be channelled to small and medium-sized enterprises, which can use it to generate employment and income. Supporters also argue that the institution has moderated its belief in free markets by accepting that, in some cases, inflows of capital need to be controlled because they can fuel credit booms and inflation, and harm competitiveness.

Sources: Stiglitz 2002; Harrigan 2010; Muuka 1998; Bretton Woods Project 2014; www.imf.org; www.brettonwoodsproject.org; Moschella 2014

Questions

1. In 2014, the IMF agreed to bail out Ukraine. Assess the conditions for the bail-out in the light of the arguments in this counterpoint box.

conducts foreign exchange operations on behalf of member states, manages their foreign reserves, and promotes the smooth operation of payments systems within the zone. It carries out the tasks typically associated with national central banks.

Private Financial Institutions

There is a whole range of other financial institutions carrying out an array of functions invaluable for business. Banks, insurance companies, pension funds, investment trusts, and unit trusts all act as intermediaries between those who wish to borrow money and those who wish to lend. Retail banks take deposits from private individuals, firms, and other bodies. Insurance companies, pension funds, and unit trusts collect longer-term savings, which they then invest in a variety of stocks and shares. By not being dependent on the shares of a single company, they offer savers the possibility of spreading risk. Investment banks (also called merchant banks) provide a range of financial services to business. They give advice in areas such as mergers and acquisitions, the disposal of businesses, and arranging issues of new shares.

Private equity funds, including venture capital companies, are another source of funding for business. These firms gather funds from private and public pension funds, charitable foundations, business, and wealthy individuals and often use them to finance smaller, sometimes start-up, companies. They usually do this in return for a share in the ownership of the company (see www.deloitte.com for information on the global outlook for venture capital).

Functions of Financial Institutions

We now look in more detail at some of the important functions performed by financial institutions for business.

Mobilizing Savings and Providing Credit

The mobilization and pooling of savings is one of the most obvious and important functions of the financial sector. Savings facilities, such as bank accounts, enable businesses and households to store their money in a secure place. In countries where secure facilities for savings are lacking, or where there is a lack of confidence in the stability of the financial sector, for example in some developing economies, people often opt to save in physical assets such as gold or jewellery, or store their savings at home. In such situations, business can find it difficult to raise finance and may have to rely on internally generated profits. By offering such facilities, the financial sector pools savings and channels them to businesses to be used productively in the economy. Interest paid on savings may increase the amount saved, giving a boost to the funds available for businesses to invest.

Financial intermediaries, by pooling the savings of firms and individuals and lending them on to business, can make it easier and cheaper for business to export and import, and to finance investment for expansion or for the introduction of new technology. Thus, the sector can help business service new foreign markets and sources of supply and can also make it easier for firms to improve competitiveness by increasing productivity or by introducing new products. The global financial crisis led to a freezing of credit making it more difficult for non-financial businesses to finance their operations.

Payment Facilities

Financial intermediaries facilitate the exchange of goods and services both in terms of domestic and cross-border transactions by providing mechanisms to make and receive payments. To be effective, payments systems need to be readily available for both domestic and foreign buyers and sellers, through bank branches or electronically, and they also need to be affordable, fast, and safe from fraud.

Good payments mechanisms free up firms to concentrate on what they do best, make goods and provide services, and this ability to specialize makes it easier for them to innovate and to increase productivity. Anything that reduces transactions costs and better facilitates the exchange of goods and services—whether that be faster payments systems, more bank branches, or improved remittance services—will help to promote business growth.

Normally, payments systems are more highly developed in the advanced economies than in poorer countries, but systems can vary from one rich country to another. The existence of multiple payments systems can raise problems of inter-operability, that is the ability of the various systems to accept payments from others. Inter-operability may be made more difficult when systems are using incompatible hardware or software systems. While this may not be such an important issue for big multinational companies, whose subsidiaries are trading with each other and where payments systems are internal to the company, it does have major implications for firms dependent on making or receiving cross-border payments from third parties.

There are various systems which operate internationally and facilitate cross-border payment:

- SWIFT: in 2013, SWIFT had around 10,500 members in 215 countries processing more than 5 billion transactions (SWIFT Annual Review 2013 www.swift.com/about_swift/publications/annual_review). Its services are used by banks, central banks, and other

---

Learning Task

Figure 10.2 shows the use of credit cards in various countries. Examine the Figure and answer the following questions.

1. Which countries have the highest and lowest use of credit cards?

   Explain Germany's position in credit card usage.

2. Now advance some explanations for credit card usage in Turkey.   ➜

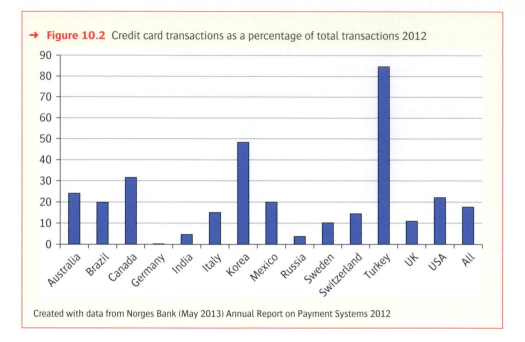

→ **Figure 10.2** Credit card transactions as a percentage of total transactions 2012

Created with data from Norges Bank (May 2013) Annual Report on Payment Systems 2012

financial institutions, such as securities brokers and dealers, investment management institutions, and money brokers, along with big MNCs such as Microsoft, GE, and DuPont.

• Continuous Linked Settlement (CLS) has 71 of the world's largest banks and more than 9,000 other institutions using the system to settle more than half of global foreign exchange transactions. It deals in the 17 main currencies used in global trade. Daily, some 800,000 transactions are carried out, totalling between US$4.5 trillion and $5 trillion (CLS Annual report 2013 www.cls-group.com/annualreport2013/).

• Visa International and MasterCard are other international organizations offering a range of cashless payment services. Visa has 14,600 financial institution customers worldwide (Visa Annual Report 2013). In the last quarter of 2013, Visa handled 16 billion transactions, equivalent to $1.2 trillion of payments, with a 12 per cent annual growth of cross-border volume (www.investor.visa.com). MasterCard dealt with over 12 billion transactions, totalling US$300 billion in value, and both together have over 3 billion cards circulating worldwide (www.corporate.visa.com; www.mastercard.com).

• PayPal and China's Alibaba are two online payments companies offering secure methods of payment for goods and services on the Web on sites such as eBay. They are not registered as banks and therefore need the support of existing financial institutions to offer their services. PayPal operates in multiple currencies in 193 countries with nearly 150 million account holders (www.paypal-media.com).

Electronic payments systems have become more widely available internationally and this has enabled firms to move their business-to-business (B2B) and business-to-consumer (B2C) activities on to the Web. Electronic payments across the European Union are now fast and cheap, and are generally more efficient than payments within the USA. In Japan, cash is used extensively compared with other industrial countries. However, Japanese businesses and consumers do also use direct debits, credit transfers, credit cards, debit cards, and bills and cheques. Electronic payments have been increasing, partly reflecting the development of a variety of access channels such as Automatic Teller Machines (ATMs), the Internet, and mobile phones. In China, online business is growing rapidly.

By contrast, in Russia, the population continues to prefer payment in cash. This is the major payment means used for retail payments for goods and services. Cash is also used for paying salaries, pensions, welfare allowances, and grants. However, the use of ATMs is growing very rapidly, as is the use of 'plastic' as a means of payment with Visa and MasterCard the main players. Compared to richer countries, the Russian payments system is underdeveloped.

In Africa, only 15–20 per cent of people have bank accounts, but 60–70 per cent have mobile phones (*The Economist* 14 September 2013). Although the majority of sub-Saharan African countries, including Nigeria, Sierra Leone, and Tanzania, still have largely cash and cheque-based economies, significant progress is being made in the regional development of electronic payment systems. East African countries, like Kenya, have moved rapidly to develop the use of mobiles for money transfers. While Latin American countries do have growing electronic payments systems, in many, because more than half of the population have no bank accounts, payments are made in cash. However, the use of debit and credit cards there is increasing quickly (www.emarketservices.com).

Reconciling Liquidity and Long-Term Finance Needs

Business investment projects often require a medium to long-term commitment of capital, whereas many savers prefer to have ready access to their savings. In other words, they like their savings to be 'liquid'. Banks and other financial intermediaries can offer finance to business for medium and long-term investment because they combine the savings of many households and businesses. Experience shows that savers do not usually all want to withdraw their money at the same time. As a result, financial institutions need only keep a proportion of their assets in a liquid form to meet the demands of those savers wishing to withdraw money while, at the same time, being able to provide medium to long-term capital for business investment.

Spreading the Risk

Savers are usually averse to risk and generally reluctant to invest all their money in a single project. They much prefer to spread the risk by investing in a range of projects. Financial intermediaries, such as banks, stock exchanges, and hedge funds, facilitate the spreading of risk by aggregating savings and then spreading them among both low and high-risk investment projects. This can enable business to get finance for high-risk projects such as those involving ground-breaking technology.

Industry Restructuring and Diversification

Financial institutions have similar objectives to other private sector commercial organizations: at the most basic level they wish to survive, but they also aim to make profits and grow. Profits are made from the commissions, charges, and interest rates levied on the financial services offered, both domestically and increasingly abroad. They also benefit from arbitrage, which involves taking advantage of price differences between markets when a financial product can be bought cheaply in, say, Tokyo and sold for a higher price in Amsterdam.

Domestic Consolidation and International Expansion

In pursuit of their objectives, financial institutions have been getting bigger through mergers and acquisitions, and also through organic growth—in other words, increasing their own output and sales. This has led to industry restructuring. The global banking system now comprises a small number of large banks operating in highly concentrated markets with relatively low rates of entry and exit. The average five bank concentration ratio in countries across the world was around 80 per cent in 2012 (see Figure 10.3). In 2011, the five biggest US banks controlled 46 per cent of the country's banking assets, whereas the corresponding figure for 2001 was 32 per cent. In Nigeria, the five bank concentration ratio for 2011 was 61 per cent, in Brazil 74 per cent, in Australia 91 per cent, and 77 per cent in the UK (World Bank www.quandl.com).

Weiss et al. (2014) report that there were 440 global bank mergers between 1991 and 2009, the majority of which occurred in the period 2004–07 (see Table 10.1). With the onset of the financial crisis, the appetite for mergers fell away (see Figure 10.4).

Fifty years ago, banks and other financial institutions tended to confine their operations to their domestic markets. Increasingly, they have expanded their operations abroad—the big

Figure 10.3 Country average five bank concentration ratio by assets – world

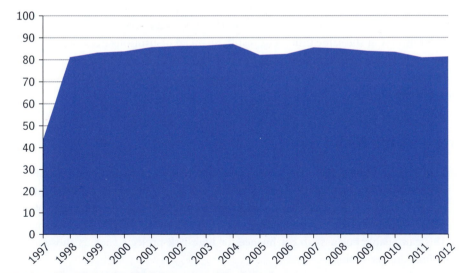

Source: Adapted from World Bank, Global Financial Development Database

Table 10.1 Regional distribution of bank mergers 1991–2009

Acquirer	Target								
	Africa	Central Asia	Eastern Europe	Latin America	North America	Pacific	South East Asia	Western Europe	Sum
Eastern Europe			1						1
Latin America				7					7
North America					313	1	1	1	316
Pacific					2	11			13
South East Asia							17		17
Western Europe	1	1	6	2	8	2	1	65	86
Sum	1	1	7	9	323	14	19	66	440

Source: Weiss et al. 2014

Figure 10.4 Bank mergers

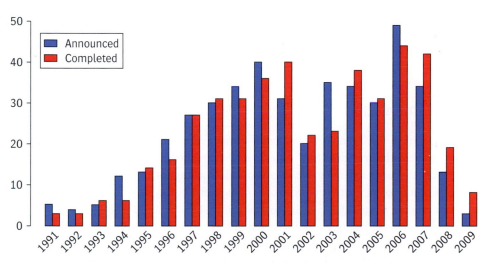

Source: Weiss et al. (2014)

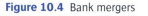

Learning Task

Examine Figures 10.3 and 10.4, and Table 10.1.

1. Which region's banks were the most active acquirers?

2. Which region's banks were the most active acquirers outside their own area?

3. Advance possible explanations for your answers to questions 1 and 2.

4. Did merger activity from 2004–07 increase market concentration? Give reasons.

German bank, Deutsche Bank offers a wide range of financial services to private and business clients in over 70 countries (www.db.com).

US banks, such as Citigroup, and European banks, like Royal Bank of Scotland (RBS), have also gone in for mergers, both at home and abroad, to get round the problem of slow-growing domestic markets. Both have made moves into China. RBS paid almost £2 billion for a 10 per cent stake in the Bank of China, while Citigroup was prepared to pay over US$3 billion for a controlling stake in the Guangdong Development Bank (*Financial Times* 19 August 2005 and 15 November 2006; Lo and Ng 2009).

The strategies pursued by financial institutions have led to a restructuring of the sector and have resulted in the creation of large financial conglomerates selling a range of products in a variety of countries.

Product Diversification

Financial institutions have also grown by expanding their product range. Traditionally, banks borrowed and lent money but did not sell insurance or trade in shares. Building societies made long-term loans on the security of private houses, but did not provide banking services such as current accounts. In their quest for profits and growth, they have diversified, and consequently have become less specialized. Big retail banks, for example, have increasingly seen their future as financial supermarkets selling a range of financial products and services. As a result, the various institutions now compete with each other over a wider product range.

Product Innovation

The financial sector has been very inventive in devising new financial products. A major development has been the growth of the hedge fund. Hedging implies action to reduce risk. While hedge funds do attempt to reduce risk, they also trade in a range of financial assets, from equities to bonds to commodities, and strive to take advantage of arbitrage opportunities. So, for example, if a currency or commodity is selling for one price in London and a higher price in New York then hedge funds will buy in London and sell in New York. Hedge funds often use complex mathematical models to make predictions of future price movements of financial assets to determine their trading strategies. Their aim is to produce good performance regardless of the underlying trends in the financial markets.

Derivatives, Swaps, and Options

In financial markets, stock prices, bond prices, currency rates, interest rates, and dividends go up and down, creating risk. Derivatives are financial products whose value is based on the value of products like shares, bonds, currencies, and commodities such as cocoa and zinc. Derivatives give the right to buy or sell these existing products in the future at an agreed price. Firms such as airlines use them to insulate themselves against increases in fuel prices. Others use them to gamble on future price changes.

Swaps are derivatives which firms can use to cover themselves against adverse movements in interest rates, inflation, exchange rates, and the possibility of borrowers defaulting on their loans. Thus, pension funds can use inflation swaps to protect the value of their assets against increases in inflation, while lenders, concerned about defaulting loans, can use credit default swaps. They work like this: two banks, one of whom has lent to General Motors and one to VW, can diversify their risk by agreeing to swap part of their liabilities. Both would then be less exposed to a default by their original borrower. This ability to spread risks may make financial institutions more willing to lend, consequently making it easier for non-financial firms to borrow.

The market in credit derivative products grew to such an extent that in December 2013 US$710 trillion was outstanding. Much of the trade in derivative products does not take place through financial markets but between individual institutions. Such trade is called over-the-counter (OTC) trading. According to the Bank for International Settlements (BIS 2013a, 2014), daily turnover in interest rate derivatives was US$2.3 trillion with contracts totalling US$584 trillion, an increase of 20 per cent over the previous year and 200 times UK GDP.

Another derivative is the option to buy or sell a specific amount of an existing product derivative at a specified price over a certain period of time. The buyer pays an amount of money for the option and the potential loss is limited to the price paid. When an option is not exercised, the money spent to purchase the option is lost. So, a firm could take out an option to borrow money at a specific rate of interest of, say, 8 per cent over a certain time, for example six months. If the interest rate rises above 8 per cent, the firm can exercise its option. If the interest rate falls below 8 per cent, then the firm borrows at the lower rate and loses the price it paid for the option.

Motives for Industry Restructuring and Diversification

Economies of scale—financial organizations hope to gain scale economies in the purchasing of supplies and savings from getting rid of duplication (a merged bank does not need more than one HQ building, one marketing department, and so on). This proclivity to merge has continued despite research literature showing that economies of scale can be exhausted by the time a bank reaches a relatively modest size. However, Hughes and Mester (2013) concluded that smaller banks benefit from large scale economies, but bigger banks experience even greater scale economies. Anderson and Joever (2012) find evidence of economies of scale particularly among the biggest banks, but note that the benefits accrue more to bankers than to investors.

Economies of scope—the idea here is that the extra costs of selling additional products alongside the old ones are small compared to the increase in revenues. So, a bank can diversify into credit cards or insurance and apply its traditional skills of selling loans to the marketing of these products. The logic is that selling extra financial products through established branch networks to existing customers offers a low cost, high productivity method of distribution.

Market share—when a bank takes over a competitor this increases its market share, reduces competition, and may, because the take-over makes it bigger, reduce the vulnerability to take-over.

Restructuring was also a response to the external environment:

- The global financial crisis caused banks to merge. For example, a number of Spanish savings banks were forced to merge by the government. In the USA, Bank of America merged with Merrill Lynch, and in the UK Lloyds TSB took over HBOS. It was also expected that the crisis would lead to increased regulatory costs and stronger capital requirements, which could force a new round of bank mergers.

- To finance the increase in international trade and investment, which grew at unprecedented rates after the Second World War.

- Economic expansion in developing nations in South East Asia led to an increased demand for financial services.

- In order to avoid regulation by the monetary authorities, financial institutions have been very clever in developing business outside regulated areas where there are profits to be made. Austrian banks, for example, faced lighter regulation than their German counterparts regarding the amount of information they had to provide on their borrowers. The Austrians attracted German clients by advertising their lax rules, leading to complaints of unfair competition by German banks (*The Economist* 19 May 2005).

- High prices for oil led to oil-producing countries having very big trade surpluses. International syndicates of banks were formed to channel the enormous sums of money from those countries to borrowers in other nations.

- Opportunities offered by the progressive deregulation of financial markets, which took place from the early 1970s. Deregulation involves the removal or reduction of certain governmental controls on financial institutions allowing them to move into other product areas and also into other countries.

The product and geographical diversification strategies followed by the financial sector have increased the international integration of financial institutions and markets. This has been facilitated by the falling cost and the cross-border diffusion of information and communications technologies. Institutions can move funds around the world to markets in different time zones easily, cheaply, and quickly. Even in the 1990s, technology was helping financial institutions 'bypass international frontiers and create a global whirligig of money and securities' (*The Economist* 3 October 1992).

Learning Task

Table 10.2 shows the assets of 10 of the biggest banks. Examine the Table and carry out the tasks below.

1. Comment on the rate of growth in the value of total assets between:
   - 1995 and 2007;
   - 2007 and 2014.

2. Advance possible explanations for your answers to Question 1.

3. Go to the map showing the geographical distribution of the world's largest banks on the **Online Resource Centre**.
   - Which countries and continents have the greatest numbers of big banks?
   - Advance some reasons for this state of affairs.

5. Explain the appearance of Chinese banks in the Table. ➔

→ **Table 10.2** World's top 10 banks by assets

Bank	Assets 1995 ($bn)	Bank	Assets 2007 ($tn)	Bank	Assets 2014 ($tn)
HSBC	352	HSBC	2.4	Industrial and Commercial Bank of China	3.2
Crédit Agricole	386	Citigroup	2.2	HSBC	2.8
Union Bank of Switzerland	336	Royal Bank of Scotland	3.8	China Construction Bank Corporation	2.6
Citicorp	257	JP Morgan Chase & Co	1.6	BNP Paribas	2.6
Dai-Ichi Kangyo Bank	499	Bank of America Corp	1.7	Mitsubishi	2.5
Deutsche Bank	503	Mitsubishi	1.8	JP Morgan Chase	2.5
Sumitomo Bank	500	Crédit Agricole	2.3	Agricultural Bank of China	2.5
Sanwa Bank	501	Industrial and Commercial Bank of China	1.2	Bank of China	2.4
Mitsubishi Bank	475	Banco Santander	1.3	Crédit Agricole	2.3
Sakura Bank	478	Bank of China	0.8	Barclays	2.3
Total assets	$4.3 trillion		$19.1 trillion		$25.7 trillion

Source: The Banker www.thebanker.com/Top-1000-World-Banks

Financial Markets

Financial institutions usually operate through markets. Markets are mechanisms for bringing together borrowers and lenders. For example, capital markets, such as the bond and stock markets, bring together organizations, both public and private, wishing to borrow and lend long-term funds in exchange for shares and bonds. The issue of new bonds and shares to raise money takes place in the primary market. Stock exchanges also enable shareholders to buy and sell existing shares in the secondary market. Non-financial organizations also purchase bonds or shares in the secondary market. Money markets, on the other hand, enable organizations to borrow and lend short term for anything up to, or just over, a year, trading in such instruments as derivatives and certificate of deposits (CDs). Companies with surplus cash that is not needed for a short period of time can earn a return on that cash by lending it into the money market.

Other financial markets include the foreign exchange market, which facilitates trading between those who wish to trade in currencies, such as importers, exporters, and speculators. A variety of institutions trade in foreign currencies, non-financial companies wishing to buy goods and services abroad, central banks trying to influence the exchange rate, commercial banks trading on their own account, financial institutions wishing to buy foreign securities and bonds, hedge funds, governments financing their military bases abroad, and so on. In fact, importers and exporters account for only a very small proportion of this trading as foreign currencies have increasingly been seen as assets in their own right. The amount of foreign exchange traded is enormous. BIS (2013) figures show that daily turnover more than doubled from almost US$2 trillion in 2004 to US$5.3 trillion in 2013, dwarfing the value of international trade in goods and services. The major currencies traded are the US dollar, the euro, and the yen while trade in the Chinese renminbi and the Mexican peso is expanding rapidly.

International banking activity has grown very rapidly since the 1960s when banks in London were permitted to accept foreign currency deposits. These banks were able to attract US dollar deposits, or eurodollars, because they faced a lighter system of regulation than banks in the USA. The eurodollar market became so large that it was described as a 'vast, integrated global money and capital system, almost totally outside all government regulation, that can send billions of "stateless" currencies hurtling around the world 24 hours a day' (Martin 1994).

The Major Markets

Modern communications and information technology allow financial institutions to operate from virtually anywhere nowadays, yet the financial sector prefers to cluster in certain locations. London and New York are the two leading global financial centres and appear to act as a magnet for finance companies. London is pre-eminent in international bond trading and leads the way in OTC derivatives, marine insurance, and trading in foreign equities. It is also the most popular place for foreign banks to locate, with 635 foreign banks operating there, compared to 120 in New York (www.cityoflondon.gov.uk; www.citidex.com). Tokyo, Chicago, Frankfurt, Singapore, and Hong Kong are other important centres.

Financial Crises

Shiller defines financial crises, so-called bubbles, as:

> A situation in which news of price increases spurs investor enthusiasm which spreads by psychological contagion from person to person, in the process amplifying stories that might justify the price increase and bringing in a larger and larger class of investors, who, despite doubts about the real value of the investment, are drawn to it partly through envy of others (*The Guardian* 19 July 2013).

There is no generally accepted theory to explain the causes of financial crises, but one thing is sure, they are a recurring phenomenon. They involve bouts of speculation when assets are bought, in the hope that the price will rise, or sold, in the expectation of a fall in price. If the price rises, those who purchased the asset can sell and make a profit. If the price falls, sellers can profit by buying the asset back at a lower price. The objects of speculation can be financial assets such as shares, bonds, currencies, or physical assets such as land, property, or works of art. Crises occur when the speculation destabilizes the market causing prices to rise or fall dramatically.

Galbraith (1990), Stiglitz (2002), and Minsky (2008) examine how destabilizing speculative episodes develop. When an asset is increasing in price, it attracts new buyers who assume that prices will continue to rise. This boosts demand for the asset and its price goes up. With prices soaring, investors charge in to take advantage of the easy profits to be made. Speculative euphoria develops as market participants come to believe that the upward movement in prices will go on indefinitely. Asset prices part company with the income they generate, whether that be rents from property or dividends on shares. As the value of the asset rises, investors are able to use it as security to borrow money from the banks to buy more of the asset. However, inevitably, there comes a tipping point, the causes of which are much debated, where some participants decide to withdraw from the market, perhaps due to an external shock, bad news, or even a rumour. Borrowers and lenders realize that debts will never be paid off: this is entitled the Minsky moment. It has been likened to the point when a cartoon character runs off a cliff and realizes it is running on thin air. The resulting fall in price sparks off panic in the market with investors rushing to off-load their assets, leading to a market collapse. Stiglitz (2002) makes the point that the excessive optimism or euphoria generated by bubbles is often followed by periods of excessive pessimism. Financial crises are contagious domestically and internationally. For example, a banking crisis can make borrowing more difficult and costly for firms and consumers. This could cause them to reduce their demand for goods and services leading to spare capacity, bankruptcies, and increasing unemployment. In an increasingly interconnected world, a financial crisis in one country can very quickly spread to others, as happened during the South East Asian crisis of the late 1990s and the credit crunch of 2007.

In summary, financial crises are characterized by:

- bouts of speculative activity, market euphoria, and rapidly rising prices;
- a tipping point which leads to panic selling, excessive pessimism, and plummeting prices;
- contagion of domestic and foreign economies.

Research by Reinhart and Rogoff (2008) shows that full-blown financial crises are deep and prolonged. House prices in real terms decline by an average of 35 per cent and share prices by 55 per cent. Output drops by over 9 per cent from the peak to the trough of the bubble, unemployment increases by over 9 per cent, while the real value of government debt explodes by 86 per cent. And problems remain after the crisis subsides. Reinhart found that growth in real incomes tended to be much lower during the decade following crises and that unemployment rates were higher, with the most extreme increases occurring in the richest advanced economies (*Financial Times* 31 August 2010).

Reinhart and Rogoff (2008a) show that financial crises have been regular occurrences in world history. In the 20 years up to 2007, many countries experienced such crises, including Sweden, Turkey, the Czech Republic, Argentina, Mexico, South Korea, Indonesia, Russia, and Japan. They claim that financial crises have repeatedly been the result of high international capital mobility and often follow when countries experience large inflows of capital.

Anatomy of the Financial Crisis 2007 Onwards

Easy Credit and Bad Loans

The main elements of the crisis can be summarized as follows. Low interest rates drove bankers to engage in a ferocious search for higher returns and the resulting higher bonuses (Financial Services Authority 2009). More than a trillion dollars was channelled into the US mortgage market, lent to the poorest, high-risk borrowers with low or uncertain incomes, high ratios of debt to income, and poor credit histories (Reinhart and Rogoff 2008). Borrowers took the loans to cash in on the boom in US house prices. These became known as **subprime loans**. Borrowers were led into taking loans by what Feldstein (2007) called 'teaser rates', unrealistically low interest rates at the start of the loan which, when they subsequently rose, became too expensive for customers to pay. Initially, borrowers only needed to pay back a minimum amount each month, which neither covered the interest nor paid back any of the capital sum. The result, in many cases, was that the size of the debt increased. This was not a great problem when interest rates were low and house prices were rising. In the five years up to 2005, house prices rose by more than half in the USA. In addition, large amounts of savings from trade surplus countries like China were being recycled into US finance markets.

Complex Financial Products and Subprime Mortgages

The boom in subprime loans was accompanied by explosive growth and complexity in financial products such as derivatives, credit default swaps, and collateralized debt obligations, many based on subprime mortgages. Lenders repackaged poor quality mortgages with more traditional and less risky financial products, like bonds, and sold them on to US and foreign financial institutions, a process called **securitization**. Ratings agencies such as Moody's and S&P gave top rating to many subprime backed securities. Buyers then used the securities as collateral to borrow more money. Financiers seeking higher returns on their investments, and driven by the prospect of massive bonuses, were misled by mathematical models indicating that the new products would diversify risk and reduce the possibility of a collapse in the financial system. Because risk was reduced, banks needed to hold less capital (Financial Services Authority 2009). Finance companies did not need to show these securities on their balance sheets, leading to a lack of information and transparency on levels of risk and on which institutions were carrying most risk. Lax regulatory systems and weak supervision of complex financial products allowed this dangerous process to occur (Naudé 2009).

Tipping Point, Impact, and Government Response

By the summer of 2007, house prices in the USA were falling and teaser rates began to expire. The rate of default on loans by subprime borrowers ballooned and the value of the assets held by the institutions plummeted. There was widespread panic and a flight from risk. This led to a **credit crunch** with institutions refusing to lend money to other finance firms fearing that they were carrying large amounts of subprime assets off the balance sheet. Facing a severe shortage of liquidity, institutions started a mass sell-off of their financial assets, which was difficult given the lack of credibility and trust in the finance industry.

In the USA, bad subprime debts and the drying up of liquidity led to the shock collapse of the giant multinational investment bank, Lehman Brothers. The government forced a fire sale of Bear Stearns to JP Morgan and a take-over of Wachovia by Wells Fargo. The government bailed out institutions such as AIG, Goldman Sachs, and Morgan Stanley to the tune of US$700 billion through its Troubled Asset Relief Programme (TARP) and nationalized Fanny Mae and Freddie Mac, two of the biggest operators in the mortgage market.

The crisis was not confined to the USA. The interconnectedness of financial markets, especially among the developed countries, meant that panic was contagious, spreading rapidly across borders. Acharya and Schnabl (2010) found that the main foreign traders of subprime securities were based in the UK, Germany, the Netherlands, and Japan. Banks had to be taken into public ownership not only in the USA but also in the UK, the Netherlands, France, Iceland, and Portugal. The Irish and Icelandic economies went into meltdown, with the former, along with Greece and Portugal, forced to accept a bail-out by the IMF and the EU and the latter also obliged to go to the IMF. The EU set up the €750 billion European Financial Stability Fund to secure financial stability by providing assistance to struggling Eurozone members (www.efsf.europa.eu).

There was a run on institutions, even those with no direct connection to the US subprime market. Northern Rock, the fifth largest British bank, unable to borrow on the money markets because of the credit crunch, had to be taken into public ownership. Although banks in developing countries were relatively unscathed by the crisis, the Bank of China was left holding nearly £5 billion of securities backed by US subprime mortgages.

Share prices on stock markets in New York, London, Paris, Frankfurt, and Tokyo plunged and financial markets became extremely volatile with share prices and currencies fluctuating violently.

The crisis meant that the value of bank assets had to be written down by US$2.3 trillion. It helped create the deepest recession in developed economies since the 1930s, led to an increase in unemployment of 30 million, and to a massive increase in government deficits (IMF 2010a; www.imf.org). Stiglitz (2010) sums up the crisis:

A deregulated market awash in liquidity and low interest rates, a global real estate bubble, and skyrocketing subprime lending were a toxic combination (2010: 1).

Learning Task

1. In the 2007 global financial crisis:
   a. In which country did the crisis have its origins?
   b. Which asset was at the root of the bubble?
   c. What role did securitization play in the crisis?
   d. What was the tipping point of the crisis?
   e. What were the effects of the crisis on non-US banks?

Central banks in the USA, Europe, and Japan went on the offensive, pumping massive amounts of financial assistance into the financial system. Allesandri and Haldane (2009) estimated total assistance at US$14 trillion, or one-quarter of global GDP. Central banks also reduced interest rates on account of fears of sharp falls in consumption and investment in their economies as a result of the crisis. Anxious to avoid a collapse in the global economy, the G20 met in 2009 and agreed to a significant increase in resources for the IMF, and they committed themselves to a US$5 trillion fiscal expansion promoting growth and jobs. (Visit the supporting **Online Resource Centre** for this book to access videos of G20 leaders commenting on the outcome of the summit.) While the USA continued its expansionary economic policies, the UK, Spain, Greece, and Ireland later introduced measures making significant cuts in public expenditure and raising taxes.

Subsequently, the US, UK, and Japanese authorities went in for a policy of quantitative easing (QE) to try to revive consumer spending and economic growth. They pumped massive amounts of money into the economy by buying assets, usually government bonds, typically from banks, insurance companies, and pension funds, with money created out of thin air. Some commentators saw this as not so much boosting economic growth, as directly fuelling a boom in stock markets and housing prices, and they were concerned that another bubble was being created (*The Economist* 14 January 2014; IMF 2014).

Counterpoint Box 10.2 The financial meltdown and the free market

Alan Greenspan, head of the Federal Reserve for 18 years up to 2006, was a great advocate of the free market. Even with the onset of the global financial crisis in 2007, he stuck to his position, 'free, competitive markets are by far the unrivaled way to organize economies' (Greenspan 2008a). Leaving financial markets free from government intervention enabled them to gather resources from savers and allocate them swiftly and efficiently to borrowers. Countries letting financial markets operate freely could grasp market opportunities more quickly and benefit from higher levels of competitiveness and growth. New financial products, such as pricing options and derivatives, helped to spread risks and to create 'a far more flexible, efficient, and hence resilient financial system' (Greenspan 2005). Therefore, governments should not regulate financial markets tightly because those markets are best able to withstand and recover from shocks when provided with maximum flexibility. Greenspan's critics assert that his free market ideology led to excessive risk-taking in the finance industry, creating an enormous bubble and ultimately resulting in a devastating financial crisis and recession.

In the USA, by March 2009, the stock market had fallen by 40 per cent in seven months and over 4 million jobs had disappeared. World output was falling for the first time since the Second World War and global unemployment had increased by 30 million between 2007 and 2009, three-quarters of which had occurred in the advanced economies. New financial products, rather than spread risk, had made economies and the global financial system much more unstable. Long before the onset of the crisis, credit derivatives were described by Warren Buffet, one of the world's most influential investors, as 'time

bombs' and 'financial weapons of mass destruction' (Berkshire Hathaway Annual Report 2002 www.berkshirehathaway.com/2002ar/2002ar.pdf), while the head of the UK Financial Services Authority referred to an 'explosion of exotic product development' and described many activities of the finance industry as 'socially useless' (*Prospect Magazine* 27 August 2009; *The Guardian* 22 September 2010).

Critics, like Johnson and Kwak (2010), argue that the finance industry in the USA is far too powerful—a financial oligarchy that has captured the institutions of US government by convincing them that 'more finance is good, more unfettered finance is better, and completely unregulated finance is best' (2010: 160). Supporters of tighter regulation of the finance industry point out that Greenspan, in an appearance before a Congressional committee in 2008, accepted that, in the face of 'a once-in-a-century credit tsunami', his belief in the self-correcting powers of the free market had been misplaced. (Visit the accompanying **Online Resource Centre** for a video link on this topic.) Critics argue that much tighter regulation of the finance industry is required if a repeat of the latest global financial crisis is to be avoided.

Sources: Greenspan 2005, 2008, 2008a; Johnson and Kwak 2010; Johnson 2009; IMF/ILO 2010

Questions

1. Compare and contrast the arguments advanced by Greenspan and his critics. Decide which side is most convincing and explain why.

Mini Case Study Northern Rock—a credit crunch casualty

Northern Rock, one of the biggest mortgage lenders in the UK, financed most of its lending by borrowing from other financial institutions and borrowed relatively little from individual savers. In the summer of 2007, liquidity in credit markets started to dry up due to the subprime mortgage crisis in the USA. As a result, Northern Rock found it increasingly difficult to raise money by selling its securitized or bundled mortgages to other financial institutions, or borrowing on the money markets. It was forced to go cap in hand to the Bank of England. When this became public, worried depositors flocked to Northern Rock bank branches to withdraw their savings, in other words there was a 'run on the bank'. The value of Northern Rock shares plummeted. The Bank of England bailed out Northern Rock to the tune of £25 billion and the government guaranteed the deposits of all the company's savers. After unsuccessfully trying to sell Northern Rock to a private buyer, the British government took Northern Rock into public ownership. Subsequently, the company shrank with between 2,000 and 3,000 Northern Rock employees losing their jobs. The case raised questions about the failure of the regulatory system to address the issue of bank liquidity and about the lack of coordination between the three responsible bodies, the Bank of England, the Financial Services Authority, and the Treasury.

Sources: *The Observer* 16 September 2007; www.telegraph.co.uk 23 January 2008; www.ft.com 17 and 20 February 2008; *The Guardian* 8 June 2010

Questions

1. Find out whether changes in UK financial regulation address the liquidity and coordination issues identified in the case.

Financial Regulation

Regulation plays an important role at both a domestic and an international level. It is a big element in the financial sector's external environment because of the effect it can have on their sales turnover, costs, and profits.

Effective regulation is also important for non-financial firms. Businesses and individuals dealing with financial institutions have an interest in those institutions being effectively regulated and supervised. Regulation can avoid hiccups in payments systems, protect customers against financial fraud, ensure financial institutions are prudent in weighing up risks, and that they have enough cash and other liquid assets on hand so that they do not go bankrupt when things go wrong.

Another major reason for regulation is the failure of countries and financiers to learn the lessons of history. Reinhart and Rogoff (2008a) see this as a widespread view that 'this time it is different', because countries and financiers claim to have learned from the mistakes made in previous crises (2008a: 53). Major crises are unlikely to occur, so it is argued, thanks to wiser macroeconomic policies, sophisticated mathematical models, and more discriminating lending practices. In response, Reinhart and Rogoff (2008) comment, 'the ability of governments and investors to delude themselves, giving rise to periodic bouts of euphoria that usually end in tears, seems to have remained a constant' (2008: 53). Galbraith (1990) talks about 'the extreme brevity of the financial memory [which means that] financial disaster is quickly forgotten' (1990: 13).

So, regulation is necessary, not simply to protect the interest of customers, but also to ensure the stability of the whole financial system. Evidence also shows that effective regulation can have a positive effect on a country's economic income and output, which could be good news for business seeking expanding markets (Levine et al. 2000; OECD 2006).

Different Systems of Regulation

Regulatory systems can vary quite considerably from one country to another. The authorities face a number of dilemmas regarding regulation. Tight regulation could reduce the attractiveness of their financial centres to banks, while too little regulation could frighten customers away.

At one extreme is a state-owned banking system in which banks are an arm of government and are never allowed to go bust, at the other is a lightly regulated system of private banks without an explicit safety-net in which bank failures are common. Either extreme faces certain dangers. Banking systems, where no bank can be allowed to fail, and depositors face no risk of loss, may breed management and depositor recklessness. At the other extreme, systems which rely only on market discipline run the risk of unnecessary bank and, possibly, systemic failure and great loss to depositors.

In many countries, the state has a major presence in the financial sector. State intervention plays an important role in both the developing and the developed world, taking various forms of intervention from explicit intervention in the banking system in China and Germany to implicit

Mini Case Study Dark pools

In June 2014, the New York regulator announced a law suit against Barclays alleging that the bank had systematically defrauded and deceived customers in the operation of its dark pool. Barclays is one of the world's largest banks and operates in 50 countries.

Dark pools, about 45–50 in number, allow institutional investors to trade large blocks of shares anonymously and away from the official stock exchanges. The deals were concealed from the public and the prices only revealed after the deals were done. This allowed huge deals to be done without affecting share prices. Reportedly, the biggest pools were run by JP Morgan, Morgan Stanley, and Credit Suisse. They were computer-driven, and cheaper than trading through conventional stock exchanges. Such pools accounted for up to 40 per cent of shares traded in the US compared with 16 per cent six years previously.

The regulator claimed that Barclays dramatically increased its share of the dark pool market by lying to clients and investors about how, and for whose benefit, it operated its dark pool. The bank, in its marketing, falsely assured customers that it had implemented special safeguards to protect them from predatory high-frequency traders (HFTs)—such traders use ultra-fast computer networks to make profits from tiny movements in prices by the aggressive buying and selling of huge volumes of shares in milliseconds. In fact, according to the lawsuit, Barclays actively sought to attract HFTs and operated its dark pool to benefit them. Internal emails revealed that the bank was 'happy

to take liberties' with the truth, but did it in order to 'help ourselves'. Barclays also misled clients by asserting that it did not favour its own dark pool when placing their orders but routed them to the best venue for the trade.

Some commentators see dark pools as parasites using data gleaned from the main stock exchanges to price their share trades. Market abuse is more likely because they operate in private, are largely unregulated, and the balance of information is uneven between the client and the pool operator. The operator possesses lots of market-moving information on trades which it could use to its own advantage; for example, using insider knowledge to buy or sell before the trade takes place.

Once the lawsuit was made public, Barclay's share price fell, knocking £2 billion off its market value. Clients like Deutsche Bank, Credit Suisse, and Royal Bank of Canada pulled business out of Barclays' dark pool.

Sources: www.ag.ny.gov/pdfs/Barclays_complaint_as_filed_June_25_2014.pdf; www.ag.ny.gov/press-release/ag-schneiderman-announces-fraud-charges-against-barclays-connection-market-ing-and; Reuters 28 June 2014; *Financial Times* 26, 28 June 2014; *The Guardian* 27 June 2014

Questions

1. Why do you think financial regulators are so concerned about dark pools?

government-sponsored enterprises in the USA. A large swathe of the German, French, and Austrian banks is publicly owned, while the banking system is in private hands in many countries, including Canada, Japan, New Zealand, the UK, and the USA—at least they were up to the financial meltdown in 2008. Up to 1991, Indian banks were nationalized and used as a source of finance for public sector spending and investment by big companies. Liberalization has since taken place only very slowly, but India, like Italy, continues to restrict foreign ownership. State intervention can also extend to insurance schemes and pension funds, but, generally, these are subject to less systematic regulation than the banks.

In the Eurozone, the ECB carries out a supervisory function in cooperation with the national central banks and regulatory bodies. The UK has a tradition of 'light-touch' regulation and the regulatory and supervisory structure is much simpler, the functions being mainly carried out by the Bank of England. Some developing countries do have regulators, but, as in the case of India, often seem to find it difficult to strike an appropriate balance between regulating the sector effectively and providing a good enabling environment for financial sector development.

The Regulatory Challenge

In the run up to the global crisis, financial markets were being transformed by a remarkable wave of cross-border growth and innovation in the form of new products such as derivatives. The tendency of financial institutions towards conglomeracy, and the increasing cross-border integration of the sector, meant that a shock in one part of the sector, or of the world, could very quickly spread and turn into a big threat to the system as a whole, as illustrated by the credit crunch of 2007. Furthermore, regulatory systems in some countries were very loose (see OECD 2006). There was also a danger that some regulators had been captured by the financial institutions they were supposed to regulate. This was reflected in their willingness to take on trust what the financial institutions told them rather than subjecting them to intensive scrutiny. Furthermore, many countries lacked any real regulation to speak of—the British Virgin Islands and the Cayman Islands being two examples. However, it was not just small island territories. The big international financial markets, London, New York, and Tokyo, all had a thriving offshore business operating safely away from the eyes of the regulator. A final issue was that regulation was not applied uniformly across the range of financial products, with some financial products being tightly regulated while others faced hardly any regulation at all.

The financial meltdown demonstrated the inability of regulation, both at national and international levels, to prevent crises. This was widely recognized during the crisis, but enthusiasm for much tighter regulation began to wane with the recovery of the financial system and the ferocious resistance from the finance sector.

Regulation has improved in the aftermath of the global financial crisis. In the major industrialized countries, higher capital requirements have been imposed, financial institutions are obliged to value their assets more conservatively, and obliged to hold more liquid assets. Banks face greater constraints on the risks they can take and must make greater provisions against bad loans.

The Basel Committee on Banking Supervision agreed a package of measures called Basel III. This nearly trebled to 7 per cent the minimum amount of equity capital banks had to hold against losses, 2.5 per cent of which was to be held as a buffer. Banks straying into the buffer zone would be subject to restrictions on share dividends and discretionary bonuses if regulators felt that they were extending credit too freely. The new rules were to be phased in from 2013 to 2019.

An official US inquiry into the crisis found that there had been dramatic failures in the corporate governance and risk management in banks (National Commission 2011). The USA, in order to avert future financial crises, imposed tighter regulations on financial firms that would have the effect of reducing their profits. It boosted consumer protection, forced banks to be more transparent and to reduce risky trading and investing activities. The transparency around derivatives was increased by obliging them to be traded on exchanges rather than over the counter. A new, more orderly process for liquidating troubled financial firms was established (Schoenholtz and Wachtel 2010). Critics argued, however, that the regulations had been watered down due to intense lobbying by the financial sector and that another financial crisis could occur before the regulations took full effect (Helleiner 2010; *Financial Times* 20 August 2010).

The EU established three new financial supervisory bodies for the banking, securities markets, and insurance and occupational pensions sectors and set up the European Systemic Risk Board (ESRB). The Commission proposed new capital requirements for the financial sector, rules governing banker pay and bonuses, and stronger rules on disclosure of financial information. It was also looking for ways to regulate credit rating agencies and auditing firms. While responsibility for financial supervision remains at national level, a new body, the European Supervisory Authorities, will act as coordinator. Measures, such as the Markets in Financial Instruments Directive (MiFID) and the Market Abuse Directive (MAD), were brought forward to promote efficiency, stability, and transparency in financial markets (see European Commission Memo/13/774 10/09/2013).

In 2014, the IMF praised efforts to make banks more secure by obliging them to hold more capital and through rules restricting risky lending. Nonetheless, it was concerned about individual countries establishing a patchwork of regulations that could be exploited by banks and might be 'mutually destructive' and recommended increased cross-border coordination of bank regulation and reform (2014: 125). It also criticized policy makers for lack of progress in failing to deal with the problem of banks that were too big to fail.

● CHAPTER SUMMARY

In this chapter we have examined the importance of the financial environment for business, whether that be in the provision of money and credit, the operation of systems of payment, providing protection against risk by the financial sector, or the impact of monetary phenomena such as inflation, interest rates, or exchange rates. We have also seen how the big financial institutions and the increasingly integrated financial markets of London, New York, and Tokyo are vital for the effective functioning of business and the economies in which it operates.

In the advanced economies, business has relatively easy access to finance through a variety of financial institutions offering a wide range of financial products. As we have seen, access to finance in developing countries is much more difficult, making it harder for businesses to start up and grow.

The financial sector has grown rapidly in terms of output and employment and has become highly internationalized. The industry has come to be dominated by a small number of very large and diversified companies operating across the globe. These big financial institutions have become very powerful actors on the world stage.

Because of their size, the extent of their diversification and internationalization, and their ability to invent new financial products, they continue to pose great challenges to the regulatory authorities. The regulation of the financial sector is fragmented within and between different countries, and can vary considerably from one state to another. Financial crises occur regularly in the system, affecting not only the country where they started, but also moving at terrifying speed across continents and markets and threatening major parts of the global economy, as we saw with the global crisis of 2007. While improvements in regulation have occurred, many critics argue that they remain inadequate and that the stability of the international finance system cannot be taken for granted.

● REVIEW QUESTIONS

1. Why is it vital for business to have confidence in the international payments system?

2. Explain the increasing internationalization of the banking system. What factors have made it easier for banks to internationalize their operations?

3. Analyse the need for effective regulation of the financial system. Explain why bankers resist the tightening of regulation.

Table 10.3 shows the extent to which payments are made by cheque and electronically in a number of countries. Examine the Table and carry out the following tasks.

1. Comment on the change in importance of cheques, e-money, and credit cards as a means of payment.

2. Compare and contrast the use of e-money as a means of payment in Germany and Singapore.

3. What are the implications of your answer to Question 2 for a German firm wishing to do business in Singapore?

Table 10.3 Payment method percentage of total number of transactions

	Cheque		E-money payments		Credit cards	
	2008	2012	2008	2012	2008	2012
Australia	6.8	3.1	nap	nap	26.0	24.1
Belgium	0.4	3.1	3.7	1.8	nav	nav
Brazil	14.8	6.1	0.1	0.2	19.3	19.8
Canada	11.5	7.5	nav	nav	29.2	31.5
China	20.7	7.0	nap	nap	nav	nav
France	22.1	15.6	0.2	0.3	nav	nav
Germany	0.4	0.2	0.3	0.2	0.2	0.2
India	31.5	15.4	nap	0.8	6.0	4.7
Italy	11.1	6.8	2.1	4.7	15.1	15.1
Korea	11.4	3.0	1.4	0.5	41.3	48.4
Mexico	24.2	12.9	nav	nav	19.2	20.0
Netherlands	nap	nap	3.7	2.5	nap	nap
Russia	0.0	0.0	0.3	3.9	1.0	3.8
Singapore	3.8	2.2	84.3	88.1	nav	nav
Switzerland	0.1	0.0	1.4	0.2	11.6	14.4
United Kingdom	9.2	4.6	nav	nav	11.7	10.9
United States	25.5	15.5	nav	nav	23.4	22.2
All	17.1	9.7	1.6	1.4	19.8	17.6

nav=not available, nap=not applicable

Source: BIS, Committee on Payment and Settlement Systems, December 2013

● ASSIGNMENT TASKS

1. You are employed in the research department of a multinational bank which advises wealthy clients on investment strategies. In 2014, numerous commentators expressed concern that policies of quantitative easing were helping create asset bubbles, for example in share prices and in the housing market. Your boss requests that you research the housing market and prepare a set of PowerPoint slides, including charts and tables, and accompanying notes that can be used to advise clients.

   a) Explain what is meant by quantitative easing and its connection with asset prices.

   b) Analyse information on changes in house prices in the US and the UK in the 20 years up to 2014.

   c) Explain what is meant by the term 'housing bubble'.

   d) Assess, on the basis of your research, whether there is a housing bubble in the UK.

   Useful sources of information: IMF Global Housing Watch; Bank of England, Financial Stability Report June 2014; Joyce et al., Bank of England Quarterly Bulletin 2011 Q3; *The Economist* 14 January 2014; Ha-Joon Chang in *The Guardian* 25 February 2014; M. Patton, www.forbes.com 28 January 2014.

2. You are a research assistant for a member of parliament (MP), who is in favour of cancelling third world debt and has agreed to a lengthy interview with a national newspaper on vulture funds. The interview has arisen because, in June 2014, a US court ruled that Argentina needed to pay debts in full to vulture funds. The MP asks you for a briefing paper on the pros and cons of vulture funds and the background to the Argentina case. Your briefing paper should address the following:

   a) explain what vulture funds do;

   b) outline the arguments for and against vulture funds;

   c) summarize the case between Argentina and the vulture funds.

   Useful sources of information: www.gregpalast.com; www.felixsalmon.com; www.bbc.co.uk; the paper by Sahay at www.imf.org; www.jubileeusa.org.

Case Study   JP Morgan, subprime mortgages, and the global financial crisis

There are a lot of banks that are actually pretty well managed—J.P. Morgan being a good example (US President Barack Obama).

This case examines the activities of the giant US multinational, JPMorgan Chase, regarding the securitization of subprime mortgages in the run-up to the financial crisis and its aftermath.

JPMorgan Chase is a giant US financial conglomerate offering banking and other financial services. It is the biggest bank in the United States, and, with total assets of US$2.5 trillion, the world's sixth largest. It has 50 million customers in around 60 countries and in 2012 earned $8.4 billion in profits.

In 2007, at the start of the crisis, bonuses at the bank were generous. Jamie Dimon, the chairman and CEO, was paid a

Source: © f9photos / istockphoto.com.   →

→ salary of $1million, but received total compensation of $27.8 million. The bank was heavily involved in the subprime mortgage market. In 2006 it was getting worried about the risks in that market. In a letter to shareholders, Jamie Dimon reassured them that the bank was protected by a 'fortress balance sheet', but went on to say:

> In hindsight, when underwriting subprime, we could have been even more conservative and less sensitive to market and competitor practices. We've now materially tightened certain underwriting standards on subprime mortgages.

Despite these changes, the company expressed further concerns in the 2007 annual report conceding that, in the face of aggressive competition, its standards had been lax and that it had underestimated the size of the housing bubble. Neither had it foreseen the magnitude of the fall in house prices:

> ...we still found ourselves having to tighten our underwriting of subprime mortgage loans six times through the end of 2007. (Yes, this means our standards were not tough enough the first five times).

The report revealed that the bank held $2.7 billion in subprime mortgage assets, and $6.4 billion in Alt-A mortgages—these were risky due either to being high relative to the property value or to the borrower's income or to inadequate income records for the borrower. Deals collapsed in 2008 when the housing market plunged and the scale of the risks was exposed, leading to the biggest financial crisis since the Depression of the 1930s.

In the first nine months of 2008, the bank took just over $7 billion in write-downs from exposure to mortgage securities and loans indebted customers used to finance acquisitions. At the height of the financial crisis, it received $25 billion in assistance through the US government's TARP. Despite calls for him to go, the CEO retained his post, and in 2010 was awarded a 51 per cent pay rise and a $5 million cash bonus.

In the years after 2007, the US authorities set out to investigate the possible mis-selling of securities which bundled various assets together with subprime mortgages. By 2013, the Department of Justice (DoJ) had reached 27 civil law financial settlements with US banks, including Goldman Sachs, Bank of America, Wells Fargo, Citigroup, and JPMorgan. The DoJ, along with several US states, agreed a $13 billion settlement with JPMorgan, the largest settlement in American history—more than three times greater than BP paid for the oil spill disaster in the Gulf of Mexico. This resolved the claims against the bank and also against Bear Stearns and Washington Mutual, crisis casualties that JPMorgan had taken over in 2008.

US Attorney General Eric Holder said:

> Without a doubt, the conduct uncovered in this investigation helped sow the seeds of the mortgage meltdown... JPMorgan was not the only financial institution during this period to knowingly bundle toxic loans and sell them to unsuspecting investors, but that is no excuse for the firm's behavior (www.justice.gov).

The Attorney for Eastern California claimed:

> Abuses in the mortgage-backed securities industry helped turn a crisis in the housing market into an international financial crisis...The impacts were staggering. JPMorgan sold securities knowing that many of the loans backing those certificates were toxic (www.justice.gov).

Also, in 2013, the bank had to pay $4.5 billion compensation to institutional investors to whom it had sold mortgage-backed securities.

JPMorgan admitted that it had seriously misrepresented various securities to its customers by claiming that they complied with underwriting guidelines. The investigation found that JPMorgan employees knew that the loans in question did not comply with those guidelines and were not otherwise appropriate for securitization, but they allowed the loans to be securitized and sold to investors.

The bank knew that over a quarter of the mortgage loans it had purchased between 2006 and 2007 were defective and did not comply with underwriting guidelines relating to, for example, high loan-to-property value ratios (some over 100 per cent), high debt-to-borrower income ratios, and inadequate or missing documentation of borrowers' income, assets, and credit history. Nevertheless, the bank decided to securitize these mortgages and sell them on to unwitting customers.

Prior to the bank acquiring the mortgage loans, an employee informed two senior executives that, due to their poor quality, the loans should not be purchased and should not be securitized. After the purchase of the loans, she wrote to another senior executive conveying her concerns about the loans. Despite these warnings, the loans were securitized and sold on to investors.

After the judgement, the bank claimed that it had not broken US law and Jamie Dimon said: 'We are pleased to have →

→ concluded this extensive agreement...' (JPMorgan News Release 19 November 2013).

Sources: JPMorgan Chase Annual Reports 2007, 2013; JPMorgan Letter to Shareholders 2006; CNN Money http://money.cnn.com/news/specials/storysupplement/ceopay/; *The Economist* 26 October 2013; www.bbc.co.uk 20 November 2013 http://www.bbc.co.uk/news/business-25009683; www.bloomberg.com; www.justice.gov/opa/pr/2013/November/13-ag-1237.html; *The Guardian* 8 April 2011, 20 November 2013; www.reuters.com 15 November 2013

Questions

1. Advance reasons for JPMorgan buying subprime mortgage loans from other financial institutions.

2. Explain the term securitization and relate this to the subprime mortgage loans bought by JPMorgan.

3. What were the concerns of JPMorgan regarding subprime mortgages in 2006 and 2007? Is there any suggestion in those concerns of the bank breaching underwriting guidelines?

4. How did the bank break the law?

5. What internal and external factors might have led to the bank breaking the law?

6. Discuss whether the penalties imposed on JPMorgan were sufficient to:
   • deter the giant bank from repeating the offence;
   • deter others from mis-selling financial products;
   • compensate society for the economic damage resulting from the financial crisis.

7. Discuss whether the case supports President Obama's view that the bank was pretty well managed.

● FURTHER READING

Castronova discusses money and the emergence of virtual money:

● Castronova, E. (2014) *Wildcat Currency: How the Virtual Money Revolution is Transforming the Economy.* New Haven: Yale University Press.

For an analysis of financial crises refer to:

● Kindelberger, C.P. and Aliber, R. (2005) *Manias, Panics and Crashes: A History of Financial Crises,* 5th edn. Hoboken: John Wiley & Sons.

● Reinhart, C. and Rogoff, K. (2008a) 'This Time is Different: A Panoramic View of Eight Centuries of Financial Crises', March. Available at: www.nber.org/papers/w13882.

For the 2007 crisis:

● Stiglitz, J.E. (2010) *Freefall: Free Markets and the Sinking of the Global Economy.* London: Allen Lane.

● Tett, G. (2010) *Fool's Gold: How Unrestrained Greed Corrupted a Dream.* London: Abacus.

● Wolf, M. (2014) T*he Shifts and Shocks: What We've Learned—And Have Still to Learn—From the Financial Crisis.* New York: Penguin.

For a critical examination of policies pursued by the IMF and the World Bank:

● Stiglitz, J.E. (2002) *Globalization and its Discontents.* London: Penguin.

For a discussion of high-frequency trading in financial markets see:

● Lewis, M. (2014) *Flash Boys: A Wall Street Revolt.* London: W.W. Norton & Company.

● REFERENCES

Acharya, V. and Schnabl, P. (2010) 'Do Global Banks Spread Global Imbalances? Asset-Backed Commercial Paper during the Financial Crisis of 2007–09'. *IMF Economic Review* 58(1).

Allesandri, P. and Haldane, A.G. (2009) *Banking on the State*. Bank of England, November. Available at: www.bankofengland.co.uk/archive/Documents/historicpubs/speeches/2009/speech409.pdf.

Anderson, R.W. and Joever, K. (2012) 'Bankers and Bank Investors: Reconsidering the Economies of Scale in Banking', *Financial Markets Discussion Group Paper* 712, September.

BIS (2013) 'Triennial Central Bank Survey: Foreign Exchange Turnover in April 2013: Preliminary Global Results', September. Available at: www.bis.org/publ/rpfx13fx.pdf.

BIS (2013a) 'Triennial Bank Survey: OTC interest rate derivatives turnover in April 2013: Preliminary Results', September. Available at: http://www.bis.org/press/p130905.htm.

BIS (2014) 'Statistical Release: OTC Derivatives Statistics at end-December 2013', May. Available at: www.bis.org/publ/otc_hy1405.pdf.

Bretton Woods Project (2014) *Follow the Money: The World Bank Group and the Use of Financial Intermediaries*, April. Available at: http://www.brettonwoodsproject.org/wp-content/uploads/2014/04/B_W_follow_the_money_report_WEB-VERSION.pdf.

Feldstein, M. (2007) 'Housing, Housing Finance and Monetary Policy', Federal Reserve Bank of Kansas City, 1 September. Available at: www.kc.frb.org.

Financial Services Authority (2009) 'The Turner Review: A Regulatory Response to the Global Banking Crisis', March.

Galbraith, J.K. (1990) *A Short History of Financial Euphoria*. London: Pelican.

Greenspan, A. (2005) 'Economic Flexibility', Remarks to the National Association for Business Economics Annual Meeting, Chicago, Illinois, 27 September.

Greenspan, A. (2008a) 'A Response to My Critics'. The Economists' Forum, FT.com, 6 April.

Greenspan, A. (2008) *The Age of Turbulence: Adventures in a New World*. London: Penguin Books.

Harrigan, J. (2010) *Globalisation, Democratisation and Radicalisation in the Arab World*. Basingstoke: Palgrave MacMillan.

Helleiner, E. (2010) 'Filling a Hole in Global Financial Governance? The Politics of Regulating Sovereign Debt Restructuring'. In Mattli, W. and Woods, N.(eds), *The Politics of Global Regulation*. Princeton: Princeton University Press.

Hughes, J.P. and Mester, L.J. (2013) 'Who Said Large Banks Don't Experience Scale Economies? Evidence from a Risk-Return-Driven Cost Function', Working Paper No. 13-13/R, federal Bank of Philadelphia.

IMF (2010) 'World Economic Outlook', October.

IMF (2010a) 'Global Financial Stability Report: Meeting New Challenges to Stability and Building a Safer System', April.

IMF (2014) 'Global Financial Stability Report', April.

IMF/ILO (2010) 'The Challenges of Growth, Employment and Social Cohesion'. Discussion Document, Oslo Conference.

Johnson, S. (2009) 'Financial Oligarchy and the Crisis'. *The Atlantic* May; and *Brown Journal of World Affairs* (2010) XVI(II Spring/Summer).

Johnson, S. and Kwak, J. (2010) *13 Bankers: The Wall Street Takeover and the Next Financial Meltdown*. New York: Pantheon Books.

Levine, R., Loayza, N., and Beck, T. (2000) 'Financial Intermediation and Growth: Causality and Causes'. *Journal of Monetary Economics* 46(1).

Lo, W.C. and Ng, M.C.M. (2009) 'Banking Reform and Corporate Governance'. *The Chinese Economy* 42(5).

Martin, R. (1994) 'Stateless Monies, Global Financial Integration and National Economic Autonomy: The End of Geography'. In Corbridge, S. et al. (eds), *Money, Power and Space*. Oxford: Blackwell.

McLeay, M., Radia, A., and Thomas, R. (2014) 'Money in the Modern Economy: An Introduction', Bank of England Quarterly Bulletin Q1.

Moschella, M. (2014) 'The Institutional Roots of Incremental Ideational Change: The IMF and Capital Controls after the Global Financial Crisis'. *British Journal of Politics and International Relations* June.

Muuka, G.N. (1998) 'In Defense of World Bank and IMF Conditionality in Structural Adjustment Programs'. *Journal of Business in Developing Nations* 2.

Minsky, H.P. (2008) *Stablizing an Unstable Economy*. New York: McGraw-Hill.

National Commission (2011) 'Financial Crisis Inquiry Report', January.

Naudé, W. (2009) 'The Financial Crisis of 2008 and the Developing Countries', Discussion Paper No 2009/01, United Nations University, January.

OECD (2006) 'Regulation of Financial Systems and Economic Growth', Working Paper 34.

Patel, R. (2009) *The Value of Nothing: How to Reshape Market Society and Redefine Democracy*. London: Portobello Books.

Reinhart, C. and Rogoff, K. (2008) 'The Aftermath of Financial Crises', paper presented at the American Economic Association meeting, 3 January 2009.

Reinhart, C. and Rogoff, K. (2008a) 'This Time is Different: A Panoramic View of Eight Centuries of Financial Crises', The National Bureau of Economic Research, March. Available at: www.nber.org/papers/w13882.

Schoenholtz, K. and Wachtel, P. (2010) *The Architecture of Financial Regulation: July 2010 Archives: Dodd-Frank and the Fed*. Available at www.stern.nyu.edu.

Stiglitz, J.E. (2002) *Globalization and its Discontents*. London: Penguin.

Stiglitz, J.E. (2010) *Freefall: Free Markets and the Sinking of the Global Economy*. London: Allen Lane.

Weiss, G.N.F., Neumann, S., and Bostandzic, D. (2014) 'Systemic Risk and Bank Consolidation: International Evidence'. *Journal of Banking and Finance* 40.

CHAPTER ELEVEN

Corporate Social Responsibility

LEARNING OUTCOMES:

At the end of this chapter you will be able to:

- Define corporate social responsibility

- Assess the free market case against corporate social responsibility

- Explain the business and moral cases for corporate social responsibility

- Identify corporate social responsibility issues in the global economy

- Discuss the implications of corporate social responsibility for business

Case Study **The Bangladesh garment industry**

In Chapter 1 we defined globalization as a process in which barriers separating different regions of the world are reduced or removed, thereby stimulating greater exchange and linkages between nations. As globalization progresses, business is confronted by important new challenges. Some of these challenges relate to the way business is done. This case looks at conditions in the Bangladeshi garment industry and brings into question who is responsible for the conditions there. Is it the government of Bangladesh for allowing such conditions? Is it the factory owners, or the multinational retailers who are supplied by these firms, or do purchasers, us, bear some responsibility? Should we care?

In April 2013, the Rana Plaza factory complex in Savar, Dhaka, collapsed killing over 1,100 people and injuring many more. Generators on the upper floors had triggered the collapse. This was not the first. In 2005, the Spectrum/Shahriyar Sweater factory collapsed killing 64 workers and injuring 80. In February 2010, a fire at the Garib & Garib Sweater Ltd factory killed 21 workers and injured 50. In another fire in December 2010, 28 workers were killed and at least 100 injured. The fire was on the ninth and tenth floors of a factory owned by the Hameem Group making clothes for Western companies such as Gap. This factory was typical of many Bangladeshi garment factories housed in multi-storey buildings not originally intended for this use. The machinery frequently overloads the electrical circuitry, often the cause of the fires. Some of the fire exits were locked, allegedly to prevent theft, so some suffocated, some jumped to their deaths, and others were trampled in the rush to the few open exits. According to *The Guardian* (8 December 2013) nearly 800 people had been injured in fires in garment factories in the previous 12 months.

The garment industry is Bangladesh's leading exporter, accounting for over 75 per cent of exports. Of those exports, 96 per cent go to North America, the UK, and Eurozone countries to retail giants including Wal-Mart, JC Penny, Zara, Tesco, H&M, IKEA, Primark, Benetton, Mango, and Marks and Spencer. Bangladesh is one of the cheapest places in the world to make

Source: © shutterstock.com.

clothes and is taking over from China as a cheap source of garments. There are an estimated 5,000 garment factories in Bangladesh employing more than 3 million workers, most of them women and some as young as 13. They work long hours, often in dangerous conditions, for a minimum wage of 5,300 taka per month (about US$68 or £1.36 per day). This has just been increased from 3,000 taka per month (about US$43) following serious labour disputes, but not all factory owners have paid up.

War on Want has undertaken a series of reports on this industry. Their latest report comments that while some see the employment of women in this industry 'as a positive step towards female emancipation the reality is that they are employed in a highly exploitative context'. They found long hours of work (32 per cent working 100–140 hours of overtime per month), low pay, late payment of wages, unpaid overtime, poor working conditions, denial of maternity leave, physical and verbal abuse, which was often of a sexual nature, and a complete lack of trade union representation.

Sources: *The Guardian* 8 December 2013; 'Stitched Up, Women Workers in the Bangladeshi Garment Sector', War on Want July 2011; *International Business Times* 25 March 2014.

Introduction

Multinational corporations are often accused of a number of abuses related to their business activities. Many have appeared in the press accused of, inter alia, bribery and corruption, abusing human rights, sanction busting, dumping, undermining governments, exploiting uneducated consumers, using forced labour, low wages, poor health and safety standards, exploiting natural resources, using child labour, and corruption. One of the many problems for business operating internationally is that standards and 'the way of doing things' differ from country to country. That is not to say this is a justification for the type of abuses listed above, but it does bring into question the very fundamental question of the role of business in society and to what extent business has any responsibility for some of the problems of society. This chapter explores the concept of **corporate social responsibility** (CSR), discusses some examples related to the concept, and looks at the implications for business.

CSR can be defined as the notion that corporations have an obligation to society to take into account not just their economic impact but also their social and environmental impact. In its renewed strategy, the European Commission defines CSR very simply as 'the responsibility of enterprises for their impacts on society'.

We use the term corporate social responsibility throughout this chapter, but it appears that business is not very keen on it. Marks and Spencer refers to its CSR activities as 'Plan A because there is no Plan B when it comes to conserving the earth's finite resources'. In other words, this is how we do business and we do not need to give it any special label. Others, such as the UK government, have dropped the 'social', which some object to as too narrow, or 'outside our remit', or as a label imposed from outside. Other labels used are 'triple-bottom-line reporting' (i.e. economic, social, and environmental), '**sustainable development**', and the most recent 'corporate citizenship'. Although there are different interpretations of these terms, they are all essentially about the obligation to society in its widest sense.

Debates about CSR

CSR is not new, and whether business has any social responsibility has been the subject of endless debate.

For some, there is only one social responsibility of business and that is, in the words of Milton Friedman (1970 [1983]), 'to use its resources and engage in activities designed to increase its profits so long as it stays within the rules of the game, which is to say, engages in open and free competition without deception or fraud'. This reflects the view that a free market society is made up of diverse entities, each with a specialist role within society. The role of business is economic and the people who run businesses are expert in that field. Their role is to combine resources to produce some product or service for sale at a profit. They compete with other firms by keeping costs as low as possible and supplying consumers with the goods and services they want at the lowest possible price. Those who are effective at doing this survive and make a profit. Those who fail go out of business. It is the drive to supply consumers with the goods and services they want, and at the same time to make as much profit as possible by driving costs down and selling as much as possible, which makes for a dynamic and efficient economy. If there are social and environmental problems, then this should not be for business people to solve because it would divert them from the role for which they are best equipped and the result would be a less efficient economy. These problems are best left to governments who can employ experts in those fields.

In this debate, and particularly in the field of international business, we are talking about a particular form of business organization and that is the 'corporation'. To become a corporation, a business has to go through a legal process which creates a body having a separate legal existence from its owners and from those who work in or manage it. Gap Inc., BP, Motorola all exist quite separately from the people who work in or manage the organization and from those who own the assets of the business, the shareholders. Shareholders change as shares are bought and sold through various stock exchanges. Managers and other workers change, but the corporation continues in existence. It is said to have perpetual succession.

In Friedman's view, the corporation should act no differently from the single owner business. Managers are employed as the agents of the principals (the owners) and should work in their interest, and that, in his view, is to make as much profit as possible. In that way, both dividends and share value increase. Managers are not experts in social welfare or in dealing with environmental problems, so how would they know how to deploy resources to deal with these problems. Nor, unlike politicians, have they been elected, so the use of funds for some purpose other than profit maximization would not only be wasteful it would be undemocratic, particularly as managers as a group do not tend to be representative of the population at large, usually being more conservative than the general population.

Counterpoint Box 11.1 Executive responsibility—to whom?

The rise in executive pay has been the subject of much public criticism in both the USA and in Western Europe. This intensified following the global financial crisis of 2007–08.

Hutton (2011) reported that the median pay for the chief executives of the 100 largest companies on the London Stock Exchange had risen to 88 times UK median earnings and 202 times the national minimum wage, up from 47 times and 124 times, respectively, in 2000. Bebchuk et al. (2010) estimate that the top executive teams of US investment banks Bear Stearns and Lehman Brothers received about US$1.4 billion and US$1 billion, respectively, from cash bonuses and equity sales during 2000–08 and suggested that this might have encouraged managers to take excessive risks, an important cause of the meltdown in the global financial system. A study by the Hay Group (2011) found no correlation between CEO pay in the UK and business performance. This is not surprising given that many studies find pay to be less of a motivator than things such as responsibility and status. Indeed Maslow's hierarchy of needs would suggest such a result.

Bebchuk and Fried (2006) argue that managers use their power to influence their compensation packages. As a result, they end up being paid excessive sums that do not lead to improved company performance and therefore do not serve shareholders' interests. They contend that executive pay is significantly decoupled from company performance. They argue

that executives owe their primary duty to shareholders but that corporate governance in the USA disenfranchises the true owners, the shareholders.

Lipton and Savitt (2007) defend multi-million dollar executive pay packages, arguing that highly paid executives have built great firms. They challenge Bebchuk's idea that corporations are the private property of shareholders. They insist that shareholders are merely owners of shares, not of the firm. Their right to exercise control over the company should be limited, but they have the right to share in the profits generated by it. They contend that it is management's prerogative to do what is in the best interest of all the corporation's stakeholders by balancing the interests of shareholders as well as other stakeholders, such as management and employees, creditors, regulators, suppliers, and consumers.

Sources: Hutton 2011; Hay Group 2011; Bebchuk and Fried 2006; Bebchuk et al. 2010; Lipton and Savitt 2007

Questions

1. Traditionally, the idea of maximizing shareholder value was supposed to lead to better economic performance, but if it just leads to increased executive pay what does this say about Milton Friedman's arguments about social responsibility?

Friedman's criticisms of CSR were not that business did not have a social role, but that its role and its obligation to society was to supply goods and services at the lowest price possible. His view was founded in a fundamental belief in the virtues of a free market economy in which each player contributed, without knowing it, to the greater good of society.

A further criticism by Friedman was the notion of a corporation, a legal creation, assuming moral responsibilities. In his words:

> What does it mean to say that 'business' has responsibilities? Only people can have responsibilities. A corporation is an artificial person and in this sense may have artificial responsibilities, but business as a whole cannot be said to have responsibilities, even in this vague sense (Friedman 1970).

There is no argument that the corporation exists as a separate legal entity with legal rights and duties. It is capable of owning and disposing of assets, employing people, entering into contracts, incurring and being owed debts, inflicting and suffering damage, suing and being sued. If it (the corporation) is held responsible for these actions, why then can it not be morally responsible for its other actions? As Goodpaster and Mathews (1982:135) point out, 'if a group can act like a person in some ways, then we can expect it to behave like a person in other ways'. We have no problem referring to a company's business strategy or its marketing plan. We would not think or refer to these examples as an individual's strategy or plan. This is because corporations have complex internal decision-making structures that arrive at decisions in line with corporate goals (French 1979). The outcome is rarely attributable to any one person, but is usually the result of a series of discussions between directors, managers, and staff. In other words, the corporation acts just like an individual. Examples from legal cases support the difficulty in identifying individuals responsible for corporate decisions. In *P & O European Ferries (Dover) Ltd* ((1991) 93 Cr App R 72) Mr Justice Turner ruled that a company may be properly indicted for manslaughter. That case, however, ended in the acquittal of the defendant company because the Crown could not show that a 'controlling mind' had been grossly negligent. The 'controlling mind' of a company is somebody who can be shown to be in control of the operations of a company and not responsible to another person. In large companies, the 'controlling mind' has proved difficult to identify, but the smaller the company the easier it is to identify. In *R v Kite and OLL Ltd*, the 'Lyme Bay' disaster, several schoolchildren, who were canoeing across Lyme Bay, died because of the poor safety standards of the company. In this case, it was possible to identify the Managing Director, Peter Kite, as the 'controlling mind' and he was successfully prosecuted for corporate manslaughter. It was because of the difficulty of identifying the 'controlling mind' that the UK strengthened legislation in this area with the introduction of The Corporate Manslaughter and Corporate Homicide Act 2007 (CMA), which came into force throughout the UK on 6 April 2008.

Another argument supporting the case for assigning moral responsibility to a company, is the existence not just of a decision-making structure but also of a set of beliefs and values guiding individual decision-making. This is commonly known as the 'culture' of the organization. Nowadays, this is more often than not enshrined in a written statement such as the one below for the HSBC group.

HSBC Values

Be dependable and do the right thing

- stand firm for what is right, deliver on commitments, be resilient and trustworthy;

- take personal accountability, be decisive, use judgement and common sense, empower others.

Be open to different ideas and cultures

- communicate openly, honestly and transparently, value challenge, learn from mistakes;
- listen, treat people fairly, be inclusive, value different perspectives.

Be connected with our customers, communities, regulators and each other

- build connections, be externally focused, collaborate across boundaries;
- care about individuals and their progress, show respect, be supportive and responsive.

Source HSBC Annual Report 2013.

Learning task

HSBC claims to put great emphasis on values empowering employees to 'do the right thing', but in 2012 they paid fines of $4.2 billion dollars for doing the wrong thing. Explain how this might happen (see Chapter 9, Case Study International banks and the law).

Some find Friedman's view of the modern corporation at odds with reality, and particularly the view that modern capitalism is at all like the classical capitalism of economics textbooks where firms have no economic or political power because they are subject to market forces. As we saw in Chapter 3, most modern markets are oligopolistic in nature, with a few very large and powerful firms dominating many markets. We also saw in Chapters 1 and 9 that these players are active politically, using their power to influence policy in their favour; for example, in removing barriers to trade and investment. The idea that the modern corporation is a passive player in the economy is far from the truth. They are powerful players in the world economy whose actions will have an impact both economically and socially, so the modern argument about CSR is not whether corporations should engage in CSR but how they do it and why they do it. In terms of how, as we shall see, there is no universal agreement about what constitutes good CSR.

The Moral Case for CSR

The moral case for CSR is that it is the right thing to do, not because it yields greater financial return, but as a good corporate citizen with the same social and environmental obligations of any other citizen, i.e. you and me.

The first stage in this argument attributes the status of 'personhood' to the corporation so that they could be considered 'moral agents' and held accountable for their actions. See the argument above (Goodpaster and Mathews (1982) and French (1979)) which likens the corporation to an individual.

The second strand of the argument emphasizes the social nature of the corporation, i.e. that it is a creation of society and should therefore serve the needs of society. Some writers (Donaldson 1982: Anshen 1970 [1983]) draw on social contract theory (the view that individuals' moral and/or political obligations are dependent upon an agreement between them to form society) to support these arguments. Anshen (1970 [1983]) argues that the agreement is one that changes as society evolves. In the 1950s, when living conditions were much worse in the West than they are now, society's expectation of business (and so their obligation to society) was to produce the goods required by society. Indeed, it is as well to remember that, from society's point of view, the basic purpose of business is to be the efficient provider of goods and services. Environmental damage, poor working conditions, and inequalities were seen as a fair price to pay for the improving standard of living. As Western societies grew richer, the trade-off between material well-being and the quality of life changed, and the expectations for business to provide safe places to work, not to damage the environment, to respect human rights, and so on, have now become the expectation confronting business.

Stakeholder theory is an offshoot of this theory, which says that business corporations are part of the wider society in which they develop relationships with groups or constituencies (to include biodiversity). These groups are said to have a 'stake' in the organization because the activities of the organization will have an effect on them and, in turn, they can impact on the organization. They are part of a social system and dependent on each other, as opposed to the Friedman view which sees them as separate entities operating at arm's length.

Other writers, such as De George (2010), reinforce this view of corporations as social institutions by emphasizing that they are indeed creations of society. They are legal creations permitted by the state. They have to go through a process of application to receive their 'charter of incorporation', which brings them into existence, and as such society can then expect these institutions to act for society as a whole. It is the corporation's 'licence to operate' that can, of course, be withdrawn if those expectations are not met. This also underpins the 'corporate citizen' view of corporations in which the corporation is regarded as an institutional citizen with rights and obligations like any other citizen.

Other arguments put forward include the following:

- Large corporations have enormous economic power and are endowed with substantial resources that they should use responsibly for the good of society.

- Business decisions will have social and environmental consequences, so corporations must take responsibility for those decisions.

- Business has been instrumental in causing many of today's problems, such as global warming and resource depletion, and therefore has a responsibility to solve these problems and avoid creating further problems.

The Business Case

The 'Business Case' refers to the underlying reasons business should engage with CSR. In other words, 'what does business get out of it'? The view of the corporation as a private body with an agent(s) acting for a principal(s) is peculiar to the UK and North America. In continental Europe and Japan, corporations are viewed much more as public bodies with obligations to a wider set of groups, investors, employees, suppliers, and customers. These countries regard corporations as social institutions with a strong public interest agenda. In these companies, managers are charged with pursuing the interests of all stakeholders whereas in the UK and North America the maximization of shareholder value is the goal. In the UK, the Companies Act 1985 extended the duties of directors to act not just in the interest of its members (shareholders) but also its employees. This has been extended in the Companies Act 2006, which includes the following section:

Duty to promote the success of the company

(1) A director of a company must act in the way he considers, in good faith, would be most likely to promote the success of the company for the benefit of its members as a whole, and in doing so have regard (amongst other matters) to—

(a) the likely consequences of any decision in the long term,

(b) the interests of the company's employees,

(c) the need to foster the company's business relationships with suppliers, customers and others,

(d) the impact of the company's operations on the community and the environment,

(e) the desirability of the company maintaining a reputation for high standards of business conduct, and

(f) the need to act fairly as between members of the company

Note that this is to 'promote the success of the company'. Rather than driving a new agenda, this is legislation catching up with reality, as most large corporations have already realized that to be successful, or at least not to court disaster, then they must, as a minimum, take into account all of their stakeholders. In the words of the UK government:

It enshrines in statute the concept of Enlightened Shareholder Value which recognises that directors will be more likely to achieve long term sustainable success for the benefit of their shareholders if their companies pay appropriate regard to wider matters such as the environment and their employees (Certified Accountants Educational Trust (London) 2011).

For the UK government, the reason for business to undertake CSR is because it makes good business sense (www.gov.uk/government/consultations/corporate-responsibility-call-for-views), although it would be difficult to sell to business in any other way. In many cases, business has come to accept CSR not because of the positive benefits it might bring but because they have awakened to the risks of ignoring it. Continuing business scandals have undermined public trust in big business. Shell's failure to consult with or to take into account the reaction of Greenpeace to their proposed sinking of a North Sea oil platform led to international protests and a damaged reputation. Nike, Gap, GlaxoSmithKline, Yahoo, BP, HSBC and other banks (see Chapter 9, Case Study International banks and the law), and many others have suffered damage to their reputations from well-publicized CSR failures. Reputation management is a critical component of corporate success and one of the reasons that, according to Porter and Kramer (2006), 'of the 250 largest multinational corporations, 64% published CSR reports in 2005'. The authors go on to say that much of this was about demonstrating the company's social sensitivity rather than a coherent framework for CSR activities. Very often, this activity is lodged in the public relations departments of these companies and is a defensive reaction focused on avoiding the disasters that have struck others. Porter and Kramer have developed their thinking and popularized the concept of shared value. They see capitalism as being under siege, with a common view that business takes a short-term view and is profiting at the expense of communities. They argue that business needs to move beyond CSR to concentrate on activities that create social value, regain trust, and which will in turn create profit and hence shared value (Porter and Kramer 2011). This is not without its critics. Crane et al. (2014) argue that this is not really a novel idea, adding little to the ideas of strategic CSR. They also argue that it ignores the tensions between economic and social goals, is naïve about the challenges of business compliance, and is based on a shallow conception of the corporation's role in society.

From the corporation's point of view, there is good reason for this focus, as the expectations of governments and people have never been higher. Moreover, modern consumers are better and more instantly informed than ever. An oil spill in Alaska, a chemical explosion in India, violation of tribal rights in Nigeria, an explosion on an oil rig in the Gulf, the collapse of a garment factory all make headline news in the Western media. Consumers want to know where the products they consume come from, under what conditions they were produced, and, more recently, what size the carbon footprint is.

Non-governmental organizations (NGOs), such as Greenpeace, Friends of the Earth, Christian Aid, Oxfam, WWF, and Amnesty International, are also watching (see, for example, www.ethicalcorp.com). There are literally hundreds of thousands, if not millions, of these organizations operating across the world, many of them exceedingly well resourced (see Crane and Matten 2010: Chapter 10 for a discussion of civil society). Greenpeace operates across more than 40 countries and has 2.8 million supporters actively financing its activities as well as receiving money from charitable foundations (www.greenpeace.org). Oxfam works in over 70 countries with an income of £367.9 million in the financial year 2012–13 (www.oxfam.org.uk).

Another reason that many large corporations have increased the size of their CSR departments is to deal with NGOs. NGOs, of course, differ in their view of business. Some, such as the World Business Council for Sustainable Business, have a membership made up of some of the world's leading companies. The council has as part of its vision 'to support the business license to operate' by being a 'leading business advocate on sustainable development' (www.wbcsd.org). So, not all NGOs are critical of business, but many are and some, such as Oxfam, have a quite different view of the world and a different set of priorities, especially in the international arena. Sensible companies try to build relationships with relevant NGOs, either through dialogue or in some cases through partnership. The World Food Programme, managed by the United Nations (UN), has a number of corporate partners including Caterpillar, LG, Unilever, and Vodafone.

As we have seen, CSR is definitely on the corporate agenda, but whether business sees this as a duty to society, in the sense implied here, is open to great doubt. The evidence presented earlier paints a picture of business reluctantly taking up CSR as a defensive reaction to protect reputation, possibly leading to a recognition that CSR activities may well improve business performance. Many commentators would contend that the argument is a distraction.

Mini Case Study Unilever and sustainability

Unilever is one of the world's largest consumer products companies with over 400 brand names worldwide, such as Persil, Pot Noodle, Bovril, PG Tips, Walls, and Ben & Jerry's. Unilever claims to recognize its responsibility to society. Its corporate purpose states, 'to succeed requires the highest standards of corporate behaviour towards our employees, consumers, and the world in which we live'.

In 2010, Unilever announced a new sustainability initiative aiming by 2020 to:

- halve the environmental impact of their footprint;
- help more than 1 billion people take action to improve their health and well-being; and
- enhance the livelihoods of millions of people as we grow our business.

For example, the Unilever Foundation partners with five leading global organizations, Oxfam, Population Services International, Save the Children, UNICEF, and the World Food Programme, to tackle some of the world's problems. They are also the primary beneficiaries in times of disaster so that Unilever can channel resources to where they are most needed. In 2013, Unilever launched 'Project Sunlight' a consumer facing campaign aimed at inspiring people to live more sustainably.

All this activity is not entirely altruistic, as Unilever recognizes the business benefits of this type of action. It will, according to Unilever:

1. Fuel innovation.
2. Help win with customers.
3. Help win in emerging markets.
4. Address consumers' needs as 'citizens'.
5. Generate cost savings.
6. Differentiate and build the Unilever brand.

As Unilever's CEO, Paul Polman, put it: 'consumers want more. They see food shortages, malnutrition and climate change, and governments are not addressing those problems. Companies that do this will get a competitive advantage. Those that do not will put themselves at risk' (*The Guardian* 15 November 2010).

For others this is all 'greenwash', i.e. advertising which presents an environmentally responsible public image, but which in reality is just aimed at promoting the company and its brands in order to increase sales. If companies were serious about saving the environment, goes the argument, then they would be encouraging consumers to buy less. They would not be planning to open new manufacturing plants in the developing world and they would be actively working to avoid the same consumption patterns as those in the West. Unilever is also the world's largest consumer of palm oil used in the manufacture of many of its products. Palm oil plantations, say the critics, come at the cost of the deforestation of native jungles and their inhabitants, both human and animal.

Sources: www.unilever.co.uk; www.chinadialogue.net/article/show/single/en/6913-Unilever-and-the-case-for-sustainable-business; www.pccnaturalmarkets.com/sc/1403/sustainable-palm-oil.html

Questions

1. Discuss the argument that Unilever is abandoning the idea of maximizing returns to shareholders by pursuing its sustainability initiative.
2. Some criticize Unilever's sustainability campaign as just a case of 'greenwash'. As a spokesperson for Unilever, how would you deal with this argument?

In the words of David Grayson (Doughty Chair of Corporate Responsibility, Cranfield School of Management):

In my experience, business leaders committed to Corporate Responsibility do it for a mixture of 'it just makes business sense and it's the right thing to do'. In practice, those percentages may vary for the same business leader depending on the topic; and certainly will vary even within a business and between businesses. I think we should stop searching for the Holy Grail of precise motivation. We would be much more sensibly employed on improving the practice of management so that whatever the particular motivation, the performance can be commercially viable ('Sense and Sustainability: Inaugural lecture 2007').

So what are those 'sound business benefits'?

Leading companies have now moved from the defensive stances of early CSR efforts to explore new ways of engaging with a range of external stakeholders. In 2010, The Doughty Centre for Corporate Responsibility undertook research for Business in the Community (www.bitc.org.uk/our-resources/report/business-case-being-responsible-business). They found 60 business benefits from being a responsible business. They clustered these benefits into the following seven categories:

- **Brand value and reputation**—brand value is strongly influenced by CSR activities. A study by the Reputation Institute in 2013 (www.reputationinstitute.com/thought-leadership/csr-reptrak-100) found that 73 per cent of 55,000 consumers surveyed were willing to recommend companies they perceived to be delivering on CSR, although of the 100 companies included in the study only five were considered to be delivering on their CSR activities compared to 12 the previous year.

- **Employees and future workforce**—just as prospective employees are put off from what are seen as bad employers, then those seen as leaders in the field of CSR will more easily attract and retain staff. Moreover, they are likely to have a more highly motivated workforce.

- **Operational effectiveness**—more efficient environmental processes can lead to operational efficiency, as can reducing waste. Better-motivated staff (see above) can also help companies reduce their operating costs.

- **Risk reduction and management**—i.e. the ability to identify and manage risks better.

- **Direct financial impact**—improved access to capital, reducing costs, and improving shareholder value.

- **Organizational growth**—many surveys show that customers are concerned about the environmental impact of the products they consume, about who made them, and under what conditions they were made. Growth can come from new markets, new product development, lateral expansion, new customers, and new partnerships.

- **Business opportunity**—the opportunities that arise from addressing stakeholder concerns such as poverty, water shortages, and poor health. Food companies, for example, can reduce the salt and fat content of food and thereby reduce costs and the use of resources, and address health concerns of the community.

They identified two other benefits which were only just beginning to emerge, but were more prominent in those companies already committed to responsible business:

- Responsible leadership—ensuring social and environmental issues are factored into the core business model. Unilever, mentioned above, is seen as a champion of sustainability and has seen growth in sales and profits.

- Macro-level sustainable development—the benefits of contributing to sustained development. The UN Global Compact and the Millennium Development Goals (see this chapter, Millennium Development Goals) are good examples of corporations engaging with macro-level issues. So, improving health care or education in a supplier country may have long-term benefits for the organization.

Global CSR

Is global CSR any different from domestic CSR? Not in principle, but the implementation is far more complex. Take the argument above that modern CSR reflects the changed expectations of society and that the trade off between growth and the negative impacts of that growth is no longer acceptable. China could justifiably argue that they are at that stage in their growth where the cost of their improved living standards, in terms of damage to the environment, is acceptable. They are, of course, growing in entirely different conditions in which global warming is a threat to everybody, but what does this mean for the global corporations operating in China? Should they be able to operate under the less stringent environmental legislation that exists in that country, or should they be working to the same standards that they work to in their home economy? Is there an obligation on the West to share new, environmentally friendly technologies with developing countries, as much of the growth of companies in the West took place in an era of less stringent environmental controls?

Countries differ not just in their environmental legislation, but also in the institutions that govern the countries that in some cases are not very effective. They also differ in their customs and their culture (see Chapter 6). Setting up operations overseas because it is cheaper might be very attractive, but why is it cheaper? Wages are lower, working hours are longer, health and safety regulations are lax and not policed very well (see this chapter, Case Study The Bangladesh garment industry). Is this acceptable? Child labour is illegal, but quite common. Would you tolerate this if these were your factories or if it was happening in your supplier's factories? If the answer is no, and an undercover investigator discovers this and reports it to the Western media, how would you react? Would you instantly close down the factory? What effect would this have on the children working there? These are the types of issues facing global companies in their everyday operations, and it is not that there is one domestic set of circumstances and one overseas set of circumstances; every country will have some differences. Shell, for example, is a global group of companies working in more than 130 countries and territories and employing 108,000 people worldwide.

Whose Standards?

Global companies have the problem of doing business in many countries in which the 'ways of doing things' differ. They therefore have the difficult task of deciding which standards to adopt. Should they take a principled stand and adopt a universal set of values wherever they operate, or take a different approach in each country and operate according to the appropriate standards of that country? The first approach appears morally attractive in that we have a tendency to assume that our own standards are the 'right' or 'best' standards and we therefore tend to judge others by those standards, but this can result in an **ethnocentric** (believing that the customs and traditions of your own nationality are better than those of others) morality which opens multinational companies to the charge of **cultural imperialism**. It would satisfy those critics who accuse MNCs of exploiting cultural differences for their own benefit, but it may offend those host cultures whose accepted practices may be very different, or it may well be impossible to operate without adopting host country practices. For example, when Google entered China it agreed to some censorship of search results to comply with the Chinese government. This offended many in the West, used to freedom of expression, but Google argued that it would be more damaging to pull out of China altogether. Google moved its operation to Hong Kong in 2010 in an attempt to bypass Chinese censorship, but its share of the Chinese search market fell to as low as 5 per cent as most users in China use the Chinese search engine, Baidu. In 2012, Google began to encrypt Web searches conducted in China in an attempt to allow users to circumvent China's 'Great Firewall' (see Chapter 7, Mini Case Study China and the Internet).

The other extreme is termed **cultural relativism** and, put simply, says 'when in Rome do as the Romans do'. This approach recognizes that countries and cultures are different and that MNCs operating in different countries should recognize and accommodate those differences. This is often used as a reason by MNCs to adopt practices that enhance their profits, such as the employment of child labour or lax health and safety standards, which would be questionable in their home country.

These extreme ethical approaches are useful to business decision-makers to the extent that they do serve to highlight the problems. Donaldson (1989) has suggested that there are some universal principles that companies and nations could agree to work toward. This entails respect for, and promotion of, some minimal rights:

- freedom of physical movement;
- ownership of property;
- freedom from torture;
- fair trial;
- freedom from discrimination;
- physical security;
- free speech and association;
- education;
- political participation; and
- subsistence.

One might argue about which rights should be included, and this may appear as a peculiarly Western set of rights, but this approach to prescribing minimum standards is the approach that has been developed, albeit in a fragmented fashion. Many companies have responded to the CSR debate by developing their own codes of conduct for their global operations and many international organizations have developed principles that seek to guide companies to best practice in CSR. The UN Global Compact is one such initiative, in which the UN and several campaigning organizations, such as Oxfam and Amnesty International, came together to agree a set of principles for CSR. There were originally nine principles in the areas of human rights, labour, and the environment, and a tenth, concerning anti-corruption, was added in 2004. This initiative was launched in 2000 and now has over 10,000 participants, including more than 7,000 businesses from over 145 countries (www.unglobalcompact.org/ParticipantsAndStakeholders/index.html0).

Learning Task

The opening case to this chapter considered conditions in the Bangladesh garment industry, which supplies many of the leading clothing retailers in the West.

1. Western retailers have no responsibility for the conditions in these factories. Discuss.

2. Primark, a subsidiary company of Associated British Foods, was one of those retailers who sourced supplies from the Rana Plaza factory. What steps have Primark taken to address the issues raised in the case?

The 10 Principles

The principles are derived from:

- The Universal Declaration of Human Rights.
- The International Labour Organization's Declaration on Fundamental Principles and Rights at Work.
- The Rio Declaration on Environment and Development.
- The United Nations Convention Against Corruption.

The Global Compact asks companies to embrace, support, and enact, within their sphere of influence, a set of core values in the areas of human rights, labour standards, the environment, and anti-corruption (see Table 11.1).

Table 11.1 UN Global Compact principles

Human Rights	Principle 1: businesses should support and respect the protection of internationally proclaimed human rights
	Principle 2: make sure that they are not complicit in human rights abuses
Labour Standards	Principle 3: businesses should uphold the freedom of association and the effective recognition of the right to collective bargaining
	Principle 4: the elimination of all forms of forced and compulsory labour
	Principle 5: the effective abolition of child labour
	Principle 6: the elimination of discrimination in respect of employment and occupation
Environment	Principle 7: businesses should support a precautionary approach to environmental challenges
	Principle 8: undertake initiatives to promote greater environmental responsibility
	Principle 9: encourage the development and diffusion of environmentally friendly technologies
Anti-Corruption	Principle 10: businesses should work against corruption in all its forms, including extortion and bribery

Source: www.unglobalcompact.org

Learning Task

Use the UN's website on the Global Compact to explain why adherence to these principles is in the best interest of business.

Four of the major weaknesses of these codes are:

1. Not many of the world's MNCs are members; 7,000 sounds like a lot, but is actually only a small proportion of the world's tens of thousands of MNCs. However, many of those who have joined are important in terms of size and reputation.

2. The codes are voluntary and the UN cannot afford to be too selective about who joins the initiative.

3. It is difficult to monitor the impact the Compact is making.

4. No effective sanctions for breaches of the code exist, although over 2,000 companies have been expelled from the Compact for failing to report progress for two consecutive years (see www.theguardian.com/sustainable-business/cleaning-up-un-global-compact-green-wash).

Companies that join are simply required to work towards implementation of the principles. They do have to report annually on their activities, through what the Compact refers to as 'Communication on Progress'. This entails a statement of continuing support, a description of practical actions, and a measurement of outcomes. In measuring outcomes, participants are encouraged to use the Global Reporting Initiative (GRI). The GRI is an attempt to produce standard sustainability reporting guidelines and make it as routine for companies as financial reporting. The GRI produces a standard format for companies to report on their economic, environmental, and social performance. Over 1,000 organizations, ranging from companies, public bodies, NGOs, and industry groups, use the guidelines, which makes it the most common framework in use. Unilever, for example, assesses progress against three indices, the UN Global Compact, GRI, and Millennium Development Goals (MDGs).

The picture, then, is of a complex global system in which the ability of the state to look after the public interest, even in relatively developed economies, is diminished. Global companies operate in many states that are weak and often corrupt. There are major world issues, such as climate change, poverty, health issues, human rights, corruption, and ecosystem problems, which are also beyond the powers of national governments and, internationally, there is a lack of effective governance. There is also a growing number of very active NGOs, often campaigning on a single issue, who are demanding action from companies. In turn, the health of companies will, in the long term, depend on the health of the global economic, social and political, and environmental systems. The case for CSR rests on a recognition by companies of this scenario and that they are in a unique position to address these issues. Many have responded, perhaps for defensive reasons, by engaging with their stakeholders and developing codes of conduct for their global activities. International organizations have also added to the drive for CSR by developing their own codes or sets of principles to which they encourage companies to adhere.

Having examined the case for CSR, we now turn to examine in more detail some of the specific issues facing global companies.

Corruption

Corruption is a major issue for international business. Corruption occurs when organizations or individuals profit improperly through their position. It occurs in both the public and the private sectors; for example, when private businesses want public contracts or licences, or when private firms wish to do business with others. Bribery is only one example of corruption. It can also include extortion, that is where threats and violence are used to get someone to act or not act in a certain way, favouritism, nepotism, embezzlement, fraud, and illegal monetary contributions to political parties (SIDA, see www.sida.se). In some cultures, corruption is accepted as the norm and many commentators, and sometimes the law, make a distinction between bribes and so-called 'facilitation payments', which are everyday small payments made to officials to 'ease the wheels of business'. International pressure groups, such as Transparency International, make no such distinction.

What's Wrong with Bribery and Corruption?

According to Transparency International, it is impossible to gauge the cost of corruption, although they present a number of informed estimates (www.transparency.org.uk/corruption/statistics-and-quotes). Global Financial Integrity calculate that in 2011 developing countries lost nearly $1 trillion to crime, corruption, and tax evasion (Kar and LeBlanc 2013) and that over the decade 2002 to 2011 this had been increasing at a rate of 10 per cent per year. This, of course, only reflects the direct financial costs and takes no account of other costs. The Rana Plaza disaster featured in the opening case study, for example, has been linked to the bribery of inspectors to overlook safety flaws (www.transparency.org/news/feature/rana_plaza_one_year_on_what_has_changed).

The cost of bribes falls mainly on the poor, whether it is through the diversion of aid money into corrupt officials' pockets or the hiking of prices when the cost of a bribe is passed on in raised prices to consumers.

- Bribery and corruption undermine the proper workings of a market economy, which can seriously reduce GDP in the poorest countries. It distorts price and cost considerations so that resources are not necessarily used in the most efficient way. Decisions are based on 'who pays the biggest bribes' rather than price, quality, service, and innovation. This raises prices for everyone, but has the greatest impact on the poor.

- Resources are often diverted away from public service projects, such as schools and hospitals, towards more high profile projects, such as dams and power stations, where there is more scope for improper payments. This again impacts most on the poor who are denied vital public services.

- Corruption is ethically wrong. It is an abuse of power, which undermines the integrity of all concerned.

- Corruption undermines the democratic process and the rule of law. Just as business has to earn its licence to operate, so does government. Politicians, government officers, and institutions all lose their legitimacy in a climate of corruption. Again, the poor are likely to be the biggest losers in such a situation.

- The environment is also likely to suffer in such a regime through the lack of environmental legislation or its non-enforcement as corrupt officials fill their pockets in return for turning a blind eye.

- For business there are several risks:
  - the risk that accusations of corruption, whether proved or not, can lead to loss of reputation;
  - a legal risk. Bribery and corruption is generally illegal wherever it occurs, but even if not, because of international pressure (the UN convention against corruption) it is becoming increasingly illegal at home (e.g. in the USA and UK) to engage in these practices elsewhere (see Chapter 9);
  - in paying bribes there is no certainty you get what you want and no recourse to any retribution or compensation if you do not;
  - if you are known as a bribe payer, then repeat demands are likely to be made;
  - it adds substantially to the cost of doing business;
  - if you cheat, so will your competitors. It makes doing business much more difficult;
  - employees and other stakeholders will lose trust in the business.

Transparency International was founded in 1993 to fight corruption. Each year, Transparency International produces the **Corruption Perceptions Index** (CPI). This index ranks 177 countries according to the level of corruption perceived to exist among public officials and politicians. A score of zero indicates highly corrupt and a score of 10 very clean.

On the map at Figure 11.1, the darker the colour the higher the perceived incidence of corruption, which is generally low in North America, Western Europe, and Australasia and high in Central and South America, Africa, Asia, and Eastern Europe.

Figure 11.1 Corruption Perceptions Index 2013

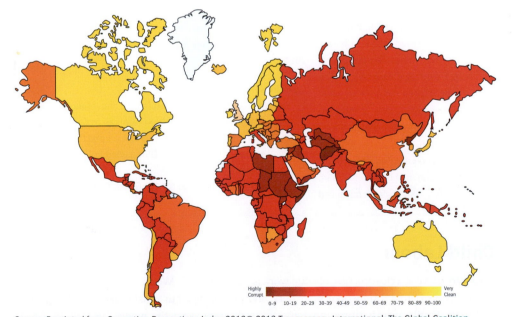

Source: Reprinted from Corruption Perceptions Index 2013© 2013 Transparency International: The Global Coalition Against Corruption. Used with permission www.transparency.org

Learning Task

Access the website of Transparency International www.transparency.org and access the Corruption Perceptions Index on which the map above is based.

1. Explain what the Corruption Perceptions Index measures.
2. Look up Table 2.1 in Chapter 2. For each of the countries plot on a graph their rank and CPI score against their GDP. What conclusions can you draw from your graph?

Mini Case Study GlaxoSmithKline (GSK)

GSK is a UK-based global pharmaceutical company. It is one of the largest drug companies in the world, employing over 97,000 people, operating in more than 100 countries, and with about 5 per cent of the world pharmaceuticals market.

China's market for drugs is growing quickly and is predicted to be $315 billion by 2020, second only in size to the USA. The Chinese government has spent billions of dollars in the last few years extending basic medical insurance to more than 90 per cent of its citizens. It plans, by 2020, to have established a universal healthcare system so that everybody can have access to drugs and medical services.

No wonder, when growth in Western markets is slowing, that pharmaceutical companies have been investing heavily in the Chinese market. But some may have gone too far. GSK has been accused by the Chinese authorities of being the 'godfather' at the centre of a network of corruption. The head of GSK's Chinese operations has been accused by the Chinese authorities of 'pressing his sales teams to bribe hospitals, doctors and health institutions'. It is claimed that they inflated the price of medicines to pay for the bribes. It is further alleged that, as the company came under scrutiny, law enforcement officers were bribed in order to try and stop the investigation.

This is not the first time GSK has been accused of unethical practices. In 2012, GSK paid $3 billion in fines in the USA. According to US attorney, Carmin Ortiz , 'GSK's sales force bribed physicians to prescribe GSK products using every imaginable form of high-priced entertainment, from Hawaiian vacations and paying doctors millions of dollars to go on speaking tours, to tickets to Madonna concerts'. They also promoted drugs for unapproved uses and held back data and made unsupported safety claims about a diabetes drug. In April of 2014, GSK announced it was investigating its business in Iraq over claims by a whistleblower that it hired 16 Iraqi government doctors to act as sales representatives. It has also been accused of bribing doctors in Poland.

In May 2014, the Serious Fraud Office in the UK announced that they were opening a criminal inquiry into GSK's sales practices. Authorities in both the UK and the US can prosecute companies for corruption committed overseas.

Sources: www.gsk.com/uk; *Financial Times* 3 April, 14 May, 27 May 2014; *The Guardian* 3 July 2012 and 7 April 2014; BBC 14 April 2014

Questions

1. Explain the terms 'cultural relativism' and 'ethnocentrism'.
2. Many claim that corruption is widespread in China and that bribing low paid doctors is common practice. If this is true then what is wrong with GSK paying bribes? Explain your answer.
3. How could a code such as the UN Global Compact help GSK?

Child Labour

Trying to arrive at a clear picture of child work is a difficult task. We are all familiar with the horror pictures of child mineworkers, soldiers, and prostitutes, but most child work takes place within the family in agriculture and domestic work, and in societies where this is often seen as

Counterpoint Box 11.2 Corruption—is it always a bad thing?

Corruption occurs on a large scale and is growing. Transparency International (2009) estimates that corrupt politicians and government officials in developing countries receive bribes believed to total some US$20 to 40 billion annually.

In 2006, Paul Wolfowitz the head of the World Bank said:

> corruption is often at the very root of why governments do not work. Today one of the biggest threats to development in many countries . . . is corruption. It weakens fundamental systems, it distorts markets, and it encourages people to apply their skills and energies in nonproductive ways. In the end, governments and citizens will pay a price, in lower incomes, in lower investment, and in more volatile economic fluctuations . . . where corruption is rampant, contracts are unenforceable, competition is skewed, and the costs of doing business becomes stifling (http://web.worldbank.org/WBSITE/EXTERNAL/NEWS/0,,contentMD K:20884956~menuPK:34463~pagePK:34370~piPK:3442 4~theSitePK:4607,00.html).

However, corruption is not always seen as a bad thing. Chang (2008) argues that bribery does not inevitably slow down economic development. For example, where a public servant takes a bribe from a firm and invests that money in a project as productive as the firm would have done, then the act of bribery may have little or no adverse effect on efficiency or growth. He also asserts that a company getting a contract through bribery may be the most efficient contender for the contract. In fact, it is likely that the most efficient firms can afford to pay the highest bribes. Some economists see corruption as rectifying market failure. A government may set a price for a good or service which does not reflect market pressures of supply and demand. A bribe could result in the authorities turning a blind eye to illegal trading on the black market, which could move the price closer to an equilibrium level thereby bringing about a more efficient allocation of resources.

Corruption, of course, is a broad term covering many different activities, including bribery. Cultural norms differ across the world and in some societies bribes are seen as part of the price paid in order to 'get things done'.

Sources: Chang 2008; Underkuffler 2009; Transparency International, Global Corruption Report 2009 http://www.transparency.org/whatwedo/pub/global_corruption_report_2009

Questions

1. Do you think it is possible to differentiate between different forms of corruption and bribery, and that not all bribery is bad? Justify your answer.

---

culturally acceptable. The International Labour Office (ILO) divides child work into three different categories:

- Economically active: a very wide category which refers to any form of productive work, paid or unpaid.

- Child labour: work that is done by a child under the specified age for work, which either deprives them of schooling, causes them to leave school early, or requires a combination of schooling and long hours of work.

- Hazardous work: the worst form of child labour, exposing children to conditions which are damaging to their mental, physical, and emotional development and which the international community has agreed to try to end.

In 2012, there were 264 million children aged between 5 and 17 who were economically active (a reduction of 42 million since 2008) with 168 million involved in child labour (215 million in 2008) and more than 85 million (115 million in 2008) undertaking hazardous work (55 million boys and 30 million girls). They do it because their survival and that of their families depend on it (International Labour Office 2013).

Not all work done by children is considered harmful and therefore in policy terms it is not just a case of eliminating all child labour. Work that does not damage health or interfere with schooling may be considered positive in contributing to personal development by developing skills and experience and preparing children for adult life, so-called 'child work'. The ILO has two conventions relating to child labour. Convention 138 allows 'child work' but aims at the abolition of child labour and stipulates that the minimum age for entry into the workforce should not be less than the minimum age for finishing school. Convention 182 calls for elimination of the worst forms of child labour for all under 18s. This includes slavery, forced recruitment for use in armed conflict, prostitution, any illicit activity, and work which is likely to harm the health, safety, and morals of children. These conventions lay down the basic principles to be implemented by ratifying countries and are tools for governments to use, in consultation with employers and workers, to draft legislation to conform with internationally acceptable standards. There are 185 ILO members, of which 179 have ratified convention 182 and 166 have ratified convention 138, but, as the figures above indicate, child exploitation is still a huge global problem.

Child labour is not simply a problem of the developing world, although most takes place there. The Asian Pacific region has the highest number of child workers with 64.4 million representing nearly 10.1 per cent of the age group. This figure had declined by 32 million since 2008. Sub-Saharan Africa has the highest incidence of child labour at 26.2 per cent, a small decrease of 2.2 per cent since 2008. A similar pattern is displayed for children in hazardous work, with 33.9 million in the Asia Pacific region and 28.8 million in the sub-Saharan Africa region, which has the highest incidence with one in ten children involved (International Labour Office 2013).

Mini Case Study Cocoa production in West Africa

The global chocolate market is worth more than US$110 billion per year. Most of that chocolate starts life in West Africa where over 70 per cent of the world's cocoa production is grown. The Ivory Coast is the largest producer with 40 per cent of world production. Here, about 1 million small, family-run farms of less than 4 hectares grow cocoa as a cash crop alongside crops grown for food. More than 6 million rely on these farms for a living. Farms are often remote and as mechanization is not appropriate, production is labour intensive.

The global supply chain is quite complex, with many intermediaries before the chocolate reaches the final consumer. Cocoa growers generally sell to a middleman for cash once or twice a year and have to take whatever price they can get. The middleman sells on to processors or exporters. Prices are ultimately determined on the London Cocoa Terminal Market and the New York Cocoa Exchange, but, like many cash crops, the farmer receives a fraction of the world price.

There is, therefore, great pressure on the farmer to keep costs down and one way of achieving this is to employ child labour. Most of the children are under 14, kept from schooling, work 12-hour days, apply pesticides, and use machetes to clear fields and split harvested cocoa pods to extract the beans. All of this falls into the ILO convention 182 of 'the worst form of child labour'.

In 2000, a British TV documentary was broadcast claiming that many children were working as slaves in the Ivory →

→ Coast. Because the demand for child labour outstrips the supply, children were purchased from the neighbouring states of Burkino Faso, Mali, and Togo. Impoverished parents would receive between £70 and £100 for each child, depending on the age. These children, some as young as six, were forced to endure harsh working conditions and long hours, and many also faced physical abuse by their masters.

An industry protocol (the Harkin-Engel protocol), signed on 19 September 2001, established the International Cocoa Initiative made up of chocolate companies, confectionery trade associations, NGOs, and trade unions to work with governments to end the worst forms of child labour. The initial deadline was 2005, but this has now been pushed back to 2020. The University of Tulane, overseeing the protocol, found that in 2009 there were 820,000 children working in cocoa in the Ivory Coast, only 40 per cent were enrolled in school, and only 5 per cent were paid for their work. Between 2001 and 2009, 8,243 children (about 1 per cent) had been reached as a result of interventions, and Tulane concluded that this was not sufficient in light of commitments under the protocol.

In 2011 and 2013, as part of their Freedom Project, CNN visited the Ivory Coast to see if conditions were improving. What they found was not very different from the picture painted above. There is a series of videos and other material on what they call 'Cocoa-nomics' at http://thecnnfreedomproject.blogs.cnn.com/category/chocolates-child-slaves/.

Sources: www.bbc.co.uk/news/world-africa-15681986: Ould et al. 2004: Robson 2010; Schrage and Ewing 2005; The University of Tulane report is available at www.childlabor-payson.org/TulaneFinalReport.pdf

Questions

1. Why do children work in the cocoa plantations of the Ivory Coast?
2. What efforts are companies making to eradicate this problem?
3. Is certification the answer, or is this just developed country morals being applied to the less developed world? Discuss.

Why do Children Work?

Reasons for child work can be divided into push and pull, or supply and demand, factors.

On the supply side, or what pushes children into work:

- Poverty—poverty remains the most important factor which pushes children into work.
- Lack of educational opportunities—poor educational facilities or expensive facilities can exacerbate the problem.
- Family breakdown—divorce, death, or illness can leave the family unit short of income. This has become a major problem in Africa because of the HIV/AIDS epidemic.
- Cultural practices—in many countries it is the practice for young children to help the family by looking after younger brothers and sisters or helping out on the land, by collecting firewood, or tending chickens, for example.

On the demand side, or what pulls children into work:

- Cheap labour—employers tend to pay children less than their adult counterparts. Some, especially domestic workers, work unpaid.
- Obedience—even where children are paid the same rate as adults, employers often prefer to employ children as they are much easier to control.
- Skills—the so-called 'nimble fingers' argument, especially in industries such as carpet weaving; probably a mythical argument, but one which is used to justify the employment of children.

- Inadequate laws—or poorly understood and policed laws, enable employers to continue employing children.
- Poor infrastructure—establishing the age of children in some countries can be difficult.

What's wrong with child labour?

- Child labour is a denial of fundamental human rights. The UN has adopted the Convention on the Rights of the Child. Article 32 says that children should not be engaged in work which is hazardous, interferes with education, or is harmful to health.
- It steals their childhood from them.
- It prevents their education.
- Children are exploited by being paid low wages or no wages at all.
- Children often work in poor conditions, which can cause long-term health problems.
- It perpetuates poverty because lack of education limits earning potential.
- It can mean lower wages for everybody, as they swell the labour supply and are usually paid lower wages than adults.
- They replace adult labour because they are cheaper to employ and easier to control.
- It is a long-term cost to society as children are not allowed to fulfil their potential as productive human beings.

Millennium Development Goals

In 2000, the 189 members of the UN adopted the Millennium Development Goals. Eight goals, with associated targets, were established for the alleviation of world poverty and general development. These goals had been developed at a number of conferences that had taken place in the 1990s, so, although they were announced in 2000, the baseline for assessing progress towards them is 1990. The target date for achieving most of these is 2015. In 2005, the targets were modified and extended to 2021 following a review of progress. The goals and targets are set out in Table 11.2.

The goals are not without their critics. See, for example, Clemens and Moss (2005 : 1) who argue that:

> Many poor countries, especially those in Africa, will miss the MDGs by a large margin. But neither African inaction nor a lack of aid will necessarily be the reason. Instead responsibility for near-certain failure lies with the overly-ambitious goals themselves and unrealistic expectation placed on aid.

Others, such as Easterly (2009), criticize the MDGs because they are unfair to Africa whose low starting point made it almost a certainty they would miss the goals. Leo and Barmeier (2010) of the Center for Global Development say that the targets were global and not supposed to be applied to regions or an individual country. Regional reporting tends to mask the fact that some countries are doing well and others not so well. China's good performance, for example, masks some poor records. Large African countries such as Nigeria, not doing so well, pull down the

Table 11.2 Millennium development goals

	Goal		Target
1	Eradicate extreme poverty and hunger	1A	Halve, between 1990 and 2015, the proportion of people whose income is less than US$1 a day
		1B	Achieve full and productive employment and decent work for all, including women and young people
		1C	Halve, between 1990 and 2015, the proportion of people who suffer from hunger
2	Achieve universal primary education	2A	Ensure that, by 2015, children everywhere, boys and girls alike, will be able to complete a full course of primary schooling
3	Promote gender equality and empower women	3A	Eliminate gender disparity in primary and secondary education, preferably by 2005, and to all levels of education no later than 2015
4	Reduce child mortality rate	4A	Reduce by two-thirds, between 1990 and 2015, the under-five mortality rate
5	Improve maternal health	5A	Reduce by three-quarters, between 1990 and 2015, the maternal mortality ratio
		5B	Achieve universal access to reproductive health
6	Combat HIV/AIDS and other diseases	6A	Have halted, by 2015, and begun to reverse the spreads of HIV/AIDS
		6B	Achieve, by 2010, universal access to treatment for HIV/AIDS for all those who need it
		6C	Have halted, by 2015, and begun to reverse the incidence of malaria and other major diseases
7	Ensure environmental sustainability	7A	Integrate the principles of sustainable development into country policies and programmes and reverse the loss of environmental resources
		7B	Reduce biodiversity loss, achieving, by 2010, a significant reduction in the rate of loss
		7C	Halve, by 2015, the proportion of people without sustainable access to safe drinking water and basic sanitation
		7D	By 2020, to have achieved a significant improvement in the lives of at least 100 million slum dwellers
8	Develop a global partnership for development	8A	Develop further an open, rule based, predictable, non-discriminatory trading and financial system
		8B	Address the special needs of the least developed countries
		8C	Address the special needs of landlocked countries and small island developing states
		8D	Deal comprehensively with the debt problems of developing countries
		8E	In cooperation with pharmaceutical companies, provide access to affordable essential drugs in developing countries
		8F	In cooperation with the private sector, make available the benefits of new technologies, especially information and communications

Source: http://unstats.un.org/unsd/mdg/Host.aspx?Content=Indicators/OfficialList.htm

regional performance and mask some who have done very well. Many of those not doing well, they note, have been devastated by conflict. They have also been criticized for being top-down (i.e. a Western agenda) with a lack of consultation with the 'bottom'. Many of these weaknesses and others were recognized in a UN review looking to set a post-2015 agenda (UN System Task Team 2012). What all seem to agree on is that the targets have focused the world's attention, generated discussion, and gained public support for aid programmes.

How close is the world to reaching these targets? For the world as a whole, the first target of halving the proportion of people living on less than US$1 a day in developing countries has been met. In 1990, 47 per cent of the world's population lived on less than $1.25 (PPP) and by 2010 this had fallen to 22 per cent, but, as noted above, a lot of this progress was due to China's rapid growth. There has been some small progress in sub-Saharan Africa, but 47 per cent were still living on less than $1.25 a day in 2010 (UN 2013). According to the UN, 1.2 billion people still live in extreme poverty. See the UN MDG website www.un.org/millenniumgoals/poverty.shtml for progress on each of the goals.

The Guardian newspaper has set up a section of their website dedicated to development, aid, and progress, and a mass of information and commentary on the MDGs can be found at (www. guardian.co.uk/global-development).

Nelson and Prescott (2003), in an article for the UN Development Programme, point out why it is increasingly in the interests of business for the MDGs to succeed. They point out three business benefits:

- Investing in a sound business environment—a healthy and competent workforce, prosperous consumers, productive companies, and a well governed economy.

- Managing direct costs and risks—environmental degradation, climate change, HIV/ AIDS, poor health education systems can add to the cost and risks of doing business.

- Harnessing new business opportunities—innovative companies are finding that the MDGs are not just a matter of responsibility, but that they provide long-term business opportunities.

Social Entrepreneurship/Intrapreneurship

Solving social and environmental problems can be seen as opportunities for business development. In their book, *The Power of Unreasonable People: How Social Entrepreneurs Create Markets and Change the World*, John Elkington and Pamela Hartigan argue that our future depends on what they refer to as 'social entrepreneurs'. Social entrepreneurs are people who look to establish social enterprises to deliver goods and services not yet met by existing market arrangements. The term entrepreneur is not new and these people are no different from the entrepreneurs of old in one sense, but the difference is that they are looking for solutions to some of the world's pressing problems. Profits are generated, but the aim is to benefit those who are the worst off and grow the business. These are not the major multinational companies, but, in the main, small and medium enterprises who are challenging the accepted ways of doing things. A good example is the UK's Belu Water, a bottled water company that donates all of its profits to WaterAid (www.wateraid.org), a charity with the aim of delivering global clean water projects. This company has changed the practices of the bottled drinks industry by using carbon-neutral packaging. By July 2013, Belu had given WaterAid £365,158, enough to transform the lives of

Mini Case Study Rwanda and the Millennium Development Goals

Rwanda is a landlocked country in east-central Africa with a population of just 10.5 million, but it is also the most densely populated country in Africa. Its capital is Kigali. It has a history of ethnic tension, and is perhaps best known for the genocide that took place in 1994 when the majority Hutus slaughtered at least 800,000 Tutsis and moderate Hutus.

It is now a stable but poor country. Its GDP per capita is estimated by the IMF to be $US783 in 2014 ($US1,646 PPP) with the economy growing at an average of about 8 per cent per annum since 2001. Predictions for growth in the next few years are around 7 per cent per annum.

Rwanda's economy is largely dependent on natural resources and commodities. The agricultural sector, although only accounting for 33 per cent of total output, employs around 73 per cent of the workforce. Productivity in this sector is low. The service sector, and in particular tourism, accounts for over 45 per cent of total output and industry 15 per cent. The government is attempting to diversify the economy and these two sectors are growing much faster than the agricultural sector.

Rwanda's relatively fast growth since 2001 has lifted about 1 million people out of poverty, but 45 per cent of the population remain below the national poverty line ($US197 per adult per year). Nearly 92 per cent of Rwanda's children now attend primary school; 91 per cent have access to health services, up from 35 per cent in 2006. The rate of infection from HIV/AIDS has been reduced by 50 per cent and maternal mortality has improved greatly from 750 to 540 deaths per 100,000 live births. There is parity between boys and girls in primary and secondary education, and Rwanda has a female majority in Parliament.

Sources: www.statistics.gov.rw/publications/all/Rwanda_in_figures 'RWANDA Annual Economic Report Fiscal Year 2012/2013', Ministry of Finance and Economic Planning, December 2013 /www.minecofin.gov.rw/fileadmin/user_upload/ECONOMIC_report_for_2012-13.pdf; www.africaneconomicoutlook.org/en/

Questions

1. To what extent has Rwanda achieved the MDGs?
2. How does this achievement compare with the average for sub-Saharan Africa?
3. What lessons can other African countries in the sub-Saharan region learn from Rwanda?

24,344 people with access to clean water, improved sanitation, and hygiene (www.belu.org/wp-content/downloads/Belu_Social_Impact_Report_2013.pdf).

A similar concept is that of the social intrapreneur. This is somebody who works within an organization, usually a big one, developing solutions to social or environmental problems. The term was first defined by Sustainability (2008) and is characterized as somebody who works inside a major organization with an 'insider-outsider mind-set' who applies the principles of social entrepreneurship within the organization. This can be thought of as what Porter and Kramer (2011) refer to as creating 'shared value' mentioned earlier in the chapter.

Similarly, Bill Gates, founder of Microsoft, made a case at the World Economic Forum in 2008 for leading businesses to 'do right by doing good' in what he calls 'creative capitalism'. In this, he urged firms to turn their attention to solve the world's big problems, and particularly the world's inequalities. It is possible to make profits in these markets, but where they could not, he hoped recognition would be an incentive. Recognizing that this may not work, he also called on governments to favour those companies adopting 'creative capitalism' and pointed out the business benefits discussed earlier in this chapter, such as attracting increasingly values-driven young workers.

One aspect of company help to the world's poor has come from an increase in international volunteering. According to Hills and Mahmud (2007), 10 years ago there was hardly any international corporate volunteering, but now 40 per cent of major American corporations send volunteers around the world to work on development projects.

One example they give is of Pfizer (one of the world's leading pharmaceutical companies) developing the Global Health Fellow programme in 2002 to send skilled employees to provide technical assistance to partners for 3–6 months in Africa, Latin America, or Asia. Since 2003, over 300 fellows had been deployed in 45 countries. This provides much improved healthcare to these countries, increases the skill level of local staff, and improves the morale and leadership skills of Pfizer employees. It also helps Pfizer's image and subsequent relationships with global health providers to be seen actively providing solutions on a voluntary basis (www.pfizer.com/responsibility/global_health/global_health_fellows).

● CHAPTER SUMMARY

In this chapter we defined corporate social responsibility as the economic, social, and environmental obligations firms have to society. Some have a view that the only obligation that business owes to society is to maximize profit, but many point out that CSR is not necessarily at odds with profit maximization as there is a strong business argument for pursuing CSR. Others argue that companies have a moral duty to pursue a wider set of objectives.

Firms operating in the international business environment face a more complex set of circumstances than those operating only in their own domestic economy, not just because of the different economic and legal context, but because of very different cultural norms. Firms must be wary of what might be seen as cultural imperialism. The UN has established the Global Compact, which seeks to guide companies to best practice in CSR.

Two areas were highlighted to be of particular concern, child labour and corruption, both still common in much of the world. The Global Compact has standards to guide companies in both of these areas. The UN announced in 2000 the Millennium Development Goals, a set of targets for the alleviation of poverty and other development goals. They recognize the interdependence between growth, poverty reduction, and sustainable development. Some progress has been made, but this has been far from uniform across the world or the goals. Their achievement will only be possible if business, together with government, makes it their business in what Bill Gates calls 'creative capitalism'. Social entrepreneurs will also contribute to these major world challenges.

● REVIEW QUESTIONS

1. Explain what commentators mean when they claim that there is only one responsibility of business and that is to make as much money as possible for their owners.

2. Social responsibility is just good public relations. Discuss.

3. Explain what is meant by child labour. What might the consequences be for a major Western firm discovered employing young children in overseas factories?

4. Differentiate between social entrepreneurship and social intrapreneurship. Explain, giving examples, how social entrepreneurs/intrapreneurs might contribute to the achievement of the Millennium Development Goals.

● ASSIGNMENT TASKS

1. Select an international company of your choice. It should be one that expresses its values on corporate social responsibility in some way. Prepare a report which:

    a) Describes the company: name, location, size, main products/services, the market it operates in, main players, and any other information you think is relevant.

    b) Outlines the CSR policies of the company.

    c) Analyses the company's activities in relation to its CSR policy.

2. You are working for a large multinational drinks company wanting to set up a bottling plant overseas. In order to obtain planning permission, you need to make a facilitation payment (bribe) to a local politician, but your company has a strict no bribes policy. The building of the plant will be subcontracted to a domestic construction company and one way round this would be to inflate the payment to this company so that they could make the facilitation payment. What would you do? Justify your decision.

Case Study Multinationals and tax avoidance

In November 2012, executives from Starbucks, Amazon, and Google appeared before the UK Public Accounts Committee to answer questions about the amount of corporation tax they paid on their operations in the UK. According to a report by Reuters (Bergin 2012), Starbucks has generated sales of over £3 billion since opening in the UK in 1998, but has paid only £8.6 million in income taxes and that largely because the taxman disallowed some deductions. In the three years up to 2012, it had paid no tax at all. Google paid about £10 million in tax on sales of £11.9 billion between 2006 and 2011. Amazon paid just £2.4 million in tax on sales of £4.2 billion. McDonald's, by comparison, paid nearly £89 million pounds in taxes on sales of £4.6 billion between 2008 and 2011.

Source: © David Henderson / Istockphoto.com.

Most taxpayers are honest and pay their fair share of taxes, but some deliberately try to evade or avoid tax. This results in what is known as the 'tax gap', the gap between what should be paid and what is paid. HM Revenues and Customs (HMRC) estimated this gap at around £35 billion in 2012–13. The Public and Commercial Services Union and Tax Research UK claim the gap is much wider and could be approaching £120 billion. Of this gap, HMRC claim just £1.4 billion is lost to tax avoidance by multinational corporations. Tax Research UK puts the figure closer to £12 billion a year.

Corporate tax revenues vary according to the level of economic activity, with revenues falling quickly in a recession and recovering slowly because of the build up of losses during the recession. They are also affected by the rate of corporation tax levied. In the UK, the rate has fallen from over 50 per cent in the early 1980s to 21 per cent in 2014–15. They are further affected by tax avoidance. According to HMRC:

> Tax avoidance is bending the rules of the tax system to gain a tax advantage that Parliament never intended. It often involves contrived, artificial transactions that serve little or no commercial purpose other than to produce a tax advantage. It involves operating within the letter but not the spirit of the law.

Global multinationals, such as those above, are able to manipulate their activities so as to reduce how much taxable →

→ profit is recorded or where their profits are taxed. For example, they can pay royalties to a subsidiary for the use of intellectual property rights or brands. According to activist group, Corporate Watch, the British payday loan company, Wonga, pays a Swiss subsidiary for the use of software and brand names to process loan applications made in the UK thereby reducing its UK tax bill. Transfer pricing refers to the prices charged for transferring goods from one part of a multinational to another. It is assumed by the tax authorities that the prices should be the same as if they were being sold to a third party, but Caterpillar in the USA, according to a Senate subcommittee, diverted more than $8 billion in profit to Switzerland and avoided $2.4 billion in tax by channelling its spare parts business through a Swiss subsidiary. Yet another way of reducing the 'tax burden' is by intra company loans such as those made by Starbucks, whose entire UK activities are funded by debt charged at a rate which seems to be higher than that charged by similar operations, e.g. McDonald's and KFC.

For some, this is just normal profit seeking business activity attempting to maximize shareholder value and in which they see no wrong. For others, there is something immoral about these activities in that businesses take advantage of the education of employees, the healthcare system, the legal system, and the transport infrastructure all necessary for the business to operate and all provided, in the main, by the state funded from taxation. There is also an argument, explored in this chapter, which says that there is a strong business case to be made from being a 'good corporate citizen'. Indeed, Starbucks own pronouncements on being 'responsible' would seem to support this idea:

> We've always believed that businesses can—and should—have a positive impact on the communities they serve. So ever since we opened our first store in 1971, we've dedicated ourselves to earning the trust and respect of our customers, partners (employees) and neighbours. How? By being responsible and doing things that are good for the planet and each other (www.starbucks.co.uk/responsibility).

In 2013, concerned about their reputation, and having 'listened to its customers', Starbucks decided to change its approach to corporation tax. It announced that it would not be claiming tax deductions for royalties or payments related to intercompany charges for interest and mark-up on the coffee it buys from other subsidiaries, and that it would be paying somewhere in the range of £10 million in the following two tax years.

See Google's evidence to the House of Commons Committee of Public Accounts at: www.publications.parliament.uk/pa/cm201314/cmselect/cmpubacc/112/112.pdf and a video of MNC personnel being 'grilled' by the Committee at: www.parliamentlive.tv/Main/Player.aspx?meetingId=11764&st=15:23:30.

Sources: Bergin 2012; www.theguardian.com/news/datablog/2012/oct/16/tax-biggest-us-companies-uk#data; *The Guardian* 31 March 2014; House of Lords 31 July 2013; HMRC March 2013; Murphy 2013

Questions

1. Differentiate between 'tax evasion' and 'tax avoidance'.
2. How do multinationals such as those mentioned in the case study avoid paying taxes?
3. Is this just good business or is their behaviour unethical?
4. Is 'tax shaming' justifiable? Explain your answer.
5. What action can governments take to ensure multinational corporations pay their 'fair share' of tax?
6. Discuss the impact of tax avoidance by multinational companies on domestic firms.

● FURTHER READING

For a textbook exploring ethics and the CSR agenda within the context of globalization read:

- Crane, A. and Matten, D. (2010) *Business Ethics—A European Perspective: Managing Corporate Citizenship and Sustainability in the Age of Globalisation,* 3rd edn. Oxford: Oxford University Press.

They also have a blog at:

- http://craneandmatten.blogspot.com/2010/12/top-10-corporate-responsibility-stories.html

For a more recent view of the case against CSR, see an article by:

- Aneel Karnani in *The Wall Street Journal,* http://online.wsj.com/news/articles/SB10001424052748703 338004575230112664504890; and

- Karnani A. (2011) 'Doing Well by Doing Good: The Grand Illusion'. *California Management Review* 1 February 2011.

For a review of social contract theory and its modern applicability, see:

- Byerly, R. (2013) 'Business in Society: The Social Contract Revisited'. *Journal of Organisational Transformation & Social Change* 10 (1): 4–20.

For a book advocating a strategic approach to CSR taking into account global stakeholders, see:

- Werther, B. and Chandler, D. (2014) 'Strategic Corporate Social Responsibility'. *Stakeholders, Globalization, and Sustainable Value Creation,* 3rd edn. London: SAGE Publications.

For a review of the Global Compact, an article critical of the Global Compact, and for a critical blog, see:

- Rasche, A., Waddock, S., and McIntosh, M. (2013) 'The United Nations Global Compact: Retrospect and Prospect'. *Business Society* 52.

- John Entine (2010) 'Ten years of "Greenwashing"'. Available at: www.jonentine.com/ethical_ corporation/2010_11_United_Nations_Global_Compact.pdf.

- http://globalcompactcritics.blogspot.com.

To read more about social entrepreneurship/intrapreneurship see:

- Elkington, J. and Hartigan, P. (2008) *The Power of Unreasonable People: How Social Entrepreneurs Create Markets and Change the World.* Boston, MA: Harvard Business Press.

- Grayson, D., McLaren, M., Spitzeck, H. (2014) *Social Intrapreneurism and All That Jazz, How Business Innovators are Helping to Build a More Sustainable World.* Greenleaf Publishing Limited.

● REFERENCES

Anshen, M. (1970 [1983]) 'Changing the Social Contract: A Roll for Business'. Reprinted in Beauchamp, T. and Bowie, N. (eds) (1983) *Ethical Theory and Business,* 2nd edn. Prentice Hall.

Bebchuk, L.A. and Fried, J.M. (2006) 'Pay without Performance: Overview of the Issues'. *Academy of Management Perspectives* 20(1).

Bebchuk, L.A., Cohen, A., and Holger, S. (2010) 'The Wages of Failure: Executive Compensation at Bear Stearns and Lehman 2000-2008'. *Yale Journal on Regulation,* 27(2).

Bergin T. (2012) 'Reuters Special Report: How Starbucks avoids UK Taxes'.

Certified Accountants Educational Trust (London) (2011) 'Shareholder Primacy in UK Corporate Law: An Exploration of the Rationale and Evidence'. Research Report No. 125.

Chang, H.-J. (2008) *Bad Samaritans: The Myth of Free Trade and the Secret History of Capitalism.* New York: Bloomsbury Press.

Clemens, M. and Moss, T. (2005) *What's Wrong with the Millennium Development Goals.* Centre for Global Development.

Crane, A. and Matten, D. (2010) *Business Ethics—A European Perspective: Managing Corporate Citizenship and*

Sustainability in the Age of Globalisation, 3rd edn. Oxford: Oxford University Press.

Crane, A., Palazzo, G., Spence L.J., and Matten, D. (2014) 'Contesting the Value of "Creating Shared Value"'. *California Management Review* 56(2): 130–53.

De George, R. (2010) *Business Ethics*, 7th edn. London: Pearson.

Donaldson, T. (1982) *Corporations and Morality*. London: Prentice Hall.

Donaldson, T. (1989) *The Ethics of International Business*. New York: Oxford University Press.

Easterly, W. (2009) 'How the Millennium Goals are Unfair to Africa'. *World Development* 37(1): 26.

Elkington, J. and Hartigan, P. (2008) *The Power of Unreasonable People: How Social Entrepreneurs Create Markets and Change the World*. Harvard Business School Press.

French, P. (1979) 'The Corporation as a Moral Person'. *American Philosophical Quarterly*, reprinted in Donaldson, T. and Werhane, P. (1983) *Ethical Issues in Business*. London: Prentice Hall.

Friedman, M. (1970) 'The Social Responsibility of Business Is to Increase it Profits'. Reprinted in Donaldson, T. and Werhane, P. (eds) (1983) *Ethical Issues in Business*. London: Prentice Hall.

Goodpaster, K. and Mathews, J. (1982) 'Can a Corporation have a Conscience?' *Harvard Business Review*, 60(1): 132 reprinted in Beauchamp, T.L. and Bowie, N.E. (1983) *Ethical Theory and Business*, 2nd edn. London: Prentice Hall.

Hay Group (2011) 'Getting the Balance Right: The Ratio of CEO to Average Employee Pay and What It Means for Company Performance'. Available at: http://www.haygroup.com/downloads/uk/Getting-the-balance-right.pdf, accessed October 2014.

Hills, G. and Mahmud, A. (2007) *Volunteering for Impact. Best Practices in Individual and Corporate Volunteering*. Boston, MA: FSG Social Impact Advisors.

HMRC (2013) 'Compliance Progress Report: Levelling the Tax Playing Field', March.

House of Lords (2013) 'Tackling Corporate Tax Avoidance in a Global Economy: Is A New Approach Needed? '. Paper 48, 31 July.

Hutton, W. (2011) 'Hutton Review of Fair Pay in the Public Sector', HM Treasury, March.

International Labour Office (2013) *Global Child Labour Trends 2008 to 2012: International Programme on the Elimination of Child Labour (IPEC)*. Geneva: ILO.

Kar, D. and LeBlanc, B. (2013) 'Illicit Financial Flows from Developing Countries: 2002-2011'. *Global Financial Integrity* December.

Leo, B. and Barmeier, J. (2010) 'Who are the MDG Trailblazers? A New MDG Progress Index'. Working Paper No. 222. Center for Global Development.

Lipton, M. and Savitt, W. (2007) 'The Many Myths of Lucian Bebclink'. *Virginia Law Review* 93(3).

Murphy, R. (2013) *Over Here and Undertaxed: Multinationals, Tax Avoidance and You*. Vintage Digital.

Nelson, J. and Prescott, D. (2003) *Business and the Millennium Development Goals, A Framework for Action*. UNDP and the International Business Leaders Forum.

Ould, D., Jordan, C., Reynolds, R., and Loftin, L. (2004) *The Cocoa Industry in West Africa: A History of Exploitation*. Anti-Slavery International.

Porter, M.E. and Kramer, M.R. (2006) 'Strategy and Society: The Link Between Competitive Advantage and Corporate Social Responsibility'. *Harvard Business Review* 84(12).

Porter M.E. and Kramer, M.R. (2011) 'The Big Idea, Creating Shared Value'. *Harvard Business Review* January/ February.

Robson, P. (2010) *Ending Child Trafficking in West Africa, Lessons from the Ivorian Cocoa Sector*. Anti-Slavery International.

Schrage, E. and Ewing, A. (2005) 'The Cocoa Industry and Child Labour'. *The Journal of Corporate Citizenship* 2005(18).

Sustainability (2008) *The Social Intrapreneur: A Field Guide for Corporate Changemakers*. Sustainability.

Underkuffler, L.S. (2009) 'Defining Corruption: Implications for Action'. In Rotberg, R.I.(ed), *Corruption, Global Security, and World Order*. Cambridge: Brookings Institution.

United Nations (2013) 'The Millennium Development Goals Report'. Available at: www.un.org/millenniumgoals/pdf/report-2013/mdg-report-2013-english.pdf, accessed October 2014.

United Nations System Task Team (2012) 'Review of the Contributions of the MDG Agenda to Foster Development: Lessons for the Post-2015 UN Development Agenda'. Discussion Note. Available at: www.un.org/millenniumgoals/pdf/mdg_assessment_Aug.pdf, accessed May 2014.

CHAPTER TWELVE

The Ecological Environment

Dorron Otter

LEARNING OUTCOMES

This chapter will enable you to:

- Examine the ecological impacts of business activity

- Describe the range of global initiatives designed to address ecological problems

- Engage in the debates as to the role of business in causing, preventing, and curing ecological damage

- Analyse the problems posed by global climate change

Case Study Fossil fuels or human fools?

The global demand for energy is predicted to rise by 56 per cent between 2010 and 2040. Table 12.1 gives the sources of global primary energy supplies in 2011.

There are the short-term immediate costs of unearthing and burning 'dirty' fossil fuels such as coal, gas, and oil, the longer term costs to the ecological environment in terms of smog, acid rain, air quality, and associated health costs, and what is now seen as the greatest global ecological problem of all, that of global climate change. For environmental campaigners, this reliance on fossil fuels will, in the end, make all of us fools if we undermine the security of the ecological environment on which we all depend.

All of us, whether in our various roles as producers, consumers, employees, entrepreneurs, householders, commuters, or tourists are intimately linked to global energy supply chains and therefore, it could be argued, we have to accept responsibility for the environmental impact of our energy production and consumption patterns.

Oil remains the single biggest source of our global energy supplies, and its production causes great political, economic, and environmental controversies. Oil spills at sea and on land have been many and have created local ecological disasters.

For the major global oil companies, there is the constant pressing need to manage both the human and the environmental risk and uncertainty involved in such an inherently dangerous business, while ensuring that they are ever mindful of the need to keep their shareholders happy by returning high profits. On top of all of this, they now need to integrate into their corporate social responsibility strategies the rise in the levels of

Source: © Photodisc

environmental awareness among their customers and meeting the environmental legal requirements of the many countries in which they are located. This can seem an impossible task.

Every oil company has had to deal with major environmental and potentially devastating PR disasters. Shell attracts the wrath of activist protestors for its operations in the Niger Delta of Nigeria. Exxon is forever bracketed with the oil tanker, the Exxon Valdez, which hit a reef and leaked oil into the pristine environment of Alaska in 1989. In 2014, Chevron was being prosecuted (but is challenging) claims that it damaged ecosystems in Ecuador and Brazil, but it is BP that has been the most recent company to have to come to global media attention as a result of its ecological impact.

This could be seen to be ironic given BPs attempt in 1997 to rebrand itself away from being British Petroleum to 'Beyond Petroleum' in recognition of the need to begin to move away from our reliance on fossil fuels and to begin to invest seriously in renewable energy sources.

These attempts to be seen as a 'green' company transcending national boundaries (the majority of BP's shareholders are no longer British), appeared to be working as there was clear market evidence that people were reacting favourably to this name and new image; however, this was undermined by an explosion at the Texas City refinery in 2005, which killed 15 people, followed by an oil spill that closed the Prudhoe Bay oilfield in Alaska in 2006.

In April 2010, an explosion ripped through an offshore oil drilling well, the Deepwater Horizon, owned by the company Transocean but leased to BP, killing 11 people and injuring ➔

Table 12.1 Sources of global primary energy supplies, 2011

Oil	31.5%
Coal	28.8%
Natural Gas	21.3%
Bio-fuels and Waste	10.0%
Nuclear	5.1%
Hydro-Power	2.3%
Other (wind, solar, geothermal)	1.0%

Source: IEA 2013

→ another 18. The location of the well was in the Gulf of Mexico, 40 miles off the Louisiana coastline of the United States. The Deepwater Horizon had been designed to operate at very low depths as increasing demand for oil pushes exploration companies to seek new sources in increasingly inaccessible places.

Trying to cap the leak proved to be an enormous technological challenge costing billions of dollars. However, on top of this cost was the cost in terms of human life and injury to the marine environment itself, as well as the damage to the economic and social lives of the fishing and tourism businesses that depended on the ecosystem of the Gulf of Mexico. By the time the leak was blocked, in September 2010, it is estimated that 4.9 million barrels of oil had leaked into the ocean, making this the biggest accidental marine spill in history.

US President Obama was clear that BP should indeed be held wholly responsible for the effects of the accident, but he also placed the accident in the wider context of our over reliance on fossil fuels and the technical challenges facing oil companies in seeking to develop increasingly inaccessible

reserves in response to ever rising global demand for energy. In July 2014, the estimated costs of the oil spill to BP was $42.7 billion.

BP itself has suffered longer term reputational and commercial damage as it is still banned by the US administration from any more drilling in the Gulf of Mexico until all court actions are resolved. In 2014, BP was still contesting a range of further claims it was facing from businesses on the shoreline of the Gulf of Mexico, claims from its shareholders that it had tried to initially hide the scale of the leak which, when revealed, led to a collapse of its share price, and a potentially further $20 billion fine from the US courts if it is found that BP behaved irresponsibly in its initial attempts to stop the leak.

Sources: Macalister 2014; US Energy Information Administration International Energy Outlook 2013 wnew.www.eia.gov/forecasts/ieo/world.cfm; *The Guardian* 2014 www.theguardian.com/environment/bp-oil-spill; BP 2014 www.bp.com/en/global/corporate/gulf-of-mexico-restoration/deepwater-horizon-accident-and-response.html

Introduction

This chapter examines the relationship between business activity and the global ecological environment, the debates as to the responsibility of business in terms of its contribution to global ecological problems, and the possible responses to dealing with these challenges.

The Ecological Problem

It is simple to outline the basic ecological problem in the context of business. We need to extract the resources that we need for production from the ecological environment. If we exploit the sources of these materials without replacing what we have taken, then we face a long-term certain problem of resource depletion. Not all resources can be replaced, especially the fossil fuels on which so much of the world's energy supplies currently depend. It is also clear that the nature of much of our productive processes results in pollution or other forms of ecological damage. Nature itself can provide ways of neutralizing these harmful by-products in the form of 'sinks' such as the oceans, forests, and plants that can absorb the pollutants, but the rising acidification of seas, deforestation, and loss of biodiversity are all undermining this. The debate provoked by attempts to quantify the 'state of the world' in terms of the rate of resource depletion and its effects on food supplies, water availability, and energy, or the 'carrying capacity' of the planet, is hotly contested.

The Economic Approach to Explaining the Ecological Problem

Economic analysis has been very influential in explaining why there is a conflict between our rational desire to increase our incomes and our ability to increase our quality of life.

While free markets in theory bring about consumer satisfaction and profits for producers, there are dangers of market failure. In relation to the external ecological environment, it may well be the case that while markets ensure that private benefits accrue to consumers and producers, there may be social costs that are incurred. Social costs, or **negative externalities,** occur as the result of the production or consumption of goods and services, but for which no individual or organization pays. They will therefore need to be identified and mechanisms devised to either reduce or eradicate them, or at least allow them to be paid for.

Consider the external environmental problems caused by motor transport. Drivers and their passengers, or the customers for whom they are driving, derive enormous benefit from this activity and are prepared to pay for the initial costs of the vehicle itself and the substantial running costs, including the cost of the (fossil) fuels needed to power the vehicles.

These private costs are not the only costs as there are substantial external environmental costs. Motor vehicles produce pollutants damaging to the environment, not least of which is the production of **greenhouse gases** (**GHGs**). This is especially the case when cars are on congested roads. The costs of lost output through time delays to people and goods are also considerable. It is argued that it is only fair that motorists sitting inside the relative comfort of their vehicles should pay for the external costs that they are imposing on society through higher road taxes, petrol duties, or even paying to use the road through 'road pricing' schemes, such as the electronic road congestion charge in London and Singapore. Of course, it might well be that the better environmental solution would be to switch away from car use to greener forms of transport such as electric cars, buses, trains, cycles, and, yes, even walking.

This market-based analysis of the externalities of production and consumption can point the way to 'correct' the environmental market failures. The simplest solution might be to devise a way whereby the agents who are responsible for the pollution pay for this. This process of 'internalizing the externality' ensures that the 'polluter pays principle' is implemented, and this can be seen as being fair in terms of forcing those responsible for environmental damage to at least pay for it and, of course, the revenue raised could be used to invest in measures to clean up the environment or 'compensate' those affected. It might also have the effect of discouraging the amount of environmentally damaging behaviour that occurs. Along the same lines, regulation could be put in place to 'permit' pollution to take place, but only in return for compensation payments.

However, critics of this approach argue that levying of environmental charges may encourage the belief that the problem is solved even though the environmentally damaging behaviour still continues. Robert Goodin sees this as the 'selling of environmental indulgences' and argues that we should simply not cause the pollution in the first place (Goodin 2007).

Furthermore, there are equity implications. Is it 'fair' to charge green taxes if more prosperous members of society or businesses can afford to pay while the poorer ones are unfairly penalized? On a global level, there is an inherent inequity in resource use, and a potential inequity in the solutions being designed to deal with environmental problems. The developed world became wealthy by being able to industrialize at a time when the environment was effectively ignored.

Now that policies are being implemented to deal with environmental issues, it would not be fair if the developing world were asked to adhere to the same levels of environmental protection. It is argued that the richer countries can afford to pay for the cost of the environmental harm they have mostly caused, and developing countries should not be asked to adopt environmental regulations at their early stage in the development process.

The analysis of ecological problems as the negative externalities of market failure has become commonly accepted, but what is contested is where the responsibility for such externalities should fall, and the range of policy measures we should adopt to address these.

Business as Usual

One of the biggest fears for those concerned about the environmental impact of businesses is that, even where they recognize potential problems, all too often they continue with 'business as usual' (BAU) behaviour. Indeed, some argue that businesses will actively seek to resist pressure to change to preserve their profits. Others argue that, given the right incentives, businesses will choose to 'go green' and that there is very often a 'business case' to be made for sustainable business practices as this will boost profitability, either through the enhanced reputation that being seen to be green brings, or through the reduction in costs resulting from a better use of resources.

There is increasing awareness among a range of pressure groups across the business, environmental, and academic communities that seek to promote and profile responsible behaviour, such as the World Business Council for Sustainable Development, the World Economic Forum (WEF) Forum for the Future, Net Impact, The Ethical Corporation, and the Globally Responsible Leadership Initiative (see www.wbcsd.org; http://reports.weforum.org/new-sustainability-champions/, www.forumforthefuture.org; www.netimpact.org; www.ethicalcorp.com, and www.grli.org). Visiting these websites will give you a good idea of the range of initiatives that are being undertaken in relation to sustainable business practices.

The WEF is the leading policy body that represents the interests of the world's biggest corporations and most wealthy individuals. In its 2014 assessment of the greatest risks for global business, the WEF puts the ecological threats to water supply (see this chapter, Case Study Economic growth and environmental risks), failure to adapt to or mitigate against climate change, food security, and unexpected weather events in its top 10 risks (WEF 2014a and WEF 2014b).

Learning Task

Look at cases which are profiled as examples of responsible business practice in relation to the ecological environment (see, for example, www.bitc.org.uk/ or www.wbcsd.org).

1. What are the problems that businesses face in addressing environmentally responsible business practice?

2. How convincing do you think the case for this is?

Perspectives on the Role of Business

Business activity is essentially the conversion of natural resources into goods and services to satisfy the needs, wants, and desires of human beings, but this generates economic growth, which creates environmental problems. Industries such as steel, cement, oil, power generation, chemicals, and transport are heavy polluters in a range of ways. There are competing perspectives about ways in which businesses should respond to the environmental challenges.

Views from the Right

For free market exponents, it is the ability of private businesses to operate in markets free from government regulation that will drive economic progress. While the indirect cost of growth might be environmental damage, there is a trade-off to be made between this and growth in living standards, and business plays a vital role in developing 'environmentally friendly' technologies—given the right incentives. Where this is not realistic, then the negative costs can be measured and businesses can be charged for the environmental damage according to the 'polluter pays principle'.

Views from the Left

There are, however, objections to this version of the secret for economic success.

Critics of business see it as being primarily interested in maximizing profits and, in cutting costs, and believe it will treat the environment as a free 'sink' for pollution.

Businesses have a vested interest in encouraging consumers to buy more and more and so are indirectly responsible for rampant consumerism. While it could be argued that businesses are simply responding to the wishes of consumers, it is the business in pursuit of profit that has every interest in fuelling consumer demand. Sheehan (2010) questions the notion of scarcity as being the basis of the economic problem. For Sheehan, while this may be the case in poorer, less developed countries, and for the poor in the developed world, what drives consumption are the demands of the rich, who live in relative abundance. Why do people who have everything still want more? Why do consumers with no room left in their wardrobes still want more clothes? Sheehan argues that the 'institution of marketing fuels this culture of consumption and helps businesses slake their thirst for ever more sales'.

A major source of disquiet is the belief that the distribution of income and wealth that results from free markets is highly unequal and that the immediate problem facing the world is not that there is not enough to go around, but that the fruits of economic growth are enjoyed by the richer members of society while the poor lose out. The biggest global problem is the gap between the living standards of the 'Global North' as opposed to the 'Global South' and that those consumers in the former are responsible for far more global environmental damage than those in the latter.

Governments need to ensure that businesses do not develop positions of monopoly power, but they frequently struggle to enforce environmental controls over powerful 'Big Business', especially when, increasingly, globalization means that corporations operate across national boundaries and, therefore, different regulatory regimes.

Green Views

The development of the modern 'green' movement can be traced to the publication of *The Silent Spring* by Rachel Carson in 1962. A biologist, Carson became very concerned about the use of pesticides in agriculture and their effects on human beings through links with cancers, and on wildlife—hence the emotive title of the book, which looks to a future where birdsong is absent (Carson 1962). Her books and articles had a huge influence on the grass roots environmental movement in the USA and resulted in the eventual ban of the pesticide DDT (Dichlorodiphenyltrichloroethane) in the USA. It also attracted a large volume of criticism from the chemical industry. This theme of environmental claim and business counterclaim will be seen again in this chapter.

Counterpoint Box 12.1 'The tragedy of the commons'

In 1968, Garrett Hardin provided a critique of what he saw as an essential problem for the future of humanity. 'The Tragedy of the Commons', published in the journal *Science,* argued that when human beings have access to commonly owned resources for which they do not have to pay, we each, as an individual, seek to get as much as we can from this shared resource, but, collectively, the result of this action will be that we will soon exhaust the resource and so all lose out.

Hardin used the example of feudal agricultural societies where farmers/peasants worked mostly on land owned by landlords, but where there might be some limited commons land available for grazing livestock. A rational farmer would seek not to over-graze land if s/he had private ownership of it, but would see the benefit in having fallow periods to allow the land to recover from potential overgrazing. The 'Tragedy of the Commons' is where, if land is not privately owned, or, in economic terms, property rights are not clearly defined, then each farmer will end up overusing the land in the fear that if they keep their animals off the land others will not.

Source: Hardin 1968

Questions

1. Discuss examples of ecological or environmental problems that might arise from 'tragedy of the commons' type situations in relation to your own living or working environment or in relation to the impact of business in general.

At the heart of 'green thinking' is the belief that we need to move away from an **anthropocentric** view of the world which sees human beings as the driving force of nature and the sole beneficiaries of the resources that are there to be exploited, to an **ecocentric** view of the world that recognizes our interdependence with nature. While there is an enormous range of opinion within the green movement, it is commonly accepted that our lives would be improved by not abusing nature, and recognizing that we need to alter the prevailing economic model of growth by accounting for environmental costs.

The Limits to Growth, another key text, focused on the key areas of population—food production, industrialization, pollution, and consumption of non-renewable resources—and predicted that growth trends would, within the next 100 years, cause sudden falls in population and industrial production unless action was taken to create ecological and economic stability based on a more equitable sharing out of the products of economic prosperity (Meadows et al. 1972).

Other influential books include *The Costs of Economic Growth* (Mishan 1969), *The Affluent Society* (Galbraith 1958), and *Small is Beautiful* (Schumacher 1973). Mishan's work was one of the first economics books to outline the costs of economic growth and the methods of cost benefit analysis that are needed when judging economic decisions, and Schumacher's focus is clear in its subtitle: *Economics as if People Mattered*. For Galbraith, writing at a time when the American post-war consumer boom was beginning to take off, the focus of economics had to be on analysing why people keep consuming even when their needs are met—a theme explored by Sheehan above and by others (see Coyle 2012; Dietz and O'Neil 2013; and Skidelski and Skidelski 2012).

In similar vein, Annie Leonard has produced a video entitled *The Story of Stuff* in which she questions why American people, who have what could be seen as enough, still want more stuff (www.storyofstuff.com). While directed mainly at schoolchildren, this short video does illustrate the views that consumer capitalism is the cause of environmental degradation.

Learning Task

Watch the video *The Story of Stuff* and think about how you react to it.

- Is it telling you anything you already know?
- Is there anything that you agree with?
- Is there anything you do not agree with?
- What is your overall reaction to this video?

Environmental Regulation

There have always been voices raised to challenge the view that economic growth represented human progress. Even at the beginning of the industrial revolution in Europe, a range of people, from poets to social activists and politicians, were anxious about the costs of economic growth. These criticisms were often centred on what they saw as the destruction of the natural environment and the effect on traditional ways of life as a result of industrialization. A fierce condemnation of the effect of the new capitalist expansion on the social environment of the poor urban working class was produced by Friedrich Engels in his *The Condition of the Working Class in England* (Engels 1844).

The dramatic success of the industrial revolution clearly had a severely damaging impact on a range of environmental factors, such as public health, pollution, and sanitation, and it was clear that there was an urgent need for governments, both local and national, to clean up the mess that was the by-product of economic growth.

In the twentieth century, it became accepted that business activity needed to be regulated in order to protect the natural environment, and that the government would have to take direct control over a range of environmental areas to deal with these externalities. Environmental legislation was seen as the responsibility of national governments, although as global trade increased, and with the rise of the multinational corporation, it is clear that not all countries have the same levels of governance and ability or willingness to enforce environmental regulations.

It has been increasingly acknowledged that if trade was to be free and fair between nations then it was important that all countries played by the same rules in terms of environmental protection to stop certain countries gaining from cheaper costs because of looser environmental compliance. Within formally agreed common markets, such as the European Union, there is an insistence that all member states adhere to the same environmental rules, so environmental legislation is determined at the EU level. However, in the absence of the political and legal structures which bind the members of the union together and form the basis of the common market, it is difficult sometimes to reconcile the rush to liberalize trade and investment across borders with the need to have commonly agreed environmental standards. Trying to develop common international environmental standards that are legally binding and enforceable is very difficult.

The World Trade Organization claims that: 'Sustainable development and the protection and preservation of the environment are fundamental goals of the WTO' (www.wto.org/english/tratop_e/envir_e/envir_e.htm).

Lack of international environmental rules can lead to trade disputes and claims of double standards. Developing countries will point to the developed world's hypocrisy in insisting on levels of environmental protection that they themselves did not have to implement as they were developing, and claim that this is simply being used as an artificial restraint on trade. Developed countries cry foul of what they perceive to be relatively poorer environmental standards in developing countries' exports, with the developing countries gaining an unfair advantage in relation to trade. Equally, there are accusations that multinational businesses are able to exploit their ability to work across boundaries by being able to avoid paying attention to the environment in the same way as they would if operating in more tightly regulated developed markets. However, this is contentious territory. Critics allege that Trafigura, the Dutch MNC trading in metals and oil, deliberately sought to avoid paying the high costs of ensuring that waste products from one of its ships were disposed of safely, by offloading this waste in a country with less stringent environmental protection laws or ability to ensure environmental compliance. Trafigura argues that this was not the case, that it cannot be blamed if the Ivorian waste disposal firm it contracted to deal with the waste acted in an irresponsible manner, and that it had sought to use a country which had signed up to the recognized international standards for disposal of hazardous ship waste.

The impact of business on the ecological environment is explicitly recognized in the environmental regulations with which businesses have to comply.

At the global level, as a result of the 1992 Rio Declaration (discussed in The Notion of Sustainable Development), the international standard, ISO 14001, was developed to provide a framework for the development of an environmental management system and the supporting audit programme (see www.iso-14001.org.uk/ for the details of how businesses can seek accreditation for this).

Binding environmental legislation is only possible at the international level if nation states agree to pool sovereignty in order to participate in custom unions, such as the EU. Various attempts have been made to enforce international environmental standards through measures such as ISO 14001 and through initiatives such as the UN Global Compact, which is an attempt to provide an enabling framework in which businesses can address issues concerning human rights, labour standards, the environment, and measures to combat corruption (see Chapter 11 for a fuller examination of this).

ISO 14001 sets out the steps that a business can take to establish an environmental management system. Successful implementation of this system means that businesses can then apply for ISO certification. To be eligible for the standard, businesses must show that they not only comply with legislation, but also that they have looked at all areas where there is an environmental impact. The underlying philosophy of the standard is that there is a clear 'business case' through a systematic ISO 14001 approach. According to the ISO, this can encompass benefits such as:

- reduced cost of waste management;
- savings in consumption of energy and materials;
- lower distribution costs;
- improved corporate image among regulators, customers, and the public; and
- a framework for continual improvement of environmental performance (www.iso.org).

In relation to the three principles that relate to the environment, the UN Global Compact is keen to impress on businesses that there need not be a conflict between preserving the environment and business success.

This could be best seen in terms of a continuum in that if businesses do not take action now to reduce their environmental impact their profits will suffer in the future. This short-term action is seen as an investment to prevent longer term costs and is referred to as mitigation. It is argued that some changes as a result of ecological damage are already upon us and so businesses will need to play their part in adapting to these changes now to save the need for greater adaptation changes in the future.

Principle 7 emphasizes the need to operationalize the precautionary principle. The basis of this principle is that we should never introduce technological change without having a full risk assessment of the effects of this change.

In Principle 8, the UN Global Compact is clear that there is a compelling case for 'environmentally responsible business practice' and outlines the following advantages to such an approach:

- cleaner production and eco-efficiency leads to improved resource productivity and lower costs;
- new economic instruments (taxes, charges, trade permits) and tougher environmental regulations will reward those companies who seek to improve eco-efficiency;
- insurance companies prefer to cover a cleaner, lower risk company, and banks are more willing to lend to a company whose operations will not burden the bank with environmental lawsuits or large clean-up bills;
- being seen to be green helps a company's brand image and employees tend to prefer to work for an environmentally responsible company;
- environmental pollution threatens human health; and
- customers are demanding cleaner products.

Source: www.unglobalcompact.org/AboutTheGC/TheTenPrinciples/principle8.html

Finally, Principle 9 asserts the important role that business can play in both developing and adopting the technologies that will enable the environment to be safeguarded.

Businesses are now urged to show their commitment to change through moving away from simply reporting their financial bottom line. It is argued that they should also report on their 'social' and 'environmental' impacts, and this has in turn produced a variety of systems to account for the environment. In 1994, John Elkington developed the concept of 'triple bottom

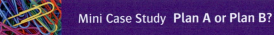

Mini Case Study Plan A or Plan B?

Marks and Spencer launched its Plan A in 2007, which mapped out a five-year programme of environmental change with 100 commitments. In March 2010, it reported that it had achieved 62 of these commitments and, in recognition of this, extended its commitments to 180 targets. This plan was supported with what they called the five pillars—Climate Change, Waste, Sustainable Raw Materials, Health, and being a Fair Partner—with a range of targets for each of these pillars.

Its 2014, their Plan A Report reflects on what it sees as the progress and obstacles to Plan A having formed the basis for transforming the company into a genuinely sustainable business. It is argued that Plan A, in its original conception, was an improvement from the narrow CSR focus on philanthropy and compliance to building a genuine business case for sustainable business practice. In 2013, before the annual general meeting, the CEO was reported as confirming that in the five years since Plan A had been introduced, its cost of £200 million had resulted in savings of £320 million. However, in 2014 the company launched Plan A 2020. At the heart of this plan is the belief that there was a need to move away from specifying sustainability as a range of targets to be hit, and simply have sustainability as being justified so long as there was a bottom line business case. The five pillars have gone as specific target areas, and sustainability is now seen as being integrated across the value chain of the business by embedding it in the core strategic values of the company, and by engaging all the company's stakeholders from employees, shareholders, suppliers, and customers into buying into the fact that sustainable practice will be at the heart of the business. For Marks and Spencer, one clear lesson from the experience of developing Plan A is that, in order for targets to be achieved, there needs to be acceptance for these goals from its wider stakeholders and that one business alone cannot change the world. For cynical critics, this could be seen as Marks and Spencer simply aiming for easy wins, like using low energy light bulbs or aiming for better fuel efficiency, and stopping short when the commitments begin to alienate shareholder support, especially in tough economic times.

We have seen that some environmental activists are cynical about the genuine commitment of businesses to move beyond 'green washing', and even where such cynicism does not exist, environmentalists such as Lester Brown (2009) argue that in order for real change to occur it is not businesses alone that can effect such change. We have seen that the Marks and Spencer report acknowledged the need for this wider engagement. Since 1974, when he founded the Worldwatch Institute, Brown has been an influential figure in the world environment movement. In 2001, he established the Earth Policy Institute to act as a more direct campaigning organization that translates research into policy proposals. For Brown, there has to be an alternative to what he terms 'Plan A' (not related to the Plan A of M&S) or the belief that, despite this range of problems, there is no alternative than to follow the 'Business as Usual' model.

In this, Brown charts both what he sees as the fundamental challenges facing us and the policies that need to be developed to combat these.

The central question that needs to be posed is the extent to which the response of businesses is such as to address fully the ecological challenges.

Sources: Marks and Spencer (2014) 'Plan A Report 2014' http://corporate.marksandspencer.com/plan-a/b6867fa1340d482da1e-bde62c099dd69; Brown 2009 www.earth-policy.org/index.php?/books/pb4/pb4_table_of_contents; Butler 2013 www.theguardian.com/business/2013/jul/07/plan-a-integral-rebirth-marks-spencer

Questions

1. In the case of a company like Marks and Spencer, what would be the business case for embarking on a programme such as Plan A?
2. Why might environmental campaigners argue that simply specifying sustainable business practice as complying with a set of environmental targets will not bring about genuine sustainability?

line accounting' as a way of highlighting the responsibility of businesses in relation to social and environmental performance as well as financial performance and this is commonly referred to as the trio of 'People, Planet and Profit' (Elkington 1994).

However, there is no commonly agreed set of procedures for doing this and instead there is a hotchpotch of approaches developed by some businesses eager to publicize their social credentials. While many leading businesses have been undertaking a range of environmental initiatives, there remains an unwillingness to be subject to government regulation to enforce compliance. Critics question the ability of self-regulation to achieve real benefits and see this desire to be 'seen to be green' as sitting uneasily with the temptation to trumpet this as a way of securing competitive advantage through 'green washing' (see Chapter 11).

Learning Task

1. In what ways do businesses potentially have a negative impact on the ecological environment?
2. In what sense do ecological problems represent a 'global tragedy of the commons'?

Global Cooperation—Establishing Effective Environmental Regimes

There is a growing recognition of the global nature of environmental problems.

What is the point of one country or area having stringent environmental safeguards if others do not, since ecological systems overlap? In other words, environmental problems are often 'trans-boundary'. National policies alone are not sufficient and put businesses at a severe competitive disadvantage if such policies are not universally applied. In the field of international relations this is a recurrent theme, namely, how can international cooperation be achieved in a world of 'anarchy', or, in other words, one in which there is no overall global authority which all countries must obey.

There are a number of global commons issues that require international cooperation if they are to be addressed. The following are examples that have been the focus of attempts to develop a global response:

- desertification;
- deforestation;
- loss of biodiversity;
- whaling;
- protection of fisheries and the marine environment;
- acid rain;
- protection of the ozone layer; and
- climate change.

In 1972 the Stockholm conference explored the causes of 'acid rain' and its effects on lakes and forests in Northern Europe and this led to the formation of the United Nations Environment Programme. The notion that pollution does not respect national borders was given direct expression when radioactivity from the Chernobyl nuclear explosion in 1984 covered most of Western Europe, and in the recognition of the effect of chloro-fluoro carbons (CFC) gases on the ozone layer (see Mini Case Study Ozone Depletion).

For effective action to be undertaken it is important to devise a system of international cooperation, and this is referred to in international relations literature as a 'regime'. To establish such regimes, multilateral treaties are required and these may be regulated either through a committee of organization or through what is referred to as the convention/protocol process, or a combination of both. The International Convention for the Regulation of Whaling makes annual schedules of catch regulations and the Convention on International Trade in Endangered Species of Wild Fauna and Flora regulates which species are to be controlled.

In the convention/protocol process, states come together and agree an initial 'framework convention' to identify the problems and ways of dealing with them, but which at first may not contain specific obligations. Once agreement is made for the convention, this is then followed by a series of meetings at which 'protocols' are negotiated which then do require member states to sign up to specific actions. The Montreal Protocol (1987) was the first global agreement to phase out those chemicals held responsible for ozone depletion. The Kyoto Protocol (1997) was the first step in developing a regime to tackle climate change, and we will return to this later.

Mini Case Study Ozone depletion

Ozone in the upper atmosphere is important as it acts as a barrier to prevent ultraviolet radiation getting through to the earth. If there is a depletion of the ozone layer then this can lead to increases in skin cancers, immune disorders for humans and other species, and crop damage. In the 1970s, it became clear that the release of CFC gases into the atmosphere was indeed causing depletion of the ozone layer. CFCs were primarily used for refrigeration and air conditioning and were also commonly found in aerosols and fire extinguishers.

What has been remarkable is the speed with which action was taken to curb the use of CFCs and other ozone depleting substances. Initially, the industries involved in the manufacture of CFCs, such as DuPont, were resistant to changing their behaviour, arguing that it was not feasible to develop substitutes for CFCs. However, a combination of consumer pressure and US government determination to take a lead in regulating against their use, once the scientific evidence became clear, was vital. At the global level, the signing of the Montreal Protocol in 1987 established a very effective international regime for cooperation to phase out CFCs. Since customers would now be obliged to use substitutes to CFCs, even if these were more expensive, and once it became clear that the market for these was now a global one, there was a real incentive for the chemical companies such as DuPont and others to spend the required research and development funds in developing substitutes.

Sources: De Sombre 2007; www.undp.org/ozone; http://ozone.unep.org/new_site/en/montreal_protocol.php

Questions

1. To what extent was there the creation of an effective international regime of cooperation to reduce the emissions of CFCs?
2. Why might such agreements be more difficult to achieve in the case of deforestation or global fisheries and the protection of the global marine environment?

The fact that states have the right to exert their own sovereignty over their own resources makes the process of environmental regime creation a complex, and at times very slow, process with conflicts between the interests of states and, of course, differences in their respective power and influence.

As well as the problems of establishing such global cooperation there are also specific problems that relate to the nature of environmental issues.

Risk and Uncertainty

The main obstacle when examining environmental problems is that, often, these problems are not immediately obvious.

Environmental policy requires people and organizations to change their behaviour in relation to resource use so that we recognize that the ecological environment is not a free good, and that we are made fully aware of the social costs of environmental damage. It is clear that across many parts of the world there has been an increase in environmental awareness and in areas such as recycling this has changed behaviour. However, a major barrier to effecting more widespread environmental improvements lies in our lack of knowledge of exactly what our ecological impact is and indeed the measures we should take to minimize this.

Environmental policies involve a 'trade-off' in that there is a conflict between short-term production and the immediate gratification of consumption and longer term well-being. While people may well be more aware of the costs of motoring and air travel, the predicted rises in the uses of these modes of transport shows that people are not prepared to alter their behaviour voluntarily.

For both consumers and producers, the costs of adapting to ecological change may appear to be too great and the task for environmental policy lies both in how to deal with this resistance and in persuading us all that the long-term benefits of preventing ecological damage are greater than the costs of taking action now to minimize it.

The Role of Science

In order for risks to be quantified, we need careful research and analysis, and this entails further problems. Scientific surveys are often very complex and contradictory and most people lack the understanding to unravel the findings. Faced with this lack of understanding, it is easy for people to simply ignore the debates and carry on as usual.

The Notion of Sustainable Development

In 1987, *Our Common Future*, a report from the United Nations World Commission on the Environment and Development (WCED) was published (commonly referred to as the Brundtland Report). This built on the work of the Stockholm Conference, which also looked at environmental concerns more widely. The publication of *Our Common Future*, and the work of the WCED, led to the 1992 Conference at Rio de Janeiro and the adoption of Agenda 21, the Rio Declaration, and to the establishment of the Commission of Sustainable Development.

At the heart of the debate about the nature of the ecological environment lies the concept of sustainable development. The commonly accepted definition of this was outlined in the Brundtland Report: 'Sustainable Development is development that meets the needs of the present without compromising the ability of future generations to meet their own needs' (WCED 1987).

This part of the statement is the bit which is most quoted and clearly shows the commitment that is made here to ensuring **intra-generational equity**, in other words that our actions today should not undermine the standards of living of the future. However, what is often left out is the full version, which goes on to say:

> it contains within it two key concepts: the concept of 'needs', in particular the essential needs of the world's poor, to which overriding priority should be given; and the idea of limitations imposed by the state of technology and social organization on the environment's ability to meet present and future needs (WCED 1987: 43).

This second statement directly argues that growth is needed if it is to ensure that inter-generational equity is achieved (helping the poor in the world today).

The 1992 Earth Summit, held in Rio de Janeiro, Brazil, was pivotal in that it formulated Agenda 21, a comprehensive programme to be adopted globally, nationally, and locally to promote sustainable development in the twenty-first century. The Rio Declaration outlined 27 key principles concerning the actions that states should take in order to safeguard the environment and these were adopted by the 178 countries that took part in the Earth Summit (http://sustainabledevelopment.un.org/content/documents/Agenda21.pdf).

It established the United Nations Framework Convention on Climate Change (UNFCCC), an international environmental treaty to deal with climate change. Every year, there is a Conference of the Parties to the Convention (COP) to monitor progress on actions to combat climate change (see this chapter, The Progress on Climate Change Action).

While the Brundtland definition of **sustainability** has become widely accepted, there is still wide disagreement as to the implications of this statement (see Kates et al. 2005). For advocates of the free market approach to dealing with ecological problems, BAU models using market prices, and, where necessary, techniques such as **cost benefit analysis** or **environmental impact analysis** to reflect environmental market failures, should normally be sufficient to allow public/private sector businesses to incorporate their environmental responsibilities into their corporate strategies. The emphasis in the free market approach is that, as far as possible, where market policies are not sufficient then businesses should be encouraged to seek to comply with environmental issues, but on a voluntary basis that will best be achieved only when there is a clear business case to be made. But, as we have seen, those on the left side, or green side, of politics, argue that markets will not be in themselves guarantors of sustainability and that there needs to be more stringent regulation and control of business. For such critics there may well be many areas where the private interests of the business to make profits do conflict with their responsibilities to people and the planet and that, therefore, they cannot be left alone to make sustainable business decisions.

Global Climate Change

There is a clear consensus that the most pressing ecological problem of our age is global climate change and that the causes of climate change are anthropogenic (that is, caused by human activity) and the result of our dependence on systems of production and consumption that rely heavily on fossil fuels in particular. Since the industrial revolution, we have continued to emit ever more GHGs into the atmosphere that have led to an increase in global average surface temperatures, which in turn create a whole series of interrelated risks for people, economies, and ecosystems. The Intergovernmental Panel on Climate Change (IPCC) was established in 1989 by the World Meteorological Office and the United Nations Environment Programme (UNEP) to provide an objective source of information about climate change, which has been published in a series of assessment reports (AR) beginning in 1990 with AR 1 (with a supplement in 1992) and further reports in 1995, 2001, and 2007 (AR4). These reports are important as they represent the views of a multinational and comprehensive range of experts assembled by UNEP about the precise role of human beings in creating climate change and its associated risks.

In advance of the full publication of AR 5 in October 2014, three separate working groups (WGs) reported in late 2013 and March/April of 2014. These reports looked at the following:

- WG1: The Physical Science Basis (www.ipcc.ch/report/ar5/wg1/).

- WG2: Impacts, Adaptation, and Vulnerability (www.ipcc.ch/report/ar5/wg2/).

- WG3: Mitigation of Climate Change (www.ipcc.ch/report/ar5/wg3/).

In terms of the physical science, WG1 AR5 was clear:

Warming of the climate system is unequivocal, and since the 1950s, many of the observed changes are unprecedented over decades to millennia. The atmosphere and ocean have warmed, the amounts of snow and ice have diminished, sea level has risen and the amount of greenhouse gases have increased (Stocker et al. 2013: 4).

GHG emissions are problematic because once emitted into the atmosphere they stay there for many, many years. They help create the 'greenhouse effect' in that they prevent the solar rays that penetrate the earth's atmosphere from going back out again, so leading to a gradual warming of the planet's surface.

Meyer illustrates the problem by using a 'bath-tap' analogy (Meyer 2007). The dominant greenhouse gas from anthropogenic sources is carbon dioxide (CO_2). Just as a bath will fill if the tap is left running, so the atmosphere fills up as emissions flow from sources such as the burning of fossil fuels for energy use. If there is no outflow from the bath, over time the constant flow will mean that the stock of water will rise. If there is a plughole with no plug, then this stock need not rise so fast, as some of the water is drained away. In relation to our CO_2 emissions, this means that if we have 'sinks' to absorb the carbon such as forests or the oceans, then not all the carbon will be added to the total stock. If, for example, the flow of water is twice the rate at which it drains away, then the net increase in the stock of water will be 50 per cent of the flow.

Ice core sampling allows CO_2 atmospheric concentration to be measured for half a million years. This has fluctuated in the band of 180 to 280 parts per million by volume (ppmv) and there is a very close correlation with these fluctuations and the changes in global temperature. During the last 200 years, there has been a rise in CO_2 concentration from 280 ppmv to a level of 391 ppmv as of January 2011. AR5 confirmed that CO_2 emissions have increased by 40 per cent since pre-industrial times and that, while the ocean has absorbed 30 per cent of the increase, this has led to ocean acidification. As more and more concentrations of GHGs occur, there is a warming of overall average global earth temperatures and AR5 confirms that, '[i]t is *extremely likely* that human influence has been the dominant cause of the observed warming since the mid 20th-century' (IPCC 2013: 17 [my emphasis]). It also shows that the last three decades are *likely* to have been the warmest 30-year period of the last 1,400 years. Figure 12.1 shows the trend in CO_2 emissions (http://climate.nasa.gov/evidence).

Up until recently, the annual increase of atmospheric CO_2 has been 1.5 ppmv. Since each additional ppmv adds 2.13 billion tonnes (gigatonnes expressed as GTC) of carbon to the atmosphere, this means that the addition to the stock of carbon retained in the atmosphere in weight terms has been

Figure 12.1 Rising CO_2 levels

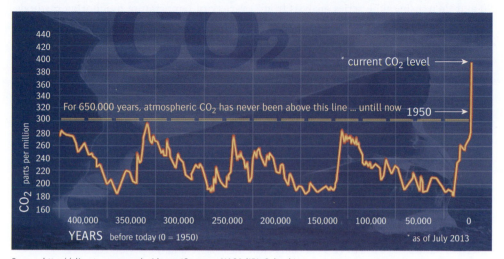

Source: http://climate.nasa.gov/evidence (Courtesy NASA/JPL-Caltech)

approximately 3.2 GTC. However, in total the annual emissions of carbon have been around 6.4 GTC, as the sinks have absorbed around 50 per cent of all emissions; although in the last 10 years, 2004–14, the rate of atmospheric increase was 2.07 ppmv (see www.co2now.org). As emissions are increasing, the sinks' ability to absorb them are decreasing, as the oceans warm and acidification occurs and forests are burned to increase land availability. This 'aggravated accumulation' will mean that the level of the bathwater will rise more quickly and is in serious danger of overflowing

Figure 12.2 shows the evidence about temperature rises on the basis of the methodology used by the Climatic Research Unit (CRU) at the University of East Anglia in the UK, whose work directly informs the IPCC.

Figure 12.2 Global air temperature

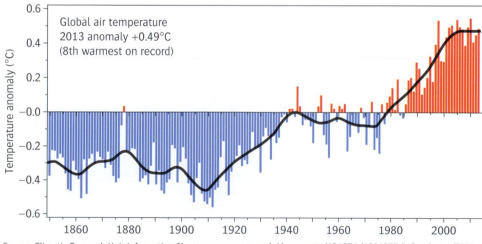

Source: Climatic Research Unit Information Sheet www.cru.uea.ac.uk/documents/421974/1301877/Info+sheet+%231. pdf/52a8dd1d-8c4d-49f7-b799-6448fff27150

This chart is drawn by taking the average global and marine temperatures in the period 1961–90 and then, using time series analysis from a variety of temperature monitoring methods, showing the variation (or anomaly) from this norm from 1850–2013.

Commenting on this data, the CRU states:

The period 2001–2010 (0.482°C above 1961–90 mean) was 0.20°C warmer than the 1991–2000 decade (0.272°C above 1961–90 average). The warmest year of the entire series was 2010, with a temperature of 0.547°C above the 1961–90 mean.

This data clearly shows the global rise in average temperatures in the last 30 years and, although the global average temperatures in the years 2011–13 have been lower than in the previous decade, they were warmer than all the years before 2001 apart from 1998.

Under the Kyoto Protocol, countries agreed to identify and quantify the sources of GHG emissions. Tables 12.2 and 12.3 show the data for the UK in 2012.

The Kyoto Protocol identified a basket of six GHGs that countries should seek to reduce and uses a base year of 1990 for CO_2, CH_4, and NO_2, and 1995 for fluorinated compounds. The UK agreed to reduce its GHGs to 12.5 per cent below the base year in the period 2008–12.

However, to illustrate the speed with which the science has begun to alter official policy responses, The UK Climate Change Act, passed in 2008, includes legally binding targets to reduce

Table 12.2 Total emissions by sector (*excluding LULUCF)

Energy Supply	35%
Transport	21%
Business	15%
Residential	15%
Agriculture	8%
Waste Management	3%
Industrial Process	2%
Public	1%

Table 12.3 Total emissions by gas (*excluding LULUCF)

Carbon Dioxide CO_2	85%
Methane CH_4	7%
Nitrous Oxide NO_2	6%
Hydro fluorocarbons	2%
Sulfur hexafluoride	0.1%

* Excluding land use, land use change, and forestry (LULUCF)
Source of Data UK GHG Inventory (UNFCCC coverage) (AEA 2012) adapted from chart at www.decc.gov.uk/assets/decc/Statistics/climate_change/1217-ghg-inventory-summary-factsheet-overview.pdf
Permission to use data from www.nationalarchives.gov.uk/doc/open-government-licence

GHGs by at least 80 per cent by 2050, and by at least 34 per cent by 2020, both below base year levels. This will be achieved by setting five-year carbon budgets to be achieved through a range of energy efficiency and carbon reduction measures, including a significant reliance on the European Emissions Trading System (Gov.UK available at www.gov.uk/government/policies/reducing-the-uk-s-greenhouse-gas-emissions-by-80-by-2050).

At the heart of the UNFCCC and Kyoto Protocol are three mechanisms designed to reduce global GHGs:

- Developed countries are set assigned amounts of GHGs in any time period and, through International Emissions trading, can trade any unused amounts with other countries (see Counterpoint Box European Emissions Trading System).

- The Clean Development Mechanism allows developed countries to fund carbon reducing projects in less developed countries in return for carbon credits.

- Joint implementation allows cooperation between developed countries where one country can help another by investing in emissions reduction projects and earn credits.

Counterpoint Box 12.2 European emissions trading system

This is a *cap and trade* system, which was first established in 2005. Having agreed to the national target of emissions, each country then allocates individual targets across businesses that are responsible for high levels of GHGs. (At the moment this covers the energy, iron, steel, mineral, wood pulp, board, and paper industries.) These allowances must then be adhered to and if a firm exceeds them then they either pay a fine or else they seek to purchase allowances from a firm that has not used all its allowances.

In principle, if the cap is set at progressively lower levels, this should produce reductions in GHGs. As market prices are set for carbon, then there will be an incentive for firms to cut back on emissions and invest in non-polluting technologies. Even if initially they cannot, revenues raised from the scheme can be used to develop renewables, act against deforestation, undertake forest plantation as well as research into and the

development of carbon capture and storage facilities, and undertake extensive energy efficiency programmes.

Businesses will be obliged to declare their emissions and submit to certificated verification procedures. The first phase was not so successful, as it is now acknowledged that initial caps were far too generous and so prices collapsed. While phase II worked better, there has been a concerted attempt to harmonize rules across all EU members in phase III, that started in 2013, and this will run till 2020 (see http://ec.europa.eu/ for more details).

Questions

Look at the details of how the scheme runs at the website above.
1. What are the strengths and weaknesses of this method of reducing GHGs?
2. What will be the impact of this scheme on the businesses involved?

Carbon reductions are occurring in many countries, but for many critics the current targets are too little and too late. It must be remembered that reductions in GHG emissions are not cuts in the amount of emissions, but simply slow the rate of flow although the overall stock of GHGs in the atmosphere rises.

For environmentalists, the implication is clear and that is that we need urgent cuts in emissions ppmv and that the current targets to stabilize emissions at 550 ppmv are simply too high and will result in runaway climate change.

The Effects of Climate Change

The Fifth Assessment Report reaffirmed the five areas of concern that had been highlighted in the Third and Fourth Assessment Reports. AR5 WGII lists these as five integrative reasons for concern (RFCs) which act as a starting point to analyse the dangerous anthropogenic interference with the climate system on people, economies, and ecosystems. These risks range from the immediate loss of life due to flooding, storms, or heat exhaustion through to rising food and water insecurity and destruction of biodiversity.

- **Unique and threatened systems**—There is high confidence that there are already some ecosystems and cultures that are at risk because of climate change and this risk grows with each 1°C increase in warming. If there is 2°C warming, then there are very high risks in relation to coral reef damage and Arctic sea ice.

- **Extreme weather events**—The risk of projected increases in droughts, heat waves, and floods, as well as their adverse consequences, is already moderate and with each additional 1°C rise in warming becomes high.

- **Distribution of impacts**—The most vulnerable people will be people in the weakest economic position, especially the poor and the elderly in both developing and developed countries alike.

- **Global aggregate impacts**—AR4 attempted to counter an often-expressed view that, while global warming may well cause problems for some, it will also equally bring benefits to others. It is easy to see how people living in cold northern climates might welcome warmer conditions. However, if global warming were to increase, AR5 confirmed that aggregate damaging impacts increase as warming increases. There will be many more losers than winners.

- **Large scale singular events**—The main concerns over the abrupt and irreversible changes that may endanger some physical systems and ecosystems are focused on coral reefs and the effect of sea level rises as a result of ice melting.

The IPCC emphasizes that adaptation (preparing now for the future problems that climate change will bring) and mitigation measures (trying to reduce the amount of GHGs and so lower potential risks) are unlikely to stop all climate change effects, but combined they can significantly reduce the risks. Conversely, delays in reducing emissions will significantly constrain the opportunities to lower stabilization levels and increase the risk of severe climate change impacts. Technology, both that which is presently available and that which is likely to become commercially available, is seen as offering a realistic hope that stabilization levels can be achieved.

In 2006, the UK government asked the respected economist, Nicholas Stern, to look at the economics of climate change. For Stern, 'Climate change presents a unique challenge for economics; it is the greatest and widest ranging market failure ever seen' (Stern 2006: i).

Stern was clear that the costs of climate change in terms of Gross National Product and quality of life would be much greater than the costs of taking action to mitigate against these now. With BAU there is a very high chance that the rise in global temperatures will exceed 2°C, and indeed there was some evidence that they may rise even as high as 5–6°C in the next century, which would 'take us into territory unknown to human experience and involve radical changes in the world around us' (Stern 2006: ix).

If this were to be the case over the next two centuries, there could be a reduction in global GNP in the range of 5–20 per cent. This is a high range of uncertainty, but for Stern this was inevitable given the difficulty of estimating such costs in general and so far into the future. In the original review, Stern argued that, in order to avoid these potential future costs, governments in the developed world would need to allocate 1 per cent of current GNP to climate mitigation and adaptation measures, but he revised this estimate upwards to 2 per cent of GNP in 2009.

Stabilizing the climate, Stern estimated, would require an 80 per cent reduction in carbon in the long run compared to current levels. As was shown above, this figure was subsequently adopted by the UK government in its Climate Change Act of 2008. The Stern Review highlighted four main policy areas that needed to be addressed if we are to be able to mitigate against the worst effects of climate change and adapt to those that will occur:

- reduce demand for emissions-intensive goods and services;
- increase resource efficiency;
- take action on non-energy emissions such as avoiding deforestation; and
- switch to low-carbon technologies for power, heat, and transport.

Stern was keen to emphasize that, while this may be seen to be a threat to BAU behaviour, in practice these changes may well provide opportunities to create markets for low-carbon energy products and to reduce costs through developing new low energy systems.

This is not going to be an easy task. At present, levels are continuing to rise, so adding to the stock of carbon, and the longer this goes on the greater the difficulty in reducing this. Stern was optimistic that it will be possible to stabilize the climate at 550ppmv by allowing annual emissions to peak in the next 10 to 20 years and then gradually cutting emissions by 1–3 per cent each year until 2050. However, since then, Stern himself has become more pessimistic and in an interview conducted while he was attending the WEF in 2013, he commented:

> Looking back, I underestimated the risks. The planet and the atmosphere seem to be absorbing less carbon than we expected, and emissions are rising pretty strongly. Some of the effects are coming through more quickly than we thought then (Stewart and Elliott 2013).

Stern is by no means alone, and fears about the potential threats of climate change have now moved to the centre of the business world. We have seen above that the WEF itself now sees climate change as one of the greatest future threats to business prosperity and at its 2014 meeting the President of the World Bank, Jim Yong Kim, stated: 'We have seen great climate leadership from countries and companies, but emissions are still rising, the poor are suffering. This is the year to take action on climate change. There are no excuses.' He went on to say: 'In 20 years, all of us will be asked the question, "What did you do to fight climate change?"…The leaders here in Davos, both from the private sector and from governments, have in their power to act in substantive ways. Now is the time to act for future generations before it is too late' (World Bank 2014).

There is concern that, without such actions to stabilize global temperature rises, the intended target of aiming to limit the average rise to 2 per cent above the 1990 norm by 2050 will be broken and that a 4°C warmer world will be likely. Under this scenario, all the RFCs above and the associated risks are extremely heightened. In 2012, the World Bank sought to establish what such a world would look like and how to avoid this (for details see World Bank 2012) as did the Organization for Economic Cooperation and Development (see OECD 2012).

The Sceptical Environmentalists

There is a small, but highly vocal, minority of critics who argue that the earth has been subject to variations in temperature before, and that this is the result of natural factors such as solar and volcanic activity. Some go further and dispute the accuracy of the data, arguing that there is now too much of a vested interest in the scientific community to prove the existence of anthropogenic climate change, which sometimes leads them to misrepresent the data.

Bjorn Lomborg, in his book *The Skeptical Environmentalist*, argues that the risks of global warming are overestimated and also that even where such risks can be proven, it is important for us not to prevent the present generations from reaping the fruits of economic growth for the uncertain prediction that unspecified groups in the future might suffer as a result of environmental damage (Lomborg 2001). In similar vein, the Nobel Prize winning economist Solow has argued, 'those who are so urgent about not inflicting poverty on the future have to explain why they do not attach even higher priority to reducing poverty today' (Solow in Rao 2000: 86). Lomborg is by no means the only critic to dispute the scientific evidence (see Booker 2009; Lawson 2008; Singer and Avery 2007).

This academic debate can often be clouded by mutual accusations of 'dirty tricks' across the spectrum of the debate. Climate change campaigners argue that there is a 'business of climate denial' with powerful business groups spending large amounts of money to lobby hard against legislation and spread disinformation to undermine the strength of the climate change evidence. One example of such a group is the Global Warming Policy Foundation established by Nigel Lawson, author and a former UK Chancellor of the Exchequer. Not only do such groups dispute the clarity of the evidence for anthropogenic climate change, but, as with Solow and Lomborg above, they also argue that the costs of putting climate change policies into action may be too high.

The Progress on Climate Change Action

The United Nations Framework Convention for Climate Change is the body that seeks to provide a framework under which all global climate change agreements are made. Since 1995, there have been annual meetings of the Conference of the Parties (COP) who participate in the UNFCCC. COP 3 in 1997 established the Kyoto Protocol, which attempted to set binding agreements in terms of carbon reduction targets and other measures discussed above only up to 2012, and mainly only on developed countries, so it was always acknowledged that further agreements would be needed. There were also objections from key parties, such as the USA and Australia, who did not sign up to the protocols. So, while it was seen as a start in framing the global response to climate change, there was a consensus that this framework needed to be strengthened. This was partly as a result of the increasing scientific evidence and its impact on public opinion as well as the growing influence of environmental pressure groups. At the global political level, the change in attitudes towards the acceptance of climate change as being real and anthropogenic in its causes by countries such as Australia and the USA gave rise to the real hope that, at the Copenhagen Climate Conference in December 2009 (COP 15), there would be a common agreement as to how to achieve the big reductions in GHGs now needed and a framework in which there could be mutual cooperation between the developed and the developing world.

In a speech in August 2009, Ban Ki-moon, the General Secretary of the UN who had championed the need for global agreements to deal with climate change, argued that climate change is 'simply the greatest collective challenge we face as a human family' (reported in the *Daily Telegraph*, 10 August 2009).

Ban had urged world leaders to make real progress at COP 15. It is widely agreed that these talks ended in failure, but also brought into stark highlight the divergences in the perceived responsibility for taking action between the developed world and the developing world. The Copenhagen accord was eventually drawn up and signed by only the USA, China, Brazil, India, and South Africa. While it acknowledged that climate change was one of the greatest challenges faced by humanity, and that actions should be taken to stabilize world average temperatures at or below a 2 per cent rise, no specific legally binding targets were given for reducing CO_2.

COP 17, which was held at Durban in South Africa in 2011, was seen to be successful in at least restoring the hope that it would be possible to develop a new set of Kyoto protocols up to 2020 and that this would be an agreement in which all countries would not only be involved, but would also agree to legally binding targets.

The main obstacles to getting the global agreements are the differences between the developed and developing countries. The rapid rise of developing countries such as the BRICS has meant that they have now become large contributors to GHGs globally, but they argue, not unreasonably, that, as newcomers to economic success, they should shoulder less of the burden for reductions in emissions compared to the rich developed world who still remain by far the biggest contributors to the stock of the GHGs that are in the atmosphere. Not only do such developing countries argue that their targets for emissions should be lower and for the developed countries higher, they also argue that there needs to be bigger transfers of money from rich nations to developed nations to subsidize and finance their investments in greener technologies and to compensate many of their poorest citizens who have suffered and will increasingly suffer from the problems of climate change which up to now have been largely caused by past emissions from the rich developed world.

All hopes are now being pinned on COP 21, which will take place in late 2015. It is hoped that COP 21 will indeed produce a global climate agreement that sets targets for all countries and that does make adequate provision for compensating the most vulnerable people and regions in relation to climate change, as well providing sufficient provision of transfers of financial and other types of support from the developed to the developing countries (for more details on the work of the UNFCC see http://unfccc.int/2860.php).

Learning Task

1. How aware are you about the science behind the debate about global warming?

2. What changes have you made, if any, to minimize your own 'ecological footprint'?

3. Have a go at measuring your own ecological footprint (see, for example, www.footprint.wwf.org.uk).

4. What reactions do you have to this footprint exercise?

● CHAPTER SUMMARY

The nature of many environmental problems is that they are trans-boundary, and if we are to avoid potential tragedies of the global commons then there needs to be concerted action at the global level, which is then translated into national and local environmental action.

It is clear that businesses have a big role to play. As converters of resources into products, attention has to be focused on their roles as sustainable businesses, not just in relation to the 'bottom' line of profit, but also in relation to their impact on people and profit. The Rio Declaration and Agenda 21 established a comprehensive set of ambitious principles for states to promote in relation to environmental policy. The UN Global Compact then translated these principles into the prescriptions for responsible business behaviour.

It is evident that there are obstacles to environmental policies. Businesses have to balance the risks of incurring the costs of environmental compliance with the risks of doing nothing. Here, there is a clear role for science and economics to specify these risks. For businesses with the short-term goal of maximizing share-holder value, it is all too easy to maintain 'business as usual', but the increasing recognition of the range of global environmental problems means that this is not a realistic possibility. Across the spectrum of business there are many examples of how individual businesses are seeking to address these concerns, but, especially in relation to climate change, it is argued that the response has not been enough. It is clear that unless businesses rise to the challenge there will be calls for tougher environmental regulation. It is also equally clear that, in order to make these changes, businesses do need external help and advice, and there is a need to then embed global responsibility into the overall business strategy.

● REVIEW QUESTIONS

1. What is the meaning of the term 'the tragedy of the commons' and how does this relate to ecological damage?

2. Explain how it is argued that market-based measures such as the 'polluter pays principle' address ecological problems.

3. Why do 'green' thinkers and left-wing activists argue that market-based measures are not, on their own, adequate to tackle the ecological problem?

● ASSIGNMENT TASKS

1. You have applied for, and been successful in obtaining, an internship for a leading newspaper. You will be working in the research team supporting the Global Environment news team. You have been asked to update the web content on its popular online pages, and, in particular, the Frequently Asked Questions section of the Climate Change web pages for which this team is responsible. At the briefing meeting, the web editor has asked you to do the background research that would enable you to provide copy to answer the following questions:

   a) What are the problems that climate change poses for the global community?

   b) Which businesses will be most affected by current and future policies to reduce emissions of greenhouse gases?

   c) In what ways will policies to reduce global GHG emissions impact on business behaviour

(For an example of a successful environment online presence from a newspaper see www.theguardian.com this is the website of *The Guardian* newspaper in the UK.) The web editor would like this in the form of a 2,000-word report together with all the references that you consulted to support your findings.

2. 'The UK Government has announced that under the Companies Act 2006 (Strategic and Directors' Reports) Regulations 2013, quoted companies are required to report their annual greenhouse gas (GHG) emissions in their directors' report... All quoted companies have to measure and report greenhouse gas (GHG) emissions. Quoted companies are those that are UK incorporated and whose equity share capital is officially listed on the main market of the London Stock Exchange; or is officially listed in a European Economic Area; or is admitted to dealing on either the New York Stock Exchange or NASDAQ.' (www.carbontrust.com/resources/guides/carbon-footprinting-and-reporting/mandatory-carbon-reporting).

Select three companies that will be affected by the reporting requirement above and compare and contrast their approaches to responding to the challenges of reducing their GHG emissions, commenting in particular on the extent to which they have identified a business case for this.

Case Study Economic growth and environmental risks

While across the world levels of absolute poverty are falling and incomes are rising, there are serious social and environmental problems associated with rapid economic growth. In countries such as China, India, and Brazil the pace of change has been extremely fast, although rates of growth have slowed since 2008 compared to those experienced in the first decade of the twenty-first century. A major feature of this economic transformation has been the speed of urbanization. China's urban population is predicted to rise from 430 million in 2001 to 850 million in 2015, and all are struggling to cope with the environmental consequences of such rapid change on housing, transport, water quality and quantity, and airborne pollution.

However, average income per capita in these countries is still low and, especially in the case of Brazil and India, a major feature of this urbanization has been the creation of vast slums. The Millennium Development Goals of the United Nations explicitly recognizes that it is the poor who often suffer the most from the environmental degradation brought about through rapid economic growth and they explicitly target the need for sustainable development to be central to growth strategies, as well as focusing attention on the need to improve the lives of slum dwellers and improve sustainable access to water.

As countries develop, it is argued that entrepreneurs need to be allowed to pursue their own interests and that their pursuit of profits will encourage them to be responsive to market needs. Simon Kuznets argued that, as countries develop, it is inevitable that the gap between high-income earners will grow relative to

Source: © leungchopan/shutterstock.com

→ the poor, but that, as countries mature, this gap will close. If you plotted the relationship between inequality and income on a diagram, as incomes rise at first so does the level of inequality, but over time this gap begins to fall. This is referred to as the 'Kuznets Curve'. As economic growth increases more and more people will be employed and governments will be able to use greater tax revenues from the higher incomes to engage in education and health programmes, raising general well-being. This is the basis of what has become called 'Trickle Down Economics'. In similar vein, it is argued that there is an environmental Kuznets Curve in that as countries develop rapidly it is inevitable that the environmental costs will increase, but that as they become richer people can afford higher levels of protection and/or invest in the new and environmentally friendly technologies.

However, the pace of change in the developing countries, coupled with the realization that global environmental problems impact more on the most vulnerable in the developing world, has led many to question this belief in the infallibility of the market. The WEF has highlighted water security as one the major risks for business in the future. (WEF 2012) These risks can stem from too much water, as in the case of flooding, or too little as the result of droughts and desertification. While events such as droughts and flooding are often local in their effects and it falls to the local or national authorities to try to deal with these, often they can have severe global effects as well. In 2010 drought in Russia led to falls in wheat production, which led to soaring food prices across North Africa and the Middle East, and for many political commentators this in turn provided the spark for the political upheavals of the Arab Spring.

Water quantity and quality directly affect business operations from agriculture to industry and, of course, is essential for maintenance of health and well-being in our households. Across the world there are problems with access to adequate water supplies and this is exacerbated by the global differences in terms of access to water as well as large income inequalities in water scarce regions that mean that poor people are always at a disadvantage. This then means that there needs to be attention paid to investing in the infrastructure that is vital for water purification and distribution, and there is intense debate as to who should pay for this, and the degree to which water should be bought and sold as a commodity or seen as a public good. Inevitably, the struggle to get adequate access to such a valuable resource, if not solved through an effective production and distribution system, has the potential to cause local and global conflicts.

Questions

1. In what ways might there be a conflict between the goals of economic growth and the concept of sustainable development?

2. Why do developing countries face particular problems in relation to environmental problems?

3. What are the main risks that face business in relation to water security?

4. If there are water security issues in relation to quantity and quality, who should take the lead for ensuring that there is universal access to adequate supplies of safe and clean water?

● FURTHER READING

This is the synthesis report of the UN Intergovernmental Panel on Climate Change and contains all the established academic evidence regarding climate change and its effects:

● IPPC (2015) Fifth Assessment Report. Available at: www.ipcc.ch/report/ar5/.

This report identifies the causes of global climate change and proposes policies to combat it:

● Stern, N. (2006) *The Economics of Climate Change—The Stern Review*. Cambridge: Cambridge University Press.

This report outlines the responses that the World Bank feels are needed to prevent catastrophic climate change:

● World Bank (2012) 'Turn Down the Heat: Why a 4°C Warmer World Must be Avoided'. Available at: http://documents.worldbank.org/curated/en/2012/11/17097815/turn-down-heat-4%C2%B0c-warmer-world-must-avoided.

This report, by the World Economic Forum's Global Agenda Council on Climate Change, focuses on the measures that business needs to take to reduce emissions of GHGs:

● World Economic Forum (2014) 'Climate Adaptation: Seizing the Challenge'. Available at: http://www3.weforum.org/docs/GAC/2014/WEF_GAC_ClimateChange_AdaptationSeizingChallenge_Report_2014.pdf.

This chapter provides a good introduction to the issues surrounding the relationship between business and sustainable development:

● Judge, E. (2014) 'The Natural Environment Global Warming, Pollution, Resource Depletion and Sustainable Development'. In Wetherly,P. and Otter,D., *The Business Environment—Themes and Issues*. Oxford: Oxford University Press.

● REFERENCES

Booker, C. (2009) *The Real Global Warming Disaster: Is the Obsession with 'Climate Change' Turning Out to be the Most Costly Scientific Blunder in History?*. London: Continuum.

Brown, L. (2009) *Plan B 4.0—Mobilizing to Save Civilization*. Washington, DC: Earth Policy Institute.

Carson, R. (1962) *The Silent Spring*. Boston: Houghton Mifflin.

Coyle, D. (2012) *The Economics of Enough: How to Run the Economy as if the Future Matters*. Princeton University Press.

Dietz, R. and O'Neill, D.W. (2013) *Enough is Enough-Building a Sustainable Economy in a World of Finite Resources*. San Francisco, CA: Berrett Koehler Publishers.

De Sombre, E. (2007) *The Global Environment and World Politics*. London: Continuum.

Elkington, J. (1994) 'Towards the Sustainable Corporation—Win-Win-Win Business Strategies for Sustainable Development'. *California Management Review* 36(2).

Engels, F. (1844) *The Condition of the Working Class in England*.

Galbraith J.K. (1958) *The Affluent Society*. New York: Houghton Mifflin Company.

Goodin, R. (2007) 'Selling Environmental Indulgences'. In Dryzek, J.S. and , Schlosberg, D., *Debating the Earth—The Environmental Politics Reader*. Oxford: Oxford University Press.

Hardin, G. (1968) 'The Tragedy of the Commons'. *Science* 162(December), American Association for the Advancement of Science.

IEA (2013) 'Key World Energy Statistics'. International Energy Agency. Available at: www.iea.org/publications/freepublications/publication/KeyWorld2013.pdf, accessed October.

Kates, R., Parris, T., and Leiserowitz, A. (2005) 'What is Sustainable Development? Goals, Indicators, Values and Practice?'. *Environment: Science and Policy for Sustainable Development* 47(3): 8–21. Available at: www.hks.harvard.edu/sustsci/ists/docs/whatisSD_env_kates_0504.pdf, accessed October 2014.

Lawson, N. (2008) *An Appeal To Reason: A Cool Look At Global Warming*. London: Duckworth.

Lomborg, B. (2001) *The Skeptical Environmentalist*. Cambridge: Cambridge University Press.

Macalister, T. (2014) "BP's Deepwater Horizon bill rises by £200 million as profits fall" at www.theguardian.com/business/2014/feb/04/bp-deepwater-horizon-bill-rises-profits-fall, accessed May 2014.

Meadows, D.H., Meadows, G., Randers, J., and Behrens, W.W. III, (1972) *The Limits to Growth*. New York: Universe Books.

Meyer, A. (2007) 'The Case for Contraction and Convergence'. In D. Cromwell and M. Levene (eds), *Surviving Climate Change—The Struggle to Avert Climate Catastrophe*. London: Pluto Press.

Mishan, E. (1969) *The Costs of Economic Growth*. London: Penguin.

OECD (2012) 'The Economics of Climate Change Mitigation: Policies and Options for Global Action Beyond 2012'. Available at: www.oecd.org/document/56/0,3746, en_2649_34361_43705336_1_1_1_1,00.html, accessed October 2014.

Rao, P.K. (2000) *Sustainable Development—Economics and Policy*. Oxford: Blackwell.

Schumacher, E.F. (1973) *Small is Beautiful—Economics as if People Mattered*. New York: Harperand Row.

Sheehan, B. (2010) *The Economics of Abundance: Affluent Consumption and the Global Economy*. Cheltenham: Edward Elgar.

Singer, S.F. and Avery, D.T. (2007) *Unstoppable Global Warming Every 1,500 Years*. Plymouth: Rowman and Littlefield.

Skidelski, R. and Skidelski, E. (2012) *How Much is Enough: Money and the Good Life*. New York: Other Press.

Stern, N. (2006) 'The Stern Review, Executive Summary— the Economics of Climate Change'. HM Treasury. Available at: www.hm-treasury.gov.uk, accessed October 2014.

Stewart, H. and Elliott, L. (2013) 'Nicholas Stern: "I Got it Wrong on Climate Change—it's Far, Far Worse"'. Available at: www.theguardian.com/ environment/2013/jan/27/nicholas-stern-climate-change-davos, accessed October 2014.

Stocker, T.F., Qin, D., Plattner, G.-K., Tignor, M., Allen, S.K., Boschung, J., Nauels, A., Xia, Y., Bex, V., and Midgley, P.M. (eds) (2013) 'Summary for Policymakers in Climate Change 2013: The Physical Science Basis: Contribution of Working Group 1 to the Fifth Assessment Report of the Intergovernmental Panel on Climate Change', IPCC, Cambridge, UK; New York, NY: Cambridge University Press.

WCED (1987) *Our Common Future*. Oxford: Oxford University Press (commonly known as the Brundtland Report).

WEF (2012) 'Global Agenda Council on Water Security'. Available at: www.weforum.org/reports/global-agenda-council-water-security-2012-2014, accessed October 2014.

WEF (2014a) 'Global Risks Report 2014'. Available at: http://www3.weforum.org/docs/WEF_GlobalRisks_Report_2014.pdf, accessed October 2014.

WEF (2014b) 'Redefining the Future of Growth: The New Sustainability Champions'. Available at: http://reports. weforum.org/new-sustainability-champions/#view/ new-sustainability-champions/report/executive-summary/, accessed October 2014.

World Bank (2012) 'Turn Down the Heat- Why a 4°C Warmer World Must be Avoided'. Available at: www-wds.worldbank.org/external/default/ WDSContentServer/WDSP/IB/2012/12/20/0003561 61_20121220072749/Rendered/PDF/ NonAsciiFileName0.pdf, accessed October 2014.

World Bank (2014) 'World Bank Group President: This Is the Year of Climate Action'. Available at: www. worldbank.org/en/news/feature/2014/01/23/ davos-world-bank-president-carbon-pricing, accessed October 2014.

Glossary

Absolute cost barriers obstacles deterring entry of new firms because the capital costs of entering are huge or where the existing firms control a vital resource, e.g. oil reserves—the company Aramco controls 98 per cent of Saudi Arabian oil reserves

Accountability the idea that organizations and people should take responsibility for their actions and their outcomes

Acquisition one firm takes over or merges with another; some authors use this term when a deal is contested

Advanced economy a country whose per capita income is high by world standards

Ageing population an increase in the average age of the population

Anthropocentric a view of the world that sees humans as being the most important species on earth

Applied research research specifically seeking knowledge that can be exploited commercially

Arbitration a process to resolve disputes that avoids using the courts

Authoritarian system one person or a group of people exercise power unrestrained by laws or opposition

Barriers to entry obstacles that prevent new firms from entering an industry and competing with existing firms on an equal basis

Basic research the pursuit of knowledge for the sake of it with no explicit aim to exploit the results commercially

Biodiversity the variety of life forms which exist on Earth. There is clear evidence that ecological changes can lead to a reduction in this

Biotechnology the use of biological systems or living organisms to make or modify products or processes

Born global refers to firms who get involved in international activities immediately after their birth

Bribery the offer of inducements in return for illegal favours

BRIC refers to Brazil, Russia, India, and China. Countries whose economies have been growing relatively rapidly in the first years of the twenty-first century and are seen as becoming major economic powers in the future

Brownfield investment where a firm expands by taking over existing production or service assets—most FDI is brownfield investment

Capital intensive where production of a good or service relies more heavily on capital, in the form of plant and equipment, than labour

Capital markets physical and electronic markets that bring together savers and investors, e.g. the stock market

Cartel firms come together to agree on a common price or to divide the market between them

Cash crop crops grown to be sold in the market for money rather than for the consumption of the producer

Centrally planned economy major economic decisions, e.g. on production, prices, and investment are made directly by government rather than being left to market forces

Civil law system based on statutes and written codes

Clientelism politicians confer favours on members of the electorate in order to obtain votes—sometimes referred to as patronage

Collectivized where the means of production are owned by the people collectively or by the state on their behalf

Common market a customs union, but with the addition that member states agree to allow free movement of goods, services, capital, and labour

Common law system accords more importance to court judgments than to written codes and statutes

Communist system usually a one-party system where the party controls the institutions of the state and owns and controls most of the production of goods and services

Comparative advantage the ability of a country to produce a good at lower cost, relative to other goods, compared to another country; even if a country is not the most efficient at producing the good, it can still benefit from specializing in producing and exporting that good

Competitive advantage strategies, skills, knowledge, or resources that allow firms to compete more effectively

Complementary product a product that is manufactured or used with another product, e.g. computers and computer software

Concentration ratio (CR) a way of measuring market concentration that takes the proportion of industry sales or output accounted for by the largest firms. A CR 5 shows the share of the five largest firms in the market

Contract a legally binding agreement between a buyer and a seller

Convention on Contracts for the International Sale of Goods (CISG) UN rules governing the sale of goods between professional buyers and sellers in different countries

Copyright the holder has the exclusive right to publish and sell literary, musical, or artistic works

Corporate social responsibility (CSR) organizations take responsibility for the impact of their activities on society including customers, suppliers, employees, shareholders, communities as well as the environment.

Corporatist social model welfare system offering relatively generous benefits and where work is seen as very important—found in countries such as Germany and Japan

Corruption where people misuse their power to enrich themselves

Corruption Perceptions Index (CPI) a ranking of countries by level of corruption carried out by Transparency International

Cost benefit analysis a technique used by economists when assessing the viability of investments (usually involving large scale investments) that seeks to measure the negative and positive externalities of these.

Creative capitalism the notion that business needs to generate profits and to solve the world's problems, e.g. use market forces to better address global poverty

Creative destruction the process by which radical new products, processes, transportation systems, and markets transform industry by destroying the old ways of doing things

Credit crunch a sudden and sharp reduction in the availability of money or credit from banks and other financial institutions

Cross elasticity of demand a measure of the extent to which customers change their purchasing patterns when one firm changes its price

Cross-border merger when a firm based in one country merges with a firm based in another

Cultural imperialism the imposition of one country's culture on another country

Cultural relativism understanding other cultures and not judging them according to one's own cultural norms and values

Culture shared beliefs, values, customs, and behaviours prevalent in a society that are transmitted from generation to generation

Customary law body of rules, values, and traditions based on knowledge gained from life experiences or on religious or philosophical principles

Customs union a free trade area, but with the addition that members agree to levy a common tariff on imports of goods from non-members

Cybercrime crime committed using computers and the Internet

Deforestation the destruction of forests either as a result of logging for timber or as people seek to clear forests so that they can farm the land

Demography the study of population in its various aspects—size, age, gender, ethnic group, and so on

Derivative in financial markets an asset whose value derives from some other asset. Buying an equity derivative does not mean buying shares, but involves taking out a contract linked to the level of share price. The contract can offer protection against adverse movements in the price of the share

Desertification the process by which once fertile areas of land become deserts. This is seen as a consequence of ecological damage

Devaluation a fall in the value of one currency against others

Developed countries see Advanced economy

Developing countries countries whose incomes are low by world standards

Directive (EU) laws that bind member states but are their responsibility to implement

Disposable income income remaining net of taxes and benefit payments available for spending or saving

Distribution of income the division of income among social groups in an economy or among countries

Diversified firm a business that operates in more than one industry or one market

DDT Dichlorodiphenyltrichloroethane, a pesticide that was widely used in agriculture in the 1950s

Dumping selling goods in a foreign market at below their costs of production or below the price in the domestic market

Ecocentric a view of the world that stresses that all species are important and that the health of the planet depends on our recognition of the mutual inter-dependence between all species

Economic growth the rate of change in GDP

Economic nationalism the state protects domestic business firms from foreign competition. They become richer and more powerful and this, in turn, increases the power of the state; same as mercantilism

Economies of scale reduction in unit costs associated with large-scale production

Economies of scope cost savings resulting from increasing the number of different goods or services produced

Embezzlement refers to the stealing of money or other assets

Emerging economy/markets an economy with low-to-middle per capita income; originally it referred to economies emerging from communism

Environmental impact analysis the use of cost benefit analysis in the form of a report undertaken by businesses when considering an investment to ensure that all the environmental costs are considered.

Equity support regime government support for innovation by buying shares and taking a stake in the ownership

Ethnocentric a belief that the values of your own race or nation are better than others

Eurozone members of the EU having the euro as their currency

Excess capacity where demand is not sufficient to keep all resources in a firm or industry fully occupied

Exchange rates the price of one currency expressed in terms of another, e.g. £1 = US$2

Executive branch implements laws, regulations, and policies and gives policy advice to government ministers

Export credits loans offered by countries, often at low cost, to buyers of exports

Export guarantees where exporters are guaranteed by governments that they will receive payment for their goods or services

Export processing zone (EPZ) an area where MNCs can invest, produce, and trade under favourable conditions such as being allowed to import and produce without paying tax

External factors components of the micro- and / or macroenvironments of business

Extortion obtaining money or other benefits by the use of violence or the threat of violence

Factors of production inputs combined by organizations to produce goods and services; the main categories are land, labour, and capital

Favouritism where a person is favoured unfairly over others, e.g. in the award of contracts

Federal system there is a sharing of significant decision-making powers between central and regional governments

Feminine society one which values highly the quality of life and human relationships

Financial markets these are mechanisms for bringing together buyers and sellers of financial assets—they can be located in one place or be dispersed

Fixed costs costs that do not vary with the level of output and are incurred whether output is produced or not

Fixed exchange rate when the exchange rate of a currency is fixed against others—in reality, a completely fixed rate is difficult to achieve

Floating exchange rate when the exchange is allowed to float freely against other currencies

Foreign direct investment (FDI) the establishment, acquisition, or increase in production facilities in a foreign country

Foreign indirect investment (FII) the purchase of financial assets in a foreign country

Franchising granting the right to an individual or firm to market a company's goods or services within a certain territory or location; McDonald's, Subway, and Domino's are examples of companies granting franchises to others

Fraud deception by those aiming to make an illegal gain

Free trade goods and services are completely free to move across frontiers—i.e. there are no tariffs or non-tariff barriers

Free trade area member states agree to remove tariffs and quotas on goods from other members of the area. Members have the freedom to set the level of tariff imposed on imports of goods from non-members of the area

GATT an international organization set up to remove barriers, particularly tariffs and quotas, to international trade; was subsumed into the WTO

GHGs greenhouse gases of which the most serious for climate change are carbon dioxide, methane, and nitrous oxide

Global income the total value of world income generated by the production of goods and services

Global integration the interconnections between countries, which increase with the reduction in barriers to the movement of goods, services, capital, and people

Global supply chains the sequence of steps that a good goes through to get from the producer of the raw materials to the final product

Globalization the creation of linkages or interconnections between nations. It is usually understood as a process in which barriers (physical, political, economic, cultural) separating different regions of the world are reduced or removed, thereby stimulating exchanges in goods, services, money, and people

Governance the structures and procedures countries and companies use to manage their affairs

Greenfield investment where a firm sets up completely new production or service facilities

Greenhouse gases see GHGs

Grey market goods sold at a lower price than that intended by the maker; the goods are often bought cheaply in one national market, exported, and sold at a higher price in another

Gross domestic product the value of all goods and services produced within the geographical boundaries of a country

Guanxi the reciprocal exchange of favours and mutual obligations among participants in a social network in China

Hedge funds financial institutions selling financial products that allow clients to reduce financial risk or to speculate in equities, commodities, interest rates, and exchange rates; they also operate on their own account

Herfindahl-Hirschmann Index (HHI) gives a measure of market concentration that includes all firms in the market. The more competitive the market, the closer the value of the index is to zero. The value of the index for pure monopoly is 10,000

Horizontal merger where a firm takes over a competitor, i.e. the merging firms are operating at the same stage of production

Human Development Indicators (HDI) used by the UN to measure human development; they include life expectancy, adult literacy rates, and GDP per capita

ICSID agency based at the World Bank that resolves international commercial disputes between businesses

Impact analysis the process of identifying the impact on business of a change in its external environment

Income inelastic when the quantity demanded of a good or services changes proportionately less than national income, i.e. the value of income elasticity is less than one

Industrial revolution a transformation from an agricultural economy to an industrialized economy with large-scale mass production carried out in factories in towns

Industry comprises all those firms who are competing directly with each other

Industry based view an organization's performance is determined by its position in relation to the external environment

Infant mortality the death rate of children in the first year of life, expressed as the number of deaths per 1,000 live births

Inflation a rise in the general price level or an increase in the average of all prices of goods and services over a period of time

Information and communications technologies (ICT) technology that is relevant to communications, the Internet, satellite communications, mobile telephony, and digital television

Information revolution the increasing importance of information and the increasing ease with which information can be accessed

Innovation the commercial exploitation of new knowledge

Intellectual property rights (IPRs) legal protection of ideas and knowledge embodied in new goods, services, and production processes

Interest rate the price paid to borrow someone else's money, sometimes called the price of money

Internal factors the internal strengths and weaknesses of the organization

International arbitration companies in different countries who are in dispute can ask that their case be resolved under the New York Convention or by referring it to ICSID at the World Bank

International Centre for the Settlement of Investment Disputes (ICSID) an international body based at the World Bank in Washington that helps to resolve disputes between governments and foreign business around investment

International Comparison Program the World Bank's programme which is developing ways of comparing relative standards of living

International Labour Organization (ILO) a UN agency promoting social justice in the workplace

International Monetary Fund (IMF) an international agency promoting monetary cooperation and stability

Inter-operability the ability of systems such as IT systems to work together

Intra-generational equity the belief that it is important that rich producers and consumers today do not impose environmental costs on the poor members of the present generation

ISIC the UN industrial classification system

Judicial branch institutions such as the police, courts, prison system, and armed forces responsible for enforcing the law

Labour intensive where production of a good or service relies more heavily on labour than on capital, i.e. plant and equipment

Legislative branch political institutions like parliaments with the power to make laws, regulations, and policies

Liberal democracy a system in which citizens have the right to elect their government and to individual freedom

Liberal social model a form of welfare system offering relatively low welfare benefits and distinguishing between those deserving welfare support and those who do not—found in North America and Australia

Liberalization the reduction of barriers to trade or of entry into a market

Licensing where a firm grants permission for another to use its assets, e.g. to produce its product, use its production processes, or its brand name

Life expectancy the average number of years that a person can expect to live from birth, which varies significantly between countries

Liquidity the ease with which assets can be turned into cash

Lisbon strategy EU 10-year plan to improve competitiveness

Lobbying attempt to influence the decisions taken by others, e.g. state institutions

Macroenvironment comprises all the political, economic and financial, socio-cultural, technological, and ecological elements in the wider environment of business

Maquiladora a factory set up in Mexico close to the US border as a result of the establishment of NAFTA

Market comprises competing goods and services, the firms producing those goods/services, and the geographical area where the firms compete

Market concentration measures the distribution of market power by market share

Market deregulation the reduction of barriers of entry into a market

Market economy an economy where prices and output are determined by the decisions of consumers and private firms interacting through markets

Market growth the change over time in the demand for a good or service

Market ideology a set of beliefs asserting that all economic decisions are best left to private individuals and firms through the market; government intervention in the market is abhorred

Market size measured by the sales turnover of a good or service in a market: the relative size of the overall economy

Masculine society one where money, incomes, promotion, and status are highly valued

Mercantilism the idea that international trade should primarily serve to increase a country's financial wealth, especially of gold and foreign currency—in this view, exports are good and imports are bad

Merger occurs where two or more companies combine their assets into a single company; some authors use the term merger only when all parties are happy to conclude the deal

Microenvironment the components of the firm's immediate environment: rivals, customers, suppliers, potential competitors, and substitutes

Migrant the UN defines migrants as people currently residing for more than a year in a country other than where they were born

Migration the movement of people across national borders from one country to another

Millennium Development Goals (MDGs) eight goals adopted by the United Nations concerning world poverty and general development

Monarchy refers to country where the monarch is the head of state

Monetary policy attempts by the authorities to influence monetary variables such as money supply, interest rates, exchange rates

Money an accepted medium of exchange for goods and services

Money laundering making illegally acquired money appear to come from a legitimate source

Money supply there are various definitions—all include the quantity of currency in circulation and then add various other financial assets such as bank current and deposit accounts

Monopolistic competition a market structure where there are many sellers producing differentiated products

Monopoly a market structure where there is only one seller

Multinational corporations (MNCs) companies who own and control operations in more than one country

NACE the EU system of industrial classification

NAFTA (North Atlantic Free Trade Area) a free trade area comprising the USA, Canada, and Mexico

NAICS the system of industrial classification used by members of NAFTA, the USA, Canada, and Mexico

Nanotechnology the science of the ultra-small

National income income generated by a country's production of goods and services—the same as GDP

Natural monopoly occurs where the market can be supplied more cheaply by a single firm rather than by a number of competitors, e.g. in the supply of water where it would not be economical to build more than one supply network

Negative externalities are the costs of either the production or consumption of goods and services that are not borne by the direct producers or consumers, but which affect society in general, e.g. exhaust fumes from vehicles pollute the air that we all have to breathe

Neo-mercantilism government policies to encourage exports, discourage imports, and control outflows of money with the aim of building up reserves of foreign exchange

Nepotism conferring favours on the members of one's family

New trade theory models of trade that incorporate market imperfections such as monopoly elements and product differentiation into their analysis

New York Convention a commercial body set up under the aegis of the UN to resolve international commercial disputes between companies

Non-governmental organization (NGO) not for profit organizations who try to persuade government and business on a variety of issues such as human rights, the environment, and global poverty

Norms rules in a culture indicating what is acceptable and unacceptable in terms of peoples' behaviour

OECD international organization comprising 30 member countries, mostly advanced: tries to promote sustainable economic development, financial stability, and world trade

Offshoring transfer of jobs abroad

Oligopoly a market structure with few sellers where the decision of one seller can affect and provoke a response from the others

Open economy a completely open economy is one where there are no restrictions on foreign trade, investment, and migration

Opportunities occur where the external environment offers business the possibility of meeting or exceeding its targets

Opportunity cost the sacrifice made by choosing to follow one course of action: the opportunity cost to a country deciding to use resources to manufacture more of a product is the benefit it gives up by not using those resources to make another good

Option the right to buy or sell an asset at an agreed price

Organizational culture comprises the values and assumptions underpinning the operation of the business; for example, regarding how authority is exercised and distributed in the firm and how employees are rewarded and controlled

Patent a patent gives the holder the exclusive right to exploit the invention commercially for a fixed period of time

Patronage see Clientelism

Per capita per head

Perfect competition a market structure with many sellers, homogeneous products, free entry and exit, and where buyers and sellers have perfect knowledge of market conditions

PESTLE a model facilitating analysis of the macroenvironment, the acronym standing for Political, Economic and Financial, Socio-cultural, Technological, Legal, Ecological

Piracy the unauthorized duplication of goods such as software or films protected by patent or copyright; robbery committed at sea usually through the illegal capture of a ship

Planned economy a system where the means of production are owned by the state on behalf of the people, and where the state plans and controls the economy

Poverty occurs where people do not have enough resources to meet their needs in absolute terms and relative to others; the World Bank uses income of US$1/US$2 a day to measure global poverty

Power distance the extent to which a society accepts hierarchical differences, e.g. inequality in the workplace

Precedent when the decision of a court binds others in subsequent cases when similar questions of law are addressed

Price leadership a situation where prices and price changes are determined by the dominant firm or a firm accepted by others as a price leader

Primary market a market where the first trading in new issues of stocks and shares occurs

Product differentiation where firms try to convince consumers that their products are different from those of their competitors through activities such as product design, branding, packaging, and advertising

Product life cycle stages of development through which a product typically moves: introduction; growth; maturity; decline

Productivity the amount of output per unit of resource input, e.g. productivity per worker; used as a measure of efficiency

Public procurement the purchase of goods and services by government departments, nationalized industries, and public utilities in telecommunications, gas, water

Purchasing power parity where the value of, for example, GDP is adjusted to take account of the buying power of income in each economy. It takes account of the relative cost of living

Qualified majority voting (QMV) EU system where any proposal must receive three quarters of the votes to be approved

Quantitative easing central banks deliberately expand the money supply by buying assets, usually government bonds, from private sector companies like pension funds. Bond prices rise and interest rates fall, hopefully promoting increases in demand and boosting economic growth

Quota limitation imposed by governments on the total amount of a good to be imported; the amount of money IMF member countries are required to subscribe to the Fund

Recession a significant decline in the rate of economic growth; technically it can be defined as a fall in GDP over two successive three-month periods

Regional trade area (RTA) barriers to movement such as tariffs and quotas are abolished among the members

Regulation rules that take their authority from statutes

Regulation (EU) laws which must be applied consistently in all member states

Religious law based on religious principles, e.g. Sharia, or Muslim, law is based on the religious principles contained in the Koran

Research and Development (R&D) the discovery of new knowledge (research) about products, processes, and services; the application of that knowledge to create new and improved products, processes, and services that fill market needs (development)

Resource based view an organization's performance is determined by its resources and capabilities

Revenue the income firms generate from their production of goods and services

Risk analysis systematic attempt to assess the likelihood of the occurrence of certain events

Rules of origin laws and regulations determining the origin of a good—this can be an issue in free trade areas where the origin of the good determines whether a tariff is imposed

Scanning a process of identifying issues in the macroenvironment that have an impact on the organization

Scenario planning using views of the future to help organizations to plan

Screening a technique to assess whether countries are attractive as a market or as a production location

Secondary market where stocks and shares are traded after their initial offering on the primary market

Securitization a process of taking several financial assets, like mortgages, and repackaging into interest-bearing securities—interest payments and repayments of the loans are received by the purchaser of the security

Shadow economy goods and services produced (legally and illegally) but not recorded in official figures—no tax is paid and laws and regulations are ignored

Social democratic model welfare benefits are generous and available to all; the system is committed to maintaining high employment and low unemployment

Social entrepreneurs where entrepreneurial/business approaches are used to deal with social problems, e.g. providing microfinance to help reduce rural poverty in developing countries

Soviet bloc the Soviet Union and its allies in Eastern Europe such as Poland, East Germany, Hungary, and Romania; the bloc started to collapse in the late 1980s

Specialization concentration on certain activities, e.g. the law of comparative advantage suggests that countries should specialize in producing those goods at which they are relatively most efficient/least inefficient

Spot rate/price the current rate or price

Stakeholder individuals or groups who have an interest in an organization and who can affect or be affected by the activities of the organization

Stakeholder map a way of prioritizing stakeholders by comparing their power against their interest

State a set of institutions having the legal power to make decisions in matters of government over a specific geographical area and over the population living there

Statutes laws passed by a legislative body such as a national or regional parliament

Strategy deciding the long-term direction of an organization

Subprime loans a mortgage loan granted to individuals with a poor credit history that renders them unable to access a conventional mortgage

Subsidies financial assistance from governments to business, often to protect it from foreign competition

Supply chain the systems and agencies involved in getting a good from the raw material supplier to the final consumer

Sustainability the ability of productive activities to continue without harm to the ecological system

Sustainable development economic development that does not endanger the incomes, resources, and environment of future generations

Swaps a means of hedging or reducing the risk of adverse price or rate changes

SWOT comprises four factors, Strengths, Weaknesses, Opportunities, and Threats, arising from a structured analysis of their internal operations (SW) and their external environment (OT)

Tariff a tax levied by countries on imports or exports

Tax avoidance exploiting legal loopholes to avoid paying tax

Tax evasion illegally avoiding paying tax

Technological advance new knowledge or additions to the pool of knowledge

Technological diffusion the spreading of new technologies within and between economies

Technology the know-how or pool of ideas or knowledge available to society

Theocratic regime religious principles play a dominant role in government and those holding political power also lead the dominant religion

Threats occur when the external environment threatens the ability of business to meet its targets

Tort an area of law concerned with injuries to people or damage to their assets

Trade surplus when the value of goods exceeds the value of imported goods

Trans-boundary processes which occur across national frontiers. Pollution in one country can often cross over into other countries. Carbon emissions are a prime example of trans-boundary pollution

Transnational Corporation synonym for MNC—a company with operations in more than one country; also used to refer to MNCs who see themselves as a global company and thus not tied to any particular country

Trillion one thousand billion, i.e. a trillion has nine zeros

UNCTAD a UN agency aimed at promoting trade and investment opportunities for developing countries and helping them integrate equitably into the world economy

Unidroit an organization trying to harmonize commercial law between countries

Uniform Commercial Code rules in force in many US states governing the sale of goods

Unitary system major decisions on policy, public expenditure, and tax rest with central government with regions having little power in these areas

Urbanization the increase in the proportion of a population living in towns and cities areas

Vertical merger a merger of firms at different stages of production of a product from raw materials to finished products to distribution. An example would be a steel manufacturer taking over a mining company producing iron ore

Vertically integrated firm a business operating at more than one stage of the production process of a good

World Bank international institution providing financial and technical help to developing countries

World Economic Forum (WEF) a think tank bringing together technical experts and business and political leaders who try to find solutions to major global economic, political, and social problems. It holds an annual meeting in Davos, Switzerland

World system the global system whose countries and regions are interconnected through a network of trade, investment, and migration linkages

World Trade Organization (WTO) international organization aimed at liberalizing world trade and investment; the successor to GATT

Index